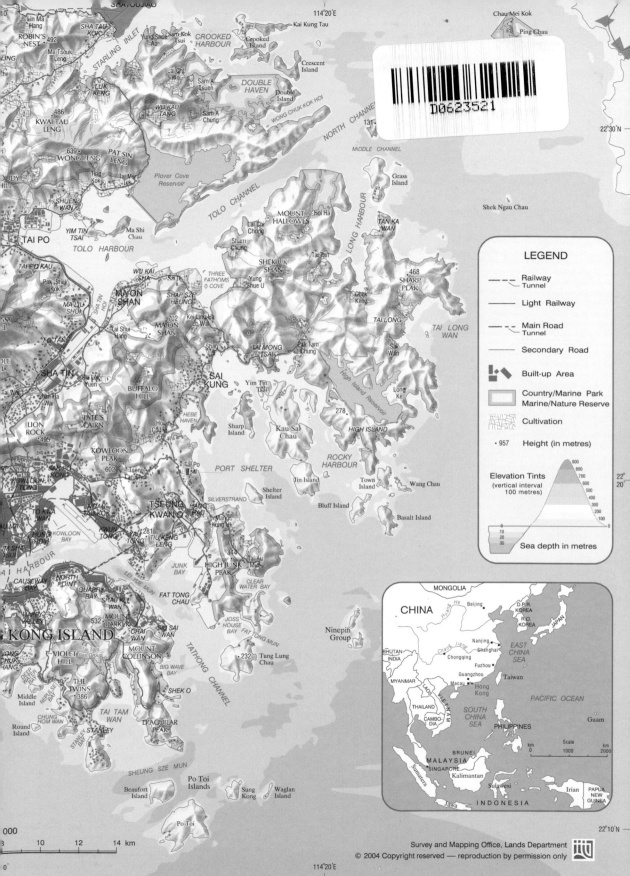

Survey and Mapping Office, Lands Department

© 2004 Copyright reserved — reproduction by permission only

Hong Kong hailed the success of China's first manned space flight in October. Large crowds turned out to greet the Delegation of the First Manned Space Mission when it made a six-day visit to Hong Kong two weeks after the epic flight. *Left:* the delegation, with spaceman Colonel Yang Liwei in the centre, being welcomed at the airport by the Financial Secretary, Mr Henry Tang, on October 31; and Colonel Yang with the Chief Executive, Mr Tung Chee Hwa, at a reception at Government House later in the evening. *Above:* enthusiastic well-wishers greeting Colonel Yang at Government House.

Colonel Yang waving to the crowd at one of the highlight events of the visit — a big welcoming gathering that community groups held at the Hong Kong Stadium. *Left:* young people eager to shake hands with Colonel Yang at Government House.

The Hong Kong Science Museum and the Hong Kong Space Museum organised special exhibitions and activities to mark the space flight. The Science Museum's exhibition, which included the Shenzhou-5 spacecraft's re-entry module that carried Colonel Yang back to Earth, attracted over 103 000 visitors in a continuous 76-hour exhibition period.

Cover Illustration
A blaze of colour erupts over the harbour
on two consecutive Sunday nights in October
as teams from Hong Kong, Italy, Japan and
the United States compete in the first Hong Kong
International Musical Fireworks Competition —
an event in which Italian artistry triumphed.

End-paper Maps
Front
The Hong Kong Special Administrative Region
Back
Hong Kong in its Regional Setting

Hong Kong: The Facts

Population: **6.803 million** (as at mid-2003)

Hong Kong Island	1.26 million	18.6%
Kowloon	2.02 million	29.7%
New Territories	3.52 million	51.7%
Marine	+	0.1%

Age structure
Median age: 38.0   Under 15: 15.7%   65 and over: 11.7%

Sex ratio
Overall: 939 males per 1 000 females
Under 15: 1 065   65 and over: 863

Overall density
6 300 people per square kilometre. The most densely populated District Council district is Kwun Tong with a density of 50 820 persons per square kilometre.

Housing
At the end of 2003, about 2.3 million people lived in public rental housing estates (managed by the Hong Kong Housing Authority and the Hong Kong Housing Society). The number of flats was 689 450.
In 2003, Hong Kong had 2.17 million domestic households: 53.1% occupied by the owners, 42.4% by tenants, and 4.5% by persons living in either rent-free accommodation or accommodation provided by employers.

Crude birth rate	Crude death rate
6.8# per 1 000 popn	5.4# per 1 000 popn

Expectation of life at birth
Male 78.6#   Female 84.3#

Nationalities
Predominantly of Chinese descent 95%
Total foreign passport-holders (end-2003): 523 880
Largest groups

Philippines	132 770	Canada	29 260
Indonesia	95 460	Thailand	28 820
USA	31 130	India	21 760
		UK	19 900
		Australia	19 600
		Nepal	17 650
		Malaysia	14 180
		Pakistan	13 750
		Japan	13 390
		Sub-total	437 670

Religion and Custom
Buddhists and Taoists make up the vast majority. Others (estimates): Christians 536 000; Muslims 70 000; Hindus 15 000; Sikhs 8 000; Jews 1 500.

Area: **1 103 square km**

Hong Kong Island & adjacent islands	81 sq. km
Kowloon	47 sq. km
New Territories—mainland	747 sq. km
New Territories—islands	228 sq. km
(Lantau 146.5 sq. km; others 81.5 sq. km)	
—Reclamation since 1887	67 sq. km

Weather

Average annual rainfall	2 214.3 mm

Wettest period

Hourly	109.9 mm (May 8, 1992)
daily	534.1 mm (July 19, 1926)
monthly	1 241.1 mm (May 1889)

Driest
10% humidity (January 16, 1959)

Highest temperature
36.1°C (August 19, 1900 and August 18, 1990)

Lowest temperature
0.0°C (January 18, 1893)

Highest wind speed (gust)
259 km/h at HK Observatory, 284 km/h at Tate's Cairn (Typhoon Wanda, September 1, 1962)

Employment
Total employment#: 3.23 million in 2003

Major Employment Sectors in 2003 #	
Wholesale, retail and import/export trades, restaurants and hotels	1 011 500 31% of total employment
Community, social and personal services	887 600 28% of total employment
Financing, insurance, real estate and business services	490 500 15% of total employment
Transport, storage and communications	361 600 11% of total employment
Construction	277 600 9% of total employment
Manufacturing	173 400 5% of total employment

Unemployment rate	7.9% in 2003
Average wages	$10,692 per month
(All selected industries)	

Notes: figures presented on this page refer to those released up to
    end-March 2004
    # provisional figures
    + less than 0.005 million

The Economy

Economic growth
Year-on-year rate of change in GDP (at constant (2000) market prices)
3.3% in 2003

Inflation affecting consumers
Year-on-year rate of change in Composite CPI:
-2.6% in 2003

Transport

Roads
The 1 934 km of roads (as at end-2003) carry 524 253 licensed vehicles, or about 271 vehicles per kilometre

Bridges
Longest: Tsing Ma suspension bridge (main span 1 377 metres) and the cable-stayed Ting Kau Bridge (two main spans totalling 923 metres)

Air movements
2003—187 508 flights; 26.75 million passengers; 2.64 million tonnes of freight

Shipping movements
2003—35 790 ocean vessel arrivals; 35 120 departures; port cargo throughput 207.6 million tonnes

Container throughput
2003—20.45 million TEUs

HONG KONG *2003*

Editorial
Information Services Department
(English edition)
Official Languages Division, Civil Service Bureau
(Chinese edition)

Photography and Design
Creative Subdivision, Information Services Department

The Information Services Department thanks all contributors and sources.

Statistical Sources
Census and Statistics Department

© **Copyright reserved**

Code No.
F30010400E0
(ISBN 962-02-0345-3)

Price
HK$106

HKSAR Government home page—http://www.gov.hk

Every effort has been made to ensure accuracy.
The Hong Kong Special Administrative Region Government
is not responsible for any inaccuracies, errors or omissions in this report,
or for any loss, action, or inaction arising from the use of, or for
advice based on, any information therein.

Published by the Information Services Department of the Hong Kong SAR Government
Printed by the Government Logistics Department
(Printed with environmentally friendly ink on paper made from woodpulp derived from sustainable forests)

Contents

*When dollars are quoted
in this report
they are Hong Kong dollars,
unless otherwise stated.
Since October 17, 1983,
the Hong Kong dollar has been
linked to the US dollar,
through an arrangement
in the note-issue mechanism,
at a fixed rate
of HK$7.8=US$1.*

*Some figures in the text are
estimated; actual figures appear
in the Appendices.*

The Hong Kong Annual Report
is obtainable from
leading bookshops throughout
Hong Kong

Government Publications
can be purchased from:

The online Government Bookstore
http://bookstore.esdlife.com

**Publications Sales Section
Information Services Department**
Room 402, 4th floor, Murray Building,
Garden Road, Central,
Hong Kong
Tel: (852) 2537 1910
E-mail: puborder@isd.gov.hk

Calendar of Events in 2003

January

8   In his annual Policy Address, the Chief Executive, Mr Tung Chee Hwa, outlines initiatives setting the direction for Hong Kong's future development and measures to eliminate the fiscal deficit.

9   The Secretary for the Environment, Transport and Works, Dr Sarah Liao, officiates at the ground-breaking ceremony for the Kowloon-Canton Railway Corporation's Lok Ma Chau Spur Line.

12   The Chief Executive joins Disney officials in a ground-breaking ceremony for the Hong Kong Disneyland project at Penny's Bay.

13   Speaking at the opening of the Legal Year, the Secretary for Justice, Ms Elsie Leung, reviews progress over the past year in legal education and the administration of justice, and outlines the challenges ahead.

17   The Lands Department announces the resumption of land at Johnston Road, Wan Chai, for a redevelopment project by the Urban Renewal Authority; five further resumptions announced later in the year involve redevelopment projects in Tai Kok Tsui, Sham Shui Po and Sai Ying Pun.

26   Round-the-clock passenger clearance services begin at the Lok Ma Chau Control Point at midnight, another milestone in enhancing cross-boundary facilities.

February

25   The Government announces it will restore civil service pay to the levels at June 30, 1997 in cash terms by two adjustments of broadly equal amount to be implemented on January 1, 2004 and January 1, 2005 respectively.

26   The National Security (Legislative Provisions) Bill, giving effect to the provisions of Article 23 of the Basic Law, is introduced into the Legislative Council for first and second readings.

   The Chief Secretary for Administration, Mr Donald Tsang, releases the Report of the Task Force on Population Policy in the Legislative Council.

March

2   The Hong Kong Observatory celebrates its 120th anniversary by laying a time capsule at its headquarters in Tsim Sha Tsui.

5 The Chief Executive attends the opening ceremony of the first session of the 10th National People's Congress in Beijing; he also attends the closing ceremony on March 18.

The 2003-04 Budget contains a series of measures aimed at reducing expenditure and raising revenue to address the fiscal deficit and as well as measures to boost the economy and promote job and training opportunities.

13 The Secretary for Health, Welfare and Food, Dr Yeoh Eng-kiong, tells a press conference the authorities are investigating a respiratory viral disease that is infecting patients and staff in the Prince of Wales Hospital; the infection is subsequently named Severe Acute Respiratory Syndrome (SARS), and proves to be deadly.

19 The Department of Health says the source of the SARS outbreak is believed to have been a visitor who stayed at a hotel in Kowloon and infected a number of other visitors there as well as a local resident who later was treated at the Prince of Wales Hospital.

20 The Secretary for Health, Welfare and Food says the number of SARS patients has risen to 165, and there have been six deaths.

21 The Government introduces the second Voluntary Retirement Scheme to facilitate the reduction in the size of civil service establishment and thereby bring about long-term savings to the Government. Civil servants in 229 designated grades with identified or anticipated surplus staff are invited to apply to leave the service voluntarily with compensation.

22 The University of Hong Kong announces that a coronavirus is the agent responsible for SARS.

25 A high-level steering committee, chaired by the Chief Executive and comprising relevant Principal Officials, is established to steer the Government response to the SARS outbreak.

27 With SARS spreading in the community, including hospitals and residential buildings, the Chief Executive announces a series of emergency measures to combat the disease, among them the temporary closure of schools. Mr Tung calls it the worst contagious disease outbreak in 50 years.

29 The Government requires all arriving passengers to fill out health declaration forms at all Immigration boundary control points — air, sea and land.

31 A severe outbreak of SARS necessitates the temporary closure of Block E of Amoy Gardens in Ngau Tau Kok; the residents are moved the next day to holiday camps designated as isolation centres for quarantine when preliminary evidence suggests that the sewerage and drainage systems might have been linked to the vertical spread of the disease in the block.

April

2   The World Health Organisation (WHO) issues a travel advisory concerning non-essential travel to Hong Kong; the tourism industry and related sectors are increasingly hard hit by the SARS outbreak.

9   The Government introduces the Betting Duty (Amendment) Bill 2003 into the Legislative Council to amend the Betting Duty Ordinance and give effect to the authorisation and regulation of football betting in Hong Kong; the council passes the bill on July 10.

11   The Government announces a proposal to construct a new two-lane boundary bridge beside the existing Lok Ma Chau boundary bridge to meet the growth in cross-boundary traffic between Lok Ma Chau and Huanggang.

     The Hong Kong Government reaches a consensus with the Guangdong Government on SARS-related matters regarding the exchange of information, medical cooperation, notification mechanism and boundary quarantine arrangements. An expert group is established to take forward the agreement.

12   The Chief Executive meets President Hu Jintao in Shenzhen, and reports on what Hong Kong is doing to combat SARS.

17   With the toll rising to some 1 300 infections and 65 deaths, the Prevention of the Spread of Infectious Disease (Amendment) Regulation 2003 is gazetted to empower authorised persons to take the body temperature of persons arriving or leaving Hong Kong, and to prohibit persons who have been exposed to the risk of SARS from leaving Hong Kong. Meanwhile, the Government announces the investigation findings of the Amoy Gardens outbreak.

23   The Government proposes a $11.8 billion package of relief measures to help the community tide over the difficulties caused by the SARS outbreak.

29   The Chief Executive attends the Special ASEAN-China Leaders' Meeting on SARS held in Bangkok, during which he reports to Premier Wen Jiabao on the situation in Hong Kong.

May

5   Heavy rain in the morning causes numerous cases of flooding and landslips throughout Hong Kong; a police officer is drowned while trying to rescue villagers in Ta Kwu Ling and schools are suspended during the day.

     The Chief Executive appoints the Chief Secretary for Administration the chairman of a special task force named Team Clean which is tasked with improving environmental hygiene and cleanliness in Hong Kong.

16   The WHO releases findings on the SARS outbreak at Amoy Gardens, which corroborates the Government's findings: a unique sequence of environmental and health events that happened simultaneously contributed to the outbreak there.

21   The Town Planning (Amendment) Bill 2003 is introduced into the Legislative Council; the bill aims at streamlining and expediting the town planning process, enhancing the transparency of the planning system and strengthening enforcement control against unauthorised developments in rural areas.

23   The WHO, which earlier praised Hong Kong for the containment measures taken against SARS, lifts its travel advisory concerning the Special Administrative Region.

27   A private sector firm is awarded the tender for preservation and development of the former Marine Police Headquarters, a monument site in Tsim Sha Tsui.

28   The Chief Executive announces an Expert Committee has been set up to review the management and control of the SARS outbreak, which caused 299 deaths among the more than 1 750 infections; the Expert Committee submits its report to the Chief Executive on October 2.

June

1   The Secretary for Constitutional Affairs, Mr Stephen Lam, launches the 2003 voter registration campaign at a ceremony in Sha Tin.

7   More than 150 representatives from women's organisations, service agencies, community groups and other sectors take part in an open forum, organised by the Women's Commission, to exchange views and experience on good practices for empowering women.

11   The last SARS case in Hong Kong is confirmed.

13   The Government announces the establishment of the Hong Kong Maritime Industry Council and the Hong Kong Port Development Council to further develop and promote the maritime and port industries; the two councils replace the Hong Kong Port and Maritime Board.

15   The Chief Executive announces that $700 million will be earmarked to create 32 000 new jobs or training places in a new plan to alleviate unemployment; the plan focuses on middle-aged unemployed people as well as on young people.

23   The WHO removes Hong Kong from its list of areas with recent local transmission of SARS.

27   The Standing Committee on Language Education and Research issues the final report of its language education review, outlining its proposals for raising language standards in Hong Kong.

29   Premier Wen Jiabao arrives for a three-day visit during which he attends ceremonies marking the sixth anniversary of the establishment of the HKSAR.

Hong Kong and the Mainland sign the Closer Economic Partnership Arrangement (CEPA). Premier Wen and the Chief Executive preside over the signing ceremony; the six Annexes to the main text are signed in Hong Kong on September 29. During his round of activities on June 30, the Premier meets key personnel involved in the fight against SARS.

The Government announces two changes in structure will take effect on July 1: the Government Logistics Department is formed by merging the Government Land Transport Agency, the Government Supplies Department and the Printing Department; and the Labour Branch of the Economic Development and Labour Bureau merges with the Labour Department.

July

1   Ceremonies marking the HKSAR's sixth anniversary begin with a flag-raising ceremony at the Golden Bauhinia Square, attended by Premier Wen Jiabao and the Chief Executive, and some 3 000 guests. Afterwards, Premier Wen attends a reception hosted by the Chief Executive in the Grand Hall of the Hong Kong Convention and Exhibition Centre.

      The Chief Executive issues a statement expressing concern at the large number of people taking part in a march on Hong Kong Island, and also expressing his understanding of their aspirations.

5   The Financial Secretary welcomes Hong Kong's continued rating as the world's freest economy in the Economic Freedom of the World 2003 Annual Report by the Cato Institute of the United States in conjunction with the Fraser Institute of Canada and some 50 other research institutes around the world.

7   The Executive Council decides to defer the resumption of the second reading of the National Security (Legislative Provisions) Bill in the Legislative Council.

      The Chief Executive accepts the resignation of Mr James Tien from the Executive Council; he subsequently appoints Mrs Selina Chow to the council on September 22.

10   A KMB double-deck bus plunges off an elevated section of Tuen Mun Road near Ting Kau, reportedly after a collision with a container lorry; the tragedy claims the lives of 20 passengers and the bus driver. Police subsequently charge a lorry driver with dangerous driving causing death.

12   Voting begins in the 2003 Village Representatives Elections and will continue every weekend until August 17; the elections are being conducted under a statutory framework for the first time.

15   Officiating at the naming and launching ceremony of 'Team Hong Kong Express', the Chief Secretary for Administration stresses the importance of public education and community support in keeping Hong Kong clean and hygienic.

16   The Chief Executive announces that he has accepted the resignations of Mr Antony Leung as Financial Secretary and Mrs Regina Ip as Secretary for Security.

19   The Chief Executive makes a duty visit to Beijing to brief Central People's Government leaders on the latest situation in Hong Kong; he meets President Hu Jintao and Premier Wen Jiabao.

24   Government Flying Services helicopters rescue 16 Mainland seamen from a container vessel adrift 30 miles northeast of Waglan Island, south of Daya Bay, during the passage of Typhoon Imbudo.

30   The Chief Secretary for Administration leads a government delegation to Beijing for a working session of the Mainland/Hong Kong SAR Conference on Coordination of Major Infrastructure Projects.

August

4   The Chief Executive announces the following appointments: Mr Henry Tang, Financial Secretary; Mr Ambrose Lee, Secretary for Security; Mr John Tsang, Secretary for Commerce, Industry and Technology; Mr Raymond Wong, Commissioner of the ICAC.

5   The Chief Executive and the Governor of Guangdong Province, Mr Huang Huahua, chair the sixth meeting of the Hong Kong/Guangdong Cooperation Joint Conference, held in Hong Kong.

18   The Immigration Department begins a region-wide Identity Card replacement exercise which will be carried out in phases over four years.

26   A Government Flying Services helicopter crashes on a Lantau hillside shortly after leaving its Chek Kap Kok base at about 10.30 pm bound for Cheung Chau on a casualty evacuation mission; both crewmen are killed.

28   The Chief Executive joins Vice-Premier Zeng Peiyan and other Mainland officials in Shenzhen to lay the foundation stone for the Hong Kong-Shenzhen Western Corridor, which will be the fourth vehicular boundary crossing.

The new Financial Secretary begins a two-day duty visit to Beijing.

September

3   Hong Kong is spared major damage during the rapid passage overnight of Typhoon Dujuan, during which the No. 9 storm signal is issued.

5   The Chief Executive announces that the Executive Council has decided to withdraw the National Security (Legislative Provisions) Bill so as to allow sufficient time for the community to study the question of its enactment.

7   The Chief Executive visits Xiamen to attend the opening ceremony of the 7th China International Fair for Investment and Trade. He has a meeting with Vice-Premier Wu Yi.

10   The Financial Secretary and the Secretary for Commerce, Industry and Technology attend the 5th Ministerial Conference of the World Trade Organisation in Cancun, Mexico.

16   The Chief Secretary for Administration leaves for the United States to promote Hong Kong's role as an international business hub and ideal strategic partner for accessing the Mainland market; he visits New York, Washington DC, San Francisco and San Jose.

October

1   The Chief Executive addresses a National Day cocktail reception marking the 54th anniversary of the founding of the People's Republic of China.

11   The Chief Executive presents honours and awards to 303 recipients at the 2003 Honours and Awards Presentation Ceremony held at Government House; the honours include Bravery Medals awarded posthumously to six front-line public sector medical staff who sacrificed their lives during the SARS outbreak.

16   On behalf of the people of Hong Kong, the Chief Executive conveys congratulations to the Central People's Government on the success of China's first manned space mission.

18   The Chief Executive arrives in Bangkok for the 11th APEC Economic Leaders Meeting on October 20 and 21.

21   Meeting in Geneva, the General Council of the World Trade Organisation announces acceptance of the offer of Hong Kong, China to host the next WTO Ministerial Conference.

24   The Secretary for Justice attends a seminar in Beijing on cooperation between Beijing and Hong Kong legal practitioners.

26   The Chief Secretary for Administration visits the Republic of Korea for a series of meetings and activities in Seoul promoting Hong Kong.

27   The Chief Executive and the Mayor of Shanghai, Mr Han Zheng, co-chair the first meeting, held in Hong Kong, of the Hong Kong/Shanghai Economic and Trade Cooperation Conference.

30   The Financial Secretary speaks at the first investment environment seminar organised in Tokyo by the HKSAR Government and the Guangdong authorities; the seminar highlights the opportunities open to Japanese companies under CEPA.

31   The Chief Executive hosts a reception at Government House in honour of the Delegation of China's First Manned Space Mission, led by Mr Hu Shixiang, and including the first spaceman, Colonel Yang Liwei; the delegation is beginning a six-day visit that includes a number of public activities.

November

2   The Chief Executive addresses a plenary session of the Boao Forum for Asia Annual Conference 2003, in Hainan.

3   The Secretary for Home Affairs, Dr Patrick Ho, welcomes the decision of the East Asian Games Association, meeting in Macau, to award the 5th East Asian Games in 2009 to Hong Kong.

4   Vice-Premier Zeng Peiyan arrives for a three-day visit at the invitation of the Chief Executive.

6   The Chief Executive and his Council of International Advisers discuss global and regional economic trends affecting Hong Kong, at the council's sixth meeting.

8 The Chief Executive leaves for visits to London and Paris, for a series of meetings with business and political leaders and to attend the Annual Dinner of the Hong Kong Trade Development Council in London; he meets the British Prime Minister, Mr Tony Blair, on November 11 and the President of France, Mr Jacques Chirac, on November 12.

17 The Financial Secretary and the Secretary for Financial Services and the Treasury, Mr Frederick Ma, officiate at the opening ceremony of the Hong Kong Exchanges and Clearing Ltd (HKEx) Representative Office in Beijing.

18 The Chief Executive announces that following approval from the State Council, the People's Bank of China will provide clearing arrangements for banks in Hong Kong to conduct personal renminbi business on a trial basis.

20 The Secretary for Justice concludes a visit to Canada in Vancouver, after first visiting Ottawa and Toronto.

23 A total of 1 066 373 people vote in the 2003 District Council Election, representing a turnout rate of 44.10 per cent for the 326 contested constituencies; candidates in 74 of the 400 constituencies are returned unopposed.

December

3 The Chief Executive briefs President Hu Jintao and Premier Wen Jiabao on latest developments in Hong Kong during a duty visit to Beijing.

7 The West Kowloon Heliport, a temporary facility located at the southern tip of the reclamation, opens for domestic helicopter services.

11 The Secretary for Justice visits Nanjing and Shanghai, where she signs cooperation agreements on legal services between the Department of Justice and the respective Justice Bureaux.

13 The Secretary for Economic Development and Labour, Mr Stephen Ip, signs the Mainland and Hong Kong Closer Tourism Cooperation Agreement with the Chairman of the Chinese National Tourism Administration, Mr He Guangwei.

18 The Financial Secretary welcomes the decline — from 8 per cent to 7.5 per cent — in the unemployment rate during the September-November quarter.

20 The Chief Executive officiates at the opening of the Kowloon-Canton Railway Corporation's West Rail that links Kowloon and the north-west New Territories.

23 The Secretary for Housing, Planning and Lands, Mr Michael Suen, in his capacity of Chairman of the Housing Authority, leads celebrations held at the Shek Kip Mei Estate to mark the 50th anniversary of Hong Kong's public housing programme.

The Chief Executive (second row, right) and other Asia-Pacific leaders at the 11th APEC Economic Leaders Meeting in Bangkok in October. *Left:* Mr Tung with President Hu Jintao at the APEC meeting.

The Chief Executive hosting the British Prime Minister,
Mr Tony Blair, at Government House in July *(top)*; meeting the
President of France, Mr Jacques Chirac, at the Elysee Palace
in Paris in November *(above centre)*; and officiating at the
launching of a Hong Kong Tourism Board promotion in London,
also in November *(above)*.

The Chief Secretary for Administration, Mr Donald Tsang, meeting the US Secretary of State, Mr Colin Powell, in Washington DC in September *(top)*; and speaking at a function in Seoul during a visit to the Republic of Korea in October *(left)*. The Secretary for Justice, Ms Elsie Leung, called on the Supreme Court of Canada during a visit to Ottawa in November *(above)*.

內地與香港關於建立更緊密經

Mainland and Hong Kon

C...r Econom...Partnership A...

The Financial Secretary and the Vice Minister of Commerce, Mr An Min, shake hands after signing the six Annexes to the Mainland and Hong Kong Closer Economic Partnership Arrangement in Hong Kong on September 29. *Right:* Mr Tang officiating at the opening of the Hong Kong Exchanges and Clearing Ltd's Representative Office in Beijing on November 17.

CHAPTER 1

Constitution and Administration

Six years after the reunification, the principles of 'one country, two systems', 'a high degree of autonomy' and 'Hong Kong people running Hong Kong' have been fully implemented. The Government is determined to ensure that this remains the case, and it remains committed to the full and faithful implementation of the Basic Law.

HONG KONG became a Special Administrative Region of the People's Republic of China (PRC) on July 1, 1997. The Basic Law of the Hong Kong Special Administrative Region (HKSAR) came into effect on the same day. The Basic Law prescribes the systems to be practised in the HKSAR.

Under the Basic Law, the HKSAR shall enjoy a high degree of autonomy except in those matters relating to defence and foreign affairs as well as other matters outside the limits of Hong Kong's autonomy. Under the Basic Law, the HKSAR shall exercise executive, legislative and independent judicial power, including that of final adjudication. The HKSAR's executive authorities and legislature shall be composed of permanent residents of Hong Kong. The HKSAR shall remain a free port, a separate customs territory and an international financial centre and may, on its own, using the name 'Hong Kong, China', maintain and develop relations and conclude and implement agreements with foreign states and regions and international organisations in the appropriate fields, including the economic, trade, financial and monetary, shipping, communications, tourism, cultural and sports fields.

Role of the Chief Executive

The Chief Executive is the head of the HKSAR. He heads the Government of the HKSAR. He is responsible for implementing the Basic Law, signing bills and budgets passed by the Legislative Council, promulgating laws, making decisions on government policies and issuing executive orders. He is assisted by the Executive Council in policy-making.

The System of Government

Executive Council

The Executive Council is an organ for assisting the Chief Executive in policy making. Under Article 56 of the Basic Law, except for the appointment, removal and disciplining of officials and the adoption of measures in emergencies, the Chief Executive shall consult the Executive Council before making important policy decisions, introducing bills into the Legislative Council, making subordinate legislation, or dissolving the Legislative Council. The Chief Executive in Council also determines appeals, petitions and objections under those ordinances which confer a statutory right of appeal. If the Chief Executive does not accept a majority opinion of the Executive Council, he shall put the specific reasons on record.

The Executive Council has 19 members. As provided for in Article 55 of the Basic Law, Members of the Executive Council are appointed by the Chief Executive from among the principal officials of the executive authorities, Members of the Legislative Council and public figures. They are Chinese citizens who are permanent residents of the HKSAR with no right of abode in any foreign country. With the implementation of the Accountability System for Principal Officials from July 1, 2002, the membership of the Executive Council now comprises 14 Principal Officials appointed under the Accountability System and five Non-Officials. Their appointment or removal is decided by the Chief Executive. The term of office of Members of the Executive Council shall not extend beyond the expiry of the term of office of the Chief Executive who appoints them.

The Executive Council normally meets once a week, and its proceedings are confidential, although many of its decisions are made public. The Chief Executive presides at its meetings. During the year, the Executive Council held a total of 48 meetings.

Legislative Council

Powers and Functions

As provided for in Article 73 of the Basic Law, the Legislative Council of the HKSAR exercises the following powers and functions:

1. To enact, amend or repeal laws in accordance with the provisions of the Basic Law and legal procedures;
2. To examine and approve budgets introduced by the Government;
3. To approve taxation and public expenditure;
4. To receive and debate the policy addresses of the Chief Executive;
5. To raise questions on the work of the Government;
6. To debate any issue concerning public interests;
7. To endorse the appointment and removal of the judges of the Court of Final Appeal and the Chief Judge of the High Court;
8. To receive and handle complaints from Hong Kong residents;
9. If a motion initiated jointly by one-fourth of all the Members of the Legislative Council charges the Chief Executive with serious breach of law or dereliction of duty and if he or she refuses to resign, the council may, after passing a motion for investigation, give a mandate to the Chief Justice of the Court of Final Appeal to form and chair an independent investigation committee. The committee shall be responsible for carrying out the investigation and reporting its findings to the council. If the committee considers the evidence sufficient to substantiate such charges, the council may pass a motion of impeachment by a two-thirds majority of all its members and report it to the CPG for decision; and

10. To summon, as required when exercising the above-mentioned powers and functions, persons concerned to testify or give evidence.

Composition

Under the Basic Law, the Legislative Council of the HKSAR is constituted by election. The election of the second term of the Legislative Council was held on September 10, 2000.

The 60 members of the council's second term comprise 24 members returned by geographical constituencies through direct elections, 30 members returned by functional constituencies representing different sectors of the community, and six members returned by an Election Committee comprising 800 elected representatives of the community. The President of the Legislative Council is elected by and from among members of the council.

The second term of office of the Legislative Council began on October 1, 2000, and in accordance with the Basic Law and the Legislative Council Ordinance, the term of office is four years (2000-2004).

Meetings of the Legislative Council

The Legislative Council normally meets on Wednesday afternoons in the Chamber of the Legislative Council Building to conduct business which includes the tabling of subsidiary legislation and other papers and reports for the council's consideration; asking of questions for replies by the Government; the introduction and consideration of bills and proposed resolutions; and debates on motions concerning matters of public interest.

All Legislative Council meetings are open to the public and are conducted in Cantonese or English with simultaneous interpretation provided. Putonghua may be used where requested by members, with simultaneous interpretation provided. The proceedings of the meetings are recorded verbatim in the Official Record of Proceedings of the Legislative Council.

During the 2002-03 legislative session (from October 2002 to September 2003), the Legislative Council held 36 meetings. Four of these were devoted to the Chief Executive's Question and Answer Sessions. The council passed a total of 34 bills and asked 615 questions and 1 006 supplementary questions. Altogether, 250 items of subsidiary legislation were tabled in the council for consideration through the negative vetting procedure. Of the items tabled, 212 were not amended, 24 were amended and two were repealed. The scrutiny of the remaining 12 items continued in the next session. The Administration moved 22 motions relating to subsidiary legislation through the positive vetting procedure and two motions under Article 73(7) of the Basic Law to endorse the appointment of judges of the Court of Final Appeal and the Chief Judge of the High Court. Members of the council moved two motions concerning the council's procedural matters, one motion to invoke the council's powers to order attendance of witnesses and production of documents under the Legislative Council (Powers and Privileges) Ordinance and 55 motion debates on issues concerning public interests. One adjournment debate was moved by a member to allow members to express their opinions on an issue concerning public interests, with a view to eliciting a reply from the Administration.

Finance Committee

The Finance Committee consists of all Members of the Legislative Council except the President. The Chairman and the Deputy Chairman of the committee are elected from among its members. The committee normally meets in public on Friday afternoons to scrutinise and approve public expenditure proposals put forward by the Government. Its work includes the scrutiny of the annual Budget presented by the Financial Secretary to the Legislative Council during the proceedings related to the Appropriation Bill, which sets out the Government's annual expenditure proposals for the following financial year. During the 2002-03 session, the committee held 18 meetings and examined a total of 70 financial proposals.

There are two subcommittees under the Finance Committee. They are the Establishment Subcommittee and the Public Works Subcommittee, both of which also conduct meetings in public. Their respective memberships are open to all members of the Finance Committee.

The Establishment Subcommittee examines and makes recommendations to the Finance Committee on the Government's proposals for the creation, redeployment and deletion of directorate posts, and for changes to the structure of grades and ranks in the Civil Service. During the 2002-03 session, the subcommittee held nine meetings and examined a total of 19 proposals put forward by the Administration.

The Public Works Subcommittee examines and makes recommendations to the Finance Committee on the Government's expenditure proposals under the Capital Works Reserve Fund for projects in the Public Works Programme and building projects carried out by or on behalf of subvented organisations. During the 2002-03 session, the subcommittee held 16 meetings and examined a total of 78 proposals put forward by the Administration.

Public Accounts Committee

The Public Accounts Committee considers reports of the Director of Audit on the accounts of the Government and the results of his value-for-money audits of government departments and other organisations that are within the purview of public audit. It may invite government officials and staff of public organisations to attend public hearings to give explanations, evidence or information, or any other persons to assist it in relation to such explanations, evidence or information. The seven members of the committee are appointed by the President of the Legislative Council in accordance with the election procedure determined by the council's House Committee.

During the session under review, the committee examined the Director of Audit's Report on the Accounts of the Government of the HKSAR for the year ended March 31, 2002, and the Director's two Reports on the Results of Value for Money Audits. The committee held 11 public hearings and 29 internal meetings during the period. The conclusions and recommendations of the committee are contained in its Report Nos. 39 and 40 tabled in the Legislative Council on February 19 and July 9, 2003, respectively.

Committee on Members' Interests

The Committee on Members' Interests considers matters pertaining to the declaration of interests and matters of ethics in relation to the conduct of Members of the Legislative Council. It is also empowered to investigate complaints regarding members' registration and declaration of interests, and make recommendations to the council relating to matters concerning members' interests. The committee examines arrangements for the compilation, maintenance and accessibility of the Register of Members' Interests. The committee comprises seven members who are appointed by the President of the Legislative Council in accordance with the election procedure determined by the House Committee. During the session under review, the committee held two meetings.

House Committee

The House Committee consists of all members except the President. The Chairman and the Deputy Chairman of the committee are elected by the members of the House Committee. The committee normally meets on Friday afternoons and is responsible for dealing with matters related to the work of the Legislative Council and preparing members for council meetings. It decides whether bills committees or subcommittees should be formed to scrutinise bills and subsidiary legislation. During the 2002-03 session, a total of 32 regular meetings of the House Committee were held.

The House Committee also holds special meetings to discuss issues of public concern. During the session under review, the committee held two special meetings to discuss with the Chief Secretary for Administration various issues of public concern.

Committee on Rules of Procedure

The Committee on Rules of Procedure is responsible for reviewing the Rules of Procedure of the Legislative Council and its committees, and proposing to the council such amendments or changes as are considered necessary. The committee consists of 12 members who are appointed by the President of the Legislative Council in accordance with the election procedure determined by the House Committee. During the session under review, the committee held a total of seven meetings.

Bills Committees

Any member, other than the President, may join a bills committee formed by the House Committee to consider the principles, general merits, and detailed provisions of a bill allocated to it for scrutiny. It may also propose amendments relevant to the bill. A bills committee usually tables a report in council after it has completed its task. It is dissolved on the passage of the bill concerned through the Legislative Council or when the House Committee so decides. During the 2002-03 session, the Legislative Council set up 30 bills committees to scrutinise bills introduced into the council, including the Betting Duty (Amendment) Bill 2003, Companies (Amendment) Bill 2002, Copyright (Amendment) Bill 2001, Landlord and Tenant (Consolidation) (Amendment) Bill 2001, National Security (Legislative Provisions) Bill, and Village Representative Elections Bill.

Subcommittees on Subsidiary Legislation

During the 2002-03 session, 26 subcommittees were formed by the House Committee to consider 44 items of subsidiary legislation tabled in council, and seven proposed resolutions presented by the Government to the council for its approval.

Panels

The Legislative Council has established 18 panels to monitor and examine the Government's policies and issues of public concern which relate to their respective policy areas. These panels also give views on major legislative or financial proposals before their introduction into the Legislative Council or the Finance Committee, and examine relevant policy matters referred to them.

Select Committees

The Legislative Council may appoint select committees to enable members to consider matters in depth. Select committees report to the council after they have completed consideration of such matters.

In response to public concern over the quality of public housing, the Legislative Council appointed a Select Committee on February 7, 2001 to inquire into the matter. The Select Committee submitted its first report to the council on January 22, 2003.

Redress System

The Legislative Council operates a redress system under which members of the public may seek assistance for redressing any grievance which resulted from implementation of government actions or policies and lodge complaints against government departments and other organisations. The redress system operates on a weekly roster with groups of six council members taking turns to receive and handle complaints and representations from the public. They also take turns to be on 'ward duty' during their duty week to meet individual complainants and to give guidance to staff in processing cases.

The Legislative Council Commission and Secretariat

The Legislative Council Commission is a statutory body independent of the Government. It is chaired by the President of the Legislative Council and consists of 12 other members. The commission's main function is to provide support and services for the Legislative Council through the Legislative Council Secretariat. It is empowered to employ staff of the Legislative Council Secretariat and oversee its work, determine the organisation and administration of support services and facilities, formulate and execute policies on their effective operation and expend funds in ways it sees fit to support these activities.

The Legislative Council Secretariat is headed by the Secretary General. Its mission is to provide efficient administrative, secretariat and research support for the council and its committees, enhance the community's understanding of the activities of the council and ensure an effective avenue for redress.

District Administration

The District Administration Scheme commenced in 1982 with the establishment of a District Board and a District Management Committee in each district. Through the scheme, the Government promotes public participation in district affairs and fosters among the people of Hong Kong a sense of belonging and mutual care. The scheme also helps to ensure that the Government is responsive to district needs and problems. Following the 1998 review of the structure and functions of district organisations, District Boards have been renamed, in English, as District Councils, to underline their important role in district administration.

The second District Council Election of the Hong Kong Special Administrative Region was held on November 23, 2003, returning 400 elected members. On January 1, 2004, the second term of the District Councils commenced. In addition to the 400 elected members, there are 27 *ex officio* members (i.e. Rural Committee chairmen in the New Territories) and 102 appointed members, making a total of 529 District Council members. The term of office of these council members is for four years starting from January 2004.

The main function of District Councils is to advise the Government on matters affecting the well-being of the people living and working in the districts as well as on the provision and use of public facilities and services within the districts. The Government also consults these bodies on a wide range of issues.

Since the establishment of District Councils in January 2000, their roles and functions have been enhanced progressively. The Government completed a comprehensive review of the District Councils in 2001 and implemented by the end of that year a package of recommendations to further enhance the roles and functions of District Councils. Funds for District Councils to implement community involvement and minor environmental improvement projects in the districts have been increased from $130 million in 1999-2000 to $205.6 million in 2003-04.

To enhance communication between District Councils and policy bureaux and departments, Policy Secretaries and Heads of Departments who deal with matters affecting people's livelihood will meet the councils regularly and these departments have assigned specific officers to provide 'one-stop' services for District Councils and to handle their complaints. Policy bureaux and departments are required to consult District Councils on policy initiatives and capital works projects affecting the well-being of the community and to reflect the views of District Councils to the approving authorities. The 18 District Councils were consulted on 385 territory-wide issues and 1 968 district issues in 2003.

To further enhance District Council members' participation in the planning and implementation of district minor works projects, the chairmanship of District Working Groups of the Rural Public Works and the Urban Minor Works Programmes has been devolved to District Council members with effect from January 1, 2003. The chairmanship of the two Steering Committees will also be devolved to District Council members in due course. The Government has also appointed more District Council members to advisory bodies, especially those connected with livelihood matters.

All the measures have helped to substantially enhance the role of District Councils as the Government's key advisers on district affairs and strengthen their ability to influence the provision, delivery and management of district services and facilities. This helps ensure that the Government remains accountable and responsive to the changing needs of the community.

Each District Council operates a meet-the-public scheme, under which residents can meet council members face to face to express their views on any district problems. The scheme has been well received by the public. It also provides District Councils a direct channel to collect public views on local matters and region-wide issues, which the councils can in turn reflect to the Government.

Each district has a District Management Committee, chaired by the District Officer, comprising the Chairman, Vice Chairman and committee chairmen of the District Council and representatives of departments providing essential services in the district.

The District Management Committee serves as a forum for inter-departmental consultation on district matters and coordinates the provision of public services and facilities to ensure that district needs are met promptly. The District Officer reports regularly the work of the District Management Committee to the District Council.

Area Committees were set up in 1972 to support the Keep Hong Kong Clean Campaign and the Fight Violent Crime Campaign. Nowadays, the functions of Area Committees are to encourage public participation in district affairs, to help organise community activities and government campaigns, and to advise on issues of a local nature.

Mutual Aid Committees are building-based resident organisations, established to improve the security, cleanliness and general management of multi-storey buildings. At year-end, there were 73 Area Committees and 3 121 Mutual Aid Committees. They provide an extensive network of communication between the Government and the people at the grassroots level.

Apart from Mutual Aid Committees, the Government also devotes time and effort to helping owners of private multi-storey buildings to form Owners' Corporations to facilitate effective management and timely maintenance of the buildings concerned. At year-end, 7 205 Owners' Corporations were registered with the Land Registry.

The Home Affairs Department has established four Building Management Resource Centres in Hong Kong, Kowloon and the New Territories to enhance its services in building management. These centres provide information, services and advice to building owners, residents, Owners' Corporations, Mutual Aid Committees and management bodies so as to assist them in improving the standards of management, safety and maintenance of their buildings. In 2003, the four centres handled a total of 36 332 visitors, 46 091 enquiries and 283 appointments for interviews with members of professional bodies.

Twenty Public Enquiry Service Centres are attached to the District Offices, providing a wide range of free services to the public. These services include answering general enquiries on government services; distributing government forms and information; administering oaths and declarations; and referring cases under the District Council members' meet-the-public scheme, the Free Legal Advice Scheme and the Rent Officer Scheme. The Public Enquiry Service Centres and the Central Telephone Enquiry Centre served a total of 2.45 million clients in 2003.

The Electoral System

Electoral System for the Legislative Council

Under the Basic Law, the Legislative Council of the HKSAR shall be constituted by elections, and the method for its formation is to be specified in the light of the actual situation in the HKSAR and in accordance with the principle of gradual and orderly progress. The Basic Law also provides that the ultimate aim is the election of all members of the Legislative Council by universal suffrage.

The composition of the first three terms of the Legislative Council as set out in the Basic Law is as follows:—

Membership	First term (1998-2000)	Second term (2000-2004)	Third term (2004-2008)
(a) elected by geographical constituencies through direct elections	20	24	30
(b) elected by functional constituencies	30	30	30
(c) elected by an election committee	10	6	—
	—	—	—
	60	60	60

The second term Legislative Council election was held successfully on September 10, 2000. A total of 155 validly nominated candidates contested the 60 Legislative Council seats. Over 1.33 million registered electors cast their votes on the polling day, representing a turnout rate of 43.6 per cent. The election was conducted fairly, openly and honestly under the supervision of the Electoral Affairs Commission.

The Basic Law provides that if there is a need to amend the method for the formation of the Legislative Council after 2007, such amendments must be made with the endorsement of a two-thirds majority of all the members of the Legislative Council and the consent of the Chief Executive, and shall be reported to the Standing Committee of the National People's Congress for the record.

(a) Geographical Constituency

Geographical constituency elections are held on the basis of universal suffrage. All eligible persons aged 18 or above have the right to be registered as electors and to vote in the elections. There are currently about three million registered electors.

For the second term Legislative Council, the HKSAR is divided into five geographical constituencies, each having four to six seats. The List Voting System operating under the Largest Remainder formula, which is a form of proportional representation voting system, is adopted. Under this system, candidates contest the election in the form of lists. Each list may consist of any number of candidates up to the number of seats in the relevant constituency. An elector is entitled to cast one vote for a list in the constituency in which he is registered. The seats for the constituency are distributed among the lists according to the number of votes obtained by the respective lists.

Any permanent resident of the HKSAR who is a Chinese citizen with no right of abode in any foreign country may stand for election in any geographical constituency, provided that he or she is a registered elector on the Final Register, has attained the age of 21, and has ordinarily resided in Hong Kong for the preceding three years.

(b) Functional Constituency

Each functional constituency represents an economic, social, or professional group which is substantial and important to the HKSAR. For the second term Legislative Council, these are (1) Heung Yee Kuk; (2) agriculture and fisheries; (3) insurance; (4) transport; (5) education; (6) legal; (7) accountancy; (8) medical; (9) health services; (10) engineering; (11) architectural, surveying and planning; (12) labour; (13) social

9

welfare; (14) real estate and construction; (15) tourism; (16) commercial (first); (17) commercial (second); (18) industrial (first); (19) industrial (second); (20) finance; (21) financial services; (22) sports, performing arts, culture and publication; (23) import and export; (24) textiles and garment; (25) wholesale and retail; (26) information technology; (27) catering; and (28) District Council. The labour functional constituency returns three Legislative Council members, while the other 27 functional constituencies return one member each.

Functional constituencies which represent professional groups have electorates based on membership of professions with well-established and recognised qualifications, including statutory qualifications. Each individual member has one vote. The electorates of functional constituencies representing economic or social groups are generally made up of corporate members of major organisations representative of the relevant sectors. Each corporate member appoints an authorised representative to cast the vote on its behalf in an election.

To become a candidate in the functional constituencies, one must satisfy the same age and residential requirements as in a geographical constituency election, be a registered elector on the Final Register, and also a registered elector of or have a substantial connection with the relevant functional constituency. To give due recognition to the significant contribution made by foreign nationals and the fact that Hong Kong is an international city and to meet the requirement of the relevant provision in the Basic Law, permanent residents of the HKSAR who are not of Chinese nationality or who have the right of abode in foreign countries may stand for election in 12 designated functional constituencies (i.e. functional constituencies No. 3, 6, 7, 10, 11, 14, 15, 16, 18, 20, 21, 23 mentioned above). Elections for functional constituencies (except functional constituencies Nos. 1 to 4) are determined by a simple majority voting system, i.e. the candidate who obtains the most votes will be elected. For functional constituencies Nos. 1 to 4, the preferential elimination voting system is used. Under this system, an elector is entitled to cast one vote. The vote is transferable among the candidates marked on a ballot paper if the elector marks his preferences for more than one candidate. A candidate who obtains an absolute majority of the votes will be elected. If no candidate obtains an absolute majority, the candidate with the least number of votes will be eliminated and that candidate's votes will be transferred to other candidates in accordance with the preferences marked on the ballot paper. The process will continue until one candidate obtains an absolute majority over other remaining candidates.

(c) Election Committee

The qualifications for candidature in the Legislative Council Election Committee election are the same as those for geographical constituency elections. The Election Committee is composed of members who are HKSAR permanent residents from four sectors: (1) industrial, commercial and financial; (2) the professions; (3) labour, social services and religious; and (4) members of the Legislative Council, Hong Kong deputies to the National People's Congress, representatives of Hong Kong members of the National Committee of the Chinese People's Political Consultative Conference, and representatives of district-based organisations. Each of these four sectors returns 200 members. Each sector is further divided into subsectors, each returning a specified number of representatives to the Election Committee by election. Members of the Legislative Council and Hong Kong deputies to the National People's Congress are *ex officio* members of the Election Committee, and the religious subsector returns its representatives to the Election Committee by nomination from designated religious bodies.

The method for returning six members to the second term Legislative Council by the Election Committee is the block vote system — each member of the Election Committee is required to cast six votes and the result is determined by a simple majority. After the end of the second term Legislative Council, the Election Committee will no longer be responsible for returning members of the Legislative Council. The six seats thus released will be filled by members returned from geographical constituencies.

Elections for the third term Legislative Council will be held in 2004. The Legislative Council (Amendment) Ordinance 2003, enacted in July 2003, provides the legal basis for the detailed arrangements of the elections. The third term Legislative Council will have a total of 60 members, with 30 members returned by geographical constituencies, and another 30 by functional constituencies.

Electoral System for the Chief Executive

Under the Basic Law, the Chief Executive is selected by election or through consultations held locally, and appointed by the CPG. The method for selecting the Chief Executive shall be specified in the light of the actual situation in the HKSAR and in accordance with the principle of gradual and orderly progress. The Basic Law also provides that if there is a need to amend the method for selecting the Chief Executives for the terms subsequent to the year 2007, such amendments must be made with the endorsement of a two-thirds majority of all the members of the Legislative Council and the consent of the Chief Executive, and shall be reported to the Standing Committee of the National People's Congress for approval. The ultimate aim is the selection of the Chief Executive by universal suffrage upon nomination by a broadly representative nominating committee in accordance with democratic procedures. Annex I to the Basic Law lays down the basic framework as to how the Chief Executive shall be selected through local election. It provides, *inter alia*, that the Chief Executive shall be elected by a broadly representative Election Committee through secret ballot on a one-person-one-vote basis.

In accordance with the Basic Law, the Election Committee responsible for electing the second term Chief Executive in 2002 is one and the same as the Election Committee that returned six members to the second term Legislative Council in 2000. *(For the composition of the Election Committee, see the relevant section under Electoral System for the Legislative Council.)* Since only one candidate, Mr Tung Chee Hwa, was validly nominated at the close of nominations, he was therefore declared elected at the 2002 Chief Executive Election by the Returning Officer in accordance with the Chief Executive Election Ordinance, on February 28, 2002. On March 4, the CPG formally announced, in accordance with the Basic Law, the appointment of Mr Tung Chee Hwa as the Chief Executive for a second term of five years.

Electoral System for the District Councils

Eighteen District Councils (DCs) are established in the HKSAR to advise the Government on district affairs and to promote recreational and cultural activities, and environmental improvements within the districts. A District Council is composed of elected members, appointed members, and, in the case of District Councils in rural areas, the chairmen of Rural Committees as *ex officio* members. The simple majority voting system is adopted for DC elections. For the first term DCs, the HKSAR was

11

divided into 390 constituencies, each represented by one elected member. Having regard to the significant increase in population in certain districts, 10 elected seats were added for the second term DCs, thus making a total of 400 seats. The election for the second term DCs was held on November 23, 2003. Over 1.06 million registered electors cast their votes on the polling day, representing a turnout rate of 44.10 per cent. The second term DCs began their four-year term on January 1, 2004.

Electoral Affairs Commission

The Electoral Affairs Commission, an independent statutory body, is responsible for ensuring that elections in the HKSAR are conducted openly, honestly and fairly. It comprises three politically neutral persons appointed by the Chief Executive and is headed by a High Court judge. The commission is responsible for making recommendations to the Chief Executive on the delineation of geographical constituencies and District Council constituencies, making regulations on practical arrangements for the Chief Executive election, the Legislative Council election, the District Council election and rural elections, and handling complaints relating to these elections. The Registration and Electoral Office, a government department headed by the Chief Electoral Officer, works under the commission's direction and carries out its decisions.

Working Relationship of the HKSARG with the MFA Office

Article 13 of the Basic Law of the HKSAR provides that:

— The CPG shall be responsible for the foreign affairs relating to the HKSAR.

— The Ministry of Foreign Affairs of the PRC shall establish an office in Hong Kong to deal with foreign affairs.

The Office of the Commissioner of the Ministry of Foreign Affairs of the PRC in the HKSAR (MFA Office) was established by the CPG to deal with foreign affairs relating to the HKSAR. Since July 1, 1997, the HKSAR Government has established effective communication channels with the MFA Office in handling the external affairs of the HKSAR, working in strict accordance with the Basic Law. The HKSAR Government liaises closely with the MFA Office in the following areas:

(*a*) Participation in international organisations and conferences — where necessary, the approval of the CPG will be sought in accordance with the Basic Law. For instance, the CPG's approval is required if the HKSAR wishes to participate in an international organisation or conference limited to states (BL 152);

(*b*) negotiation and conclusion of international agreements with foreign states and regions — where necessary, the CPG's authorisation will be obtained in accordance with the relevant provisions of the Basic Law. For example, the CPG's specific authorisation is required for the negotiation and conclusion of Air Services Agreements with foreign states (BL 133); and

(*c*) matters relating to the establishment of consular missions in the HKSAR — the establishment of foreign consular and other official or semi-official missions is a matter for the MFA Office (BL 157). The HKSAR Government is responsible for the day-to-day management of the consular corps, such as the issue of consular identity cards, actual provision of privileges and immunities and ensuring the security of consular premises.

HKSAR's External Affairs

The HKSAR continues to play an active role in the international arena and maintains close contact with its international partners.

Since July 1, 1997, the HKSAR Government has, on its own, concluded 10 international agreements with foreign states and regions on matters such as customs cooperation, cooperation in information technology and avoidance of double taxation in accordance with Article 151 of the Basic Law. It has also obtained the CPG's authorisation to conclude 73 bilateral agreements with foreign states in accordance with the relevant provisions of the Basic Law, comprising 34 on air services, 11 on visa abolition, three on readmission of persons, 23 on reciprocal juridical assistance, one on investment promotion and protection, and one on avoidance of double taxation. More than 200 multilateral conventions are applicable to the HKSAR, about 75 of which do not apply to the Mainland.

In 2003, representatives of the HKSAR Government participated as members of delegations of the PRC about 80 times in international conferences limited to states, including those organised by the International Telecommunication Union, World Intellectual Property Organisation, International Monetary Fund, Universal Postal Union and International Labour Organisation. Representatives of the HKSAR Government, using the name 'Hong Kong, China', also participated more than 560 times in inter-governmental conferences not limited to states, including those organised by the Asia-Pacific Economic Cooperation, Pacific Economic Cooperation Council, World Trade Organisation, World Customs Organisation and World Meteorological Organisation. Active participation in international activities has enabled the HKSAR to maintain its status as an international financial, trade, civil aviation and shipping centre.

In 2003, the HKSAR played host to a number of prominent events, including the BusinessWeek CEO Conference, the Conference on International Cooperation for Tourism Development under a New Paradigm and the ICAC-Interpol Conference.

At year-end, a total of 114 foreign states maintained an official or semi-official presence in the HKSAR, including 56 consulates general, 53 honorary consuls and five semi-official (mostly trade) missions. In addition, international organisations — such as the Bank for International Settlements, the European Union, the United Nations High Commissioner for Refugees, the International Monetary Fund, the International Finance Corporation and the World Bank — have set up offices in the HKSAR.

Working Relationship with the Mainland Authorities

Since reunification, the HKSAR Government has made significant progress in developing and maintaining a cordial working relationship with the CPG and other Mainland authorities. Through a wide range of exchanges, including visits, meetings, seminars and training programmes, various bureaux and departments of the HKSAR Government have enhanced mutual understanding with their Mainland counterparts. Some have also made arrangements to underline the commitment of both sides to cooperate in such areas as postal services, marine conservation and the fight against intellectual property piracy.

The Hong Kong and Macao Affairs Office (HKMAO) of the State Council plays the role of a facilitator and provides assistance to the HKSAR Government in developing official contacts with Mainland authorities. Liaison with the HKMAO is

13

maintained on arrangements of visits by HKSAR Government officials and on other matters of mutual concern.

Article 22 of the Basic Law provides that no department of the CPG and no province, autonomous region, or municipality may interfere in the affairs which the HKSAR administers on its own in accordance with the Basic Law. The HKMAO continues to play the role of a 'gate-keeper' to ensure that the Mainland authorities at all levels conduct business with the HKSAR in line with this principle.

As the closest Mainland province, Guangdong has probably the most extensive network of communication with the HKSAR. For 22 years, the Cross-boundary Liaison System has provided an effective mechanism for Hong Kong and Guangdong to discuss and resolve practical issues of mutual concern, including the fight against cross-boundary crime and the regulation of the Shenzhen River. Cooperation with Guangdong was further strengthened with the establishment of the Hong Kong/Guangdong Cooperation Joint Conference (Joint Conference) in March 1998 by the HKSAR Government and the Guangdong Provincial Government in conjunction with the HKMAO. It provides a high-level forum to explore and coordinate major initiatives in cooperation between Hong Kong and Guangdong. On August 5, the Joint Conference held its Sixth Plenary meeting and announced a new cooperation framework and a structured long-term cooperation agenda. Under the new framework, the Plenary is to be chaired by the Chief Executive of the HKSAR and the Governor of Guangdong, and the implementation of cooperation initiatives to be spearheaded by the Chief Secretary for Administration and the Executive Vice-Governor of Guangdong. Both sides will work towards a common objective to turn the Pearl River Delta region into one of the world's most vibrant economic hubs in the next two decades. To achieve this objective, 15 expert groups have been set up to take forward various cooperation initiatives which cover such matters as the implementation of the Mainland/HKSAR Closer Economic Partnership Arrangement (CEPA), control point operation, infrastructure, tourism, innovation and technology, education, intellectual property rights and environmental protection. Alongside the 15 expert groups, there are the Hong Kong Guangdong Strategic Development Research Group (Research Group) and the Greater Pearl River Delta Business Council (Business Council). The Research Group undertakes to conduct research into subjects which have a significant bearing on Hong Kong/Guangdong cooperation while the Business Council is set up to facilitate discussion and exchanges between Hong Kong and Guangdong enterprise, trade and business associations.

Apart from the Joint Conference, the HKSAR Government and the CPG set up the Mainland/HKSAR Conference on the Coordination of Major Infrastructure Projects in January 2002 (Coordination Conference). The Coordination Conference is co-chaired by the Chief Secretary for Administration and the Vice-Chairman of the National Development and Reform Commission to enhance coordination and cooperation between the Mainland and the HKSAR in transport and major infrastructure projects. It has held four meetings so far and has embarked on studies on the Guangzhou-Shenzhen-Hong Kong Express Rail Link, logistics cooperation and the Hong Kong-Zhuhai-Macao Bridge. *(See Chapter 13: Transport for more details of these projects)*

In October, the HKSAR Government and the Shanghai Municipal Government established the Hong Kong/Shanghai Economic and Trade Cooperation Conference to foster closer economic and trade ties between the two places, particularly to leverage on opportunities brought about by CEPA. This newly established forum, chaired by the Chief Executive of the HKSAR and the Mayor of Shanghai, held its first meeting on October 27. The two sides exchanged views on eight areas of cooperation and would continue to liaise closely to follow up on implementation of the cooperation initiatives.

Office of the HKSAR Government in Beijing

The Beijing Office was established in March 1999 in accordance with Article 22 of the Basic Law. Its main role is to further enhance liaison and communication between the HKSAR Government and the CPG and other Mainland authorities.

Through its liaison work, the Beijing Office provides an accurate and up-to-date picture of the HKSAR to the CPG, other Mainland authorities, non-governmental bodies and Mainland residents. It keeps the relevant bureaux and departments of the HKSAR Government informed about the latest developments in the Mainland. This enables the HKSAR Government to have a better understanding of the policies and practices in the Mainland and to evaluate their possible implications for Hong Kong. Acting on instructions of the bureaux and departments of the HKSAR Government, the Beijing Office takes necessary action with the Mainland authorities on specific issues. The Beijing Office also provides logistical support to visiting delegations of the HKSAR Government. The office handles enquiries, and also requests for assistance concerning Hong Kong residents in the Mainland. In 2003, the office handled a total of 609 trade, economic and general enquiries and requests for assistance.

The Beijing Office regularly organises activities to promote Hong Kong in the Mainland with a view to enhancing the Mainland's understanding of Hong Kong's systems and latest developments, strengthening trade and economic links, and facilitating exchanges between Hong Kong and the Mainland. In 2003, the Beijing Office organised two large-scale promotional events in Fujian and Zhejiang, to project Hong Kong's image and assist its business and professional sectors in exploring opportunities in the Mainland market.

During the outbreak of SARS, the Beijing Office collected and disseminated, to Hong Kong and to relevant contacts in the Mainland, useful information affecting Hong Kong residents living or doing business in the Mainland, and assisted in the post-SARS economic relaunching of Hong Kong in the Mainland. Major efforts included promotional campaigns in Beijing, Fujian and Zhejiang, as well as nation-wide publicity drives through the mass media.

With the support of the China National Radio, the Beijing Office continued to broadcast a weekly radio programme to keep the residents in the southern part of the Mainland abreast of the latest situation in Hong Kong. The programme, in Cantonese, is estimated to have reached an audience of at least 1.5 million in that area.

In addition, the Beijing Office handles immigration matters. It processes applications for entry to Hong Kong and conducts negotiations on visa-free access with foreign diplomatic missions in Beijing. The office also provides practical assistance to Hong Kong residents in distress in the Mainland, and on request handles cases involving the detention of Hong Kong residents in the Mainland. During the year, the office handled 219 such cases.

Advisory and Statutory Bodies

The network of advisory and statutory bodies is a distinctive feature of the system of government. It seeks to obtain, through consultation with interested groups and individuals in the community, the best possible advice on which to base decisions or to perform statutory functions.

Advisory bodies give advice to the Government through a Principal Official or a Head of Department. A few advisory bodies tender their advice directly to the Chief Executive. Their areas of activities are wide-ranging. Some of the advisory bodies, such as the Telecommunications Standards Advisory Committee, deal with the interests of a particular industry. Others advise on a particular area of government policy, such as the Transport Advisory Committee. Some advisory bodies, such as the District Fight Crime Committees and Area Committees, deal essentially with district affairs. Statutory bodies perform their functions according to the relevant legislation. Some of them, such as the Hospital Authority, perform executive functions.

Government officials and members of the public are represented in these bodies. Over 5 000 members of the public are serving on about 500 bodies. These people are appointed in view of their specialist knowledge or expertise, their record or interest in contributing to community service, and the specific needs of the concerned bodies. Many of them are also nominees or representatives from organisations in different sectors.

The Government oversees the operation of the advisory and statutory bodies to ensure that they meet the needs of the community. A reasonable turnover of membership is generally maintained to keep up the inflow of new ideas. The Government will continue to enhance participation of various sectors in the work of advisory and statutory bodies as well as promote the public's understanding of their work through a number of transparency measures.

Structure of the Administration

The Chief Executive is the head of the Government of the HKSAR. The Chief Secretary for Administration, the Financial Secretary or the Secretary for Justice are to deputise for the Chief Executive during his temporary absence.

There are currently 11 bureaux, each headed by a Director of Bureau, which collectively form the Government Secretariat. There are 64 departments and agencies whose heads are responsible to the Directors of Bureaux for the direction of their departments and the efficient implementation of approved policies. The exceptions are the Audit Commission, the independence of which is safeguarded by having the Director's report submitted directly to the Legislative Council; and the Independent Commission Against Corruption and the Office of The Ombudsman, whose independence is safeguarded by having the Commissioner's and The Ombudsman's reports submitted directly to the Chief Executive.

Following the implementation of the Accountability System for Principal Officials on July 1, 2002, the Chief Secretary for Administration, the Financial Secretary, the Secretary for Justice and the 11 Directors of Bureaux are no longer civil servants. They are directly responsible to the Chief Executive and accountable to him for matters falling within their respective portfolios as assigned to them by the Chief Executive. They are appointed to the Executive Council. Together with five non-official members of the Executive Council, they assist the Chief Executive in policy-making.

The Government has conducted a review of the Accountability System for Principal Officials one year after its implementation. The review concluded that, in overall terms, the implementation of the Accountability System is an important step forward in constitutional development in Hong Kong and a step in the right direction. However, the Government recognises that its first year of operation was not entirely smooth. The system will take time to evolve and develop.

Role of the Chief Secretary for Administration

The Chief Secretary for Administration is the leading Principal Official of the HKSAR Government. He is the most senior among the three Secretaries of Departments available to deputise for the Chief Executive.

The Chief Secretary for Administration assists the Chief Executive in supervising the policy bureaux as directed by him and plays a key role in ensuring harmonisation in policy formulation and implementation. This is particularly important in areas which cut across policy bureaux.

The Chief Secretary for Administration also covers specific priority areas of the Chief Executive's policy agenda, and is responsible for forging a closer and more effective working relationship with the Legislative Council and for drawing up the Government's legislative programme. The Chief Secretary for Administration exercises statutory functions vested in him by law, such as those concerning certain public bodies and the handling of appeals.

Role of the Financial Secretary

The Financial Secretary reports directly to the Chief Executive. Working closely with the relevant Directors of Bureaux, he oversees policy formulation and implementation in financial, monetary, economic, trade and employment matters. He also chairs several important committees, including the Exchange Fund Advisory Committee and the Banking Advisory Committee.

The Financial Secretary is responsible under the Public Finance Ordinance for laying before the Legislative Council each year the Government's estimates of revenue and expenditure. In his annual budget speech, he outlines the Government's budgetary proposals and moves the Appropriation Bill, which gives legal effect to the annual expenditure proposals contained in the Budget.

Central Policy Unit

The Central Policy Unit provides advice on policy issues to meet the special requirements of the Chief Executive, the Chief Secretary for Administration and the Financial Secretary, and reports direct to them.

The unit consults widely with business and professional circles, political organisations and concern groups and the academic community. It undertakes in-depth examination of complex policy issues, analyses options, takes soundings of community feedback and recommends solutions for the Government's internal consideration. The unit is responsible for coordinating the annual Policy Address exercise. It also provides secretariat support for the Commission on Strategic Development, which is chaired by the Chief Executive.

Efficiency Unit

The Efficiency Unit reports directly to the Chief Secretary for Administration and is tasked with pursuing the Government's commitment to transforming the management and delivery of public services so that the community's needs are met in the most effective and efficient manner. The unit works in partnership with client bureaux and departments across the Government to identify opportunities for performance enhancement, design practical solutions, develop compelling business cases, and secure effective implementation.

The unit has played a major role in many important reform initiatives: the creation of trading funds; customer service improvements, including the development of the performance pledge programme; and the design and implementation of an integrated call centre. Other major aspects of the unit's work include greater involvement of the private sector in delivering public services, for example, through outsourcing and public private partnerships; and the undertaking of major re-engineering projects particularly where this is required to make real gains from the adoption of new technology and best management practice. All the work of the unit is focused on enhancing the quality of public services at the same time as seeking greater efficiency in the use of limited public resources.

Sustainable Development Unit

The Sustainable Development Unit, established under the Chief Secretary for Administration's Office, promotes sustainable development in both the Government and the community, and provides secretariat support to the Council for Sustainable Development.

The council was appointed by the Chief Executive in March 2003 to promote sustainable development in Hong Kong.

One of the unit's major tasks is to implement a sustainability assessment system within the Government to facilitate the integration of sustainability considerations in the decision-making process. All bureaux and departments are required to conduct sustainability assessments of their major initiatives and programmes, and explain the sustainability implications in their submissions to the Executive Council.

The unit also provides secretariat support to the Sustainable Development Fund.

The Civil Service

The Civil Service employs about 4.7 per cent of Hong Kong's labour force. It provides staff for all government departments and other units of the Administration. At December 31, the total strength of the Civil Service was 164 700 (excluding about 1 500 ICAC and judicial officers).

Overall policy responsibility for the management of the Civil Service lies with the Civil Service Bureau of the Government Secretariat. It includes policies on matters such as appointments, pay and conditions of service, staff management, manpower planning, training and discipline. The bureau is also the focal point for consultation with major staff associations and its General Grades Office manages the 26 800 executive, clerical and secretarial staff. Management of the Civil Service is governed mainly by three important instruments: the Public Service (Administration) Order, the Public Service (Disciplinary) Regulation, and the Civil Service Regulation, all made with the authority of the Chief Executive.

The Public Service Commission is an independent statutory body set up in 1950 under the Public Service Commission Ordinance to advise the Chief Executive on appointment, promotion and disciplinary matters in the Civil Service. The Government is also advised on matters relating to pay and conditions of service by four independent bodies: the Standing Committee on Directorate Salaries and Conditions of Service (directorate officers excluding judicial officers and the disciplined services); the Standing Committee on Judicial Salaries and Conditions of Service (the judicial officers); the Standing Committee on Disciplined Services Salaries and Conditions of Service (the disciplined services); and the Standing Commission on Civil Service Salaries and Conditions of Service (all other civil servants).

In accordance with the Basic Law, Principal Officials must be Chinese citizens who are permanent residents of the HKSAR with no right of abode in any foreign country and have ordinarily resided in Hong Kong for a continuous period of not less than 15 years. It is also a Basic Law requirement that new recruits to the Civil Service on or after July 1, 1997 should normally be permanent residents of the HKSAR, save for certain exceptions, for example to fill professional and technical posts.

Subject to the above policy, appointment to the Civil Service is based on open and fair competition which aims to recruit the 'best person for the job'. Promotion is performance-based and is not a reward for long service. As the largest employer in Hong Kong, the Government takes the lead in employing people with a disability to help them integrate into the community and ensure that they are given equal opportunity in recruitment to the Civil Service.

The Government monitors closely the turnover in the Civil Service for manpower planning purposes. Overall wastage in the Civil Service in 2002-03 was 3.6 per cent. Following the introduction of the Voluntary Departure Scheme (VDS) and the first Voluntary Retirement Scheme (VRS) in March and July 2000 respectively, the wastage rate had risen to 5.7 per cent in 2001-02. With the departure of participants in the above two schemes, the wastage rate began to level out at 3.6 per cent in 2002-03. The VDS was implemented to enable civil servants in designated grades in the Housing Department to leave the service voluntarily to facilitate a phased transfer of Housing Authority estate management and maintenance services to the private sector. The first VRS was launched to allow eligible civil servants in designated grades with identified or anticipated surplus staff to retire from the service voluntarily with retirement benefits and compensation. Given the importance of continuity at the management level, the Government has a well-established staff planning mechanism to review succession planning of senior staff and to identify and groom officers with potential for advancement to senior management, in order to develop a pool of talent for senior positions.

The Government values regular communication and consultation with staff. There are four consultative councils at the central level: Senior Civil Service Council, Model Scale 1 Staff Consultative Council, Disciplined Services Consultative Council and Police Force Council. More than 80 consultative committees operate at the departmental level. A Civil Service Newsletter is published regularly to provide an added link with serving and retired civil servants.

Staff commitment and contributions are recognised in various forms including appreciation letters, commendations and honours or awards. Long Service Travel Awards, Long and Meritorious Service Awards and retirement souvenirs are given to staff having long and meritorious service. An Outstanding Customer Service Award Scheme was launched in 2003 to recognise the efforts and achievement of bureaux and departments and their staff in providing quality customer service to the public and to further promote a customer-focused culture in the Civil Service.

Civil Service Reform

In March 1999, the Government released a Consultation Document on Civil Service Reform. The main objective was to put forward proposals to modernise the administration of the Civil Service so as to make it more flexible and prepare staff to face the changes and increasingly demanding challenges in the years ahead and meet the demands of society. As a result of feedback received during the consultation, the Government has drawn up more detailed proposals in the various policy areas for detailed discussion with the Staff Sides and department/grade management through working groups that have staff representatives.

Following are the highlights of reform initiatives in four main areas:

1. Entry and Exit

On June 1, 2000, the Government introduced a new entry system and terms of appointment for new recruits to the Civil Service to increase the flexibility of its appointment system.

In June 2003, the Government implemented a Civil Service Provident Fund Scheme to replace the pension schemes as the retirement benefits system for officers who are offered appointments to the Civil Service on or after June 1, 2000 under the new entry terms and when they subsequently progress onto permanent terms of appointment.

In 2003, the Government set the target to reduce the civil service establishment to around 160 000 by 2006-07. To help achieve this target, a general recruitment freeze was imposed with effect from April 1, 2003.

In July 2000, the Administration introduced a Voluntary Retirement Scheme (VRS) to enable staff of 59 designated grades with an identified or anticipated staff surplus to retire from the service voluntarily with compensation and pension payments. About 9 800 applications were approved. In March 2003, the Administration introduced the second VRS to enable identified or potential surplus staff in specified ranks/streams of 229 designated grades to leave the service voluntarily so as to reduce the civil service establishment and bring about long-term savings to the Government. About 5 300 applications were approved.

The Administration has since September 2000 introduced a Management-Initiated Retirement Scheme to provide for the retirement of directorate civil servants on permanent and pensionable terms to facilitate improvement in the government organisation.

2. Pay

The current pay policy for the Civil Service is to offer sufficient remuneration to attract, retain, and motivate staff of a suitable calibre to provide the public with an effective and efficient service. Such remuneration should be regarded as fair by both civil servants and the public they serve. Within these parameters, broad comparability with the private sector is an important factor in setting civil service pay.

As part of ongoing efforts to modernise the management of the Civil Service and to address public comments on the existing civil service pay adjustment mechanism, the Government has embarked on an exercise to develop an improved pay adjustment mechanism for long-term adoption in the service. The objective of the exercise is to put in place an improved mechanism which reflects the civil service pay policy and upholds the principle of maintaining broad comparability between civil service pay and private sector pay. The exercise includes the conduct of a pay level survey, improvement to the methodology for the conduct of annual pay trend surveys and the development of an effective means for implementing both upward and downward pay adjustments.

In April 2003, the Civil Service Bureau established a steering committee and a consultative group to provide professional input and staff views to the exercise. In November, the Civil Service Bureau issued a progress report setting out the policy considerations as well as the timetable for taking forward the exercise. The aim is to complete the whole exercise, including the conduct of a pay level survey, in the second quarter of 2005.

3. Conduct and Discipline

In April 2000, the Government introduced measures to streamline the disciplinary procedures and set up an independent Secretariat on Civil Service Discipline to handle disciplinary cases in a prompt, impartial and equitable manner.

4. Training and Development

Training and development programmes are used extensively to support the implementation of the reform initiatives. The Government acquired funding of $50 million to introduce a Three-year Training and Development Programme from 2001-02 to 2003-04. The programme focuses on three main themes, namely, training for staff affected by the Voluntary Retirement exercise, training to equip staff with the requisite skills and knowledge to implement the Civil Service Reform initiatives and promoting a continuous learning culture in the Civil Service.

Since 2001-02, more than 2 600 seminars and courses on various subjects have been offered to about 72 000 staff. Most of them are junior staff. In support of the second VRS launched in March 2003, the Three-year Training and Development Programme will be extended to 2004-05 to provide training to staff affected by the scheme, thereby assisting them in adapting to the new working environment.

Civil Service Training and Development

The Government is committed to providing civil servants with training programmes that will equip them with the skills and knowledge necessary for providing quality service to the public. The Civil Service Training and Development Institute (CSTDI) is the Government's central training and development agency. The institute provides general training and advisory services to bureaux and departments, and it also promotes a culture of continuous learning in the Civil Service.

To encourage departments and grades to think and plan ahead so that their corporate goals can be more effectively supported by training and development activities, the institute has for some years been promoting the formulation of departmental training and development plans. By 2003, all departments and grades had drawn up their own detailed plans. In the coming years, the institute will continue

21

to assist departments and grades in deriving full benefits from the annually rolled forward training and development planning process.

The CSTDI continued to accord priority to leadership development in 2003. A 'Directorate Leadership Scheme' to strengthen the leadership capacity of senior officers and a 'Leadership In Action' Programme designed to groom senior officers with high potential for further career development were launched. Also, a series of seminars was held jointly with three private sector organisations to facilitate the exchange of ideas and best practices in corporate leadership. A forum on 'Continuous Improvement Through People' was held for about 300 professional officers from different bureaux and departments to facilitate the sharing of experience in implementing continuous improvement and service enhancement initiatives.

Building on the cyber-learning infrastructure put in place since 2000, the institute has made sustained efforts to enrich the content and to upgrade the functions of the Government's e-learning portal, the Cyber Learning Centre Plus (CLC Plus). The portal provides a one-stop access to a wide spectrum of training and development information and learning resources for staff at different levels. The number of registered users grew to over 35 000 in 2003.

Continuous emphasis has been placed on national studies programmes, including staff exchange programmes with Mainland institutions. Besides the programmes offered by the Tsinghua University and the National School of Administration, the Peking University has been commissioned to organise programmes on national affairs for senior civil servants, starting from 2004. During the year, the CSTDI also arranged a series of seminars to help civil servants better understand the opportunities and challenges that the Closer Economic Partnership Arrangement with the Mainland provides for Hong Kong. Updated and more comprehensive job-related reference materials were added to the CLC Plus to help keep civil servants abreast of latest developments in the Greater Pearl River Delta region. A variety of courses and promotional activities were organised on a continuing basis to enhance civil servants' knowledge of the Basic Law.

During the year, the Administration completed a review of the CSTDI's operations with a view to rationalising service delivery. Starting from April 2004, the institute will be subsumed under the Civil Service Bureau, in the interests of achieving greater efficiency and economy in operation. The institute will continue to focus on its core business of delivering cost-effective training and development and consulting services to its clients.

Official Languages

Chinese and English are the official languages of Hong Kong. It is the Government's policy to develop and maintain a Civil Service that is proficient in both written Chinese and English and conversant in Cantonese, Putonghua and spoken English. While reports and publications of public interest issued by the Government are available in both languages, correspondence with the public is in the language appropriate to the recipients. The Official Languages Division of the Civil Service Bureau implements the Government's language policy in the Civil Service. It provides language-related services to all government bureaux and departments. In addition to providing translation and interpretation services, its Official Languages Officers also draft speeches and edit important documents in Chinese for senior officers.

Simultaneous interpretation services are provided by its Simultaneous Interpreters at official meetings when necessary.

The division also provides research and support services. It has been promoting the wider use of Chinese in the Civil Service through a wide range of activities including seminars and lectures on Chinese language and culture. It runs a Helpdesk which answers telephone enquiries from civil servants on the use of official languages. The division develops writing aids and reference materials, such as guidebooks on official Chinese writing and English-Chinese glossaries of terms commonly used in government departments. In order to arouse the interest of civil servants in Chinese and English, it publishes a quarterly newsletter entitled *Word Power*. These publications and reference materials can be accessed at the Civil Service Bureau's home page.

Government Records Service

The Government Records Service (GRS) manages government records and provides a full range of records and archival management services.

The GRS develops and oversees the implementation of the government records management system. It operates two Records Centres as central repositories for storage of inactive government records. In light of the growing demand for electronic records management, a new office was established in October 2003 in support of new government initiatives and practices in this area.

The GRS also contributes to the protection of Hong Kong's archival heritage through proper preservation and conservation of government archival holdings. Its microfilm centre, being an ISO 9001:2000 certified unit, provides microfilm services for government agencies to an international standard.

In maintaining one of the largest local sources of information for historical and other studies relating to Hong Kong, the GRS appraises and acquires records of enduring value from government and private sources and makes them available for public access through its Central Preservation Library for Government Publications and online services. A wealth of archival records is kept, including government publications, reports, newspapers, printed materials and monographs on Hong Kong. Members of the public may visit the purpose-built Hong Kong Public Records Building in Kwun Tong or use the online service at *http://www.grs.gov.hk*.

Office of The Ombudsman

The Office of The Ombudsman is an independent statutory authority, set up in 1989 under The Ombudsman Ordinance, to provide an avenue for reports and investigation of grievances arising from administrative acts or omissions, decisions and recommendations.

Since December 2001, the Office has been established as a corporation sole, thus severing linkage with the Administration. It has set up its administrative systems and recruits contract staff on its own remuneration packages. For longer-term economy, it is now accommodated at its purchased permanent office in Sheung Wan.

Directly responsible to the Chief Executive, The Ombudsman serves as the community's monitor on government departments and public bodies specified in the schedule to the ordinance. The aim is to ensure that:

- bureaucratic constraints do not interfere with administrative fairness;

- public authorities are readily accessible to the public;
- abuse of power is prevented;
- wrongs are righted;
- facts are pointed out when public officers are unjustly accused;
- human rights are protected; and
- the public sector continues to improve quality, transparency and efficiency.

Two exceptions to the monitoring system are the Hong Kong Police Force and the Independent Commission Against Corruption, both of which have their own separate body for dealing with public complaints.

The 17 major public organisations in the schedule are: the Airport Authority, Employees Retraining Board, Equal Opportunities Commission, Hong Kong Arts Development Council, Hong Kong Examinations and Assessment Authority, Hong Kong Housing Authority, Hong Kong Housing Society, Hong Kong Monetary Authority, Hong Kong Sports Development Board, Hospital Authority, Kowloon-Canton Railway Corporation, Legislative Council Secretariat, Mandatory Provident Fund Schemes Authority, Office of the Privacy Commissioner for Personal Data, Securities and Futures Commission, Urban Renewal Authority and Vocational Training Council.

Apart from investigating complaints, The Ombudsman may initiate direct investigations of her own volition into matters of public interest and widespread concern, and publish the reports. This proactive and preventive approach aims at addressing problems affecting a broad spectrum of the community. The direct investigations are particularly useful in redressing administrative flaws of a systemic nature and addressing fundamental problems or underlying causes for complaint.

Since 1994, when The Ombudsman was empowered to undertake direct investigations, 45 such investigations have been completed — six of them in 2003. These six concerned the following subjects:

* the monitoring of charitable fund-raising activities by the Social Welfare Department and the Television and Entertainment Licensing Authority;
* the prevention of abuse of the Comprehensive Social Security Assistance Scheme operated by the Social Welfare Department;
* the Education and Manpower Bureau's enforcement of the Education Ordinance in respect of universal basic education;
* the role of the Home Affairs Department in facilitating the formation of Owners' Corporations;
* the assistance provided by the Home Affairs Department to owners and Owners' Corporations in managing and maintaining their buildings; and
* the operation of the Integrated Call Centre by the Efficiency Unit of the Chief Secretary for Administration's Office of the Government Secretariat.

The reports of all direct investigations have been published and are available for public scrutiny at the Office's Resource Centre.

The Ombudsman Ordinance also empowers The Ombudsman to investigate complaints of non-compliance with the Code on Access to Information against government departments, including the Hong Kong Police Force and the Independent

Commission Against Corruption. The Ombudsman is also empowered to act as an independent review body in respect of an alleged breach of the code.

The Office received 12 320 enquiries and 4 352 complaints in 2003, compared with 15 207 enquiries and 4 662 complaints in 2002. The areas attracting substantial numbers of complaints were related to error, wrong advice or decision, failure to follow procedures or delay, negligence or omission, disparity in treatment, lack of response to complaints, staff attitude and ineffective control. The departments or organisations receiving the most complaints were: Housing Department, Home Affairs Department, Lands Department, Department of Health, Food and Environmental Hygiene Department, Correctional Services Department, Buildings Department, Hospital Authority, Transport Department and Social Welfare Department. The very nature of their services has a closer impact on the community and they have more direct, frequent and extensive contact with members of the public.

Although The Ombudsman has no authority to enforce her recommendations, over 95 per cent of the recommendations made have been accepted by the organisations concerned.

Office of the Director of Audit

The Audit Commission is established under the Basic Law, which provides that the Audit Commission shall function independently and be accountable to the Chief Executive of the HKSAR. The Audit Commission is one of Hong Kong's oldest departments. The first Auditor-General was appointed in 1844.

The Audit Ordinance, enacted in 1971, provides for the audit of the Government's accounts by the Director of Audit and for the submission of his report to the President of the Legislative Council. The Director also audits the accounts of the Exchange Fund, the Hong Kong Housing Authority, five trading funds and more than 60 statutory and non-statutory funds and other public bodies. Furthermore, the Director reviews the financial aspects of the operations of the multifarious government-subvented organisations.

The Director of Audit carries out two types of audit: regularity audits and value-for-money audits. Regularity audits are intended to provide an overall assurance of the general accuracy and propriety of the financial and accounting transactions of the Government and other audited bodies. The Audit Ordinance gives the Director statutory authority to conduct regularity audits.

Value-for-money audits are intended to provide independent information, advice and assurance about the economy, efficiency and effectiveness with which any bureau of the Government Secretariat, department, agency, other public body, public office or audited organisation has discharged its functions. Except for some public organisations where the Director of Audit has obtained statutory authority to conduct value-for-money audits in the respective ordinances, value-for-money audits are carried out according to a set of guidelines tabled in the Provisional Legislative Council by the Chairman of the Public Accounts Committee in 1998.

After the Director of Audit's report has been submitted to the President of the Legislative Council and laid before the council, it is considered by the Public Accounts Committee. In 2003, the Director submitted three reports: one on the audit certification of the Government's accounts for the preceding financial year and two on the results of value-for-money audits.

The Director of Audit's reports on the accounts of other public bodies are submitted to the relevant authority in accordance with the legislation governing the operation of these bodies.

Home Pages

Administration Wing, Chief Secretary for Administration's Office: http://www.gov.hk/admwing
Civil Service Bureau: http://www.csb.gov.hk
Constitutional Affairs Bureau: http://www.gov.hk/cab
Home Affairs Bureau: http://www.hab.gov.hk
Legislative Council: http://www.legco.gov.hk
Office of The Ombudsman: http://www.ombudsman.gov.hk

CHAPTER 2

The Legal System

In November 2001, the Legislative Council of the HKSAR called for a comprehensive review of the community's legal needs and how those needs were being met. The Solicitor General chairs a consultative committee which has been set up in 2003 to oversee a Hong Kong research project. The committee comprises representatives from the legal services sector and other professional, academic and community bodies interested in promoting access to justice. A three-year consultancy study to carry out the research will commence in early 2004.

THE legal system of the Hong Kong Special Administrative Region (HKSAR) is based on the rule of law and the independence of the Judiciary. Under the principle of 'one country, two systems', the HKSAR's legal system differs from that of the Mainland, and is based on the common law.

The constitutional framework for the legal system is provided at the international level by the Sino-British Joint Declaration, which was signed in December 1984. It is provided at the domestic level by the Basic Law — a law enacted by the National People's Congress (NPC) of the People's Republic of China (PRC) under Article 31 of the Chinese Constitution. Both the Joint Declaration and the Basic Law guarantee the continuance of the legal system that was in place before China resumed the exercise of sovereignty over Hong Kong on July 1, 1997.

Continuation of the Legal System

A central theme of the Joint Declaration and the Basic Law is one of continuity. Common law principles, and nearly all the 600 or so ordinances that were in force before July 1, 1997 continue to apply in the HKSAR. Some ordinances required adaptation to bring them into line with the Basic Law and to reflect Hong Kong's new status as a Special Administrative Region of the PRC, and the Government has introduced over 50 bills to make the necessary textual amendments to the legislation. Most of the ordinances have now been adapted. Ordinances that have not yet been adapted require further consideration of the policy issues involved.

The courts and tribunals that had previously been in existence were re-established on July 1, 1997 (though some were renamed) and the Hong Kong Court of Final Appeal was established on that date. This replaced the Judicial Committee of the Privy Council as the highest court of appeal for Hong Kong. All judges who were in service immediately before July 1, 1997 were reappointed by the Chief Executive of the HKSAR. These reappointments were made in accordance with the recommendations of an independent commission — the Judicial Officers Recommendation Commission. All judicial proceedings that had been instituted before July 1, 1997 were continued by virtue of the Hong Kong Reunification Ordinance.

Law in the HKSAR

The laws in force in the HKSAR are:

(1) the Basic Law;

(2) national laws listed in Annex III to the Basic Law;

(3) the laws in force before July 1, 1997 that were adopted as laws of the HKSAR by the Standing Committee of the NPC; and

(4) laws enacted by the legislature of the HKSAR.

National laws relating to defence and foreign affairs, as well as other matters outside the limits of the HKSAR's autonomy, may be applied locally by way of promulgation or legislation by the HKSAR. Currently, 11 national laws apply in the HKSAR.

All ordinances in force in the HKSAR are bilingual, and their Chinese and English texts are equally authentic. Those ordinances, and the subsidiary legislation made under them, are published in both a hard-copy loose-leaf edition and in electronic form freely available on the Internet. All new legislation is published in the *Government Gazette.*

The Law Drafting Division of the Department of Justice is responsible for drafting legislation in both official languages. From time to time, the division publishes an English-Chinese glossary of legal and relevant terms appearing in legislation and the third edition, containing about 30 000 entries, was published in September 1998. A Chinese-English Glossary of Legal Terms, containing around 11 500 terms, was published in December 1999. Both publications are available in electronic form via the Internet, and in hard copy format.

Court Challenges Under the Basic Law

Since the Basic Law came into effect on July 1, 1997, Hong Kong has, for the first time, a detailed written constitution. Litigants are able to base their arguments on provisions of the Basic Law, and challenge actions that they believe are inconsistent with them.

Legal challenges based on the Basic Law have been launched in a wide variety of cases. One significant group of cases focused on the right of abode in Hong Kong of various categories of persons, including Chinese citizens born in Hong Kong, Mainland-born children of Hong Kong permanent residents, children adopted in the Mainland by Hong Kong permanent residents and foreign nationals having ordinarily resided in Hong Kong for a continuous period of not less than seven years. Other constitutional challenges have included the conditions of employment of civil servants, the election of village representatives in the New Territories, the transfer of sentenced persons, the registration of social workers, the assessment of government rent, the abolition of the Provisional Urban Council and the Provisional Regional Council, the right to use the Chinese language in courts, the freedom to travel and enter the HKSAR, the determination by the Chief Executive of the minimum term of an indeterminate sentence, the offence of misconduct in public office and the

A large procession, from Causeway Bay to Central, took place on July 1 in connection with public concerns in a number of matters, including draft legislation to implement Article 23 of the Basic Law.

The Government organises wide-ranging activities to promote the Basic Law among all sectors of the community to enhance understanding and knowledge of the HKSAR's constitutional document. The activities in 2003 included a roving exhibition *(left)*, a photo exhibition and a civic education quiz *(above)*, and an inter-school competition to design a souvenir postal cover *(top)*.

i選票
ionable
Papers

The Chief Executive
ceremonially helping to
empty a ballot box prior
to counting of votes in the
District Council Election
on November 23, in which
more than one million
people voted. *Right:*
teams of young volunteers
manned registration
booths during the voter
registration campaign.

protection of private property rights. The gradual development of a body of jurisprudence on the Basic Law serves to reinforce its effectiveness in determining the rights, obligations, powers and privileges guaranteed to the people of Hong Kong.

Arbitration and Alternative Dispute Resolution

Arbitration has been a popular method of dispute resolution in the HKSAR for some time. It is governed by the Arbitration Ordinance, which has two distinct regimes — a domestic regime derived from English law and an international regime which reflects the UNCITRAL Model Law, the model law adopted by the United Nations Commission on International Trade Law.

Awards made in the HKSAR can be enforced in more than 135 jurisdictions that are signatories to the New York Convention on the Recognition and Enforcement of Foreign Arbitral Awards. Since July 1, 1997, the HKSAR's membership has been by virtue of the fact that the PRC is a signatory to the New York Convention and has applied it to Hong Kong. A system for reciprocal enforcement of arbitration awards between the HKSAR and the Mainland, based on the spirit of the New York Convention, has been in place since January 2000. In June 2000, the summary enforcement of other awards (e.g. from Taiwan and Macau) was introduced.

The Hong Kong International Arbitration Centre (HKIAC) was established in 1985 to act as an independent and impartial focus for the development of all forms of dispute resolution in the HKSAR and the Asia-Pacific region. The HKIAC provides information on dispute resolution and arbitration both in the HKSAR and overseas. It operates panels of international and local arbitrators, and maintains lists of accredited mediators. The HKIAC's premises are in Exchange Square in Central, with 10 hearing and conference rooms and full support facilities. The number of cases involving the HKIAC has substantially increased in recent years. It is expected that there will be a further increase in such cases, not only because of the increased popularity of arbitration and mediation as a means of dispute resolution, but also because of the growth of the HKSAR as a regional dispute resolution centre.

The Secretary for Justice

The Secretary for Justice heads the Department of Justice, and is the Chief Executive's legal adviser and a member of the Executive Council. The Secretary for Justice chairs the Law Reform Commission and the Committee on Bilingual Legal System, and is also a member of the Judicial Officers Recommendation Commission and the Operations Review Committee of the Independent Commission Against Corruption.

The Secretary for Justice is the representative of the HKSAR Government in all actions brought by, or against, it and is also responsible for the drafting of all government legislation.

The Secretary for Justice is responsible for all prosecutions in the HKSAR, with responsibility for deciding whether a prosecution should be instituted in any particular case, and, if so, for instituting and conducting the prosecution.

The Department of Justice provides legal advice to all government departments and bureaux. The department consists of the Secretary for Justice's Office and six divisions, five of which are each headed by a Law Officer to whom the Secretary for Justice delegates certain powers and responsibilities. The remaining division, headed by the Director of Administration and Development, handles departmental administration. The Secretary for Justice's Office provides legal and administrative support to the Secretary for Justice in respect of her many functions.

The Civil Division, headed by the Law Officer (Civil Law), provides legal advice to the Government on civil law, drafts commercial contracts and franchises and conducts civil litigation, arbitration and mediation, on behalf of the Government. The division also provides counsel to the Market Misconduct Tribunal.

The International Law Division, headed by the Law Officer (International Law), advises the Government on issues relating to public international law. Lawyers in this division also participate in the negotiation of agreements and arrangements with other jurisdictions and, as members of the Chinese delegation, at the Hague Conference on Private International Law. The division also handles requests to and from the HKSAR for international legal cooperation.

The Law Drafting Division, headed by the Law Draftsman, is responsible for drafting all legislation, including subsidiary legislation, in Chinese and English, and assists in steering legislation through the Executive and Legislative Councils. It is also responsible for compiling the loose-leaf edition of the Laws of Hong Kong and for maintaining the computer database of Hong Kong's legislation known as the Bilingual Laws Information System (BLIS), which is freely available on the Internet.

The Solicitor General heads the Legal Policy Division, which includes the Law Reform Commission Secretariat. The division provides legal input — with emphasis on legal policy values — on a wide variety of topics being considered by the Government, and also advises on issues affecting the administration of justice, human rights, constitutional law, China law and the Basic Law.

The Prosecutions Division is headed by the Director of Public Prosecutions. Counsel from this division conduct most criminal appeals, including those to the Court of Final Appeal. They also conduct the majority of trials in the Court of First Instance and the District Court and, when necessary, they prosecute in the Magistrates' Court. The division also provides legal advice to law enforcement agencies and other government departments.

In order to enhance civil servants' understanding of the Basic Law, the Civil Service Training and Development Institute (CSTDI) has been organising regular seminars on the subject since 1995. Besides university lecturers and officers from relevant government departments, counsel of the Department of Justice have also been invited to be speakers in these seminars. Specific training courses for particular bureaux and departments are arranged as necessary. The Basic Law is also covered in the curriculum of some China studies courses organised by the institute, such as the foundation course taught at the Tsinghua University in Beijing.

Since 2001, the Legal Policy Division and the CSTDI have co-published the *Basic Law Bulletin* on a regular basis in order to promote greater awareness and knowledge of the Basic Law among civil servants. In 2002, the department assisted the institute in the production of a new Basic Law web course as well as in the organisation of various Basic Law promotional activities.

The Law Reform Commission

The Law Reform Commission was established in January 1980. It considers and reports on such topics as may be referred to it by the Secretary for Justice or the Chief

Justice of the Court of Final Appeal of the HKSAR. Its membership includes academics, practising lawyers and prominent community members.

Since its establishment, the commission has published 45 reports covering subjects as diverse as commercial arbitration, divorce, sale of goods and supply of services, fraud and hearsay in civil proceedings. The recommendations in 26 of these reports have been implemented, either in whole or in part. The commission is currently considering references on privacy, domicile, hearsay in criminal proceedings, privity of contract, conditional fees, criteria for service as a juror and decision-making for persons in a coma.

The Legal Profession

The legal profession in Hong Kong is divided into two distinct branches — barristers and solicitors. Solicitors have limited rights of audience before the courts whereas barristers have unlimited rights of audience in all courts. Lawyers practising within one branch of the profession are not, at the same time, allowed to practise within the other branch.

Hong Kong has more than 5 300 practising solicitors and 650 local law firms, plus some 34 foreign law firms, 630 registered foreign lawyers and seven registered associations between foreign law firms and local law firms in Hong Kong.

The Law Society is the governing body for solicitors and foreign lawyers and foreign law firms. It has wide responsibilities for maintaining professional and ethical standards and for considering complaints against these legal professionals.

Around 380 solicitors are also notaries public, and are members of the Hong Kong Society of Notaries, providing notarial service to different sectors of the community.

Hong Kong has more than 840 practising barristers, whose governing body is the Hong Kong Bar Association. The Code of Conduct for the Bar of the HKSAR governs their conduct and etiquette.

In 2003, the Bar of the HKSAR was involved in many events of legal importance to the public, the most notable one being the discussion over Article 23 of the Basic Law. Apart from taking part in forums and interviews organised by other institutions, the Bar in conjunction with the University of Hong Kong and the City University of Hong Kong organised a two-day open forum on Article 23. The forum was well attended and broadcast world-wide through the Internet.

As in the past, the Bar in 2003 continued to be involved actively in the legal education reform in Hong Kong through participation in various boards of the University of Hong Kong and the City University of Hong Kong. Further, through its Free Legal Service Scheme, the Bar in 2003 also continued to provide free legal service to the public, with satisfactory results.

While maintaining amicable relationship with international legal institutions, the Bar in 2003 also strengthened its ties with lawyers' associations in the Mainland. The signing of the Mainland/Hong Kong Closer Economic Partnership Arrangement (CEPA) in June 2003 has also provided impetus to bring the Bar closer to the Mainland.

The Judiciary

A key element in the success and continuing attraction of the HKSAR is that its judicial system operates on the principle, fundamental to the common law system, of the independence of the judiciary from the executive and legislative branches of government. The courts make their own judgments, whether disputes before them involve private citizens, corporate bodies or the Government itself.

The Court of Final Appeal is the highest appellate court in the HKSAR. The court is headed by the Chief Justice. There are three permanent judges and a panel of eight non-permanent Hong Kong judges and 10 non-permanent judges from other common law jurisdictions. In hearing and determining appeals, the court will consist of five judges, and the court may, as required, invite a non-permanent Hong Kong judge or a non-permanent judge from other common law jurisdictions to sit on the court. The Chief Justice is the head of the Judiciary. He is assisted in the overall administration by the Judiciary Administrator.

The High Court, comprising the Court of Appeal and the Court of First Instance, is headed by the Chief Judge of the High Court. Sitting in the High Court, in addition to the Chief Judge are nine Justices of Appeal and 25 Judges of the Court of First Instance. The Registrar, Senior Deputy Registrars and Deputy Registrars of the High Court serve as Masters of the High Court in civil trials in the Court of First Instance.

The Court of Appeal hears civil and criminal appeals from the Court of First Instance and the District Court. The Court of First Instance's jurisdiction is unlimited in both civil and criminal matters. Civil matters are usually tried by Court of First Instance Judges sitting without juries, although there is a rarely used provision for jury trials in certain cases, including defamation. For criminal trials, they sit with a jury of seven, or sometimes nine on special direction of the Judge.

The District Court is one level below the Court of First Instance. It has a Chief District Judge and 33 Judges, who sit without a jury in both criminal and civil cases. The Court's Registrar and Deputy Registrars serve as Masters of the District Court to deal with interlocutory and taxation matters. The District Court tries the more serious criminal cases except murder, manslaughter and rape. The maximum term of imprisonment is seven years. The District Court's civil jurisdiction is limited to disputes with a monetary value of up to $1,000,000, or recovery of possession of land of rateable value up to $240,000. It has jurisdiction over employees' compensation cases. Its family jurisdiction involves divorce, custody and adoption matters. It also has an appellate jurisdiction over stamp duty appeals.

The Magistrates' Courts process about 90 per cent of the cases in Hong Kong annually. Led by the Chief Magistrate, the team consists of eight Principal Magistrates, 67 Permanent Magistrates and nine Special Magistrates sitting in nine different locations.

Magistrates exercise criminal jurisdiction over a wide range of offences. In general, their sentencing power is limited to two years' imprisonment and a fine of $100,000. Specific statutory provisions empower magistrates to impose sentences up to three years' imprisonment and a fine of $5 million. Magistrates also handle cases in the Juvenile Courts, which deal with offences, except homicide, committed by children and young persons below 16 years of age. Special Magistrates handle minor offences such as littering and traffic contraventions. Their sentencing power is limited to a maximum fine of $50,000 or as specified in their warrants of appointment.

In addition, there are five tribunals. The Lands Tribunal handles tenancy claims, rating and valuation appeals, applications for the compulsory sale of buildings for redevelopment, and compensation assessments when land is resumed by the Government or reduced in value by development. The Labour Tribunal handles claims arising from contracts of employment. The Small Claims Tribunal handles civil claims up to $50,000. The Obscene Articles Tribunal determines whether articles are obscene or indecent. It also classifies articles submitted by people, such as authors and publishers. The Coroner's Court conducts inquests and inquires into the causes of and circumstances connected with a death.

In accordance with the Basic Law and the Official Languages Ordinance, the courts can use either or both of the official languages in any proceedings.

Legal Aid

Eligible applicants receive legal aid through the provision of the services of a solicitor and, if necessary, a barrister in court proceedings to ensure that a person who has reasonable grounds for pursuing or defending a legal action is not prevented from doing so by lack of means. Publicly funded legal aid services are provided through the Legal Aid Department and the Duty Lawyer Service.

Legal Aid Department

The Legal Aid Department provides legal aid services to any person in Hong Kong, resident or non-resident, who satisfies the criteria for legal aid.

Ordinary Legal Aid Scheme for Civil Cases

The Ordinary Legal Aid Scheme is available for representation in civil proceedings in the Court of Final Appeal, Court of Appeal, Court of First Instance and District Court covering proceedings relating to major areas of the livelihood of the community at large, including family and matrimonial disputes, personal injury claims, employment disputes, tenancy disputes, contractual disputes, immigration matters and professional negligence claims.

An applicant must pass the means and merits tests to qualify for legal aid. For the means test, the applicant must show that his financial resources, i.e. annual disposable income and total disposable capital assets after deduction of certain statutory allowances, do not exceed $169,700. The Director of Legal Aid may waive the upper financial eligibility limit in meritorious cases where a breach of the Hong Kong Bill of Rights Ordinance or an inconsistency with the International Covenant on Civil and Political Rights as applied to Hong Kong is an issue. For the merits test, the applicant must satisfy the Director of Legal Aid that he has reasonable grounds for bringing or defending the civil proceedings. A legally aided person is required to pay a contribution depending on his financial resources and in the event that property is recovered or preserved on his behalf in the proceedings.

An applicant who is refused civil legal aid may appeal to the Registrar of the High Court, or in Court of Final Appeal cases, to a Review Committee. The decision of the Registrar or the Review Committee is final.

During the year, 21 643 applications for legal aid were received, and legal aid was granted to 10 694 applicants. The Legal Aid Department's expenditure on civil cases was $343 million and $769 million was recovered for the aided persons.

Supplementary Legal Aid Scheme

This scheme provides legal assistance to applicants whose financial resources exceed the ceiling stipulated in the Ordinary Legal Aid Scheme but do not exceed $471,600. Under this scheme, legal aid is available for cases involving personal injury or death as well as medical, dental or legal professional negligence, where the claim for damages is likely to exceed $60,000. The scheme also covers claims under the Employees' Compensation Ordinance irrespective of the amount of the claim.

The scheme is self-financing and is funded by legal aid contributions and damages or compensation recovered. In 2003, 106 applications for legal aid were received and legal aid was granted to 79 applicants. Expenditure was $23 million and $61 million was recovered on behalf of the aided persons.

Legal Aid in Criminal Cases

In criminal cases, legal aid is available for representation in proceedings in the Court of First Instance and the District Court, in committal proceedings in the Magistrates' Court, in appeals from the Magistrates' Courts, and in appeals to the Court of Appeal and the Court of Final Appeal.

Legal aid is granted to applicants who pass the means test and if the Director of Legal Aid is satisfied that legal aid is desirable in the interests of justice.

The Director of Legal Aid has the discretion to grant legal aid in a criminal case even where the applicant's financial resources exceed the financial eligibility limit if he is satisfied that it is desirable in the interests of justice to do so, subject to payment of a contribution.

There is no provision for appeal against the Director of Legal Aid's refusal to grant legal aid in criminal cases on grounds of means or merits (except for appeals to the Court of Final Appeal). Appeals against refusal of legal aid for appeals to the Court of Final Appeal are heard by a Review Committee chaired by the Registrar of the High Court and comprising of a barrister appointed by the Chairman of the Hong Kong Bar Association and a solicitor appointed by the President of the Law Society of Hong Kong.

An applicant may apply to a judge for legal aid to be granted to him provided he satisfies the means test. However, applicants charged with or convicted of murder, treason or piracy with violence may apply to a judge for legal aid for the trial or appeal and for exemption from the means test or payment of a contribution.

During the year, 4 411 applications for criminal legal aid were received and legal aid was granted to 2 803 applicants. Total expenditure on criminal cases was $89 million.

Duty Lawyer Service

The Duty Lawyer Service operates the Legal Advice Scheme, the Duty Lawyer Scheme and the Tel-Law Scheme. It is subvented by the Government but independently administered by the legal profession of Hong Kong. The Hong Kong Bar Association and the Law Society of Hong Kong each nominate four members to sit on the council of the Service, which manages and administers its operations. Three lay members have also been invited to sit on the council.

The Legal Advice Scheme provides free advice to members of the public without means testing, at nine advice centres located in the District Offices. Members of the public can make appointments to see volunteer lawyers through one of the 27 referral agencies (with over 100 branches), which include all District Offices, Caritas Services Centres and the Social Welfare Department; 940 volunteer lawyers participate in the scheme. A total of 6 036 people were given legal advice during the year.

The Duty Lawyer Scheme provides legal representation to virtually all defendants who are charged in the magistracies. To be eligible for legal representation under the scheme, an applicant has to pass a means test: if his gross annual income does not exceed $127,330, he is eligible for assistance under the scheme. However, the Administrator of the Duty Lawyer Service has a discretion to grant legal representation to defendants whose gross annual income exceeds this limit, if she considers that it is in the interests of justice to do so. Applicants are also subject to a merits test. The prime consideration is whether the defendant is in jeopardy of losing his liberty or whether a substantial question of law is involved.

The scheme assigns barristers and solicitors to advise defendants facing extradition and to represent persons who are at risk of criminal prosecution as a result of giving incriminating evidence in Coroners' inquests. They are also assigned to represent hawkers at the hearing of their appeals to the Municipal Services Appeals Board. With effect from October 1, the Duty Lawyer Scheme was expanded to cover Care or Protection Proceedings in the Juvenile Court. Legal representation is offered to those children/juveniles in Care or Protection Proceedings who are detained in a gazetted place of refuge and whose parents/guardians have consented to such representation.

More than 1 384 barristers and solicitors were on the duty lawyer roster and 50 172 persons were assisted under the Duty Lawyer Scheme in 2003.

The Tel-Law Scheme offers taped legal information to the public in Cantonese, Putonghua and English. The tapes cover various aspects of law including matrimonial, landlord and tenant, criminal, financial, employment, environmental and administrative law. They are updated regularly and new tapes are added when new subjects are identified as being of interest to the public. During the year, 78 topics were available and 44 145 calls were received.

Legal Aid Services Council

The Legal Aid Services Council is an independent statutory body established to advise the Chief Executive of the HKSAR on legal aid policies. It also supervises the provision of legal aid services by the Legal Aid Department without interfering with its day-to-day operation. Chaired by a non-official who is not in the legal profession, the council's members include lawyers, lay members and the Director of Legal Aid. During the year, it continued to conduct reviews of legal aid issues and of the services provided by the Legal Aid Department. The council discussed with the Government the annual and biennial review of financial eligibility limits of legal aid applicants, the five-yearly review of the criteria for assessing financial eligibility of legal aid applicants, and the operation of the Legal Aid Services Council Ordinance.

The Legal Aid Services Council also operates a scheme under which a legal aid applicant seeking to appeal to the Court of Final Appeal may apply for a counsel's certificate for a review of the Director of Legal Aid's refusal to grant legal aid on merits grounds.

In 2003, aid was granted in respect of 94 applications, comprising 86 criminal cases and eight civil cases, with a total financial commitment of $2,544,000.

The council has drawn up its work plan covering the period from 2003 to 2008.

The Official Solicitor

The Director of Legal Aid was appointed the Official Solicitor under the Official Solicitor Ordinance which took effect on August 1, 1991.

The Official Solicitor's main duties are to act as guardian *ad litem* or next friend in legal proceedings for persons under disability of age or mental capacity, as representative of deceased persons' estates for the purpose of legal proceedings, as Official Trustee and Judicial Trustee, to act as committee of the estate of mentally incapacitated persons, to represent any party in care or protection proceedings and to act on behalf of a person committed to prison for contempt who is unable or unwilling to apply on his own behalf for release.

The Official Solicitor's case-load for 2002-03 was 262, an increase of 16 per cent over the previous financial year.

Director of Intellectual Property

The post of Director of Intellectual Property was established in 1990 as a statutory office by the Director of Intellectual Property (Establishment) Ordinance. The Intellectual Property Department operates the Trade Marks, Patents, Designs and Copyright Licensing Bodies Registries. The department is also responsible for making recommendations on policy and legislation related to intellectual property protection, provision of civil intellectual property legal advice to the Government, and promotion of public awareness of, and respect for, intellectual property rights.

The Rights of the Individual

Article 39 of the Basic Law provides that the provisions of the International Covenant on Civil and Political Rights (ICCPR) and the International Covenant on Economic, Social and Cultural Rights (ICESCR) as applied to Hong Kong shall remain in force. Additionally, the HKSAR continues to abide by the major international conventions on human rights. These include the International Convention on the Elimination of All Forms of Racial Discrimination (ICERD), the Convention against Torture and Other Cruel, Inhuman or Degrading Treatment or Punishment (CAT), the Convention on the Rights of the Child (CRC), and the Convention on the Elimination of All Forms of Discrimination against Women (CEDAW).

The HKSAR's second report in the light of the ICESCR was submitted, as part of China's first report under the covenant, to the United Nations (UN) in June 2003. The HKSAR's first report under the CRC was submitted to the UN as part of China's second report under the convention, also in June.

The Hong Kong Bill of Rights Ordinance, enacted in 1991 to give effect in domestic law to the provisions of the ICCPR, remains in force.

In 2003, the Government decided in principle to introduce a bill into the Legislative Council to prohibit racial discrimination in certain areas. A public consultation paper on the legislative proposals will be published in 2004. If all proceeds smoothly, the bill will be introduced into the Legislative Council in the 2004-05 legislative session.

To improve government services for the ethnic minorities, a Race Relations Unit was established in June 2002. Its work includes devising and producing publicity materials in minority languages[1], maintaining a hotline for enquiries and complaints, outreach work to schools, and providing secretariat services to the Committee on the Promotion of Racial Harmony. The committee is an advisory body comprising non-government members with an active interest in race issues, and relevant government

---

[1] The Race Relations Unit has published a guidebook *Your Guide to Services in Hong Kong* in eight languages — English, Indonesian, Filipino, Thai, Sinhalese, Hindi, Nepali and Urdu — in order to help minority communities, both established and newly arrived, to adapt to life in Hong Kong.

departments. The committee's functions include formulating proposals for race-related public education and publicity, and vetting Funding Scheme applications.

In 2003, an Ethnic Minorities Forum and a Human Rights Forum were established to strengthen the links between the Government and relevant NGOs.

The Steering Committee on New Arrival Services is a high level body that seeks to ensure that new arrivals — whatever their origin — know what services are available to them, that those services are delivered, and that the services so provided remain appropriate to the needs of the committee's target clientele. The committee is chaired by the Permanent Secretary for Home Affairs. Its members comprise representatives of government departments that provide key services and an NGO.

Equal Opportunities Commission

The Equal Opportunities Commission (EOC) was established as an independent statutory body under the Sex Discrimination Ordinance in May 1996 and started full operation in September that year. The commission is tasked to oversce the implementation of the Sex Discrimination Ordinance, the Disability Discrimination Ordinance and the Family Status Discrimination Ordinance. The functions of the commission include handling complaints, encouraging conciliation, providing assistance to aggrieved persons, and undertaking public education, research and training programmes to promote equal opportunities in the community. In 2003, the commission handled 13 626 enquiries and 1 348 complaints relating to the three anti-discrimination ordinances; 233 complaint cases were conciliated.

Office of the Privacy Commissioner for Personal Data

The Personal Data (Privacy) Ordinance provides for the appointment of a Privacy Commissioner for Personal Data to monitor, supervise and promote compliance with the ordinance. The Office of the Privacy Commissioner for Personal Data (PCO) began full operation in December 1996.

In 2003, the PCO handled 15 782 enquiries and 1 176 complaints, and conducted eight compliance checks in relation to the ordinance.

Following a public consultation and discussions with the banking industry, in January 2003 the PCO issued the report on the broader sharing of consumer credit data and gazetted in May the revised Code of Practice on Consumer Credit Data which took effect from June 2. The revised Code of Practice was intended to address the community's concerns about the probable loss to the local economy caused by the rising trend of personal bankruptcy and consumer debt.

In December, the PCO issued the Report on the Public Consultation in Relation to the Draft Code of Practice on Monitoring and Personal Data Privacy at Work. Apart from reporting on the feedback collected, the PCO also responded to concerns raised during the consultation and set out the future course of action on the subject with a view to striking a balance between the interests of both employers and employees.

To enhance the general public's understanding of the ordinance, the PCO had continued to produce several newsletters and pamphlets. The office also undertook a variety of activities to foster a culture of respecting one another's privacy. The activities included public seminars, plenary meetings of the Data Protection Officers' Club, workshops for semi-finalists in the *Privacy Protection in Action: TV Advertisement Competition* and a drama performance.

Home Pages

Administration Wing, Chief Secretary for Administration's Office:
http://www.gov.hk/admwing
Department of Justice: http://www.doj.gov.hk
Judiciary: http://www.judiciary.gov.hk
Legal Aid Department: http://www.gov.hk/lad
Home Affairs Bureau: http://www.hab.gov.hk

CHAPTER 3

The Economy

In 2003, the Hong Kong economy grew by 3.3 per cent, faster than the 2.3 per cent growth in 2002. This was notwithstanding a severe setback in the second quarter upon the impact of SARS. Growth impetus came mainly from a sustained strong expansion in export trade throughout the year, yet a distinct revival in domestic demand during the second half of the year also contributed. The labour market continued to be slack in overall terms, but showed a notable improvement in the latter part of the year. Consumer prices drifted lower for the fifth consecutive year, albeit with a markedly narrowed decrease towards the year-end.

THE Hong Kong economy began the year on a strong note, with the Gross Domestic Product (GDP) increasing by 4.5 per cent in real terms in the first quarter over a year earlier. Growth in the second quarter was abruptly derailed by the spread of Severe Acute Respiratory Syndrome (SARS), with GDP relapsing to a 0.5 per cent decline. Nevertheless, economic activity soon staged a broad-based recovery in the third quarter after the waning of SARS, and the upswing was sustained well into the fourth quarter upon a further lift in local sentiment. Reflecting this, GDP bounced up strongly to 4.0 per cent and 5.0 per cent growth respectively in these two quarters. Thus, even with the severe setback caused by SARS earlier in the year, the Hong Kong economy still attained an appreciable growth of 3.3 per cent in real terms for 2003 as a whole, which compared favourably with that of 2.3 per cent in 2002. On a seasonally adjusted quarter-to-quarter comparison, GDP shrank by 0.5 per cent and 2.6 per cent respectively in real terms in the first and second quarters of 2003, but reverted to increases by 6.6 per cent in the third quarter and 1.5 per cent in the fourth quarter.

In the external sector, inbound tourism and the travel-related sectors suffered a drastic downturn in the second quarter of 2003 upon the impact of SARS, but regained strength swiftly in the third quarter and advanced further in the fourth quarter. The remarkable turnaround was backed by a strong rebound in visitor arrivals from the Mainland, especially after the launch of the Individual Visit Scheme in late July. As to merchandise exports and offshore trade, they both displayed highly robust growth throughout 2003, bolstered by continued strong expansion in the Mainland economy, a visible revival in the global economy, as well as a surge in intra-regional trade. Enhanced competitiveness of Hong Kong's exports, backed by a distinct weakening in the US dollar and further domestic cost adjustments, as well as deriving from increasing competitiveness of Mainland products in the world market, rendered an additional boost to the export growth.

In the domestic sector, consumer spending likewise underwent a severe setback in the second quarter of 2003, but was progressively resurrected in the third and fourth quarters. Consumer sentiment appeared especially upbeat towards the end of the year, boosted by the rally in the local stock market, a more active property market, and progressive improvement in the unemployment situation. Investment spending on machinery and equipment also turned up to a notable growth in the latter part of 2003, on the back of improved economic conditions and brighter business outlook, especially after the signing of the Closer Economic Partnership Arrangement (CEPA) between Hong Kong and the Mainland. Yet building and construction output was weak throughout.

The labour market weakened substantially during the first half of 2003 upon the abrupt fall-off in economic activity caused by SARS, with labour demand shrinking most visibly in the consumption and tourism-related sectors. Then, as the economy revived, employment and vacancies showed renewed increases in the latter part of the year. The seasonally adjusted unemployment rate, having surged from 7.2 per cent in the fourth quarter of 2002 to a high of 8.7 per cent in May-July 2003, fell back appreciably to 7.3 per cent in the fourth quarter. The underemployment rate likewise surged, from 3.1 per cent in the fourth quarter of 2002 to a high of 4.3 per cent in the second quarter of 2003, as many employees in the SARS-affected sectors were temporarily suspended from work at that time. This was nevertheless followed by a notable decline to 3.3 per cent in the fourth quarter, as these employees gradually resumed work and as the overall work intensity rose again along with the recovery in economic activity. Labour earnings eased further by 1.8 per cent in money terms in the third quarter of 2003 over a year earlier.

The property market had clearly turned around in late 2003, after the languishing performance earlier in the year. On residential property, trading activity, having plunged in the second quarter, rebounded appreciably in the latter part of the year amidst growing optimism for the economy. Flat prices staged a distinct upturn in the fourth quarter, while flat rentals seemed to have bottomed out towards the year-end. On commercial property, the market for office space likewise picked up towards the end of the year, as manifested by a notable surge in the prices of office space and a narrowed decline in office rentals. As to the market for shopping space, the improvement in performance was even more distinct, with prices lifted visibly and rentals ceased declining. Regarding industrial property, while demand remained generally weak, keener interest came from certain end-users in converting some of the existing industrial sites into hotel use.

On consumer prices, the downtrend in the Composite Consumer Price Index (CPI) continued in 2003, as local prices were held down by the generally slack domestic demand and profit margin squeeze especially during the course of the SARS outbreak, as well as by the lower wages and rentals. The rates concession and waiver of water and sewage charges, as part of the Government's special relief measures, also dragged down the CPI for some months later in the year. Yet as the downward effect of these relief measures was lessened, and as price discounts and other concessions on many of the consumer items were reduced along with steadily improving demand, the year-on-year decline in the Composite CPI tapered visibly to 2.3 per cent in the fourth quarter of 2003, having widened from 2.0 per cent in the first quarter to 2.5 per cent and 3.6 per cent respectively in the second and third quarters. Also partly contributing were firmer prices of retained imports amidst a weaker US dollar and rising world commodity prices. For 2003 as a whole, the Composite CPI fell by 2.6 per cent, narrowed from the 3.0 per cent drop in 2002.

The GDP deflator, as a broad measure of overall price change in the economy, however, exhibited a more pronounced decline by 5.1 per cent in 2003, as against a 3.0 per cent fall in 2002. This was due in large part to a worsening in the terms of trade, aside from downward price pressure in the domestic economy. Consequential to the enlarged decrease in the GDP deflator, nominal GDP had a larger fall in 2003 than in 2002, by 2.0 per cent as against 0.8 per cent.

Structure and Development of the Economy

With its strategic location at the doorway to the Mainland and on the international time zone that bridges the time gap between Asia and Europe, the HKSAR has been serving as a global centre for trade, finance, business and communications. Hong Kong is now ranked the 11th largest trading entity in the world. It operates the busiest container port in the world in terms of throughput, as well as one of the busiest airports in terms of number of international passengers and volume of international cargo handled. In addition, it is the world's 12th largest banking centre in terms of external banking transactions, and the seventh largest foreign exchange market in terms of turnover. Its stock market is Asia's second largest in terms of market capitalisation.

Hong Kong is characterised by a high degree of internationalisation, business-friendly environment, rule of law, free trade and free flow of information, open and fair competition, well-established and comprehensive financial network, superb transport and communications infrastructure, sophisticated support services, and a skilled and well educated workforce complemented by a pool of effective and enterprising entrepreneurs. Added to these are the substantial amount of fiscal reserves and foreign exchange reserves, a fully convertible and stable currency, and a simple tax system with a low tax rate. On these virtues, Hong Kong is widely regarded as amongst the freest and most competitive economies in the world. The US Heritage Foundation ranks Hong Kong as the world's freest economy for the 10th year in a row in 2004. The Cato Institute of the United States, in conjunction with the Fraser Institute of Canada and other research bodies around the world, also consistently ranks Hong Kong as the freest economy in the world.

Over the past two decades, the Hong Kong economy has more than doubled in size, with GDP growing at an average annual rate of 5.0 per cent in real terms. This outpaces considerably the growth of the world economy and the Organisation for Economic Cooperation and Development (OECD) economies. Over the same period, Hong Kong's per capita GDP doubled at constant price level, giving an average annual growth rate of 3.7 per cent in real terms. At US$23,300 in 2003, this per capita GDP was amongst the highest in Asia, next only to Japan (*Chart 1*).

In line with increased external orientation of the Hong Kong economy, trade in goods expanded by eight times and trade in services by almost three times in real terms over the past two decades. In 2003, the total value of visible trade (comprising re-exports, domestic exports and imports of goods) reached $3,543 billion, corresponding to 287 per cent of GDP. This was distinctly larger than the ratios of 156 per cent in 1983 and 230 per cent in 1993. If the value of exports and imports of services is also taken into account, the ratio is even greater, at 331 per cent in 2003, as compared to 192 per cent in 1983 and 267 per cent in 1993.

41

Chart 1 **Gross Domestic Product**
(year-on-year rate of change in real terms)

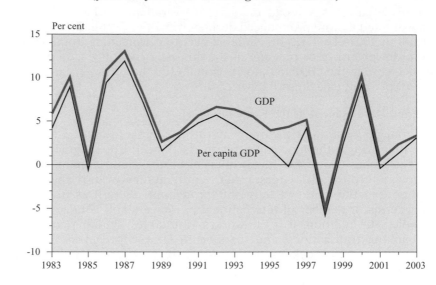

Over the past two decades, the Hong Kong economy grew at an average annual rate of 5.0 per cent in real terms, outpacing the corresponding growth rate of 2.8 per cent for OECD economies as a whole. In 2003, the economy still attained a 3.3 per cent growth in real terms, despite the impact of SARS.

As another indication of the high degree of external orientation, the stock of inward direct investment in Hong Kong amounted to $2,622 billion in market value at end-2002, equivalent to 208 per cent of GDP. Hong Kong is the second most favoured destination for inward direct investment in Asia, next only to the Mainland. The corresponding figures for the stock of outward direct investment in Hong Kong were likewise substantial, at $2,413 billion and 192 per cent of GDP, much larger than those for many other economies in Asia. As a major financial centre in the region with huge cross-territory fund flows, Hong Kong's external financial assets and liabilities were also substantial, at $8,033 billion and $5,355 billion respectively at end-2002. The corresponding ratios to GDP in that year were 638 per cent and 425 per cent. Reflecting Hong Kong's sound international investment position, net external financial assets amounted to $2,677 billion at end-2002, equivalent to 213 per cent of GDP. As to gross external debt, which is the sum of the non-equity liability components in international investment, it stood at $2,803 billion at end-2003, equivalent to 227 per cent of GDP. Yet a major proportion of it arose from normal operations of the banking sector, and the Government incurred no external debt at all.

The Gross National Product (GNP), comprising GDP and net external factor income flows, stood at $1,269 billion in 2003. This was higher than the corresponding GDP by 2.8 per cent, owing to sustained net inflow of external factor income. In gross terms, inflows and outflows of external factor income remained substantial in 2003, at $329 billion and $294 billion respectively, equivalent to 27 per cent and 24 per cent of GDP. This was related to the huge volume of both inward and outward investment in Hong Kong.

Contributions of the Various Economic Sectors

Primary production (including agriculture, fisheries, mining and quarrying) is insignificant in Hong Kong, in terms of both value added contribution to GDP and share in total employment. This reflects the predominantly urbanised nature of the economy.

Secondary production (comprising manufacturing, construction, and supply of electricity, gas and water), which constituted a significant contributor to GDP up to the early 1980s, has diminished in relative importance since then. Within this broad sector, the value added contribution from manufacturing shrank from 21 per cent in 1982 to 14 per cent in 1992 and distinctly more to only 5 per cent in 2002, consequential to ongoing relocation of the more labour-intensive production processes to the Mainland. For the construction sector, its contribution to GDP edged lower from 7 per cent in 1982 to 5 per cent in 1992, and further to 4 per cent in 2002. As to supply of electricity, gas and water, the corresponding share held relatively stable, at around 2-3 per cent over the past two decades.

The open door policy and economic reform in the Mainland have not only provided an enormous production hinterland and market outlet for Hong Kong's manufacturers, but have also created abundant business opportunities for a wide range of service activities. These activities include specifically freight and passenger transport, travel and tourism, telecommunications, banking, insurance, real estate, and professional services such as financial, legal, accounting and consultancy services. In consequence, the Hong Kong economy has become increasingly service-oriented since the 1980s.

Reflecting this, the share of the tertiary services sector (comprising the wholesale, retail and import/export trades, restaurants and hotels; transport, storage and communications; financing, insurance, real estate and business services; community, social and personal services; and ownership of premises) in GDP went up visibly, from 69 per cent in 1982 to 79 per cent in 1992 and further to 88 per cent in 2002 *(Chart 2)*.

The profound change in the economic structure was also borne out by a broadly similar shift in the sectoral composition of employment. Over the past two decades, the share of the services sector in total employment followed a continuous uptrend, rising distinctly from 52 per cent in 1983 to 73 per cent in 1993 and further to 85 per cent in the first three quarters of 2003. On the other hand, the corresponding share for the manufacturing sector kept on shrinking, from 38 per cent in 1983 to 18 per cent in 1993 and further to only 5 per cent in the first three quarters of 2003 *(Chart 3)*.

The Services Sector

The services sector has not only flourished but also diversified in types of activities, concomitant with the structural transformation of the economy. Trade-related and tourism-related services, community, social and personal services, and finance and business services such as banking, insurance, real estate and a host of related professional services, have all grown distinctly over the past two decades. Strong expansion was also observed in information technology in the more recent years, especially those pertaining to telecommunications services and Internet applications, in line with the shift in economic structure more towards knowledge-based activities.

Chart 2   **Gross Domestic Product by broad economic sector**

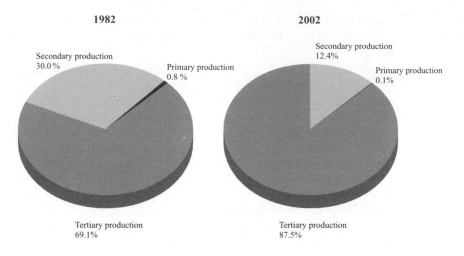

1982

Secondary production
30.0%

Primary production
0.8 %

Tertiary production
69.1%

2002

Secondary production
12.4%

Primary production
0.1%

Tertiary production
87.5%

Along with a profound shift in economic structure, the share of the tertiary services sector in GDP continued to increase, while the share of the secondary sector dwindled further over the past two decades.

Chart 3   **Employment by broad economic sector**

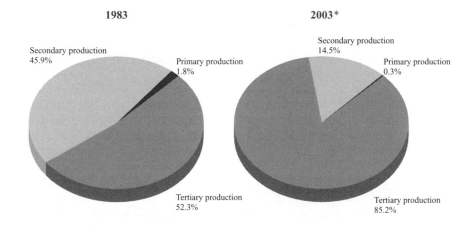

1983

Secondary production
45.9%

Primary production
1.8%

Tertiary production
52.3%

2003*

Secondary production
14.5%

Primary production
0.3%

Tertiary production
85.2%

Consequential to the ongoing relocation of the less skill-intensive and lower value added manufacturing processes to the Mainland, as well as the strong growth in service activities in Hong Kong, the tertiary services sector has expanded markedly and has overtaken the secondary sector to become the largest employer in the economy since 1981.

* Average of Q1 to Q3 2003.

On trade in services, exports and imports of services both grew by an annual average of 7 per cent in real terms over the past two decades. In 2002, civil aviation, travel and tourism, trade-related services, and various financial and banking services were the largest components of trade in services. Within exports of services, offshore trading and merchandising services have overtaken transportation as the most important component in 2002, accounting for 35 per cent of the total value in that year. For transportation, the corresponding share was 30 per cent. This was followed by travel and tourism (with a share of 17 per cent), and financial and banking services (6 per cent). As to imports of services, travel and tourism remained the largest component, accounting for 50 per cent of the total value in 2002. Transportation was in the second place (with a share of 26 per cent), followed by offshore trading and merchandising services (7 per cent), and financial and banking services (3 per cent).

Net output or value added of the services sector as a whole rose visibly, by an annual average of 6 per cent in value terms between 1992 and 2002. Amongst the major constituent sectors, net output of community, social and personal services had the fastest growth (at an average annual rate of 9 per cent). This was followed by transport, storage and communications (6 per cent); the wholesale, retail and import/export trades, restaurants and hotels (5 per cent); and financing, insurance, real estate and business services (4 per cent).

In terms of value added contribution to GDP, the wholesale, retail and import/export trades, restaurants and hotels continued to be the largest in 2002, with a share of 27 per cent. This was followed by community, social and personal services (22 per cent), financing, insurance, real estate and business services (22 per cent), and transport, storage and communications (11 per cent) *(Chart 4)*.

Chart 4   Gross Domestic Product by major service sector

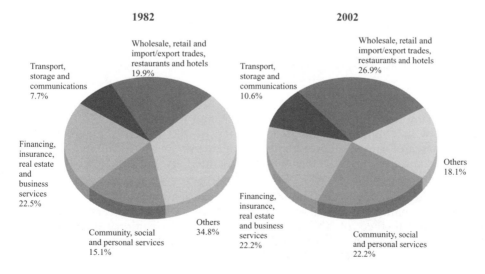

Over the past two decades, community, social and personal services had a more distinct increase in net output than other major service sectors. Yet ranked in terms of value added contribution to GDP, the wholesale, retail and import/export trades, restaurants and hotels remained the largest service sector in 2002.

45

In terms of employment, the wholesale, retail and import/export trades, restaurants and hotels was again the largest sector, accounting for 31 per cent of the total employment in the first three quarters of 2003. This was followed by community, social and personal services (with a share of 28 per cent), financing, insurance, real estate and business services (15 per cent), and transport, storage and communications (11 per cent) (*Chart 5*).

Chart 5   **Employment by major service sector**

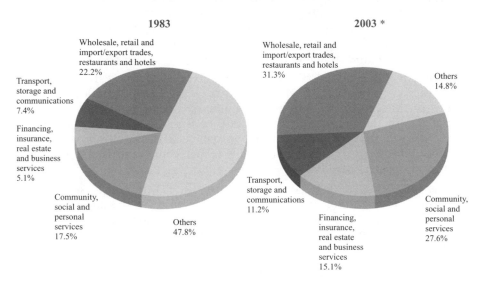

Over the past two decades, financing, insurance, real estate and business services showed the fastest employment growth. But in terms of employment size, the wholesale, retail and import/export trades, restaurants and hotels continued to be the largest employer in the economy in 2003.

* Average of Q1 to Q3 2003.

The Manufacturing Sector

Manufacturing firms in Hong Kong are renowned for their versatility and flexibility in coping with changing demand conditions in the overseas markets. Moreover, through increased outward processing arrangements in the Mainland, Hong Kong's productive capacity has effectively been expanded by multiples, which has helped uphold the price competitiveness of its products.

Besides relocating the more labour-intensive production processes to the Mainland, Hong Kong's manufacturers have also been striving hard to diversify their products and markets, in face of the challenges from globalisation of trade and keen competition from other export producers. Concurrently, productive efficiency and product quality have been continuously upgraded by incorporating more advanced skills and technology.

Within the local manufacturing sector, textiles and clothing remain the most important industries, notwithstanding continued decline in their relative significance over the years. Other major industries include machinery and equipment, electronics, printing and publishing, food processing and metal products. Generally speaking, those manufacturing operations still remaining in Hong Kong are more knowledge-based with a higher value added and a greater technology content. Between 1993 and 2003, labour productivity in the local manufacturing sector, as measured by the ratio of the industrial production index to the manufacturing employment index, rose visibly, by an annual average of around 6 per cent.

In 2003, the United States and the Mainland were the two largest markets for Hong Kong's domestic exports, accounting for 32 per cent and 30 per cent respectively of the total. Other major markets included the United Kingdom (6 per cent), Germany (4 per cent), Taiwan (3 per cent), Japan (2 per cent), and the Netherlands (2 per cent). In the more recent years, new markets have been developed for Hong Kong's exports, including markets in the Middle East, Eastern Europe, Latin America and Africa.

Increasing Economic Links between the HKSAR and the Mainland

Since the Mainland adopted its economic reform and open door policy in 1978, economic links between Hong Kong and the Mainland have gone from strength to strength. This has brought substantial economic benefits to both places.

Visible trade between Hong Kong and the Mainland has expanded rapidly since 1978, at an average annual rate of 22 per cent in value terms. But the pace of growth moderated in the more recent years, to an annual average of 8 per cent during 1993-2003, partly due to increased direct shipment of goods into and out of the Mainland upon enhancement of port facilities and simplification of customs procedures there. The Mainland remained Hong Kong's largest trading partner in 2003, accounting for 43 per cent of the total trade value in Hong Kong. The bulk (specifically, 91 per cent) of Hong Kong's re-export trade was related to the Mainland, making it the largest market for as well as the largest source of Hong Kong's re-exports. Reciprocally, Hong Kong was the Mainland's third largest trading partner in 2003 (after Japan and the United States), accounting for 10 per cent of the Mainland's total trade value (Chart 6).

In the more recent years, there has been an increasing shift in the mode of Hong Kong-Mainland trade from re-exports to offshore trade. Between 1990 and 1995, Hong Kong's exports of trade-related services grew at an annual average rate of 5 per cent in real terms, much slower than the growth in re-exports involving the Mainland, at an annual average rate of 22 per cent. The growth pattern was reversed during 1995 to 2003, when exports of trade-related services surged at an average annual rate of 15 per cent in real terms, outpacing the growth in re-exports involving the Mainland, at an average annual rate of 7 per cent.

Over the past two decades, there has also been a sharp increase in people, service and investment flows between Hong Kong and the Mainland. Hong Kong is a major service centre for the Mainland generally and South China in particular, providing a wide array of financial and other business support services like banking and finance, insurance, transport, accounting and sales promotion.

Hong Kong is also a principal gateway to the Mainland for business and tourism. Between 1993 and 2003, the number of trips made by Hong Kong residents to the Mainland grew at an average annual rate of 9 per cent to 53 million trips, and the number of trips made by foreign visitors to the Mainland through Hong Kong at an average annual rate of 4 per cent to 2.7 million trips. Yet, mainly due to the outbreak of SARS in the region in the first half of the year, these two particular types of trips decreased by 6 per cent and 21 per cent respectively in 2003.

Chart 6   **Visible trade between Hong Kong and the Mainland**

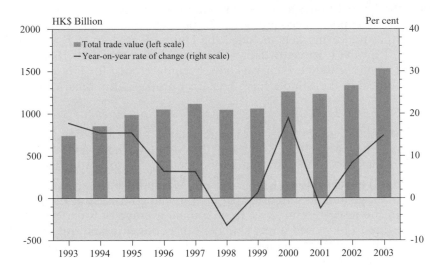

Since the Mainland adopted its economic reform and open door policy in 1978, there has been a rapid expansion in merchandise trade, especially re-export trade, between Hong Kong and the Mainland.

Moreover, Hong Kong is a major source of external direct investment in the Mainland. The cumulative value of Hong Kong's realised direct investment in the Mainland amounted to US$218 billion at end-September 2003, accounting for about half of the total inward direct investment there. Over the years, there has been a noticeable shift in the composition of Hong Kong's direct investment across the boundary, from industrial processing to a wider spectrum of business ventures, such as hotels and tourist-related facilities, real estate and infrastructure development. Relative to other places in the Mainland, Hong Kong's economic links with Guangdong are the most intimate. At end-2002, the cumulative value of Hong Kong's realised direct investment in Guangdong was US$86 billion, accounting for 69 per cent of its total inward direct investment. According to a survey conducted by the Federation of Hong Kong Industries in December 2003, 11 million Mainland workers were employed directly or indirectly in the Mainland by industrial ventures with Hong Kong interests, of whom 10 million were in Guangdong. This is about 57 times the size of Hong Kong's own manufacturing workforce.

In the opposite direction, there has likewise been a sizeable flow of investment capital from the Mainland to Hong Kong over the past years. By end-2002, the Mainland had invested a total of US$76 billion in Hong Kong, making it the largest source of external direct investment here. Over 2 000 Mainland enterprises currently operate in Hong Kong, with total assets amounting to US$220 billion. Mainland enterprises take up a significant role in such major economic sectors as banking, insurance, shipping and tourism, reportedly accounting for about 25 per cent of the market shares in those sectors. Mainland enterprises also maintain high investment stakes in other lines of business such as the import/export trade, the wholesale/retail trade, warehousing, real estate and infrastructure development.

In tandem with the upsurge in cross-boundary business activities, financial links between Hong Kong and the Mainland have strengthened substantially over the past years. Hong Kong's authorised institutions' external claims on and liabilities to entities in the Mainland were generally on the rise over the period. Comparing end-2003 with a year earlier, external liabilities of Hong Kong's authorised institutions to entities in the Mainland grew by 13 per cent to $326 billion, and their external claims on entities in the Mainland even faster by 41 per cent to $179 billion.

The Bank of China (Hong Kong) Limited is the second largest banking group in Hong Kong, after the HSBC Group. It is also one of the note-issuing banks in Hong Kong, besides the Hongkong Bank and the Standard Chartered Bank. As to the other three state-owned commercial banks, namely the China Construction Bank, the Agricultural Bank of China, and the Industrial and Commercial Bank of China, they have all been granted banking licences to operate in Hong Kong since 1995. On the other hand, the HSBC Group, the Bank of East Asia and the Standard Chartered Bank are amongst the best-represented foreign banks in the Mainland.

Hong Kong has been serving as a major funding centre for the Mainland. Besides being a direct source of funds, it also provides a window through which foreign funds can be channelled efficiently into the Mainland for financing development projects there. While syndicated loans remain the most important means for Mainland-related enterprises to raise funds in Hong Kong, issuance of securities has become increasingly popular in the more recent years. In 2003, listing activities by Mainland enterprises continued to be a prominent feature in Hong Kong's stock market, especially so in the latter part of the year when the market staged a visible upturn amidst improved investor sentiment. By end-2003, a total of 64 state-owned enterprises in the Mainland had been listed on the Main Board of Hong Kong's stock market, raising a total equity capital of $191.3 billion. Amongst them, 10 were listed in 2003, raising $46.8 billion. In addition, another 72 non-state-owned Mainland enterprises had likewise been listed by end-2003, raising a total equity capital of $590.4 billion. Of these, one was listed in 2003, raising $4.7 billion. On the Growth Enterprise Market, there were 28 state-owned enterprises, raising a total equity capital of $4.0 billion. All these listings have helped broaden the base of Hong Kong's stock market, and entrench further Hong Kong's position as a major fund raising centre in the region.

The signing of CEPA on June 29, followed by the signing of its six Annexes on September 29, serve to expand further business opportunities between Hong Kong and the Mainland, by enlarging the scope for cross-boundary trade, service and investment flows. Under CEPA, the Mainland will accord zero tariff as from January 1, 2004 for exports from Hong Kong meeting the rules of origin requirement in 374 Mainland product codes. On services, Hong Kong companies will be allowed to have earlier entry and wider market access, as well as to form wholly-owned or majority-owned subsidiaries in 18 service sectors in the Mainland. CEPA also facilitates trade and investment between Hong Kong and the Mainland through promoting cooperation in customs clearance, electronic commerce, transparency in laws and regulations, and other procedures.

With continuing reform and liberalisation of the Mainland economy, particularly after China's entry into the World Trade Organisation, more foreign investment can be expected to flow into the Mainland. Hong Kong's service hub role for the Mainland will continue to strengthen. Hong Kong possesses a strong niche in partnering with as well as in providing various business support services to foreign enterprises seeking to enter the Mainland market. In the other direction, as more Mainland enterprises seek to extend their business outward, Hong Kong can also help them to gain access to the overseas markets.

The Economy in 2003

External Trade

External trade was buoyant throughout 2003, sustaining strong growth in all four quarters of the year. This was attributable to the generally improved global economic environment during the year, enhanced price attractiveness of Hong Kong's exports stemming from the exchange rate movements and the domestic cost adjustments, as well as the rising competitiveness of Mainland products as the main source of Hong Kong's re-exports to the overseas markets. The war in Iraq and the outbreak of SARS had inflicted only brief and limited impact on Hong Kong's exports. The growth in exports in the third and fourth quarters remained distinct even against a higher base of comparison in the same period a year earlier.

Total exports of goods (comprising re-exports and domestic exports) surged by 14.0 per cent in real terms in 2003, after an already notable growth of 8.6 per cent in 2002. Performance was favourable all through the year, with year-on-year increases by 19.1 per cent, 14.3 per cent, 9.8 per cent and 14.2 per cent respectively in real terms in the four quarters. On a seasonally adjusted quarter-to-quarter comparison, total exports of goods rose by 3.4 per cent, 1.9 per cent and 1.5 per cent respectively in real terms in the first three quarters of 2003, and then picked up more sharply to a 6.2 per cent leap in the fourth quarter. Analysed by major market, the Mainland remained the largest market for Hong Kong's total exports of goods, accounting for 43 per cent of the total value in 2003. This was followed by the United States (with a share of 19 per cent), Japan (5 per cent), the United Kingdom (3 per cent), and Germany (3 per cent).

Re-exports remained the key driver of the overall export growth, surging by 16.1 per cent in real terms in 2003, considerably up from the already impressive growth at 10.9 per cent in 2002. Double-digit increases took place in all four quarters of 2003. On the other hand, the ongoing structural shift towards re-exports and offshore trade continued to impinge upon domestic exports, which contracted further by 7.4 per cent in real terms in 2003, though more moderate than the 11.3 per cent plunge in 2002.

Imports of goods were likewise robust, soaring by 12.8 per cent in real terms in 2003, also sharply exceeding the 7.8 per cent rise in 2002. Year-on-year growth was most distinct in the first quarter of 2003, at 18.7 per cent in real terms. It remained strong in the second quarter, at 10.6 per cent, upon sustained expansion in re-export trade and even with the spread of SARS severely dampening import intake for local use. Then, with the moderation in re-export growth in the third quarter partly offsetting a revival in import intake for local use, imports of goods had a slower growth by 7.9 per cent in the third quarter. This was followed by a re-accelerated growth at 15.0 per cent in the fourth quarter, as re-exports picked up again while import intake for local use rebounded noticeably. On a seasonally adjusted quarter-to-quarter comparison, imports of goods rose by 2.9 per cent in real terms in the first quarter of 2003, yet moderating to a 0.9 per cent increase in the second quarter, before turning up again to increases by 2.6 per cent and 7.0 per cent respectively in the third and fourth quarters. Analysed by major source, the Mainland continued to be the largest source of Hong Kong's imports of goods, accounting for 44 per cent of the total value in 2003. This was followed by Japan (with a share of 12 per cent), Taiwan (7 per cent), the United States (5 per cent), Singapore (5 per cent), and the Republic of Korea (5 per cent) *(Chart 7)*.

Chart 7

Hong Kong's visible trade
(year-on-year rate of change in real terms)

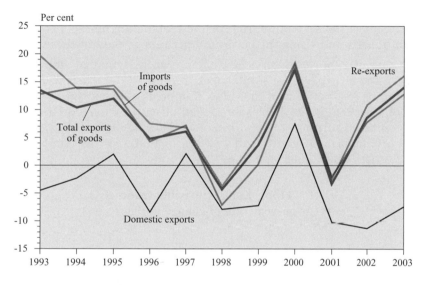

Total exports of goods, including in particular re-exports, continued to surge in real terms in 2003, as did imports of goods.

Yet, with a larger rise in import prices than in export prices, the value of imports of goods grew at a faster pace than that of total exports of goods in 2003. As a result, the visible trade deficit reckoned on a GDP basis widened in absolute terms, to $45.0 billion (or 2.5 per cent of the value of imports of goods) in 2003, from $39.4 billion (2.5 per cent) in 2002.

On invisible trade, exports of services maintained a strong growth momentum in the first quarter of 2003, but they were dented severely by the spread of SARS in Hong Kong in the second quarter. Nevertheless, backed by a swift rebound in the third quarter and a further pick-up in the fourth quarter, exports of services still attained an appreciable growth at 5.5 per cent in real terms in 2003, albeit milder than the 12.2 per cent surge in 2002. On a year-on-year comparison, exports of services leaped by 12.7 per cent in real terms in the first quarter of 2003, before falling abruptly by 12.0 per cent in the second quarter as inbound tourism and related business plummeted upon the SARS impact. As such business bounced up strongly thereafter, exports of services increased again, by 7.8 per cent in the third quarter, and then distinctly more by 11.8 per cent in the fourth quarter. On a seasonally adjusted quarter-to-quarter comparison, exports of services rose by 0.9 per cent in real terms in the first quarter of 2003, before plummeting by 19.7 per cent in the second quarter. A sharp turnaround ensued, with a 33.5 per cent jump in the third quarter and a further 2.2 per cent increase in the fourth quarter.

Imports of services were likewise badly hit by SARS in the second quarter. Notwithstanding the subsequent rebound, imports of services still went down by 4.4 per cent in real terms in 2003, following a meagre 0.2 per cent rise in 2002. On a year-on-year comparison, imports of services shrank in both the first and second quarters of 2003, by 3.9 per cent and 19.6 per cent respectively in real terms, outweighing the increases by 0.5 per cent and 4.2 per cent respectively in the third and fourth quarters. On a seasonally adjusted quarter-to-quarter comparison, imports of services contracted by 3.8 per cent in real terms in the first quarter of 2003 and then plunged by 17.8 per cent in the second quarter, before rebounding markedly by 27.8 per cent in the third quarter and rising further by 2.9 per cent in the fourth quarter.

As the value of exports of services went up whereas that of imports of services moved lower, the invisible trade surplus reckoned on a GDP basis widened further to $161.1 billion or 85.1 per cent of the value of imports of services in 2003, from $144.5 billion or 74.7 per cent in 2002. This more than offset the enlarged visible trade deficit to yield a combined surplus of $116.1 billion in 2003, equivalent to 5.9 per cent of the total value of imports of goods and services in that year, as compared to $105.1 billion or 5.9 per cent in 2002 *(Chart 8)*.

Chart 8　　　　　　　　　**Hong Kong's invisible trade**
(year-on-year rate of change in real terms)

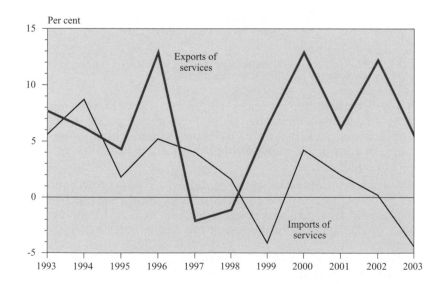

Notwithstanding the severe setback upon the SARS impact in the second quarter, exports of services still attained an appreciable growth in 2003, albeit slower than that in 2002. Imports of services were affected more by SARS, relapsing to a decline in 2003, after a mild increase in 2002.

Domestic Demand

Local consumer spending faced a severe blow in the second quarter of 2003 upon the spread of SARS. Then, with the epidemic brought under control, local consumer spending recuperated progressively in the third quarter, followed by an even more visible pick-up in the fourth quarter. Added to this was a strong resurgence in inbound tourism. For 2003 as a whole, although the volume of retail sales still decreased marginally by 0.6 per cent, this compared favourably with the 2.6 per cent dip in 2002. Private consumption expenditure (PCE) likewise staged a notable turnaround after the waning of SARS. On a year-on-year comparison, PCE went down by 1.8 per cent and 3.5 per cent respectively in real terms in the first two quarters of 2003, but increased again by 1.6 per cent in the third quarter, for the first time since end-2001. As consumer sentiment improved further in tandem with the upturn in the economy, a rally in the local stock market and a rebound in the property market, PCE growth accentuated to 3.6 per cent in the fourth quarter. For 2003 as a whole, PCE showed virtually no change in real terms, having contracted by 1.2 per cent in 2002. The pick-up in consumer spending in late 2003 occurred across almost all the major consumer goods and services. On a seasonally adjusted quarter-to-quarter comparison, PCE fell by 0.1 per cent and 1.4 per cent respectively in real terms in the first two quarters of 2003, and then bounced up by 3.9 per cent and 1.2 per cent respectively in the third and fourth quarters.

Amidst the fiscal restraint, government consumption expenditure (GCE) reckoned on a national accounts basis registered only modest growth in the first three quarters of 2003, by 1.3 per cent, 0.4 per cent and 0.5 per cent respectively in real terms over a year earlier. While the growth rate re-accelerated to 5.6 per cent in the fourth quarter, this was due in part to a low base of comparison a year earlier. Also contributing were the one-off compensatory payments made to those civil servants retiring under the Second Voluntary Retirement Scheme. For 2003 as a whole, GCE edged up by 1.9 per cent in real terms, still slower than the 2.4 per cent growth in 2002. On a seasonally adjusted quarter-to-quarter comparison, GCE increased throughout the four quarters of 2003, by 1.0 per cent, 0.1 per cent, 1.3 per cent and 3.0 per cent respectively in real terms.

Overall investment spending, as represented by gross domestic fixed capital formation (GDFCF), regained some strength in the latter part of 2003, after the setback amidst the SARS impact in the earlier months. GDFCF still grew by 3.5 per cent in real terms in the first quarter of 2003 over a year earlier, but relapsed to a sharp decline by 5.7 per cent in the second quarter as business conditions worsened upon the spread of SARS. Then, with the ensuing recovery in economic activity, the decline in GDFCF narrowed to a mere 0.6 per cent in the third quarter, and rebounded to a 2.5 per cent rise in the fourth quarter. For 2003 as a whole, GDFCF fell only marginally by 0.1 per cent in real terms, much improved from the 4.3 per cent dip in 2002.

There was a clear resurgence of interest in acquisition of machinery and equipment during most of the year, other than the brief relapse in the second quarter. On a year-on-year comparison, expenditure on machinery, equipment and computer software soared by 11.9 per cent in real terms in the first quarter of 2003. After a temporary decrease by 2.0 per cent in the second quarter, the expenditure surged ahead by 4.9 per cent in the third quarter and even more by 10.2 per cent in the fourth quarter as the business outlook brightened. The intake of several aircraft in the second half of the year also helped. For 2003 as a whole, expenditure on machinery, equipment and computer software rose by 6.1 per cent in real terms, reversing the 9.1 per cent decline in 2002.

On the other hand, building and construction output remained subdued in overall terms throughout the year. Expenditure on building and construction fell back by 6.9 per cent in real terms in 2003, after a modest increase by 1.2 per cent in 2002. On a year-on-year comparison, the decreases were 3.5 per cent, 8.4 per cent, 6.7 per cent and 9.3 per cent respectively in real terms in the four quarters of 2003. The slump was mostly attributable to a distinct fall-off in private sector building work, despite a rise in consents for new building projects during the year. The increase in private sector civil engineering work rendered only a marginal offset. Public sector expenditure on building and construction was also slack in the first half of the year, upon the winding down of work on the KCR West Rail and Ma On Shan Extension. Nevertheless, it regained some momentum in the second half of the year, upon commencement of several new infrastructural projects including the Hong Kong section of the Hong Kong-Shenzhen Western Corridor and the Deep Bay Link *(Chart 9)*.

Chart 9   **Main components of domestic demand**
(year-on-year rate of change in real terms)

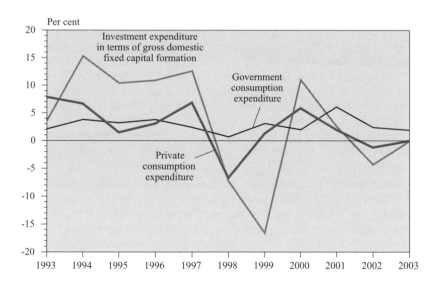

Consumer spending suffered a severe blow in the second quarter of 2003 upon the impact of SARS. Yet it staged a distinct turnaround in the third and fourth quarters, as the SARS impact dissipated and as overall economic activity turned around. Overall investment spending also picked up in the latter part of the year, amidst renewed interest in acquisition of machinery and equipment. As to government consumption expenditure, there was only a modest growth amidst continued fiscal restraint.

Net Output or Value Added by Economic Activity

As reflected in quarterly GDP by major economic sectors at constant prices, net output or value added for all the service sectors taken together went higher by an average of 3.7 per cent in real terms in the first three quarters of 2003 over a year earlier, slightly exceeding the 3.5 per cent gain in 2002. Analysed by constituent sector and on a year-on-year comparison in real terms, net output in the wholesale, retail and import/export trades, restaurants and hotels rose strongly by 9.5 per cent in the first three quarters of 2003. This was attributable to a marked increase in net output in the import/export trade, more than offsetting the declines observed in the wholesale and retail trades and in restaurants and hotels owing to the SARS impact in the second quarter. Meanwhile, net output in financing, insurance, real estate and business services moved up by 3.6 per cent, mainly underpinned by improved performance of banking services and also buoyancy in stock brokerage amidst an upsurge in stock market turnover. On the other hand, net output in transport, storage and communications as well as in community, social and personal services shrank by 0.2 per cent and 1.0 per cent respectively. These largely reflected the downturn in air and land transport services and in recreation and entertainment services, upon the spread of SARS in the second quarter.

Net output in the local manufacturing sector was reduced distinctly, by an average of 10.2 per cent in real terms in the first three quarters of 2003 over a year earlier, further to a 9.8 per cent fall in 2002. The weak performance of domestic exports and ongoing relocation of production processes outside Hong Kong largely contributed. As to the construction sector, net output dropped by an average of 4.3 per cent in real terms in the first three quarters of 2003 over a year earlier, after a 0.8 per cent fall in 2002. This was mainly due to winding down of some major railway projects earlier in the year and generally slack building activity.

The Labour Market

The labour market slackened visibly in the first half of 2003, but underwent a progressive improvement in the second half, as the economy recovered from the severe setback inflicted by SARS earlier in the year. Indicative of this, the seasonally adjusted unemployment rate rose from 7.2 per cent in the fourth quarter of 2002 to 7.5 per cent in the first quarter of 2003, and markedly further to 8.6 per cent in the second quarter and then to a peak of 8.7 per cent in May-July. Nevertheless, along with the upturn in economic activity, the seasonally adjusted unemployment rate fell back to 8.3 per cent in the third quarter and notably further to 7.3 per cent in the fourth quarter. For 2003 as a whole, the unemployment rate averaged 7.9 per cent, which however was still considerably higher than that in 2002, at 7.3 per cent. Furthermore, there was a clear lengthening in the median duration of unemployment, from 90 days in the fourth quarter of 2002 to 109 days in the fourth quarter of 2003, as well as a surge in the proportion of persons unemployed for six months or more, from 30 per cent to 36 per cent.

The underemployment rate exhibited a broadly similar profile. It jumped to a peak of 4.3 per cent in the second quarter of 2003, after a modest decline from 3.1 per cent in the fourth quarter of 2002 to 2.9 per cent in the first quarter of 2003. Conceivably, this was due to a significant proportion of employees having been temporarily suspended from work or asked to take no-pay leave during the SARS period. Yet as SARS waned and the affected employees gradually returned to their jobs, the underemployment rate came down again, to 3.6 per cent in the third quarter and further to 3.3 per cent in the fourth quarter. For 2003 as a whole, the underemployment rate averaged 3.5 per cent, which however was also appreciably above that in 2002, at 3.0 per cent *(Chart 10)*.

55

Chart 10   **Unemployment and underemployment rates**

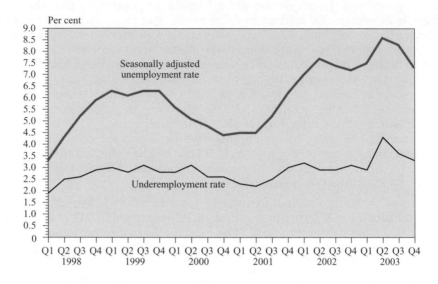

Both the unemployment rate and the underemployment rate surged to record highs in the summer of 2003, consequential to an abrupt economic downturn under the impact of SARS. Yet they came down visibly afterwards, in tandem with a distinct rebound in overall economic activity.

For the employed persons, work intensity dwindled noticeably during the second quarter of 2003, amidst the spread of SARS. The median hours of work were reduced to 45 hours per week in the second quarter, from 48 hours per week in both the fourth quarter of 2002 and the first quarter of 2003. Yet in line with the revival in economic activity, work intensity rose again to 48 hours per week in the third and fourth quarters. For 2003 as a whole, the median hours of work stood at 48 hours per week, the same as in 2002. The proportions of employed persons working for 50 hours or more per week and for 60 hours or more per week, at 41 per cent and 25 per cent respectively in the fourth quarter of 2003, were even slightly higher than those of 40 per cent and 24 per cent in the fourth quarter of 2002.

Total employment as enumerated from households contracted by 0.3 per cent in 2003, yet this was smaller than the 0.6 per cent decrease in 2002. On a year-on-year comparison, employment growth slowed down from 0.8 per cent in the first quarter of 2003 to 0.5 per cent in the second quarter, and then turned negative in the third quarter with a decline of 1.7 per cent amidst the SARS impact. In the fourth quarter, the decrease narrowed visibly to 0.6 per cent, in line with improved performance of the economy after SARS waned. Total labour force expanded only mildly by 0.4 per cent per cent in 2003, lesser than the 1.8 per cent rise in 2002. This was entirely attributable to a decline in the labour force participation rate, especially that for persons aged 15-19 and aged 50 and above. On a year-on-year comparison, labour force growth moderated over the course of 2003, turning from increases of 1.3 per cent and 1.5 per cent respectively in the first and second quarters to decreases of 0.7 per cent and 0.5 per cent in the third and fourth quarters *(Chart 11)*.

Chart 11 **Total labour force and total employment**
(year-on-year rate of change)

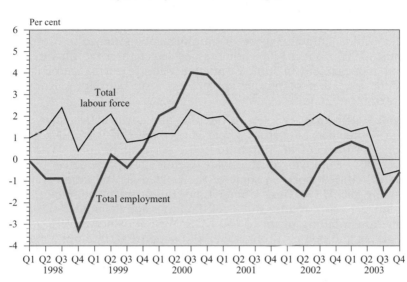

In the first three quarters of 2003, labour force growth continued to outpace employment growth. Yet the difference between these two growth rates was markedly reduced in the fourth quarter, mainly due to relatively improved employment on the back of a pick-up in overall economy activity. As a result, the unemployment rate fell back visibly by the year-end.

Employment as enumerated from business establishments shrank by 3.3 per cent in September 2003 from a year earlier, following decreases of 2.5 per cent in March and 3.8 per cent in June. For the first nine months of 2003 as a whole, the decrease averaged at 3.2 per cent, exceeding that of 1.6 per cent in 2002. On a seasonally adjusted quarter-to-quarter comparison, total employment nevertheless edged up by 0.1 per cent in September 2003, after declining by 1.7 per cent in March and 1.6 per cent in June. The downtrend since mid-2001 was thus arrested. Increased labour demand, alongside the turnaround in business activity after the waning of SARS, largely contributed.

Taking all the service sectors surveyed together, employment was 2.6 per cent down in September 2003 from a year earlier, further to decreases of 1.4 per cent in March and 2.2 per cent in June. Analysed by major constituent sector, employment in storage and communications continued on a marked decline, by 13.0 per cent in September 2003 from a year earlier, amidst more downsizing and lay-offs in the telecommunications sector, predominantly in the early part of the year. Yet employment in restaurants and hotels had a moderated decrease as compared to a few months earlier, by 8.7 per cent, aided by the surge in inbound tourism and revival in local consumer spending. Employment in the retail trade likewise went down, by 6.4 per cent, notwithstanding the generally improving business conditions. Employment in water transport, air transport and services allied to transport was reduced by 4.4 per cent, with more distinct decreases seen in air transport services and in air ticket and travel agents. Employment in the wholesale and import/export trades contracted by 4.3 per cent, mainly reflecting a higher base of comparison a year earlier.

57

Employment in financing, insurance, real estate and business services had a smaller reduction, by 0.5 per cent. On the other hand, employment in community, social and personal services increased by 3.9 per cent, underpinned by strong demand for the relevant services.

As to the local manufacturing sector, employment continued to drop, by 9.1 per cent in September 2003 from a year earlier, albeit lesser than the dips of 9.4 per cent in March and 13.8 per cent in June. Continued weak performance of domestic exports and ongoing relocation of production processes outside Hong Kong remained the major contributory factors.

Employment of manual workers at building and construction sites dwindled by 8.5 per cent in September 2003 from a year earlier, yet this was much smaller than the plunges of 13.3 per cent in March and 20.2 per cent in June. Within the total for September 2003, employment at private sector sites plummeted by 10.2 per cent, partly due to reduced work on some of the residential and commercial development projects along the MTR Tung Chung Line. Employment at public sector sites was down by 6.0 per cent, amidst still slack building activity under the Public Housing Programme and winding down of the KCR West Rail project. Taking into account off-site workers and related professional and support staff, employment in the entire building and construction sector was lower by 9.0 per cent in the third quarter of 2003 than a year earlier, following declines of 3.5 per cent in the first quarter and 5.4 per cent in the second quarter.

Overall labour earnings in the private sector eased further by 1.8 per cent in money terms in the third quarter of 2003 over a year earlier, after a decrease of 2.0 per cent in the first quarter, and an enlarged drop of 2.5 per cent in the second quarter owing to the SARS impact. Discounting a larger decline in consumer prices as reflected by the Composite CPI, overall labour earnings were nevertheless up by 1.9 per cent in real terms in the third quarter of 2003 over a year earlier, after virtually nil change in the first quarter and a fall of 0.1 per cent in the second quarter. For the first three quarters of 2003 as a whole, overall labour earnings were reduced by an average of 2.1 per cent in money terms from a year earlier, exceeding the 1.1 per cent decrease in 2002. In real terms, labour earnings increased much less for the first three quarters of 2003 as a whole, by an average of 0.6 per cent over a year earlier, as against the 2.0 per cent rise in 2002. On a seasonally adjusted quarter-to-quarter comparison, overall labour earnings rose marginally by 0.2 per cent in money terms in the third quarter of 2003, having been down by 1.0 per cent in the first quarter and 0.7 per cent in the second quarter. The downtrend over the preceding seven quarters was thus reversed. In real terms, overall labour earnings picked up more, by 1.5 per cent in the third quarter of 2003, after recovering from a fall of 0.6 per cent in the first quarter to a rise of 0.5 per cent in the second quarter.

Overall labour wages in the private sector likewise continued to fall, by 2.1 per cent in money terms in September 2003 over a year earlier, following a decrease of 1.5 per cent in March, and a larger decrease of 2.5 per cent in June due to the SARS impact. Discounting an enlarged decline in consumer prices as measured by the CPI(A), overall labour wages increased by 0.7 per cent in real terms in September 2003 over a year earlier, having risen by 0.3 per cent in March and then edged down by 0.1 per cent in June. For the first nine months of 2003 as a whole, overall labour wages fell by an average of 2.1 per cent in money terms over a year earlier, but edged up by an average of 0.3 per cent in real terms. In 2002, there was a decline of 1.0 per cent in money terms, yet an increase of 1.3 per cent in real terms (Chart 12).

Chart 12

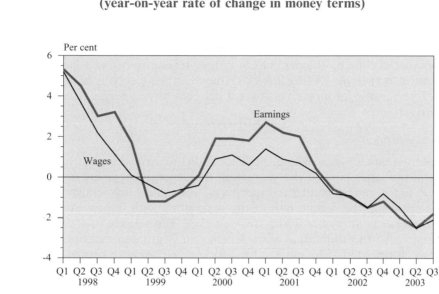

Earnings and wages
(year-on-year rate of change in money terms)

Amidst the slackened labour market conditions, overall labour earnings and wages continued on a decline in money terms in 2003. The decline nevertheless showed some narrowing since mid-year.

Analysed by economic sector, labour earnings in money terms fell virtually across-the-board. For all the service sectors surveyed taken together, labour earnings went down by 2.0 per cent in money terms in the third quarter of 2003 over a year earlier, further to declines of 2.1 per cent in the first quarter and 3.0 per cent in the second quarter. Yet, discounting the decrease in consumer prices, labour earnings still gained by 1.6 per cent in real terms in the third quarter of 2003 over a year earlier, as against falls of 0.1 per cent in the first quarter and 0.6 per cent in the second quarter. Analysed by major constituent sector, earnings in community, social and personal services and in restaurants and hotels were slashed by 5.7 per cent and 5.2 per cent respectively in money terms, or 2.2 per cent and 1.7 per cent in real terms, in the third quarter of 2003 over a year earlier. Earnings in transport, storage and communications, in the wholesale, retail and import/export trades, and in financing, insurance, real estate and business services decreased to a lesser extent, by 0.6-1.8 per cent in money terms. In real terms, there were nevertheless increases, by 1.8-3.1 per cent. As to the local manufacturing sector, labour earnings were down by 3.6 per cent in money terms in the third quarter of 2003 from a year earlier, lesser than the decrease of 5.1 per cent in the first quarter but larger than the decrease of 2.2 per cent in the second quarter. In real terms, labour earnings in this sector edged lower by 0.1 per cent in the third quarter of 2003 from a year earlier, as compared to a fall of 3.2 per cent in the first quarter and a rise of 0.3 per cent in the second quarter.

As to labour wages in the service sectors, those in restaurants and hotels and in personal services were lower by 5.0 per cent and 4.1 per cent respectively in money terms in September 2003 than a year earlier. In real terms, the corresponding decreases were 2.3 per cent and 1.3 per cent. Wages in transport services and in the wholesale, retail and import/export trades fell less, by 1.6 per cent and 1.5 per cent respectively in money terms. In real terms, there were still increases by 1.1 per cent and 1.3 per cent. Wages in financing, insurance, real estate and business services had an even smaller decline by 0.3 per cent in money terms, and thus a larger increase by 2.5 per cent in real terms. As to the local manufacturing sector, wages continued to fall, by 3.7 per cent in money terms or 1.0 per cent in real terms in September 2003 over a year earlier.

The Property Market

The property market as a whole showed a distinct turnaround in 2003, mostly occurring in the latter part of the year, from the general sluggishness in the past few years. The markets for residential property and shopping space both staged a noticeable upturn in the second half of the year, along with improved performance of the overall economy and rally in the stock market. The signing of CEPA in June and implementation of the Individual Visit Scheme for Mainland visitors to Hong Kong in July also contributed. The market for office space likewise turned better towards the end of the year.

More specifically, the sales market for private residential property remained sluggish in the first half of 2003, but rebounded distinctly in both transaction volume and prices in the second half of the year. Following the Government's promulgation of nine policy measures to stabilise the housing market in late 2002, transactions had a brief pick-up in early 2003, but slackened subsequently amidst renewed worries over job security and income stability. Acquisition interest was curtailed further during the period from mid-March to early June, upon the impact of SARS. The ample supply of new flats in the mass market continued to cause a drag. Nevertheless, market sentiment started to improve in early June, boosted by an improved outlook for the economy and a more sanguine global economic environment. This was particularly so after the signing of CEPA in June and implementation of the Individual Visit Scheme for Mainland visitors to Hong Kong in July. The announcement by the Government in October of further measures to engender steady development of the housing market also helped. Developers actively resumed sales in the primary market, which generally received a good response. This led many developers to reduce or withdraw the price discounts and other concessions offered earlier. Meanwhile, activity in the secondary market also took a notable upturn. Flat prices bottomed out in the third quarter, and bounced up visibly in the fourth quarter. In the luxury end of the market, strong buying interest re-emerged in the latter part of the year, leading to a more pronounced rebound in prices. The Government's new policy measure to attract investment immigrants to Hong Kong may have rendered some lift to this segment.

On a quarter-to-quarter comparison, flat prices on average drifted lower by 4 per cent, 5 per cent and 1 per cent respectively in the first three quarters of 2003, but rebounded to an increase of 8 per cent in the fourth quarter. For 2003 as a whole, while flat prices on average still fell by 1 per cent, this was much narrowed from the 12 per cent drop in 2002. Yet, compared with the peak level in the third quarter of 1997, flat prices in the fourth quarter of 2003 remained substantially lower, by an average of 62 per cent.

As to the rental market for private residential flats, leasing activity likewise turned more active in the second half of 2003, after remaining quiet in the first half of the year. Flat rentals, having eased during most of 2003, tended to stabilise in the fourth quarter. On a quarter-to-quarter comparison, private housing rentals on average declined by 3 per cent, 4 per cent and 2 per cent respectively in the first three quarters of 2003, but were broadly stable in the fourth quarter. For the year as a whole, there was on average a fall of 9 per cent, lesser than the 14 per cent dip in 2002. Against the peak level in the third quarter of 1997, private housing rentals were significantly down in the fourth quarter of 2003, by an average of 48 per cent *(Chart 13)*.

Chart 13   **Prices and rentals of residential property**
(1999=100)

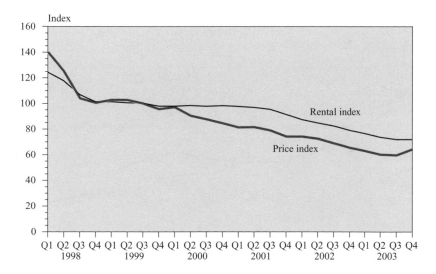

Having fallen during most of 2003, flat prices picked up visibly in the fourth quarter, while rentals tended to stabilise, amidst a distinct improvement in the overall economic performance and outlook.

On commercial property, the rental market for office space weakened further during most of 2003, but became more active towards the end of the year. The abundant supply of new and existing office space, coupled with the SARS impact, exerted much downward pressure on rentals in the first half of the year. Yet, after the waning of SARS, such downward pressure on rentals tended to dwindle in the second half. With rentals for Grade A office space having fallen to a more attractive level and with an upturn in business sentiment, leasing demand for office space strengthened somewhat in the latter part of the year. Also, more tenants were willing to relocate their offices from buildings which were older or in secondary locations to better ones. On a quarter-to-quarter comparison, office rentals declined on average by 4 per cent, 6 per cent and 3 per cent respectively in the first three quarters of 2003, but rose back by 2 per cent in the fourth quarter. For 2003 as a whole, the decrease on average was 12 per cent. As to the sales market, activity remained subdued in the first half of 2003. But investor interest was rekindled markedly in the second half of the year, stimulated in part by the signing of CEPA in June and perhaps more so by the better economic outlook. On a quarter-to-quarter comparison, prices for office space on average went down by 4 per cent and 5 per cent respectively in the first and second quarters of 2003, yet rebounded by 4 per cent in the third quarter and further by 7 per cent in the fourth quarter. For 2003 as a whole, there was on average a slight increase of 2 per cent. Against their respective peak levels in 1994, prices and rentals for office space in the fourth quarter of 2003 plunged by an average of 72 per cent and 62 per cent respectively *(Chart 14)*.

Chart 14   **Prices and rentals of office space**
(1999=100)

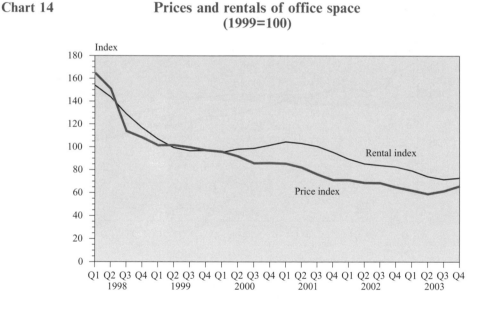

Rentals for office space continued to decline during most of 2003, yet rose again mildly in the fourth quarter. Prices showed a distinct upturn in the second half of the year, amidst a resurgence of buying interest.

The rental market for shopping space, having remained bleak in the first quarter and then hard hit by the spread of SARS in the second quarter, revived in the remainder of the year. This was supported by the pick-up in local consumer demand, as well as in inbound tourism particularly following implementation of the Individual Visit Scheme in July. However, there was a mixed performance amongst different retail premises amidst the revival, depending on location and management quality. Retail premises in popular locations and in better-managed shopping malls fared much better. On a quarter-to-quarter comparison, rentals for shopping space, on average having fallen by 3 per cent and 6 per cent respectively in the first and second quarters of 2003, rose back by 1 per cent and 3 per cent in the third and fourth quarters. For 2003 as a whole, there was on average a 5 per cent decline. The sales market performed better, as investor interest grew keener in the second half of the year. There were reportedly a number of transactions involving short-term re-sale with profits. On a quarter-to-quarter comparison, prices for shopping space on average went higher by 1 per cent, 2 per cent and 9 per cent respectively in the second, third and fourth quarters of 2003, after a 2 per cent decrease in the first quarter. For 2003 as a whole, there was on average an increase of 10 per cent. Compared with the peak levels in the third quarter of 1997, prices and rentals for shopping space in the fourth quarter of 2003 plummeted by an average of 53 per cent and 30 per cent respectively.

On industrial property, the rental market remained generally depressed in 2003. Demand for conventional flatted factory space continued to be undermined by the further contraction in local manufacturing activity. Modern industrial premises that could be used as back-up service centres also faced competition from office space in the fringe areas, as rentals for such office space fell to an even lower level. On a quarter-to-quarter comparison, rentals for industrial space on average eased by 2 per cent, 7 per cent and 3 per cent respectively in the first three quarters of 2003, but rose again by 3 per cent in the fourth quarter. For 2003 as a whole, rentals for industrial space on average dipped by 9 per cent. As to the sales market, support came mainly from projects involving the conversion of industrial sites to hotel use amidst the rebound in inbound tourism. On a quarter-to-quarter comparison, prices for industrial space on average went up by 1 per cent and 3 per cent respectively in the third and fourth quarters of 2003, after nil change in the first quarter and a decline of 3 per cent in the second quarter. For 2003 as a whole, prices for industrial space were on average virtually unchanged. Against their respective peak levels in 1994, prices and rentals for industrial space in the fourth quarter of 2003 slumped by an average of 68 per cent and 51 per cent respectively.

On supply of new property, completions of private residential flats decreased by 14 per cent to 29 115 units in 2003, in stark contrast to the 30 per cent increase in 2002. Completions of new office space increased substantially further by 80 per cent to 299 000 square metres in 2003, after a surge of 117 per cent in 2002. On the other hand, completions of shopping space shrank by 15 per cent to 118 000 square metres in 2003, after a 5 per cent rise in 2002. As to industrial property, there was no completion of conventional flatted factory space in 2003, following a plunge of 91 per cent to 3 000 square metres in 2002. Completions of industrial-cum-office space amounted to 15 000 square metres in 2003, after no completion in 2002.

Overall property transactions, as measured by agreements for sale and purchase of property registered with the Land Registry, rose by 2 per cent both in number and total value in 2003. These reversed the corresponding decreases of 3 per cent and 4 per cent in 2002. The increase was concentrated in the second half of the year, reflecting revival in the property market. Analysed by main type of property, transactions in residential property fell slightly by 2 per cent in number but were unchanged in total value in 2003. Meanwhile, transactions in non-residential property increased both in number and total value, by 22 per cent and 15 per cent respectively *(Chart 15)*.

Chart 15   **Sale and purchase agreements by broad type of property**

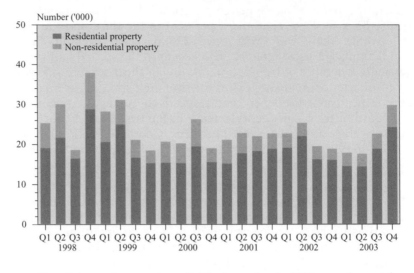

Overall transactions went up slightly in number in 2003, as a decrease in transactions of residential property was more than offset by a concurrent increase in transactions of non-residential property.

Price Movement

Overall consumer prices, whilst still coming down for the fifth consecutive year since late 1998, had a smaller decrease in 2003 than in 2002. The moderation in the price decline took place in the first and fourth quarters of 2003, outweighing the accentuated falls in the second and third quarters, which were mainly brought about, first, by the severe impact of SARS on consumer demand, and, then, by the special relief measures granted by the Government to alleviate the SARS impact. The moderation was more appreciable towards the year-end, when both property rentals and labour wages tended to stabilise amidst the generally improved economic conditions. Also, in face of the surge in inbound tourism and revival in local consumer spending, some of the local retailers and service providers reduced the price discounts and other concessions on their goods and services, and some others even raised the prices modestly. A rebound in the prices of retained imports over the past year, amidst a weaker US dollar and an uptrend in world commodity prices, should have contributed as well.

For 2003 as a whole, the Composite CPI went down by 2.6 per cent, smaller than the 3.0 per cent decline in 2002. The year-on-year decrease actually narrowed to 2.0 per cent in the first quarter of 2003, from 2.9 per cent in the fourth quarter of 2002, although this was largely attributable to a low base of comparison owing to the rates concession by the Government in 2002. The decrease then widened to 2.5 per cent in the second quarter under the impact of SARS, and further to 3.6 per cent in the third quarter on account of the new rates concession as well as the waiver of water and sewage charges granted as relief measures by the Government. The decrease narrowed again, to 2.3 per cent in the fourth quarter, upon firming up in retail prices of some of the goods and services, and lapse of the special relief measures.

Analysed by sub-index, the CPI(A) and CPI(B) likewise had lesser declines in 2003, by 2.1 per cent and 2.7 per cent respectively, than in 2002, by 3.2 per cent and 3.1 per cent. As to the CPI(C), the decrease however widened slightly, from 2.8 per cent to 2.9 per cent. This was mainly due to lower rentals for private housing and reduced charges for package tours during the past year, which tended to benefit the higher-income households more. The quarterly profiles of these sub-indices were nevertheless similar, characterised in general by enlarged declines in the second and third quarters yet moderated falls in the first and fourth quarters.

The GDP deflator, as a broad measure of overall price change in the economy, dipped by 5.1 per cent in 2003, distinctly larger than the 3.0 per cent decrease in 2002. Yet the year-on-year decline in the fourth quarter of 2003, by 4.8 per cent, was narrowed from the widening declines in the second and third quarters, by 5.4 per cent and 5.7 per cent respectively, though still exceeding the decline in the first quarter, by 4.6 per cent. The larger fall in the GDP deflator in 2003 than in 2002 was mainly attributable to a worsening in the terms of trade in goods and services as well as an accentuated decline in the price deflator for government consumption expenditure, which more than offset moderated declines in the price deflators for gross domestic fixed capital formation and private consumption expenditure. Within the GDP deflator, the domestic demand deflator and the total final demand deflator nevertheless had lesser decreases in 2003 than in 2002, by 3.8 per cent and 2.4 per cent respectively as against 4.5 per cent and 3.5 per cent *(Chart 16)*.

Chart 16   **Main inflation indicators**
(year-on-year rate of change)

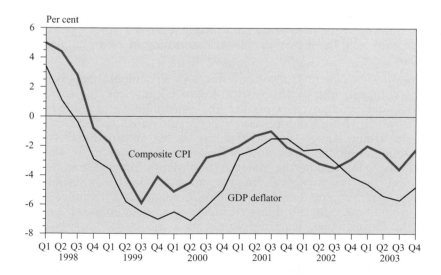

Both the Composite CPI and the GDP deflator continued to decline in 2003, but the decline narrowed visibly towards the year-end.

Economic Policy

Under the 'one country, two systems' principle, the HKSAR shall continue to adopt economic, social and political systems distinct from those in the Mainland following reunification in July 1997. The Basic Law, as the constitutional law of the HKSAR, gives a firm protection to this principle. The HKSAR shall continue to uphold the rule of law, maintain an effective executive-led Government, sustain an efficient and clean Civil Service, foster free enterprise and free trade, render a sound financial system and a robust monetary regime, practise prudent public finance, and keep a simple and predictable tax system with low tax rate. This serves to provide a favourable overall business environment and helps instil confidence for foreign investors coming to Hong Kong.

The Government firmly believes that the market can allocate and utilise resources more effectively and has a greater capacity to foster creativity, provide economic impetus and create employment opportunities. Moreover, the Government is determined to enhance those areas of strength instrumental to upholding Hong Kong's competitiveness as a premier business hub in the region, as well as to remove obstacles to the economic growth process. The guiding principle is the 'market leads and government facilitates', as this ensures optimal resource usage and greater efficiency. Primarily it is market forces that drive the overall economy forward. The role of government is to create the best environment for business, and to facilitate the smooth functioning and promote the healthy development of the market. Throughout the past few years, the Government has taken proactive moves to reduce rigidities in the economy, redefine its role, and minimise bureaucratic 'red tape'.

Meanwhile, faced with the challenges posed by globalisation and closer integration with the Mainland, Hong Kong needs to restructure and re-position itself, in order to stay competitive and attain sustainable growth. Hong Kong by itself can hardly compete purely in cost terms. The strategy to enhance competitiveness is to go up the value chain through speeding up structural transformation to a knowledge-based economy, through pursuing education reform and population policy to amass the pool of talent, as well as through leveraging on the immense business opportunities in the Mainland. The vision is to build Hong Kong as Asia's world city, by consolidating its unique position in the region as well as reinforcing its role as a pivotal gateway to the Mainland.

Focusing on areas where Hong Kong has a clear comparative advantage is key in competing with the rest of the world. Financial services, logistics, tourism, and professional and producer services are the four high value added sectors in the economy in which Hong Kong possesses a competitive edge. The Government strives to maintain Hong Kong's competitiveness as an international financial centre, through streamlining the rules and procedures to attract more financial product issuers, through increasing the breadth and depth of the market, and through strengthening the infrastructure for the market. On the logistics industry, the Government has support measures including reinforcing facilities to expand sea transport and liberalising air rights to create a broader mass in air transport. On tourism, the Government, working closely with the trade, pursues a strategy that enhances the attractiveness of Hong Kong and entrenches its markets. As for producer and professional services, the Government continues to remove business barriers, streamline licensing procedures, and provide upgraded services for the business sector. CEPA is of much significance in enabling the various professional services to gain a better foothold in the Mainland economy.

Proximity to the Mainland is a key advantage that should be well capitalised on. This is to be done through earnestly increasing the cross-flows between Hong Kong and the Mainland. On flow of people and goods, key measures include improving existing boundary crossings and building new ones, shortening customs processing time, and enabling more Mainland visitors to come to Hong Kong. On flow of capital, Hong Kong is currently the Mainland's largest source of foreign direct investment as well as major funding centre, and this role is expected to be enhanced even further. Moreover, CEPA will help accentuate all these flows even more.

On upgrading the quality of the workforce, the Government is committed to education reform, and will continue to invest substantially in education, training and retraining for advancing knowledge and skills. These measures are aimed at facilitating Hong Kong's economic restructuring and enhancing individuals' capability to gear in with the requirements for a knowledge-based and skill-intensive economy. Apart from nurturing local talent, the Government also strives to attract talent from all over the world to live and work in Hong Kong. The population policy has eased restrictions on the entry of Mainland talents and professionals. With more professionals coming to Hong Kong, the vitality of the economy will be engendered further, and this in turn will create more job opportunities for the local workforce.

A high priority is attached to tackling the fiscal deficit. The Government has set out to do this through containing public expenditure, through introducing practical revenue measures, and through revitalising the economy to yield better revenue growth. The Government is determined to reduce its operating expenditure to $200 billion, to restore fiscal balance, and to keep public expenditure to 20 per cent of GDP or below by 2008-09.

Public Finance

Structure of Government Accounts

The Government controls its finances through a series of fund accounts. The General Revenue Account is the main account for day-to-day departmental expenditure and revenue collection. There are eight other funds established by resolutions of the Legislative Council for specific purposes such as to finance capital works expenditure or government loans and investments. They are the Capital Works Reserve Fund, Capital Investment Fund, Civil Service Pension Reserve Fund, Disaster Relief Fund, Innovation and Technology Fund, Land Fund, Loan Fund and Lotteries Fund.

The Capital Works Reserve Fund finances the public works programme, land acquisitions, capital subventions, major systems and equipment items, computerisation and the payment of redemption money in respect of land exchange entitlements. Its income is derived mainly from land premia and appropriation from the General Revenue Account.

The Capital Investment Fund finances the Government's capital investments, such as equity injections in the Airport Authority, the Kowloon-Canton Railway Corporation and the MTR Corporation Limited, and capital investments in the Hong Kong Housing Authority and the Urban Renewal Authority. Its income is derived mainly from appropriation from the General Revenue Account and dividends.

The Civil Service Pension Reserve Fund acts as a reserve to meet payment of civil service pensions in the unlikely event that the Government cannot meet such liabilities from the General Revenue Account. Its income is derived from appropriation from the General Revenue Account and investment income.

The Disaster Relief Fund finances grants for humanitarian aid in relief of disasters that occur outside Hong Kong. Its income is derived mainly from appropriation from the General Revenue Account.

The Innovation and Technology Fund finances projects that contribute to innovation and technology upgrading in the manufacturing and service industries, as well as those that contribute to the upgrading and development of the manufacturing and service industries. Its income is derived mainly from investment income.

The Land Fund was established on July 1, 1997 to enable the investments held by the former Trustees of the HKSAR Government Land Fund to be formally brought into the Government's account. Its income is derived from investment income.

The Loan Fund finances loan schemes such as housing loans and student loans. Its income is derived mainly from loan repayments and interest.

The Lotteries Fund finances welfare services through grants and loans. Its income is derived mainly from the sharing of the proceeds of the popular Mark Six lotteries.

Management of Public Finances

The principles underlying the Government's management of the public finance are set out in the Basic Law: to keep expenditure within the limits of revenues in drawing up the budget, to strive to achieve a fiscal balance, to avoid deficits and to keep the budget commensurate with the growth rate of its gross domestic product. The Budget presented by the Financial Secretary to the legislature each year is developed against the background of a medium-range forecast to ensure that full regard is given to the longer-term trends in the economy.

Public Expenditure

In accounting terms, public expenditure is taken to include government expenditure from the General Revenue Account and the other funds except loans and investment from the Capital Investment Fund, plus expenditure by the Housing Authority, the Lotteries Fund and government trading funds. Government grants and subventions to institutions in the private or quasi-private sectors are included, but not spending by organisations in which the Government has only an equity stake (such as the MTR Corporation Limited, the Kowloon-Canton Railway Corporation and the Airport Authority). Similarly, loans and equity injections by the Capital Investment Fund are excluded as they do not reflect the actual consumption of resources by the Government.

The Housing Authority, operating through the Housing Department, is financially autonomous. The Government provides the Authority with capital and land on concessionary terms to finance housing loans to eligible families and to build public housing for rent and for sale. However, as part of the measures to stabilise the property market, the Government announced in November 2002 that the production and sale of subsidised Home Ownership Scheme flats would cease indefinitely from 2003 onwards.

A trading fund is an accounting entity enabling a department to provide services on a commercial or quasi-commercial basis. Unlike a vote-funded department, departments operating on a trading fund are allowed to retain revenue generated to meet its expenditure and to finance future expansion.

Financial Results

Public expenditure in 2002-03 totalled $263.5 billion. The Government itself accounted for $236.2 billion. The growth rate over the preceding year was 2.2 per cent in nominal terms or 0.2 per cent in real terms. Some $51.8 billion, or 19.7 per cent of the public expenditure in 2002-03, was of a capital nature. An analysis of expenditure by function is at *Appendix 6, Table 6*. The growth rate of public expenditure is compared with the rate of economic growth at *Table 7*.

Total government revenue in 2002-03 amounted to $177.5 billion. The consolidated cash deficit for the year was $61.7 billion. Details of revenue by source and of expenditure by component for 2002-03 and 2003-04 (Revised Estimate) are at *Table 8*.

The Government's consolidated account recorded a deficit of $61.7 billion in 2002-03. The accumulated balances at the end of 2002-03 stood at $311.4 billion. These balances form the Government's fiscal reserves and are available to meet any calls on its contingent liabilities and enable it to cope with any short-term fluctuations in expenditure relative to revenue.

Revenue Sources

Hong Kong's tax system is simple and relatively inexpensive to administer. Tax rates are low, and the Government accords a high priority to curbing tax evasion and minimising opportunities for tax avoidance. The major sources of revenue are profits tax (22 per cent) and salaries tax (19 per cent). Other significant sources include revenue from investment returns (7 per cent), utilities, fees and charges for services provided by the Government (7 per cent), land transactions (6 per cent), betting duty (6 per cent), rates (5 per cent), stamp duties (4 per cent) and duties on dutiable commodities (4 per cent). *(For major sources of revenue, see Appendix 6, Chart 2)*

The Inland Revenue Department collects about 52 per cent of total revenue, including profits tax, salaries tax, property tax, stamp duty, betting duty, estate duty and hotel accommodation tax. Profits, salaries and property taxes, which together accounted for about 39 per cent of total revenue in 2002-03, are levied under the Inland Revenue Ordinance. Persons liable to these taxes may be assessed on three separate and distinct sources of income: business profits, salaries and income from property.

Profits tax is charged only on net profits arising in or derived from Hong Kong, from a trade, profession or business carried on in Hong Kong. In 2002-03, profits of unincorporated businesses were taxed at 15 per cent and profits of corporations at 16 per cent. The respective rates for 2003-04 are 15.5 per cent and 17.5 per cent. For 2004-05, profits of unincorporated business will be taxed at 16 per cent while that of corporations will remain at 17.5 per cent.

Profits tax is paid initially on the basis of profits made in the year preceding the year of assessment and is subsequently adjusted according to profits actually made in the assessment year. Generally, all expenses incurred in the production of assessable profits are deductible. There is no withholding tax on dividends paid by corporations. Interest income, other than that received by financial institutions, and dividends received from corporations are exempt from profits tax. In 2002-03, the Government received about $38.8 billion in profits tax, or about 22 per cent of total revenue.

Salaries tax is charged on emoluments arising in, or derived from, Hong Kong. The basis of assessment and method of payment (including provisional payments) are similar to the system for profits tax. Tax payable in 2002-03 was calculated on a sliding scale that progressed from 2 per cent, 7 per cent and 12 per cent on the first, second and third segments of net income (that is, income after deduction of allowances) of $35,000 each, respectively, and then to 17 per cent on the remaining net income. No one, however, needed to pay more than the standard rate of 15 per cent of his or her total income. The respective rates for 2003-04 are 2 per cent, 7.5 per cent, 13 per cent and 18.5 per cent with segments of $32,500 each and a standard rate of 15.5 per cent. For 2004-05, the respective rates will be 2 per cent, 8 per cent, 14 per cent and 20 per cent with segments of $30,000 each and a standard rate of 16 per cent. The earnings of husbands and wives are reported and assessed separately. However, where either spouse has allowances that exceed his or her income, or when separate assessments would result in an increase in salaries tax payable by the couple, they may elect to be assessed jointly. Salaries tax contributed some $29.7 billion, or about 17 per cent of total revenue, in 2002-03. Owing to generous personal allowances under Hong Kong tax law, only 37 per cent of the workforce had to pay salaries tax.

As part of a package of relief measures to help the community tide over the difficulties due to the outbreak of SARS and revive the economy, a 50 per cent rebate of 2001-02 final tax on salaries tax and personal assessment, subject to $3,000 per case, was made in July 2003. The rebate cost approximately $2.3 billion with around 1.3 million taxpayers benefiting from it.

Owners of land or buildings in Hong Kong were charged property tax in 2002-03 at the standard rate of 15 per cent of the actual rent received, less an allowance of 20 per cent for repairs and maintenance. The standard rates for 2003-04 and 2004-05 are 15.5 per cent and 16 per cent respectively. There is a system of provisional payment of tax similar to that for profits tax and salaries tax. Property owned by a corporation carrying on a business in Hong Kong is exempt from property tax (but profits derived from ownership are chargeable to profits tax). Receipts from property tax accounted for about 1 per cent of total revenue, or about $1.2 billion in 2002-03.

The Stamp Duty Ordinance imposes fixed and ad valorem duties on different classes of documents relating to assignments of immovable property, leases and share transfers. The revenue from stamp duties accounted for about 4 per cent of total revenue, or about $7.5 billion, in 2002-03.

A duty is imposed on bets on horse racing administered by the Hong Kong Jockey Club, on proceeds of Mark Six lotteries and on gross profits of the Hong Kong Jockey Club's football betting operation — the only legal forms of betting in Hong Kong. The rate of duty on betting proceeds from horse racing was 12 per cent on standard bets and 19 per cent on exotic bets in 2002-03. The rate on exotic bets was increased to 20 per cent with effect from August 1, 2003. The duty on football betting, which was introduced on August 1, 2003, is charged at a rate of 50 per cent of gross profits. The yield from betting duty in 2002-03 totalled some $10.9 billion, and accounted for about 6 per cent of total revenue.

In 2002-03, estate duty was imposed on estates valued at over $7.5 million, at levels ranging from 5 per cent to a maximum of 15 per cent, while a hotel accommodation tax of 3 per cent was imposed on expenditure on accommodation by guests in hotels and guesthouses.

Under the Dutiable Commodities Ordinance, duties are levied on only four types of commodities — hydrocarbon oil, alcoholic beverages, other alcohol products (i.e. methyl and ethyl alcohol) and tobacco products, both locally manufactured and imported. The Customs and Excise Department is responsible for collecting these duties. In 2002-03, the department collected duties worth $6.6 billion or about 4 per cent of total revenue.

The Rating and Valuation Department is responsible for the billing and collection of rates, which are levied on landed properties at a specified percentage of their rateable value. For the 2003-04 financial year, the rates charge is 5 per cent.

The rateable value of a property is an estimate of its annual rent in the open market as at a designated date. In order to better reflect prevailing market rents, revaluation of rateable values is now conducted on an annual basis. The current Valuation List took effect on April 1, 2003 with rateable values reflecting rental values at October 1, 2002. The Valuation List as at March 31, 2003 contained about 2 089 000 assessments. In 2002-03, the revenue from rates was $8.9 billion, accounting for about 5 per cent of total revenue.

A one-off concession was granted to all ratepayers as a relief measure to help the community tide over the difficulties due to the outbreak of SARS. The concession was equivalent to the actual rates payable for the July to September 2003 quarter, subject to a ceiling of $5,000 for each non-domestic property or $1,250 in the case of domestic property. About 90 per cent of ratepayers were not required to pay any rates in the July to September 2003 quarter, while the remaining 10 per cent of ratepayers had their rates bills reduced by the full concession amount of $5,000 or $1,250, as the case might be. The concession produced a total saving of $2 billion for ratepayers.

The Rating and Valuation Department is also responsible for the billing and collection of government rent which is payable from July 1, 1997 for land leases granted on or after May 27, 1985, and on the extension of non-renewable land leases. The latter group comprises all land leases in the New Territories and New Kowloon north of Boundary Street which were renewed on June 28, 1997. Government rent is levied at 3 per cent of the rateable value of the lot and is adjusted in step with any subsequent changes in the rateable value. There were about 1 535 000 assessments in the Government Rent Roll as at March 31, 2003. The total government rent collected in 2002-03 was $4.3 billion.

The Government derives significant amounts of revenue from other sources. Fees and charges for services provided by government departments generated about $9.7 billion, or about 6 per cent of total revenue, in 2002-03. It is government policy that fees should in general be set at levels sufficient to recover the full cost of providing the services. Certain essential services are, however, subsidised by the Government or provided free of charge. Government-operated public utilities generated about $2.1 billion which accounted for about 1 per cent of the total revenue; the most important of these, in revenue terms, is water charges. The Government has frozen most government fees and charges since February 1998 to ease the burden on the community at a time of economic setback. Owing to the outbreak of SARS, the Government announced a package of relief measures in April to help the community tide over the difficulties and revive the economy. As part of the package of relief measures, the Government provided some one-off concessions by reducing water and sewage charges and trade effluent surcharge for a four-month billing period and waiving certain licensing fees for a maximum of one year. In addition, the

Government announced that it would not propose any further upward adjustment to fees and charges until the end of October 2003. All these concessions produced total savings of $0.8 billion for households and businesses.

Also, in 2002-03, the Government collected $17.6 billion, amounting to about 9.9 per cent of the total revenue, from investments and interest income on the fiscal reserves.

Lastly, some $11.5 billion, or about 6.5 per cent of the total revenue in 2002-03, was generated from land transactions. All revenue from land transactions is credited to the Capital Works Reserve Fund to help finance the Public Works Programme.

Need to Broaden Tax Base

The Government has identified two major problems besetting the public revenue. First, the tax base is narrow. Only about 37 per cent of the workforce pay tax on their salaries. Among them, only 100 000 contribute about 60 per cent of the salaries tax. Similarly, as few as 500 corporations, only about 1 per cent of the total number of profit-making corporation, contribute 60 per cent of the profits tax.

The second problem is the stability of the revenue. Many of the existing taxes are easily affected by the ups and downs of the economy. Owing to the economic downturn and deflation brought about by the financial crisis and the slump in the property market, the recurrent revenue has dropped from $201.6 billion in 1997-98 to an estimated $149.2 billion in 2003-04, representing a decrease of $52.4 billion or 26 per cent. Hence it is necessary to explore stable and broad-based revenue sources in the long term to improve the Government's revenue structure, thereby laying down a solid foundation for the public finances. In this connection, a broad-based Goods and Services Tax (GST) is considered to be a reasonable and equitable way of smoothing out bumps in the revenue stream. However, the Government is not contemplating the introduction of a GST in a deflationary environment. This would only be levied against the backdrop of a healthy and growing economy. An internal committee has been set up to study the feasibility of a GST.

Government Logistics Department

The Government Logistics Department was established on July 1, 2003 upon merging of the then Government Supplies Department, Government Land Transport Agency and Printing Department.

Purchases of goods and related services required by government departments are undertaken centrally by the Government Logistics Department. These goods and related services are normally obtained by competitive tendering, without giving preference to any particular source of supply, to ensure that users' needs are met at the best possible price, having regard to life-time cost and reliability of supply. Helping users to derive the best value in their purchases, the department formulates a specific strategy for each type of purchase based on market conditions, focusing on meeting requirements for high-value and critical items by cost-effective and reliable means.

'Hong Kong, China' is a signatory to the World Trade Organisation Agreement on Government Procurement (WTO GPA). Government procurement is undertaken in accordance with the principles of openness, transparency, fairness and non-discrimination. Public tender procedures are widely used for general and common items. Restricted or single tender procedures are used where open competitive tendering would not be an effective means such as in cases involving compatibility with existing equipment, or patented/proprietary items, or unforeseen urgency. For complex and critical purchases, suppliers may be required to undergo a prequalification exercise before tendering to ensure that they are capable in terms of financial and technical standing and reliability in performance. To facilitate sourcing and market research, the department maintains and regularly updates the Supplier Lists which comprise local and overseas suppliers for different categories of commodities and services.

Invitations for public and prequalification tenders are published in the Government of the Hong Kong Special Administrative Region *Gazette* and local newspapers. Firms on the department's Supplier Lists and in the case of procurements covered by WTO GPA, consulates and overseas trade commissions, are also informed. To allow easy access by suppliers outside Hong Kong, the department also puts its tender invitations and related information on the Internet. The Electronic Tendering System, which was introduced in April 2000 and enabled subscribers to download tender documents and to submit tender offers by electronic means, has been running smoothly with the number of subscribers rising steadily.

In 2003, the department awarded contracts at a total value of $7.35 billion, purchasing items from 35 different territories. Major items of purchase included computer equipment and software, pharmaceuticals, telecommunications equipment and spares, medical consumables, books and marine equipment and spares.

Supplies of common-user goods and essential and emergency items are purchased in bulk and held in the purpose-built Government Logistics Centre in Chai Wan which came into operation in 1996. The operations are assisted by a modern computerised system with international bar-coding functions that provides, among other services, online communication with customers. In 2003, the total values of stock items acquired and issued to customers were $223 million and 236 million, respectively. The department has progressively transferred the common-user items to allocated term contracts for direct delivery from the contractors to user departments on an as and when required basis with a view to avoiding stocking and double handling.

The department also deploys supplies staff to other departments to ensure there is a professional approach to procurement and maintenance of stores and equipment.

Home Pages

Economic Analysis and Business Facilitation Unit, Financial Secretary's Office: http://www.gov.hk/fso/eabfu/eng/
Financial Services and the Treasury Bureau: http://www.gov.hk/fstb
Government Logistics Department: http://www.gld.gov.hk

CHAPTER 4

Financial and Monetary Affairs

The financial services sector is one of the pillars of Hong Kong's economy. Encompassing key services such as banking, securities, insurance, fund management and other related services, the sector employs above 5 per cent of Hong Kong's working population, or about 180 000 people. Being a high value-added sector, its activities account for a disproportionately high, around 12 per cent share of GDP.

HONG KONG is an international financial centre with an integrated network of financial institutions and markets. The Government's policy is to maintain and further develop an appropriate legal, regulatory, infrastructural and administrative framework, with the aim of providing a level playing field for all market participants, maintaining the stability of the financial and monetary systems and enabling Hong Kong to compete effectively with other major financial centres.

Major achievements in 2003 are highlighted below:—

- Hong Kong is the world's 12th largest banking centre in terms of external assets and seventh largest centre for foreign exchange trading.

- Hong Kong's stock market ranks 10th world-wide in terms of market capitalisation.

- The Hong Kong dollar debt market continued to grow in 2003. The total outstanding amount of Hong Kong dollar debt securities reached $558 billion at year-end, compared with $533 billion a year earlier.

- The new Securities and Futures Ordinance (SFO), which consolidates 10 previous ordinances governing the securities and futures markets into a composite piece of legislation, came into effect on April 1, 2003 to keep the regulatory regime on a par with international standards and practices.

- Total assets of Mandatory Provident Fund (MPF) schemes grew to about $89.4 billion at year-end. About 95 per cent of employers, 96 per cent of relevant employees and 82 per cent of self-employed persons have enrolled in MPF schemes.

Hong Kong as an International Financial Centre

A favourable geographical position, bridging the time gap between North America and Europe; strong links with the Mainland and other economies in South-East Asia and excellent communications with the rest of the world; rule of law; a level playing field as well as a sound regulatory regime have all helped Hong Kong develop into both a leading international financial centre in the region and the premier capital formation centre for the Mainland. The absence of any restrictions on capital flows into and out of Hong Kong is another important strength.

Hong Kong's financial markets are characterised by a high degree of liquidity. They operate under effective and transparent regulation which fully meets international standards. A highly educated workforce and ease of entry for professionals from outside Hong Kong further contribute to the development of financial markets in Hong Kong.

In late 2002, Hong Kong participated in the Financial Sector Assessment Programme (FSAP), a joint International Monetary Fund (IMF)-World Bank initiative designed to promote financial stability and assess compliance with key international codes and standards covering various financial services sectors. The FSAP exercise was concluded in June 2003 with the issuance of a final report, which confirmed that the financial system of Hong Kong is fundamentally sound and that the market infrastructure is robust and efficient.

Hong Kong has a very strong presence of international financial institutions. Of the world's top 100 banks, 75 have operations in Hong Kong. As at December 2003, there were 121 foreign-owned licensed banks. Apart from these, some foreign institutions also operate as restricted licence banks and deposit-taking companies through their subsidiaries, related companies or branches in Hong Kong. A further 87 foreign banks have local representative offices.

The interbank money market is well-established. Wholesale deposits are traded actively among local authorised institutions (AIs), and between local and overseas institutions, with an average daily turnover of $168 billion in 2003.

Hong Kong also has a mature and active foreign exchange market, which forms an integral part of the global market. The link with overseas centres enables foreign exchange dealings to continue 24 hours a day with the rest of the world. The last triennial survey coordinated by the Bank for International Settlements in April 2001 shows that the daily average foreign exchange turnover in Hong Kong is US$66.8 billion, which represents 4 per cent of the world's total transactions and makes Hong Kong the world's seventh largest foreign exchange market.

With a total market capitalisation of $5,547.8 billion as at year-end, the Hong Kong stock market ranked 10th in the world and second in Asia, following Japan[1]. The daily turnover (including $154 million on the Growth Enterprise Market) averaged $10.4 billion in 2003. At year-end, 1 037 public companies (including 185 on the Growth Enterprise Market) were listed on the Stock Exchange of Hong Kong Limited (SEHK), a wholly-owned subsidiary of the Hong Kong Exchanges and Clearing Limited (HKEx). The 73 (including 27 on the Growth Enterprise Market) newly-listed companies raised a total of $59.1 billion from initial public offerings (of which $2.1 billion was raised in the Growth Enterprise Market). Besides new share issues, funds were also raised in the secondary market, with a total amount of $154.5 billion. Funds raised in H-shares and red-chips markets amounted to $53.2 billion, some 25 per cent of the total funds raised in the Hong Kong market during the year.

The stock market is an important fund-raising centre for Mainland enterprises. As at end-2003, of the 93 Mainland incorporated enterprises listed outside the Mainland

---

(H shares), 92 were quoted on the SEHK. The daily turnover of these H-shares and red chips accounted for 38.7 per cent of the total market turnover. In 2003, about $50.4 billion was raised in new listings of H-shares and red chips in Hong Kong, accounting for some 85 per cent of the total funds raised in initial public offerings (IPO) on the SEHK. The market capitalisation of H-shares and red chips accounted for about 29 per cent of the total market capitalisation. During 2003, the H-share index surged by 152 per cent. It is expected that Mainland issuers will continue to be a major growth driver of the securities market of Hong Kong in the future.

The average daily turnover of Hang Seng Index Futures and Mini-HSI Futures traded on the Hong Kong Futures Exchange (HKFE) increased from 19 602 contracts and 4 522 contracts in 2002 to 27 588 contracts and 5 064 contracts in 2003, respectively, representing increases of 41 per cent and 12 per cent. The average daily turnover of Hang Seng Index Options also increased to 8 596 contracts in 2003, compared with 4 369 in 2002, representing an increase of 97 per cent. The average daily turnover of Mini-HSI Options was 130 contracts, whereas that of H-share Index Futures launched in December 2003 reached 3 196 contracts. Apart from Index futures and options, the HKFE also traded 33 stock futures contracts with an average daily turnover of 76 contracts in 2003. As regards stock options, contracts in respect of a total of 34 stocks were traded in the market by year-end. The average daily turnover of stock options was 17 122 contracts in 2003.

The Hong Kong fund management industry is characterised by its strong international flavour, both in terms of the presence of global fund managers and authorised funds. In a survey conducted by the Securities and Futures Commission (SFC) in 2003, there were 192 companies that provided fund management or advisory services and that derived gross operating income from such activities at the end of 2002, an increase of 12 per cent from 172 a year earlier. Total assets under management amounted to $1,491 billion (US$191.2 billion)[2] as at December 31, 2002, representing a growth of 0.4 per cent over the previous year.

The number of authorised unit trusts and mutual funds was 1 862 at the end of 2003 (excluding Mandatory Provident Fund-related unit trusts).

Hong Kong operates one of the most active physical gold markets in the world. Spot gold can be traded through two closely related yet independent markets in the city — the Chinese Gold and Silver Exchange Society and the Loco-London gold market.

The society, established in 1910, provides trading of both tael bars and kilo bars in Hong Kong dollars[3]. Prices closely follow those in the other major gold markets in London, Zurich and New York. Loco-London gold quotation is made in US dollars per troy ounce of gold.

Hong Kong continues to be one of the most open insurance centres in the world. Among the 188 authorised insurers at year-end, 94 were insurers from 22 overseas countries or the Mainland. Twelve of the world's top 20 insurers are authorised to carry out insurance business in Hong Kong either directly or through a group company. There are 23 professional reinsurers, including most of the top reinsurers in the world. Gross premium income in 2002 was $89.0 billion, approximately 7.1 per cent of Hong Kong's Gross Domestic Product (GDP).

---

[2] Excluding assets under pure investment advice.

[3] Tael bars are of 99 per cent fineness and weighted in taels (one tael equals approximately 1.20337 troy ounces). Kilo bars are of 999.9 parts per thousand fineness and weighted in kilograms.

Premier Wen Jiabao being warmly welcomed at the Hong Kong International Airport on June 29, on his arrival for a three-day visit for the 6th Anniversary celebrations of the HKSAR.

Medical staff of the Prince of Wales Hospital and the chairman of the hospital's governing committee bid farewell to Premier Wen after he visited the hospital which had been at the centre of the battle against SARS. *Left:* a poignant occasion as the Premier visits a family in Amoy Gardens which lost its mother to SARS; and meeting experts researching the disease at the Genetic Research Centre of the University of Hong Kong.

Well-wishers greeting Premier
Wen outside the Hong Kong
Convention and Exhibition
Centre where many people had
gathered for the flag-raising
ceremony on July 1 at the
Golden Bauhinia Square.
Right: a visit to a supermarket
in New Town Plaza, Sha Tin,
acquainted the Premier with
aspects of daily life in
Hong Kong.

Financial Services in Hong Kong

Banking Sector

Main Features

Hong Kong maintains a three-tier system of deposit-taking institutions, namely, licensed banks, restricted licence banks and deposit-taking companies. They are collectively known as authorised institutions (AIs) under the Banking Ordinance. The Hong Kong Monetary Authority (HKMA) is the licensing authority for all three types of AIs.

Only licensed banks may conduct full banking services, including in particular the provision of current and savings accounts and acceptance of deposits of any size and maturity. Restricted licence banks may take deposits of any maturity of $500,000 or above. Many deposit-taking companies are owned by, or otherwise associated with, licensed banks. Deposit-taking companies may take deposits of $100,000 or above with an original maturity of at least three months.

Hong Kong has one of the highest concentrations of banking institutions in the world. As at December 2003, there were 134 licensed banks, 42 restricted licence banks and 39 deposit-taking companies, which included operations of banks from 32 countries around the world. These 215 AIs maintained an extensive network of 1 308 local branches. In addition, there were 87 representative offices of overseas banks in Hong Kong. A local representative office is not allowed to engage in any banking business. Its role is confined to liaison work between the bank and its customers in Hong Kong.

The total deposit liabilities of all AIs to customers and the total loans and advances extended by these institutions at year-end were $3,566 billion and $2,035 billion, respectively. The total assets of all AIs amounted to $6,506 billion.

Hong Kong has a robust interbank payment system, which operates through the Real Time Gross Settlement (RTGS) system. The Hong Kong Dollar RTGS system has a single-tier settlement structure with all banks maintaining settlement accounts with the HKMA. All RTGS payment transactions are settled in real time across the books of the HKMA. Intraday liquidity can be obtained by the banks through the use of their Exchange Fund Bills and Notes for intraday repurchase (repo) agreements with the HKMA.

Leveraging on the experience with the Hong Kong Dollar RTGS system, the HKMA introduced the US Dollar RTGS system in August 2000. The system allows participants to settle US dollar transactions real-time in the Asian time zone and thereby to reduce or eliminate foreign exchange settlement risk caused by any time gap. Since its full implementation, the system has been operating smoothly and has attracted an increasing number of participants. As at December 2003, there were 67 direct participants and 160 indirect participants. Among the indirect participants, 113 were from overseas. Turnover of the system grew to 4 000 transactions per day with a total value of over US$4.9 billion.

With a view to further enhancing the financial infrastructure in Hong Kong, the HKMA launched a Euro RTGS system in April 2003. Similar to the technology used for the Hong Kong dollar and US dollar RTGS systems, the Euro RTGS system is built on the same infrastructure and offers a range of advanced and sophisticated clearing functions. The key functions include the real-time gross settlement for Euro payments and for payment versus payment (PvP) between Euro and US dollar or Euro and Hong Kong dollar foreign exchange transactions. The system also maintains a seamless interface with the Central Moneymarkets Unit (CMU) to cater for the delivery versus payment (DvP) of Euro denominated debt securities and repo facilities.

The CMU Service, established in 1990, is operated by the HKMA to provide a clearing and custodian system for Exchange Fund Bills and Notes, as well as private sector debt issues. There are 172 CMU members, most of which are financial institutions in Hong Kong. At year-end, there were 1 255 issues with a total value of $217.7 billion equivalent lodged with the CMU. The CMU system accepts both Hong Kong dollar and foreign currency denominated debt instruments. It has been fully integrated with the interbank payment systems, and is linked up with the international central securities depositories like Euroclear and Clearstream to enable overseas investors to trade CMU securities. It also has established links with the regional central securities depositories in Australia, New Zealand and the Republic of Korea.

Through a seamless interface with the US Dollar and Euro RTGS systems, the CMU enables members to settle US dollar and Euro securities on a DvP basis, thereby enhancing settlement efficiency and eliminating settlement risk. The interface also enables automatic intraday repo to provide intraday liquidity to participants of the US Dollar and Euro RTGS systems.

Hong Kong Monetary Authority

The HKMA was established in April 1993. The Exchange Fund (Amendment) Ordinance 1992 provides for its establishment.

The HKMA's policy objectives are to maintain currency stability, within the framework of the Linked Exchange Rate System, through sound management of the Exchange Fund, monetary policy operations and other means deemed necessary; to ensure safety and stability of the banking system through the regulation of banking business and the business of taking deposits, and the supervision of AIs; and to promote efficiency, integrity and development of the financial system, particularly payment and settlement arrangements.

The HKMA is an integral part of the Government, but can employ staff on terms different from those of the Civil Service to attract personnel of the appropriate experience and expertise. Its staff and operating costs are charged directly to the Exchange Fund instead of the general revenue. The HKMA is accountable to the Financial Secretary, who is advised by the Exchange Fund Advisory Committee on matters relating to the control of the Exchange Fund.

The HKMA seeks advice on policy matters routinely from the Banking Advisory Committee and the Deposit-Taking Companies Advisory Committee. Both committees are established under the Banking Ordinance. They are chaired by the Financial Secretary and comprise members from the banking industry and other relevant professions. Members of the committees are appointed by the Financial Secretary under the authority delegated by the Chief Executive.

The Banking Ordinance provides the legal framework for banking supervision in Hong Kong. Under the ordinance, the HKMA is the licensing authority responsible for the authorisation and revocation of all AIs, as well as the approval and revocation of money broker licences. The HKMA seeks to maintain a regulatory framework that is fully in line with international standards. The objective is to devise a prudential supervisory system to help preserve the general stability and effective working of the banking system while at the same time providing sufficient flexibility for AIs to make commercial decisions. Hong Kong's framework of banking supervision is in line with the Core Principles for Effective Banking Supervision promulgated by the Basel Committee.

The HKMA's supervisory approach is based on a policy of 'continuous supervision' through a combination of on-site examinations, off-site reviews, prudential meetings, cooperation with external auditors and meetings with boards of directors. Since 2000, the HKMA has been using a risk-based supervisory framework for all AIs. This approach puts emphasis on evaluation of the quality of risk management practices and internal controls in respect of various types of risks faced by AIs. On-site examinations are typically focused on areas of higher risk at AIs.

On the international front, the HKMA continues to promote cooperation among central banks in the region, principally through the Executives' Meeting of East Asia-Pacific Central Banks (EMEAP), whose activities cover supervisory liaison and cooperation, development of financial markets and infrastructure, and various areas of central bank operations. The HKMA currently chairs the EMEAP Working Group on Financial Markets, and has just completed a two-year term (from 2002 to 2003) as chairman of the South-East Asia, New Zealand and Australia (SEANZA) Group of Central Bank Governors, as well as the SEANZA Forum of Banking Supervisors. To facilitate supervisory training in the region, the HKMA is active in organising seminars for regional banking supervisors in collaboration with the BIS Financial Stability Institute. In addition, Hong Kong is an active member of both the Financial Action Task Force (FATF), and the Asia/Pacific Group on anti-money laundering, which are inter-governmental bodies charged with the objective of developing and promoting legal, law enforcement and financial regulation policies to combat money laundering.

Recent Developments

In line with its policy of adhering closely to international regulatory standards, the HKMA is committed to adopting the New Capital Accord in Hong Kong. In view of the complexity of the New Accord, the HKMA will work closely with the industry with a view to agreeing on an implementation approach that is both practicable and appropriate for Hong Kong. The HKMA issued for industry consultation in July 2003 its preliminary implementation proposals, and will carefully consider the industry's feedback and other supervisory priorities before finalising the implementation plans. Recognising the importance of cross-border supervisory cooperation to implementation of the New Accord, the HKMA will continue to take an active part in liaison with other regional supervisors and monitor closely developments in relation to the New Accord and the manner in which it is being implemented in different jurisdictions. Besides, the FSAP exercise concluded in June 2003 noted that Hong Kong had a very high degree of compliance with international best practices in banking regulation and supervision, including the Basel Core Principles for Effective Banking Supervision.

With the commencement of the Banking (Amendment) Ordinance 2002 and the Securities and Futures Ordinance on April 1, 2003, banks are subject to a new securities regulatory framework which, among other things, upholds a level playing field between banks and non-bank intermediaries in the securities market. The HKMA has been reinforcing its role as front-line supervisor of banks through day-to-day co-operation with the SFC to ensure a consistent supervisory approach in accordance with the new Memorandum of Understanding between the two regulators. An electronic register containing the names and relevant particulars of banks' securities staff is made available for public inspection at the HKMA website.

The HKMA continued to implement the policy initiatives contained in the reform programme announced in 1999. A bill to implement the proposed Deposit Protection Scheme was introduced into the Legislative Council in April 2003, and the council has formed a Bills Committee to consider it. Good progress has also been made in the establishment of a Commercial Credit Reference Agency (CCRA) in Hong Kong. The banking industry has identified a service provider to operate the CCRA and is working with the service provider to finalise the implementation details. It is expected that the proposed CCRA would be up and running in 2004. Meanwhile, the Code of Practice on Consumer Credit Data was revised in June 2003 to allow a wider range of positive consumer credit data to be shared among AIs and other credit providers. This has helped strengthen the credit management systems of AIs and thus is conducive to the maintenance of the stability of the banking system.

The HKMA continued to enhance its electronic banking (e-banking) and technology risk management supervisory framework. In this connection, the HKMA rolled out an automated control self-assessment process to 40 AIs, and also completed over 20 on-site examinations on e-banking, technology risk management and business continuity planning in 2003. In addition, the HKMA issued a guideline note on general principles for technology risk management and a series of circulars to AIs to help strengthen their information technology control environment.

In 2003, the HKMA noted a spate of fake bank websites and e-mail cases in Hong Kong and overseas. To ensure that members of the public in Hong Kong are adequately protected from these frauds, the HKMA issued a circular in May 2003 to recommend AIs to take certain preventive and detective measures, and also a number of press statements to alert people to these cases. The HKMA, the Hong Kong Police Force and the Hong Kong Association of Banks have also been cooperating since February 2003 to launch a multi-channel consumer education programme (for example, issuance of an educational leaflet, production of various episodes played on television and radio) to promote awareness of e-banking security precautions among the general public.

The HKMA received a number of reports on suspected Automatic Teller Machine (ATM) fraud cases during the second half of 2003. The HKMA has been taking the matter seriously and issued a circular in October 2003 to AIs to set out its expectation on the related precautionary measures that should be undertaken and the way in which customer complaints in this relation should be handled. AIs have been actively enhancing their precautionary measures for their ATMs. The HKMA will continue to assess the adequacy of individual AIs' measures, and also to ensure that customers' complaints are being dealt with fairly and fully in a satisfactory manner.

One of the functions of the HKMA is to promote and encourage high standards of conduct and sound and prudent business practices among AIs, primarily by way of the Code of Banking Practice. The code is issued by the industry associations and endorsed by the HKMA. It sets out the minimum standards to be followed by AIs in their dealings with personal customers. In 2002, the industry established the Code of Banking Practice Committee, in which the HKMA is represented, to provide guidance on the interpretation of the code and to undertake future review from time to time.

Following an in-depth review, the committee recommended new provisions be added to the code in 2003 to address the problem of guarantors and third party security providers being held liable for the borrower's additional debts without their consent or knowledge.

On developing financial infrastructure, following implementation of the outbound link from CMU to Euroclear in November 2002 to provide a two-way link, an outbound link from CMU to Clearstream was similarly implemented in January 2003 to provide a two-way link between CMU and Clearstream. These real-time links enable Asian investors to hold and settle Euroclear and Clearstream eligible securities directly via their CMU accounts, thus significantly improving settlement efficiency.

At year-end, the Government introduced the Clearing and Settlement Systems Bill into the Legislative Council. The objectives of the proposed legislation are to provide express statutory backing for the oversight role of the Monetary Authority in relation to important clearing and settlement systems in Hong Kong, in line with concerns expressed by the International Monetary Fund; and for the finality of settlements effected through such systems, so as to facilitate the inclusion of the Hong Kong dollar in the Continuous Linked Settlement System which is a global clearing and settlement system for cross-border foreign exchange transactions. Many major international currencies have been admitted to the Continuous Linked Settlement System and it is hoped that the Hong Kong dollar can be admitted in 2004.

Securities and Futures Sector

Main Features

The securities and futures markets in Hong Kong are operated by the SEHK and the HKFE, respectively. Both the SEHK and the HKFE are wholly-owned subsidiaries of the HKEx. At year-end, there were 499 corporate and individual exchange participants on the SEHK and 129 exchange participants on the HKFE.

At year-end, there were 852 companies listed on the Main Board of SEHK with a total market capitalisation of $5,477.7 billion, raising an aggregate of $209.0 billion within the year.

New products continued to be launched in 2003. To meet market demand created by the growth of the H-shares market and to offer an effective trading and hedging instrument for investors in H-shares, the HKEx launched the H-shares Index Futures in December 2003. At about the same time, the H-share Exchange Traded Fund was also listed on the SEHK.

The Hong Kong Securities Clearing Company (HKSCC), a wholly-owned subsidiary of the HKEx, operates the Central Clearing and Settlement System (CCASS) for the clearing and settlement of securities transactions at the SEHK. The CCASS is an automated book-entry system. In addition to brokers and custodians, CCASS services are also available to retail investors.

Securities transactions on the HKEx's securities market are executed by the Third Generation Automatic Order Matching and Execution System (AMS/3) which provides facilities and investor access channels that make securities trading more accessible. The system has maintained 100 per cent uptime record for three consecutive years since its launch in October 2000. The AMS/3 provides an electronic platform for trading of equities, debt securities, exchange traded funds, unit trusts/mutual funds, derivative warrants and equity linked instruments.

The HKEx rolled out the final phase of the CCASS/3 in May 2003 by introducing the Participant Gateway, which provides a direct electronic interface between the CCASS/3 and the CCASS Participants' back office systems. The CCASS/3 network connection provides integrated access to FinNet, which was built to connect financial institutions in Hong Kong to effect straight-through processing of financial transactions.

The HKEx upgraded the software of its electronic trading system for futures and options in October 2003. The upgrade raised the performance and stability capabilities of the Hong Kong Futures Automated Trading System (HKATS) and paved the way for the introduction in 2004 of an integrated clearing and settlement system for the HKEx's derivatives market to increase efficiency.

Securities and Futures Commission

The SFC was established in May 1989 following enactment of the Securities and Futures Commission Ordinance (SFCO). This represented the first important phase in the overhaul of the regulation of securities and futures markets in Hong Kong, and the implementation of one of the most important recommendations made by the Securities Review Committee in May 1988.

The regulatory objectives of the SFC, as set out in the SFO that came into effect on April 1, 2003, include:—

- to maintain and promote the fairness, efficiency, competitiveness, transparency and orderliness of the securities and futures industry;
- to promote the understanding by the public of the operation and functioning of the securities and futures industry;
- to provide protection for members of the public investing in or holding financial products;
- to minimise crime and misconduct in the securities and futures industry;
- to reduce systemic risks in the securities and futures industry; and
- to assist the Financial Secretary in maintaining the financial stability of Hong Kong by taking appropriate steps in relation to the securities and futures industry.

Established as an autonomous statutory body outside the Civil Service, the SFC is responsible for regulating the securities and futures markets in Hong Kong. The SFC at present has a governing body of 13 directors (six of them executive) appointed by the Chief Executive. The Government is not involved in the day-to-day regulation of the securities and futures industry.

The SFC is funded by the market. No government funding has been sought since 1993. The revised estimate of its operating expenditure budget for 2003-04 was $408 million.

The SFC seeks advice on policy matters from its Advisory Committee, which comprises three executive directors of the SFC and 11 independent members. The independent members are appointed by the Chief Executive and are broadly based and representative of market users.

Exercise of powers by the SFC is subject to a range of checks and balances. For instance, decisions relating to matters concerning the licensing of persons and intervention in their business are subject to appeal to the independent full-time

Securities and Futures Appeals Tribunal (SFAT), which has replaced the previous part-time Securities and Futures Appeals Panel. A much wider range of the SFC's decisions are now subject to appeal to the tribunal. In November 2000, a Process Review Panel (PRP) was established to undertake an ongoing review of the fairness and consistency of the SFC's internal operational procedures. Members of the PRP are appointed by the Chief Executive. The Government published the PRP's second Annual Report in May 2003. The PRP could not identify any serious deficiency in the SFC's operational process. Yet, there were certain areas where the PRP has made recommendations for improvement. The SFC has been positive in adopting the recommendations of the PRP.

Broadly speaking, the SFC's work involves licensing, supervision and monitoring of intermediaries; regulation of the public marketing of unit trusts, mutual funds and other collective investment products; regulation of takeovers, mergers and other corporate activities; listing regulation under the dual filing system for IPO applicants and issuers; supervision of markets including the exchanges and clearing houses; enforcement of securities laws and rules; and investor education.

As at year-end, there were 20 103 licensed persons, including securities brokerage firms, futures dealers, and securities margin financiers, as well as their representatives, and 98 registered institutions, such as banks, engaging in regulated activities like dealing and advising on securities and futures.

The SFC considers investor education the first important step to investor protection. It maintains an Electronic Investor Resources Centre (eIRC), which is a web-based collection of investor education materials and links. It aims to assist investors in making informed investment decisions.

During the year, the SFC continued its active campaign to educate investors on various investment related subjects. Easy-to-understand leaflets and feature articles were published online and in hard copies on investing basics, bonds, portfolio planning, pooling risk in margin trading, hedge funds, exotic warrants, commodity futures and index tracking exchange traded funds.

As in previous years, the SFC also organised a series of investor education workshops for secondary school teachers of Economics, Commerce and related subjects to facilitate their teaching work. It also partnered with the Open University and the HKEx to organise investor education lectures for the public free of charge.

In the meantime, the SFC remained active in external relations and international activities. In June 2003, it signed a Declaration on Co-operation and Supervision of Cross-Border Investment Management Activity with the Australian Securities and Investments Commission (ASIC). The MoU enables the SFC and the ASIC to exchange information and offer assistance to each other concerning the activities of fund managers licensed in their respective jurisdictions.

The SFC continued to participate in different aspects of the work of the International Organisation of Securities Commissions (IOSCO), including the work on the regulation of securities analysts and rating agencies. Hong Kong was selected by the IOSCO Executive Committee to host the 31st Annual Conference of IOSCO in 2006. This will be the first time that Hong Kong has hosted the IOSCO Annual Conference.

Insider Dealing Tribunal and the Market Misconduct Tribunal

The Insider Dealing Tribunal has been an important feature of the regulatory framework for the securities market in Hong Kong. Established under the Securities (Insider Dealing) Ordinance, the tribunal looks into cases involving suspected insider dealing referred to it by the Financial Secretary. Since the commencement of its operation in 1994, the tribunal has concluded 14 cases.

With the commencement of the SFO on April 1, 2003, the Insider Dealing Tribunal has been replaced by a Market Misconduct Tribunal (MMT), which covers five other types of market misconduct (namely false trading; price rigging; disclosure of information about prohibited transactions; disclosure of false or misleading information inducing transactions; and stock market manipulation) in addition to insider dealing. The MMT decides cases on the civil standard of proof and can impose a range of civil sanctions, such as ordering the disgorgement of profits, banning a person from trading in SFC regulated financial products and disqualifying a person from directorship or management of a company.

The MMT inquires into market misconduct which occurs on or after April 1, 2003. The Insider Dealing Tribunal continues in existence to inquire into cases of insider dealing that occurred before April 1, 2003.

As an alternative to civil proceedings, market misconduct is subject to criminal prosecution, which, if successful, may result in more severe penalties on conviction, including up to 10 years' imprisonment or a fine of up to $10 million.

Recent Developments

The Government, together with the SFC, strives to continue to provide a favourable environment for introducing new financial products, and for its intermediaries.

The SFC published in July 2003 a Code on Real Estate Investment Trusts (REITs) following market consultation. Market respondents welcomed the code which facilitates new product development. The SFC also concluded the review of Chapter 20 of the Listing Rules of HKEx for streamlining the listing of SFC-authorised collective investment schemes. The HKEx announced the amendments in August and the new Chapter 20 became effective on September 1, 2003.

The SFC consultation on the draft guidelines for regulating Exchange Traded Index Tracking Funds (ETFs) ended in May 2003. The new guidelines, which provide for streamlined requirements on investment restrictions and risk disclosure requirements, suitable disclosure of trading information and streamlined recognition of overseas ETFs, were gazetted and became effective in October 2003.

With the liberalisation of commission rates in April 2003, brokerage commissions are now freely negotiable between brokers and their clients. The Government convened a Working Group on the Business Environment of the Stockbroking Industry in a bid to enhance the competitiveness of small and medium sized brokerage firms. The Working Group engaged the industry actively and completed its deliberations in April 2003. It put forward a number of recommendations, including enhancing transparency of brokerage commissions and other service fees; promoting image building of brokers and market awareness among investors; and enhancing training opportunities for brokers. The SFC, the HKMA, the HKEx and various industry associations have been following up on these recommendations.

The SFC Working Group on Review of Financial Regulatory Framework for Licensed Corporations, which was established in May 2002 to review the arrangements for securities margin finance providers (SMF providers) to pool and re-pledge clients' securities as well as the need to tailor regulatory capital requirements, has made good progress in examining the various risks arising from the operation of securities firms. The SFC plans to conduct public consultation in relation to these measures in 2004.

The SFO has also given the SFC greater flexibility and powers to pursue and combat market crimes and misconduct. In implementing the new SFO, the SFC has refocused its enforcement resources in the last year to address three areas of high risk in the financial markets in Hong Kong: corporate misconduct, serious misconduct by intermediaries, and market misconduct. These areas will continue to be the SFC's enforcement priorities in the coming year. The SFC is also taking a tougher stance towards such misconduct.

Insurance Sector

Main Features

Hong Kong is one of the most open insurance centres in the world. At year-end, there were 188 authorised insurers, 94 of which were incorporated in Hong Kong and the remaining 94 were incorporated in 22 overseas countries or the Mainland, with the United States taking the lead followed by the United Kingdom.

Notwithstanding the economic slowdown, the total gross premiums of the insurance industry reached $89.0 billion in 2002, representing a 16.6 per cent growth over 2001. Gross premiums of the general insurance sector increased by 20.6 per cent to $23.4 billion in 2002. General Liability, Property Damage, Motor Vehicle and Accident and Health business have attained significant premium growth. Underwriting performance improved from a loss of $473 million in 2001 to a profit of $1,243 million in 2002.

The long term insurance business continued to attain a double-digit annual growth from 1991 to 2002, with office premiums increasing by 15.2 per cent to $65.5 billion in 2002. The office premiums in force of Individual Life business amounted to $49.6 billion, accounting for 75.7 per cent of the total office premiums. The number of Individual Life policies in force grew by 5.9 per cent to 5.2 million in 2002.

At year-end, there were 32 099 insurance intermediaries, including 31 635 agents (of whom 1 973 are agency firms) and 464 brokers.

Insurance Authority

The Commissioner of Insurance, appointed by the Chief Executive as the Insurance Authority (IA), has the principal function (under the Insurance Companies Ordinance (ICO)) to regulate and supervise the insurance industry for the promotion of the general stability of the insurance industry and for the protection of existing and potential policy holders.

The ICO, which prescribes a comprehensive regulatory framework for all classes of insurance business, has the two main objectives of ensuring the financial stability of all insurers authorised in Hong Kong and the fitness and propriety of their management. These objectives are achieved through the prescription of, *inter alia*, the minimum share capital and the solvency margin requirements, and the requirement for directors and controllers of insurers to be fit and proper persons.

A general business insurer is also required to maintain assets in Hong Kong to meet the claims of Hong Kong policy holders. For life insurance business, a fully-fledged appointed actuary system has been implemented to ensure that the insurer would be able to meet its obligations.

Prudential supervision of insurers is carried out mainly through examination of the financial statements, reports of actuaries and other returns submitted by insurers and regular on-site visits. The IA may take appropriate action against an insurer, under the ICO, to safeguard the interests of policy holders. These measures include the limitation of premium income, placing of assets in the IA's custody, assumption of control by a manager appointed by the IA or petitioning for the winding-up of the insurer.

Insurance intermediaries have been brought under the regulation of the ICO since 1995. An insurance agent must be properly appointed by an insurer and an insurer is required to comply with the Code of Practice for the Administration of Insurance Agents in appointing and controlling its agents. An insurance broker must meet certain minimum requirements before he can be authorised.

Self-regulatory measures are in place to strengthen the market discipline in the insurance industry. These measures, formulated by the insurance industry in consultation with the IA, include the adoption of a Code of Conduct for Insurers governing the writing of insurance contracts and insurance benefit illustration standards for life insurance policies.

As a member of the International Association of Insurance Supervisors (IAIS), Hong Kong endeavours to ensure that its supervisory standards are in line with the principles and standards developed by the association. It has also established an Insurance Advisory Committee with representatives from the industry as members. The committee was set up pursuant to section 54 of the ICO for advising the Government on matters relating to the administration of the ICO and the carrying on of insurance business in Hong Kong.

Recent Developments

The IA reviews from time to time the regulatory regime of the insurance sector, in the light of operational experience, market development and the international trends to ensure its effectiveness. In the process, it maintains close liaison with industry bodies and overseas regulators. In 2003, the IA issued a number of guidelines for further enhancement of the different aspects of the regulatory regime. For instance, the IA issued in February a Guidance Note on Classification of Class C-Linked Long Term Business (GN11) and in June a Guidance Note on Reinsurance with Related Companies (GN12). GN11 was issued to clarify the classification of long term business between Class A (Life and Annuity) and Class C (Linked Long Term). GN12, on the other hand, was issued to specify the criteria for adequate reinsurance arrangements with related reinsurers and how to address the supervisory concern arising from inadequate reinsurance arrangements.

Having regard to the latest international regulatory developments, the IA also issued in June 2003 a Supplement to the Guidance Note on Prevention of Money Laundering and a Guideline on the Combat of Terrorist Financing.

The existing self-regulatory system for insurance intermediaries has been in operation since 1995. In recent years, there have been rapid developments in the industry such as the growing numbers of insurance intermediaries and the increasing sophistication of insurance products. There is also a rising public expectation for better protection for the insured. The IA considers that there is a need to enhance the existing system. The relevant self-regulatory organisations (SROs) were consulted on possible improvements to the existing regulatory regime. On the basis of the industry's comments, the IA is in the process of liaising with the SROs to implement a number of proposals. Some items of the proposed improvements have been implemented, such as the disclosure of registration number to facilitate identification of insurance intermediaries, and reinforcement of the requirements relating to policy replacement. The IA will continue to liaise with the industry and parties concerned to enhance the regulatory system for insurance intermediaries and further protect the interests of the insuring public.

In January 2003, legislation has been made to introduce a definition of 'Hong Kong Long Term Insurance Business' and a requirement to submit annual returns of such business. Besides promoting market transparency, and the integrity and comprehensiveness of the relevant statistics, this would also enable the IA to monitor the operation of long term insurers more effectively.

In the light of international regulatory trends and developments of the insurance industry, the Government is reviewing the institutional set-up of the IA. The review entails a study on turning the IA into a regulatory agency independent of the Government. Relevant stakeholders are being consulted.

The IA had commissioned a consultancy study on the need and feasibility of establishing Policyholders' Protection Funds (PPFs) in Hong Kong. Stage 1 of the study which comprises a review of the existing regulatory regime and a feasibility study on establishing PPFs was largely completed. The IA issued in December 2003 a consultation paper inviting public comments by the end of March 2004. The Government is keeping an open mind on the PPF concept.

To examine the need for enhancing the supervisory framework of the assets of long term business insurers, the IA commissioned another consultancy study in September 2003. The study focuses on the appropriate framework for asset valuation and the need for a mechanism that better safeguards the interest of Hong Kong policy holders in the event of failures of long term insurers. The first stage of the study would be completed by early 2005. It would include a review of the existing regulatory framework as well as the international practice. Stakeholders will be consulted in the process.

Retirement Protection Schemes: Mandatory Provident Fund Schemes and Occupational Retirement Schemes

Main Features

On December 1, 2000, the Mandatory Provident Fund (MPF) System was implemented to help encourage the workforce to save and invest for their retirement protection. The system, which was formulated after extensive consultation, is a privately managed, employment-related mandatory system of provident fund schemes. Unless exempted, employees and self-employed persons aged between 18 and 65 are required to participate in MPF schemes.

The MPF system provides for joint contributions by the employer and employee, each contributing 5 per cent of the employee's relevant income to a registered MPF trust scheme, subject to the maximum and minimum levels of income for contribution purposes. The accrued benefits are fully vested in the scheme members and can be transferred from scheme to scheme when employees change employment or cease to be employed. A self-employed person has to contribute 5 per cent of his or her relevant income. In normal circumstances, benefits must be preserved until the scheme member attains the retirement age of 65.

By year-end, about 95 per cent of employers (i.e. about 218 000), 96 per cent of relevant employees (1 733 000) and 82 per cent of self-employed persons (299 000) had enrolled in MPF schemes. The total MPF assets amounted to about $89.4 billion, with monthly MPF contributions amounting to around $2 billion.

Unlike the compulsory MPF schemes, occupational retirement schemes (ORSO schemes) registered under the Occupational Retirement Schemes Ordinance (ORSO) are voluntary schemes established by employers. The objective of the ORSO is to regulate such schemes through a registration system to ensure that they are properly administered and funded. All registered schemes must meet certain requirements, including asset separation, independent trusteeship, restricted investments, funding, independent audit, actuarial reviews, information disclosure and the submission of audited financial statements to the Registrar of Occupational Retirement Schemes.

To tie in with the implementation of the MPF System, ORSO schemes that fulfilled certain conditions were exempted from MPF requirements. Members of such schemes may choose to remain in the existing scheme or join a MPF scheme. At year-end, there were 5 554 MPF-exempted ORSO schemes covering over 500 000 employees.

Mandatory Provident Fund Schemes Authority

The Mandatory Provident Fund Schemes Authority (MPFA) was set up in September 1998 under the Mandatory Provident Fund Schemes Ordinance (MPFSO). It is tasked with the responsibility of regulating and supervising the MPF System and ensuring compliance with the MPFSO. Two statutory committees, the MPF Schemes Advisory Committee and the MPF Industry Schemes Committee, have been established to advise the MPFA on the overall operation of the MPFSO and the Industry Schemes respectively. The MPF Schemes Appeal Board has also been set up under the MPFSO to hear appeals against the relevant decisions of the MPFA.

To ensure that the interests of MPF scheme members are protected, the MPFA closely monitors the operation of MPF trustees and other service providers, investigates complaints about non-compliance and takes enforcement actions accordingly. Proactive inspections are carried out at business premises to ensure compliance of employers in enrolling their employees in MPF schemes and making contributions. The MPFA also educates the public on the need for retirement protection and on the MPF System, with an emphasis on investor education. Some of the educational activities were held in conjunction with other bodies (for example, the Hong Kong Investment Funds Association and labour unions).

The MPFA also acts as the Registrar of Occupational Retirement Schemes.

Recent Developments

In order to further enhance the effectiveness and efficiency of the MPF System, the MPFA continued to review the MPF legislation in the light of operational experience. The MPF Schemes Operation Review Committee (SORC), comprising representatives of employer and employee bodies, service providers, professional organisations, the

Government and the MPFA, was set up in 2001 for this purpose. The SORC has so far completed three phases of its work. Following the coming into force of the provisions relating mainly to raising the minimum relevant income level for making MPF contributions and other scheme administration measures in February 2003, all the provisions arising from the first phase of review have become operational. The proposals resulting from the second and third phases of its review cover issues relating to investment regulation, scheme administration and enforcement. The Government is aiming to put these proposals through the legislative process.

The MPFA has also initiated a project since late 2002 to review and improve the disclosure of information about fees, charges and fund performance of MPF products, with a view to enabling scheme members to make informed investment decisions. Key proposals have been developed in consultation with industry bodies and other regulators, and the details are being worked out progressively. The proposals will be implemented in phases from 2004 to 2006. Public education programmes will be developed to tie in with the different stages of implementation.

Financial Links between Hong Kong and the Mainland

Hong Kong provides Mainland enterprises with an efficient access to international capital through its banking, equity and debt markets. Nevertheless, the cross-boundary capital flows have by no means been one-way. Hong Kong's banks have maintained a strong presence in the Mainland. The financial links between Hong Kong and the Mainland will be further strengthened with China's accession to the World Trade Organisation (WTO), which will over time generate increasing demand for a wide range of financial support services for increasing trade and investment flows between the Mainland and the rest of the world. The arrangements for banks in Hong Kong to conduct renminbi (RMB) business signify an important step forward for the development of the banking sector and open a new channel for the flow of renminbi funds between Hong Kong and the Mainland through the banking system.

Cross-boundary funds were flowing steadily among financial institutions in both places. Over the years, the Mainland has accumulated a substantial amount of funds in Hong Kong dollars from trading activities and inward investment. These funds are placed with financial institutions in the Mainland and are subsequently channelled back to Hong Kong through the inter-bank market.

AIs' external liabilities to and claims on financial institutions in the Mainland at end-December were $226.6 billion and $157.1 billion, respectively. The amounts represented 15 per cent and 5.8 per cent, respectively, of AIs' total liabilities to and claims on banks outside Hong Kong.

Many banks from Hong Kong have established a strong presence among businesses in the Mainland. A total of 15 locally incorporated banks have established 46 branches and 29 representative offices there by year-end. Hong Kong's banks, with their long-established financial links with the Mainland and their well-developed global financial expertise, should be able to further expand their scope of business in the Mainland as well as to help Mainland entities to reach out following China's accession to the WTO.

The joint clearing facility for Hong Kong dollar cheques, agreed between the HKMA and the Guangzhou Branch of the People's Bank of China (PBoC), was introduced in September 2000 to expedite the processing of Hong Kong dollar cheques issued by banks in Hong Kong and presented in Guangdong. This was the second agreement of its kind: a similar cheque clearing facility was established between Hong Kong and Shenzhen in January 1998. In September 2001, an agreement was reached for the cross-boundary joint clearing facility for Hong Kong dollar cheques, drawn upon banks in Hong Kong and presented in Guangdong (including Shenzhen), to be extended to cover cashier's orders and demand drafts.

In June 2002, the joint cheque clearing facility was further extended to clear Hong Kong dollar cheques drawn on banks in Guangdong, including Shenzhen, and presented in Hong Kong. Under this arrangement, the time required for clearing is reduced to two working days. In 2003, about 250 000 cheques totalling $22 billion were cleared through the two-way joint clearing facilities. Furthermore, in order to expedite cross-boundary payments between Hong Kong and Shenzhen, Hong Kong dollar and US dollar RTGS links between Hong Kong and Shenzhen to enable banks on both sides to make Hong Kong dollar and US dollar RTGS payments were implemented on December 12, 2002 and November 17, 2003 respectively.

The Chief Executive announced on November 18, 2003 that, following approval from the State Council, the PBoC had agreed to provide clearing arrangements for personal RMB business in Hong Kong. The scope of such RMB business includes deposit-taking, exchange, remittances and RMB cards. This arrangement will help promote economic integration between Hong Kong and the Mainland, and facilitate cross-border tourist spending. In addition to meeting the demands of the market and the public, the Hong Kong banking sector will also be able to develop new areas of business. This will enhance the competitiveness of the banks in Hong Kong and the attractiveness of Hong Kong as an international financial centre.

Portfolio investment in the form of 'China funds' is popular. By year-end, 79 China or Greater China equity funds[4] had been authorised by the SFC and they invested in Hong Kong companies, H-shares, red-chips listed on the Hong Kong Stock Exchange, B-shares listed on the Shanghai and Shenzhen Stock Exchanges, Taiwanese companies listed on the Taiwan Stock Exchange, or other Greater China related securities listed in overseas markets.

Hong Kong as an International Capital Formation Centre for the Mainland

The Government is committed to making full use of the favourable conditions of the Hong Kong market, including higher liquidity, a robust legal system, efficient information flow, availability of professional expertise, and closer proximity to the Mainland market to provide better services to Mainland enterprises seeking listing in an international financial centre.

The rapidly expanding Mainland market represents a massive opportunity. The presence of Mainland issuers has increased both the breadth and depth of Hong Kong's securities and futures markets. Hong Kong's equity market has evolved from one highly concentrated in properties and finance businesses into a market with a great diversity of constituent stocks and a wide range of products.

Hong Kong has established itself as the most important international fund-raising centre for Mainland enterprises. At year-end, about 260 Mainland enterprises were listed in Hong Kong. Significantly, 92 out of the 93 Mainland-incorporated enterprises which had listed outside the Mainland (H-shares) have chosen to list on

---

[4] Excluding guaranteed funds, hedge funds, index funds, money market funds, etc., that invest in Greater China.

the SEHK. These 92 enterprises had raised a total of more than $195.3 billion directly and indirectly through Hong Kong as at end-2003, including $48.3 billion raised in 2003.

In 2003, the three largest IPOs on the SEHK all concerned Mainland issuers. These three IPOs alone already accounted for 62 per cent of funds raised in the whole year. In particular, the China Life Insurance Company Limited was reported to be the largest IPO in the world in 2003 and was the third largest in Hong Kong's history.

Apart from the equity market, Mainland enterprises raise capital in Hong Kong through issuance of bonds, project financing and loan syndication. Mainland enterprises also have easy access in Hong Kong to investment banking services such as mergers and acquisitions, and consultancy on restructuring.

In a bid to further strengthen communication and enhance cooperation, the SFC had regular meetings with the China Securities Regulatory Commission (CSRC), the two exchanges in Shanghai and Shenzhen, and the HKEx to discuss issues of mutual interest.

Mainland and Hong Kong Closer Economic Partnership Arrangement (CEPA)

The signing of the main parts of CEPA and its Annexes, in June and September 2003 respectively, has offered greater market access and flexibility for Hong Kong's financial services suppliers and professionals in the Mainland. It is envisaged that the coming into operation of CEPA on January 1, 2004 will not only enhance Hong Kong's attractiveness to market users, but also strengthen its competitiveness as an international financial centre and the premier capital formation centre for Mainland enterprises.

In the banking sector, the substantial lowering of the total asset requirement from US$20 billion to US$6 billion would enable seven additional Hong Kong banks to set up branches in the Mainland. This makes it possible for Hong Kong banks to set up branches in the Mainland as early as 2004 to become acquainted with the Mainland market and to make early preparation for conducting renminbi business.

Under CEPA, when applying for conducting renminbi business, Mainland branches of Hong Kong banks are only required to demonstrate profitability for two consecutive years vis-à-vis three years for other foreign banks. More importantly, in conducting profitability assessment the relevant authorities will base their assessment on the overall profitability of all branches of the Hong Kong bank in the Mainland vis-à-vis the profitability of individual branches for a foreign bank.

CEPA also provides special advantages for the insurance sector. Hong Kong has taken a great step forward by raising the maximum allowed equity participation by Hong Kong insurers in a Mainland insurance company to 24.9 per cent, compared with 10 per cent for other foreign insurers. Besides, Hong Kong insurance companies would have greater opportunities to enter the Mainland insurance market through the formation of groups. CEPA also allows Hong Kong residents to engage in the relevant insurance services after obtaining the Mainland's insurance qualifications and being employed or appointed by a Mainland insurance institution.

In the accounting sector, the Government has welcomed the arrangements that Hong Kong accountants, who have already qualified as Chinese Certified Public Accountants (CPAs) and practised in the Mainland (including partnership), are treated on a par with Chinese CPAs in respect of the requirement for annual residency in the Mainland. The validity period of the 'Temporary Auditing Business Permit' applied by Hong Kong accounting firms to conduct temporary auditing services in the Mainland is also extended from six months to one year.

With respect to the securities industry, as provided under CEPA, the HKEx set up a representative office in Beijing in November 2003. Moreover, the CSRC and the SFC reached a consensus on the implementation of the CEPA provision on simplification of procedures for Hong Kong professionals applying for the Mainland securities and futures industry qualifications, and signed the 'Mainland/Hong Kong CEPA-Arrangements relating to Qualifications of Securities and Futures Industry Practitioners' in December 2003. The Arrangements also apply to Mainland professionals who want to obtain the Hong Kong qualifications.

Under the Arrangements, Hong Kong professionals having passed the examination on relevant Mainland laws and regulations may be granted industry qualifications by the Mainland's Securities Association of China or China Futures Association; while Mainland professionals may be deemed by the SFC as having satisfied the requirements for industry qualifications in Hong Kong. Subject to satisfying other requirements, these professionals may practice in the Mainland or be licensed in Hong Kong.

Initiatives to Enhance Hong Kong's Competitiveness

The Government is determined to strengthen Hong Kong's status as an international financial centre and the premier capital formation centre for the Mainland. To this end, a Financial Market Development Task Force was set up in December 2001 to provide a high-level forum to coordinate new initiatives in promoting the development of Hong Kong's financial markets. The Task Force brings in expertise and professional input from the regulators and market participants.

The individual regulators will continue to further enhance Hong Kong's regulatory framework in the light of international experience and standards. The objective is to have an effective regulatory framework that will ensure sound business standards and confidence of the market but without unnecessary impediments.

Major initiatives to enhance Hong Kong's competitiveness as an international financial centre are outlined in the following paragraphs.

Implementation of the Securities and Futures Ordinance

The SFO, which consolidates and modernises 10 ordinances governing the securities and futures markets into a composite piece of legislation, strengthens the quality of the regulatory framework and keeps the regulatory regime on par with international standards and practices. It seeks to: facilitate development of a fair, orderly and transparent market to promote investors' confidence; secure appropriate investor protection; reduce market malpractice and financial crime; and facilitate market innovation and competition. The commencement of the SFO, on April 1, 2003, enhances Hong Kong's position as an international financial centre and the premier capital formation centre for the Mainland.

Main features of improvement under the new regulatory regime include:—

(a) greater accountability of the SFC;

(b) streamlined and enhanced regulation of market intermediaries and levelling the playing field between brokers and banks in their conduct of securities business and other regulated activities;

(c) facilitating market innovation;

(d) greater effectiveness in combating market misconduct;

(e) greater market transparency;

(f) enhanced investor compensation arrangements; and

(g) provision of a responsive regulatory framework through prescribing the detailed and technical regulatory requirements in subsidiary legislation.

Implementation of the SFO has been smooth since April 1, 2003. The SFC has endeavoured to provide continuous guidance to the market to assist practitioners in their understanding of the new law. Apart from posting relevant materials in connection with the SFO on its website to facilitate easy access by market participants and providing dedicated hotlines and e-mail boxes to answer questions from the industry, the SFC also organised or participated in more than 67 seminars to introduce the new law to the industry.

Migration of financial intermediaries to the new single licensing regime gathered pace. Around 7 420 intermediaries, representing 42 of all those who would migrate, had either migrated or lodged their migration applications as at year-end. More than 4 400 have already received their new licences.

Company Law and Corporate Governance Reform

The Standing Committee on Company Law Reform (SCCLR), established in 1984, meets regularly to consider amendments to the Companies Ordinance to ensure that it meets the changing needs of the business community. The Companies Registry provides secretariat support for the SCCLR.

The Overall Review of the Companies Ordinance by the SCCLR has resulted in 62 recommendations for reform, including a mix of amendments to specific sections of the Companies Ordinance, topics which require further research and study, and major structural proposals such as rewriting and restructuring the Companies Ordinance. Virtually all the proposals regarding amendments to specific sections of the Companies Ordinance have been included in the Companies (Amendment) Ordinance 2003 which was enacted in July 2003. Work on topics requiring further research and study has been undertaken in the context of either the SCCLR Corporate Governance Review or independently by the SCCLR. The results of some of this work are contained in the Companies (Amendment) Bill 2003. This bill, which was introduced into the Legislative Council in June 2003, is being scrutinised by a Bills Committee. Consideration is now being given as to how the recommendation to rewrite and restructure the Companies Ordinance can best be taken forward.

The Corporate Governance Review by the SCCLR, which aims to identify and bridge any gaps in Hong Kong's corporate governance regime, making it a benchmark in the region, has continued to make good progress. A consultation document on the Phase II of the review setting out a large number of proposals on directors' duties and responsibilities, shareholders' rights and the disclosure of corporate information was published for public consultation on June 11, 2003. Depending on the outcome of the review, appropriate amendments will be made to the Companies Ordinance, the Listing Rules and the Code of Best Practice.

The Government published in January 2003 a Corporate Governance Action Plan. The roll-out of the SFO is one of the major initiatives under the Action Plan.

In May 2003, the SFC and the HKEx jointly consulted the market on strengthening the regulation of sponsors and independent financial advisers. Responses to the consultation were being considered to develop measures to strengthen the present regulatory regime.

The HKEx issued the consultation conclusions on Proposed Amendments to the Listing Rules relating to Corporate Governance Issues in January 2003. Taking into account the responses to the consultation, the HKEx is in the process of amending its Listing Rules. It is also working on a Code on Corporate Governance Practices which will be released for public consultation in early 2004.

The Government published a Consultation Paper on Proposals to Enhance the Regulation of Listing in October 2003, following the issuance of a report by the Expert Group to Review the Operation of the Securities and Futures Market Regulatory Structure in March. Public views were sought on proposals to give statutory backing to certain fundamental listing requirements and on ways to improve the regulatory structure governing the performance of listing functions. The Government will consider carefully the public views received and work closely with the SFC and the HKEx to draw up appropriate measures to improve the regulatory regime for listing.

Enhancement of the Financial Infrastructure

As part of the three-pronged strategy announced in the Budget Speech in March 1999 for reforming the securities and futures markets in Hong Kong, the Financial Secretary appointed a Steering Committee on the Enhancement of the Financial Infrastructure in Hong Kong (SCEFI) to study and recommend the necessary improvements to the financial infrastructure in Hong Kong. The objective is to enhance the competitiveness of Hong Kong as an international financial centre in terms of risk mitigation, efficiency enhancement and cost reduction. The SCEFI recommended the development of a single clearing arrangement for securities, stock options, futures and other exchange-traded transactions; straight-through processing and a scripless securities market. The Government, together with the SFC, the HKMA and the HKEx, is pressing ahead with the implementation of various SCEFI recommendations.

In 2002, the SFC consulted the public on the proposed scripless securities market. The consultation conclusions were published in September 2003. The scripless initiative was broadly accepted by the industry. Following this, the HKEx published in October 2003 a separate consultation paper on proposed operational details of the scripless model. Comments received from the securities and futures industry are being analysed by the HKEx and conclusions will be published in 2004.

Human Resources Development

A robust physical infrastructure cannot function effectively without the input of trained persons of the right calibre. Hong Kong needs to have a workforce that is adaptable and well-equipped to meet future challenges and to reap the benefits offered by new opportunities. The Advisory Committee on Human Resources Development in the Financial Services Sector was established in June 2000, tasked with the mission to develop a vision on human resources development in the financial services sector. Activities organised or coordinated by the committee include opinion surveys, seminars and an internship programme. The committee has also sought the assistance of the Vocational Training Council in compiling more statistics on the manpower situation in the banking and finance industry.

Hong Kong Dollar Debt Market

The Hong Kong dollar debt market continued to grow in 2003. Outstanding Hong Kong dollar debt securities increased by 5 per cent to $558 billion at year-end. The Exchange Fund accounted for about 22 per cent of total outstanding debt. Other issuers included AIs, statutory bodies or government-owned corporations, multilateral development banks (MDBs), non-MDB overseas borrowers and local corporations.

New issuance of Exchange Fund paper, mainly for rollover purposes, amounted to $213 billion in 2003, accounting for about 56 per cent of the total new issuance. Demand for Exchange Fund Notes remained steady, with an average over-subscription rate of about 4.6 times in 2003. The Hong Kong dollar Exchange Fund Notes yield curve shifted upward with the US Treasuries yields amid the brightening US economic outlook. The yield on 10-year Exchange Fund Notes rose to 4.39 per cent at the end of 2003 from 4.27 per cent in 2002. Nevertheless, as the yield on the Exchange Fund Notes was rising at a slower pace, the yield spread tightened to about eight basis points at the year-end, as compared with 44 basis points in 2002. The average daily turnover of Exchange Fund papers amounted to $21 billion in 2003.

Issuance activities of non-Exchange Fund paper decreased in the year. Hong Kong dollar debt issues launched in 2003 totalled $170 billion, compared with $180 billion in 2002. Of this amount, $61 billion or 36 per cent was issued by AIs, $86 billion or 50 per cent was issued by non-MDB overseas borrowers, and $16 billion or 9 per cent was issued by statutory bodies or government-owned corporations. Despite the decline in issuance activity, the product range continued to expand. The year saw the launch of a significant number of structured deals, such as step-up bonds with callable features, extendable notes and fixed-floating rate bonds. The Government also encouraged public corporations to take the lead in launching debt issuance programmes, including Hong Kong dollar bonds with longer maturity periods and particularly at the retail level. Recent examples included 7 to 15 year bonds issued by the Airport Authority, the Kowloon-Canton Railway Corporation and the MTR Corporation Limited in 2003. Retail interest was strong. The Kowloon-Canton Railway Corporation successfully launched a 10-year issue, the longest maturity so far for retail investors in Hong Kong. Ford Credit, the financing arm of the US-based car producer Ford Motor, issued the first retail bond by a foreign company in Hong Kong. Besides, a number of banks continued to issue retail certificates of deposit.

Fixed-rate debt still dominated the market and constituted about 87 per cent of total new issues in 2003. The average maturity profile of all outstanding fixed-rate debts at year-end increased slightly compared with the previous year.

The HKMA launched on August 1, 2003 a one-year pilot scheme for promoting Exchange Fund Notes in the retail market. The scheme introduced a new arrangement, whereby a portion of each quarterly issue of 2-year and 3-year Exchange Fund Notes will be made available for non-competitive tender by retail investors through the Retail Exchange Fund Notes Distributors ('Distributors'), namely Bank of East Asia, DBS Bank (HK) and Wing Lung Bank. In the first three non-competitive tenders conducted in August, October and November 2003,

Exchange Fund Notes totalling $241 million were sold to retail investors. In addition to providing the non-competitive tender service, the Distributors agreed to adhere to a number of unified standards in the distribution of Exchange Fund Notes to retail investors in the secondary market to enhance pricing transparency and facilitate comparison by retail investors.

Along with the launch of the scheme, the HKMA added a new section, 'Exchange Fund Notes: Information for Investors', to its website to educate retail investors on bond investment. An updated pamphlet was also distributed to the public to promote awareness of the retail Exchange Fund Notes programme.

The Financial Secretary announced in his Budget Speech on March 5, 2003 that income from Qualified Debt Securities[5] with a maturity period of seven years or more, which were previously eligible for a 50 per cent profits tax concession, would be totally exempted from profits tax. In addition, the Government relaxed the minimum maturity requirement on the current 50 per cent tax concession in respect of Qualified Debt Securities from five years to three years.

The Government is implementing measures to overhaul the existing regulatory framework for offers of shares and debentures under a three-phased approach. Measures under Phase I involved the issuance of various guidelines by the SFC in February 2003, permitting awareness advertisements, putting in place an alternative 'dual prospectus' structure, and allowing faxed copies of expert consent letters and bulk print proofs of prospectuses for the purpose of registration. They also included a 'two class' exemption[6] by the SFC in relation to prospectuses for offers of debentures, which came into operation in May 2003. Phase II involved the Companies (Amendment) Bill 2003, which was introduced into the Legislative Council in June. It proposed, among other things, to simplify procedures for registration and issue of prospectuses. In Phase III, the SFC will conduct a comprehensive review of all local laws and procedures governing public offers of securities as well as regulatory reforms introduced in other leading jurisdictions, with a view to putting in place a framework that provides the most efficient, competitive and fair environment for issuers and investors alike. The SFC has started the review and aims to put forward proposals for public consultation by September 2004.

Development of a Secondary Mortgage Market

A well-developed secondary mortgage market plays a useful role in channelling long-term funds, such as insurance and pension funds, to meet the rising demand for long-term home financing. The Hong Kong Mortgage Corporation (HKMC), wholly

---

[5] Qualified debt securities (QDSs) are debt paper (a) issued to the public in Hong Kong, (b) with an original maturity of not less than five years, (c) with a minimum denomination of HK$50,000 or its equivalent in a foreign currency, (d) lodged with and cleared by the Central Moneymarkets Unit in its entirety, and (e) for papers issued by non-statutory bodies or non-government owned corporations, they would need to have at all relevant times a credit rating from a recognised rating agency acceptable to the HKMA [e.g. currently BBB- or above from S&P's].

[6] The 'two class' exemption includes:

    a. prospectuses relating to offers of listed and unlisted debentures will be exempted, subject to certain conditions of the Third Schedule to the Companies Ordinance on the basis that the SFC considers they are irrelevant for the purposes of making an informed investment decision and/or unduly onerous for companies to comply with; and

    b. prospectuses relating to offers of listed debentures will be exempted from those contents requirement that are the same as or similar to those requirements under the applicable listing rules (provided no waiver, modification or other dispensation has been granted from such requirements).

owned by the Government through the Exchange Fund, was incorporated in March 1997 with a mission to develop this market.

The HKMC's business is being developed in two phases. The initial phase involves the purchase of mortgage loans for its own portfolio and the funding of the purchases largely through the issuance of unsecured debt securities. In the second phase, the HKMC securitises the mortgages into Mortgage Backed Securities (MBS) and offers them for sale to investors.

Since its commencement of business in October 1997, the HKMC has proceeded smoothly with its Mortgage Purchase Programme. Through effective marketing and the introduction of innovative products, the outstanding principal balance of the HKMC's retained mortgage portfolio reached $34.6 billion as at year-end.

The HKMC introduced the Mortgage Insurance Programme (MIP) in March 1999 to promote home ownership in Hong Kong. It enables the banks to lend home mortgage loans above the 70 per cent loan-to-value ceiling set by the HKMA without incurring additional risk. In 2000, the MIP was expanded to cover mortgage loans with a loan-to-value ratio from 85 per cent to 90 per cent. In 2001, the MIP was expanded to cover equitable mortgage loans on residential properties under construction with loan-to-value ratio of up to 90 per cent. The loan size ceiling for mortgage loans on residential properties under construction with loan-to-value ratio of up to 85 per cent was increased from $8 million to $12 million in December 2003. The streamlined pricing arrangement (commonly known as 'one-stop' 90 per cent mortgage service) for mortgages covered by the MIP was well received since its introduction in late 2002. Since its inception in 1999, the MIP has steadily been gaining acceptance by home buyers and increasing market penetration through product diversification and effective promotion. The total number of applications received since launch amounted to 31 000 and the penetration ratio of the programme had reached a level of 13.6 per cent for the first 10 months of 2003.

One of the missions of the HKMC is to promote the development of the MBS and debt markets in Hong Kong. The HKMC launched a back-to-back MBS Programme in October 1999. The back-to-back structure allows banks to effectively 'repackage' their mortgage portfolios into more liquid portfolios and to maintain the majority of the cash flow if they hold the MBS in their own investment portfolio. The HKMC's guarantee on the timely payment of principal and interest serves to make the MBS a safe and attractive investment for investors. The HKMC has securitised $2.84 billion of MBS with three of its key business partners. The corporation also launched a multi-currency conventional bond-style MBS Programme in December 2001. Under the programme, two issues of $2 billion and $3 billion were launched in March 2002 and November 2003, respectively.

Debt issuance is the mainstay of the HKMC's funding sources. Through debt issuing activities, the HKMC is able to achieve the objective of promoting the development of the Hong Kong dollar debt capital market. In 2003, the HKMC successfully launched 54 debt issues for a total amount of $10.9 billion under an enlarged Debt Issuance Programme (programme size increased from $20 billion to $40 billion) and through the retail bond issuance scheme, making it the most active corporate issuer of fixed rate debt securities in Hong Kong. At year-end, the HKMC had 112 issues of debt securities with a total amount of over $33.1 billion outstanding. The HKMC debt securities were well received by financial institutions, as well as institutional and retail investors. To help develop the retail debt market, the

HKMC pioneered the issue of retail bonds through banks as placing agents in October 2001. Since then the HKMC has issued 16 retail bonds for a total amount of over $7.5 billion. Banks and other corporations adopted the same mechanism to issue retail debt securities with an aggregate issued amount of over $38.6 billion in the same period.

Companies Registry

The Companies Registry administers and enforces the major part of the Companies Ordinance. The Registry incorporates local companies, registers overseas companies, registers documents required to be submitted by registered companies and provides facilities for search of company records. It also administers and enforces several other ordinances including the Trustee Ordinance, insofar as it relates to trust companies, the Registered Trustees Incorporation Ordinance and the Limited Partnerships Ordinance. The Registry is also responsible for a wide range of legal, policy and regulatory issues, including the ongoing work under the Companies Ordinance and corporate governance reviews.

Since 1993, the Companies Registry has operated as a trading fund department. Therefore, the Registry can keep most of its income and deploy it flexibly, having regard to its needs, business turnover and its customers' demands and expectations. The department achieved a surplus of $40.4 million in the 2002-03 financial year. The substantial surplus generated over the past years has built up a healthy reserve, protected the department from the adverse impact of the economic downturn and helped finance the department's development projects.

The Registry has continued with its implementation of the Strategic Change Plan (SCP) to transform the department into a fully computerised Registry by early 2006 and enable electronic delivery of services in filing, processing, storing and obtaining documents or information. The implementation of the SCP will lead to a significant reduction in the time taken to process documents, more timely updating and disclosure of company information, improved quality of information, enhanced data security and integrity and higher productivity at reduced operating costs. The core initiative of the SCP is the development of an Integrated Companies Registry Information System (ICRIS) in two phases. The first phase includes the replacement of the existing computer systems, document imaging, conversion of microfilm records and online searches on current data and digitised images of registered company documents kept in the Registry's database. The second phase will include the implementation of online document registration and company incorporation. Development of Phase I of ICRIS is under way. It is anticipated that Phase I of ICRIS will be implemented in the third quarter of 2004.

In 2003, 50 049 new companies were incorporated. During the year, the total nominal capital of new companies registered was $49.08 billion and 5 778 companies increased their nominal capital by $681.41 billion. At year-end, 497 406 local companies were on the register, compared with 503 111 in 2002.

Companies incorporated overseas must register certain documents with the Registry within one month of establishing a place of business in Hong Kong. During 2003, 724 of these were registered. At year-end, 6 983 companies from 82 countries were registered.

Money Lenders

Under the Money Lenders Ordinance, anyone wishing to carry on business as a money lender must apply to a licensing court for a licence. The ordinance does not apply to authorised institutions under the Banking Ordinance.

Licence applications are, initially, submitted to the Registrar of Companies as Registrar of Money Lenders. A copy is also sent to the Commissioner of Police who may object to the application. The application is advertised, and any member of the public who has an interest in the matter has the right to object. During the year, 774 applications were received. Altogether, a total of 711 licences were granted, involving both new applications and outstanding applications brought forward from the previous year. At year-end, there were 775 licensed money lenders, including those whose applications for renewing their licences had yet to be approved.

The ordinance provides penalties for offences such as carrying on an unlicensed money-lending business. It also provides that any loan made by an unlicensed money lender shall not be recoverable by court action. With certain exceptions (primarily authorised institutions under the Banking Ordinance), any person, whether a licensed money lender or not, who lends or offers to lend money at an interest rate exceeding 60 per cent per annum commits an offence. Any agreement for the repayment of any such loan, or security given in respect of such loan is unenforceable.

Bankruptcies, Individual Voluntary Arrangement and Compulsory Winding-up

The Official Receiver's Office administers the estates of individuals adjudged to be bankrupt by the court. The estates of companies ordered to be wound up by the court are administrated by insolvency practitioners from the private sector.

The Official Receiver or the insolvency practitioner appointed by him under a tendering scheme becomes the receiver of an individual debtor or provisional liquidator of a company when a bankruptcy order against the property of the debtor is made or a winding-up order against the company is made. Where the assets of an estate do not exceed $200,000, the Official Receiver or the insolvency practitioner appointed by him is usually appointed the trustee or the liquidator by way of a summary procedure order. In other cases, a meeting of creditors in bankruptcy, or meetings of creditors and contributories in compulsory liquidations, will be convened to decide whether the Official Receiver, the insolvency practitioner appointed by him or some other fit persons from the private sector should be appointed the trustee or liquidator.

When acting as the trustee or liquidator, the Official Receiver or the insolvency practitioner appointed by him investigates the affairs of the bankrupt or the wound-up company, realises assets and distributes dividends to creditors. The Official Receiver also prosecutes certain offences set out in the Bankruptcy and Companies Ordinances, applies for disqualification orders against unfit company directors, supervises the work of outside liquidators and trustees, and monitors the funds held by liquidators in both compulsory and voluntary liquidations.

During the year, the court made 24 922 bankruptcy orders, 2 743 interim orders in individual voluntary arrangements and 1 248 winding-up orders. The assets realised by the Official Receiver during 2003 amounted to $136.4 million, while $115.9 million in dividends was paid to creditors in 1 690 insolvency cases. There were 1 207 cases assigned under the scheme for contracting out of summary winding-up cases.

The Companies (Corporate Rescue) Bill, which was introduced into the Legislative Council in May 2001, aims to put in place a statutory corporate rescue procedure for companies in financial difficulty. The Legislative Council has set up a Bills Committee to examine the bill. In the light of the comments expressed by the Bills Committee, the Government has conducted a further round of consultation with concerned parties and is considering possible changes to certain provisions in the bill.

Professional Accountancy

Hong Kong had 21 835 registered professional accountants at year-end. Of these, 3 242 were certified public accountants (CPAs) or public accountants, who are in public practice and entitled to perform statutory audits. There were 1 099 CPA firms and 139 corporate practices registered at year-end.

The Hong Kong Society of Accountants (HKSA) is a self-regulatory body established under the Professional Accountants Ordinance with a wide range of responsibilities for registering professional accountants, maintaining accounting, auditing and ethical standards for the profession and conducting training programmes and examinations to qualify professional accountants.

In response to the Secretary for Financial Services and the Treasury's request in December 2002, the HKSA put forward proposals to reform the regulatory regime with the opening up of its governing body (the Council) and the two Disciplinary and Investigation Committees. The HKSA proposed that the latter two committees would in future comprise a majority of lay members. Action is in hand to amend the law to take forward the 'opening up' proposals. The HKSA also proposed the establishment of an Independent Investigation Board to tackle public interest cases. The Administration has published a consultation paper on this proposal in September 2003 and will decide the way forward in due course.

Monetary Policy

Hong Kong's monetary policy objective is to maintain currency stability. Given the highly externally oriented nature of the Hong Kong economy, this objective is further defined as a stable external value of the currency of Hong Kong, in terms of its exchange rate in the foreign exchange market against the US dollar at around HK$7.80 to US$1. This clear monetary policy objective is achieved through the linked exchange rate system, which was introduced in October 1983 after a nine-year period during which the Hong Kong dollar floated and the exchange rate was volatile.

The linked exchange rate system is characterised by currency board arrangements, requiring the Hong Kong dollar monetary base to be at least 100 per cent backed by, and changes in it to be 100 per cent matched by corresponding changes in, US dollar reserves held in the Exchange Fund at the fixed exchange rate of HK$7.80 to US$1. In Hong Kong, the monetary base includes the amount of currency notes and coins issued, the Aggregate Balance (which is the sum of the clearing balances of banks held with the HKMA for the purpose of effecting the clearing and settlement of transactions between banks themselves and also between the HKMA and banks), and the outstanding amount of Exchange Fund Bills and Notes.

Since the inception of the linked exchange rate system in October 1983, note-issuing banks are required to hold Certificates of Indebtedness (CIs) issued by the Exchange Fund to provide backing for bank note issuance. The issuance and redemption of CIs are made against US dollars at the convertibility rate of HK$7.80 to US$1 for the account of the Exchange Fund. Similarly, the issue and withdrawal of government-issued currency notes and coins in circulation are conducted against US dollars at the fixed exchange rate of 7.80.

When the linked exchange rate system was introduced in October 1983, there was no institutional arrangement whereby banks in Hong Kong maintained clearing accounts with the currency board. Thus, that part of the monetary base represented by the clearing balances of the banking system was initially not subject to the discipline imposed by a currency board system. Action was taken to correct this in 1988 through arrangements that required the Management Bank of the Clearing House of the HKAB to maintain a clearing account with the Government's then Monetary Affairs Branch for the account of the Exchange Fund. This was replaced by another arrangement, when the RTGS system was introduced, for interbank transactions in Hong Kong towards the end of 1996. Since then, all licensed banks have had to maintain direct clearing accounts with the Exchange Fund.

By assuming responsibility for the interbank clearing system, the HKMA also became responsible for the provision of lending to any banks experiencing day-to-day shortages of liquidity. A Liquidity Adjustment Facility (LAF) was set up in 1992 for this purpose. This was replaced in September 1998 by the Discount Window arrangement under which banks have unrestricted access to day-end liquidity through repurchase agreements using Exchange Fund Bills and Notes as collateral. A two-tier structure of Discount Rates has been adopted to ensure that interest rates are adequately responsive to capital flows, while avoiding excessive interest rate volatility if liquidity shortages are only modest.

Under the currency board system, Hong Kong dollar exchange rate stability is maintained through an interest rate adjustment mechanism. The monetary base increases when the foreign currency (in Hong Kong's case, US dollars) to which the domestic currency is linked is sold to the currency board for the domestic currency (inflow into the Hong Kong dollar). It contracts when the foreign currency is bought from the currency board (outflow from the Hong Kong dollar). The expansion or contraction in the monetary base leads interest rates for the domestic currency to fall or rise, respectively, creating the monetary conditions that automatically counteract the original capital movements, ensuring stability of the exchange rate.

To strengthen the institutional framework for the operation of the currency board system in Hong Kong, a Subcommittee on Currency Board Operations was established under the Exchange Fund Advisory Committee (EFAC) in August 1998. The subcommittee has been entrusted with the responsibility of overseeing the operation of the currency board system in Hong Kong and may, where appropriate, recommend to the Financial Secretary through the EFAC measures to enhance the robustness and effectiveness of Hong Kong's currency board arrangements.

The HKMA pursues a policy of transparency to ensure that the financial industry and the wider public are fully informed of the currency board operations. To this end, the Aggregate Balance and forecast changes to the Aggregate Balance attributable to the currency board's foreign exchange transactions are disclosed on a real-time basis. In addition, the size of the monetary base and its components are published on a daily basis, while the Currency Board Account is published on a monthly basis. The records of the meetings of the Subcommittee on Currency Board Operations are also published within six weeks of each meeting.

The Government is fully committed to the maintenance of the linked exchange rate system, which is a cornerstone of Hong Kong's monetary and financial stability, and to the strict discipline of the currency board arrangement under that system.

Monetary Situation

The Hong Kong dollar exchange rate stayed close to the linked rate of 7.80 during the first three quarters of 2003, but strengthened markedly to 7.70 in early October before easing to 7.7631 at the end of 2003. In response to banks' bids, the HKMA has sold a cumulative $31.9 billion of Hong Kong dollars since late September 2003. The notable strengthening of the Hong Kong dollar reflects improved prospects of the economy, the US dollar weakness, and the international pressure for the renminbi to appreciate.

Hong Kong dollar interest rates were on a downtrend during the year, with a brief increase in April-May on worries about the negative impact of the SARS outbreak. Domestic interest rates have dropped below the US dollar counterparts since August 2003. In terms of one-month money, Hong Kong dollar interbank interest rate (HIBOR) closed the year at 0.07 per cent, 99 basis points below the corresponding euro-dollar rate, owing in part to a larger Aggregate Balance. The best lending rate quoted by major banks in Hong Kong was unchanged at 5.0 per cent during the year, while the savings deposit rate quoted by major banks dropped marginally from 0.03 per cent to 0.01 per cent.

The yields on Exchange Fund paper largely followed those on US Treasuries, with 7-year and 10-year Notes closing the year at 3.73 and 4.37 per cent respectively. The yield curves of Exchange Fund papers steepened during the year, mainly reflecting decreases in short term interest rates. The yield differentials between the Exchange Fund Notes and US Treasuries decreased during the year, to -50 basis points and 12 basis points respectively for 7-year and 10-year paper.

The overall exchange value of the Hong Kong dollar, as measured by the trade-weighted Effective Exchange Rate Index (EERI), was predominantly affected by the exchange rate of the US dollar vis-à-vis other major currencies. Largely reflecting a weakening of the US dollar against other major international currencies, the EERI decreased from 102 at the end of 2002 to 99 at the end of 2003.

Growth of Hong Kong dollar narrow money (HK$M1) and broad money (HK$M3) accelerated notably from mid-2003. Narrow money (seasonally adjusted) increased by 35.8 per cent during the year, while broad money rose by 5.9 per cent. The brisk growth of narrow money was attributable in part to a low opportunity cost of holding non-interest bearing monetary assets as well as a significant rebound in stock market activity in the second half of 2003. The pick-up in growth of broad money reflected a revival in economic activity although it was still restrained by record-low deposit rates. For example, the estimated return on broad money, which is a weighted average of the yields of its components, was close to zero, and much lower than yields on longer-term US Treasuries.

Loans for use in Hong Kong shrank for the third consecutive year by 1.4 per cent in 2003, as credit demand continued to be affected by sluggish private investment, the weak property market and slack in the labour market. Analysed by economic use, residential mortgage loans, and loans for building, construction, property development and investment fell further in 2003. In other sectors, outstanding credit card advances continued to decrease in 2003, although the rate of decline moderated in the second half. Notwithstanding a pick-up in consumer spending, the drop in credit card advances reflected mainly a tightening of credit card issuance and lending policies by banks, write-offs and restructuring of credit card receivables during the year. Trade financing remained robust, alongside strong external trade performance. Lending to stockbrokers and financial concerns increased in the second half of the year, attributable to active stock market activity. The contraction in Hong Kong dollar loans, coupled with an expansion in Hong Kong dollar deposits led to a fall in the Hong Kong dollar loan-to-deposit ratio to 81.5 per cent at the end of 2003, from 88.5 per cent a year earlier.

Exchange Fund

The Exchange Fund was established by the Currency Ordinance of 1935 (later renamed as the Exchange Fund Ordinance). Since its establishment, the Fund has assumed the role to back the bank note issuance of Hong Kong. In 1976, the Fund's role was expanded. The backing for coins issued and the majority of the foreign currency assets held in the Government's General Revenue Account, were transferred to the Exchange Fund. Meanwhile, the Government began to transfer the fiscal reserves of its General Revenue Account (apart from the working balances) to the Fund to centralise the investment management of its financial assets. Through this transfer, the bulk of the Government's financial assets are placed with the Fund. The Coinage Security Fund was merged with the Exchange Fund on December 31, 1978.

Prior to April 1, 1998, fiscal reserves were placed with the Exchange Fund as deposits on which market interest rates were paid by the Fund to the General Revenue. As the official reserves have grown significantly over the years, it was decided that the fiscal reserves placed with the Exchange Fund should seek to achieve a higher long-term real rate of return. With effect from April 1, 1998, the return on the fiscal reserves placed with the Exchange Fund is linked to its overall return.

Upon the establishment of the Hong Kong Special Administrative Region on July 1, 1997, the assets of the Land Fund Trust were vested in the Hong Kong SAR Government. The Chief Executive of the Hong Kong SAR appointed the Financial Secretary as the public officer to receive, hold and manage the Land Fund, as part of the Hong Kong SAR Government reserves. Subsequently, the Land Fund was established by resolution made and passed by the Provisional Legislative Council under section 29 of the Public Finance Ordinance. Between July 1, 1997 and October 31, 1998, under the direction of the Financial Secretary, the Land Fund was managed by the HKMA as a portfolio separated from the Exchange Fund. Effective from November 1, 1998, the assets of the Land Fund, which itself has still remained as a separate government fund, were merged into the Exchange Fund and managed as part of the Investment Portfolio of the Exchange Fund.

The Land Fund will continue to be administered in accordance with the Resolution of the Provisional Legislative Council of July 1997. Following an investment decision taken by the Financial Secretary under the terms of the Resolution, the placement of the entire Land Fund, along with the fiscal reserves, with the Exchange Fund, yields a return that is the same as that of the Exchange Fund. In 2003, a Resolution was made and passed by the Legislative Council under the Public Finance Ordinance to authorise the transfer of $120 billion from the Land Fund to the General Revenue Account to meet the Government's expenditure requirement. The Exchange Fund's primary statutory role, as defined in the Exchange Fund Ordinance, is to affect the exchange value of the Hong Kong dollar. Its functions were extended on the enactment of the Exchange Fund (Amendment) Ordinance 1992 by introducing a secondary role of maintaining the stability and integrity of the monetary and financial systems, with a view to maintaining Hong Kong as an international financial centre.

The HKMA manages the Exchange Fund. Apart from ensuring that the Fund meets its statutory roles, the HKMA's principal activity is the day-to-day management of the Fund's assets. These are invested mainly in OECD bonds and equities. To meet the Government's operational needs, part of the Exchange Fund is also held in Hong Kong dollar denominated assets.

To meet the objectives of preserving capital, providing liquidity to maintain financial and currency stability and generating an adequate long-term return, the Exchange Fund is managed as two distinct portfolios. The first is a Backing Portfolio which ensures that the monetary base related to the currency board operations is fully backed by highly liquid, primarily short-term, US dollar denominated debt securities. The second is an Investment Portfolio which preserves the Fund's value for future generations of Hong Kong. The long term asset allocation strategy of the Exchange Fund is guided by the investment benchmark, which defines the bonds and equities mix as well as the overall currency composition of the Fund. The management of the Fund and the investment style adopted are set out and explained in the HKMA's annual report.

On December 31, 2003, the Exchange Fund's total assets stood at $1,011.6 billion, of which foreign currency assets amounted to $929.6 billion (or US$119.7 billion). The accumulated surplus of the Exchange Fund amounted to $384.9 billion. The Fund's financial position from 1998 to 2003 inclusive is shown in the *Appendices*. With a view to demonstrating the Government's continued commitment to greater openness and transparency, foreign currency asset figures have been published monthly since January 1997. In addition, an abridged balance sheet of the Exchange Fund and a set of Currency Board accounts are published monthly.

Another function related to the Exchange Fund is currency issuance. Bank notes in denominations of $20, $50, $100, $500 and $1,000 are issued by the three note-issuing banks: the Standard Chartered Bank, the Hongkong and Shanghai Banking Corporation Limited and the Bank of China (Hong Kong) Limited. The note-issuing banks may issue currency notes only by surrendering non-interest-bearing US dollar backing at a fixed exchange rate of 7.80. Thus the Fund enjoys the seigniorage from the notes.

Through the HKMA, the Government issues the new $10 currency note and coins of $10, $5, $2, $1, 50 cents, 20 cents and 10 cents denominations. Sufficient quantities of the $10 note and all denominations of coins have been maintained for injection into the market when required. The total of notes and coins in circulation at year-end was $140.3 billion. The new $100 and $500 banknotes issued by the three note-issuing banks began to circulate in December (the new $20, $50 and $1,000 banknotes will be available by the second half of 2004). This is the first comprehensive redesign of banknotes for almost 10 years. The security features used in the new banknotes and the colour schemes of each denomination are standardised. On top of the security features used in the existing banknotes, the new banknotes contain a number of new features to enhance the security of the Hong Kong currency.

Home Pages

Financial Services and the Treasury Bureau: http://www.gov.hk/fstb
Office of the Commissioner of Insurance: http://www.gov.hk/oci
Official Receiver's Office: http://www.gov.hk/oro
Companies Registry: http://www.gov.hk/cr
Hong Kong Monetary Authority: http://www.gov.hk/hkma
Securities and Futures Commission: http://www.hksfc.org.hk
Mandatory Provident Fund Schemes Authority: http://www.mpfahk.org
Hong Kong Exchanges and Clearing Limited: http://www.hkex.com.hk
Electronic Investor Resources Centre: http://www.hkeirc.org

CHAPTER 5

Commerce and Industry

Strong economic ties with the Mainland, especially with the Pearl River Delta (PRD), now form one of Hong Kong's fundamental strengths. The branching out of production processes to the Mainland in the last two decades has triggered a remarkable transformation in the economy of both Hong Kong and the PRD and brought about the development of Hong Kong into an international financial centre and services hub. The Mainland is Hong Kong's largest trading partner, accounting for 43 per cent of its total trade in 2003. Hong Kong accounted for nearly half of the Mainland's foreign direct investment as at the end of June 2003. Of the 3 200 regional headquarters and offices established in Hong Kong in mid-year, more than 80 per cent are responsible for overseeing their Mainland businesses.

HONG KONG is a leading international trading and services hub as well as a high value-added manufacturing base. It is widely recognised as one of the freest economies in the world, and the gateway to the Mainland market.

In 2003, Hong Kong's total merchandise trade amounted to $3,548.2 billion. Over 288 000 business establishments in a wide range of services and manufacturing sectors are operating in Hong Kong, and the vast majority are small and medium enterprises (SMEs). There is also a strong presence of international businesses in Hong Kong. At the end of 2002, Hong Kong had about 9 000 enterprise groups with inward direct investment.

Hong Kong's continuing economic success owes much to a simple tax structure and low tax rates, a versatile and industrious workforce, an excellent infrastructure, free flow of capital and information, the rule of law, and the Government's firm commitment to free trade and free enterprise.

The Government sees its task as facilitating commerce and industry within the framework of a free market. It maintains no tariffs and no regulatory measures impinging on international trade other than those required to discharge its international obligations or to protect health, the environment and access to high technology. The HKSAR also practises an open and liberal investment policy and actively encourages inward investment.

The Government's industrial policy aims to promote industrial development by creating a business-friendly environment and providing adequate support services.

The Government zones land for general and specialised industrial use. It also maintains and develops advanced education and training facilities, ensures a modern legislative and regulatory environment, and supports industry in enhancing productivity and quality through technology and management improvement. The Government, however, does not subsidise any specific industries.

With the weight of the Hong Kong economy shifting towards knowledge-based and higher value-added activities, the Government puts increasing emphasis on promoting innovation and technological improvement in industry and business. It aims to strengthen support for technology development and application, develop a critical mass of fine scientists and engineers, skilled technicians and venture capitalists, and encourage the development of a significant cluster of technology-based businesses.

Merchandise Trade Performance

With continued growth in the Mainland economy and a visible pick-up in the global economy, Hong Kong was witness to a notable growth in external trade in 2003. Total merchandise trade increased by 11.6 per cent to $3,548.2 billion. Domestic exports dropped by 7 per cent to $121.7 billion, while re-exports rose by 13.4 per cent to $1,620.7 billion. Imports increased by 11.5 per cent to $1,805.8 billion. The year recorded a trade deficit of $63.4 billion, greater than the corresponding deficit of $58.9 billion in 2002. The *Appendices* provide summary statistics of external trade.

In 2003, Hong Kong's largest trading partners were the Mainland of China (the Mainland), followed by the United States of America (USA) and Japan.

In 2003, Hong Kong was the world's 11th largest trading entity in terms of value of merchandise trade.

Imports

Imports of raw materials and semi-manufactures, at $654.5 billion in 2003, constituted the largest share of total imports. This was followed by consumer goods ($573.9 billion), capital goods ($481.1 billion), foodstuffs ($53.4 billion) and fuels ($35.4 billion).

In 2003, the Mainland, Japan and Taiwan were Hong Kong's major suppliers, accounting for 43.5 per cent, 11.9 per cent and 6.9 per cent of the total value of imports, respectively.

Domestic Exports

Articles of apparel and clothing accessories continued to be the largest component of domestic exports, valued at $63.9 billion or 52.5 per cent of the total value of domestic exports in 2003. At $10.2 billion, electrical machinery, apparatus and appliances, and electrical parts thereof came second. Other major exports items included textile yarn, fabrics, made-up articles and related products; office machines and automatic data processing machines; and plastics in primary form.

In 2003, the USA, the Mainland and the United Kingdom were Hong Kong's largest markets, absorbing 32.2 per cent, 30.2 per cent and 6.4 per cent of the total value of domestic exports, respectively.

Re-exports

In 2003, principal commodities re-exported were electrical machinery, apparatus and appliances ($303.1 billion or 18.7 per cent of the total value of re-exports), as well as telecommunications and sound recording and reproducing apparatus and equipment ($218.8 billion or 13.5 per cent of the total value of re-exports). The Mainland, Japan and Taiwan were the main origins of the re-exports, while the Mainland, the USA and Japan were the main destinations.

The Manufacturing Sector

Innovation, technology and relocation of lower value-added operations to the Mainland have accelerated the development of more knowledge-based and higher value-added manufacturing activities, as well as manufacturing-related services or producer services. Expansion of manufacturing activities offshore since the 1980s has turned Hong Kong into a strategic control centre of an increasingly globalised production network. In spite of Hong Kong's economic restructuring, the manufacturing sector remained an important sector of the economy, providing employment to 168 300 persons (7.6 per cent of the total private sector employees) in December 2003.

The printing and publishing industry was the largest employer in the manufacturing sector in 2003, followed by the clothing industry. *Chart 1* shows the breakdown of employment within the manufacturing sector in 2003.

Chart 1: Number of Persons Employed by the Manufacturing Sector as at September 2003

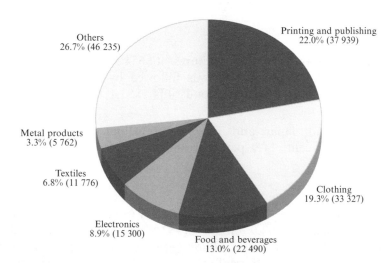

The manufacturing sector remains export-oriented and its excellent performance contributed to Hong Kong's ranking as one of the world's leading exporters of textiles, clothing, watches and clocks, toys and jewellery. Domestic exports amounted to $122 billion in 2003 with clothing, electronics, textiles, chemical products and jewellery being the major export items. *Chart 2* shows the value breakdown of domestic exports in 2003.

The electronicAsia exhibition *(left)* and concurrent Hong Kong Electronics Fair *(above)* at the Hong Kong Convention and Exhibition Centre in October attracted thousands of buyers from around the world, with a diverse range of products for use in industry, telecommunications, entertainment and other fields.

HONG
KONG

a's world city

See You
Next Year

Hong Kong
HOUSEWARE
香港家庭用品展 Fair
21 - 24/4/2004

Hong Kong
GIFTS & PREMIUM
香港禮品及贈品展 Fair
28/4 - 1/5/2004

Graham Uden – courtesy of Hong Kong Trade Development Council

The Hong Kong Convention and Exhibition Centre celebrated its 15th anniversary in November, and has been the venue for around 30 000 events with the total attendance exceeding 40 million people. The events in 2003 included the combined Hong Kong Houseware Fair and Hong Kong Gifts and Premium Fair *(left)* and the Hong Kong Book Fair *(above)*, which were held in July.

The Hong Kong Watch and Clock Fair *(above)* in September and the Hong Kong Optical Fair *(right)* in November both drew large attendances.

courtesy of Hong Kong Trade Development Council

Chart 2: Value of Domestic Exports of the Manufacturing Sector in 2003

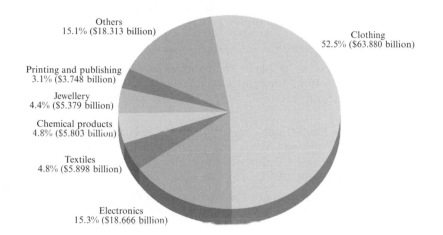

Others
15.1% ($18.313 billion)

Clothing
52.5% ($63.880 billion)

Printing and publishing
3.1% ($3.748 billion)

Jewellery
4.4% ($5.379 billion)

Chemical products
4.8% ($5.803 billion)

Textiles
4.8% ($5.898 billion)

Electronics
15.3% ($18.666 billion)

The manufacturing sector is dominated by SMEs. Of the 16 270 manufacturing establishments in 2003, 16 060 (98.7 per cent) employed fewer than 100 persons, accounting for 64 per cent of Hong Kong's total manufacturing employment. Many SMEs are linked with larger factories through an efficient and flexible sub-contracting network. This arrangement has enabled the manufacturing sector to respond swiftly to market changes.

The Services Sector

The services sector grew significantly in the past two decades. Its share in Hong Kong's Gross Domestic Product (GDP) rose from 67.2 per cent in 1984 to 87.5 per cent in 2002. In 2003, 85.3 per cent of total employment was in the services sector. Hong Kong has become one of the most service-oriented economies in the world. Much of this growth was fuelled by the demand for producer services by Hong Kong's globalised production network and the trend to source goods and services globally.

Like manufacturing, the services sector is dominated by SMEs. In 2003, 98.3 per cent of Hong Kong's 272 000 service establishments were SMEs (fewer than 50 persons). Together, they employed 1.2 million persons (60.2 per cent of employment in selected service industries in the private sector).

In 2003, Hong Kong's total services trade amounted to US$69.3 billion, making it the world's 15th largest trading entity in terms of value of services trade. In the same year, Hong Kong exported US$45 billion worth of services, bearing a ratio of 28.4 per cent of GDP. Hong Kong ranked third after Japan and the Mainland in the region in terms of absolute value of exports of services. In the global league table of exports of services, Hong Kong ranked 10th in 2003.

Hong Kong's exports of services comprise mainly merchanting and other trade-related services, transportation and travel services, which accounted for 37 per cent, 30 per cent and 16 per cent respectively of the total value in 2003. The corresponding share for exports of financial services was 6 per cent, and that for exports of insurance and other services was 11 per cent.

In addition to being a net exporter of services in overall terms, analysed by component of services trade, in 2003 Hong Kong recorded a surplus in merchanting and other trade-related services (US$15 billion), transportation services (US$6.8 billion) and financial services (US$2 billion).

External Investment

Hong Kong's attractiveness as a place to do business is reflected by two major indicators, namely the inflow of foreign direct investment (FDI), and the number of foreign-owned regional headquarters and regional offices of companies incorporated outside Hong Kong.

A Census and Statistics Department survey shows that Hong Kong's FDI inflow in 2002 amounted to US$9.7 billion. According to the 'World Investment Report 2003' released by the United Nations Conference on Trade and Development, Hong Kong was the second largest recipient of FDI in Asia in 2002.

Hong Kong had 8 978 enterprise groups[1] with inward direct investment at the end of 2002, comprising 380 in the manufacturing sector and 8 598 in the non-manufacturing sectors. The market value of the stock of inward direct investments amounted to $2,622.3 billion. *Chart 3* shows the major economic activities of these enterprise groups while *Chart 4* shows source countries/territories of the inward direct investments. Regarding employment, more than 69 per cent of them were enterprise groups employing fewer than 20 persons *(Chart 5)*.

Chart 3: Position of Inward Direct Investment in Hong Kong at Market Value by Major Economic Activity of Hong Kong Enterprise Group at end-2002

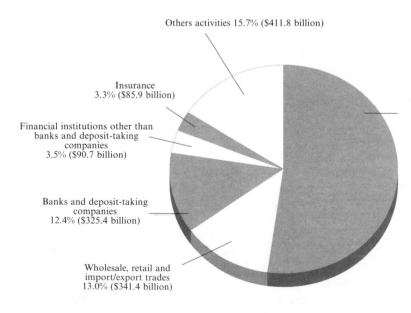

Others activities 15.7% ($411.8 billion)

Insurance 3.3% ($85.9 billion)

Financial institutions other than banks and deposit-taking companies 3.5% ($90.7 billion)

Banks and deposit-taking companies 12.4% ($325.4 billion)

Wholesale, retail and import/export trades 13.0% ($341.4 billion)

Investment holding, real estate and various business services 52.1% ($1,367.0 billion)

---

[1] An enterprise group may consist of a parent company, its subsidiaries, associates and branches.

Chart 4: Position of Inward Direct Investment in Hong Kong at Market Value by Major Investor Country/Territory at end-2002

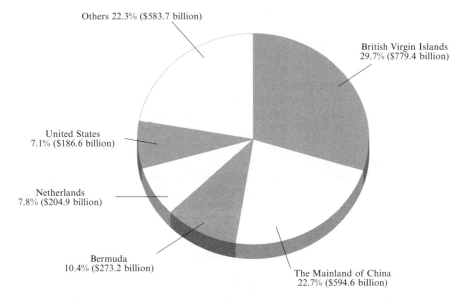

Others 22.3% ($583.7 billion)

British Virgin Islands
29.7% ($779.4 billion)

United States
7.1% ($186.6 billion)

Netherlands
7.8% ($204.9 billion)

Bermuda
10.4% ($273.2 billion)

The Mainland of China
22.7% ($594.6 billion)

Remarks: British Virgin Islands, Bermuda and Cayman Islands are important offshore financial centres commonly used by investors to channel inward direct investment funds to Hong Kong.

Chart 5: Number of Hong Kong Enterprise Groups (HKEGs) with Inward Direct Investment by Employment Size in mid-2002

No. of HKEGs

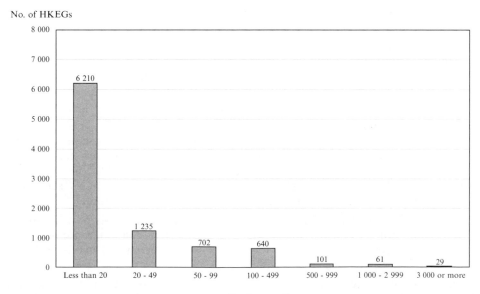

Employment Size

According to the survey conducted by the Census and Statistics Department, on June 2, 2003, there was a total of 3 207 regional headquarters and regional offices in Hong Kong of companies incorporated outside Hong Kong. Compared with the corresponding figure of 3 119 recorded for 2002, there was an increase of 2.8 per cent.

The Institutional Framework

Commerce and Industry Branch

The Commerce and Industry Branch of the Commerce, Industry and Technology Bureau is responsible for the formulation and coordination of policies and strategies in relation to Hong Kong's external commercial relations, inward investment promotion and intellectual property protection. It also oversees the development of policies and programmes for the industrial and trade sectors, including SMEs, as well as the business and services promotion. The branch is assisted in its work by a number of departments, namely the Trade and Industry Department, the Invest Hong Kong, the Customs and Excise Department and the Intellectual Property Department. It is also supported by a network of Economic and Trade Offices outside Hong Kong.

Trade and Industry Department

The Trade and Industry Department is responsible for handling the HKSAR's commercial relations with its trading partners, implementing trade policies and agreements, including the issue of certificates of origin and export and import licences, as well as providing general support services for the industrial sector and SMEs.

Invest Hong Kong

Invest Hong Kong is the government department established on July 1, 2000 to spearhead Hong Kong's efforts to attract inward investment. Its Head Office in Hong Kong works closely with the Economic and Trade Offices and consultants in North America, Europe, Asia, Middle East, and Australia to offer solution-oriented investment promotion, facilitation and after-care services to ensure that foreign companies have the support required to establish or expand their operations in the HKSAR, the Mainland and the Asia-Pacific region. Invest Hong Kong also provides information to facilitate the making of informed investment decisions by investors in setting up regional headquarters and regional offices in Hong Kong.

Invest Hong Kong adopts a proactive investment promotion strategy by focusing on economic sectors where Hong Kong has an edge over other cities. The targeted sectors are financial services, trade related services, transportation, telecommunications, media and multimedia, business and professional services, information technology, technology (especially electronics and biotechnology), and tourism and entertainment. In addition, Invest Hong Kong seeks to strengthen its after-care service with a view to retaining and expanding investments already made.

From January 1, 2003 to December 31, 2003, Invest Hong Kong assisted 142 foreign companies in completing 142 investment projects in Hong Kong, an increase of 21 per cent compared with 2002. The total amount of investment generated exceeded $2.49 billion, and over 2 400 new jobs were created.

Investment promotion activities included sponsoring and participating in several major international conferences. BusinessWeek's CEO Forum in November featured leading business executives and government officials, including Vice Premier Zeng Peiyan and former US President Bill Clinton, and attracted over 600 delegates. Invest Hong Kong supported other major events in 2003, such as the 21st Pacific Insurance Conference with 300 senior executives from the life and health insurance industry; CASBAA (The Cable & Satellite Broadcasting Convention 2003) with 91 speakers and some 1 100 delegates from around the world.

Invest Hong Kong's work in promoting Hong Kong's advantages was recognised at the Asia Pacific Investment Promotion Agency (IPA) Awards 2003 organised by *Strategic Direct Investor* magazine, a Euromoney Institutional Investor publication. Invest Hong Kong won awards for the Best Overall Managed IPA, Best North Asia IPA, Best IPA in Creating Partnerships and Best IPA in Attracting Financial Services Investment.

Hong Kong Economic and Trade Offices

The Hong Kong Economic and Trade Offices seek to promote economic and trade interests by enhancing understanding of the HKSAR among opinion-formers; closely monitoring developments that might affect the HKSAR's economic and trading interests, such as proposed legislation; and liaising closely with the business and commercial sectors, politicians, think tanks and the news media. They also organise events to promote Hong Kong's image. In addition, most of these offices seek to attract direct investment into Hong Kong. One of the means is to actively promote Hong Kong's enhanced business advantages and environment under the Closer Economic Partnership Arrangement.

The offices are located in Brussels, Geneva, London, New York, San Francisco, Singapore, Sydney, Tokyo, Toronto, Washington and Guangdong.

The Brussels Office represents Hong Kong's economic and trade interests in dealings with the European Union (EU). It also monitors and promotes bilateral relations with the EU and its member states except the United Kingdom.

The Geneva Office represents Hong Kong, China, as a member of the World Trade Organisation (WTO), and represents Hong Kong as an observer on the Trade Committee of the Organisation for Economic Cooperation and Development (OECD).

The London Office promotes Hong Kong's economic and trade interests in the United Kingdom and non-EU countries including Switzerland, Norway and Russia as well as the Central and Eastern European countries that will acede to the EU in May 2004. Hong Kong's representative to the International Maritime Organisation is also based in the office.

The offices in Sydney, Tokyo and Toronto are responsible for bilateral economic and trade relations in their host countries. The Sydney Office is also responsible for promoting Hong Kong's economic and trade interests in New Zealand. The Singapore Office is responsible for Hong Kong's commercial relations with the member states of the Association of South-East Asian Nations (ASEAN). It also serves as a direct point of contact with the Secretariats of the Asia-Pacific Economic Cooperation (APEC) and the Pacific Economic Cooperation Council (PECC), which are located in Singapore.

The Washington Office focuses on monitoring and liaising with the US Administration, Congress and think tanks on legislation and government policies that may have implications for Hong Kong's trade with the United States. The New York Office and the San Francisco Office are responsible for promoting economic and trade relations between Hong Kong and individual US states and also seek to attract direct investment into Hong Kong.

The Guangdong Office, which came into operation in July 2002, is situated in Guangzhou City. Its main duties are to promote trade and economic relationships between Hong Kong and Guangdong Province, to provide better support services for Hong Kong businesses operating in Guangdong, especially the Pearl River Delta, and also to provide free advisory service and assistance to enterprises in the province, which are looking for direct investment opportunities in Hong Kong. It is also the first Economic and Trade Office to be established in the Mainland.

Customs and Excise Department

The Customs and Excise Department is responsible for enforcing various trade control systems, including the certification of origin system, the textiles import and export control system, the strategic commodities control system and the import and export declaration system. These systems aim to protect and facilitate legitimate trade. The department is also responsible for enforcing the criminal law for the protection of copyright and trade marks, as well as enforcing consumer protection legislation relating to the safety of various commodities, the integrity of weights and measures, and the marking of precious metals. In addition, to ensure that Hong Kong has an adequate supply of rice, which is an essential foodstuff for the local population, at a reasonably stable price, the department monitors the local stock of rice. Since January, the department has also taken on a new responsibility of enforcing the certification scheme for rough diamonds. Its aim is to stop trade in 'conflict diamonds' from fuelling armed conflicts, activities of rebel movements and illicit proliferation of armaments. Upon the signing of the Mainland and Hong Kong Closer Economic Partnership Arrangement, the department has also taken up the responsibility of enforcing the relevant control system through conducting factory inspections, consignment checks, costing verifications, blitz checks and investigations to ensure that goods exported under the Arrangement meet the requisite rules.

Intellectual Property Department

The Intellectual Property Department runs the Trade Marks, Patents, Designs and Copyright Licensing Bodies Registries, advises on policy and legislation related to intellectual property protection, provides civil intellectual property legal advice to the Government, and promotes public awareness of and respect for intellectual property rights.

External Commercial Relations

Regional Trade Agreements

Notwithstanding the Government's commitment to the primacy of the multilateral trading system under the WTO, it is accepted that free trade agreements (FTAs) may contribute to multilateral trade liberalisation if they are fully WTO-consistent. The Government is, therefore, prepared to consider negotiating FTAs with trading partners so long as these would be in Hong Kong's interests and contribute to multilateral trade liberalisation.

Mainland and Hong Kong Closer Economic Partnership Arrangement

The HKSAR Government and the Central People's Government (CPG) signed the main text of the Mainland and Hong Kong Closer Economic Partnership Arrangement (CEPA) on June 29, 2003, and concluded the six Annexes on September 29, 2003. Under CEPA, the Mainland has agreed to eliminate import tariff for 374 Hong Kong products under its 2004 tariff codes and to give preferential market access to Hong Kong service suppliers in 18 services sectors[2]. Both sides have also agreed to enhance cooperation in trade and investment facilitation. CEPA came into full operation on January 1, 2004. It adopts a building block approach and provides a mechanism for further liberalisation measures. A Joint Steering Committee, jointly led by Financial Secretary of the HKSAR Government and the Vice Minister of Commerce of the CPG, is responsible for overall coordination of CEPA.

The establishment of the CEPA under the framework of the WTO will further promote trade and investment flows, as well as exchanges of talent, capital and technology, between Hong Kong and the Mainland, which would be mutually beneficial and conducive to sustained economic growth. Since the announcement of CEPA, the Government has launched a strong awareness and publicity campaign to promote the business opportunities brought about by CEPA to local, foreign and Mainland investors.

Hong Kong and New Zealand Closer Economic Partnership Agreement

Negotiations with New Zealand on a free trade agreement continued. The negotiations encompassed a wide-ranging scope with emphasis on trade and investment liberalisation and facilitation. The two sides have achieved good progress on many issues and are committed to concluding the negotiations as soon as possible to achieve a high-quality agreement that is beneficial to both economies.

Hong Kong's Participation in the WTO

The HKSAR is a founding member of the WTO. Its separate membership reflects Hong Kong's autonomy in the conduct of its external commercial relations, which is guaranteed under the Basic Law.

The WTO provides a fair, predictable and rules-based multilateral trading system for trade in goods, services and trade-related intellectual property rights. It promotes the liberalisation of international trade and serves as a forum for multilateral trade negotiations and dispute settlement among its members. Active participation in the WTO's multilateral trading system is the cornerstone of the HKSAR's external trade policy.

As a small and totally open economy, the HKSAR's participation in the WTO is guided by two objectives: firstly, to sustain the momentum of trade liberalisation, especially in areas of interest to the HKSAR, such as tariffs and services; secondly, to strengthen and update the multilateral rule-based trading system so that it remains an effective framework to promote trade expansion and liberalisation, as well as to protect Hong Kong against any arbitrary and discriminatory actions taken by its trading partners.

---

[2] These include management consulting, convention and exhibition, advertising, accounting, real estate and construction, medical and dental, distribution, logistics, freight forwarding, storage and warehousing, transport, tourism, audiovisual, legal, banking, securities, insurance and telecommunications services.

The HKSAR participates actively in the new Round of multilateral trade negotiations launched at the WTO's Fourth Ministerial Conference in Doha, Qatar, in November 2001. Its priority in this round of trade negotiations is to seek greater market access for its services sectors and industrial goods.

In September 2003, the HKSAR took part in the Fifth Ministerial Conference held in Cancun, Mexico, which aimed to take stock of the progresss of negotiations and give further instructions to take them forward. The conference ended without consensus on the direction of the negotiations due to members' divergent positions on some of the key issues. However, by the end of 2003, WTO members had already demonstrated a strong sense of re-engagement for continuous negotiations. The new Round of negotiations is scheduled for completion by January 1, 2005. Hong Kong's business community will benefit from the positive outcome of further multilateral trade negotiations.

As a further demonstration of its commitment to the WTO, the HKSAR has offered to host the Sixth WTO Ministerial Conference. The offer was unanimously accepted by the WTO members in October 2003 although the date has yet to be decided. Besides enhancing Hong Kong's involvement in all key negotiations, hosting of the conference will help raise its international profile, induce considerable economic benefits in the form of tourist receipts, and attract future overseas tourists, international conferences and other business opportunities.

Regional Economic Cooperation

As an integral part of the Asia-Pacific economy and an important services, financial and trading centre, Hong Kong continued to play an active role in enhancing regional economic cooperation. Its economic links with the region remained strong. In 2003, some 83 per cent of Hong Kong's total external trade was conducted with the other 20 member economies of APEC. Hong Kong participates as a full and separate member in APEC and PECC under the name Hong Kong, China.

APEC is a regional forum set up in 1989 for high-level government-to-government dialogue and cooperation on trade and economic issues. Hong Kong joined the forum in 1991. In October, the Chief Executive represented the HKSAR at the 11th APEC Economic Leaders Meeting held in Bangkok, Thailand. The meeting was preceded by the 15th APEC Ministerial Meeting, at which the Secretary for Commerce, Industry and Technology represented the HKSAR.

APEC pursues its goal of free and open trade and investment by 2010 for industrialised economies and 2020 for developing economies through work in three areas — trade and investment liberalisation, trade and investment facilitation, and economic and technical cooperation. Hong Kong participates actively in all three. It has been a Vice-Chair of APEC's Committee on Trade and Investment (CTI) since 1996.

Thailand, as the APEC Chair for 2003, has set the overall theme as 'A World of Differences: Partnership for the Future', with five sub-themes: knowledge-based economy for all; promoting human security; financial architecture for a world of differences; new growth enterprises: SMEs and micro business; and act on development pledge. Hong Kong had its 2002 Individual Action Plan reviewed by other APEC members in August and was commended for its continued openness and commitment to free and open trade and investment.

PECC, founded in 1980, is a non-governmental regional forum comprising government officials, business leaders and academics who work in their personal capacity on practical policy issues to enhance trade, investment and economic development in the Pacific region. Hong Kong joined this forum in May 1991. The Hong Kong Committee for Pacific Economic Cooperation, established in March 1990 to advise on and coordinate Hong Kong's participation in and input to the PECC process, continues to play an active role in PECC's various fora, task forces and project groups.

Observer Role in the OECD

The HKSAR is an observer on the Trade Committee and the Committee on Financial Markets of the Paris-based OECD, which are important fora for discussions on policy matters in respect of trade and financial services. Ideas introduced in these committees are often followed up in other international organisations such as the WTO and eventually translated into binding multilateral agreements or codes.

Liaison with the Mainland

China formally acceded to the WTO on December 11, 2001. It is generally expected that China's broad market-opening commitments for accession to the WTO, as well as the enhanced accessibility to overseas markets as provided for under the WTO agreements, will boost the Mainland's overall economic growth. The Mainland is Hong Kong's largest trading partner and there is a strong economic link between the two places. The Mainland's accelerated economic growth is expected to usher in enormous business opportunities for Hong Kong. The anticipated surge in trade flow and the improvement of the investment environment in the Mainland brought about by China's accession to the WTO should help boost Hong Kong's external trade and intermediary services. In addition, CEPA will open up many business opportunities in the Mainland for Hong Kong businessmen, and enhance the attractiveness of Hong Kong to overseas investors.

The Government is committed to facilitating businessmen's efforts in tapping the Mainland market, particularly the opportunities brought about by China's accession to the WTO and CEPA. It maintains close contact with the Mainland authorities at different levels through various government bureaux and departments, the Beijing Office of the HKSAR Government, the Hong Kong Economic and Trade Office in Guangdong as well as quasi-government bodies like the Hong Kong Trade Development Council (TDC). Regular high-level communication is also achieved through mechanisms such as the Hong Kong/Guangdong Cooperation Joint Conference, the Hong Kong/Shanghai Economic and Trade Cooperation Conference and the CEPA Joint Steering Committee.

Trade in Textiles

Hong Kong's textiles exports to the European Union, Canada and the United States are subject to certain quantitative restrictions. In accordance with the WTO Agreement on Textiles and Clothing (ATC), these quantitative restrictions are being phased out over 10 years, in four stages from January of 1995, 1998, 2002 and 2005, respectively. All quantitative restrictions will have been eliminated from January 1, 2005. Hong Kong has been closely monitoring the implementation of the ATC and the operation of the Textiles Monitoring Body, the ATC's supervisory body. Through cooperation with the International Textiles and Clothing Bureau (of which Hong

117

Kong, China was the Chairman from January 1999 until September 2002), Hong Kong and a group of developing country exporters of textiles have been working together to ensure that the liberalisation process under the ATC is on course and to explore possibilities for further liberalisation.

Hong Kong continues to cooperate with its trading partners in combating illegal transhipment of textiles. Among other things, to promote understanding of Hong Kong's anti-transhipment efforts, Hong Kong Customs officers conduct joint factory observation visits in conjunction with US Customs representatives. Such visits are not acts of law enforcement. In 2003, one round of a joint factory observation visit was conducted.

To combat false declarations of origin and values of goods and illegal transhipment of textiles, the Customs and Excise Department in 2003 carried out 96 063 factory and consignment inspections and 1 284 investigations. The department also conducted 976 'blitz' check operations on textile consignments at various import and export control points. It successfully prosecuted 820 offenders, resulting in the imposition of fines amounting to $18.87 million. It operates a monetary reward scheme to elicit information on textiles origin fraud.

Trade in Strategic Commodities

To ensure that Hong Kong has continued access to advanced products and technologies to sustain its economic development and that Hong Kong will not be used as a conduit for illicit diversion of strategic commodities, the Government maintains a comprehensive import and export control system to monitor the flows of strategic commodities through Hong Kong. The licensing control system for strategic commodities is administered by the Trade and Industry Department with the support of vigorous enforcement action by the Customs and Excise Department. Hong Kong maintains close cooperation with its trading partners to keep itself abreast of the developments in the international arena on strategic trade control matters, and to make sure that its control arrangement is complementary to those of its trading partners.

The Chemical Weapons (Convention) Ordinance, which was passed by the Legislative Council in July, enables the Government to fully implement the Chemical Weapons Convention in Hong Kong. It underlines Hong Kong's commitment to internationally agreed arrangements on the ban of chemical weapons and on the monitoring of activities involving sensitive chemicals. It also helps enhance Hong Kong's international reputation in the area of strategic trade control, and helps ensure its continued access to a full range of chemicals needed for local industrial, medical, research and trading purposes.

In 2003, the Customs and Excise Department investigated 251 cases of unlicensed import and export of strategic commodities and prosecuted 51 offenders, resulting in fines amounting to $2.28 million. Goods valued at $2.78 million were seized and confiscated.

Bilateral Investment Promotion and Protection Agreements

Hong Kong has bilateral investment promotion and protection agreements with 14 economies: Australia, Austria, Belgium/Luxembourg, Denmark, France, Germany, Italy, Japan, Republic of Korea, the Netherlands, New Zealand, Sweden, Switzerland

and the United Kingdom. A primary objective of these agreements is to assure overseas investors of the stable investment environment in Hong Kong.

Customs Cooperation

Hong Kong Customs plays an active role in the work of the World Customs Organisation (WCO), which aims to enhance the effectiveness and efficiency of customs administrations and facilitate trade by achieving harmony and uniformity of customs procedures among its members and the Sub-committee on Customs Procedures (SCCP) of APEC, which is tasked to simplify and harmonise customs procedures to facilitate cross-border trade in the Asia-Pacific region. As at December, the WCO has a world-wide membership of 162 Customs administrations, and APEC has 21 member economies.

In the WCO forum, the department works closely with the WCO Vice-Chairman representing the Asia-Pacific region on regional matters, and is a co-coordinator of regional activities on enforcement programmes in the areas of security, commercial fraud, smuggling and intelligence, customs-business partnership and integrity.

In the APEC SCCP forum, the department works closely with member economies on trade facilitation work, and is a co-coordinator of SCCP Collective Action Plans on Public Availability of Information, Customs Integrity and Customs-Business Partnership.

To promote counter-terrorism work, the department participates actively in the WCO Task Force on Security and Facilitation of the International Trade Supply Chain and the APEC Counter-Terrorism Task Force.

The department maintains a close liaison with the WCO Regional Intelligence Liaison Office (RILO) in Tokyo. Since Tokyo started hosting the RILO in 1999, the department has seconded two officers to support intelligence analysis and coordination among members in the Asia-Pacific region.

The RILO office will be relocated to Beijing with effect from 2004. The department will continue to provide full support to the project by seconding an officer to the Beijing Office in order to enhance the regional intelligence network by exchanging timely intelligence and offering investigative assistance to regional members.

Recognising the importance of international cooperation with other customs administrations and law enforcement agencies in combating transnational customs crimes, the department maintains a good working relationship and close liaison with the customs attachés and the representatives of other law enforcement agencies stationed in 12 consular missions in Hong Kong. Through regular bilateral meetings, the department has enhanced mutual cooperation with the Mainland and other customs administrations in building up a strong network for combating transnational customs crimes.

Container Security Initiative

In the aftermath of the September 11, 2001 incident, the US Bureau of Customs and Border Protection proposed the Container Security Initiative (CSI) to address the perceived risks of terrorist attacks associated with ocean-going containers destined for the United States. Under the CSI, the customs authority of a participating foreign port will work with the US Customs officers stationed abroad to identify containers that carry a high risk of being exploited for terrorist attacks. The customs authority of the participating port will scan or inspect the identified containers before the containers depart the port for the United States. Following careful consideration and discussion with the local exporting and shipping communities, Hong Kong agreed to join the CSI, and the Hong Kong and US Customs signed a 'Declaration of Principles' on this in September 2002. Hong Kong's participation in the CSI would help ensure the smooth flow of US-bound cargo that originated from Hong Kong, and enhance the security of the global maritime trading system. Both are vital to Hong Kong as a major trading entity and as the world's busiest container port. A CSI pilot scheme was launched in Hong Kong on May 12, 2003.

Small and Medium Enterprises

SMEs are the driving force of economic growth. There are over 283 000 SMEs in Hong Kong, representing about 98.2 per cent of all local enterprises. They employ more than 1.31 million people. The Government is committed to helping SMEs grow and develop.

Four SME funding schemes were established in December 2001/January 2002 to help SMEs secure loans for acquiring business installations and equipment, and meeting working capital needs, expand overseas markets, upgrade human resources, and enhance overall competitiveness. They are, respectively, the SME Loan Guarantee Scheme, the SME Export Marketing Fund, the SME Training Fund and the SME Development Fund. Over 32 800 SMEs have so far benefited from these schemes and the total government guarantee/grant involved is about $4.3 billion.

Following a comprehensive review on the effectiveness of the four funding schemes, the Small and Medium Enterprises Committee recommended a number of improvement measures, which were accepted by the Chief Executive and implemented in February and March 2003. To help SMEs rise to the challenges brought about by the SARS outbreak early in the year, further improvement measures for the funding schemes were introduced in June.

The Support and Consultation Centre for SMEs (SUCCESS) of the Trade and Industry Department is the Government's first-stop SME support centre which provides a comprehensive range of free information and consultation services to business start-ups and SMEs. SUCCESS regularly runs various activities for its clients to enhance their competitiveness, for example, seminars, workshops and company visits. SUCCESS also publishes an SME newsletter and operates a reference library. SMEs may visit SUCCESS to seek experts' advice on their specific business problems through the 'Business Advisory Services' or join the 'Mentorship Programme' under which each participant will be assigned a mentor from whom to seek guidance on business operation for a period of nine to 12 months.

Promotion of Innovation and Technology

Innovation and Technology Commission

To promote the development of innovation and technology, the Innovation and Technology Commission (ITC) under the Communications and Technology Branch is tasked with the mission of spearheading Hong Kong's drive to become a world-class, knowledge-based economy. The commission formulates and implements policies and measures to promote innovation and technology; supports applied research, technology transfer and application; promotes technological entrepreneurship; facilitates the provision of technology infrastructure and development of human resources; and promotes internationally accepted standards and conformity assessment services to underpin technological development and international trade. The commission works closely with its partners in the Government, industry, business, tertiary education institutions and industrial support organisations.

To make Hong Kong a regional centre for innovation and technology, the Government has been implementing various initiatives to drive forward innovation and technology. It offers a range of infrastructure and funding support for applied research and development activities.

Council of Advisors on Innovation and Technology

The Council of Advisors on Innovation and Technology (CAIT) is a high-level standing advisory body reporting directly to the Chief Executive. Its role is to advise and make recommendations to the Chief Executive on matters relating to innovation and technology so as to optimise their contributions to Hong Kong's economic development.

The CAIT comprises a total of 17 members; 15 of them are non-official members mainly from the business and academic sectors, either locally or externally. All are experts in their respective fields covering finance, economics, electronic engineering as well as telecommunications technology and services. Two Special Advisors, renowned in their fields, have also been appointed to provide expert advice to the council.

Innovation and Technology Fund

The $5 billion Innovation and Technology Fund supports projects that will help upgrade the technology level and promote innovation in the manufacturing and service industries. By year-end, the fund had provided financial support of some $1,432 million to 506 projects undertaken by industrial support bodies, trade and industry associations, higher education institutions, professional bodies and locally incorporated companies.

Promoting Technological Entrepreneurship

Major efforts have been made to promote technological entrepreneurship. A $750 million Applied Research Fund was established in March 1998, replacing two previous schemes to provide equity finance for technology ventures in the private sector. In November 1998, private venture capital firms were appointed as managers for the fund. Besides selecting technological ventures for investment, the venture capital firms provide management and networking advice to the investee companies. By year-end, $382 million in financial support had been provided to 23 companies through these fund managers.

Hong Kong Applied Science and Technology Research Institute Company Limited

The publicly funded Hong Kong Applied Science and Technology Research Institute Company Limited (ASTRI) has been in operation since September 2001. It performs relevant and high quality research and development for transfer to industry for commercialisation with a view to upgrading the technology level of industry and stimulating the growth of technology-based industry in Hong Kong. The ASTRI's current research programmes focus on photonic technologies, integrated circuit design, wireless communications, Internet software and biotechnology.

121

Hong Kong Jockey Club Institute of Chinese Medicine Limited

The Hong Kong Jockey Club Institute of Chinese Medicine Limited (HKJCICM), incorporated in May 2001 as a subsidiary company of the ASTRI, will take forward the vision to position Hong Kong as a world centre for the development of health food and pharmaceuticals based on Chinese medicine. Its mission is to spearhead the development of Chinese medicine as a high value-added industry for Hong Kong through promotion and coordination of related activities and strategic support for scientific and evidence-based development programmes. The Hong Kong Jockey Club Charities Trust has pledged to donate $500 million to support the HKJCICM's research and development programmes. The institute has set its programme directions to steer Chinese medicine development embracing standardisation, technology and product development, safety appraisal and evidence-based clinical studies.

Hong Kong Design Centre

The establishment of the Hong Kong Design Centre (HKDC) was proposed by four leading design professional bodies in Hong Kong with a view to promoting the design industry and its competitiveness in the region as a service industry. With a grant and support from the Government, and a donation from the Hong Kong Jockey Club Charities Trust, the HKDC commenced operation in September 2002. It is a multi-disciplinary design centre which aims to promote design as a value-added activity, raise design standards and foster design-related education, and raise the profile of Hong Kong as an innovative and creative hub.

Publicity and Promotional Events

The ITC organised the Hong Kong Student Science Project Competition, coordinated the State Science and Technology Awards and took the lead in coordinating Hong Kong's participation in the China Hi-Tech Fair 2003 held in Shenzhen. All these publicity and promotional events helped foster an innovation and technology culture in the community.

Protection of Intellectual Property Rights

The Government's commitment to protecting intellectual property rights is evidenced by its dynamic legislative programme, vigorous law enforcement and continuous public education. Hong Kong has in place an intellectual property regime which is in full compliance with international standards.

Registration

Registration activities have taken on a new focus to deliver Internet online search for trade marks (available since January 2003), patents and designs (to be launched in the first quarter of 2004). By November 2003, 10 months into online search of trade marks, the United States emerged as the top user of this search service. Registration in a 90 per cent paperless environment and online filing for trade marks, patents and designs is scheduled to be in place by the first quarter of 2004.

Another focus for registration activities is customer relationship management. Forty-five briefings, workshops, 'walk-throughs' and visits were conducted for filers and stakeholders.

Trade Marks

The Trade Marks Registry is responsible for the registration of trade marks in respect of goods and services. On April 4, 2003, the new Trade Marks Ordinance came into effect. The new ordinance increases the range of signs that can serve as trade marks and simplifies the registration procedures. More user-friendly features such as multi-class applications, reduction of the number of forms from 42 to 15 have also been introduced. In addition, there has been a substantial reduction in registration fees.

In 2003, 20 382 applications were received, comprising 16 017 single-class applications and 4 365 multiple-class applications. During the period, 20 359 marks were registered, an increase of 25.4 per cent compared with 16 240 in 2002. Out of the total of 80 countries filing applications, the principal places from which applications originated were:

HK, China	7 374	France	758
USA	3 489	United Kingdom	680
Japan	2 116	Switzerland	547
Germany	969	British Virgin Islands	475
China	888	Italy	319

The register had a total of 171 140 marks as at December 31, 2003.

Patents

The Patents Ordinance provides for the grant of standard patents based on patents granted in the State Intellectual Property Office of China, the United Kingdom Patent Office or the European Patent Office (in respect of patents designating the United Kingdom). It also provides for the grant of short-term patents. In 2003, the Patents Registry received 9 102 standard patent applications and 3 075 were granted. During the period, there were also 398 applications for grant of short-term patents, and 335 were granted.

Registered Designs

The Registered Designs Ordinance enables designs to be registered independently in the HKSAR. In 2003, the Designs Registry received 2 339 applications for registration of 3 327 designs, comprising 1 933 single-design applications and 406 multiple-design applications. During the period, 3 310 designs were registered.

Copyright

The Copyright Ordinance provides protection for literary, dramatic, musical and artistic works, typographical arrangements of published editions, sound recordings, films, broadcasts, cable programmes, and performers' performances irrespective of the domicile of the copyright owners. In line with international standards, there is no requirement to register copyright.

The Copyright (Amendment) Ordinance 2003, which took effect on November 28, removed civil and criminal liabilities pertaining to parallel importation of and subsequent dealing in articles commonly known as computer software products. However, if the principal attraction of a computer software product is musical or visual recordings, movies, television dramas, e-books, or a combination of them, then restrictions continue to apply.

Enforcement

The Customs and Excise Department is responsible for enforcing the criminal sanctions for the protection of copyright and trade marks. It investigates reports of copyright infringement and trade mark counterfeiting, and takes action against the manufacture, distribution, sale, import and export of pirated and counterfeit goods. The department also takes action against the possession of infringing copies of computer programmes, movies, television dramas and music recordings in business as well as unauthorised possession of video recording equipment in a place of public entertainment used primarily as a cinema, theatre or concert hall.

The department maintains stringent control on all optical disc and stamper factories to prevent them from engaging in copyright piracy activities. Optical disc and stamper manufacturers are required to apply for a licence from the Commissioner of Customs and Excise. At year-end, 113 licensed stamper and optical disc factories, 738 optical disc production lines and 21 stamper production units were registered with the department.

During the year, the department processed 10 341 cases and arrested 1 288 persons in connection with copyright piracy activities. The total quantity of items seized amounted to 7.08 million, with a value of $229.46 million. The department also processed 760 cases relating to counterfeit goods and goods bearing false trade descriptions. A total of 743 persons were arrested and 39.46 million pieces of counterfeit goods, valued at $258.4 million, were seized.

During the year, the department detected 23 corporate software end-user piracy cases, resulting in the arrest of 38 persons and the seizure of infringing copies of computer software with a market value of $2 million, as estimated by the copyright owners. It also received one report of unauthorised possession of video recording equipment in a cinema and conducted a criminal investigation into the reported criminal activity.

As an initiative to help young people to keep away from copyright pirates, the Customs and Excise Department and the Social Welfare Department jointly established in April 2002 a referral system under which juvenile offenders apprehended in piracy cases can be given assistance and counselling as circumstances warrant. Since the implementation of the system, a total of eight juvenile offenders have been referred to the Social Welfare Department for such services.

The Special Task Force of 147 Customs officers continued to take vigorous enforcement action against illicit manufacturing and retailing of optical discs. Its main enforcement objective is to carry out repeated and focused operations at 'black spot' retail outlets and their storage facilities to suppress the sale of pirated optical discs.

As a result of the department's vigorous enforcement action, large-scale illicit optical disc manufacturing activities, for which expensive replicating machines were used, had been successfully stamped out, and no such large-scale activity was detected in 2003. Copyright pirates have turned to smaller scale operations by setting up copying workshops equipped with CD-writers to manufacture pirated discs. During the year, the department neutralised 28 such illegal workshops, with the seizure of 481 CD-writers and the arrest of 57 persons.

The department also takes action against copyright piracy activities on the Internet. Since its establishment in early 2000, the department's Anti-Internet Piracy Team has detected 31 Internet piracy cases, resulting in the seizure of pirated goods and equipment valued at $2.04 million, and the arrest of 53 persons.

Public Education

During the year, the Intellectual Property Department continued to keep up the momentum of public education. Consumers and retailers were encouraged to join the ongoing campaigns, 'I Pledge' and 'No Fakes', to show their commitment to buy, use and sell genuine goods.

In 2003, the department continued its programme of visiting secondary schools. Visits to 23 schools with a total of 6 830 students were made. Several teaching aids were produced including a comic book and a three-dimensional computer game.

The department has produced several Announcements in the Public Interest to promote respect for intellectual property rights and a TV programme on *Making Intellectual Property Your Business — A Wealth Creation Series*. This eight-episode programme conveyed to the public the message that intellectual property is a prime driver of economic growth. In cooperation with trade and professional organisations, the department also organised several seminars for SMEs to help them understand the importance of intellectual property and explain to them the systems for protecting such assets in Hong Kong.

Following the Sixth Guangdong/Hong Kong Joint Conference held on August 5, the Guangdong/Hong Kong Expert Group on the Protection of Intellectual Property Rights was set up to enhance the cooperation between the two places in the area of protection of intellectual property rights. The first meeting was held in Hong Kong on December 3. In December, the Guangdong-Hong Kong-Macau Intellectual Property Database was launched to help enterprises operating in the three places, particularly SMEs, to understand their respective intellectual property laws and systems. The database can be accessed at *http://www.ip-prd.net/*. The department partnered with the Trade Development Council and its counterparts in Guangdong in organising seminars and briefing sessions to promote understanding of the respective systems.

Participation in International Organisations

The Intellectual Property Department continued to participate in the activities of the WTO Council for Trade-Related Aspects of Intellectual Property Rights (TRIPS) in 2003. Representatives of the department also attended conferences at the World Intellectual Property Organisation (WIPO), including the meeting of the Assemblies of the Member States, and the conferences held by various committees, such as the Standing Committee on Copyright and Related Rights. The department also represented Hong Kong, China at other international and regional intellectual property symposia and conferences, including the 16th meeting of the APEC Intellectual Property Experts Group held in Christchurch, New Zealand, in March and the 17th meeting held in Vancouver, Canada, in July.

Business and Services Promotion

The Government launched the Helping Business Programme in 1996, with the aim of creating a more business-friendly environment and maintaining Hong Kong's position as one of the best places in the world for doing business. Measures were initiated under the programme to cut government red tape and eliminate over-regulation; reduce costs of compliance to business; and introduce new and improved services.

During the year, 10 studies and projects were completed under the Helping Business Programme and some 50 recommendations were identified. Helping business initiatives introduced by various government agencies in the year included implementation of an Open Bond System to provide flexibility and reduce the operating costs for the dutiable commodity trade; launch of on-screen fillable forms on the Government Forms website (*http://www.info.gov.hk/forms*) to provide alternatives for the public to access and fill in government forms electronically; streamlining the Transport Department's processes and operations and enhancing its communication with the trade; and identifying opportunities to streamline the regulatory procedures and shorten the processing time for issue of licences and permits for the construction industry.

To promote services, the Government organised different publicity activities such as the 'Soar Over Hong Kong' scheme, 'Quality Customer Services' programme and other projects to promote among the community a better understanding of Hong Kong's services economy and awareness of the importance of quality service.

Specific efforts were also made by Government to promote Hong Kong's professional services. These included the $100 million Professional Services Development Assistance Scheme, which was launched in February 2002 to provide funding support, on an equal matching basis, for the eligible professional service sectors to organise projects which aim to enhance the external competitiveness and standard of Hong Kong's professional services. Media publicity was also launched in the Pearl River Delta area to promote Hong Kong's professional services there.

Trade Documentation

As a free port, the HKSAR maintains minimal import and export documentation requirements. Most products do not need licences to enter or leave Hong Kong. Licences or notifications are only required if the HKSAR needs to fulfil its international obligations, to protect public health, safety, environment, or intellectual property rights, or to ensure Hong Kong's unrestricted access to high technologies and hi-tech products. Products that require import or export licences include textiles and clothing, strategic commodities, rice, chilled or frozen meat and poultry, pharmaceutical products and medicines, pesticides, radioactive substances and irradiating apparatus, left-hand-drive vehicles, ozone-depleting substances, and optical disc mastering and replication equipment.

The HKSAR maintains a certification of origin system to facilitate its exports to overseas markets. The Trade and Industry Department administers this system and issues certificates of origin. In addition, the Government has designated five organisations to issue certificates of origin — the Hong Kong General Chamber of Commerce, the Federation of Hong Kong Industries, the Indian Chamber of Commerce Hong Kong, the Chinese Manufacturers' Association of Hong Kong, and the Chinese General Chamber of Commerce.

Government Electronic Trading Services (GETS)

To maintain Hong Kong's competitiveness in the global business community, the Government has been promoting the wider adoption of electronic commerce in the trading community since the early 1990s.

Global e-Trading Services Limited and Tradelink Electronic Commerce Limited are currently the service providers providing front-end services for the electronic submission and processing of certain official trade-related documents. Such services are known as the Government Electronic Trading Services (GETS) and are available for seven government-related trade documents: restrained textiles export licence, import and export declaration, production notification, certificate of origin, dutiable commodities permit, cargo manifest (excluding road mode of transport), and notification under the Textiles Trader Registration Scheme.

Hong Kong Awards for Industry/Services

To promote and honour the pursuit of excellence by companies in both the manufacturing and services sectors, the Trade and Industry Department — in collaboration with the Hong Kong Productivity Council, major trade and industrial associations and industry support bodies — organises the annual Hong Kong Awards for Industry and the Hong Kong Awards for Services. The former promotes industrial excellence in product design, productivity, quality, environmental performance, export marketing and technological achievement, while the latter promotes services excellence in innovation, productivity, customer service, tourism services and export marketing.

Trade and Industrial Support Organisations

Hong Kong Trade Development Council

The Hong Kong Trade Development Council (TDC), a statutory body established in 1966, is responsible for promoting and expanding Hong Kong's external trade in goods and services. With a global network of more than 40 offices in major business centres around the world, the TDC helps its customers, mainly local SMEs, develop marketing opportunities, trade contacts, market knowledge and competitive skills. It also seeks to project and uphold a positive image of Hong Kong as the international trade platform in Asia. To this end, it organised more than 350 promotional events in and outside Hong Kong in 2003.

Among its promotional events in 2003, the TDC organised 18 international trade fairs (seven of which were the biggest in the region), three public exhibitions and two special fairs for SMEs and CEPA. These events attracted more than 15 500 exhibitors and over 1.2 million visitors, including about 150 000 from overseas. The TDC also organised participation by Hong Kong companies in major trade events around the world.

In its product and services promotions, the TDC placed particular emphasis on the Mainland. Apart from treating the Mainland as a fast growing market, the TDC also promoted Hong Kong as a professional services centre, trade services platform and partner for Mainland businesses seeking global opportunities as well as for overseas firms targeting the Mainland market. It also emphasised the combined strengths of Hong Kong and the Pearl River Delta area, which overseas manufacturers can tap into for locating their production facilities in the Mainland.

The TDC sought to enhance and promote the competitive advantages of Hong Kong's SMEs through a wide range of business matching and information support services, as well as more than 140 business training courses and workshops for SMEs in 2003. Its internet trade portal provided a cyber marketplace for comprehensive trade information, e-commerce facilities and other value-added services, most of which were available free of charge. The portal was significantly enhanced with the launch of a multimedia broadcast platform to provide timely market information in concise audio and video clips, as well as portal interfaces for non-English speaking overseas buyers.

In addition, the TDC maintained a global databank of about 620 000 business contacts, which was useful to users world-wide for the purposes of sourcing and finding business partners. It also produced more than 100 research publications, an online product catalogue, 15 trade magazines and numerous supplements.

The TDC sought to expand its global network and strengthen the advocacy for Hong Kong through high-level business seminars in the world's business capitals, roadshows, speaking engagements at international events, global advertising campaigns in the world's top business and trade publications, and its online business newspaper *Hong Kong Trader* (which was sent electronically to over 230 000 senior corporate executives and decision-makers around the world). The TDC serviced three high-level bilateral business committees to help foster stronger economic ties between Hong Kong and the United States, the European Union and Japan. To facilitate partnership and cooperation between Hong Kong SMEs and their overseas counterparts, the TDC also maintained close liaison with nearly 30 Hong Kong Business Associations around the world and the global federation of these business associations, i.e. the Federation of Hong Kong Business Associations Worldwide which connected over 9 000 SMEs that have close links with Hong Kong.

Hong Kong Export Credit Insurance Corporation

The Hong Kong Export Credit Insurance Corporation (ECIC) was created by statute in 1966 to provide export credit insurance facilities for Hong Kong exporters of goods and services against non-payment risks arising from commercial and political events. The corporation is wholly owned by the Government, which also guarantees its maximum contingent liability, currently standing at $12.5 billion.

The ECIC aims at encouraging and supporting export trade through the provision of professional and customer-oriented services. It provides a wide range of insurance facilities to Hong Kong exporters of goods and services for payments on credit terms. The Comprehensive Cover Policy, which covers exports, re-exports and external trade business for credit terms up to 180 days, is the most commonly used insurance policy. Tailor-made policies and endorsements are also available to cater for the specific needs of exporters in different sectors.

The corporation's total insured business in 2003 amounted to $29 billion, representing an increase of 5 per cent over the previous corresponding period. Gross premium income grew by 4 per cent to $141 million. Cash claims payments decreased by 18 per cent on 2002 to $42 million.

During the year, the corporation continued to strengthen its support to the exporting community, especially the SMEs. It worked closely with various trade associations and institutions in organising workshops and seminars to enhance exporters' understanding of credit management. The insurance policy was generally accepted by banks as useful collateral in granting export financing to exporters, especially the SMEs.

During the SARS outbreak, the corporation introduced a series of initiatives to help exporters tide over the difficult times. These measures included the 'Free Credit Check' service on overseas buyers from March to September, and the refund of annual policy fees received during 2002-03, which totalled $3.81 million, to the policy holders. In addition, the corporation devoted extra resources to help exporters capture the opportunities arising from CEPA and integration with the Pearl River Delta area.

On the international front, the corporation continued to maintain close cooperation with members of the International Union of Credit and Investment Insurers (Berne Union) through visits, meetings and workshops.

Hong Kong Science and Technology Parks Corporation

The Hong Kong Science and Technology Parks Corporation (HKSTPC) was established in May 2001 to offer one-stop infrastructural support services to technology-based companies and activities in a synergistic manner. It is a statutory body formed by merging the former Hong Kong Industrial Estates Corporation, Hong Kong Industrial Technology Centre Corporation and Provisional Hong Kong Science Park Company Ltd. It offers a comprehensive range of services to cater for the needs of industry at various stages. These services range from nurturing technology start-ups through the incubation programme and providing premises and services in the Science Park for applied research and development activities to the provision of land and premises in the industrial estates for production purposes.

The Science Park, being developed by the HKSTPC at Pak Shek Kok, will provide a total area of 22 hectares. Built under the concept of clustering, it will provide an effective working environment and support services to facilitate collaboration and synergy among its tenants and ultimately enhance Hong Kong's long-term economic success. The four clusters are electronics, information technology and telecommunications, biotechnology, and precision engineering. Phase 1 of the Science Park was officially opened in June 2002.

The HKSTPC operates three industrial estates with 214 hectares of land, in total. Developed land is provided at cost to companies with new or improved technology and processes that cannot operate in multi-storey buildings. The industrial estates have helped broaden the industry base and upgrade the technology level of Hong Kong. The industrial estates in Tai Po and Yuen Long are practically full while the one in Tseung Kwan O is half-full.

Through its business incubation programme, the HKSTPC nurtures technology-based start-up companies by providing low-cost accommodation as well as management, marketing, financial and professional business services in the critical initial years of these companies.

Hong Kong Productivity Council

The Hong Kong Productivity Council (HKPC) promotes excellence in productivity to enhance the value-added content of products and services.

In view of the rapid changes in recent years in the international environment, restructuring in the local industry scene and in southern China, and the resultant challenges to its mission, the HKPC commissioned a consultancy study in June 2001 on its role, management and operation. Pursuant to the consultancy study, HKPC has repositioned its service focus to provide integrated support to innovation and growth-oriented Hong Kong firms across the value chain. Its principal sectoral focus is on manufacturing, particularly in Hong Kong's foundation industries, and related service activities. The main geographical focus is Hong Kong and the Pearl River Delta.

Other Trade and Industrial Organisations

The local business community has a strong and well-established culture in forming trade and industrial associations to represent their interests. The Federation of Hong Kong Industries, the Chinese Manufacturers' Association of Hong Kong, the Hong Kong General Chamber of Commerce and the Chinese General Chamber of Commerce are among the oldest and the most influential trade and industrial associations in Hong Kong. There are also numerous other associations, representing specific sectors or interests. In addition, there are various overseas chambers of commerce representing the interests of businesses from, for example, Australia, Canada, India, Japan, the United Kingdom and the United States.

The Federation of Hong Kong Industries is a statutory body established in 1960 to promote and foster the interests of Hong Kong's industrial and business communities. It has more than 3 000 member companies. Major services include the issuing of certificates of origin, organisation of overseas study missions, promotion and endorsement of products with the Hong Kong Quality Mark, and the provision of English Language Skills Assessment Tests. The federation categorises its members into 25 groups covering major industries and services. It also organises the annual Young Industrialist Awards of Hongkong and the consumer product design category of the Hong Kong Awards for Industry.

The Chinese Manufacturers' Association of Hong Kong (CMA), established in 1934, is a member of the International Chamber of Commerce and has a membership of nearly 3 700. Services provided include the issue of certificates of origin and the organisation of industrial and trade promotion activities. It runs the Testing and Certification Laboratories which provide technical back-up services, including materials, consumer product and environmental testing, pre-shipment inspection, and technical consultancy services. Since 1989, the CMA has been the organiser of the machinery and equipment design award category of the Hong Kong Awards for Industry.

The Hong Kong General Chamber of Commerce is the oldest business association in Hong Kong. Founded in 1861, it has around 4 000 corporate members. It issues certificates of origin and is the local issuing authority for the International Association Temporarie Admission Carnets. It also organises trade missions. The chamber is represented on many official advisory committees/bodies. It founded both the Hong Kong Article Numbering Association and the Hong Kong Coalition of Service Industries. The chamber also sponsors the Hong Kong Committee of the Pacific Basin Economic Council.

Established in 1900, the Chinese General Chamber of Commerce has over 6 000 members. Services provided include issuing certificates of origin, providing Electronic Trading Access Service, organising trade delegations, and promoting business information exchange. The chamber maintains close contacts with trade organisations in the Mainland and world-wide.

Standards and Conformance Services

The Innovation and Technology Commission's services in the areas of metrology, documentary standards and accreditation provide the technical foundation for Hong Kong's standards and conformance infrastructure.

The Standards and Calibration Laboratory (SCL) is the official custodian of Hong Kong's physical measurement standards. It provides a comprehensive calibration service traceable to the International System of Units (SI). The SCL is a signatory to the Global Mutual Recognition Arrangement for National Measurement Institutes and its services are internationally recognised and accepted.

The Product Standards Information Bureau (PSIB) offers a comprehensive range of standards information services. Apart from its reference standards library which is open to the public, the PSIB also provides a free advisory service on standards, and a standards sales service. It is the Enquiry Point and Notification Authority for Hong Kong under the WTO Agreement on Technical Barriers to Trade. The PSIB also coordinates Hong Kong's input to APEC on standards and conformance matters.

The Hong Kong Accreditation Service (HKAS) provides a comprehensive range of accreditation services for conformity assessment bodies including testing and calibration laboratories, certification and inspection bodies. In 2003, accreditation services were expanded to Chinese medicine testing and certification of construction products. The HKAS is a signatory to the Mutual Recognition Arrangements of the International Laboratory Accreditation Cooperation and the Asia Pacific Laboratory Accreditation Cooperation. It has also concluded a bilateral Mutual Recognition Arrangement with the multilateral agreement group of the European Cooperation for Accreditation. As a result of these arrangements, the test and calibration reports issued by HKAS-accredited laboratories are recognised by 46 other accreditation bodies world-wide.

Human Resources, Technical Education and Industrial Training

Success in the knowledge-based economy of the 21st century depends heavily upon the availability of talent and skilled manpower at all levels.

Higher-level education and training are provided by the tertiary education institutions. The Vocational Training Council (VTC) provides technical education and industrial training. In addition, it administers the New Technology Training Scheme which provides financial assistance to employers for training their staff in new technologies and those technologies that are not yet widely applied locally but the application of which will significantly benefit Hong Kong. The Clothing Industry Training Authority (CITA) runs two training centres for the clothing and footwear industries. The Trade and Industry Department is represented on the VTC and the CITA whereas the ITC is represented on the VTC committees concerned with the New Technology Training Scheme

The Government also implements the Admission Scheme for Mainland Talents and Professionals. The scheme aims at attracting talented persons and professionals from the Mainland to work in Hong Kong in order to meet local manpower needs and enhance Hong Kong's competitiveness in the globalised market.

Consumer Protection

Consumer Council

The Consumer Council is a statutory body established in April 1974 for protecting and promoting the interests of consumers of goods and services and purchasers of immovable property. The council comprises a chairperson, a vice-chairperson and 20 members appointed by the Government from a wide spectrum of the community. It forms committees and working groups to deal with specific consumer protection tasks. The council office is headed by a chief executive, and has seven functional divisions and a staff of 124.

The council carries out its functions through its consumer policy work, complaint and advice service, research and survey programmes, publications and consumer education activities.

The council's testing and survey programmes seek to provide consumers with objective and up-to-date information so that they can make informed choices. During the year, 46 product tests, 52 in-depth studies and 16 survey projects were completed. Most products were tested mainly for their safety, performance, convenience, durability and environmental impact. The tests and surveys covered a wide range of products and services, from home theatre components (DVD players, loudspeakers) and cosmetics to information disclosure by mandatory provident fund scheme service providers. In regard to products, digital cameras have been continuously tested in the light of their rising popularity. In view of the sluggish economy, the council also conducted a series of studies on consumer credit such as debt relief solutions, charges and services of professionals for voluntary insolvency. As a member of the International Consumer Research and Testing Ltd, a testing body of consumer organisations, the council shares its test results and collaborates with members on international comparative tests, producing quality reports in a more cost-effective manner.

The council provides complaint and advice services to the community through an extensive network of telephone hotlines and 11 Consumer Advice Centres. It acts as mediator between consumers and the traders concerned. During the year, 26 501 consumer complaints and 140 484 consumer enquiries were received, the highest figure on record. Telecommunications services continued to top the list of consumer complaints.

In view of the importance of competitive markets to consumer welfare, the council conducts research, disseminates information and tenders advice on competition-related issues. The council's chief executive is a member of the Competition Policy Advisory Group, and the council made a number of submissions in response to public consultation papers that raised issues affecting competition. The council also published a research study on the state of competition in the retailing of foodstuffs and household necessities, and disseminated an advisory guideline on how to identify and prevent the anti-competitive practice of 'bid-rigging', for use by parties seeking tenders.

The council is practically in daily contact with the mass media on all matters of consumer interest and concern. Its monthly magazine, *CHOICE*, regularly publishes findings of comparative product tests and service surveys providing useful and practical information, advice and viewpoints to the public. The magazine's reach extends far beyond its average monthly circulation of 31 298, penetrating virtually all sectors of the community through extensive media coverage and press statements published at the council's website. The Consumer Rights Reporting Awards 2003 continued to attract entries of high quality from journalists in all sectors of the media. The award presentation ceremony of this annual event was held on the World Consumer Rights Day, which falls on March 15 every year.

The fourth Consumer Culture Study Award organised during the year encouraged secondary school students to conduct their own studies of the local consumer culture.

A total of 360 teams, comprising 2 300 students from 91 schools, participated in this programme.

The Consumer Council Resource Centre in Tsim Sha Tsui, which has been operating since 2002, provides consumer complaint and advice services, a resource library and multimedia computers by which visitors can access educational resources. Talks, visits and workshops were also organised at the centre.

The Consumer Legal Action Fund aims to give greater consumer access to legal remedies and to provide legal assistance to consumers with meritorious cases. The fund, with the council as its trustee, is administered by a board of administrators underpinned by a management committee with members appointed by the Government. Since its establishment in 1994, the fund has considered 58 groups of cases, with the number of applicants in each case ranging from one to more than 800.

In networking, the council is an executive and a council member of the Consumers International (CI), of which its chief executive is former President. The CI is a federation of 271 consumer organisations in 123 countries dedicated to the protection and promotion of consumer interests. The council also maintains regular contacts with its counterparts overseas and in the Mainland. During the year, 293 officials from various parts of the Mainland visited the council's office as part of their training programmes and there were also visitors from other consumer organisations and international bodies.

Enforcement of Consumer Protection Legislation

The Customs and Excise Department carries out spot checks and investigations to ensure that toys, children's products and consumer goods supplied in Hong Kong are safe. It also has responsibilities in protecting consumers from fraudulent traders who offer goods of deceptive weights and measures or products made of gold and platinum that have deceptive markings. In 2003, the department carried out 3 563 spot checks and 1 062 investigations. It also organised talks for traders to promote their awareness of product safety.

In the area of consumer protection, the Government Laboratory continues to support the Customs and Excise Department in enforcing the product safety legislation. In 2003, the Laboratory undertook more than 21 000 tests to determine whether or not the various tested items including toys, children's products and consumer goods were in compliance with relevant safety standards. In particular, urgent hygienic tests on a large number of personal protective products such as face masks, disposable towels and latex gloves were carried out. Assessments of potential hazards posed by commodities that failed the safety tests were also conducted. In the investigation of fraudulent trade practices, the Laboratory continued its role in verification of measuring equipment for use by traders and determination of fineness of gold and platinum articles.

Trade in Endangered Species

Imports, exports or possession of endangered species are regulated by the Animals and Plants (Protection of Endangered Species) Ordinance, which implements the Convention on International Trade in Endangered Species of Wild Fauna and Flora (CITES). Licensing policy follows the CITES principles closely. Commercial imports and exports of highly endangered species are prohibited, and international trade in less endangered species is subject to licensing requirements.

The ordinance is administered by the Agriculture, Fisheries and Conservation Department (AFCD), and enforced by both the AFCD and the Customs and Excise Department (C&ED). It provides for penalties of up to a maximum fine of $5 million and imprisonment for two years.

Hong Kong's exemplary efforts to combat illegal trade in endangered species was recognised in March 2003 when the CITES Secretary-General awarded the Secretary-General's Certificates of Commendation to the AFCD and the C&ED. Hong Kong thus became the first recipient of the certificate, which was introduced in 2002. The Secretary-General also commended Hong Kong's long history of commitment to the implementation of the convention and its support of the secretariat's work.

Home Pages

Commerce, Industry and Technology Bureau: http://www.gov.hk/citb
(links to related departments and agencies)
Consumer Council: http://www.consumer.org.hk

CHAPTER 6

Employment

With the advent of a global knowledge economy, Hong Kong is going through a process of economic restructuring. While the transformation holds promises of new opportunities, it also poses challenges for the workforce. Employees therefore have to adapt to the changing environment, and continually upgrade their skills in order to remain competitive in the labour market. The Government for its part is doing everything it can to facilitate employment through training/retraining and enhanced employment services, safeguard employees' rights and benefits, foster harmonious employer/employee relations and promote occupational safety and health in this changing landscape.

MANPOWER is Hong Kong's most treasured asset. The Hong Kong Special Administrative Region (HKSAR) Government aims to ensure that there is a dynamic, well-motivated, adaptable and skilful workforce contributing to Hong Kong's economic competitiveness.

In 2003, the Government continued to devote much effort to facilitating employment. Chaired by the Financial Secretary, the Task Force on Employment has devised a wide range of measures to boost the economy and promote employment since its inception in 1998. The Task Force, comprising senior officials and representatives of the business, employees, training and academic sectors, serves as a high-level forum to tap the views of the community on ways to improve the employment situation. It was expanded in 2002 to include representatives of political parties.

The Government has continued to offer extra help to enhance the employability of the more vulnerable groups in the community. During the year, the Employees Retraining Board offered over 114 400 training places (the capacity being more or less the same as in 2002) to assist eligible workers, especially those displaced or unemployed ones, to re-enter the labour market.

In addition, the Government has continued its efforts to assist young people to enhance their employability through the Youth Work Experience and Training Scheme which provides on-the-job training of six to 12 months to young people.

At the same time, the Government recognises the need to promote good employer-employee relations, enhance the rights and benefits of employees in a way commensurate with Hong Kong's socio-economic development, and protect the safety and health of employees at work.

Measures in Response to SARS Outbreak

In response to the outbreak of SARS and to prepare for the entry of school leavers into the labour market in the summer, two employment/training packages, coordinated by the Labour Department, were introduced in May and July to create a total of 53 550 employment-related and training openings, at the cost of $1.15 billion. Of these openings, 17 000 were training places offered under the Skills Enhancement Project to provide trade-specific and generic training to employees of industries hard-hit by SARS — such as catering, retail, tourism, hotel, passenger transport, building decoration, real estate, and airport and related industries.

As part of the SARS-related employment packages, the 'Special Incentive Allowance Scheme for Local Domestic Helpers (LDHs)' was launched, through the 'Integrated Scheme for LDHs' administered by the Employees Retraining Board, in June. The incentive scheme aims to promote the service of LDHs for household cleaning and to address the mismatch in supply and demand in the LDH market arising from geographical locations and working hours. A sum of $60 million has been earmarked to provide an allowance to qualified LDHs who are willing to work in a district different from the one in which they reside or during 'unsocial hours' (i.e., 5 pm to 9 am). It is estimated that some 8 000 LDHs will benefit from the scheme.

To help needy employers in the worst-hit industries — including the tourism, restaurants, retail and entertainment businesses — to tide over the difficult time and to preserve jobs, the Government established a low-interest Loan Guarantee Scheme, with a commitment of $3.5 billion. The department assisted in administering and publicising the scheme. A total of 1 802 applications had been received at the close of applications on July 31. Of these, 1 559 applications with a total loan amount of $499,204,781 were approved. The successful applicants employed 18 236 staff altogether.

To help resolve labour relations issues arising from the outbreak of SARS, the Labour Department mapped out enlightened human resources strategies in collaboration with the various industry-based tripartite committees and Human Resource Managers' Clubs. The department also published guidelines and distributed reference materials to employers and employees through newspapers and the electronic media.

Labour Market Situation

In the fourth quarter of 2003, Hong Kong's labour force decreased by 0.5 per cent over the corresponding period of 2002. The labour force stood at 3.5 million, of whom 56.1 per cent were males and 43.9 per cent were females. The seasonally adjusted unemployment rate for the fourth quarter of 2003 was 7.3 per cent while the underemployment rate was 3.3 per cent, as compared with 7.2 per cent and 3.1 per cent, respectively, a year earlier.

Of those employed, the majority (85.5 per cent) were engaged in the service sectors — 31.5 per cent in wholesale, retail and import/export trades, restaurants and hotels; 27.2 per cent in community, social and personal services; 15.5 per cent in financing, insurance, real estate and business services; and 11.3 per cent in transport, storage and communications. Only 5.2 per cent worked in the manufacturing sector.

Owing to a structural shift in employment during the past decade, the number of persons engaged in the service sectors is now over 10 times as many as in the manufacturing sector. In December 2003, 1 988 500 persons were engaged in selected industries in the service sectors, which was 0.7 per cent lower than the corresponding figure in 2002. Only 168 300 persons were engaged in the manufacturing sector, a decrease of 8.8 per cent compared with a year earlier.

The printing and publishing industry was the largest manufacturing industry, engaging 37 900 persons in December 2003, followed by the wearing apparel industry (excluding footwear), the textiles industries and the food manufacturing industry, which engaged 22 500, 20 300 and 19 400 persons, respectively. Details of the distribution of establishments and persons engaged by selected major industry groups are given in the *Appendices*.

Employment Situation

The labour market worsened abruptly in the first half of 2003, mainly affected by the outbreak of SARS. The seasonally adjusted unemployment rate increased from 7.5 per cent in the first quarter of 2003 to an all-time high of 8.7 per cent in May-July 2003. However, the labour market improved somewhat thereafter in tandem with the gradual recovery of business activities. The seasonally adjusted unemployment rate decreased to 7.3 per cent in the fourth quarter of 2003. Vacancies registered with the Labour Department rose from 209 570 in 2002 to 225 106 in 2003. The department also placed 66 100 job-seekers in employment during the year.

Wages

Wage rates are calculated on a time basis, either daily or monthly, or on an incentive basis according to the volume of work performed. The average wage rate for employees up to the supervisory level, including daily-rated and monthly-rated employees, decreased by 1.5 per cent in money terms between December 2002 and December 2003. After discounting changes in consumer prices, the average wage rate decreased by 0.3 per cent in real terms.

In December 2003, the average monthly wage rate for the supervisory, technical, clerical and miscellaneous non-production workers in the wholesale, retail and import/export trades, restaurants and hotels sector was $11,552. Based on the wage indices, the average wage rate for this group decreased by 2.1 per cent in money terms, or by 0.8 per cent in real terms, compared with December 2002.

Over the same period, the average wage rate in the manufacturing sector decreased by 2.2 per cent in money terms, or by 0.9 per cent in real terms. The overall average daily wage was $325 for craftsmen and operatives.

Labour Administration and Services

The Labour Department is headed by the Permanent Secretary for Economic Development and Labour (Labour) who also assumes the role of the Commissioner for Labour. It formulates and implements labour policies, enforces labour legislation, promotes harmonious labour relations and responsible trade unionism, safeguards employees' rights and benefits and protects the safety, health and welfare of the workforce. It also provides free employment services to employers and job-seekers.

Labour Legislation

The Labour Department administers labour laws in force in the HKSAR. Labour legislation has been enacted which, supplemented by administrative measures, enables Hong Kong to maintain internationally accepted labour standards.

Eight items of labour legislation were enacted in 2003. Among them, the Occupational Deafness (Compensation) Ordinance was amended to improve the benefits provided to employees under the Occupational Deafness Compensation Scheme. The Employees Compensation Assistance Ordinance was amended to make it clear that in the event of insurer insolvency, the Employees Compensation Assistance Fund Board may assist employers regarding legal costs in relation to proceedings brought by their employees for employment-related injuries.

The Construction Sites (Safety) Regulations (CSSR) were amended to improve the safety performance of construction subcontractors by holding both the principal contractor and the subcontractor jointly and severally liable for safety offences. Consequential amendments were also made to the Factories and Industrial Undertakings (Lifting Appliances and Lifting Gear) Regulations, the Factories and Industrial Undertakings (Suspended Working Platforms) Regulation and the Factories and Industrial Undertakings (Loadshifting Machinery) Regulation to reflect the changes arising from the CSSR amendment.

During the year, there were 5 424 prosecutions for breaches of various ordinances and regulations administered by the Labour Department. Fines totalling $29,898,996 were imposed.

International Labour Affairs

The international labour conventions of the International Labour Organisation (ILO) prescribe standards on matters such as labour administration, employment, and occupational safety and health as models for member states. These conventions have a significant influence on the formulation of the HKSAR's labour legislation. On August 8, 2003, the Worst Forms of Child Labour Convention, 1999 (No. 182) came into force in the HKSAR. Currently, 41 conventions are applied here. This number compares favourably with most member states of the ILO in the Asia-Pacific region.

The HKSAR continues to participate in the activities of the ILO. In 2003, representatives from the HKSAR participated in the 91st Session of the International Labour Conference as advisers to the delegation of China. The HKSAR also participated in the 17th International Conference of Labour Statisticians as members of China's delegation.

Labour Relations

The state of labour relations in Hong Kong remained harmonious. In 2003, the Labour Relations Division of the Labour Department provided conciliation service in 427 trade disputes, a decrease of one per cent over 2002. There was only one work stoppage, resulting in the loss of 150 working days. The average loss was 0.05 working day per 1 000 salaried employees and wage-earners, which is among the lowest in the world. During the year, the division handled 33 689 claims for wages and other employment-related benefits or entitlements. This represented a decrease of three per cent over 2002. About 65 per cent of the disputes and claims in 2003 were settled through conciliation by the division — a record high since 1997.

The Labour Department organises a wide variety of activities to promote harmonious labour relations in Hong Kong. To enhance public understanding of the Employment Ordinance, promotional activities such as seminars and talks are organised and a wide range of publications is produced for free distribution to the public. Also, the information is widely publicised through the department's website and the mass media.

At the enterprise level, the department promotes good labour management practices and effective communication. A network of 18 Human Resources Managers' Clubs has been established and experience-sharing sessions and briefings are organised for human resources practitioners. The department also promotes tripartite dialogue at the industry level through the setting up of committees comprising representatives of employers, employees and labour officials. With the assistance of the department, nine tripartite committees have been formed, covering the catering, construction, theatre, warehouse and cargo transport, property management, printing, hotel and tourism, cement and concrete, and retail industries.

Trade Unions

Trade unions must be registered under the Trade Unions Ordinance, which is administered by the Registrar of Trade Unions. Once registered, a trade union becomes a body corporate and enjoys immunity from certain civil suits.

During the year, 29 new unions were registered. At year-end, 689 unions (comprising 644 employee unions, 23 employers' associations, and 22 mixed organisations of employees and employers) and three trade union federations were registered under the ordinance.

About half of the employee unions are affiliated to the following four major labour organisations registered under the Societies Ordinance: the Hong Kong Federation of Trade Unions (149 affiliated unions), the Hong Kong and Kowloon Trades Union Council (40 unions), the Hong Kong Confederation of Trade Unions (57 unions), and the Federation of Hong Kong and Kowloon Labour Unions (51 unions).

Labour Advisory Board

The Labour Advisory Board is a non-statutory body set up to advise the Permanent Secretary for Economic Development and Labour (Labour) on matters affecting labour, including legislation and conventions and recommendations of the ILO. The Labour Advisory Board comprises 12 members. Six of them represent employers, and another six represent employees. The Permanent Secretary for Economic Development and Labour (Labour), is the *ex officio* chairman.

The board has set up five committees and one working group on special subjects which cover employees' compensation, employment services, occupational safety and health, labour relations, the implementation of international labour standards and the processing of applications for labour importation under the Supplementary Labour Scheme.

Protection of Wages on Insolvency Fund

The Protection of Wages on Insolvency Fund is financed by an annual levy of $600 on each business registration certificate with effect from May 2002. Employees who are owed wages and other employment termination benefits by insolvent employers may apply to the fund for an *ex gratia* payment.

The fund covers arrears of wages not exceeding $36,000 accrued during a period of four months preceding the applicant's last day of service; wages in lieu of notice for termination of employment up to $22,500 or one month's wages, whichever is less; and severance payment up to $50,000 plus 50 per cent of any entitlement in excess of $50,000. In 2003, out of 22 042 applications processed, the fund disbursed a total of $468.2 million to 19 794 applications.

Employees' Rights and Benefits

The Employment Ordinance provides for various employment-related benefits and entitlements for employees. On top of the statutory requirements, employers and employees are free to negotiate on the terms and conditions of their employment.

Since December 2000, all relevant employers have to enrol their employees in MPF schemes in accordance with the Mandatory Provident Fund (MPF) Schemes legislation. The participation rate of the relevant employers in MPF schemes, which are regulated by the Mandatory Provident Fund Schemes Authority, reached 95.4 per cent by year-end.

Labour Conditions

The employment of children under 15 years of age is generally prohibited. Subject to stringent requirements, children aged 13 and 14 may be employed in non-industrial establishments. Young persons aged 15 to 17 may work in industrial establishments, subject to regulations governing their employment conditions. Specific provisions under labour legislation protect their safety, health and welfare.

Labour inspectors conduct rigorous workplace inspections to monitor employers' compliance with the various provisions of labour legislation to safeguard the statutory rights and benefits of local and imported workers, and to ensure that employers possess valid insurance policies covering their liabilities for work injuries of their employees. Labour inspectors also check employees' proof of identity to help combat illegal employment.

Employees' Compensation

In Hong Kong, the employees' compensation system adopts the no-fault principle whereby compensation is payable irrespective of whether the injury, the occupational disease or death was caused by the employee's fault. The Employees' Compensation Ordinance covers injuries or death caused by accidents arising out of and in the course of employment or by specified occupational diseases. An employer must be in possession of a valid insurance policy to cover his liabilities under the ordinance and at common law.

The Employees' Compensation Division of the Labour Department, which administers the Employees' Compensation Ordinance, assists injured employees and family members of deceased employees to obtain compensation from their employers. It also administers a scheme to provide interest-free loans to those injured employees and family members of deceased employees who need financial assistance as a result of a work-related accident.

Payment of compensation under the Pneumoconiosis (Compensation) Ordinance is administered by the Pneumoconiosis Compensation Fund Board. Pneumoconiosis sufferers who were diagnosed before 1981 are not covered by the ordinance. They receive *ex gratia* benefits from the Government under the Pneumoconiosis Ex Gratia Scheme.

The Occupational Deafness Compensation Scheme compensates employees suffering from noise-induced deafness due to employment in specified noisy occupations. It is administered by the Occupational Deafness Compensation Board. The Occupational Deafness (Compensation) (Amendment) Ordinance 2003, which came into effect on May 16, 2003, has introduced improvements to the scheme and additional benefits to persons who are entitled to occupational deafness compensation, including the reimbursement of expenses in relation to hearing assistive devices and rehabilitation services.

The Employees Compensation Assistance Scheme provides a safety net for injured employees or family members of deceased employees so that they can receive compensation from the scheme in cases where employers default payment of compensation for work-related injuries or insurers become insolvent. The scheme is financed by a levy imposed on all employees' compensation insurance policies taken out by employers.

Minor Employment Claims Adjudication Board

The Minor Employment Claims Adjudication Board adjudicates claims under the Employment Ordinance and in accordance with individual employment contracts. The board hears and determines employment claims involving not more than 10 claimants for a sum of money not exceeding $8,000 per claimant. During the year, the board concluded 2 763 cases and made awards amounting to $6.6 million.

Labour Tribunal

The Labour Tribunal is part of the Judiciary and provides a quick, inexpensive and informal method of adjudicating various types of disputes between employees and employers which are not within the exclusive jurisdiction of the Minor Employment Claims Adjudication Board.

In 2003, there were 11 263 cases filed in the tribunal of which 11 232 were initiated by employees and 31 by employers. Of these cases, 91.9 per cent were referred by the Labour Relations Division of the Labour Department after unsuccessful conciliation attempts. During the year, the tribunal dealt with a total of 11 385 cases and made awards amounting to more than $705 million.

Stepping Up Enforcement Against Wage Offences

To expedite investigation and prosecution concerning wage offences, the Labour Department has a dedicated unit to conduct in-depth investigations into suspected breaches of the Employment Ordinance at the earliest instance. In 2003, the department secured convictions for 445 summonses on wage offences, representing a significant increase of 220 per cent compared with 139 summonses in 2002. The department has taken swift action to detect wage offences through inspections of targeted workplaces. It has also strengthened its educational and promotional efforts to remind employers of their statutory obligation to pay wages on time and to educate employees on the right to lodge claims and the importance of serving as prosecution witnesses.

Occupational Safety and Health

The Occupational Safety and Health Branch of the Labour Department administers the Occupational Safety and Health Ordinance, the Factories and Industrial Undertakings Ordinance and their subsidiary legislation to protect the safety and health of employees at work in almost all economic sectors.

Enforcement of the legislation is carried out through routine inspections of workplaces and special campaigns. To arouse safety awareness among employers and employees and to facilitate compliance with the law, the department promotes the Occupational Safety Charter, publishes a wide variety of guidebooks and codes of practice and undertakes other activities such as organising safety campaigns and award schemes, exhibitions and seminars.

Boilers and Pressure Vessels Safety

The Boilers and Pressure Vessels Division of the Labour Department administers the Boilers and Pressure Vessels Ordinance to ensure the safe use and operation of pressure equipment. The division conducts regular spot checks on pressure equipment. It also conducts examinations for the issue of Certificates of Competency, investigates accidents and undertakes activities to promote safety.

In 2003, the division processed 1 537 applications for registration of equipment, conducted 6 494 inspections, and issued 425 Certificates of Competency and endorsements.

Occupational Health

The Occupational Health Service of the Labour Department aims to protect the health of workers from hazards in the workplace environment. The service sets occupational health standards, monitors occupational hygiene practice in the workplaces and enforces occupational health and safety legislation. It undertakes medical examinations for radiation workers and government employees engaged in hazardous occupations, provides clinical consultation for employees with a work-related illness, investigates occupational diseases, arranges medical assessments for injured employees, and conducts health educational and promotional programmes for workers. The service also provides hyperbaric oxygen therapy for treatment of decompression sickness in divers.

In 2003, the service enhanced its inspection of hospitals, homes for the elderly and workplaces undergoing cleaning and disinfection to ensure the adequate provision and training in the use of personal protective equipment for workers.

Occupational Safety and Health Council

The Occupational Safety and Health Council was established in 1988 to foster a safe and healthy working environment in Hong Kong through training, promotion, consultancy, information services and research.

Training and promotional initiatives for high-risk industries are the council's priorities. A total of 15 000 persons attended the 650 training courses organised by the council in 2003. Classroom training was strengthened with practical sessions on gas welding, forklift truck operation, working in a confined space, working at a height, abrasive wheel operation, and use of fire extinguishers. The council also provided training on the application of psychology in safety management and occupational rehabilitation to enable employers to assist injured employees to return to work. It organised regular technical seminars on topical issues such as safe working on scaffolding, outdoor work under extreme weather, and health and hygiene at construction sites.

In view of increasing public demand, the council published the first Hong Kong Occupational Safety and Health Products and Services Suppliers Directory, providing detailed information on OSH products, services and suppliers.

The council hosted the 'Safety and Health Expo and the 12th International Conference on Safe Communities' in March. There were exchanges of international expertise and an exhibition displaying a wide range of occupational safety and health products and services. A milestone at the Expo was the World Health Organisation's accreditation of Tuen Mun and Kwai Tsing as the first designated safe communities in Hong Kong. As the sixth affiliate 'safe community support centre' of the World Health Organisation, the council continued to promote safety and health at the district and community levels.

With the support of trade unions and related organisations, the council launched a campaign on 'Workplace Protection against SARS' in May to educate high-risk employee groups on the effective use of personal protective equipment and prevention of biological hazards. This was done by means of seminars, videos and publications as well as the distribution of protective equipment. In July, the council launched a 'Workplace Hygiene Charter' to promote a clean and hygienic working environment. A series of workplace exercises was designed for construction workers, health care workers, cleaners and professional drivers to help them improve personal health.

The council's OSH Enhancement Scheme for Small and Medium Enterprises (SMEs) was enhanced during the year by the introduction of an accredited list of safety consultants. The scheme provides technical support to SMEs.

Employment Services

The Labour Department provides diversified modes of free employment and recruitment services to job-seekers and employers through a network of 11 district-based Job Centres (two of which are Employment and Guidance Centres for New Arrivals), a Telephone Employment Service Centre, a Central Recruitment Unit and a Job Vacancy Processing Centre. In addition, special recruitment activities are held regularly to assist job-seekers in finding jobs and employers in recruiting staff. Job-seekers can make use of facilities such as vacancy search terminals, telephones, fax machines and computers with an Internet connection in Job Centres to complete the whole job-hunting process at one stop. Moreover, employment services are also available on the Internet round-the-clock through the Interactive Employment Services (iES) website (*http://www.jobs.gov.hk*).

During the year, 233 070 job-seekers registered with the Labour Department, 225 106 vacancies were received and a record high of 66 100 placements was achieved.

Re-employment Training Programme for the Middle-aged

The Re-employment Training Programme for the Middle-aged was launched in April to assist job-seekers who are aged 40 or above and have been unemployed for three months or more find jobs. A training allowance of $1,500 per month for each trainee for not more than three months is granted to employers who engage the middle-aged unemployed and provide them with on-the-job training.

Helping the Disabled Find Jobs

The Selective Placement Division of the Labour Department helps people with a disability integrate into the community through open employment. It provides a free employment counselling and placement service for the hearing impaired, sight impaired, physically handicapped, chronically ill, ex-mentally ill and mentally handicapped. In 2003, the division launched a series of activities to promote the employment of people with a disability. It recorded 4 309 job-seekers with a disability and achieved 2 442 placements.

Employment Agencies

The Employment Agencies Administration of the Labour Department enforces Part XII of the Employment Ordinance and the Employment Agency Regulations. It monitors the operation of employment agencies through licensing, inspection and investigation of complaints. In 2003, it issued 1 393 employment agency licences, revoked four such licences, refused to renew one licence and refused to issue two licences.

Employment Outside Hong Kong

The External Employment Service of the Labour Department administers the Contracts for Employment Outside Hong Kong Ordinance to safeguard the interests of local employees engaged to work outside Hong Kong for foreign employers. All employment contracts involving manual employees, or non-manual employees with monthly wages not exceeding $20,000, must be attested by the Commissioner for Labour.

Telephone Enquiry Service

The Labour Department's Telephone Enquiry Service handles general enquiries on labour legislation and on services offered by the department. Guided by an interactive voice processing system, callers can listen to pre-recorded messages and obtain fax information 24 hours a day by making a selection from a wide range of topics. The service is supplemented by staff operators handling more complicated enquiries during office hours. The service handled 1 187 809 calls in 2003.

Preparing People for Work

Careers Guidance

The Careers Advisory Service of the Labour Department, through the promotion of careers education, helps young people to choose a career best suited to their talents, interests and abilities and also supports careers teachers with back-up information. The public can also access careers information published by the service through its website.

Throughout the year, the service arranged student group visits to its Careers Information Centres and various commercial and industrial establishments. Its Education and Careers Expo 2003 attracted 184 359 visitors and a total of 159 037 students took part in its Careers Quiz 2003.

Skills Upgrading Scheme

The Finance Committee approved in June 2001 the allocation of $400 million for the provision of focused skills training for workers with secondary, or below, education. By December 31, 2003, the number of industry sectors brought under the Skills Upgrading Scheme had increased from six in 2001 to 17. These were: Printing, Chinese Catering, Retail, Import and Export Trade, Transportation, Wearing Apparel and Textile, Hotel, Tourism, Hairdressing, Property Management, Insurance, Electrical and Mechanical Engineering, Real Estate Agents, Building Maintenance and Decoration, Beauty Care, Passenger Transport, and Elderly Care. By year-end, 55 703 trainees from 3 088 classes had completed training.

Youth Pre-employment Training Programme

The Youth Pre-employment Training Programme was first launched in 1999 to enhance the employability of school leavers aged 15 to 19 through a wide range of employment-related training, workplace attachment, careers counselling and support services. The fourth programme was concluded in June, with about 10 300 trainees taking part.

The fifth programme, for 2003-04, is being delivered in two phases. The first phase, which commenced in September, attracted some 6 500 participants.

Youth Work Experience and Training Scheme

To enhance the employability of young people, the Government allocated $400 million to launch the Youth Work Experience and Training Scheme in July 2002. Administered by the Labour Department, it aims at providing on-the-job training of six to 12 months' duration for young people aged 15 to 24, with an education attainment below degree level.

The Labour Department canvasses training vacancies from various industries in the private sector as well as the public sector. In addition, special employment projects tailor-made for different trades and occupations are launched to provide diversified training opportunities for trainees under the scheme.

Non-governmental organisations (NGOs) have been commissioned to offer induction training and case management service to trainees. Case managers, who are registered social workers from NGOs, assist trainees to formulate career plans, identify suitable training vacancies, prepare for selection interviews, review their job search strategy, and adapt to the work environment after they are placed into employment.

The target of the scheme is to provide 10 000 training places by July 2004. This target was achieved in November, eight months ahead of schedule. By year-end, 10 971 trainees were successfully placed in training vacancies under the scheme. In addition, 7 632 trainees were placed in other jobs in the open employment market with the advice and assistance of their case managers.

Feedback from trainees, employers and NGOs on the scheme is highly favourable. Independent consultants from the Centre for Social Policy Studies of the Hong Kong Polytechnic University have also confirmed the effectiveness of the scheme in enhancing the employability of young people in a mid-term review conducted in 2003.   145

Employees Retraining Scheme

The Employees Retraining Scheme (ERS) was launched in 1992 to provide retraining to eligible workers to assist them in taking on new or enhanced skills so that they can adjust to changes in the economic environment. It is administered by the Employees Retraining Board (ERB) which is a statutory body set up under the Employees Retraining Ordinance, comprising representatives from employers, employees, persons related to vocational training and retraining or manpower planning as well as the Government. In addition to regular income from a levy collected under the labour importation schemes, the Government provided a recurrent subvention of $378 million in 2003-04.

The ERS focuses on assisting displaced workers who have experienced difficulties in seeking alternative employment. The main target group of the scheme is displaced workers aged 30 or over with no more than lower secondary education. The scheme offers a wide variety of full-time and part-time courses delivered through a network of more than 50 approved training bodies. The courses broadly fall into seven categories: courses on job search skills, job-specific skills, general skills (computer and vocational languages), courses for the elderly, courses for people with disabilities, tailor-made courses and self-employment courses.

During the year, 60 600 full-time and 56 900 part-time retraining places were provided under the ERS. The two Retraining Resource Centres, in Yau Ma Tei and Lok Fu, continued to provide self-learning facilities, job market information and other supporting services to all graduate retrainees. The objective is to reinforce the effectiveness of the ERS and foster the concept of lifelong learning.

The 'Integrated Scheme for Local Domestic Helpers (LDHs)', an initiative launched in May 2002 to provide a one-stop service comprising job placement, referral and follow-up service for employers and graduate retrainees of domestic helper courses, has been running with success. To enhance the quality of training, the ERB set up in October 2002 a Practical Skills Training and Assessment Centre to administer a standard skills assessment for graduate retrainees of domestic helper courses. Retrainees who pass a practical skill assessment test will be issued a 'competency card' in recognition of the skills standard they have achieved. To further promote the service of LDHs and to address the mismatch in supply and demand in the LDH market, the 'Special Incentive Allowance Scheme for LDHs' was introduced in June as part of the SARS-related employment packages. (*More details of the incentive scheme are given at the start of this chapter, in the paragraphs on action taken during the SARS outbreak*).

Imported Workers

General Policy on Entry for Employment

The Immigration Department controls the entry of foreigners for employment. Foreigners may work or invest in Hong Kong if they possess a special skill, knowledge or experience of value to and not readily available in Hong Kong and are employed with a remuneration broadly commensurate with the market level, or if they can make a substantial contribution to the economy.

The department applies the policy in a flexible manner. Genuine business persons and entrepreneurs are welcome to establish a presence in Hong Kong, bringing with them capital and expertise. Qualified professionals, technical staff, administrators and managerial personnel are also admitted with the minimum formalities. During the year, 15 774 foreign professionals and persons with technical, administrative or managerial skills from more than 100 countries/territories were admitted for employment.

Importation of Labour

Apart from the above, a Supplementary Labour Scheme is operated for the importation of workers who do not fall under the general policy on entry for employment. The Government's policy on importation of labour is based on two cardinal principles:

(*a*) local workers must be given priority in filling job vacancies available in the job market; and

(*b*) employers who are genuinely unable to recruit local workers to fill their job vacancies should be allowed to import workers.

This scheme commenced in February 1996. All applications are considered on a case-by-case basis. To ensure priority of employment for local workers, each application for imported workers has to pass three tests before it is submitted to the Labour Advisory Board for consideration and to the Government for a decision. These tests are advertising in newspapers, job-matching by the Labour Department for four weeks, and tailor-made retraining course for workers, if appropriate. In all, 758 visas/entry permits were approved during the year and a cumulative total of 10 324 visas/entry permit applications had been approved by year-end.

Admission Scheme for Mainland Talents and Professionals

The new Admission Scheme for Mainland Talents and Professionals was implemented on July 15, 2003, replacing the Admission of Talents Scheme and the Admission of Mainland Professionals Scheme. The new scheme aligns the conditions for admitting Mainland people for employment with those applicable to foreigners. It aims at attracting talented persons and professionals to work in Hong Kong in order to meet local manpower needs and enhance Hong Kong's competitiveness in the globalised market. (*Further details of this scheme are given in Chapter 20*).

Admission of Mainland Students Graduated from University Grants Committee (UGC)-funded Institutions in Hong Kong

With effect from August 1, 2001, Mainland students who have graduated from UGC-funded institutions since 1990 may be admitted for employment, provided that they possess a special skill, knowledge or experience of value to and not readily available in Hong Kong and are employed with a remuneration broadly commensurate with the market level. The objective of this arrangement is to attract outstanding Mainland students who have completed full-time studies at the bachelor degree level or above to re-enter Hong Kong for employment after graduation so as to increase the territory's competitiveness in the knowledge-based global economy.

Foreign Domestic Helpers

Foreign domestic helpers (FDHs) may be admitted subject to the conditions that they have relevant experience, that their employers are bona fide Hong Kong residents who are prepared to offer reasonable terms of employment including suitable accommodation and wages not lower than a minimum level set by the Government, and that the employers are willing to provide for the maintenance of the helpers in Hong Kong as well as to meet the costs of repatriation of the helpers to their country of origin. Employers must also satisfy requirements on income and assets.

In general, demand for FDHs has increased over the past two decades but the number decreased in 2003. By year-end, there were 216 863 such helpers in Hong Kong, a decrease of 8.5 per cent compared with the number of 237 104 in 2002. About 58.4 per cent of the FDHs in Hong Kong were from the Philippines and 37.4 per cent from Indonesia.

Following a review of the policy on FDHs in the context of formulating a population policy, the Government has imposed an Employees Retraining Levy of $400 per month for the contract period on the employers of FDHs to generate funds for training and retraining the local workforce. The levy, imposed under the Employees Retraining Ordinance, took effect on October 1, 2003.

Home Pages

Economic Development and Labour Bureau: http://www.edlb.gov.hk
Education and Manpower Bureau: http://www.emb.gov.hk
Security Bureau: http://www.gov.hk/sb
Labour Department: http://www.labour.gov.hk
Occupational Safety and Health Council: http://www.oshc.org.hk

CHAPTER 7

Education

The Government has been investing heavily in education to enhance Hong Kong's competitiveness in a knowledge-based and globalised economy. Approved recurrent public expenditure and total public expenditure on education in the 2003-04 financial year amounted to $49.3 billion and $61 billion respectively, representing 23.8 per cent of both recurrent and total government expenditure.

SINCE October 2000, the Government has implemented a comprehensive education reform for various stages of education from early childhood to tertiary and continuing education. The overall objective of the reform is to promote all-round education for all and to inculcate in young people the motivation and ability for lifelong learning so that they can keep up with the pace of change in the new millennium.

The reform covers a wide range of initiatives, including reform of the curriculum, teaching practices, admission systems and assessment mechanisms. Measures have also been introduced to increase opportunities for senior secondary and post-secondary education, provide more choice and diversity; empower schools and in return, increase the transparency and accountability of schools; and step up the professional development of principals and teachers as well as support for them.

It is generally observed that since the abolition of the Academic Aptitude Test, children are happier at school and they now have more chance to attain deeper understanding through project work and experiential learning activities; that good practices and knowledge generated through action research in professional learning communities are shared more widely within and among schools; and that parents are more involved in their children's learning and are volunteering their services more actively in support of the schools.

Key Achievements in 2003

Curriculum Reform

The curriculum reform is the core component of the education reform. It aims to motivate students to learn, to enhance their knowledge and abilities, and develop in them positive values and attitudes to establish a solid foundation for lifelong learning and whole-person development.

In response to the need for curriculum development in schools, the Curriculum Development Council (CDC) developed in 2002 a 'Basic Education Curriculum Guide' setting out the themes essential for whole-school curriculum development.

School curriculum leaders have been appointed to support primary school heads to lead curriculum development in primary schools for a period of five years. The initiative is being phased in over three years from the 2002-03 school year.

In addition, secondary and primary schools, university academics and curriculum development experts worked together, under a series of Seed (Research and Development) Projects, to generate useful knowledge and experiences in the context of learning and teaching for other schools' reference. Among these projects, the Chinese Language and English Language projects had an obvious impact on students' reading habits and communication skills. A range of learning and teaching resources was also developed to support the new curricula, including packages for reading and for catering to students' learning diversity, and electronic curriculum planners.

Through various advisory services, collaborative lesson preparation, and action research, schools were able to build up their curriculum reform capacity and adopt more effective practices to enhance school-based curriculum development, including more flexible time-tabling and curriculum continuity and assessment.

Enhancing the Capacity of Teachers

To ease the workload of teachers, the Government has provided schools with the Capacity Enhancement Grant starting from the 2000-01 school year. Schools can make use of the grant to employ additional staff or hire outside services so as to ease teachers' workload. The feedback from schools confirmed that the grant had helped ease the workload of teachers and had enhanced the effectiveness of teaching and learning. Approval was obtained from the Finance Committee of the Legislative Council in June to refine the rate structure of the grant with effect from the 2003-04 school year. The maximum provision to a school is $526,000 for a primary school with 24 or more classes or a special school with 19 or more classes, and $430,000 for a secondary school with 24 or more classes.

Professional Development

The Advisory Committee on Teacher Education and Qualifications released its report entitled *Towards A Learning Profession — The Teacher Competencies Framework and the Continuing Professional Development of Teachers* in November. The report was a landmark document that laid the foundation for professionalising the teaching force in Hong Kong. The Advisory Committee recommended, among other things, to institutionalise the practice of continuing professional development (CPD) among teachers. As an indicative target for teachers in a three-year trial period, teachers were encouraged to pursue 150 hours of CPD in meeting school needs and personal development goals. It was a major step forward in upgrading the quality of education and students' learning. It also gave due recognition to teachers who were already engaged in lifelong learning. To facilitate the planning and review of CPD by teachers and schools, the Advisory Committee also formulated a Generic Teacher Competencies Framework that builds upon a set of core professional values indicative of a teacher's level of professional maturity.

Quality Education Fund

To provide financial support for worthwhile initiatives in basic education, the Government established the Quality Education Fund in 1998 with an allocation of $5 billion. The projects funded include those for the furtherance of effective learning, all-round education, school-based management, education research, application of information technology in education and schemes that recognise excellence in the performance of schools. By year-end, the fund had made six rounds of grants amounting to $2.9 billion for 4 900 projects, and closed its call for the seventh round with about 800 applications. As a supporting measure for the education reform, the fund also promotes and disseminates good practices distilled from funded projects through various means such as experience-sharing sessions, briefings, seminars and project expositions.

Improvement in Assessment Mechanism

Basic Competency Assessments are being introduced at key stages of learning for Chinese, English and Mathematics. Under the Basic Competency Assessments, the Student Assessment helps teachers better understand the learning needs of students as well as the areas requiring improvement, so that timely assistance can be provided to enhance their learning effectiveness. The Territory (System) Assessment provides the Government and school management with useful information on students' standards at the levels of Primary 3, Primary 6 and Secondary 3 on a territory-wide and school basis.

In June, the Hong Kong Examination Assessment Authority introduced the computer-aided Student Assessment programme to all primary schools and connected it to the supportive learning and teaching materials through the Internet. Views were also collected from schools on the basic competencies which students were expected to attain for the three subjects of Chinese, English and Mathematics.

Increase in Post-secondary Opportunities

To upgrade Hong Kong's human capital to cope with the requirements of a knowledge-based economy, the Chief Executive announced in his 2000 Policy Address that 60 per cent of the 17-20 age group should have access to post-secondary education by the 2010-11 school year. To provide the impetus, the Government offers interest-free start-up loans, accreditation grants and land to providers of post-secondary education and new financial assistance for students. The overall post-secondary participation rate for the 17-20 age group has increased from 32 per cent in 2000-01 to 48 per cent in 2003-04.

Improvement in Language Education

The language policy of the Government is to enable students and the working population to be biliterate (in Chinese and English) and trilingual (in Cantonese, Putonghua and English).

In early 2001, the Standing Committee on Language Education and Research (SCOLAR) began a review of the language education policy in Hong Kong. The Standing Committee has reviewed academic and official literature on the subject, conducted school visits and held in-depth discussions with key stakeholders as well as carrying out a survey of students' motivation for language learning. In January, the Standing Committee issued a consultation document entitled *Action Plan to Raise Language Standards in Hong Kong*. A total of 193 submissions were received from education-related bodies, schools, tertiary institutions, political parties, and individual members of the public.

Having regard to the feedback received, the SCOLAR finalised and released its recommendations in June, and these were generally supported by the public.

Specifically, it recommended that basic competencies in Chinese and English expected of students, university graduates and working professionals should be specified, and that the Hong Kong Examinations and Assessment Authority should develop standards-referenced public examinations in Chinese and English for assessing Secondary 5 and Secondary 7 students from 2007 and 2009, respectively.

The Standing Committee also recommended that school management, teachers, parents, the mass media, and the Government should work together to create a more motivating language learning environment for students and working adults, and that all English Language and Putonghua teachers should meet the Language Proficiency Requirement within the time frame specified by the Government.

The Government has supported the Action Plan set out by the SCOLAR. Two key support measures are being implemented. An incentive grant scheme will be set up in the first quarter of 2004, to encourage serving Chinese and English Language teachers to pursue professional development and upgrade their qualifications. A Task Force on Language Support will also be formed to provide local schools with on-site and/or district-based professional support to enhance the curriculum development and pedagogical capability of the Chinese and English language panels.

International Recognition

In July, the findings of the Programme for International Student Assessment placed Hong Kong students first in mathematics, third in science and sixth in reading literacy among 43 economies. More importantly, the study found that students of different socio-economic backgrounds in Hong Kong have similar access to, and benefit from, the education system. The study sought to measure how well 15-year-old students performed when they approached the end of compulsory education. Tests and background questionnaires were administered to a large representative sample of students in each of the 43 participating economies. The results were a confidence booster to the educators and provided evidence-based data on the strengths of Hong Kong's education system.

Combating SARS

The Education and Manpower Bureau played the role of a leader, an adviser, as well as a partner with schools in combating SARS when the disease broke out early in the year. It was committed to ensuring that all schools had put in place an effective mechanism, with implementation strategies, to guard against the disease.

A Central Task Force on SARS was set up at the outset to facilitate the formulation of counter measures and to monitor the situation. The bureau worked in close collaboration with relevant government departments, in particular the Department of Health, in formulating a series of effective counter measures. These included requiring schools to report any cases of SARS, drawing up contingency plans for an emergency situation, disinfecting school premises, home confinement of affected persons, suspension and resumption of classes, and special holiday arrangements. Parents were also required to check their children's temperature before they left home for school.

To answer public enquiries, eight telephone hotlines were set up at the peak of the outbreak. A reporting mechanism was also put in place to enhance effective communication between the bureau, the schools and the Department of Health. Furthermore, to ensure that schools would maintain a state of heightened awareness at all times, a comprehensive *Handbook on Prevention of SARS in Schools* was compiled and uploaded to the bureau's website. This provided schools and parents a ready reference to all related anti-SARS measures as well as to guidelines on such aspects as environmental hygiene and personal hygiene and the need to keep school buses clean.

The bureau rendered a wide range of support and assistance to schools and students. Special funding was obtained to assist schools in taking all necessary precautionary measures against the spread of SARS such as the purchase of masks, ear thermometers and chlorine tablets. To facilitate self-learning by students at home during the period when classes were suspended, the bureau, in collaboration with various institutions and organisations, provided web-based self-access learning materials and programmes. In addition, to educate students in the context of the SARS outbreak, teaching kits were produced to enable students to heighten their awareness and strengthen their ability in crisis management as well as to enhance their commitment to the community. A set of guidance activities to help pupils to cope with the situation and build up a school culture against adversity was also provided. To enhance communication, meetings were held with school councils as well as the Committee on Home-School Co-operation and the federations of Parent-Teacher Associations to exchange views. Before classes resumed, briefings were also arranged to ensure schools and parents were prepared for the students' return.

The concerted efforts of schools, parents and the bureau proved effective: no students or staff members contracted SARS in the schools during the outbreak.

Major Challenges Ahead

Academic Structure Reform for Senior Secondary Education and Undergraduate Programmes

The Government will consult the community in 2004 on the three-year academic structure for senior secondary education and four-year undergraduate programmes, including the conditions, financing and development of supporting measures. The reform was recommended by the Education Commission in its *Review of the Academic Structure for Senior Secondary Education* and its *Interface with Higher Education Report* published in May. Its major objective is to remove the major constraints of the senior secondary and university curriculum, and address related problems in senior secondary education which at present is largely examination-oriented. The reform is expected to reinforce whole-person development and widen the knowledge base of students.

Review of the Medium of Instruction (MOI) and Secondary School Places Allocation (SSPA) System

To enable students to learn effectively without language barriers, the Government has adopted a MOI policy since the 1998-99 school year. Under this policy, schools are required to use the appropriate MOI having regard to student ability, teacher capability and language learning-support strategies and programmes for students. Since the appropriate MOI for most students is their mother tongue, 293 aided and government secondary schools have been using Chinese as the MOI for junior secondary classes. There are 112 secondary schools which adopt English as the MOI.

In 2000, the Education Commisison put forward recommendations to reform the SSPA system. With effect from the 2000-01 school year, the Academic Aptitude Test (AAT) was abolished and an interim SSPA mechanism introduced. The interim mechanism basically retains the various elements in the old SSPA system, except with the increase of the percentage of discretionary places from 10 per cent to 20 per cent, the abolition of the AAT and the reduction of the allocation bands from five to three. In mid-2003, the Education Commission set up a Working Group to review the interim SSPA mechanism and the existing MOI policy for secondary schools, with a view to recommending a long-term SPA mechanism and MOI arrangements, which are educationally sound and beneficial to students. Public consultation would be conducted in 2004 with a view to gauging the public's views on the issues.

Curriculum Reform

The Government is continuing with other aspects of the education reform, which include the curricula and teaching methods, and the assessment mechanism to help enhance learning and teaching effectiveness. On school curriculum reform, the Government is capitalising on past achievements in taking forward projects on curriculum planning, effective pedagogy and assessment. More resources in learning, teaching and assessment will be developed to support the primary and secondary curricula. For instance, the Curriculum Development Council will develop, in collaboration with the Hong Kong Examinations and Assessment Authority, combined Curriculum and Assessment Guides for more examination subjects to align assessment with curriculum, and learning with teaching. A pilot scheme of Career-Oriented Curriculum for senior secondary students is also under way. Its intention is to promote diversity in school curricula to meet the needs of students who would benefit from learning in areas with specific career orientation alongside more academic studies.

Overall Education Landscape

Education Commission

The Education Commission (EC) is responsible for advising the Government on the overall educational objectives and policies, and the priorities for implementation as well as coordinating the work of all other major education-related advisory bodies on the planning and development of education at all levels. Following the merger of the Education and Manpower Bureau and the Education Department, the EC and the Board of Education, which advised the department on educational matters, were merged in early 2003 to streamline the advisory structure. After the merger, the EC also advises the Government on implementation issues with important policy implications to ensure better synergy between policy formulation and implementation.

Early Childhood Education

In September 2003, 137 000 children were enrolled in 768 kindergartens. All of them are privately run.

The Government plays an important role in promoting the development of quality kindergarten education through various means. They include upgrading the qualifications of kindergarten principals and teachers; providing financial support to kindergartens in the form of rent reimbursement and a subsidy scheme to employ more qualified teachers without increasing kindergarten fees substantially; conducting quality assurance inspections and promoting, in the longer term, school self-evaluation and an external monitoring mechanism.

School Education

Free and universal basic education is provided for children aged six to 15 to enjoy six years of primary education plus three years of basic secondary education. Admission to Primary 1 in aided and government schools is through a centralised system, and at the end of Primary 6 all students are provided with secondary school places. Most secondary schools offer three-year basic and two-year senior secondary courses leading to the Hong Kong Certificate of Education Examination as well as a two-year sixth-form matriculation course leading to the Hong Kong Advanced Level Examination. All Secondary 3 students who are willing and able to continue with their study are given the opportunity to receive subsidised Secondary 4 education or vocational training. About one-third of Secondary 5 leavers may further their studies in subsidised Secondary 6 and 7 school places.

In September 2003, 418 300 children were enrolled in government and aided primary schools and 411 600 children in government and aided secondary schools. Government and aided school places made up about 90 per cent of the school places. To inject more diversity into the school system and give parents wider choices, the Government in 1999 introduced various measures to facilitate the development of Direct Subsidy Scheme (DSS) schools and non-profit-making private independent schools. These measures include allocating government-built school premises for operation of DSS schools, and allocating land at a nominal premium with a capital grant for construction of DSS/non-profit-making private independent schools. In September, there were 51 DSS schools, offering 4 per cent of the school places. A total of 10 more non-profit-making private independent schools are scheduled to commence operation in phases by 2007.

Fifty-five international schools and 15 schools operated by the English Schools Foundation were operating in Hong Kong in September. These schools form an important social infrastructure to maintain Hong Kong's status as an international business centre and a vibrant cosmopolitan city. They offer different non-local curricula, namely, American, Australian, British, Canadian, French, German-Swiss, International Baccalaureate, Japanese, Korean and Singaporean, and provide a total of 32 600 places.

Special Education

The Government's main policy objective is to integrate children with special educational needs into the community through coordinated efforts by non-governmental organisations with government support. In the 2003-04 school year, 117 mainstream schools adopted a whole-school approach to supporting about 700 students with special educational needs or with a mild disability. In addition, 62 special schools are operated for those with severe or multiple disabilities, of which 19 provided boarding facilities. Together, they provide 8 500 day places and over 1 000 boarding places. Fifteen special schools are also serving as resource centres providing professional and resource support for ordinary schools which have admitted students with special education needs.

In addition, the Government also provides support services for gifted students to develop their potential. For instance, there are relevant training courses for teachers and resource packages to support school-based gifted education.

155

Vocational Education

The Vocational Training Council (VTC) was established in 1982 to provide and promote a cost-effective and comprehensive system of vocational education and training for school leavers and adult learners to acquire skills and knowledge for lifelong learning and enhanced employability.

The VTC provides high quality and internationally recognised full-time pre-employment education and training courses, at various levels ranging from the craftsman level to higher diploma level, through its Hong Kong Institute of Education, VTC School of Business and Information Systems, training and development centres. It also operates industry-wide training schemes and a voluntary trade testing and certification scheme.

A self-funded Continuing Professional Development Centre has been set up to promote continuing professional education by providing short courses and organising professional examinations such as the Insurance Intermediaries Qualifying Examination and the Mandatory Provident Fund Schemes Examination.

Altogether, some 147 000 full-time and part-time places were available during 2003 for both school leavers and people in employment.

Technical Training

The Construction Industry Training Authority provides training for the construction industry. It operates three construction training centres as well as a management training centre, a trade testing centre and a safety training centre. The Authority is funded by a levy of 0.4 per cent on the value of all construction works exceeding $1 million. It offered a total of 4 264 full-time and 130 221 part-time training places in the 2003-04 training year. In addition, the Authority conducts trade tests for construction workers to assess the standards of skills achieved, and certification tests for operators of construction plants.

The Clothing Industry Training Authority provides training courses for the clothing and footwear industries. It is financed by a levy of 0.03 per cent on the Free-on-Board value of clothing and footwear items produced in and exported from Hong Kong. It operates two training centres to deliver both full-time and part-time courses at technician and craftsman levels. In 2003-04, the Authority provided training to 480 full-time and 5 570 part-time students.

Five skills centres, three run by the VTC and two by non-governmental organisations, prepare people with a disability for open employment or mainstream vocational education and technical training. Collectively, they provide 1 362 full-time places, 310 of them residential, for the 2003-04 training year.

Post-secondary Education

Many higher education institutions have responded positively to the Chief Executive's policy initiative to provide more post-secondary education opportunities to secondary school leavers by offering self-financing programmes.

In 2003-04, more than 120 accredited self-financing programmes are offered by 18 post-secondary institutions, providing some 12 000 full-time places at sub-degree level or above. These are in addition to some 9 500 publicly funded places at sub-degree level offered by the City University of Hong Kong, the Hong Kong Polytechnic

University, the Hong Kong Institute of Education, the VTC and the Hong Kong Academy for Performing Arts.

Higher Education

Hong Kong has 11 degree-awarding higher education institutions, eight of which are publicly funded through the University Grants Committee (UGC). The other three not funded by the UGC are the publicly funded Hong Kong Academy for Performing Arts, the self-financing Open University of Hong Kong and the Hong Kong Shue Yan College.

The UGC is appointed by the Chief Executive to advise on the development and funding of higher education and administer public grants to eight publicly funded higher education institutions. It comprises non-local academics, local academics and local professionals and businessmen. Civil servants staff its secretariat.

The UGC also plays a major role in quality assurance and promotion of excellence. Major initiatives include the Teaching and Learning Quality Process Reviews and Areas of Excellence scheme. The former enhances the institutions' awareness of the importance of teaching and learning quality, and the latter aims to identify existing areas of strength in the institutions and develop them further through concentration of efforts and resources.

Each of the eight higher education institutions funded through the UGC is an autonomous statutory body with its own ordinance and governing body. They are free to manage their own affairs within the parameters of the law. Seven of the eight are universities and the remaining one is a teacher education institution. They all have distinctive and complementary roles that reflect their varying origins, missions and the way they have responded to Hong Kong's complex and evolving needs. Following a comprehensive review of the higher education sector, the UGC will take a more strategic approach to the higher education system, by developing an interlocking but differentiated system whereby the whole higher education sector is viewed as one force in the regional and international arenas of higher education, with each institution fulfilling a unique role based on its strengths.

At present, 14 500 first-year first-degree places are available in institutions funded by the UGC, covering about 18 per cent of the 17-20 age group. On top of this, a further 30 per cent of people in the same age group have access to other local higher education opportunities (for example, sub-degree programmes and vocational training) or go to universities overseas. To enhance the global outlook of local students, the institutions are encouraged to enrol non-local undergraduates and taught postgraduates, who may number up to 4 per cent of the institutions' approved targets for publicly funded places. In view of the enthusiastic response to the institutions' enrolment campaigns, institutions are allowed to enrol an additional 4 per cent of non-local students using private funding with effect from 2005-06. As for research postgraduates, the institutions are no longer subject to any quota in enrolling non-local students.

Degrees up to doctorate level awarded locally are widely recognised by institutions of higher learning around the world. Academic standards are guaranteed by the institutions' appointment of external examiners from prominent overseas universities and colleges and the monitoring of teaching and learning quality assurance processes by the UGC. The Hong Kong Council for Academic Accreditation validates courses and programmes offered by higher education institutions that are not self-accrediting.

Adult Education

The Government commissioned school operators to run evening courses at primary to senior secondary levels for 6 073 adult learners in the 2003-04 school year. It also subvented a variety of adult education programmes operated by non-governmental organisations, offering a total of 17 124 places.

Project Yi Jin

The Government launched Project Yi Jin in October 2000 to provide an alternative route to expand the continuing education opportunities for secondary school leavers and adult learners. The programme aims to upgrade students' knowledge in biliteracy, trilingualism, and information technology application through combining academic pursuits with practical skills training. Successful completion of the programme will lead to a qualification comparable to five passes in the Hong Kong Certificate of Education Examination for employment and continuing education purposes. The programme is run by member institutions of the Federation for Continuing Education in Tertiary Institutions, and has both full-time and part-time modes. In the 2003-04 school year, over 3 600 full-time and part-time students enrolled in the programme.

Qualifications Framework

To improve the quality of the manpower through lifelong learning, the Government proposes to set up a qualifications framework (QF) and an associated quality assurance mechanism. In its simplest form, a QF is a hierarchy of qualifications organised into different levels. It will provide clear information on standards of courses and providers in the academic and vocational and continuing education sectors. With clear and flexible progression pathways, learners can draw up their own road maps to upgrade themselves and acquire higher qualifications. Given a transparent quality assurance mechanism and through the major stakeholders' participation in the process, qualifications in the QF will be given wide recognition.

The Government has consulted the public on the proposal and examined the feedback. It has also conducted a number of pilot studies on the framework. The Government proposes to develop the QF step by step with the advice of the Manpower Development Committee, which was set up in October 2002 to advise on policies for developing Hong Kong's human resources.

Regulatory Framework and Governance Structure

The Government's Role and Organisation

The Secretary for Education and Manpower, who heads the Education and Manpower Bureau of the Government Secretariat, formulates and reviews education policy, secures funds in the government budget, and oversees the effective implementation of educational programmes. The Permanent Secretary for Education and Manpower assists him in formulating, coordinating and implementing education policies with the support of the bureau. The bureau merged with the former Education Department in January, and had an establishment of 6 255 at year-end. The reorganisation has brought about better synergy between policy formulation and implementation, improved communication and enhanced efficiency.

Education Ordinance

School education services come under the Education Ordinance. School operators must comply with the provisions of the ordinance and the subsidiary legislation covering areas such as registration of schools, teachers and managers, health and safety requirements, fees and charges and teacher qualifications.

Vocational Training Council Ordinance

The Vocational Training Council Ordinance provides for the establishment, functions and management of the VTC, which is the main body responsible for vocational education and technical training. Its membership comprises representatives from the industry, commerce and service sectors, employee representatives and government officials.

Post-Secondary Colleges Ordinance

The Post-Secondary Colleges Ordinance covers institutions offering post-secondary courses. There are currently two approved post-secondary colleges registered under the ordinance, namely the Hong Kong Shue Yan College and the Caritas Francis Hsu College.

Non-local Higher and Professional Education (Regulation) Ordinance

The Non-local Higher and Professional Education (Regulation) Ordinance took effect in June 1997 to protect Hong Kong consumers by guarding against the marketing of substandard non-local courses conducted in Hong Kong.

Management of Schools and Tertiary Institutions

School-based Management

All public sector schools have started to implement school-based management (SBM) with effect from 2000. To facilitate schools' implementation of SBM, the Education and Manpower Bureau has streamlined administrative procedures, devolved more responsibilities and given greater flexibility to schools. In return, schools have to be more transparent and accountable for their performance and the use of public funds. Each school draws up its annual school plan, compiles a school report and a school profile for the information of parents and members of the public. Also, schools have put in place a staff appraisal system. The Education (Amendment) Bill 2002 on the school-based management governance framework provides for the participation of key stakeholders in schools' decision-making processes and the incorporation of school management committees. Once the bill is enacted, there would be a transition period before schools are required to comply with the requirements.

Quality Assurance Inspections

The implementation of SBM since 2000 has been accompanied by an increasing emphasis on internal school self-evaluation processes to assist schools to improve the quality of learning of students. The Quality Assurance Inspections (QAIs) conducted by the Education and Manpower Bureau provide an external impetus for schools to set priorities for improvement in the coming years. QAIs are being transformed into a new mode of external school review. By phases, all schools will be supported in their self-evaluation processes for sustained development, and in their self-assessment of performance relative to previous standards and the performance of other schools in

Hong Kong. The self-assessment will then be reviewed by an expert external review team once every four years. This process identifies areas in which the school does well and allows each school to set out its direction for improvement.

Governing Bodies of Tertiary Institutions

Each tertiary institution has its own structure of governance, set out in its ordinance. The structure includes a governing body (called the council or the court), a body to regulate academic affairs (called the senate or the academic board) and, in some cases, an executive body.

The Chief Executive of the HKSAR, in his capacity as Chancellor of the universities, is empowered by the ordinances to appoint the chairman of each governing body, as well as a prescribed number of members. This ensures a balanced distribution of members from the industrial, commercial and academic fields.

Curriculum Development

Curriculum Development Council

The Curriculum Development Council (CDC) is an advisory body that makes recommendations to the Government on all matters relating to school curriculum development from kindergarten to senior secondary forms. Its membership includes heads of schools, practising teachers, parents, employers, academics from tertiary institutions, professionals from related fields or related bodies, representatives from the Hong Kong Examinations and Assessment Authority and the Vocational Training Council, as well as officers from the Education and Manpower Bureau.

Curriculum

The school curriculum in Hong Kong is defined in terms of the five essential learning experiences, i.e. moral and civic education, intellectual development, community service, physical and aesthetic development and career-related experiences for lifelong learning and whole-person development of students. Henceforth, all students are entitled to the five learning experiences that correspond to ethics, intellect, physique, social skills and aesthetics.

In 2001, the CDC developed an open, coherent and flexible curriculum framework that enables students to meet the challenges of a knowledge-based society. The framework is composed of three interconnected components: Key Learning Areas[1], Generic Skills[2] and Values and Attitudes[3]. The Key Learning Areas serve as the major knowledge domain of subjects providing contexts for the development of generic skills and values and attitudes. By making use of the curriculum framework, schools are now offering their students a broad and balanced curriculum.

The school curriculum is sufficiently diversified, providing students at all levels with a variety of options to cater for their different aptitudes, abilities and learning needs.

---

[1] Existing subjects are grouped into eight Key Learning Areas: Chinese Language Education; English Language Education; Mathematics Education; Science Education; Technology Education; Personal, Social & Humanities Education; Arts Education; and Physical Education.

[2] Nine Generic Skills helping students to learn how to learn in the areas of collaboration, communication, critical thinking, creativity, information technology, numeracy, problem-solving, self-management, and study.

[3] For example: national identity, responsibility, perseverance, respect for others, commitment, trust, and modesty.

The orientation of the subjects under the relevant key learning areas could be academic, social, practical and/or vocational at the appropriate level of schooling.

Information Technology in Education

The Government launched the Five-year Strategy on Information Technology (IT) in Education in 1998 to enhance students' access to IT and the Internet, provide training and support for all teachers, use IT to support teaching in the school curriculum, and foster a community-wide culture that helps promote IT in education. By the end of 2003, all schools had been provided with the necessary IT infrastructure and had broadband connection to the Internet, with over 60 per cent of them having fibre access and enjoying 10 to 100 megabytes-per-second bandwidth. By August, all teachers had completed IT training at different levels. Professional support for schools in the application of IT in education had been strengthened.

To support primary schools in implementing IT learning targets set in the curriculum, a computer awareness programme has been developed. The Curriculum Reform has reinforced the role of IT as a tool to support the reform measures. In the past years, the Education and Manpower Bureau assumed the dual role of forerunner and facilitator in the production of curriculum resources for IT education.

Supported by the Quality Education Fund, the Hong Kong Education City (HKEdCity) was launched in August 2000 to promote quality education and IT for lifelong and life-wide learning. It quickly became one of the most popular education portals in Hong Kong with over 1.3 million registered users and an average daily hit rate reaching about three million. The HKEdCity was corporatised in 2002 and continues to receive support from the Government to develop into an e-learning and e-business platform for teachers, parents and students. In 2003, the HKEdCity improved its IT infrastructure and search engine. It also continued to build partnerships with various entities and improve its web services.

During the year, expositions, activities and competitions continued to be held to promote community participation in the use of IT in education. Tertiary institutions conducted various studies to evaluate the pedagogical and other impacts of IT in education. The Government is reviewing the overall effectiveness of the first five-year strategy and mapping out the direction of the next five-year strategy.

Language Education

The Standing Committee on Language Education and Research (SCOLAR) was set up in 1996 to advise the Government on language education issues in general. The Standing Committee identifies research and development projects necessary for the enhancement of language proficiency, and advises the Trustee of the Language Fund on the policy and procedures governing the operation of the fund, which was set up in 1994. By year-end, the Language Fund had disbursed about $756.8 million for 283 approved projects aimed at enhancing the language proficiency of the population. These language learning, public education, resource development, teacher training and research projects are conducted by a range of organisations, including local tertiary institutions, post-secondary colleges, schools, educational and professional bodies and government departments.

Native-speaking English Teacher Scheme

The Native-speaking English Teacher (NET) Scheme has been implemented in all public sector secondary schools since 1998. It was extended to government-funded primary schools in 2002. In addition to teaching, NETs also help change teaching practices by working with local English teachers to make the learning of English more interesting. At present, about 470 NETs are serving in secondary schools, and some 310 in primary schools. Primary schools that were not allocated a NET are provided with a grant for hiring native-speaking English Language Teaching Assistants.

Teachers' Professional Development

The Advisory Committee on Teacher Education and Qualifications (ACTEQ) will continue with its comprehensive review of teacher education to enhance the overall standard and professionalism of the teaching force in Hong Kong. Working in close collaboration with the stakeholders through specific task forces, the ACTEQ will study the changing demands on teachers in the context of the education reform; explore with various teacher education institutions the ways to enrich the initial teacher education curriculum; strengthen induction support for beginning teachers and work to sustain the momentum for teachers' and principals' continuing professional development.

Principals' Professional Development

To better equip and support principals in their work, the Government has organised a wide range of professional development programmes for serving and newly appointed principals, vice principals and senior teachers aspiring to become principals. To systematically address the diverse maturity and developmental needs of principals at various career junctures, the Government has introduced a professional development framework for principals after thorough consultation with the education sector. All serving principals are required to undertake 50 hours of continuing professional development every year, adding up to a minimum of 150 hours in a three-year cycle so as to set a good role model for teachers in pursuing lifelong learning. From the 2004-05 school year, persons aspiring to become principals will need to attain the Certification of Principalship before they could be considered for appointment to principals.

Hong Kong Teachers' Centre

The Hong Kong Teachers' Centre (HKTC) was set up in 1989 to promote professionalism and a sense of unity among teachers. Working either independently or in collaboration with other educational bodies, the HKTC organised 1 260 professional or personal development activities for 75 000 participants to promote the curriculum reform, quality teaching and learning. It also disseminates information on current educational issues by distributing newsletters and other resource materials to teachers. It has also taken various measures to enhance professional exchanges and experience sharing among teachers, including the organisation of an educational conference annually.

Council on Professional Conduct in Education

The Council on Professional Conduct in Education was set up in 1994 to enhance teachers' professionalism. With a composition of 23 elected members from schools/educational organisations and three members nominated by the Permanent

Secretary for Education and Manpower, it advises the Permanent Secretary on matters relating to professional conduct in education. It also draws up operational criteria defining the conduct expected of an educator and advises, where necessary, on cases of dispute or alleged professional misconduct.

Student Finance

To ensure that no students are deprived of education for lack of financial means, the Student Financial Assistance Agency (SFAA) provides financial assistance to needy students. Subject to a means test, the assistance available takes various forms such as fee remissions, grants and/or low-interest loans for pre-primary to tertiary education. The agency also administers non-means tested schemes of assistance and privately funded scholarships awarded on the basis of academic merit.

Means-tested Financial Assistance

Kindergarten pupils receive assistance in paying tuition fees up to the weighted average of the fees charged by non-profit-making kindergartens or the actual fee, whichever is the less. In the 2002-03 school year, 62 609 pupils were granted fee remission totalling $512.1 million.

Assistance for needy primary and secondary school students takes the form of grants for the purchase of textbooks, subsidies for home-school travel and remission of tuition fees for those studying at Secondary 4 to 7 in public sector schools. In the 2002-03 school year, $505.2 million was provided to 386 019 students to purchase essential textbooks. A further $336.6 million was disbursed for travel subsidies to 208 313 students. In addition, 97 115 Secondary 4 to 7 students had their tuition fees waived, either fully or by one half. For students taking the Hong Kong Certificate of Education Examination and the Hong Kong Advanced Level Examination, 12 277 had their examination fees paid on their behalf at a cost of $12.7 million.

At the post-secondary and tertiary level, grants, low-interest loans and travel subsidies are made available to needy, full-time students pursuing eligible courses at UGC-funded institutions, the Hong Kong Institute of Vocational Education of the VTC, the Prince Philip Dental Hospital and the Hong Kong Academy for Performing Arts. In the 2002-03 academic year, $880.1 million in grants and $525.1 million in loans were provided to 35 694 students of these institutions. For eligible persons pursuing accredited, self-financing post-secondary education programmes leading to a sub-degree qualification, the means-tested assistance is in the form of a grant or a loan to cover tuition fees. In the 2002-03 academic year, $51.4 million in grants and $50.9 million in loans were provided to 3 547 such students. In addition, 441 full-time students of the Hong Kong Shue Yan College were provided $3.1 million in grants and $7.1 million in loans. Travel subsidies totalling $102.2 million were also provided to 35 768 students of the above institutions.

Non-means Tested Financial Assistance

Financial assistance for meeting tuition fee payments and living expenses, as appropriate, may also take the form of non-means tested loans. These loans are interest-bearing on the basis of no-gain no-loss to the Government. Access to these loans is open to any person pursuing eligible full-time or part-time publicly funded or self-financing local award-bearing programmes as well as professional or continuing education courses provided in Hong Kong by registered schools, non-local universities and recognised training bodies. In the 2002-03 academic year, 23 372 persons obtained non-means tested loans amounting to $800.2 million.

Scholarships and Other Assistance Schemes

The SFAA administers many privately funded scholarships and assistance schemes for school students. Scholarships are mainly merit-based and are provided for both local studies and studies at overseas institutions.

Tuition Fee Reimbursement for Project Yi Jin (PYJ) Students

The Government provides a 30 per cent reimbursement of tuition fees to PYJ students who have successfully completed a module. Starting from the 2002-03 school year, needy students who pass a means test will be eligible for reimbursement of the tuition fees paid for each module that has been completed satisfactorily.

Continuing Education Fund

A $5 billion Continuing Education Fund was launched in June 2002 to subsidise adults with learning aspirations to pursue continuing education and training courses in specified sectors. Eligible applicants are reimbursed 80 per cent of their fees, up to $10,000, on successful completion of a reimbursable course or module forming part of the course. With effect from September 2003, the eligibility of the fund has been relaxed to include degree holders. Over 70 000 applications had been received by the end of 2003.

Community's Participation in Education

Home-school Cooperation

Promotion of home-school cooperation is a vital element in quality education. With the continued efforts of the Committee on Home-School Co-operation set up in 1993 on the recommendation of the Education Commission, the number of Parent-Teacher Associations had increased to about 1 451 in December. 'Deepening home-school cooperation, propelling education betterment' was the theme in 2003 for the purpose of enhancing home-school cooperation and school education.

In June 2001, $50 million was set aside to strengthen parent education and to encourage parents to participate in educational affairs. By December 2003, about 2 300 applications for funding support had been approved. Education programme materials for parents, featuring children's physical, psychological and intellectual development, have been developed and distributed. About 300 parent education organisers and 300 peer counsellors had attended relevant training courses by year-end.

Professional Bodies' Involvement as Advisers to Schools

The Government supports business involvement in schools to enable students to have an early understanding of the business world. Under the 'School-Company Partnership' programme organised by the Young Entrepreneurs Development Council, a non-profit-making organisation, 'ambassadors' from the participating companies work with their partner school in providing career talks, entrepreneur workshops and business case studies for the students. The programme introduces entrepreneurship to youngsters at the early stage of career planning and provides them with an insight into the business world.

A similar programme is offered to senior secondary students by the Junior Achievement Hong Kong (JAHK), another non-profit-making organisation. With the assistance of volunteers from the business sector, the JAHK organises sharing sessions, trade fairs and workshops to provide students with hands-on business learning experience.

Committee on the Promotion of Civic Education

The Committee on Promotion of Civic Education was set up in 1986 for the purpose of advising on matters relating to promoting civic education, as well as implementing activities in conjunction with the Government and concerned parties in promoting civic education outside schools with a view to enhancing civic awareness and civic responsibility in all sectors of the community.

In 2003, the committee focused its efforts in promoting good citizenship, civic responsibilities, building a caring and harmonious society, family cohesiveness, volunteer services, respect for human rights and the rule of law, as well as better understanding of Chinese culture and heritage and the Basic Law.

The committee launched a series of television animation programmes and a website to promote various civic education themes. Other promotional activities included telephone hotline stories, special features in newspapers and an interactive drama on the Basic Law. Civic education reference materials including newsletters for young school children, a comic series on civic education, a magazine produced by secondary students and a 2004 calendar on good citizenship were produced during the year.

In response to the SARS outbreak, the committee produced a number of Announcements in the Public Interest (APIs) to promote civic responsibility in maintaining community hygiene and published a book entitled *You light up my life — a record of SARS outbreak in Hong Kong* to sustain the resilience, vigilance and unity shown by Hong Kong people in fighting the disease.

The committee continued to implement the Community Participation Scheme to encourage community organisations to arrange civic education activities at the district level.

In late 2003, the committee reviewed its role and functions, in conjunction with the Government, in the light of latest community developments. As a result, it decided to strengthen its strategic planning and research work; to focus more efforts in promoting civic responsibilities targeting young adults and the working population; to revamp the Community Participation Scheme; as well as to enhance collaboration with district-based civic education committees, the education sectors, the media and professionals in its promotional efforts.

Commission on Youth

The Commission on Youth was established in 1990. Its main objectives are to advise on matters pertaining to youth, initiate studies and research, promote cooperation and improvement in the provision of youth services and serve as a focal point of contact with other international youth organisations regarding exchange programmes. The Government has been working closely with the commission in achieving these objectives.

Expressing concern about young people who were unemployed and unable to pursue further studies, the Chief Executive asked the commission in July 2002 to develop a plan to provide the young people with pluralistic options in terms of both training and employment opportunities. The commission submitted its final report to the Chief Executive in March.

During the year, the commission organised the third Youth Summit with the objective of exploring ways to enhance the social participation of young people in Hong Kong. Youth delegates from Shanghai, Singapore, Seoul and Phnom Penh were also invited to attend the event. The proposals that arose from the Youth Summit were subsequently forwarded to the commission, the Government, and other concerned parties for consideration.

The commission also published the report *Youth in Hong Kong — A Statistical Profile 2002*, with commentary based on statistical data, which provided broad and useful references on six youth-related issues: poverty, substance abuse, unemployment, human capital, cultural capital and social capital.

The commission launched a first-ever benchmarking survey of civic engagement and social networks of youth in Hong Kong. This would establish a baseline for future studies and surveys on this subject, and develop a set of useful indicators for evaluating youth services.

The commission continued to implement youth development programmes that seek to realise the full potential of young people. These included the International Youth Exchange Programme that aimed at broadening the horizon and international perspective of young people. In 2003, four groups comprising 67 youth delegates visited Japan (twice), Britain and Ireland under the programme. The commission also received 22 young people from Britain and Ireland making return visits to Hong Kong.

In addition, the commission continued to implement three funding schemes to encourage more youth groups and community organisations to participate in community-based projects. The Youth Leadership Training Funding Scheme aims to sponsor non-governmental organisations in organising leadership training programmes for youth. The Community Participation Scheme for Organising Study Tours to the Mainland enables young people to cultivate a sense of belonging among themselves and enhances their understanding of the history and culture of China. The Youth Community Service Funding Scheme encourages more young people to serve the community through voluntary work. In 2003, the commission sponsored 162 leadership training programmes, 205 study tours to the Mainland and 137 projects for voluntary work.

The Charter for Youth enunciates principles and ideals in youth development. To encourage more youth organisations and individuals to subscribe to the Charter, the commission continued to promote it through broadcasting an API in 2003.

Home Pages

Education and Manpower Bureau: http://www.emb.gov.hk
Home Affairs Bureau: http://www.hab.gov.hk

CHAPTER 8

Health

Life expectancy at birth is projected to reach 82 for men and 88 for women in 2031, one of the longest in the world. This is a remarkable achievement for Hong Kong's health care services. The Government will continue to provide affordable lifelong holistic care to each individual and strive to further improve the health status of the community.

ONE of the cornerstones of the Government's health care policies is that no one should be denied adequate medical treatment through lack of means. The public health care sector provides a range of services and facilities to meet the health care needs of the community.

Health of the Community

Hong Kong's health indices compare favourably with those of most developed countries. The infant mortality rate, one of the most important indicators of health, has been declining over the past two decades and reached as low as 2.3 per thousand live births in 2003. The maternal mortality ratio has remained low for the past two decades. In 2003, there were only two cases of maternal death reported, giving a maternal mortality ratio of 4.2 per hundred thousand live births. Longevity has also improved significantly for Hong Kong people over the years. On average, a baby boy born in 2003 could expect to live 78.6 years and a baby girl 84.3 years. Life expectancy at birth is projected to reach 82 for men and 88 for women in 2031.

Organisational Framework

The Health, Welfare and Food Bureau is responsible for, among other matters, the policy formulation and resource allocation for health in Hong Kong. It also oversees implementation of policies to protect and promote public health, to provide comprehensive and lifelong holistic care to each citizen, and to ensure that no one is denied adequate medical treatment due to lack of means.

The Department of Health is the Government's health adviser and agency to execute health care policies and statutory functions. It safeguards the community's health through a range of promotional, preventive, curative and rehabilitative services. It also works with the private sector and teaching institutions to protect public health.

The Hospital Authority is a statutory body established in 1990 under the Hospital Authority Ordinance to manage all public hospitals. It provides medical treatment and rehabilitation services to patients through hospitals, general out-patient clinics, specialist clinics and outreaching services.

There were 33 994 hospital beds in Hong Kong in 2003, representing 5.0 beds per thousand population: 28 007 beds in hospitals run by the Hospital Authority, 2 902 in private hospitals, 2 352 in nursing homes and 733 in correctional institutions.

Primary Health Care Services

Family Health

The Family Health Service of the Department of Health provides a comprehensive range of health promotion and disease prevention services for children from birth to five years and women aged 64 or below. The service operates through 50 Maternal and Child Health Centres (MCHCs) and three Woman Health Centres (WHCs). Anticipatory guidance on child-care and parenting are provided for parents and care-givers to bring up healthy and well-adjusted children. Immunisation, health assessment and developmental surveillance services are offered to children at MCHCs. Antenatal, postnatal and family planning services are provided for women of child-bearing age. About 44 per cent of expectant mothers and 94 per cent of newborns attended MCHCs in 2003. The Woman Health Service is available in the three WHCs and 10 MCHCs, providing health education, counselling and appropriate screening service to women aged 64 or below.

The government-subvented Family Planning Association of Hong Kong runs eight clinics, three youth health care centres, a mobile clinic, a mobile library, a reference library and seven women's clubs. The services encompass fertility regulation, women's health check-up, pre-marital and pre-pregnancy preparation, menopause service, subfertility service, youth counselling and men's health check-up. A Cervical Disease Clinic was opened in 2003. The association also offers family life education and sexuality education, and organises outreaching activities and publicity campaigns to advocate and promote responsible parenthood, and sexual and reproductive health among individuals, families and the community.

Student Health

The Student Health Service of the Department of Health places emphasis on health promotion, disease prevention and continuity of care. Its 12 student health service centres and three special assessment centres provide health assessment, health education and individual health counselling to all primary and secondary school students. The Adolescent Health Programme was introduced in the 2002-03 school year to promote psychosocial health in secondary schools. School health inspectors visit schools regularly regarding environmental hygiene and sanitation. School health officers and nurses advise on the control of communicable diseases and organise immunisation campaigns.

Elderly Health

The Department of Health provides Elderly Health Services through 18 elderly health centres and 18 visiting health teams to enhance primary health care for the elderly, improve their self-care ability, encourage healthy living and strengthen family support so as to minimise illness and disability. Elderly health centres provide an integrated health service including health assessment, physical check-up, counselling, curative treatment, and health education to people aged 65 and above. Visiting health teams reach into the community and residential care settings to conduct health promotion activities for the elderly and to provide training to carers to enhance their health knowledge and skills in caring for the elderly.

Clinics

The Department of Health operates 20 methadone clinics, 19 tuberculosis and chest clinics, 10 social hygiene clinics, five dermatology clinics, three clinical genetic clinics, seven child assessment centres and other clinic services. About 10 million visits to clinics were recorded in 2003. During the year, 59 general out-patient clinics operated by the department were transferred to the Hospital Authority to enhance integration of primary and specialist care.

Apart from public service facilities, members of the community may seek medical treatment from the private sector, which includes medical practitioners working in private practices and 178 clinics registered under the Medical Clinics Ordinance.

Dental Health

Preventive services are delivered through the School Dental Care Service of the Department of Health which provides annual dental examination and basic dental care to about 436 000 children annually. A 24-hour interactive voice response system at the telephone hotline provides voice and fax information on the service and on oral health. The public can also visit the School Dental Care Service home page *(http://www.schooldental.gov.hk)* for updated information. The Department of Health monitors the level of fluoridation in the communal water supply in order to reduce dental decay among the population.

Specialist oral health care services are provided to hospital patients and those with special oral health needs. In addition, there are 11 designated dental clinics which provide emergency dental service to the public.

Hospital and Development Programmes

Demand for hospital services remained high in 2003. There were 739 000 discharges, 5 648 000 specialist out-patient attendances and 4 348 000 general out-patient attendances. Accident and emergency departments of major public hospitals had 1 816 000 attendances, or 4 962 per day.

The international trend has been to focus on the development of ambulatory and community care programmes. In line with this development, starting from 2001-02 the allocation of public funding for public hospital services has been changed from the facility-based approach to a population-based approach so as to encourage the mobilisation of resources from institutions to community settings. The new funding arrangement has facilitated the further development of the Hospital Authority's ambulatory and community outreach programmes.

In 2003, the Hospital Authority continued to step up training for family physicians, community paediatricians, community physicians, general practitioners and community allied health practitioners to support development of the community mode of health care delivery. It introduced a Visiting Medical Officer Scheme for residential care homes for the elderly to improve the quality of care and to reduce hospital admission for elders. It also rolled out a number of pilot schemes, such as the community allied health services schemes and the community drug compliance and counselling service, to enhance the level of care in the community setting. In order to strengthen its ambulatory services, the Hospital Authority is in the process of remodelling the Tang Shiu Kin Hospital into an ambulatory care centre, which is due for completion in late 2004.

Projects in the hospital development programme progressed satisfactorily. Phase I redevelopment of both the Caritas Medical Centre and the Kowloon Hospital was completed. Several other hospitals were undergoing redevelopment or major refurbishment/remodelling.

Health Promotion

Health Promotion Programmes

Central Health Education Unit

The Central Health Education Unit of the Department of Health continued to take a leading role in providing the direction and health education resources to promote the health of the people. The unit comprises experts in different disciplines to facilitate the provision of knowledge-based, needs-driven and effective health promotion.

The unit organised a variety of health promotion activities in 2003, involving all levels of the local community as well as international organisations. These activities included the Healthy Exercise for All Campaign, the World Health Organisation Technical Meeting on Evidence of Health Promotion Effectiveness, and health campaigns to observe the World Health Day, World No Tobacco Day and World Breastfeeding Week.

The unit also recognises the importance of research and evaluation in health promotion. In 2003, the unit conducted population surveys to assess the public's awareness of the anti-SARS (Severe Acute Respiratory Syndrome) campaign and the region-wide anti-dengue fever campaign, and also their knowledge, attitudes and practice regarding recommended preventive measures. A randomised controlled trial to examine the efficacy of exercise prescription in the primary health care settings in Hong Kong was completed. Another study was also undertaken to examine the feasibility and efficacy of a campaign to promote stair climbing in public housing estates in Hong Kong.

Oral Health Education Unit

Educational and promotional activities are organised throughout the year by the Oral Health Education Unit of the Department of Health to enhance the community's general level of oral health awareness. These activities include outreaching programmes delivered through the 'Oral Health Education Bus', and target-specific programmes delivered through MCHCs, kindergartens and pre-school centres to more than 193 000 pre-schoolers every year. Information on oral health education is accessible to the public through the Oral Health Education home page, *http://www.toothclub.gov.hk*, and the 24-hour interactive Oral Health Education telephone hotline.

For the first time, Hong Kong held a 'Love Teeth Day' on September 20 to coincide with the annual 'National Love Teeth Day' organised by the Mainland authorities. Based on the findings of the Oral Health Survey Report published by the Department of Health in 2002, the gum health of the community gives cause for concern. Hence, the focus of the 2003-04 campaign is on the promotion of healthy gums.

Smoking and Health

Tobacco Control Office

The Tobacco Control Office was set up in 2001 under the Department of Health to coordinate the Government's tobacco control efforts and to promote a smoke-free culture in Hong Kong through intersectoral collaboration and community mobilisation.

Recognising the complexity of tobacco control issues, the office has adopted a multi-pronged approach to achieve its goals. One of the priority areas is to assist managers and staff working in statutory no-smoking areas to comply with and enforce the Smoking (Public Health) Ordinance. In 2003, the Tobacco Control Office organised 114 workshops for 2 078 venue management staff of no-smoking areas. In addition, 444 restaurants and 78 shopping malls were visited by the officers of the Tobacco Control Office and the legal requirements were explained to managers of these no-smoking areas.

Under the ordinance, tobacco advertisements are prohibited in printed publications distributed in Hong Kong. The office screened 2 417 issues of printed publications and issued 66 warning letters concerning tobacco advertisements during the year. The office also organises health education activities by itself or in collaboration with other organisations to increase public awareness of the harmful effects of tobacco and second-hand smoke.

Hong Kong Council on Smoking and Health

The Hong Kong Council on Smoking and Health is an independent statutory body, established in 1987 to acquire and disseminate information on the hazards of using tobacco products, and to advise the Government on matters related to smoking, passive smoking and health.

During the year, the council conducted publicity and community involvement campaigns with particular emphasis on discouraging smoking in public and in workplaces. The council also continued its school health education programmes. In addition to 139 health talks delivered to primary and secondary schools, the council arranged a tour of a newly developed interactive education drama in 95 primary schools. The council also operates a telephone hotline to receive enquiries, suggestions and complaints from members of the public on matters related to smoking and health.

Disease Prevention and Control

Non-communicable Diseases

Health problems in Hong Kong are mostly associated with lifestyle-related chronic degenerative diseases. Among the leading causes of death, cancers, diseases of heart and cerebrovascular diseases together accounted for about 56 per cent of all deaths during the year. These diseases affect mainly elderly people and will continue to dominate the mortality statistics as the population ages.

In 2003, cancers were the top killer in Hong Kong and claimed more than 10 000 lives. A Cancer Coordinating Committee has been established to formulate comprehensive strategic plans and make recommendations for the effective prevention and control of cancer in Hong Kong.

To reduce the number of women developing and dying from cervical cancer, the Department of Health, in collaboration with other health care providers, has been planning for the introduction of a Cervical Screening Programme in 2004. It is recommended that women aged 25 to 64 years receive three-yearly cervical smears following two consecutive yearly negative smears. In 2003, a Cervical Screening Information System was under development by the department to collect and analyse data on cervical smears.

Communicable Diseases

Severe Acute Respiratory Syndrome (SARS)

In early 2003, infections caused by a previously unknown coronavirus broke out in Hong Kong. The disease was later named as SARS by the World Health Organisation (WHO). It proved to be a major new threat to international public health. The epidemic in Hong Kong lasted for a period of three months and infected 1 755 individuals, 299 of whom died.

The Government put in place comprehensive public health measures to bring the epidemic under control. It declared SARS a statutory notifiable disease and conducted a comprehensive public education programme to heighten awareness of the SARS symptoms so that potential cases were taken to medical facilities as early as possible. The Government also stepped up health checks at boundary and immigration control points, through health declarations and temperature screening, to prevent SARS being spread by the travelling public.

Modern technology such as the online e-SARS database developed by the Hospital Authority and the Major Incident Investigation and Disaster Support System of the Hong Kong Police Force were utilised to provide timely contact tracing of SARS patients as well as to expand the scope of such tracing. To stop the spread of SARS in the community, the Director of Health also required the close contacts of suspected and confirmed SARS patients to undergo home confinement and medical surveillance for a maximum of 10 days.

The Government established a multi-disciplinary response team to carry out immediate investigation and undertake prompt remedial action in buildings where SARS cases were reported so as to minimise the risk of environmental transmission within the community.

Hospital infection control measures were heightened through giving health care staff training in infection control and providing staff with adequate protective gear. A region-wide cleansing and disinfection campaign was also launched in late March to clean up public places and to encourage all members of the community to clean their environment.

During the fight against SARS, the Government maintained close liaison with the WHO and other national authorities, and held daily press briefings to keep the local and international communities informed of the latest developments concerning the epidemic. It also improved the notification mechanism between Hong Kong and Guangdong Province and extended it from May to cover Macau.

With the concerted efforts of the community, the epidemic in Hong Kong, regarded by WHO as one of the hardest to contain because of the region's high population density and extensive cross-boundary travel, was successfully controlled. On June 23, the WHO removed Hong Kong from the list of areas with recent local transmission.

The Chief Secretary for Administration, appointed after the outbreak of SARS to head a newly formed environmental task force named Team Clean, distributing cleansing materials to a storekeeper in Central during a 'Territory-wide Cleansing Day' on April 19. *Left:* Mr Tsang being briefed on street cleanliness in the area.

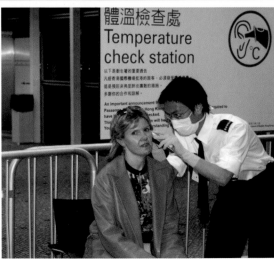

As part of anti-SARS measures, an Infrared Thermal Imaging System was installed at the Lo Wu Control Point to check that passengers travelling between Hong Kong and the Mainland did not have a fever. *Left:* checking the temperature of passengers at the airport.

Top right: primary school pupils washing their hands before class —
regular washing of hands was one of many preventive measures adopted
throughout the community after SARS struck. *Above:* residents
returning to a housing block that the authorities evacuated because of
the disease. *Far right:* during the outbreak, numerous events were held
to rally public morale such as this community function at which
hundreds of goodwill messages were displayed. *Right:* in November,
an exercise was held to test preparedness for any future outbreak.

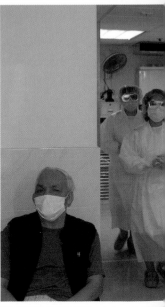

The World Health Organisation's Executive Director for Communicable Diseases, Dr David Heymann, giving a presentation on SARS in Hong Kong on June 15; and *(below right)* visiting the Amoy Gardens housing estate in Ngau Tau Kok where one block had to be evacuated. *Above right:* the WHO Director-General, Dr Gro Harlem Brundtland, speaking to reporters at the airport after inspecting quarantine and health control facilities there during a one-day visit to Hong Kong on June 19.

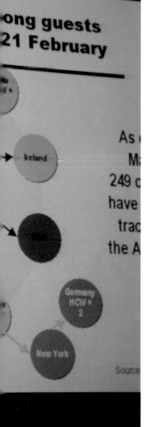

ong guests
21 February

Ireland

Germany
HCW +
2

New York

Children at a school in Tai Po celebrating finally being able to take off their anti-SARS face masks; showbusiness personality Kelly Chan, Hongkong Post's Philatelic Ambassador for 2003-04, helping to launch a 'Hello from Hong Kong' postcard campaign, signifying that the adversity had been overcome.

The epidemic highlighted the urgent need to review the capacity of the health care system, and to better prepare for any future outbreak. The Chief Executive of the HKSAR announced on May 28 the setting up of a SARS Expert Committee to conduct a review. Members of the Expert Committee were selected for their wide range of experience in their respective fields, which included health systems, public health, epidemiology and communicable disease control, medical expertise, and hospital management and operation.

The Expert Committee reviewed the work of the Government, including the Hospital Authority, in the management and the control of the outbreak. It examined and reviewed the capabilities and structure of the health care system in Hong Kong and the organisation and operation of the Department of Health and the Hospital Authority in the prevention and management of infectious diseases such as SARS. The Expert Committee also identified lessons to be learnt, and made recommendations on areas requiring improvements in order to better prepare the system for any future outbreak.

The Expert Committee released its report on October 2, and proposed a comprehensive set of improvement measures. The Government attaches much importance to full and timely implementation of these recommendations. In November, the Chief Executive appointed a Monitoring Committee to oversee the implementation of the recommendations. The Monitoring Committee will make periodic reports to the Chief Executive on the progress of implementation.

Other Communicable Diseases

Hong Kong now lists 28 statutory notifiable infectious diseases, including three quarantinable diseases, namely cholera, plague and yellow fever. During the year, 15 885 cases of notifiable infectious diseases were reported, of which 38.3 per cent were due to tuberculosis.

Children in Hong Kong are immunised against tuberculosis, hepatitis B, poliomyelitis, diphtheria, tetanus, pertussis, measles, mumps and rubella. Owing to high vaccine coverage, diseases such as diphtheria and poliomyelitis have been eradicated and the incidence of other vaccine-preventable infectious diseases among children is relatively low.

As at year-end, the cumulative number of HIV (human immunodeficiency virus) infection and AIDS (Acquired Immune Deficiency Syndrome) cases reported had exceeded 2 200 and 650, respectively. Each year, about 200 new cases of HIV infection are reported. Sexual transmission remained the most common mode of spread of the infection, though in recent years there has been growing concern over reports of HIV infection among injection drug users.

Centre for Health Protection

On May 5, the Chief Executive announced that the Administration had begun a study on establishing a Centre for Disease Control type of organisation in Hong Kong to strengthen its capacity to combat communicable diseases. This initiative was echoed in the SARS Expert Committee's report issued on October 2. The committee recommended, among other things, that a Centre for Health Protection (CHP) with responsibility, authority and accountability for prevention and control of communicable diseases be set up within the Government and its existing public health infrastructure.

The Administration has taken active steps to move forward the Chief Executive's undertaking and the Expert Committee's recommendations. An advisory committee chaired by the Permanent Secretary for Health, Welfare and Food and comprising health care professionals in the public and private sectors and academics from four local universities was formed in November to help establish the CHP. The committee was tasked to advise on the organisational framework and functions of the CHP and to monitor the progress of its development.

Health Regulatory Activities

Port Health

The Port Health Office of the Department of Health enforces measures in the Quarantine and Prevention of Disease Ordinance and the International Health Regulations to prevent the introduction of quarantinable diseases into Hong Kong by air, land or sea. No cases of plague or yellow fever were reported during the year.

Responding to the SARS outbreak, the Port Health Office has strengthened the control and preventive measures at entry control points since March 2003. Travellers, both entering and leaving Hong Kong, are required to declare their health status and have their body temperature screened. During the year, over 68 million and 74 million travellers were screened by health declarations and body temperature checking, respectively.

Radiation Health

The Radiation Health Unit of the Department of Health is the Government's adviser on radiation safety and protection. It advises the Government on the protection of public health in the event of a nuclear incident, on the management of radioactive materials and wastes, and the effects on health of radiation exposure. The unit also serves as the executive arm of the Radiation Board, which is the statutory authority set up under the Radiation Ordinance, to control the import, export, sale, possession and use of radioactive substances and irradiating apparatus. It safeguards public health against ionising radiation through licensing control and inspection of premises where radioactive substances or irradiating apparatuses are present. In addition, the unit conducts radiation monitoring measurements for occupationally exposed persons and maintains the radiation dosimetry metrology standards for environmental and protection level radiation dosimetry measurements for Hong Kong.

In 2003, the unit assessed and issued 8 375 licences and permits and provided monitoring service to 8 353 occupationally exposed persons. The average radiation exposure of occupationally exposed persons was 0.07 mSv against an annual statutory limit of 20.

Chinese Medicine

The Chinese Medicine Council of Hong Kong, established in September 1999, is responsible for devising and implementing regulatory measures for Chinese medicine.

Subsidiary legislation for the registration of Chinese medicine practitioners was enacted in June 2000. In 2003, the Chinese Medicine Council of Hong Kong conducted the Registration Assessment and the first Licensing Examination. By year-end, 4 738 and 3 227 Chinese medicine practitioners were registered and listed, respectively, with the Chinese Medicine Council of Hong Kong.

The subsidiary legislation on Chinese medicines was passed by the Legislative Council in January 2003. Applications for Chinese medicine trader licences and for registration of proprietary Chinese medicines have been open since May and December 2003, respectively.

Western Medicines

The regulation of Western medicines in Hong Kong is stipulated under the Pharmacy and Poisons Ordinance. Acting on the authority of the Pharmacy and Poisons Board, the Department of Health registers and approves the marketing of pharmaceutical products, issues licences to drug manufacturers, importers, wholesalers and retailers, and takes action against illegal sale of controlled drugs in collaboration with the Hong Kong Police Force. Legislative controls are also enforced on poisons, antibiotics and dangerous drugs.

During the year, 3 906 applications for registration of pharmaceutical products were approved. At year-end, there were 20 415 pharmaceutical products registered in Hong Kong.

Health Care Professionals

Under existing legislation, 12 types of health care professionals are required to be registered with their respective boards or councils before they are allowed to practice in Hong Kong. In December, the professionals registered with their respective boards and councils numbered: 11 016 doctors, 1 848 dentists, 4 738 Chinese medicine practitioners, 43 782 nurses (including registered and enrolled nurses), 4 791 midwives, 1 457 pharmacists, 67 chiropractors, 1 758 physiotherapists, 1 073 occupational therapists, 2 519 medical laboratory technologists, 1 921 optometrists and 1 551 radiographers.

Medical Charges

In the Health Care Reform Consultation Document published in December 2000, one of the strategic directions on health care financing was to revamp the fee structure of Hong Kong's public health care sector, so that the public subsidies could be targeted to areas of most need, and inappropriate use and misuse of services could be reduced.

Following a comprehensive review to examine how the relative priorities of services provided may be reflected in the subsidy level, the Administration announced its decision to revamp the fee structure of the public health care system in November 2002. All revised charges had taken effect from April 1, 2003. Following the fee restructuring, charges continue to be affordable to the public. Overall, the government subsidy still represents a high level of 96 per cent of costs.

It has been the Government's policy that no one will be denied adequate medical care due to lack of means. To ensure that this principle is upheld after the introduction of charges for accident and emergency service at public hospitals in November 2002, recipients of Comprehensive Social Security Assistance (CSSA) have been exempted from payment of the charges. In addition, an enhanced medical fee waiver mechanism has been implemented to enable vulnerable groups other than CSSA recipients, including low-income patients, chronically ill patients and elderly patients in economic hardship, to be granted a fee waiver for accident and emergency and other public medical services.

Training of Medical and Health Personnel

The University of Hong Kong and the Chinese University of Hong Kong provide basic training of doctors. They took in 141 and 140 medical students, respectively, in 2003. During the year, seven doctors holding professional qualifications obtained outside Hong Kong had passed the Licensing Examination conducted by the Medical Council of Hong Kong. Training in dentistry is available at the University of Hong Kong, which enrolled 40 dentists in 2003.

The Hong Kong Academy of Medicine is an independent statutory body with the authority to approve, assess and accredit specialist training within the medical and dental professions. Its 15 colleges conduct training and examinations to award specialist qualifications to qualifying candidates.

The University of Hong Kong, the Chinese University of Hong Kong, the Hong Kong Polytechnic University and the School of General Nursing of the Queen Elizabeth Hospital of the Hospital Authority provide basic training of Registered Nurses. The three universities recruited 385 nursing students into their four-year general nursing degree programmes in 2003. In addition, the Hong Kong Polytechnic University and the School of General Nursing of the Queen Elizabeth Hospital enrolled 280 nursing students into their three-year higher diploma nursing programmes. During the year, 37 nurses with professional nursing qualifications obtained outside Hong Kong passed the Licensing Examinations for Registered Nurses or Enrolled Nurses conducted by the Nursing Council of Hong Kong.

Government Laboratory

The Government Laboratory offers a comprehensive range of analytical and advisory services to support the Government in upholding its various commitments in the protection of public health.

In 2003, a total of 92 052 tests on a wide range of food samples were carried out for surveillance and for compliance with the statutory standards. The scope of analytical services for the testing of veterinary drug residues in food animal products and live food animals for surveillance and statutory purposes has been further extended to facilitate the second phase enforcement of the Public Health (Animals and Birds) (Chemical Residues) Regulation and Harmful Substances in Food Regulations. The Laboratory has also continued to participate actively in technological exchanges with Mainland counterparts with a view to strengthening technical capabilities in ensuring food safety and protecting public health.

The Laboratory has continued to provide a comprehensive analytical service to assure the quality of Western and Chinese medicines that constitute an indispensable part of the health care system. During the year, 40 129 tests were carried out on Western pharmaceutical products for compliance with the international or other acceptable standards in quality and safety; and 58 268 tests were made on proprietary Chinese medicines and herbal medicines for their heavy metal and pesticide residue content, and adulteration with Western drugs or controlled substances. In addition, the Laboratory undertook method development and research work pertaining to the examination of toxic Chinese herbal medicines and actively participated in the development of regulatory standards for commonly used Chinese herbal medicines.

The Laboratory sustained the year-round surveillance of tar and nicotine yield in cigarettes, with results published for public information and affirmation of the data declared by tobacco traders.

Auxiliary Medical Service

The Auxiliary Medical Service (AMS) is a government-financed volunteer organisation established under the Auxiliary Medical Service Ordinance. Its main role is to augment the regular medical, health and ambulance services during an emergency and to supplement these services in non-emergency situations. The AMS has an establishment of 4 418 volunteer members, who come from all walks of life. The Director of Health is the Commissioner of the AMS, and is responsible to the Chief Executive for the efficient operation of the service, which has an establishment of 100 civil servants.

Under the health surveillance programme drawn up to combat the SARS outbreak, the AMS assisted the Department of Health in screening the temperature of all inbound and outbound visitors and other travellers at the Hong Kong International Airport. This temperature screening service was subsequently extended to cover all visitors arriving at land and sea immigration control points, where on average 350 AMS members were deployed daily until mid-November. At the peak of the SARS outbreak, the AMS also mobilised members for duty at the medical stations set up in the Amoy Gardens private housing estate, where they carried out temperature checks on residents and also distributed SARS-related information. In addition, AMS members reinforced the staff at the four designated medical centres and the three isolation centres established under the mandatory medical surveillance programme for persons who had had close contact with SARS patients and the Amoy Garden residents who were required to undergo the 10-day period of quarantine.

During weekends and public holidays, the AMS continues to deploy a first-aid bicycle team on the 11-kilometre cycling track between Tai Wai and Tai Po, under the Volunteer Service Programme. These first-aid teams are able to treat most injured cyclists on the spot in minutes, making it unnecessary for injured persons to be taken to hospital by ambulance. First-aid bicycle teams are also on duty at a number of major events such as the annual Hong Kong Marathon as well as the Walk for Millions, the Trailwalker and other fund raising activities.

In other activities, the AMS assists the Education and Manpower Bureau in running the Youth Pre-employment Training Programme that encompasses various training modules such as basic first aid skills, physical fitness training and team building. In 2003, 14 courses were organised and 360 youngsters completed the training programme.

Home Pages

Health, Welfare and Food Bureau: http://www.hwfb.gov.hk
Department of Health: http://www.gov.hk/dh
Hospital Authority: http://www.ha.org.hk
Auxiliary Medical Service: http://www.gov.hk/ams

CHAPTER 9

Food Safety, Environmental Hygiene, Agriculture and Fisheries

Given Hong Kong's population density and the variety of food consumed here, ensuring food safety and a high standard of environmental hygiene and animal health is a major challenge. The Government is committed to meeting this challenge. It is also dedicated to helping the local agriculture and fisheries industries to enhance the safety and quality of their products so as to stay competitive.

IN the face of new challenges and potential hazards arising from the changing environment and the use of new technology, the Government has devoted much effort to ensuring that the food the community consumes is safe and that quality environmental hygiene and veterinary services are in place to provide a living environment comparable to other major international cities. It is also the Government's policy objective to facilitate the sustainable development of the agriculture, fisheries and aquaculture industries.

Organisational Framework

The Health, Welfare and Food Bureau is responsible for, among other matters, the policy formulation and resource allocation for food safety, environmental hygiene, animal health, and agriculture and fisheries. It also oversees implementation of policies to protect and promote food safety and animal health, to achieve a high standard of environmental hygiene, and to enhance the competitiveness of the agricultural and fisheries sectors.

The Food and Environmental Hygiene Department (FEHD) was set up on January 1, 2000, to serve the people of Hong Kong in the area of food safety and environmental hygiene.

The Agriculture, Fisheries and Conservation Department (AFCD) is responsible for implementing agricultural and fisheries policies, including the provision of infrastructural and technical support to facilitate the development of the two industries. It provides wholesale marketing facilities and animal disease diagnostic services, and administers agricultural and fisheries loans. The department is also the Government's adviser on veterinary services.

Public Cleansing Services

The FEHD has been providing effective and efficient public cleansing services, such as street cleansing services, waste collection and provision of public toilets.

The department provides manual street sweeping services in all urban and rural areas. The frequency of sweeping varies from once to eight times daily, depending on the need in each area.

Waste is collected daily throughout the year, except on Lunar New Year's Day when only major refuse collection points are opened for collection of domestic waste and junk. The department has 259 refuse collection vehicles for collecting domestic waste and junk. In 2003, about 5 899 tonnes of domestic waste were collected every day.

To meet growing public expectations, the department has taken various measures to improve public toilet facilities, including stationing cleaners in toilets with high usage rates. Under a regular refurbishment programme, 51 public toilets were renovated during the year.

Being responsible for the provision of public cleansing and environmental hygiene services, the FEHD was directly involved in the wide-ranging actions taken to combat SARS. In addition to enhancing street cleansing and washing services in order to provide a cleaner and more hygienic city environment, the department, as a member of the Multi-disciplinary Response Team, played a key role in the proactive investigation of SARS cases. The department carried out extensive pest control duties and investigations, demonstrated effective disinfection methods to all households in which SARS had occurred, and inspected the cleanliness of common areas, such as lift lobbies, in SARS-affected buildings. The FEHD also disinfected the 264 residential units in an evacuated block, and assisted in providing emergency cleansing and waste collection services at the designated isolation centres.

In collaboration with the Information Services Department, the Housing Department and the Home Affairs Department, the FEHD distributed to all residential units and management agencies leaflets that gave guidelines on household disinfection and on inspection and disinfection of the common areas in residential buildings.

To demonstrate the determination of the Government and the community in combating SARS, a community participation event — a 'Territory-wide Cleansing Day' organised by the Home Affairs Department — was held on April 19 and 20.

Working in collaboration with other departments and participating communities, the FEHD provided cleansing services at streets, public places, rear lanes and environmental hygiene 'black spots'; inspected buildings including old tenements; disseminated health education messages on the importance of environmental hygiene; and took stringent enforcement action. It cleared 220 hygiene 'black spots', collected or removed about 160 tonnes of junk and refuse, inspected more than 3 300 buildings, issued over 300 statutory notices and administered some 800 verbal warnings.

Clean Hong Kong Programme

In an effort to improve environmental hygiene, the Government launched the Clean Hong Kong Programme in December 2000 to address Hong Kong's environmental hygiene conditions and to bring about improvements. The FEHD continued to take the leading role in the programme during the year.

179

After the outbreak of SARS, the Chief Executive appointed a special task force, called 'Team Clean', in May to develop a comprehensive strategy and formulate new means to improve the cleanliness of the living environment. The FEHD was involved in spearheading the implementation of a wide range of new environmental hygiene improvement measures. The department carried out measures such as enhancing cleansing and washing of public places, environmental 'black spots', private lanes and common areas of old tenement buildings; intensifying rodent and pest control work; and enhancing the collection of bagged refuse at on-street dumping spots.

In order to stamp out the irresponsible and unhygienic acts of littering and spitting, the Government proposed, and the Legislative Council approved, an increase in the fixed penalty against common cleanliness offences (that is, littering, spitting, unauthorised display of bills or posters and fouling of street by dog faeces) from $600 to $1,500, with effect from June 26, 2003, to enhance the deterrent effect of the legislation. All enforcement departments, including the FEHD, adopted a 'zero tolerance' approach in administering the law. By December 31, over 9 100 fixed penalty notices of $1,500 had been issued.

On the publicity and public education front, Clean Hong Kong messages were disseminated to the public through television and radio Announcements in the Public Interest (APIs), posters and banners, and advertisements on public transport and at large-scale publicity functions. Educational efforts were also directed at various target groups, for example tourists and road users. Clean Hong Kong messages were incorporated in school curricula, and extra-curricular activities and school talks were organised for over 30 000 students. In community involvement, community groups have been invited to organise activities to promote public awareness in keeping the environment clean.

The FEHD runs the Clean Hong Kong Funding Scheme, providing a maximum subsidy of $15,000 for each project. During the year, 93 organisations were allocated funds to arrange activities. District Councils and District Clean Hong Kong Committees also organised 280 district promotional, educational and physical clean-up activities. Moreover, 3 463 voluntary helpers were appointed Clean Hong Kong Ambassadors and District Hygiene Squad members to help disseminate the Clean Hong Kong message and monitor district hygiene conditions.

The multi-pronged approach of enhancing cleansing operations, enforcement action, public education and publicity, as well as community and district involvement, has brought about visible improvement in the overall cleanliness of Hong Kong.

Abatement of Sanitary Nuisances

Accumulation of refuse, choked or defective plumbing systems, water dripping from air-conditioners, and water seepage inside private premises are common sanitary nuisances. To tackle these problems, the FEHD issues statutory notices that require abatement of the nuisance. Prosecution will be initiated against those who fail to comply with the notice within a specified period. During the year, the department issued 3 387 statutory notices and initiated four prosecutions.

Pest Control

Prevention of vector-borne diseases is an important public health function carried out by the FEHD. The department constantly reviews the methodology used in pest control to enhance effectiveness and efficiency. Anti-rodent and anti-mosquito campaigns were mounted throughout Hong Kong during the year.

A surveillance programme has been put in place for monitoring the dengue fever vector, and taking prompt action to eliminate breeding sites. In September, mosquito control measures were strengthened immediately upon confirmation of a local dengue fever case in Yuen Long. The prompt response successfully controlled the disease without any spread.

Throughout the year, 24 372 construction sites and 64 491 village-type houses were inspected by anti-mosquito squads, and 48 496 mosquito breeding grounds were eliminated. The AFCD assisted with 7 015 inspections of livestock farms to seek out and eliminate mosquito breeding areas. The anti-mosquito efforts will continue in order to reduce the risk of dengue fever.

Cemeteries and Crematoria

As land is a limited resource in Hong Kong, it is the Government's policy to encourage cremation of the dead. Normally, human remains buried in public cemeteries have to be exhumed after six years and be either cremated or reinterred in an urn cemetery.

The FEHD operates six government crematoria and 11 public cemeteries, and oversees the management of 28 private cemeteries.

Food and Other Trade Licensing

The FEHD is the authority responsible for licensing food businesses and issuing permits for the sale of restricted foods including frozen confections, sushi and sashimi. It also issues licences to places of public entertainment such as theatres, cinemas and entertainment machine centres. In addition, it issues trade licences for commercial bathhouses and offensive trades as well as for private swimming pools. The FEHD also provides support to the Liquor Licensing Board, which is an independent statutory body constituted for the purpose of issuing liquor licences. Board members are appointed by the Chief Executive. The board meets about four times a month to consider applications.

During the year, the department received and processed 2 437 applications for food business licences, 864 for restricted food permits, 890 for places of public entertainment licences, 60 for other trade licences and 711 for liquor and club liquor licences.

Alfresco dining has been gaining in popularity in recent years. Since 2002, the FEHD has streamlined application procedures to provide a 'one-stop-shop' service to applicants. During the year, the department approved 47 applications.

From January, the department took up the responsibility for issuing karaoke establishment permits for karaoke establishments that are situated in premises that have a restaurant licence.

The FEHD also develops and puts forward new initiatives in consultation with the Legislative Council and the trade to further improve hygiene in food premises, and thereby enhance food safety. In February, the Public Health and Municipal Services (Amendment) Ordinance 2002 came into effect to speed up the closure of food premises that pose immediate health hazards or are being operated without licences. A total of six food premises were closed under these new provisions. Moreover, with

181

effect from November, the department put in place a new streamlined sanction system for issuing warning letters in cases where licensing conditions are breached. The FEHD is also formulating a loan scheme to provide financial assistance to operators of food premises so that they can improve kitchens, toilets and other facilities.

Food Safety and Labelling

The FEHD is tasked to ensure that the food available for human consumption is safe and properly labelled. It also aims to safeguard public health through the testing and control of live food animals.

Under the food surveillance programme, 54 451 samples were taken in 2003 for chemical, microbiological and/or radiological testing to ensure that food was fit for human consumption.

A total of 69 538 and 42 667 vehicles carrying food (vegetables and other food) and live food animals (pigs, cattle and poultry) were inspected at the Man Kam To Food Control Office and 235 620 blood and 65 687 urine and tissue samples were taken from food animals for testing for diseases and veterinary drug residues as prescribed by the law. The Government Laboratory provides a comprehensive range of analytical and advisory services to support the Government in upholding its commitments in protecting public health. During the year, a total of 92 052 tests on a wide range of food samples were carried out for surveillance and for compliance with the statutory standards. The Laboratory continued to participate in technological exchanges with its Mainland counterparts with a view to strengthening technical capabilities in ensuring food safety and protecting public health.

The Government proposes to implement a labelling system to ensure that the declaration of nutritional information is consistent across the range of prepackaged food on sale in Hong Kong and to protect consumers from false claims. The public, the food trade and other organisations were consulted on the labelling proposals in late 2003. The Government will take full account of the views received before finalising the details of the labelling requirements.

A regulatory impact assessment study was completed during the year to assess the possible economic impact of introducing a labelling scheme on prepackaged genetically modified (GM) food in Hong Kong. The study result was made available to the public. After considering the results of the study, the Government proposed to introduce a pre-market safety assessment to be supplemented by a voluntary labelling system for such GM food. The details of the pre-market safety assessment requirement and the proposed voluntary labelling guidelines will be drawn up for consultation in due course. Meanwhile, the department continues to provide the community with factual and unbiased information on GM food through a multitude of channels including its website, newsletters, teaching kits, and seminars for students and teachers.

Enhanced Measures Against Avian Influenza

Following the evaluation of a one-year trial programme on selected chicken farms, the AFCD implemented a region-wide H5 vaccination and surveillance programme for all chicken farms in Hong Kong in June as a supplementary measure against the recurrence of avian influenza. During the year, an agreement was reached with the Mainland authorities on the vaccination of chickens for export to Hong Kong to ensure similar levels of protection are provided to both imported Mainland chickens and locally produced chickens. By mid-January 2004, all birds available in the local market will have been vaccinated against H5 avian influenza. The need for continuous vaccination of chickens will be closely monitored.

During the year, the AFCD continued to upgrade the biosecurity standards at local farms to prevent the introduction of the virus there. By the end of April, 36 biosecurity measures had been implemented on all chicken farms. These included the requirements for farmers to install birdproofing facilities in their chicken sheds and disinfecting baths or other disinfecting equipment at their farm gates, segregate the chicken production area from the areas for delivery of feed and its storage, separate different batches of chickens, and designate special areas for loading chickens for transport to market. An additional measure requiring a 500-metre separation for new farms was also introduced. These measures are monitored regularly by the AFCD.

Since March, in order to reduce the virus load in retail markets, the FEHD has designated two 'rest days' every month (from once a month previously) at live poultry retail outlets. On these days, all trading in live poultry is temporarily suspended to facilitate thorough cleansing and disinfection of the outlets. Prior to the 'rest days', all live poultry in the retail outlets has to be slaughtered.

With a view to minimising the risk of an avian flu virus spreading on premises selling live poultry, the department prescribed additional conditions for operators of fresh provision shops and market stalls selling live poultry. These conditions require the operators to surrender to the department for disposal any dead poultry and live poultry infected with disease, and to remove live poultry to another cage for temporary storage pending the cleansing and disinfection of the cages where the live poultry was originally kept.

In addition to the continuing H5 surveillance programme covering local chicken farms, imported chickens, the wholesale market and retail outlets, the AFCD has extended its surveillance to wild birds, waterfowl in recreational parks and pet birds on sale in the market. This has further strengthened its capability to detect the presence of any H5 viruses in the environment and the possible reassortment of the viruses, and enables appropriate and timely measures to be taken.

Markets and Cooked Food Markets

The FEHD operates 105 public markets (including 24 free-standing cooked food markets) with about 12 300 occupied stalls selling commodities ranging from fresh food to household items.

To improve the cleanliness of public markets, the department enhanced the intensive cleansing of common areas and facilities and inspection of their cleanliness. A monthly cleansing day was introduced from November under which stall tenants are required to thoroughly cleanse their own stalls to a level acceptable to the FEHD. A new streamlined system of sanction took effect in November, whereby warning letters are issued to operators who have breached tenancy conditions.

Hawkers

The FEHD maintains control over hawking activities in Hong Kong. During the year, 90 503 raids were carried out and 18 867 convictions secured in the courts for offences related to hawking.

As a means to further improve environmental hygiene, options that include an *ex gratia* allowance or relocation are offered to itinerant and cooked food stall hawker licence holders who surrender their licences.

Since mid-2003, the department has also assisted the Housing Department in clearing illegal cooked food hawker 'black spots' in public housing estates. The two departments carried out a total of 516 joint operations which resulted in 89 arrests and 687 seizures of abandoned hawker equipment and goods.

Slaughterhouses

At present, fresh meat in Hong Kong is supplied from three privately operated slaughterhouses: Sheung Shui Slaughterhouse, Tsuen Wan Slaughterhouse and Cheung Chau Slaughterhouse. The FEHD assumes the role of the managing authority to monitor and oversee the operation of these slaughterhouses.

During the year, to enhance food safety and public health protection, 35 978 animal health certificates and 27 639 admission forms for local pigs were verified and 65 667 urine and tissue samples were collected from slaughterhouse animals for testing for veterinary drug residues. A total of 2 156 864 pigs, 45 318 cattle and 4 267 goats were slaughtered and examined in the three slaughterhouses. Meat supplied from slaughterhouses is subject to inspection by health inspectors and only meat fit for human consumption is released for sale in the market.

Since its formation in January, the department's Intelligence Unit has achieved encouraging results in cracking down on illegal slaughtering activities. As a result of covert surveillance, six successful raids were mounted against such activities, leading to the arrest of six culprits and the seizure of 1 800 kilograms of pork.

With regard to meat smuggling, staff of the Intelligence Unit worked jointly with the Customs and Excise Department in conducting 15 large-scale raids, resulting in 15 arrests and the seizure of 38 947 kilograms of smuggled meat.

Public Education

The FEHD operates the Health Education Exhibition and Resource Centre in Kowloon Park, Tsim Sha Tsui and the Communication Resource Centre at the Public Health Laboratory Centre in Shek Kip Mei to educate the public on the importance of food safety and environmental hygiene through multimedia interactive exhibits and library materials.

Outreaching programmes, including talks and various health education activities, are organised to disseminate messages on personal hygiene, food safety and measures that help to maintain a hygienic living environment. During the year, more than 2 700 health talks were given for food handlers, school children, foreign domestic helpers, the elders, new arrivals and other members of the public.

Primary Production

Agriculture and fisheries industries are relatively small sectors in Hong Kong. The Government does not give direct subsidies to the local agriculture and fisheries industries or attempt to protect them from the free operation of market forces. Instead, the AFCD focuses on helping the industries to improve the quality of their output and enhance their productivity and competitiveness.

During the year, the total production of the industries was valued at $2,699 million. It accounted for 5 per cent of vegetables, 39 per cent of cut flowers, 23 per cent of live pigs, 31 per cent of live poultry, 6 per cent of freshwater fish and 31 per cent of seafood sold locally. Approximately 18 980 people were employed directly in the industries. The overall output of the local agriculture and fisheries industries has remained relatively stable over the past few years.

Agriculture Industry

Local agriculture is directed towards the production of high quality, fresh food crops through intensive land use. Farming is largely undertaken in the New Territories and just 2 per cent of the land area is under cultivation. Overall, the most common crops cultivated are vegetables and cut flowers, and production was valued at about $272 million in 2003. Pigs and poultry are the principal animals reared for food and the value of locally produced pigs amounted to $529 million and that of poultry, including chickens and pigeons, to $251 million.

As a result of limited supply of farm land and labour, competition from imports, raised environmental standards and calls for improved farm hygiene and safe produce, the local agriculture industry has to adapt rapidly to sustain its long-term development.

The AFCD encourages crop farmers to target specific niche markets and enhance their competitiveness by cultivating safe as well as quality vegetables. The department has cooperated with the local organic farming organisations and the Vegetable Marketing Organisation to develop organic farming and the market for organic vegetables in Hong Kong. So far, farmers from four local farming districts have joined the Organic Farming Conversion Scheme. The AFCD also promotes the use of greenhouse technology for intensive high-value crop production. During the year, two new vegetable varieties suitable for local production — jade Chinese kale and strawberry — were introduced to farmers for production.

The voluntary Accredited Farm Scheme operated by the AFCD and the Vegetable Marketing Organisation since 1994 aims to supply clean and safe vegetables. This programme has continued to expand with an additional six farms accredited. The organisation continued to use a 'Good Farmer' cartoon logo to promote accredited produce.

Fisheries Industry

Fresh fish constitute one of Hong Kong's most important primary products. Productions from capture and culture fisheries in 2003 were estimated at about 157 400 tonnes and 3 840 tonnes respectively, with a total value of $1.6 billion.

The Hong Kong fishing fleet comprises some 4 630 vessels which are manned by around 10 100 local fishermen and 3 800 Mainland deckhands. The predominant fishing method is trawling, which accounted for 84 per cent of the catch, or 131 700 tonnes. Other fishing methods include lining, gill netting and purse-seining. The 157 400 tonne total fish catch had an estimated wholesale value of $1.5 billion. Discounting the catch landed or sold outside Hong Kong, some 63 000 tonnes of the catch were supplied for local consumption.

Under licence from the AFCD, 1 157 mariculturists operate in 26 designated fish culture zones. They supplied 1 490 tonnes of live marine fish valued at $76 million.

Freshwater and brackish water fish are cultured in fish ponds covering some 1 030 hectares, most of which are located in the north-western New Territories where they form part of the wctland system of conservation interest. With the increasing urbanisation of the New Territories, commercial fish pond production has gradually declined. Pond fish culture yielded some 2 110 tonnes, or 6 per cent, of freshwater fish for local consumption.

To promote sustainable development of the fishing industry and to conserve fisheries resources in Hong Kong waters, the AFCD continued to pursue a number of fisheries management and conservation measures and to strengthen enforcement against destructive fishing practices. An artificial reef deployment project, started in 1996, has been completed in 2003. Altogether, artificial reefs with a total volume of 158 300 cubic metres have been deployed at Hoi Ha Wan and Yan Chau Tong Marine Parks, Port Shelter and Long Harbour.

Over 220 species of fish, including many high-valued species such as groupers, breams, snappers and sweetlips, have been using the reefs for feeding, shelter and as spawning and nursery areas. The AFCD also started a trial on releasing shrimp fry in the Sha Chau and Lung Kwu Chau Marine Park with a view to assessing its effectiveness in enriching Hong Kong's marine resources. Following the completion of the consultancy study on the feasibility of developing an offshore fishing industry in 2002, the department continued to assist fishermen in developing offshore fishing through provision of technical support, liaison services and credit facilities.

To enhance public awareness of the importance of conserving fisheries resources, the AFCD has set up a Fisheries Education Centre in Aberdeen. The centre enables visitors to gain a better understanding of the local fishing industry, fisheries resources and fisheries management measures through exhibits, interactive games and a video show. The Mainland fisheries authorities continued to enforce a fishing moratorium in the South China Sea between June 1 and August 1 to conserve fisheries resources. Apart from gill-netting, long-lining, hand-lining and cage trapping, all fishing operations were banned during this period. About 1 400 Hong Kong fishing vessels were affected. The Government continued to assist affected fishermen to cope with the fishing moratorium through the provision of low-interest loans, supporting services and vocational training.

With the aim of enhancing the sustainability of the local aquaculture industry, the AFCD conducts adaptive development studies and provides technical services to fish farmers. A fish health management programme is in place to help fish farmers minimise losses due to fish disease. Under the programme, departmental staff make regular visits to fish farms to educate farmers on measures to prevent and detect disease, and to provide a fish disease diagnostic service in case of an outbreak. Improved culture techniques and good management practices are also introduced to farmers through seminars, on-farm demonstrations and advisory leaflets.

Traditionally, marine cultured fish are fed with trash fish. In recent years, with the AFCD's support, an increasing number of marine fish farmers have switched to moist or dry pellet feed which reduces pollution and improves both feed efficiency and fish health.

To provide a wider choice of species for culture, the department is identifying new species with good market potential that can be recommended to farmers. A trial culture of high-finned grouper indicated that a fairly good growth rate could be obtained under cage culture conditions and the winter survival rate enhanced with a diet enriched with vitamin C. Techniques for culturing high-finned grouper have been introduced to mariculturists at technical seminars. Two new freshwater fish species, jade perch and tench, have been identified as suitable for culture in Hong Kong waters, and have better market potential. Collaborative culture trials of these two species with fish farmers have been conducted.

To mitigate the impact of mariculture on the surrounding environment, the AFCD, in collaboration with the City University of Hong Kong, is conducting a study on using specially designed artificial reefs known as biofilters to provide a hard substratum for growing filter-feeders, such as green-lipped mussels, to trap and remove organic wastes, thereby improving the water quality. The trial biofilters were placed in the Kau Sai fish culture zone in 2002. Preliminary findings showed that the biofilters have led to the establishment of a rich fish community and a significant reduction in organic waste in the sediments within the fish culture zone. In response to a growing public demand for angling facilities and the wish of some mariculturists to open their fish rafts for recreational fishing, the AFCD began a trial scheme in recreational fishing on fish culture rafts in two fish culture zones in August 2002. Subsequently, the scheme has been extended to six more fish culture zones.

The department continues to implement its red tide monitoring and management measures with a view to minimising the impact of red tides on mariculture. The monitoring effort includes proactive phytoplankton monitoring before the formation of a red tide and rapid risk assessment of red tide incidents that are reported. A computerised system using Geographic Information System technology helps visualise the spatial and temporal distribution of red tides and provides a quick analysis of their development and movement. Red tide warnings are disseminated to mariculturists and the public through the red tide support groups set up in fish culture zones, press releases and the AFCD website.

Marketing

Much fresh food produce is sold in wholesale markets managed by the AFCD, the Vegetable Marketing Organisation and the Fish Marketing Organisation. The Western Wholesale Food Market and the Cheung Sha Wan Wholesale Food Market Phase I are the two biggest market complexes developed and managed by the department. Each is an integration of several markets. The Western Wholesale Food Market, for example, accommodates markets for freshwater fish, vegetables, fruit, poultry and eggs and allows buyers to purchase a variety of fresh food produce under one roof.

Apart from these market complexes, the AFCD also manages two temporary wholesale markets, one in North District and the other in Cheung Sha Wan, for vegetables and poultry respectively.

During the year, the Government's wholesale markets handled 290 000 tonnes of vegetables, 63 000 tonnes of poultry, 35 000 tonnes of freshwater fish and fisheries products, 113 000 tonnes of fruit and 51 000 tonnes of eggs. The total value amounted to $4.2 billion.

The Vegetable Marketing Organisation is established as a non-governmental body providing vegetable wholesale marketing facilities. It operates a vegetable wholesale market at Cheung Sha Wan, set up under the Agricultural Products (Marketing) Ordinance on a non-profit-making basis. It charges commission on the vegetables sold and in return provides trading facilities, transport, accounting, and pesticides residue testing services to farmers and traders. Any surplus is ploughed back into the development of farming and the provision of scholarships for farmers' children. In 2003, the organisation handled 251 000 tonnes of vegetables valued at $779 million.

The Fish Marketing Organisation is a statutory body established under the Marine Fish (Marketing) Ordinance. It provides orderly marketing services at its seven wholesale markets. Revenue comes from charging commission on the proceeds of sales. Surplus earnings are channelled back into the industry through the provision of low-interest loans to fishermen, improved services and facilities in the markets and scholarships for fishermen and their children. During the year, 41 850 tonnes of marine fish valued at $740 million were sold through the organisation.

Veterinary Services and Animal Management

The AFCD closely monitors animal health in Hong Kong. In 2003, staff of the department made over 10 700 visits to livestock and poultry farms to monitor conditions, test for the presence of diseases, and check on the use of veterinary drugs. To enhance its preventive capacity, the department not only advises farmers on proper husbandry practices but also provides them with vaccines so that newly imported breeding pigs can be inoculated against major animal diseases such as foot and mouth disease and swine fever.

The new RRT-PCR ('real-time reverse transcribed-polymerase chain reaction') technology for avian influenza evaluated in 2002 was shown to be useful in early detection and monitoring for H5N1 avian influenza virus infection during and after outbreaks in December 2002 to January 2003. Introduction of new, rapid, molecular diagnostic testing procedures for H5 avian influenza viruses has been extended to diagnosis of other avian, swine and fish diseases of significance to Hong Kong.

The second and third phase implementation of Public Health (Animals and Birds) (Chemical Residues) Regulation in 2003 required the introduction of screen testing for an increased range of chemical residues in animal urine/serum samples. The scope of analytical services for the testing of veterinary drug residues in food animals products and live food animals for surveillance and statutory purposes has been further extended by the Government Laboratory and the AFCD's Veterinary Laboratory to facilitate the second phase enforcement of the Public Health (Animals and Birds) (Chemical Residues) Regulation and the Harmful Substances in Food Regulations.

Although Hong Kong has achieved a rabies-free status with the aid of vaccination, the AFCD has strict measures in place to prevent a recurrence of the disease. Dog keepers are required to have their dogs licensed, implanted with microchips for identification and vaccinated against rabies by the time their dogs reach five months of age. In 2003, some 45 000 dogs were vaccinated against rabies. As part of the rabies prevention strategy, continual action is taken to reduce the risk of a rabies reservoir developing in the stray animal population. Over 13 500 stray dogs were caught in the year. The department also deploys manpower to catch other stray animals that may cause a nuisance in local communities.

The AFCD is the licensing authority for all pet shops in Hong Kong. No one is allowed to trade in pets unless they are licensed under certain conditions. In 2003, there were over 275 licensed pet shops selling a wide range of animals including dogs, cats, birds, turtles and some exotic animals. The department inspects the shops regularly to ensure that their operations are in line with the licensing conditions, monitor the animal health conditions and prevent cruelty to the animals.

Home Pages

Health, Welfare and Food Bureau: http://www.hwfb.gov.hk
Food and Environmental Hygiene Department: http://www.fehd.gov.hk
Agriculture, Fisheries and Conservation Department: http://www.afcd.gov.hk

CHAPTER 10

Social Welfare

The Government is committed to building an efficient, effective, accountable and sustainable social welfare system. To address challenges posed by a fiscal deficit, unemployment due to economic restructuring, growing demand on social security support and weakened family solidarity, the Government continues to focus on encouraging self-reliance and self-betterment so as to build up social capital and strengthen social cohesion. In 2003, major work objectives of the Social Welfare Department included the strengthening of support for families in need; intensifying self-reliance among able-bodied recipients under the Comprehensive Social Security Assistance Scheme; and re-engineering of community services for elders. The department also participated actively and extensively in various aspects of work relating to combating the SARS outbreak.

HONG KONG devotes much effort to caring for and supporting those least able to take care of themselves. Social welfare forms an important component in the Government's responsibility for social development. In 2003, the Government continued to provide a well-resourced safety net to look after the physical and psychological well-being of the elderly, the infirm and the disabled; to assist the disadvantaged, the poor and the unemployed with an emphasis on enhancing, not impeding, their will to be self-reliant; and to encourage those with sufficient means to show concern for others in the community.

The Government is advised by the Social Welfare Advisory Committee on social welfare policy, the Rehabilitation Advisory Committee on matters of rehabilitation, and the Elderly Commission on services for elders and the Women's Commission on a strategic overview of women's issues. The responsibility for formulating and carrying out policies on social welfare rests with the Secretary for Health, Welfare and Food and the Director of Social Welfare, respectively. The Social Welfare Department (SWD) maintains a close working partnership with non-governmental organisations (NGOs) which, with subventions provided by the Government, are the main providers of social welfare services.

In 2003, expenditure on social welfare amounted to $32.4 billion: this comprised $22.9 billion (70.7 per cent) on financial assistance payments, $6.9 billion (21.3 per cent) on subventions, $0.5 billion (1.5 per cent) on contract services and $2.1 billion

(6.5 per cent) on services provided by the SWD. Social welfare accounted for 15.2 per cent of the total recurrent public expenditure.

Major Achievements

Strengthening Support for Families in Need

Based on the findings of the evaluative study of 15 pilot Integrated Family Service Centre (IFSC) projects which adopted the 'child-centred, family-focused and community-based' approach, a consensus was reached between the SWD and the social service sector that the IFSCs represent an effective mode of service delivery in terms of service accessibility, ability to reach out to at-risk families, partnership with community organisations and agencies, and users' participation and satisfaction. The department is poised to fully re-engineer the family services by converting Family Services Centres into IFSCs in order to better meet the changing needs of the community.

Measures to enhance the provision of timely services for individuals or families in crisis situations were also put in place. These measures include setting up a three-year pilot Suicide Crisis Intervention Centre providing round-the-clock outreaching service and intervention for those in a crisis or at high/moderate suicidal risk. In addition, a quick link has been provided between the Departmental Hotline Service Unit and the Family Crisis Support Centre. To further facilitate timely intervention in family violence cases, the department and the Hong Kong Police Force implemented a new referral procedure in January so that domestic violence cases can be brought to the department's attention for early intervention. Publicity and public education based on the central theme of *Strengthening Families and Combating Violence* continued during the year.

Intensifying Support for Self-reliance

Under the impact of the SARS outbreak and the continuing economic downturn, the number of unemployment cases receiving Comprehensive Social Security Assistance (CSSA) surged from 40 513 at end-2002 to 50 118 at end-2003. While the Government is committed to providing a safety net for those least able to help themselves, to ease the significant rise in CSSA unemployment cases, intensified measures were introduced to strengthen the Support for Self-reliance Scheme. Employable CSSA recipients are provided with more targeted employment assistance including direct job matching. Community work requirements have been further enhanced to help recipients develop work habits and to contribute to society. More NGOs have been commissioned to run intensive employment assistance projects. To encourage CSSA recipients to find and stay in employment and to increase the incentive to work, the maximum level of disregarded earnings under the CSSA scheme has been raised.

Re-engineering of Community Support Services for Elders

To provide greater service integration and eliminate duplication, and provide a service infrastructure that will be more responsive to the changing needs of elders, a major exercise to re-engineer community support services for elders was launched in August 2002. As a result, a range of community units was upgraded with effect from April 1, 2003 to provide expanded functions and integrated services. These units now comprise 40 District Elderly Community Centres, 110 Neighbourhood Elderly Centres and 60 district-based Integrated Home Care Services Teams.

Combating the SARS Outbreak

The department participated actively and extensively in various aspects of work in combating the SARS outbreak, ranging from promoting environmental hygiene in welfare services units to offering assistance to individuals and families directly affected.

Guidelines to promote environmental hygiene and to advise on contingency arrangements in case of an infection were drawn up and distributed to residential social services. As part of the precautionary measures against SARS, face masks were distributed to vulnerable groups, through services units. With a special funding allocation, resources were utilised to assist elderly day service units, residential care homes for elders and persons with disabilities, drug treatment centres as well as child care centres in taking measures to prevent the spread of SARS, and to improve environmental hygiene.

Operation CARE was among the initiatives taken by the Administration to relieve the impact of SARS on the economy through the creation of temporary jobs while strengthening social cohesiveness and fostering a spirit of mutual care within the community. This project aimed at improving the general household environment of elders and other vulnerable groups so as to boost their resistance against contagious diseases by having their homes cleansed, and minor household repairs done, by a force of mainly young workers engaged on a short-term basis. Some 4 500 job opportunities were created for this task. A total of 42 NGOs, local bodies and labour federations, comprising 73 units, were commissioned to take part in the operation. Over 150 000 elders and vulnerable groups benefited from the household cleansing service, and over 70 000 elders and vulnerable families-in-need received the household repairs service.

In addition, assistance and support in the form of counselling and urgent financial assistance were rendered by social workers and clinical psychologists to SARS patients and their families. The department also provided transitional residential placements for children and elders without adequate support upon hospitalisation of their care-givers and temporary accommodation for discharged SARS patients who could not return home immediately.

The department also oversaw the provision of both tangible and psychosocial support to people placed under confinement in their own homes or in the holiday camps designated as isolation centres. The wide range of support rendered by the department and some NGOs included delivery of meals, provision of daily necessities, arrangements for child care, emergency financial assistance, and psychological support/intervention through hotlines. The department was designated to administer a $150 million Trust Fund for SARS which the Government established in November to provide special *ex gratia* assistance on compassionate grounds for individuals or families affected by the unprecedented outbreak between March and June. Besides providing special *ex gratia* relief payment for eligible families of deceased SARS patients, the Trust Fund also provides special *ex gratia* financial assistance for eligible recovered SARS patients or eligible 'suspected' SARS patients treated with steroids who are suffering from longer term effects, attributable to SARS (including the effects of medication received), which might have resulted in some degree of relevant dysfunction. By year-end, a total of 188 applications had been approved, involving $64.6 million. The department has also been entrusted to administer two non-government funds, namely the 'Business Community Relief Fund for Victims of

SARS' and the 'We Care Education Fund' initiated by the business sector and the civil service sector respectively, and to allocate grants to eligible individuals or families.

Social Welfare Programmes

Family and Child Welfare

The overall objective of the family and child welfare programme is to preserve and strengthen the family as a unit through assisting individuals and families to identify and deal with their problems, or to prevent problems from arising, and to provide for needs which cannot be met from within the family. A comprehensive network of family and child welfare services is provided by the department and NGOs.

Services for Families

The department adopts a three-pronged approach to provide a continuum of services to support families.

At the primary level, prevention of problems and crises is effected through publicity, education, empowerment and early identification. The publicity campaign on *Strengthening Families and Combating Violence* continues. Twenty Family Support and Resource Centres set up in community centres provide drop-in service, mutual support and early identification and referral of cases in need of intensive casework service. These services are supplemented by the department's 24-hour hotline service that provides information on social welfare services. A Family Helpline manned by social workers provides immediate telephone counselling for individuals and families facing a crisis.

At the secondary level, a range of support services, from developmental programmes to intensive counselling, is provided through a network of 66 Family Services Centres and Integrated Family Service Centres, staffed by 746 social workers who handled a total of 87 912 cases during the year. There are also five Single Parent Centres and eight Post-migration Centres.

At the tertiary level, specialised services and crisis intervention are provided through five Family and Child Protective Services Units, the Family Crisis Support Centre, the Suicide Crisis Intervention Centre and two projects on prevention and handling of elder abuse and another on elderly suicide. In addition, four Refuge Centres provide 162 short-term residential places for individuals in need, including battered spouses and their children; they accept admission on a 24-hour basis.

The problem of street-sleeping is tackled through a continuum of outreaching, counselling and referral services provided by the department's outreaching teams and family services centres, together with temporary shelters, urban hostels and day relief centres operated by NGOs. The 'Three-year Action Plan to Help Street Sleepers', targeting street sleepers who are younger and in good health, has assisted 529 street sleepers to live off the street since April 2001.

Services for Children

The department provides a wide range of child welfare services. The adoption service arranges permanent homes for children abandoned by their parents or whose parents are unable to maintain them. Residential child care services are provided for children and young people who need care or protection because of family crises or their behavioural or emotional problems. At year-end, there were 745 places in foster care service, 952 places in small group homes and 1 331 places in children's homes, boys' and girls' homes and hostels.

Child care centres provide day care services for children under the age of six years. At year-end, there were 28 978 aided day nursery places, 960 aided day creche places, 717 occasional child care places and 1 672 extended hour places provided in 272 centres. All child care centres have to register under the Child Care Services Ordinance and Regulations. A fee assistance scheme helps low-income families with social needs to pay fees for child care centres.

An inter-bureau/departmental working group has been working on the details for implementing the harmonisation of pre-primary services currently provided by child care centres and kindergartens.

The Administration introduced the Adoption (Amendment) Bill 2003 into the Legislative Council in June to further improve the local adoption arrangements and give effect in Hong Kong to the Hague Convention on Protection of Children and Cooperation in respect of Intercountry Adoption. The council was expected to form a Bills Committee in January 2004 to study the bill, and to complete the legislative proceedings during its 2003-04 session.

The Administration commissioned the Duty Lawyer Service to run the Legal Representation Scheme — with effect from October 1, 2003 — for children and juveniles involved in care or protection proceedings who are deprived of liberty and detained in a gazetted place of refuge under the Protection of Children and Juveniles Ordinance.

Social Security

The Comprehensive Social Security Assistance (CSSA) Scheme and the Social Security Allowance (SSA) Scheme form the mainstay of Hong Kong's social security system. They are supplemented by three accident compensation schemes: the Criminal and Law Enforcement Injuries Compensation Scheme, the Traffic Accident Victims Assistance Scheme, and Emergency Relief.

The CSSA Scheme

The CSSA Scheme is non-contributory but means-tested. The scheme provides cash assistance to people suffering from financial hardship, enabling them to meet basic needs. Applicants should satisfy the stipulated residence requirement. To help able-bodied unemployed CSSA recipients and other socially disadvantaged groups overcome barriers to work and become self-reliant, the department continued to implement the comprehensive package of employment-related services and introduced measures to intensify the Support for Self-reliance Scheme (*see Major Achievements above*). At year-end, there were 290 206 CSSA cases, compared with 266 571 in 2002. Total expenditure on the CSSA during the year amounted to $17.33 billion, representing an increase of 9.9 per cent over the previous year.

The SSA Scheme

The non-contributory SSA Scheme provides allowances to meet the special needs of the severely disabled and elderly persons. The scheme covers Normal Disability Allowance, Higher Disability Allowance, Normal Old Age Allowance and Higher Old Age Allowance. At year-end, 563 880 people were receiving social security allowances, compared with 561 078 in 2002. Total expenditure during the year was $5.27 billion, representing a decrease of 0.9 per cent over the previous year.

Deflationary Adjustment

To restore social security benefits to their originally intended buying power in view of the deflation over the last four years, the Chief Executive in Council approved in February proposals to adjust the standard payment rates under the CSSA Scheme and those of the Disability Allowance (DA) under the SSA Scheme downwards in accordance with the movement of the Social Security Assistance Index of Prices. With the enactment of the 2003 Appropriation Ordinance, the CSSA standard rates for able-bodied recipients and the DA rates were reduced by 11.1 per cent from June, and the CSSA standard rates for the elderly, the disabled and those who are medically certified to be in ill-health were first reduced by 6 per cent in October, to be followed by a second-phase reduction a year later. Other standard payment rates and asset limits under the CSSA Scheme were reduced from June in accordance with the established mechanisms.

Accident Compensation Schemes

The Criminal and Law Enforcement Injuries Compensation Scheme offers *ex gratia* payments on a non-means-tested basis to innocent victims injured or to dependants of those killed in crimes of violence or through the action of a law enforcement officer using a weapon in the execution of his duties. During the year, a total of $9.68 million was paid out in 635 cases, compared with $9.60 million in the previous year. The Traffic Accident Victims Assistance (TAVA) Scheme offers early financial assistance for people injured or for dependants of those killed in traffic accidents on a non-means-tested basis, regardless of the element of fault leading to the occurrence of the accident. During the year, a total of $154.70 million was paid out in 7 939 cases, compared with $150.18 million in 2002.

Emergency relief in the form of cooked meals or cash grants in lieu of cooked meals and other essential relief articles is provided to victims of natural and other disasters. Grants from the Emergency Relief Fund are paid to these victims (or to their dependants in cases of death). Emergency relief was given to 104 victims on 20 occasions during the year.

Social Security Appeal Board

The Social Security Appeal Board considers appeals against the SWD's decisions concerning the CSSA, SSA and TAVA. It heard a total of 147 appeals during the year. The department continued to strengthen the function of the Special Investigation Section and further tighten measures to reduce fraud and abuse of welfare benefits. At the same time, a risk management approach was being adopted in the administration of the social security schemes.

Services for Elders

The basic principle underlying services for elders is to provide senior citizens with a sense of security, a sense of belonging and a feeling of health and worthiness. The aim is to promote the well-being of those persons aged 60 and above in all aspects of their life through provision of services that will enable them to remain active members of the community for as long as possible, and, to the extent necessary, to provide residential care suited to their varying needs.

The department has been operating an *Opportunities for the Elderly Project* since 1999 to provide subsidies to community organisations to plan and implement programmes to promote a sense of worthiness among elders and enhance community care for them. During the year, 274 programmes were implemented, with the approved grants amounting to $2.68 million. These programmes were complementary to the three-year *Healthy Ageing Campaign* launched by the Elderly Commission in 2001.

In November, the department implemented a Central Waiting List for subsidised long-term care services. Applications for and allocation of subsidised long-term care services, including residential care services and community care services, are centrally coordinated by the department under the auspices of the Long Term Care Services Delivery System. Applicants will be given a standardised assessment to ascertain their care needs and matched with appropriate services in accordance with the assessment results.

Community Support Services

Community support services are provided to elders who require assistance to continue living at home. Support is also provided for their care-givers. At year-end, there were 40 district elderly community centres, 60 district-based integrated home care services teams, one home help team, 18 enhanced home and community care services teams, 49 day-care centres/units for elders, 60 social centres for elders, 114 neighbourhood elderly centres, 40 support teams for the elderly and one holiday centre for elders. Under the Senior Citizen Card Scheme, 908 063 Senior Citizen Cards were issued by year-end. A total of 8 070 companies, organisations, government departments with 14 614 units and outlets, and 1 767 medical units with 1 972 branches participated in the scheme to provide concessions, discounts and priority services to senior citizens.

An *in situ* expansion exercise was conducted in day care centres for the elderly to strengthen their allied health support and caring capability to provide a continuum of care for elders with different levels of frailty and dementia. A total of 220 additional day care places have been created in this exercise since April.

Residential Care Services

Residential care is provided for elders who need care in their daily living and are unable to live at home for various reasons. At year-end, there were 97 subsidised hostel places, 7 343 subsidised home for the aged places, 5 931 bought places from private residential care homes for the elderly, 11 499 subsidised care-and-attention home places and 1 699 subsidised nursing home places.

The Residential Care Homes (Elderly Persons) Ordinance, which provides legislative control over all residential care homes for the elderly (RCHEs), has been in full operation since June 1, 1996. Upon all RCHEs meeting the required licensing standard in 2002, a number of service improvement measures have been taken to further upgrade the service quality, particularly that of private homes. These initiatives include provision of subsidised training for RCHE staff, dissemination of information to the public and stepping up prosecution action against non-compliant homes.

To further promote the quality of residential care services for elders, the department commissioned the Hong Kong Association of Gerontology in July 2002 to conduct a two-year pilot programme on the development and establishment of an accreditation system for residential care services for elders. The pilot programme will be completed in mid-2004, and the Government will consider the way forward, taking into account the recommendations of the association.

Rehabilitation Services

Rehabilitation services are provided by government departments and NGOs with the objective of integrating people with disabilities into society and helping them to fully develop their capabilities. These services are coordinated by the Commissioner for Rehabilitation on the advice of the Rehabilitation Advisory Committee.

Services for Children with Disabilities

At year-end, the NGOs provided 1 716 integrated programme places in ordinary child care centres, 1 341 special child care centre places (inclusive of 108 residential places) and 1 749 early education and training centre places for pre-school disabled children. For autistic children, an enhanced training programme with input from clinical psychologists was provided in special child care centres. In addition, there were 96 small group home places for school-age mentally handicapped children requiring residential service.

Services for Adults with Disabilities

The Marketing Consultancy Office (Rehabilitation) assists in the marketing and business development of sheltered workshops and supported employment services. With a view to promoting integration of people with disabilities into society, 1 810 supported employment places were provided in 2003 for those who were able to work in open settings with the necessary counselling and support service. For those who were not yet ready to compete in the open job market, 7 417 sheltered workshop places were provided to help them develop work skills. In addition, 453 places in the integrated vocational training centres provided a continuum of vocational rehabilitation services in a one-stop setting. There were 3 881 day activity centre places for mentally handicapped persons and 230 training and activity centre places for ex-mentally ill persons to help them become more independent in daily living. Five social clubs for ex-mentally ill persons and 17 social and recreational centres for other groups of people with disabilities were set up to encourage their participation in the community through various leisure activities.

As for residential services, there were 5 501 hostel and home places, and 241 supported hostel places for people with disabilities who could neither live independently nor be adequately cared for by their families. For aged blind people who were unable to look after themselves adequately, or in need of care and attention, 899 places were provided in homes for the aged blind and in care-and-attention homes. For chronic and ex-mentally ill patients, there were 980 long stay care home places and 1 349 halfway house places.

Professional Back-up and Support Services

Professional back-up services from clinical psychologists, occupational therapists and physiotherapists are provided for people with disabilities in rehabilitation day centres and hostels. Speech therapy service is also provided for disabled children attending pre-school rehabilitation centres. Various support services are provided in the community. These include home-based training and support service for mentally handicapped persons, a community mental health link and after-care service for dischargees of halfway houses, and a community rehabilitation network for persons with a visceral disability or chronic illness. Furthermore, a respite service for handicapped persons, occasional child care service for disabled pre-schoolers and six parents resource centres are provided to meet the special needs of families with disabled members.

Medical Social Services

Medical social workers provide patients and their families with individual and group counselling, financial aid, housing assistance or referral to other community resources to facilitate their treatment, rehabilitation and reintegration into society. To provide easy access to patients and their family members, medical social workers are stationed in public hospitals and specialist clinics so that immediate advice and assistance can be given to those in need. During the year, 137 681 cases received services from 349 medical social workers.

Services for Offenders

To help offenders become law-abiding citizens and reintegrate into the community, the department discharges statutory functions under related ordinances and provides community-based and residential services for the offenders. Under the Juvenile Offenders (Amendment) Ordinance, which took effect on July 1, 2003, the minimum age of criminal responsibility has been raised from seven to 10 and the age of offenders placed in rehabilitation programmes run by the department has been revised accordingly.

Probation officers assess the offenders' suitability for probation supervision and make recommendations to the courts. They also supervise probationers to monitor their compliance with probation orders. During the year, 2 591 offenders were placed on probation. Officers also prepare reports on long-term prisoners, for consideration of early release, and on prisoners who submit petitions for early release.

Offenders aged 14 or above and convicted of an offence punishable by imprisonment may be placed on Community Service Orders to perform unpaid work of benefit to the community under statutory supervision. During the year, 1 659 offenders were put under such orders.

Seven residential homes, with a total capacity of 440 places, provide educational, prevocational and character training for young offenders and children and juveniles with behavioural or family problems.

The Young Offender Assessment Panel, jointly operated by the department and the Correctional Services Department (CSD), provides the courts with coordinated professional views on sentencing options for young offenders aged 14 to under 25.

The Post-Release Supervision of Prisoners Scheme, another joint service of the department and the CSD, assists discharged prisoners in their rehabilitation and reintegration into the community. During the year, 441 ex-prisoners were placed under supervision. One NGO is subvented to provide hostel and supportive services for ex-prisoners and ex-offenders.

Services for Young People

The overall objective of welfare services for young people is to help those aged between six and 24 years to develop into mature, responsible and contributing members of society through the provision of a range of preventive, supportive and remedial services.

At year-end, 131 Integrated Children and Youth Services Centres (ICYSCs) were providing children and youth service, outreaching social work service, school social work service and, where possible, family life education under one management to address the changing needs of youth in an integrated, holistic manner. During the year, joint funding from the Hong Kong Jockey Club Charities Trust and the Lotteries Fund was approved for a total of 34 ICYSCs throughout the territory to undergo modernisation. Through improving the physical environment and the provision of modern furniture and equipment, these centres have been made more appealing to contemporary youth.

At year-end, 473 secondary schools were each provided with one school social worker unit, which identifies and helps students with academic, social and emotional problems, maximises their educational opportunities, develops their potential and prepares them for responsible adulthood. Sixteen District Youth Outreaching Social Work Teams provide services to address the needs of high-risk youth and also deal with juvenile gang issues.

For early identification of the developmental needs of students and, where necessary, timely intervention with a primary preventive programme, the *Understanding the Adolescent Project* was implemented in 308 secondary schools in the 2003-04 school year.

The Community Support Services Scheme (CSSS) assists young people who have broken the law or are at-risk. By year-end, six CSSS teams, one operated by the department and five by NGOs, had served 4 343 young people.

In order to strengthen support for young offenders, the SWD and the Police Force jointly developed a formalised system of conducting a 'Family Conference' for juveniles cautioned under the Police Superintendent's Discretion Scheme. Implemented in October, the 'Family Conference' aims at engaging relevant professionals at an early stage, together with family members, to decide on appropriate intervention strategies to meet the needs of young offenders.

With the aim of helping young drug abusers abstain from drug-taking habits and reintegrate into the community, a multi-modality approach is adopted to provide drug treatment and rehabilitation services. At year-end, the department was subventing 15 voluntary drug treatment and rehabilitation centres/halfway houses, five counselling centres for psychotropic substance abusers and two social clubs for ex-drug abusers. Under the requirements of the Drug Dependent Persons Treatment and Rehabilitation Centres (Licensing) Ordinance, 44 certificates of exemption and one licence valid for drug dependence treatment centres had been issued or renewed by year-end.

To enhance cooperation among relevant youth services, 18 Local Committees on Services for Young People, chaired by the District Social Welfare Officers, coordinate the provision of youth services at district level.

Clinical Psychological Services

The department and NGOs employ a total of 69 clinical psychologists who provide a range of services to family casework, rehabilitation and correctional units in the social service sector. These services include psychological assessment, treatment, consultation, staff training and public education services. During the year, a total of 3 722 cases were served, and 2 585 assessments and 16 218 treatment sessions conducted.

Volunteerism

The Steering Committee on Promotion of Volunteer Service held a series of promotional and publicity programmes to promote volunteerism among students and youth, corporations and community organisations. To capitalise on the momentum already gained, the *Campaign Evergreen 2003*, one of the major initiatives of the Volunteer Movement, was organised to further cultivate the volunteer spirit and help in revitalising Hong Kong after the SARS outbreak. At year-end, 1 111 organisations and 442 710 individuals had registered to participate in volunteer service.

Staff Development and Training

In 2003, the department's Staff Development and Training Section organised 531 in-service training programmes for a total of 15 686 participants from the department and NGOs. In addition, to continue the promotion of cyber learning within the department, an upgraded version of the e-Learning Centre was launched in March, featuring a fully functional Learning Management System with more course-ware and other learning resources made accessible to all staff in the department.

Research and Statistics

The department conducts surveys and research studies, develops and maintains data systems and undertakes statistical compilation and estimation for the monitoring, planning, development and review of social welfare services.

Subvention and Service Monitoring

By year-end, recurrent subvention and capital grants had been given to 180 NGOs for the provision of social welfare services in accordance with government policies. Funding allocation for capital grants was administered by the department on the advice of the Lotteries Fund Advisory Committee.

To facilitate the smooth implementation of the continuing subvention reform, a Lump Sum Grant Steering Committee (with the Director of Social Welfare as Chairperson) advises on measures to achieve continuous improvement. The performance monitoring aspects of the reform have been implemented progressively since 1999 under the Service Performance Monitoring System. This assesses service performance on the basis of a set of well-defined Service Quality Standards and a Funding and Service Agreement developed for each specific service.

Information Technology

The Technical Infrastructure (TI) and the Client Information System (CIS) are the most significant information technology (IT) initiatives being taken by the department. The TI involves a corporate-wide network to support deployment of IT applications and joined-up initiatives. The CIS will provide a workflow-based database which collects and shares client data across the department for operational, management and planning purposes.

Information Technology Development Projects

At year-end, Lotteries Fund grants totalling about $202 million had been approved for implementing 27 IT projects in the department and a number of NGOs. The scope of these applications includes the development of Core Applications in Human Resource Management and Financial Management as well as the development of a management information system, a knowledge management system, eServices through websites, and a digital voice library for the blind and visually impaired.

Community Building and Promoting Mutual Care

Several government departments and NGOs contribute towards the community-building programme which serves to foster among the people of Hong Kong a sense of belonging, mutual care and civic responsibility.

Community-building efforts involve providing purpose-built facilities for group and community activities, the formation of citizens' organisations, encouraging community participation in the administration of public affairs, solving community problems and improving the quality of community life in general. The Home Affairs Bureau has policy responsibility for the programme and the Home Affairs Department and the SWD are principally responsible for its implementation. The Home Affairs Department, through its network of district offices, is primarily concerned with encouraging participation in community service and promoting mutual care and community spirit through local organisations such as area committees, mutual aid committees, rural committees, charitable organisations, social service groups, kaifong associations and women's organisations.

The SWD and NGOs, through the provision of group and community work activities, promote social relationships and cohesion within the community and encourage individuals to solve community problems.

Enhancing Social Capital: Community Investment and Inclusion Fund

In his 2001 Policy Address, the Chief Executive announced the plan to set up the $300 million Community Investment and Inclusion Fund (CIIF) to encourage mutual concern and aid, promote community participation, and support cross-sectoral programmes. The CIIF Committee was established in April 2002 to handle applications for funding. Three batches of projects have been called, with over 470 proposals received and processed. By year-end, 31 projects had been selected, involving total funding support of $23.1 million. In addition, over 32 briefings have been held, involving around 2 715 participants from 1 772 different groups and organisations to promote the social capital concept embodied in this new fund. An Inaugural CIIF Sharing Forum was held in October 2003 to mark the CIIF's first anniversary. National and international experts shared experiences in social capital development, and members of local project teams that had been granted funding support also shared experiences in implementing their projects.

Women's Commission

The Women's Commission was set up on January 15, 2001 as a central mechanism to promote the well-being and interests of women in Hong Kong. It is tasked to identify all women's needs and address matters of concern to women in a holistic and systematic manner. It has developed a long-term vision and strategy for the development and advancement of women in Hong Kong. The Women's Commission takes a strategic overview of women's issues, advises the Government on policies and initiatives that are of concern to women and seeks to ensure that women's perspectives are factored in (or mainstreamed) during policy formulation.

Chaired by a non-official member of the Legislative Council, and comprising another 21 members, the commission's mission is 'To enable women in Hong Kong to fully realise their due status, rights and opportunities in all aspects of life.' The commission performs three strategic functions in championing women's causes; inspiring and catalysing changes; and mobilising community resources. It has identified three priority areas of action: gender mainstreaming, empowerment of women and public education. Special task forces have been set up to take forward work in these areas. During the year, the commission continued to focus efforts on an overarching theme of capacity building.

In respect of gender mainstreaming, the aim is to integrate women's needs and perspectives in formulation and implementation of public policies, programmes and legislation. The commission has secured the Administration's agreement to introduce gender mainstreaming in different policy areas incrementally. It has developed a checklist as an analytical tool to facilitate gender sensitive analysis. Most government bureaux and departments have already designated a directorate officer as the 'Gender Focal Point' within their establishments to promote gender awareness. To facilitate the taking into account of women's perspectives in the policy-making process, training is provided for civil servants to enhance their sensitivity towards gender issues and women's concerns. Workshops have been organised for staff of the Social Welfare Department, Education Department and the Police Force, as well as for newly recruited Administrative Officers. About 100 civil servants attended such training in 2003.

In the empowerment of women, the Women's Commission aims to better equip women for life's challenges and to create a more enabling environment for women to develop themselves. The commission has reviewed and suggested improvements to a number of services for women to ensure their appropriateness, adequacy and quality. It promotes development of new service models (such as setting up a mutual child care service using a membership model and organising women cooperatives) and good empowerment practices. The commission has published a booklet to publicise and promote good practices and organised a session for beneficiaries to share their experience with other women. To enhance women's participation in advisory and statutory bodies, the commission has obtained the Administration's agreement to take gender composition into account in making appointments to these bodies. Government bureaux and departments are urged to reach out, identify and cultivate women candidates for appointment. A major effort in the capacity building of women is the development of an innovative and flexible learning mode, namely the Capacity Building Mileage Programme, that seeks to enhance women's all-round abilities, and also promotes positive life skills. The programme is being implemented on a three-year pilot basis in partnership with a local tertiary institution and a radio station with funding support from the Lotteries Fund and supplementary learning activities organised by NGOs.

A public education and publicity campaign (including TV and radio announcements of public interest, a TV drama series and radio programmes) has been launched to enhance public knowledge of the commission's work and to reduce gender prejudices and stereotyping as well as to raise public awareness of women-related issues. Results have been positive.

To achieve a better understanding of the situation of women in Hong Kong, the Women's Commission initiated — in liaison with the Health, Welfare and Food Bureau and the Census and Statistics Department — the first ever large-scale household survey on the use of time by women and men in Hong Kong. The survey looked into the average amount of time spent daily by different people on different activities, and their pattern of participation in various aspects of life such as housework, voluntary work, and cultural, recreational/sports and social activities. The different time use patterns of the two genders were quantified and analysed and the results were released in August.

Another survey completed during the year found that the publicity and public education campaign undertaken by the Women's Commission had significantly increased public awareness of its work.

In order to achieve the maximum impact on society, the commission has developed a 'Framework of Collaboration' with substantive input from women's groups and interested parties. The commission will step up collaboration with the non-governmental sector in promoting the realisation of women's full potential and elimination of gender prejudices, and striving for a more prosperous and better future for all.

Home Pages

Health, Welfare and Food Bureau: http://www.hwfb.gov.hk
Social Welfare Department: http://www.info.gov.hk/swd
Women's Commission: http://www.women.gov.hk

CHAPTER 11

Housing

Under the new policy framework, the provision of assistance to those in genuine need continues to lie at the heart of the Government's housing policy. The Government will work to ensure that all those who cannot afford adequate accommodation in the private market have the opportunity to have access to subsidised public rental housing. It is committed to maintaining the average waiting time for public rental housing at around three years and ensuring that there is an adequate supply of public rental housing through a rolling construction programme run by the Hong Kong Housing Authority.

THE year of 2003 marked the 50th year of public housing development in Hong Kong. About one third of the population in Hong Kong now lives in public rental housing with another 20 per cent in subsidised home ownership flats. The total housing stock in Hong Kong in December amounted to 2 363 410 flats, comprising 689 450 public rental housing (PRH) flats[1], 394 630 subsidised home ownership flats and 1 279 330 flats in the private sector.

The revised estimate of public expenditure on housing in 2003-04 was $27.9 billion and reached 10 per cent of total public expenditure.

Housing Policy

The Statement on Housing Policy delivered by the Secretary for Housing, Planning and Lands on November 13, 2002 set out three major guiding principles of the Government's housing policy. Firstly, the focus of the Government's subsidised housing policy should be on the provision of assistance to low-income families who cannot afford private rental accommodation. Secondly, the Government should minimise its intervention in the private property market. Thirdly, the Government should maintain a fair and stable operating environment for the private property market by ensuring adequate land supply and provision of efficient supporting infrastructure.

Since the Government's announcement on the repositioning of its housing policy, the Hong Kong Housing Authority (HKHA)[2] has realigned its activities with the new

---

[1] Including public rental housing and interim housing flats operated by the Hong Kong Housing Authority and public rental housing flats operated by the Hong Kong Housing Society.

[2] The HKHA, established in 1973, is a statutory body responsible for implementing the majority of Hong Kong's public housing programmes. It plans and builds public housing for renting to low-income people. It manages public rental housing estates, interim housing, transit centres, flatted factories and ancillary commercial and community facilities.

policy agenda and priorities to focus on the provision of public rental housing. It has ceased the sale and construction of the Home Ownership Scheme (HOS) flats, initiated studies on the disposal arrangements for the surplus subsidised sale flats, undertaken to review the Home Assistance Loan Scheme (HALS) and put in place a concrete action plan for divesting its retail and car parking facilities.

Institutional Framework

Following a comprehensive review of the institutional framework for housing policy, the former Housing Bureau and the Housing Department merged on July 1, 2002 to form the new Housing Department. The reconstituted Housing Department integrates the policy and operational responsibilities in the provision of public housing, the procurement of services from the private sector and the assessment of eligibility for public housing assistance. It continues to provide secretariat and executive support to the HKHA and its committees to enable them to discharge their duties effectively. The reconstituted Housing Department also monitors developments in the private housing market, and oversees policy matters relating to the regulation of estate agents.

Under the Accountability System for Principal Officials implemented on July 1, 2002, the Secretary for Housing, Planning and Lands is the Principal Official responsible for overall housing matters. He was appointed as Chairman of the HKHA on April 1, 2003 to help forge a closer collaboration between the HKHA and the Government in the provision of housing services. The Secretary for Housing, Planning and Lands is underpinned by the Permanent Secretary for Housing, Planning and Lands (Housing), who also heads the Housing Department.

Public Rental Housing

Under the new policy framework, the provision of assistance to those in genuine need continues to lie at the heart of the Government's housing policy. The Government would work to ensure that all those who cannot afford adequate accommodation in the private market have the opportunity to have access to subsidised PRH. It is committed to maintaining the average waiting time for PRH at around three years and ensuring that there is an adequate supply of public rental housing through a rolling construction programme run by the HKHA. The actual quantum of PRH units to be built will be adjusted regularly taking account of the housing demand of low-income families and the turnover in PRH tenancies. To maximise the cost-effectiveness in the construction process, the HKHA has reviewed the design standards and finishes for new public rental housing in support of the concept of a 'Functional and Cost-effective' design.

At present, about 2 130 200 people or 31 per cent of Hong Kong's population live in public rental housing estates managed by the HKHA or the Hong Kong Housing Society[3]. At December, there were 90 240 households on the Waiting List for PRH. The current average waiting time for PRH is 2.1 years.

Rent Policy

The affordability of tenants is the prime factor in determining rent levels of public rental flats. Other factors taken into consideration include estate value, maintenance

---

[3] The HKHS is an independent, not-for-profit organisation established in 1948. It plans and builds quality housing for rent to specific target groups at affordable rents

and management charges, rates and general household incomes. At present, public housing rents are inclusive of rates and management and maintenance expenses. Public housing tenants pay, on average, 48 per cent of the assessed market rent (inclusive of rates) for the flats they live in.

The HKHA has established an Ad Hoc Committee on Review of Domestic Rent Policy to conduct a comprehensive review of its domestic rent policy. The objective is to map out a rent adjustment mechanism that is more flexible, draws a closer link with tenants' affordability and promotes the long-term sustainability of the public housing programme.

Rent Assistance

Public housing tenants facing temporary financial hardship may apply for a 50 per cent rent reduction under the Rent Assistance Scheme operated by the HKHA. The scheme was revised in October 2002 and the eligibility criteria for elderly households were relaxed. Tenants affected by redevelopment were also allowed to apply for rent assistance immediately upon rehousing. By year-end, 20 903 households had benefited from this scheme since its implementation in 1992.

Better-off Tenants

Better-off tenants are required to pay higher rents. At December 31, there were 14 879 households paying the higher rents. The subsidy saved through charging under this scheme amounted to $164 million in 2003. In addition, tenants living in estates for more than 10 years with both household income and assets exceeding the prescribed limits, or choosing not to declare household assets, are required to move out. In 2003, some 962 better-off tenants, including 503 households which acquired their own flats under the HOS, the Private Sector Participation Scheme (PSPS) or the HALS, returned their public rental housing flats to the HKHA.

Allocation

In 2003, 40 091[4] rental flats were allocated by the HKHA and the HKHS to various categories of applicants. Of these flats, 19 944 were new and 19 966 refurbished: 70.11 per cent were allocated to Waiting List applicants, 1.56 per cent to tenants affected by the HKHA's Comprehensive Redevelopment Programme, 0.88 per cent to families affected by clearances, 2.46 per cent to junior civil servants, 24.92 per cent to sitting tenants for transfers including overcrowding relief, and the remainder to victims of fire and natural disasters and compassionate cases recommended by the Social Welfare Department.

Flats are allocated in accordance with the order of registration and applicants' choices of district. Applicants are required to satisfy comprehensive means tests (covering income and assets), not to own any domestic property and to meet the residence rule in Hong Kong before being admitted into public rental housing. To speed up the letting of some less popular flats, the HKHA launched the Express Flat Allocation Scheme and invited all eligible applicants on the Waiting List to select a flat from among the vacant flats, with prolonged vacancy periods, in all districts. During the year, 1 100 households were successfully rehoused under this scheme.

4 Including 181 Rent Allowance for Elderly Scheme cases.

Rent Allowance Schemes

The Rent Allowance for Elderly Scheme was launched as a pilot scheme in August 2001 to give elderly applicants an arrangement to receive cash rent allowances to lease private accommodation in lieu of PRH allocation. Upon implementation, the pilot scheme attracted only a lukewarm response. Out of the total quota of 1 100 allowances in the two-year trial period, only about 620 were utilised. The HKHA therefore decided to phase out the scheme in September 2003 by ceasing to accept new applications. Existing beneficiaries, upon expiry of the current private leases, can opt for PRH units or continue to receive cash rent allowances provided that they still meet the prevailing eligibility criteria.

Divestment of Commercial Properties

To concentrate on its primary mission of providing subsidised public rental housing to people in need, the HKHA announced a plan to divest its retail and car parking facilities in 2004-05. Proceeds from the divestment would help the Authority to tide over its financial difficulties resulting from the cessation of the HOS, thus allowing it to pursue various measures to improve its finances in the longer term.

Home Ownership

Sale of Subsidised Flats

Since 1978, over 422 000[5] subsidised sale flats have been sold to households of eligible families/persons at discounted prices under the Government's various subsidised home ownership schemes. Among these were the HOS, the PSPS and the Tenants Purchase Scheme (TPS) under the HKHA. Given the significant changes in the economy and property market over the past few years, the Government believes that home ownership should essentially be a matter of personal choice and affordability. In this respect, the Government has come to the view that it should withdraw from its previous role as direct housing provider and refrain from competing with the private residential market. Furthermore, it should facilitate eligible families/persons to become home owners through the more flexible and well tested means of loans. Accordingly, the HKHA has decided that, with the exception of a limited number of unsold and returned HOS/PSPS flats to be sold to Green Form applicants, the production and sale of HOS/PSPS flats would cease indefinitely from 2003 onwards, and the TPS would halt following the sale of the TPS Phase 6. In November 2003, the HKHA further accepted the Government's proposal for not putting up the above unsold and returned HOS/PSPS flats for sale before the end of 2006 in order to give a clear signal of the determination to minimise the Government's intervention in the property market.

Home Assistance Loan Scheme

Following the withdrawal from the direct provision of subsidised sale flats, the HALS has become the principal means for offering assistance to eligible families/persons aspiring to become home owners. The HALS, with a quota of 10 000 for 2003-04 equally split between White and Green Form applicants, provides home purchase assistance towards down payment and related expenses, in the form of an interest-free

---

[5] Of the 422 000 flats sold since 1978, 46 900 flats can be traded in the open market as at-end December 2003. These flats are not counted as subsidised sale flats under the current definition.

loan or monthly mortgage subsidy[6], to those who cannot afford to buy a reasonable flat in the private market.

The HKHA will conduct a review of the future of the HALS in the light of enhanced affordability of eligible HALS applicants as a result of availability of competitive mortgage loans in the market and the downward adjustment of property prices since the HALS was conceptualised.

Housing for Groups in Special Need

The Elderly

An elderly person who prefers to live alone can apply under the Single Elderly Persons Priority Scheme and be allocated a public rental flat within three years. The Government has pledged to reduce the average waiting time of elderly singletons who wish to live by themselves to two years by 2005. Two or more elderly persons who are willing to live together may apply under the Elderly Persons Priority Scheme, and be allocated flats within two years.

There are two priority schemes for public rental flats which encourage households to live with and take care of their elderly members. Applicants with elderly parents or dependent relatives aged 60 or above under the Families with Elderly Persons Priority Scheme are allocated flats three years in advance at most of normal allocation in the district of their choice. Alternatively, they may also apply under the Special Scheme for Families with Elderly Persons for two separate flats in the same estate in new towns two years at most in advance of normal allocation.

To help low-income elderly households living in non-self-contained private flats or temporary structures, the Government pledged in the 2000 Policy Address to help eligible elderly people to apply for public housing. All eligible elderly households which submitted applications by the end of March 2001 have been offered public rental flats by the end of 2003.

Under its Senior Citizen Residences Scheme (SEN), the HKHS has been implementing two projects, one in Tseung Kwan O and the other in Jordan Valley, for developing purpose-built housing with integrated health care facilities for senior citizens in the middle-income group. The units in the projects are to be leased to eligible senior citizens on a 'lease-for-life' basis, thereby providing security of tenure in line with the concepts of 'healthy ageing' and 'ageing in place'. The project in Tseung Kwan O was completed in late 2003, whereas the one in Jordan Valley is expected to be ready for occupation around mid-2004.

Squatters

The numbers of squatters and squatter structures have been reduced in recent years as a result of rehousing and clearance programmes. There are now approximately 216 600 people living in about 7 200 squatter structures in the urban areas and about 389 900 squatter structures in the New Territories. Squatter control is maintained by

---

6 The three forms of financial assistance available under HALS are as follows—

	Family rate	Singleton rate
(1) Basic loan repayable over 20 years	$390,000	$195,000
(2) Higher loan repayable over 13 years	$530,000	$265,000
(3) Monthly mortgage subsidy for 48 months	$3,800	$1,900

regular patrols and hut inspections. About 740 illegal structures and extensions were demolished during the year.

Rooftop Structures

In April 2001, the Buildings Department drew up a seven-year clearance programme to clear 12 000 illegal rooftop structures on 4 500 single-staircase buildings. Rooftop dwellers are encouraged to register on the Waiting List for public rental housing. Occupants affected by enforcement action against illegal rooftop structures will be rehoused to public rental housing, including interim housing, according to their cligibility. In 2003, about 2 600 people affected by rooftop clearance were relocated.

Redevelopment

In 2003, the rehousing of some 4 220 households living in seven domestic housing blocks at Lower Ngau Tau Kok Estate (I) was completed. Since the launching of the HKHA's Comprehensive Redevelopment Programme (CRP) in 1988, 531 housing blocks have been redeveloped to improve the living conditions of some 181 730 households.

Housing Supply

Flat production in 2003 was 42 500. This comprised 26 400 flats in the private sector, 11 600 public rental housing flats and 4 500[7] subsidised home ownership flats.

Monitoring Demand for and Supply of Land for Housing

The Government will ensure an adequate supply of land for residential development. A comprehensive monitoring system together with an alert mechanism to adjust land supply and land production have been put in place so that the market demand is met in a timely manner.

Supporting Infrastructure

Provision of the bulk of infrastructure to support housing developments has always been carried out in a programmed and structured manner. To avoid delay of housing developments due to lack of infrastructure facilities, the Government has adopted fast-tracking measures to deliver these projects if needed. From 1995 to 2003, there are 57 such projects and 44 have already been completed. The remaining 13 projects are at various stages of implementation with a total project estimate of about $5.8 billion.

Private Sector Housing

Private Residential Property Prices

Owing to the outbreak of SARS, both private residential property prices and transaction volume hit a low point in the second quarter of 2003. The market, however, had been improving since the third quarter. The average property price in the fourth quarter had returned to the pre-SARS level. The price level in December was

---

[7] Including the flats under the HKHS's SEN. The production and sale of HOS flats has ceased indefinitely since 2003, except for a small number of unsold and returned flats which will be sold to Green Form applicants. For those HOS flats that are completed or under construction, these will be disposed of through market-friendly means.

10 per cent higher compared with July. The number of residential property transactions in the fourth quarter saw an increase of 29 per cent over the third quarter, and an increase of 51 per cent over the fourth quarter in the previous year.

Tenancy Control

As one of the measures to help revitalise the private housing market, the Government announced in November 2002 that it would seek to remove the security of tenure restrictions currently imposed on landlords of rented premises with a view to restoring the free operation of the private rental market.

Under existing security of tenure provisions in Part IV of the Landlord and Tenant (Consolidation) Ordinance, if a tenant seeks to renew the tenancy and is willing to pay the prevailing market rent, the landlord would have to agree to the tenancy renewal. Only on certain statutory grounds can the landlord refuse to renew the tenancy. Given the ample supply of rental units in the market and the drastic reduction in rentals, such protection in favour of tenants is no longer justified. The Government therefore considers it timely to remove the security of tenure provisions for domestic tenancies.

A public consultation was conducted in March 2003 on the proposal to relax security of tenure. The majority of the respondents were in favour of the proposal. In June 2003, the Government introduced into the Legislative Council the Landlord and Tenant (Consolidation) (Amendment) Bill 2003 to, among other things, remove the security of tenure restrictions for domestic tenancies.

Estate Agents

The Estate Agents Authority (EAA) was established on November 1, 1997 to devise licensing arrangements and practice directions for estate agents. The Estate Agents (Licensing) Regulation became operational on January 1, 1999. All estate agents are now required to obtain a licence to practise.

The Estate Agents Practice (General Duties and Hong Kong Residential Properties) Regulation and the Estate Agents (Determination of Commission Disputes) Regulation took effect on November 1, 1999. The former stipulates rules relating to the conduct, duties and practice of licensed estate agents. The latter prescribes rules and procedures for the EAA to assist in the mediation of disputes between an agent and a client. The Estate Agents (Registration of Determination and Appeal) Regulation, which came into operation on March 1, 2000, prescribes the procedural rules for the EAA to adjudicate in disputes on the amount of commissions payable to estate agents and for aggrieved parties to lodge appeals.

Consumer Protection

In order to ensure the provision of comprehensive and sufficient sales information of local uncompleted residential properties to potential purchasers, a committee set up by the Government in August 2001 has been monitoring information contained in sales brochures on local uncompleted residential flats to enhance consumer protection. The committee comprises representatives from the Legislative Council, the Consumer Council, the Real Estate Developers Association, the HKHA, the HKHS, and the legal, surveying and building professions. Views about sales descriptions of local uncompleted residential properties are collected through the website and the bilingual telephone hotlines of the Housing, Planning and Lands Bureau.

Home Pages

Housing, Planning and Lands Bureau: http://www.hplb.gov.hk
Hong Kong Housing Authority/Housing Department:
http://www.housingauthority.gov.hk

CHAPTER 12

Land, Public Works and Utilities

Major studies have been undertaken with the aim of setting out a long-term strategy for land use and infrastructure development in Hong Kong as well as to enhance synergy with the Pearl River Delta. These initiatives will serve as a blueprint for building on the fine record of accomplishment in the extensive Public Works Programme. With an excellent track record of having constructed nine new towns that now house about 46 per cent of the population, the Government has plans to undertake new projects and to implement an urban renewal programme in older areas. Emphasis is placed on sustainable development, and people's well-being.

TO meet the needs of the community and sustain Hong Kong's position as a world city in Asia, the Government is committed to maintaining a robust investment in building new infrastructure and improving existing facilities. It will spend about $31 billion on capital works in 2003-04. In the next few years, it will maintain an average annual capital works expenditure of about $29 billion.

Government works projects are implemented by the Works Departments under the Public Works Programme. In 2001, the Government simplified the administrative procedures and as a result reduced the overall pre-construction period of a typical engineering project from six years to less than four years. The Environment, Transport and Works Bureau further re-engineered in 2003 the methodology for the planning and implementation of infrastructural projects to improve efficiency and cost-effectiveness in the delivery of projects.

The Government commenced in 2003 the construction of a number of major projects which included the third phase of the Central Reclamation, the second stage of Penny's Bay reclamation, Hong Kong-Shenzhen Western Corridor, Deep Bay Link, the territory-wide rehabilitation of trunk watermains and the remaining works of the school improvement programme. In order to help boost the economy, the expenditure on minor works to improve various public facilities has also been increased in the past two years to alleviate the unemployment situation in the construction industry. The increased minor works have created over 6 000 additional new jobs for construction workers since October 2001.

With the concerted effort of all, the accident rate for public works contracts in 2003 continued on a downward trend to 19 accidents per thousand workers per year, representing a decrease of 24 per cent compared with 2002. With the success on site safety, the Government is taking steps to integrate health, safety and environmental protection into one portfolio to improve the overall performance of construction sites. The 'Pay for Safety and Environment Scheme' was introduced during the year to encourage contractors to improve site environmental performance in addition to health and safety. Additional measures were also introduced to enhance site cleanliness and hygiene, including the surroundings, to improve the site environment. Furthermore, regulatory action against contractors convicted of site safety offences was extended to cover environmental protection and mosquito breeding offences.

The Government and the Provisional Construction Industry Coordination Board achieved notable progress in implementing many of the recommendations made by the Construction Industry Review Committee. In order to strengthen communication with other stakeholders, the board has produced since April 2003 a quarterly leaflet outlining its major achievements and activities to complement information available at its website (*http://www.pcicb.gov.hk*).

Building upon the momentum generated by promulgation of the *Guidelines on Subcontracting Practice*, the board successfully launched in November the Primary Register, an initial phase of the voluntary subcontractor registration scheme. After securing a critical mass of registered subcontractors, this platform will evolve into a grading mechanism of individual capability and specialty.

Regarding employees' compensation insurance, the Hong Kong Federation of Insurers has revised its code of best practice to ensure proper coverage for all genuine employees working in construction sites, complemented by a set of guidelines formulated by the Labour Department to clarify the judicial criteria adopted in determining the requisite employment status. Furthermore, a premium rebate scheme has been rolled out as a driver of good safety performance based on prescribed indicators governing claims ratios, accident rates and outcome of audit inspections.

Based on a proposal submitted by the board, law drafting is in hand to introduce new legislation for establishment of the Construction Industry Council as an umbrella organisation to drive forward industry reform and promote self-regulation.

As part of the Government's comprehensive Slope Safety Strategy, a 10-year Landslip Preventive Measures (LPM) Programme, with a budget of about $9 billion, was launched in April 2000 to systematically upgrade substandard government slopes and carry out safety screening of private slopes. In addition, about $700 million will be spent in 2003-04 to maintain government slopes. For private slopes, a revised loan scheme on building safety improvement was set up in July 2001 to provide assistance to owners who need financial assistance to maintain their slopes. To further enhance visual harmony with the surroundings, landscaping will be included in upgraded or newly formed government slopes.

Organisational Framework

The primary objective of the Government's lands policy is to facilitate Hong Kong's continual development through a steady and sufficient supply of land, effective planning and use of land, and efficient registration of land.

The Secretary for the Environment, Transport and Works is responsible for the delivery of public works projects in a cost-effective manner, the formulation of policies on slope safety, water supply, flood control and construction site safety. She also oversees, and has policy responsibility for, the activities of the seven Works Departments: Architectural Services Department, Civil Engineering Department,

Drainage Services Department, Electrical and Mechanical Services Department, Highways Department, Territory Development Department and Water Supplies Department. In addition, she oversees the operation of the Electrical and Mechanical Services Trading Fund.

The Secretary for Housing, Planning and Lands, supported by the Permanent Secretary for Housing, Planning and Lands (Planning and Lands), oversees the operation of four departments: Buildings Department, Lands Department, Planning Department and Land Registry. He also oversees part of the work of the Civil Engineering Department, Electrical and Mechanical Services Department and Territory Development Department.

The Permanent Secretary for Housing, Planning and Lands (Planning and Lands) is chairman of both the Committee on Planning and Land Development (CPLD) and the Town Planning Board (TPB). The CPLD is responsible for considering and endorsing land use plans and major development proposals. The TPB is a statutory body, established under the Town Planning Ordinance, responsible for making town plans, and considering planning applications for individual projects in Hong Kong.

Review of the Town Planning Ordinance

The existing Town Planning Ordinance was first enacted in 1939. There is a need to revise the legislation from time to time to meet the requirements of the changing social and economic environment in Hong Kong.

The Town Planning Bill proposing an overhaul of the statutory planning system was introduced into the Legislative Council in February 2000. Owing to the complexity of the issues involved, the council's Bills Committee was not able to complete consideration of the bill within the 1998-2000 term, and it was dissolved after nine meetings. Since then, the Administration has taken the opportunity to review the bill's proposals in the light of the comments received and the changing socio-economic conditions.

While there is a general consensus on the need to streamline the planning procedures and to promote public participation, views on certain complex policy issues are diverse. These issues need to be resolved after further consultation with the stakeholders. Since there is a strong demand in the community to improve the efficiency and effectiveness of the present planning system, the Administration has decided to propose amendments to the Town Planning Ordinance in stages, giving priority to those amendments which have general consensus and would produce more immediate benefits to the community.

The first-stage amendments have been included in the Town Planning (Amendment) Bill 2003 which was introduced into the council in May. The main objectives of the amendment bill are to streamline the plan-making process and planning approval procedures, enhance the openness and user friendliness of the planning system and strengthen planning enforcement control in the rural New Territories.

Hong Kong Planning Standards and Guidelines

The *Hong Kong Planning Standards and Guidelines* is a government document of planning criteria and guidelines for determining the quantity, scale, location and site requirements of various land uses and facilities. It applies to planning studies and the preparation or revision of town plans. The document is under constant review to take account of changes in government policies, demographic characteristics and social and economic trends. During the year, planning standards and guidelines for residential densities, industry, parking provisions and urban design were formulated, updated or being revised.

The document is available for sale to the public on a chapter-by-chapter basis and uploaded to the Planning Department's website to promote public awareness of its content and to facilitate its application by non-governmental bodies.

Territorial Development Strategy

The Territorial Development Strategy (TDS) is the highest tier of planning in the hierarchy of town plans in Hong Kong. It provides a broad land use, transport and environmental framework for planning and development. It also serves as a basis for preparation of sub-regional plans and more detailed district plans.

The last review of the TDS was completed in 1996. Taking into account the emergence of new factors having strategic planning implications, a new round of review, the Hong Kong 2030: Planning Vision and Strategy, commenced in 2000. The study is to assess Hong Kong's future development needs in a wider regional perspective and for a longer time horizon.

The stage one and two public consultations were undertaken in 2001 and 2002, respectively. The stage three public consultation, focusing on the building of scenarios and formulation of development options, was launched in late 2003.

Sub-regional Development Strategies

These strategies serve as a bridge between the TDS and district plans. They translate the territorial goals into more specific planning objectives for the five sub-regions of Hong Kong, namely the Metro Area, North-East New Territories (NENT), North-West New Territories (NWNT), South-East New Territories (SENT) and South-West New Territories (SWNT). Extensive public consultation has been carried out to collect views on these strategies in view of their significant implications for the long-term planning framework for the respective sub-regions.

The Metroplan Review Study is intended to produce an updated planning framework for the development and redevelopment of the Metro Area for 2016 and beyond. The study includes a review of the 1993 Kowloon Density Study. The review study was completed in March 2003. In parallel, the Planning Study on the Harbour and its Waterfront Areas which aims at developing a planning framework for guiding future developments around Victoria Harbour was also completed in March.

The integrated planning and development studies on NENT and NWNT have been completed. The studies have identified and established the feasibility of developing Kwu Tung North, Fanling North and Hung Shui Kiu as the new development areas.

To follow up the recommendations of the SWNT Recommended Development Strategy, promulgated in 2001, an integrated planning and engineering feasibility study for Mui Wo and South Lantau is being carried out to formulate a preferred land use scheme for the area which would balance development and conservation needs in accordance with the principle of sustainable development.

The SENT Development Strategy Review was also completed in 2001. It provides a broad planning framework for the long-term development of SENT with a view to enhancing the sub-region as the 'Leisure Garden of Hong Kong' by promoting conservation, enhancing visitor attractions and achieving a sustainable level of development. Detailed planning based on the strategic planning framework at district level is being undertaken.

District Planning

Development projects are implemented in accordance with statutory or departmental district plans. These plans aim to regulate and provide guidance to development in terms of land use, building density and development characteristics, and to ensure that they are in line with planning objectives of the districts.

Statutory Planning

The Town Planning Board is set up under the Town Planning Ordinance to prepare statutory plans to show the broad land use framework of specific areas, including major roads and other transport systems, and provide statutory planning controls through land use zoning and specification of development parameters. Two types of statutory plans are prepared: outline zoning plans (OZPs) and development permission area (DPA) plans.

DPA plans are similar to OZPs but they are interim plans covering rural areas of the New Territories and would be eventually replaced by OZPs. Development scheme plans (DSPs) prepared by the former Land Development Corporation and its successor, the Urban Renewal Authority, also require approval by the board.

In 2003, two new OZPs and one new URA DSP were published by the board. The board also amended 60 statutory plans. At year-end, there were 105 OZPs, two DPA plans, eight LDC DSPs and one URA DSP.

Under the Town Planning Ordinance, any person affected by statutory plans on exhibition for public inspection, including DSPs, may lodge objections with the board. In 2003, there were 94 objections. The board gave preliminary consideration to 87 objections and further consideration to 80 objections (including those brought forward from previous years). Draft plans, together with objections not withdrawn and amendments made to meet objections, will be submitted to the Chief Executive in Council (CE in C) for approval. In 2003, 33 statutory plans were submitted to the CE in C for approval. The CE in C also referred 70 approved plans and one draft plan back to the board for amendment.

A set of notes is attached to each statutory plan, indicating the uses in particular zones that are always permitted and those uses for which the board's permission must be sought. In 2003, the board considered 883 applications for planning permission and reviewed its decisions on 139 planning applications.

Applicants who are aggrieved by the decisions of the board on review may lodge appeals with the independent Town Planning Appeal Board. The Appeal Board heard eight cases in 2003: seven were dismissed and one was allowed.

The Town Planning Board also promulgates guidelines for applications for developments in areas covered by statutory plans. In 2003, it promulgated seven sets of revised guidelines. Altogether, 21 sets of guidelines were in force.

Departmental Plans

Apart from statutory plans, the Planning Department prepares departmental outline development plans (ODPs) and layout plans (LPs) for individual districts or planning areas to show the planned land uses, development restrictions and transport networks in greater detail. There were 77 ODPs and 299 LPs covering Hong Kong in 2003.

Enforcement

Under the Town Planning Ordinance, no person shall undertake or continue a development in a development permission area (DPA) unless the development was a use in existence before the gazetting of the relevant Interim DPA or DPA plans, or is permitted under the DPA plan or the replacement OZP, or has obtained permission from the board. Development not satisfying these criteria is an 'unauthorised development (UD)' subject to enforcement and prosecution action. Currently, about 19 800 hectares of land in the rural area are covered by DPA plans or the replacement OZPs.

The Planning Authority may serve statutory notices on the respective landowners, occupiers and/or responsible persons, requiring them to discontinue the UD by a specified date unless planning permission for the development is obtained, or demanding a reinstatement of the land. It is an offence in law not to comply with the requirements of the notices.

In 2003, 282 new UDs were detected in the rural area. Most were related to uses such as open storage of vehicles, containers and construction machinery/materials; workshops; and container vehicle/trailer parks. The Director of Planning issued 998 warning letters for 246 cases, 673 enforcement notices for 128 cases, and 660 compliance notices for 120 cases. As for prosecution, 18 defendants in 16 cases were convicted. The average fine imposed was $30,117, with a range of $2,000 to $50,000. During the year, enforcement action resulted in the discontinuation of 197 UDs covering 55 hectares of land, and regularisation through the planning application system of another 226 UDs covering 80 hectares of land.

Urban Renewal

The Chief Executive announced in his 1999 Policy Address the setting up of the Urban Renewal Authority (URA) to replace the Land Development Corporation and to expedite urban renewal. The URA was established in May 2001 to undertake a 20-year urban renewal programme. In November 2001, the Government promulgated the Urban Renewal Strategy (URS) after wide public consultation, setting out the policy guidelines for the URA in the implementation of the urban renewal programme.

The purpose of urban renewal is to improve the environment of the older urban areas and the living conditions of the residents therein through a comprehensive and holistic approach comprising the redevelopment of dilapidated buildings, the promotion of the rehabilitation of older buildings, the revitalisation of old districts and the preservation of buildings of historical, cultural or architectural interest.

The Government has put in place a financial support package for the URA to enable it to launch the urban renewal programme on a sound financial footing. In May 2002, the Executive Council approved in principle land grants at nominal premium for urban renewal sites. The Finance Committee of the Legislative Council also approved in June 2002 a commitment of $10 billion for equity injection into the URA in phases from 2002-03 to 2006-07. A total of $4 billion had been injected into the URA by year-end.

To facilitate the implementation of the urban renewal programme, the Housing, Planning and Lands Bureau keeps under close review the delivery of the programme in the annual examination of the URA's five-year Corporate Plan and annual Business Plan; provides the necessary support and policy guidance to the URA; monitors and facilitates the implementation of individual projects, including vetting development projects having regard to any objections raised under the statute; oversees land resumption and clearance exercises to be undertaken by the Lands Department; and will review the URS regularly to take account of the community's changing needs.

The Planning Department supports the operation of the URA from the planning perspective so as to optimise the community benefits of URA projects and to ensure compliance with the statutory planning requirements. The department undertakes planning studies to assist in the formulation and review of the URS and will develop a comprehensive geographical information system to allow for the sharing of information on building conditions among various government departments for the purpose of drawing up and updating the rehabilitation and urban renewal programme. In addition, the department is involved in processing development schemes and master layout plans submitted by the URA for the Town Planning Board's consideration; and coordinating the provision of infrastructure, government, institution or community facilities and open space in URA projects.

The URA has made steady progress in taking forward a comprehensive urban renewal programme. By December, it had launched 13 redevelopment projects, two of which are carried out by the Hong Kong Housing Society (HKHS) under the URA/HKHS strategic partnership in urban renewal. In October, the URA extended its voluntary building rehabilitation pilot scheme whereby material incentives and technical assistance are provided to owners of old buildings to encourage them to undertake preventive maintenance. The URA also began a number of revitalisation projects during the year to renew the environment and economic fabric of old districts.

Planning Studies

Studies completed by the Planning Department during the year included: Metroplan Review Study; Planning Study on the Harbour and its Waterfront Areas; Focus Study on Aberdeen Harbour; Planning and Development Study on Hong Kong Island South and Lamma Island; Planning and Development Studies on NENT and NWNT; Setting Up of a 3-Dimensional Digital Model for the Main Urban Area of Hong Kong; and the Study on Urban Design Guidelines for Hong Kong.

The ongoing studies carried out by the Planning Department include Hong Kong 2030: Planning Vision and Strategy; Study on Planning for Pedestrians; Landscape Value Mapping of Hong Kong; and a Study to Examine Ways to Centralise and Disseminate Planning Data.

Studies commenced during the year included: Cross Boundary Travel Survey 2003 and Assignment on Provision of Transport Consultancy Services for Model Enhancement.

The department also worked on several major development proposals, notably, South-East Kowloon Development; the Central Reclamation Phase III; Wan Chai Development Phase II; Further Development of Tseung Kwan O Feasibility Study; and the Penny's Bay Development to facilitate Hong Kong Disneyland Phase I.

Urban Development Areas

Construction works and feasibility studies on new urban development areas generally follow the broad pattern of land use and guidelines in the Metroplan, and integrate with the replanning and redevelopment of adjoining old areas in a coordinated manner. The Territory Development Department (TDD) is conducting detailed design of several major reclamation projects to provide new land for growth, to decant existing population and to provide or upgrade facilities to allow for the redevelopment of old and run-down areas.

Hong Kong Island

The Central and Wan Chai Reclamation extends along the waterfront from Sheung Wan to Causeway Bay. Three of the five reclamation phases have been completed — the Central Reclamation Phases I and II, and the Wan Chai Reclamation Phase I. The comprehensive feasibility study for the Wan Chai Development Phase II was completed in August 2001.

The construction of the Central Reclamation Phase III commenced in February. This phase, together with the other phases of the Central and Wan Chai Reclamation, will accommodate strategic road and rail links along the north shore of Hong Kong Island between the Central and Eastern Districts. The TPB has requested the Government to undertake a comprehensive planning and engineering review of the reclamation under the Wan Chai Development Phase II as a result of the High Court's judgement on the judicial review of the TPB's decision in respect of the draft Wan Chai North Outline Zoning Plan.

On the eastern side of Hong Kong Island, the Aldrich Bay development has produced some 28 hectares of land for private and public housing, open space and other uses to house about 30 000 people. Construction of roads and major infrastructure was completed in late 2003.

The Cyberport, Hong Kong's information technology flagship, is being developed on 24 hectares of land at Telegraph Bay in the Southern District of Hong Kong Island. The Cyberport is a comprehensive development providing 100 000 square metres of Grade A office accommodation for IT and IT-related companies, a specially designed shopping arcade covering 27 000 square metres and a five-star hotel providing 173 rooms. Phase I and II of the Cyberport were completed in April 2002 and February 2003 respectively, and the remaining two phases will be completed in early and late 2004 respectively. The ancillary residential development, to be completed between 2004 and 2007, will provide about 2 900 units for sale in the open market.

The Southern Access Road and the public transport interchange were opened to the public in April 2002 to coincide with the completion of the first phase of the Cyberport. The other access road, connecting the northern end of the Cyberport with Sha Wan Drive, will be completed in the third quarter of 2004.

Kowloon

The West Kowloon Reclamation provides a total of 340 hectares of land for strategic transport links, commercial development and housing development. It has a current population of about 56 800 which is expected to rise to about 192 000 by 2016. Infrastructure works have been substantially completed, and the final phase of reclamation to provide 13 hectares of land is near completion and remaining roadworks are in progress.

The Comprehensive Feasibility Study for the Revised Scheme of the South-East Kowloon Development (SEKD) was completed in September 2001. The further reduction in the total reclamation area to some 133 hectares and the adoption of environmentally friendly measures have been welcomed by the public. The scheme was translated into two Outline Zoning Plans that were gazetted in July 2001 and authorised in June 2002. The new development area of the SEKD comprises the former Kai Tak airport apron and runway (280 hectares) and new reclamation areas (133 hectares). Detailed design work for some of the infrastructure in the SEKD began in January 2002. However, in the light of the High Court's judgement on the judicial review of the TPB's decisions in respect of the draft Wan Chai North Outline Zoning Plan, the Government has started to review the reclamation scheme of the SEKD to ensure that it meets legal requirements.

New Towns and Rural Townships

The development of new towns in the New Territories continued in 2003. At year-end, about 3.2 million people were housed in the new towns and the nearby rural townships, enjoying a wide range of community and recreational facilities, including schools, markets, shopping centres, parks and open spaces and convenient transport links.

Railway development continued to add convenient mass transit connections between the new towns and the urban areas. The KCR West Rail, commissioned in December, links the new towns of Tsuen Wan, Yuen Long, Tin Shui Wai and Tuen Mun with West Kowloon. The new town of Tseung Kwan O has been served by the MTR Tseung Kwan O Line since August 2002.

Engineering design and construction works on land formation and infrastructure of the development are overseen and coordinated by the TDD.

Landscape Design and the Natural Environment

Extensive landscape works continued to be implemented in conjunction with the developments, providing a green framework to the new neighbourhoods. Trees are planted along roadsides to provide shade and colour, and attention is given to the provision and design of sitting-out areas and walkways for the enjoyment of the public. Ecological restoration works have also been undertaken in accordance with the recommendation of the environmental impact assessment studies to mitigate the impact of engineering works.

Apart from the tree planting associated with the developments, large-scale afforestation programme continued in the hinterland of the new towns and urban development areas, reducing soil erosion due to water run-off from hillsides, preventing siltation of drainage systems and enhancing the countryside. More than 12 million trees and shrubs have been planted over the last five years, with about three million planted in 2003.

Tsuen Wan

Tsuen Wan new town embraces the areas of Tsuen Wan, Kwai Chung and Tsing Yi Island, covering a total development area of about 2 400 hectares. It has a current population of about 772 000, which is expected to rise to about 816 000 by 2012. The new town has Hong Kong's container terminals in its midst in Kwai Chung Area. In addition, the Container Terminal 9 is under construction in southeast Tsing Yi.

Major highway projects are being constructed or planned to further extend and reinforce the main road network. Construction is proceeding on part of the rationalised Route 8 (previously part of Route 9) between Tsing Yi and Cheung Sha Wan, and the section of Route 5 between Shek Wai Kok and Chai Wan Kok.

Sha Tin

Sha Tin new town embraces the areas of Sha Tin and Ma On Shan. It covers a total development area of about 2 000 hectares and is already home to about 641 000 people.

Construction work is under way on the Sha Tin Heights Tunnel and Approaches, which now form part of the rationalised Route 8 (and were previously part of Route 9) linking Sha Tin to Cheung Sha Wan, and on the Road T3, which will connect with the Sha Tin Heights Tunnel. Both projects will be completed in 2007.

The construction of Trunk Road T7, which will bypass the Ma On Shan Town Centre and improve traffic conditions there, is due for completion in mid-2004.

Tuen Mun

Tuen Mun new town, in the western New Territories, is developed mainly on land reclaimed from Castle Peak Bay and on platforms built in the valley between Castle Peak and the Tai Lam Hills. It covers a total development area of about 1 900 hectares. The new town's current population is about 485 000, and this is forecast to rise to about 535 000 in 2012.

In south-west Tuen Mun, the River Trade Terminal operates as a consolidation point for containers and bulk cargoes shipped between Hong Kong and the Pearl River Delta ports. The reclamation for special industrial use has been completed. To cope with the increasing traffic demand in association with these developments, Lung Fu Road (Foothills Bypass) has been opened to traffic.

Tai Po

Tai Po has grown from a small market town into a new town with a population of around 282 000. The new town, covering about 1 270 hectares, is well developed with the major infrastructure in place.

The Pak Shek Kok Development includes the development of a Science Park and residential and recreation uses. The advance engineering infrastructure works for the development have been substantially completed to facilitate the inauguration of the initial phase of the Science Park. The Stage I works for the remaining infrastructure continued during the year and are scheduled for completion in early 2005 whereas the Stage 2 works are programmed to commence in early 2004 for completion in end-2006 to tie in with the Science Park's development programme.

Fanling and Sheung Shui

Fanling and Sheung Shui are former traditional market towns which now have a population of about 246 000. The total development area is about 780 hectares. The new town's population is expected to reach around 269 000 in 2012.

The river training works at the River Indus Basin to relieve the risk of flooding in the Fanling and Sheung Shui areas were substantially completed in mid-2003.

Yuen Long

Yuen Long new town has a current population of about 177 000 and this is expected to grow to around 206 000 by 2012. It covers a development area of about 1 170 hectares.

Development in the new town is being extended southward and along the Tuen Mun-Yuen Long Corridor. Infrastructure works for the southern extension area commenced in end-2002 for completion in 2006.

The river training works for the upper reaches of the Kam Tin River and the Ngau Tam Mei Catchment are in progress. Works on the San Tin Eastern Main Drainage Channel and the Yuen Long Bypass Floodway commenced in end-2002 and early 2003 for completion in 2005 and 2006, respectively. These works will alleviate flooding problems.

Tseung Kwan O

Tseung Kwan O new town has a current population of around 311 000 and covers a development area of about 1 005 hectares.

In external transport, the new town is served by Po Lam Road, Clear Water Bay Road and the Tseung Kwan O Tunnel. Further external road links under planning include the Western Coast Road and widening of Hang Hau Road/Clear Water Bay Road to dual-carriageway standard.

The Tseung Kwan O Industrial Estate is located north of Fat Tong Chau. A total of about 95 hectares of land has been formed and serviced for development of high-technology industries or industries requiring large amounts of land. The reclamation of about 104 hectares in Fat Tong O for further industrial developments and potentially hazardous installations is substantially completed.

The feasibility study on further development of Tseung Kwan O continued and is targeted for completion in late 2004. The objective of the study is to formulate a comprehensive development plan and to improve the overall design of Tseung Kwan O and heighten its living environment.

Tin Shui Wai

Tin Shui Wai new town has been built on land reclaimed from low lying areas off Deep Bay. An initial Development Zone of 220 hectares has been developed with major infrastructure works and a full range of community facilities completed. The new town now houses about 200 000 people. The opening of the KCR West Rail and the Light Rail Transit extension, as well as new roads linking the new town to the trunk road network, provide good communications with the Yuen Long and Tuen Mun districts and the urban areas beyond.

Engineering works for the Reserve Zone, covering 210 hectares, are in an advanced stage and targeted for completion in mid-2004. The overall population of the new town will increase to around 289 000 in 2012.

Tung Chung

Construction works for Phase 1 of Tung Chung new town were completed in 1997, providing facilities for an initial community of around 20 000. Engineering works for Phase 2 development were completed in 2001 to serve an intended population of about 67 000. In 2003, the population had risen to about 41 000. Reclamation for Phase 3A development was completed early in the year.

The new town is linked to the rest of Hong Kong by the North Lantau Highway as well as the MTR Tung Chung Line.

In December, the Government granted a franchise to the MTR Corporation Limited for the finance, design, construction, operation and maintenance of a cable car system linking Tung Chung and Ngong Ping. This is expected to become an important tourism facility.

North-East New Territories and North-West New Territories New Development

The planning and development studies on North-East New Territories (NENT) and North-West New Territories (NWNT) have been completed. The studies have established the feasibility of developing Kwu Tung North (497 hectares) and Fanling North (192 hectares) in NENT as New Development Areas to house populations of 100 000 and 80 000, respectively, and developing Hung Shui Kiu (450 hectares) in NWNT as a New Development Area to accommodate a population of about 160 000. The development of these New Development Areas will be triggered when the need arises.

Building Development

The Private Sector

There was increased activity in private building development during the year. The number of building sites where superstructure works started increased from 124 in 2002 to 266 in 2003, involving a total gross floor area of 1.17 million square metres and 2.07 million square metres, respectively. In 2003, a total of 785 buildings, with a total gross floor area of 2.87 million square metres, were completed at a total cost of $33.1 billion. This compared with 1 132 buildings, with a total gross floor area of 3.88 million square metres, built at a total cost of $45.7 billion, in 2002.

Major construction works in progress at year-end included the residential part of the Cyberport development in Pok Fu Lam, the Hong Kong Disneyland theme park and the associated Penny's Bay Rail Link, the Lok Ma Chau Spur Line, the Ma On Shan Rail and the Tsim Sha Tsui Extension of the East Rail.

As a continuing exercise to promote client-oriented service, the third *Joint Practice Note for Authorised Persons and Registered Structural Engineers* was issued in August, describing new measures to streamline the process of landscape master plans and the provision of pre-submission enquiry services.

The Buildings Department continued to rationalise the control on supervision of building works by building professionals. A working group, set up to review all site supervision requirements under the Buildings Ordinance, has prepared a draft proposal for an integrated site supervision system.

During the year, 25 816 reports on unauthorised building works (UBWs) were processed; 24 003 removal orders issued; and 49 556 UBWs removed. A total of 714 prosecutions were instituted against offenders for erecting UBWs or failing to comply with removal orders. These resulted in 461 convictions with fines totalling $1.95 million.

To tackle the problem of UBWs, the Buildings Department continued to embark on 'blitz' clearance operations, to demolish in one exercise all external UBWs on a number of buildings in the same district. A total of 1 000 buildings were targeted for 'blitz' clearances in 2003. The programme to remove all illegal rooftop structures on 4 500 single staircase buildings that pose a serious fire hazard gathered momentum. Enforcement action against 713 buildings with illegal rooftop structures was completed, compared with 402 and 632 in 2001 and 2002, respectively.

The SARS outbreak raised public awareness of the importance of proper maintenance of drainage systems in buildings. The Buildings Department inspected the external drainage pipes of about 11 000 private buildings without Owners Corporations (OCs) or Mutual Aid Committees (MACs). For the other 18 000 buildings with OCs, MACs or management companies, the department advised them to inspect their drains. A total of 1 811 drainage repair orders were issued and 1 913 buildings had defects rectified.

A Working Group on Building Design for a Clean and Healthy Environment was set up to review the existing relevant regulations, identify new and improved building design standards and propose ways to achieve a clean and healthy built environment.

As part of the Government's newly formed Team Clean's measures to improve environmental hygiene, the Buildings Department took part in a joint operation with other relevant departments to clean up 85 priority district 'black spots' and launch six pilot projects to rectify environmental hygiene problem in target areas. A total of 839 UBWs and 494 drainage defects were removed or rectified in these operations.

Under the Fire Safety (Commercial Premises) Ordinance, joint inspections with the Fire Services Department were made to improve fire safety in commercial premises built before 1987. For prescribed commercial premises (banks, betting centres, jewellery shops, shopping arcades, supermarkets), 194 Fire Safety Directions were issued to 120 premises requiring the owners concerned to remedy infractions. For specified commercial buildings (built before 1987), 3 537 Fire Safety Improvement Directions were issued to 140 buildings requiring upgrading of fire safety standards and facilities.

The recently enacted Fire Safety (Buildings) Ordinance requires the upgrading of essential fire safety provisions in composite and domestic buildings built before 1987. When the ordinance comes into operation, 9 000 composite buildings designed for both domestic and commercial uses will be required to upgrade fire service installations and fire safety construction. The upgrading programme will then be extended to cover the remaining 3 000 domestic buildings in which the fire risk involved is lower.

Under the Building Safety Loan Scheme, 2 588 applications with a total loan amount of $77.76 million were approved during the year.

Starting from November 2002, a total of 550 buildings were selected for action under the Coordinated Maintenance of Buildings Scheme. Owners of 300 buildings were motivated to take up their maintenance responsibilities, and repair or other improvement works were completed on 131 of these buildings.

The department began a comprehensive review of the Buildings Ordinance and its regulations in 2000. As a result of the review, legislative amendments have been proposed to rationalise the building control regime, strengthen safety requirements, facilitate law enforcement, and improve service to the public.

The proposed legislative amendments were included in the Buildings (Amendment) Bill 2003, which was introduced into the Legislative Council in April.

The Public Sector

The Architectural Services Department acts as Government's architect in providing full professional, technical and financial management services for the development and maintenance of public buildings (other than public housing) in three main areas:—

(i) technical advice and monitoring services to all bureaux and departments on their projects subject to government subvention and on government projects entrusted to or in joint venture with the private sector. About 900 projects, valued at $58 billion, were monitored during the year;

(ii) professional and technical services for project management, design and supervision of the construction of building projects in the Public Works Programme and those of the Hospital Authority (HA). During the year, the department's rolling programme covered 339 projects at a total value of about $56 billion; and

(iii) building maintenance services, including the provision of general maintenance for all public buildings and facilities as well as those of the HA, covering a total floor area of approximately 27.4 million square metres. The department also undertakes conservation and restoration of listed buildings and gazetted monuments, and emergency and major repairs to all subvented schools outside public housing estates.

Under the re-engineering programme, the department will focus on its strategic roles as the building authority for and steward of government buildings, and as the Government's corporate professional adviser on architectural policies, building planning and maintenance matters. The bulk of the building and maintenance works currently undertaken by the department will be gradually outsourced to the private sector. During the year, the level of outsourcing increased to 59 per cent.

In 2003, the actual expenditure on building projects undertaken or monitored by the department was $11.67 billion, with a further expenditure of $2.32 billion on routine maintenance and minor alteration works. The building projects undertaken by the department were in the following categories:—

Education

The construction of 27 schools was completed in 2003, and works on 27 schools were under way for completion in 2004 and 2005. The design for the school projects will be site and user-specific whenever the necessary lead time is available in the programme.

In the continued development of environmental and 'green' aspects, a building integrated photovoltaic system was installed in one of the schools completed as a pilot scheme to save energy and to raise students' awareness of the merits of natural energy.   225

The department has completed improvements to 450 schools in recent years, including 62 schools in 2003. Improvement works began at 94 schools during the year, bringing the number of schools undergoing improvements to 235.

Disciplined Services

Sha Tau Kok Fire Station, Lau Fu Shan Fire Station and Ambulance Depot, the Police Dog Unit and Force Search Unit Complex at Sha Ling, and the remaining works under the 'Police Stations Improvement Project' programme were completed during the year.

Construction work was in progress on a variety of projects. These included the Fire Stations and Ambulance Depots in Braemar Hill and Penny's Bay, Mong Kok and Kwai Chung Ambulance Depots and Fire Services Department Regional Command Headquarters, and the Reprovisioning of Civil Aid Service and Fire Services Department Facilities at Site 17 of the West Kowloon Reclamation. Other projects were the Immigration Service Training School and Perowne Immigration Centre in Tuen Mun, Phase 3 Redevelopment of Police Headquarters at Arsenal Street in Wan Chai, and the New Territories South Regional Police Headquarters and Operational Base in Tsuen Wan.

Preparatory work was under way for the construction of the Marine Police Outer Waters District Headquarters and Marine Police North Division at Ma Liu Shui, Independent Commission Against Corruption Headquarters building in North Point, and reprovisioning of Victoria Prison at the site of the old married quarters at the Correctional Services Department's Lai Chi Kok Reception Centre.

An earlier project completed by the department was the conversion of the Married Officer Quarters of the Correctional Services Department at Stanley into the Hong Kong Correctional Services Museum.

Science and Research

The development of the Science Park at Pak Shek Kok was in progress. The Science Park is delineated into different zones for housing tenants of sizes ranging from small incubator firms to multinational conglomerates within a park-like environment. The buildings are equipped with comprehensive infrastructure facilities, and advanced technological and environmental systems.

Phase 1 of the Science Park comprises 10 buildings. The first three buildings were completed in 2002. During the year, three more buildings were completed, including the Photonic Centre, the Wireless Centre and the Innovation Centre for research and development facilities. Construction of the remaining four buildings was under way.

Medical and Health

During the year, construction was in progress on a number of projects, including the Castle Peak Hospital Redevelopment (Phase 2), the establishment of a Radiotherapy Centre and the redevelopment of the Accident and Emergency Department at Princess Margaret Hospital, the remodelling of Tang Shiu Kin Hospital into an Ambulatory Care Centre, and the redevelopment of Staff Quarters for the establishment of a Rehabilitation Block at Tuen Mun Hospital. Works were also progressing on the remodelling of the Tuen Mun Polyclinic Building for the establishment of an Ophthalmic Centre, the enhancement of infection control facilities in the public hospital system, and construction of a Public Mortuary at Area 26E, Kwai Chung.

Recreation and Culture

Projects completed during the year included the Jordan Valley Playground (Phase 2, Stage 2), local open space in Area 44 of Tuen Mun and improvement works to Victoria Park.

Works commenced on eight open space projects, Hammer Hill Road Park, Stanley Complex, Water Sports Centre in Stanley Main Beach, and Tung Wan Beach Building in Cheung Chau. Improvement to Lok Wah Playground in Kwun Tong and renovation of the YMCA Wu Kai Sha Youth Village in Ma On Shan were also under way.

Construction was in progress on the Tai Kok Tsui Complex, Ma On Shan Sports Ground (Phase 2), Kowloon Bay Recreation Ground, local open spaces in Areas 18 and 21 of Fanling, and Indoor Recreation Centre/Library in Area 100, Ma On Shan.

The Public Square Street Garden in Yau Tsim Mong District, refurbished in Chinese style with special features like a 'Nine-dragon Wall' and a 'Pai Lau', attracts the patronage of both local residents and tourists.

Tourism

Construction of the Hong Kong Wetland Park and the Visitor Centre in Tin Shui Wai continued. This is the first pilot project to use recycled aggregates in structural concrete under the Government's policy on construction and demolition waste management.

As part of the overall initiatives to improve the townscape of Sai Kung, improvement works to the Sai Kung Waterfront area were completed during the year. The department also managed streetscape and signage projects in districts popular with tourists.

Boundary Crossing Facilities

The enhanced boundary crossing facilities for both cargo and passengers traffic at Lok Ma Chau were substantially completed during the year.

Improvement works to the Lo Wu Terminal Building were in progress for completion by early 2005. Installation of an air-conditioning system at the Lo Wu Cross Boundary Footbridge began in October.

Expansion of customs and immigration facilities at the Sha Tau Kok Control Point was under planning.

Design for the development of boundary crossing facilities at the Hong Kong-Shenzhen Western Corridor proceeded in cooperation with the Shenzhen Port Affairs Office.

Initiatives in Sustainable Development

The department continued its efforts in promoting and practising sustainability in the building industry.

Steps are taken to ensure that all building designs are compatible with the surrounding environment, efficient in utilising 'land', 'energy' and 'material' resources, and easy to 'operate', 'service' and 'maintain'. To encourage staff and consultants to adopt a holistic approach to environmental design, environmental performance assessments including the Hong Kong Building Environmental Assessment Method (HK-BEAM) were conducted on the projects concerned.

Provision of a healthy built environment for users and public is a key objective. All projects were designed with the aim of attaining the 'Excellent' class of Indoor Air Quality (IAQ) as defined under the IAQ Certification Scheme for Offices and Public Places, which was launched during the year. The 'Overall Energy Approach' was used to achieve a healthy indoor environment in a cost-effective and energy-efficient manner.

The department continued to take the lead in implementing energy efficient technologies in building services installations. These included the installation of water-cooled air-conditioning systems, total energy heat pumps, and demand control systems, resulting in an estimated annual saving of 300 million megajoules of energy.

Use of renewable energy is promoted effectively. During the year, 3 300 square metres of photovoltaic panels with a total electrical capacity of 300 kilowatts were installed in new projects. The Hong Kong Wetland Park's Visitor Centre, to be completed in 2005, will be the first building in Hong Kong that utilises geothermal energy for operating its air-conditioning system.

The efforts of the department in promoting sustainability have been recognised by various bodies. Awards received included the 'Commendation for Environmental Reporting' from the Association of Chartered Certified Accountants Hong Kong Environmental Reporting Awards 2002, and the Hong Kong Institute of Architects 2002 Annual Award under the category of 'Special Architectural Award — Sustainable Design' for the Veterinary Laboratory at Tai Lung in Sheung Shui.

Land Administration

The Lands Administration Office of the Lands Department consists of the headquarters, 14 District Lands Offices and various specialist sections. Its main functions are land acquisition, land disposal, land management and lease enforcement.

Land Acquisition

When private land is acquired in the public interest, usually to implement public works projects, it may be acquired either by negotiation or by resumption under the relevant ordinances, which provide for payment of compensation based on the value of the property and for business loss, at the date of acquisition. If agreement cannot be reached on the amount of compensation, either party can refer the claim to the Lands Tribunal for adjudication. Apart from statutory compensation, there is an alternative system of *ex gratia* zonal compensation to provide a simplified compensation procedure and early payments relating to land resumption in the New Territories.

A total of 513 066 square metres of private land, comprising 511 874 square metres of agricultural land and 1 192 square metres of building land, were acquired in 2003. Most of the acquired area was to provide land for implementation of road improvement works and river training projects. The improvement works included the construction of roads for the Deep Bay Link and the widening of Yuen Long Highway between Lam Tei and the Shap Pat Heung Interchange. The river training projects included the rehabilitation works at Ping Yuen River, the main drainage channels for the Tin Tsuen Channel and drainage improvement works for Pat Heung in the Yuen Long District.

More than $1.434 billion was paid out territory-wide in compensation payments in 2003.

The Lands Department was also involved in the resumption of land for implementation of urban renewal projects undertaken by the Urban Renewal Authority. During the year, statutory compensation totalling $65 million was paid to owners of 60 resumed properties affected by 11 urban renewal projects in Mong Kok, Yau Ma Tei, Sham Shui Po, Wan Chai, Kennedy Town, Tsuen Wan and Tsim Sha Tsui.

The Lands Department continued to resume and clear land for implementation of railway projects. By year-end, $131 million was paid out in respect of the West Rail project and $65 million for the KCR East Rail extensions which included the Lok Ma Chau Spur Line and the extension from Hung Hom to Tsim Sha Tsui.

Land Disposal

All land within the HKSAR is state property, and the Government is responsible for its disposal and management. Government land for private development is normally disposed of by way of public auction or tender. Land is also made available by private treaty grant at a nominal land premium to non-profit making educational, medical and charitable institutions for operating schools, hospitals and social welfare and other community facilities. Land grants at full market value premium are made to public utility companies for their installations.

New government land leases are normally granted at a premium for 50 years from the date of grant and subject to an annual rent equivalent to three per cent of the rateable value of the property at the date of grant, adjusted in step with any changes in the rateable value thereafter.

As part of a package of measures implemented since November 2002 to restore public confidence in the property market, scheduled land auctions had stopped and the Application List system was suspended until the end of 2003.

Sites sold by public tender in 2003 included a heritage site for commercial development and preservation of historic buildings, with a total area of 1.23 hectares, and four sites, for petrol filling stations, with a total area of 0.8 hectares.

In addition to land supply from the Government, existing privately held land leases can be amended, normally at a premium, on lease-holders' initiatives to provide for a more intensive or different type of development in accordance with the prevailing planning intentions. These amendments are effected by either lease modification or land exchange. During the year, 152 such transactions were concluded, involving a total of 1 515 hectares.

Land Control and Estate Management

The Task Force (Black Spots) (TFB) was set up in 1994 to clean up environmental 'black spots' that arose in the 1980s as a result of the massive conversion of agricultural land into open storage sites, container depots and vehicle parking/repairing sites in the New Territories. During the year, 286 sites covering

28.09 hectares were improved, making a cumulative total of 2 309 sites comprising 275.40 hectares of land.

The TFB provided support in the identification of suitable new sites for uses relating to container freight/open storage activities and during the year disposed of two sites by way of public tender. It also promoted improvements to the infrastructure in areas zoned for open storage related uses and coordinated government departmental action in the prevention and control of illegal dumping of waste.

The Property Management Unit manages properties that are resumed, surrendered or lease-expired. During the year, nine properties were taken over for management, making a cumulative total of 462. Thirteen properties were sold and 19 let on a short-term basis.

Important advances continue to be made in the area of slope safety maintenance. Identification of the parties responsible for maintenance of registered man-made slopes is an ongoing exercise that is associated with the slope registration system operated by the Geotechnical Engineering Office of the Civil Engineering Department. The public can use the Internet (at the Lands Department's website) to identify the parties responsible for the maintenance of registered man-made slopes. The Slope Maintenance Responsibility Information System on the Internet has been enhanced with an option to display information in simplified Chinese characters in addition to traditional Chinese characters and English.

The Lands Department is responsible for maintaining about 16 900 registered man-made slopes on government land that are not allocated to other maintenance departments. The department's Slope Maintenance Section, with the assistance of private consultants, carries out regular inspections of these slopes and employs contractors to undertake routine maintenance works and, where required, stabilisation works. The works are prioritised according to the level of risk posed to life and property in the event of landslides. During the year, routine works were carried out on 3 400 slopes and stabilisation works on 116 slopes.

In order to improve the environment and the state of housing in New Territories villages, District Lands Offices grant indigenous villagers permission to build small houses and approve the rebuilding of old village houses. They also issue short-term tenancies or short-term waivers and government land licences for rebuilding temporary domestic structures.

In control and enforcement, the Lands Department implements measures to prevent illegal use of unallocated government land, such as unauthorised occupation, dumping, excavation, cultivation or trespassing. Apart from taking preventive measures, such as fencing-off of vacant government land or deploying security guards at 'black spots', the District Lands Offices take enforcement action against offenders under the Land (Miscellaneous Provision) Ordinance and the Summary Offences Ordinance. Clearance action to maintain and improve the environment of government land is also taken regularly.

A scheme to better manage the display of non-commercial publicity materials at roadsides was implemented jointly by the Lands Department and the Food and Environmental Hygiene Department in April. The objective is to provide an efficient arrangements for display of such materials without compromising traffic safety or the streetscape. At year-end, 21 215 designated spots for displaying banners in public places were under the administrative aegis of the Lands Department.

Government Conveyancing

The Legal Advisory and Conveyancing Office of the Lands Department provides professional legal services to the Government in respect of all government land transactions and associated matters. It is responsible for the drafting of all government land disposal and acquisition documents, the apportionment and recovery of arrears (by re-entry or vesting action) of government rents, other than those payable under the Government Rent (Assessment and Collection) Ordinance.

It provides conveyancing services to The Financial Secretary Incorporated for the extension of non-renewable leases, The Secretary for Home Affairs Incorporated for the purchase of accommodation for welfare purposes in private developments and other government departments in relation to certain loan schemes.

The office also processes applications for the sale of units in uncompleted developments that are subject to the Lands Department Consent Scheme. In the latter half of 2003, the office conducted a review of the Consent Scheme with a view to further strengthening its operation and to improving protection for flat purchasers. The Lands Department will implement the improvement measures in 2004-05.

The office is also responsible for the approval of Deeds of Mutual Covenant which, among other things, set out the rights and obligations between the manager and co-owners of a development. During the year, 32 applications for the sale of units in uncompleted developments, involving 17 813 residential units, and 44 Deeds of Mutual Covenant were approved.

Survey and Mapping

The Survey and Mapping Office provides various survey and mapping services for land, building and engineering developments in Hong Kong. Specifically, it provides maps and aerial photographs, land boundary survey service for land administration, and aerial survey and photogrammetric service for specific purposes in addition to general mapping. It also establishes and maintains the territory-wide Geodetic Network which provides a unique geographical positioning reference system. It administers the Land Survey Ordinance, which governs the conduct and practice of Authorised Land Surveyors, and controls the standard of land boundary survey in land subdivision. It is delegated with the authority to name roads and streets under the Public Health and Municipal Services Ordinance, and to name geographical places on request. To fulfil these functions effectively and efficiently, the office has set up a Land Information Centre housing a computerised land information system and its sub-systems and databases. The Basic Mapping System provides the 1:1 000 basic digital mapping covering all of Hong Kong. The Cadastral Information System records all land boundaries for identifying land parcels.

During the year, the office established a Territorial Continuous Global Positioning System Array with six GPS reference stations for accurate and efficient 3-D positioning. Six more of these stations will be set up in the near future. When fully operational, the system will greatly facilitate survey operations.

The Basic Mapping System contains updated digital map databases of graphic map features with attribute information. Licences and permits are issued to private organisations to use the databases to develop their own applications, map products and websites. Utility companies, engineering consultants, computing system consultants and education institutes use the databases for applications involving

231

automated mapping, facilities management, customer support and geographical information systems.

The Computerised Map Archives Retrieval System enables people to search and inspect map and aerial photograph archives. Two kiosks have been set up for public use at the headquarters of the Survey and Mapping Office. More kiosks will be installed at other map sales outlets.

Moreover, the office has developed a new series of digital orthophoto images covering the entire territory. This is a technology that enables map users to see a close to reality simulation. (*Details of the office's map products and services can be accessed at the Lands Department's website*).

In December, the office acquired ISO 9001:2000 certification accredited by the Hong Kong Quality Assurance Agency.

Land Registration

In Hong Kong, the security given by legal title to property is at present provided by a deeds registration system operated by the Land Registry under the Land Registration Ordinance. This legislation was first enacted in 1844 and is the oldest local law still in force in Hong Kong. Around $1,000 billion in loans is currently extended to families and businesses in Hong Kong against the security of registered property. In 2003, 102 313 matters were registered.

The Land Registry has some 500 staff members. It is organised into the Urban Land Registry, serving Hong Kong Island and Kowloon, and eight New Territories Land Registries. A single document imaging centre serves all the registries and there is also a Reports on Title Office. The department is responsible for registering documents affecting land and keeping land records for public inspection. The department operates on a Trading Fund basis, under which it has to meet its operating costs out of its revenues from fees and charges, and finance investments in service improvements.

The Land Registration Ordinance provides that documents affecting land have priority according to their respective dates of registration. Registration is not mandatory but the benefit that it gives through protecting interest in land creates a strong incentive for matters to be registered.

A land document is registered by delivering it to the appropriate land registry with a memorial, which contains the essential particulars of the document, and the prescribed fee. These particulars are then entered into a computerised land register for the relevant piece of land or property. The registered land document is scanned and stored as an electronic image on an optical disc.

Each land register provides a record of transactions affecting a property, starting from the grant of the relevant government lease. The registers, memorials and related land documents are available for search by members of the public at every search office, on payment of a fee. Subscribers and customers may conduct a one-stop search for properties anywhere in Hong Kong at their own offices and at every search office in the registry through the introduction of the Direct Access Services and the Cross District Search Service, respectively.

The Land Registry is implementing a strategic change plan to improve the security of title that is provided and further enhance the efficiency of its services. The plan involves re-engineering of business practices and organisation structure as well as introduction of new technology and new legislation.

The first elements of the plan were put in place in 2002. Amendments to the Land Registration Ordinance were passed that allowed the department to plan for major organisational changes. The new legislation allows the department to offer a unified registration and information service for the whole territory in place of the separate Urban and New Territories registries. On passage of the legislation, a contract was signed for development of the Integrated Registration Information System (IRIS). This will replace several separate information systems currently in use in the department. It will support the organisational change and help to improve service quality. Development and initial testing of the IRIS was carried out during the year.

The scrutiny of the Land Titles Bill commenced in March in a Legislative Council Bills Committee. This legislation will provide the basis for changing Hong Kong's registration system from a deeds-based system to a title registration system. The advantage of this is that the ownership of property and the existence of charges, easements, covenants and other rights affecting land can be established by reference to the title register itself rather than by time consuming and inconclusive research of historical documents. To facilitate the scrutiny of the bill by the Legislative Council, the Land Registry held extensive discussions with the Law Society of Hong Kong and other professional bodies to seek their input into the process. Deliberations on the bill continued at year-end.

The IRIS is expected to be put into operation in the third quarter of 2004. At the same time, the department will be reorganised to replace the Urban and New Territories registries with a unified registry serving the whole territory. Internet access to information services will be provided, one-stop counter services introduced and the department aims to achieve shorter business processing times for all services. The IRIS system will continue to be developed to further improve services and support the introduction of title registration, subject to enactment of the Land Titles Bill.

Drainage Services

Flood Prevention Infrastructure

The Drainage Services Department is implementing a series of major flood control projects in the New Territories and in West Kowloon, costing about $12 billion.

In the north-western New Territories, improvement works to about 20 kilometres of the major river network have been completed. These cover the lower and middle reaches of the Shan Pui River, the lower and middle reaches of the Kam Tin River near Yuen Long Nam San Wai, the Ngau Tam Mei main drainage channel, and the upper reaches of the Kam Tin River near Kam Tin San Tsuen and Shek Wu Tong. As a result, the flood risk in the surrounding areas has been relieved.

Construction of the Yuen Long Bypass Floodway commenced in January. Upon its completion in 2006, the flooding problem in Yuen Long new town areas will be resolved. Construction of the San Tin eastern main drainage channel commenced in 2002 and, upon its completion in late 2005, the flood risk in San Tin will be reduced. Design work for the San Tin western drainage channel is under way.

In the northern New Territories, the critical flood mitigation undertakings include the Shenzhen River Regulation Project and the rehabilitation of the River Ganges, which are aimed at improving the downstream outlets for rivers in the Sheung Shui

233

and Ta Kwu Ling areas. The first undertaking is a joint project between the HKSAR Government and the Shenzhen Municipal Government, and the Stage I and Stage II works on the Shenzhen River have been completed. These works, together with the completion of river training works in the lower and mid-stream of the River Indus and the River Beas, have basically eliminated the risk for formerly flood-prone villages in the Lo Wu, Tin Ping Shan and Ho Sheung Heung areas.

The Stage III works in the Shenzhen River project have commenced in phases since 2001 and are scheduled for completion in early 2006. These works include the training of four kilometres of the river's channel from Lo Wu to its confluence with the River Ganges.

To tackle the flooding problem in the Ta Kwu Ling area, a drainage rehabilitation scheme for 1.7 kilometres of the River Ganges is under way for completion at the end of 2005. Design work for another 21.5 kilometres of drainage channels in the northern New Territories is also in hand, including the upstream portions of the rivers Ganges, Beas and Indus, and the Ma Wat and Kau Lung Hang channels. On completion of these remaining river training works, the regional flooding problem in the northern New Territories will have been overcome.

In addition to the river training works, village flood pumping schemes have been implemented to protect low-lying villages from flood hazards. These schemes involve construction of bunds around villages and pumping of stormwater from within the bunded area to an outside channel during rainstorms. Construction of a village flood pumping scheme for Chuk Yuen Tsuen and Ha San Wai, near Fairview Park in Yuen Long, was completed in March, eliminating the flood risk in this 'black spot'. Altogether, 21 schemes are now in operation. Similar schemes for Ma Tin and Shui Pin Wai are under construction for completion in early 2004. Two more schemes at Wang Chau, and Mai Po Lo Wai and Mai Po San Tsuen are under construction. Another two schemes, at Shui Pin Tsuen and Tai Kiu, are at the detailed design stage.

In West Kowloon, the Stage I drainage improvement works, which commenced in 1998, were completed in mid-year. These works included laying about 10 kilometres of stormwater drains in Yau Ma Tei, Mong Kok, Kowloon Tong, Sham Shui Po and Lai Chi Kok. Drainage improvement works have also been completed at Nathan Road between Boundary Street and Nullah Road, providing initial relief to the flooding problem in Mong Kok.

The Stage II works, which commenced in phases in late 1999 and 2001, are scheduled for completion in 2004. These works include improvements to about 23 kilometres of stormwater drains in Tsim Sha Tsui, Yau Ma Tei, Mong Kok, Sham Shui Po, Cheung Sha Wan and Lai Chi Kok. This stage also includes the construction of large flood storage tank underneath the Tai Hang Tung Recreation Ground in Mong Kok and a 1.5-kilometre stormwater transfer tunnel from Kowloon Tong to Kai Tak Nullah. The Stage III works also are under way for completion in 2007. These works include laying about 11 kilometres of stormwater drains in Yau Ma Tei.

The department has completed seven Drainage Master Plan (DMP) Studies to review the condition and performance of the existing stormwater drainage systems in various flood-prone areas throughout Hong Kong. Phase I of the drainage improvement works as recommended in the Studies commenced in December 2001 in Yuen Long areas. Further packages of drainage improvement works for other regions have been included in the Public Works Programme and are at different planning and detailed design stages. Another DMP Study for southern Hong Kong Island commenced in September 2002 for completion in 2004, aiming at devising long-term and short-term measures to upgrade the stormwater drainage system so as to cope with current and future development needs.

Under a preventive maintenance programme, the public drainage system is regularly inspected and desilted before and during the rainy seasons. These preventive measures ensure that stormwater is discharged effectively, and prevent blockages and overflows which may cause flooding and nuisance to the public.

In 2003, the department maintained about 3 223 kilometres of watercourses, river channels and drains, from which about 60 000 cubic metres of silt were removed. To provide effective drainage services, the department operates a 24-hour drainage hotline service to receive complaints from the public on blocked drains. It also operates an Emergency and Storm Damage Organisation to ensure that emergency situations are dealt with speedily and efficiently.

The department has completed a series of aesthetic improvement works to the open nullahs in East Kowloon as part of the Government's efforts in 'greening' the environment. In March 2002, it began the construction of a planter parapet to replace the granite wall along the Kai Tak Nullah in the Wong Tai Sin District, and over 10 000 shrubs were planted on the parapet to provide a green environment for residents. The project, costing $1.4 million, was substantially completed in June.

The importance of flood prevention is promoted through various public education activities. Promotional pamphlets and advisory notes are published and distributed to villagers and to property management offices before the rainy season. In addition, the department has organised site visits for District Councillors and the media to promote their understanding of the department's work and thereby enhance public awareness of what is being done to prevent flooding.

Civil Engineering

Geotechnical Engineering

The Civil Engineering Department (CED) manages a comprehensive slope safety system, which has brought about a substantial improvement in the safety of slopes in Hong Kong. This has been achieved by improving slope safety standards and technology, ensuring the safety of new slopes, improving the safety of existing slopes, and providing public warnings, information, education and community advisory services on slope safety.

The department audits the adequacy of the design and construction of all geotechnical works by the private sector, public authorities and government departments to ensure their long-term safety. In 2003, it audited 13 666 geotechnical design proposals and inspected 2 890 active construction sites.

The department maintains a continuing Landslip Preventive Measures (LPM) Programme to rectify the safety of existing slopes. In 2003, a total of about $920 million was spent on the LPM Programme. Upgrading works were completed on 260 government slopes, and all were landscaped to blend them with the surrounding environment. In addition, safety screening was completed on 320 private slopes.

The department inspects hillside squatter villages to identify huts vulnerable to landslides, recommends rehousing of the affected squatters and advises the occupants to seek safe shelter during heavy rain. In 2003, it inspected about 70 squatter villages.

With the availability of the Slope Maintenance Responsibility Information System on the Internet, members of the public can have ready access to information on slopes under their responsibility. Other slope-related information is also available in the Slope Information System. A bilingual version of the system has been uploaded to the Internet at the CED's Hong Kong Slope Safety website. The website has become an important source of reference for the public in obtaining slope-related information.

The Catalogue of Slopes has been made even more comprehensive. The department has done this by systematically examining the latest topographic plans and using aerial photograph interpretation techniques in order to identify and register slopes which meet the registration criteria but have not been included in the catalogue. The number of registered slopes in the catalogue has subsequently increased from 54 000 to 57 000.

In sustaining public awareness of slope safety, the department promotes and disseminates slope safety and slope maintenance messages to the public, and organises slope safety talks at schools and roving exhibitions in the community. In addition, a major exhibition will be held in the Central Library in April 2004 to show the history of landslide disasters in Hong Kong. A pamphlet on *Maintenance of Buried Services Affecting Slopes* is being prepared to remind slope owners to inspect and maintain underground water-carrying services. As part of efforts to improve the living environment, an open competition for the 'Best Landscaped Slope' was launched in June to encourage slope owners to maintain and beautify their slopes. The response was excellent.

The department's Community Advisory Unit provides useful advice to private slope owners to help them maintain and improve the condition and appearance of their slopes. In order to assist private slope owners to discharge their slope maintenance responsibility, a simple guide to 'Dangerous Hillside Orders' has been published to provide a step by step approach to undertaking the requirements of a Dangerous Hillside Order (an order issued under the Buildings Ordinance) promptly and effectively.

The Slope Maintenance Audit Section helps maintenance departments to improve their performance in discharging their slope maintenance responsibilities. Audits of government slope works indicate a continuous improvement in the overall state of maintenance.

The department maintains a 24-hour year-round emergency service to provide geotechnical advice to government departments on actions to be taken to protect the public against landslide danger. The computerised information system and telecommunication facilities have been upgraded to enhance efficiency in handling landslide information and emergency calls.

The department conducts various studies to improve the knowledge and methodology of dealing with natural terrain landslide hazards. It has developed techniques in dating natural terrain landslides, assessing the mobility of landslide debris and applying Geographic Information System technology to hazard studies. Natural terrain hazard mitigation works are being arranged for five sites in developed areas, while studies are being carried out in respect of four other sites.

During the year, the department continued to produce geotechnical guidance documents to disseminate new technological development findings and improved design and construction practice. In particular, the third edition of the *Guide to Slope Maintenance* and a revised *Layman's Guide to Slope Maintenance* were published.

Guidance on new vegetation mixes and new planting techniques for greening slopes was also given.

The Geotechnical Information Unit in the Civil Engineering Library houses the largest collection of geotechnical data in Hong Kong. The library is open to the public, and served more than 26 500 users during 2003.

The department provides specialist geotechnical services to government departments, including the provision of ad hoc geotechnical advice and conducting feasibility studies, detailed investigations, design and construction supervision for a wide range of public works projects. The projects handled by the department during the year included site formation works at Kong Sin Wan Tsuen, Pok Fu Lam; slope upgrading works at the former Victoria Barracks, Kennedy Road; site formation works for the Yam O Tuk Fresh Water Service Reservoir on Lantau Island, and the Ping Che Fresh Water Service Reservoir in Fanling; geotechnical works for the drainage project at San Tin; and geotechnical works for Stage III of the Shenzhen River Regulation Project. In addition, the department also provides construction material testing and ground investigation services to support public works projects. The testing service is provided by the Public Works Laboratories. During the year, some 880 000 tests were carried out, and 20 000 metres of soil and rock were drilled.

Mining and Quarrying

The department enforces legislation relating to mining, quarrying and explosives, and administers quarrying contracts. It processes applications for the manufacture, storage, conveyance and use of explosives, and inspects stone quarries, blasting sites and explosives stores.

Hong Kong consumed 16.3 million tonnes of aggregates and other rock products in 2003. About 50 per cent of its demand for aggregates and rock products was met locally, with the balance imported from the Mainland.

One quarrying contract and two quarry rehabilitation contracts were in force during the year. The rehabilitation contracts require the operators to rehabilitate the quarries within a specified period, in return for the granting of rights to process and sell surplus rock excavated during the course of the works. The rehabilitation works involve recontouring and extensive planting to blend the quarries with the surrounding hillsides.

The department manages two government explosives depots (one at Kau Shat Wan on Lantau Island and the other at Piper's Hill, Sha Tin) which provide bulk storage facilities for imported explosives. It also undertakes the delivery of explosives from the depots to blasting sites and issues shotfirer certificates. About 2 100 tonnes of explosives were consumed in 2003, being used mostly for quarrying and site formation works.

The department also provides technical support to the Home Affairs Bureau and the Marine Department in assessing applications for fireworks displays.

Fill Supply and Mud Disposal

The Marine Fill Committee (MFC) is responsible for identifying and managing the supply of marine fill resources for development projects, and for managing disposal facilities for dredged and excavated sediment. The Public Fill Committee (PFC) has the duty to manage construction and demolition (C&D) materials and utilisation of

237

land-based fill reserves. Both committees are responsible to the Secretary for the Environment, Transport and Works.

About 10.9 million cubic metres of C&D materials were generated by local construction activities in 2003. Of this, about 9.6 million cubic metres of inert materials were re-used as fill in public filling areas including Tseung Kwan O Area 137, Tuen Mun Area 38, North Tsing Yi and Penny's Bay, or stockpiled at the fill banks in Tuen Mun Area 38 and Tseung Kan O Area 137.

The PFC explores ways to minimise the generation of C&D materials and reduce their disposal at landfills. The construction industry is encouraged to adopt construction methods and materials that reduce the generation of C&D materials at source. The temporary recycling facility at Tuen Mun Area 38 recycles suitable C&D materials into aggregates for re-use. In 2003, the recycling facility produced about 0.2 million tonnes of recycled aggregates for use in government projects.

The MFC maintains a Fill Management Database on fill requirements, mud disposal and surplus excavated materials from major public and private projects. Its purpose is to help the construction industry coordinate sources of fill materials and make the best use of surplus materials. All project data is available at the CED's home page.

The department manages mud disposal facilities. In 2003, about seven million cubic metres of uncontaminated mud and 0.5 million cubic metres of contaminated mud were generated from various works projects and maintenance works on navigational channels in the harbour. Uncontaminated mud was disposed of at open sea floor disposal grounds or exhausted marine sand borrow pits. Contaminated mud was placed in specially selected and closely monitored exhausted sand borrow pits, which were then capped with clean mud on completion of filling to isolate the contaminants from the environment. The use of exhausted sand borrow pits for mud disposal is preferred as it has the dual benefits of providing much needed disposal capacity and restoring the seabed to its natural profile and state.

In connection with the management of Hong Kong's fill resources and mud disposal capacity, the department, on behalf of the MFC, continues to undertake a series of geotechnical, environmental and ecological studies and monitoring to examine the effect of the dredging and disposal activities, and to investigate possible ways to avoid or minimise the impact on the marine environment.

Hydraulic Studies

Coastal engineering projects may affect the flow of water, sediment transport and wave activity in the harbour. The department employs sophisticated computer hydraulic models to analyse the likely effects of proposed schemes, both during and after the construction phases, to ensure that their impacts are minimised to within acceptable limits. The models are used for reclamation layout planning, design of marine structures, waterway studies and assessment of future maintenance dredging requirements. A digital tidal stream atlas and a wave atlas were also developed by the department in 2001 to provide average tidal and extreme wave information. These atlases are being updated to reflect the latest shoreline and seabed profiles and to enhance the accuracy of the information.

Water Supplies

Water from Guangdong

The rivers in Guangdong are Hong Kong's major source of raw water. Hong Kong began to receive raw water from Guangdong when a scheme was completed in 1960 for receiving a piped supply of 22.7 million cubic metres a year.

In 1989, an agreement was concluded with the Guangdong provincial authorities for a long-term water supply. Dongjiang (East River) water is now delivered to Hong Kong via the Shenzhen Reservoir through a transfer system, covering about 80 kilometres, which is commonly known as the Dongshen Water Supply System.

In recent years, due to rainfall being much above average together with the declining demand from local industry, the demand for raw water from Guangdong has decreased. The Government reached an agreement with the Guangdong provincial authorities in July 1998 whereby the annual increase stipulated in the 1989 agreement was to be reduced from 30 million cubic metres to 10 million cubic metres for the years from 1998 to 2004. As a result, the total intake for the seven years will be reduced by 560 million cubic metres. Under the agreement, the supply quantity for 2003 was 810 million cubic metres, rising to 820 million cubic metres in 2004, compared with the system's present designed maximum capacity of 1 100 million cubic metres per year. The annual supply quantity beyond 2004 will be subject to further review.

The Dongshen Water Supply System initially had an open channel design. However, to eliminate pollution of the water within the system, a closed aqueduct was built. The first section of the closed aqueduct was commissioned in January, and resulted in a significant improvement in the raw water quality. The completion of the entire closed aqueduct in June was a milestone in the work to improve the quality of Dongjiang water. The raw water quality data obtained after the full commissioning indicated further improvements.

Water Storage and Consumption

Full supply was maintained throughout the year. At year-end, the water in storage amounted to 446 million cubic metres, compared with 442 million cubic metres a year earlier. Hong Kong's two largest reservoirs, High Island and Plover Cove, held a total of 402 million cubic metres. Rainfall of 1 942 millimetres — 12.29 per cent lower than the annual average of 2 214 millimetres — was recorded in 2003.

A peak daily consumption of 2.91 million cubic metres was recorded on July 14, compared with the 2002 peak of 2.83 million cubic metres. The average daily consumption throughout the year was 2.67 million cubic metres, compared with the 2002 average of 2.6 million cubic metres. The consumption of potable water totalled 974 million cubic metres, compared with 949 million cubic metres in 2002. In addition, 241 million cubic metres of sea water were supplied for flushing, compared with 235 million cubic metres in 2002.

Water Works

The first stage of the Tai Po Water Treatment Works, with a daily capacity of 250 000 cubic metres, was commissioned in June. Work is progressing on the first stage of the 20-year programme for the replacement or rehabilitation of some 3 050 kilometres of watermains. This work began in December 2000. Construction is under way for the additional service reservoirs, pumping stations and water supply networks in Kowloon West and East, Hong Kong Island, Pok Fu Lam (including the Cyberport), Tseung Kwan O, Ngong Ping, Sha Tin, Tai Po, North District, Tuen Mun, Yuen Long, Tin Shui Wai and North Lantau (for Hong Kong Disneyland). Major improvement works on the sea water supply system for Central Kowloon and Tsuen Wan continue.

Continuing planning work is in hand to increase the water supply capacity to meet demands from new developments and redevelopment in Central, Wan Chai, western and south-western areas on Hong Kong Island; Kwun Tong in Kowloon; and Tsuen Wan, Kwai Tsing, Yuen Long, Hung Shui Kiu, North Lantau, Tseung Kwan O, and the north-eastern and north-western New Territories. Major design work is focused on the provision of additional service reservoirs, pumping stations and water supply networks in North Point, Quarry Bay, Wan Chai; Kowloon East, West Kowloon Reclamation, Cha Kwo Ling, Tuen Mun, Sha Tin, Yuen Long, Tai Po, Tin Shui Wai, Tseung Kwan O and North Lantau.

As part of the strategy to encourage proper maintenance of internal plumbing systems in buildings, a voluntary Fresh Water Plumbing Quality Maintenance Recognition Scheme was launched in July 2002. The scheme received encouraging public support and more than 870 certificates of compliance were issued under the scheme, benefiting more than 190 000 customers.

Water Accounts and Customer Relations

The number of consumer accounts continues to rise at a rate of about 1.6 per cent per year and the consumer account base expanded to approximately 2.58 million accounts at year-end. To provide greater convenience to customers, applications for change of consumership, change of mailing address, and change of water bill language for a domestic account can be made online. The Water Supplies Department continues to act as an agent to collect general sewage charges on behalf of the Drainage Services Department.

To heighten both customer service and operational efficiency, the department rolled out the first stage of its Customer Care and Billing System (CCBS) in December and the entire system will be completed by the end of 2004.

Electricity

The Hongkong Electric Company Limited (HEC) supplies Hong Kong Island and the neighbouring islands of Ap Lei Chau and Lamma; CLP Power Hong Kong Limited (CLP Power) supplies Kowloon and the New Territories, including Lantau and several outlying islands. The supply to consumers is at 50Hz alternating current while the voltage is 220 volts single-phase and 380 volts three-phase.

The two supply companies are investor-owned. The Government monitors their performance through mutually agreed Scheme of Control Agreements. Current agreements with CLP Power and HEC came into effect on October 1, 1993, and January 1, 1994, respectively. Both will last for 15 years. The first and second five-yearly interim reviews were completed in early 1999 and late 2003, respectively. The agreements require each company to seek the approval of the Government for certain aspects of their financial plans, including projected tariff levels. The agreements do not grant the companies any exclusive rights. They are not franchises, nor do they define a supply area for either company or exclude new entrants to the market.

Electricity for HEC's supply areas is supplied from the Lamma Power Station. At year-end, total installed capacity (i.e. rated power output of generators) at the Lamma Power Station was 3 420 megawatts (MW). In May 2000, the Government approved HEC's new power station at the Lamma Extension and the installation of the first 300MW gas combined-cycle generator. The unit was scheduled to be commissioned in 2004. Subsequent to the review conducted at end-2003, the Government agreed with HEC's proposal to defer the commissioning of the unit to 2006. HEC's transmission system operates at 275 kilovolts (kV), 132kV and 66kV and distribution is effected mainly at 22kV, 11kV and 380 volts.

The Castle Peak Power Company Limited (CAPCO), which is 60 per cent owned by ExxonMobil Energy Limited (formerly known as Exxon Energy Limited) and 40 per cent by CLP Power, supplies electricity to CLP Power from its Black Point (1 875MW), Castle Peak (4 108MW) and Penny's Bay (300MW) power stations, with the total installed capacity being 6 283MW. Two more 312.5MW generators are scheduled to be commissioned at the Black Point power station during 2005-06.

The associated transmission and distribution systems are wholly owned by CLP Power. Its transmission system operates at 400kV and 132kV, and distribution is effected mainly at 33kV, 11kV and 380 volts.

The CLP Power and HEC transmission systems are interconnected by a cross-harbour link. This provides emergency back-up and achieves cost savings to consumers through economic energy transfers between the two systems and a reduction in the amount of generating capacity that needs to be kept as spinning reserve against the tripping of other units. The interconnection link, commissioned in 1981, currently has a total capacity of 720 megavolt-amperes (MVA) (i.e. 720 000 kilovolt-amperes (kVA)).

CLP Power's transmission system is also interconnected with the electricity network in Guangdong Province which facilitates the export and import of electricity to and from the province. The electricity sales to Guangdong are made from existing reserve generating capacity of CLP Power and are governed by an agreement with the Government, signed in March 1992, under which CLP Power's consumers receive priority of supply and 80 per cent of the profit from the sales.

In 1985, the Hong Kong Nuclear Investment Company Limited (a wholly-owned subsidiary of the CLP Holdings Limited) and the Guangdong Nuclear Investment Company Limited (now wholly owned by the China Guangdong Nuclear Power Holding Company Limited) established the Guangdong Nuclear Power Joint Venture Company Limited, to build and operate the Guangdong Nuclear Power Station at Daya Bay in Guangdong. This station comprises two 984MW pressurised water reactors which went into commercial operation in February and May 1994, respectively. CLP Power undertook to buy about 70 per cent of the station's power to meet part of the longer-term demand for electricity in its supply area.

Through its affiliated company, the Hong Kong Pumped Storage Development Company Limited, CLP Power has the right to use 50 per cent of the 1 200MW capacity of Phase 1 of the Guangzhou Pumped Storage Power Station, at Conghua. Off-peak electricity from the CAPCO system and the Guangdong Nuclear Power Station is used to pump water from a lower reservoir to an upper one. The water is allowed to flow downhill during the day to generate electricity to meet Hong Kong's peak demand.

Three-year Demand Side Management (DSM) Agreements between the Government and the two power companies expired in June 2003. The DSM programmes included rebate schemes for lighting and air-conditioning systems for non-residential customers, as well as other education and information schemes. All rebate schemes ended on June 30 and education and information schemes were completed by year-end.

The Electricity Ordinance, with its subsidiary regulations, is the main enabling legislation on electrical safety. It sets out the legal framework encompassing all the areas within which the concerned legislation shall apply, including the registration of electrical contractors/workers and competent persons, the safety standards and requirements for electricity supply, electricity supply lines, electrical wiring and products.

The 2003 edition of the Code of Practice for the Electricity (Wiring) Regulations was issued in December, and served to give new and revised guidelines on technical requirements for compliance with the Electricity (Wiring) Regulations.

Since 1990, the regulations concerning registration of electrical contractors and workers, the safety of electrical wiring, the supply of safe household electrical products, and the protection of electricity supply lines from third party damage have come into effect in stages. At December 2003, some 8 700 electrical contractors and 59 000 electrical workers held valid registration. Also, some 880 competent persons had been approved for locating underground electricity cables.

During enforcement of the Electricity Ordinance in 2003, the Government conducted 13 000 site inspections to check the safety standards of electrical installations and electrical product supply outlets, and prosecution action was initiated in 207 cases.

Gas

Towngas and liquefied petroleum gas (LPG) are the two main types of fuel gas widely used throughout Hong Kong for domestic, commercial and industrial purposes. In addition, LPG is used as a fuel for LPG taxis and light buses, and natural gas is used for electricity generation.

Hong Kong has about two million gas customers in the domestic, commercial and industrial sectors. In 2003, Towngas accounted for 80 per cent of the total fuel gas sold in energy terms, and LPG for 20 per cent.

Towngas is manufactured at plants in Tai Po and Ma Tau Kok, both using naphtha as feedstock. They have output capacities of 8.4 and 2.6 million cubic metres per day, respectively. Towngas is supplied through an integrated distribution system to about 1.52 million customers. The mains network extends throughout Hong Kong via a 127-kilometre high-pressure pipeline and some 2 978 kilometres of distribution mains.

LPG is imported into Hong Kong by sea and stored at five terminals on Tsing Yi Island before being distributed to approximately 754 000 customers and LPG vehicle filling stations. In 2003, about 22 per cent of total sales was supplied in cylinders by some 222 appointed gas distributors (operating 603 cylinder wagons), about 14 per cent was distributed to bulk storage installations providing piped LPG supplies to residential and commercial developments, and the remaining 64 per cent to vehicle filling stations as fuel for more than 18 000 LPG taxis and light buses. Cylinder LPG is now used in less than 24 per cent of domestic dwellings.

Natural gas is currently used for power generation at the Black Point and Castle Peak power stations. It is imported from the Yacheng 13-1 gas field off Hainan Island in southern China via a 780-kilometre high-pressure submarine pipeline.

The Gas Safety Ordinance regulates the importation, manufacture, storage, transport, supply and use of fuel gas. All gas supply companies, gas installers and contractors must be registered with the Gas Authority (the Director of Electrical and Mechanical Services) in order to carry out their operations. At year-end, there were seven registered gas supply companies, 2 901 registered gas installers and 421 registered gas contractors.

Home Pages

Environment, Transport and Works Bureau: http://www.etwb.gov.hk
Housing, Planning and Lands Bureau: http://www.hplb.gov.hk
Economic Development and Labour Bureau: http://www.edlb.gov.hk

CHAPTER 13

Transport

Twelve million commuter trips are made in Hong Kong every day. Nine out of 10 trips are made on public transport. With an accident fatality rate of 0.0297 per 1 000 population, Hong Kong has one of the safest road networks in the world. The number of fatal accidents in 2003 was 173, which was among the lowest figures in the past 43 years.

WITH a growing population and continuous development, moving people and goods around in Hong Kong has always been a great challenge. The Government has to ensure that this is carried out in accordance with sustainable development principles. It involves the planning and implementation of the further expansion and improvement of the transport infrastructure, with emphasis on railways; further promoting the use of public transport services by maintaining their quality and improving their coordination; effectively managing road use to reduce congestion and promote safety; and continuing to support environmental improvement measures in transport-related areas.

There were significant achievements in railway development in 2003. The West Rail project and the Light Rail Tin Shui Wai Extensions project of the Kowloon-Canton Railway Corporation (KCRC) were completed in December. Steady progress was made on building the KCRC's Ma On Shan to Tai Wai Rail Link and the Hung Hom to Tsim Sha Tsui Extension. Both projects are targeted for completion in 2004. Construction of the MTR Corporation Limited's (MTRCL) Penny's Bay Rail Link is targeted for completion in 2005. The construction of the Sheung Shui to Lok Ma Chau Spur Line is also on schedule for completion before mid-2007 to meet the growing demands of cross-boundary passenger traffic and to ease congestion at Lo Wu.

The preliminary planning and design of the Shatin to Central Link and detailed planning and design of the Kowloon Southern Link are ongoing. In January, the Government decided that the completion of the North Hong Kong Island Line of the Island Line Extensions should be deferred to beyond 2016. The MTRCL was also invited to proceed with further planning on the West Hong Kong Island Line Phase 1 from Sheung Wan to Belcher of the Island Line Extensions including a possible link with the South Hong Kong Island Line.

During the year, construction of several major road projects began, including the Deep Bay Link, Hong Kong-Shenzhen Western Corridor, a new boundary bridge between Lok Ma Chau and Huanggang and Trunk Road T3. There has also been significant development in the planning of a road transport link between Hong Kong and Pearl River West. The joint study commissioned by HKSAR and Mainland authorities has been completed, confirming the urgency of and the need for such a link. The Governments of Hong Kong, Macau and Guangdong have set up a Hong Kong-Zhuhai-Macao Bridge Advance Work Co-ordination Group to take forward the preparatory work for the bridge.

The new bus franchises of Citybus Limited (North Lantau and Airport bus network), Long Win Bus Company Limited and New World First Bus Services Limited took effect in mid-2003, for a period of about 10 years, upon expiry of their previous franchises.

In traffic management, a comprehensive Intelligent Transport Systems (ITS) Strategy, which sets out a plan for the deployment of advanced information and telecommunication technologies to enhance the safety, efficiency, reliability, user and environmental friendliness of the transport system in Hong Kong, was finalised in 2001. The ITS Strategy features two core projects — a Transport Information System currently under development and the Journey Time Indication System which has been put into operation. (*See later section on Use of Information Technology in Transport*)

Coordinated Action Against SARS

When the outbreak of SARS was reported in March, the Transport Department coordinated action on the transport front to help prevent the spread of the disease. The department stepped up publicity efforts to increase public transport operators' awareness of SARS and, in consultation with the Department of Health, issued guidelines on SARS prevention to public transport operators and passengers. Public transport operators increased the frequency of cleansing and disinfection of their fleets and gave instructions to their drivers and operational staff concerning the wearing of masks and the adoption of precautionary measures when handling passengers suspected to have SARS symptoms. The department also monitored the preventive measures taken by the operators and developed contingency transport plans in the event of a spread of SARS within individual public transport organisations.

During the outbreak, the average daily public transport patronage fell by 10.9 per cent from 11 million in the first quarter of 2003 to 9.8 million in the second quarter. It picked up gradually in the third quarter after the outbreak waned. The average daily public transport patronage returned to the normal level of about 11.3 million in the fourth quarter.

To assist the public transport sector in coping with the difficult time, the Government implemented the following measures: (a) three-month concessionary parking charges for taxis and 'nanny vans'; (b) one-year waiver of licence fees for taxis, public light buses and coaches; (c) temporary relaxation of restricted zones for taxis; (d) lifting of 4-5 pm restricted zones for all transport modes; and (e) relaxation of restricted zones at specific locations for public light buses.

The outbreak seriously affected cross-boundary passenger traffic at the land crossings in the period from mid-March to June. However, freight traffic was more or less unaffected. The overall passenger figure fell by 22 per cent from an average daily of 323 400 before the outbreak to 251 600. The steepest decline of 32 per cent was recorded in April when the daily average was only 220 900. Patronage of through trains plunged by 48 per cent while the trains to Lo Wu carried 32 per cent fewer passengers. The decreases in respect of the crossings at Lok Ma Chau, Man Kam To and Sha Tau Kok were 30 per cent, 29 per cent and 23 per cent, respectively. Patronage started to pick up in July and the total passenger flow eventually returned to the pre-SARS level.

Patronage of cross-boundary ferry services also dropped significantly during the outbreak. Compared with the same months in the previous year, the number of passengers fell by about 20 per cent in March, and some 50 per cent in April and May. The situation continued until August, when the patronage rose again and exceeded 1 908 000, which actually represented a 2.3 per cent increase over the same month in 2002.

Upon the outbreak being reported in March, the Marine Department issued an early warning to shipowners, agents and people in the industry notifying them to take precautionary measures. The department also issued notices to all visiting vessels to report on crew members' state of health when they submitted their Pre-arrival Notification. Other means included consultative committee meetings with port operators and the local shipping community.

A Malaysian-registered cargo ship, which departed from Thailand for Guangdong, entered Hong Kong waters in May after its captain suspected 10 of its 24 crew members might be infected with SARS. Hong Kong rendered assistance on humanitarian grounds. The 10 crew members were later confirmed to be free from SARS at hospital.

Administrative Framework

The Environment, Transport and Works Bureau of the Government Secretariat, headed by the Secretary for the Environment, Transport and Works, is responsible for, among other matters, the overall policy formulation, direction and coordination of land transport and ferry services. The Secretary is assisted by the Transport Advisory Committee, which advises the Chief Executive in Council on major transport policies and issues. The committee has 18 appointed members, including the chairman and three government officials. A Transport Complaints Unit is established under the committee, and in 2003 this unit received 15 118 complaints and suggestions on traffic and transport matters. On local transport matters, the Government is advised by the District Councils and their traffic and transport committees.

The Environment, Transport and Works Bureau is supported by the Transport Department and the Highways Department. The Transport Department is headed by the Commissioner for Transport. The Highways Department is headed by the Director of Highways. The Transport Department is the authority for administering the Road Traffic Ordinance and legislation regulating public transport operations. Its responsibilities cover transport planning, road traffic and tunnel management, carparks and metered parking spaces, regulation of roads, railways and waterborne public transport, licensing of drivers and the registration, licensing and inspection of vehicles. The Highways Department is responsible for the overall design and construction of highways, and their repair and maintenance. The department also studies new railway proposals, monitors their construction, and helps resolve any interfacing problems they may have with other works projects.

The Hong Kong Police Force is the principal agency for enforcing traffic legislation and prosecuting offenders. The Prosecutions Unit of the Transport Department handles prosecutions involving safety defects on buses, disqualification under the Driving-offence Points System, and breaches of vehicle safety regulations, government tunnel regulations and Tsing Ma Control Area regulations. In September, the unit expanded its purview to coordinate the enforcement and regulatory actions of the department concerning illegal transport. The name of the unit was also changed to Prosecution and Regulation Unit.

Transport Tribunals, set up under the Road Traffic Ordinance with a chairman and members appointed from among the public, provide a channel of appeal against decisions made by the Commissioner for Transport in respect of the registration and licensing of vehicles, the issue of hire car permits and passenger service licences, and the designation of car-testing centres, vehicle emission testing centres, driving schools and driving improvement schools. The Transport Department also operates an Emergency Transport Coordination Centre, which provides a focal point for liaison with public transport operators on traffic and transport arrangements during serious traffic and transport disruptions, rainstorms and typhoons.

Policy Objective and Transport Strategy

The Government aims to provide a safe, efficient, reliable and environmentally friendly transport system that meets the economic, social and recreational needs of the community, and is capable of supporting sustainability and future development of Hong Kong. It does this by:

- expanding and improving the transport infrastructure in a timely manner;
- improving the quality and coordination of public transport services; and
- managing road use to reduce congestion and promote safety.

In pursuing the transport objective of facilitating the mobility of people and goods in Hong Kong, the Government also ensures that this is achieved in an environmentally sustainable manner by seeking and supporting environmental improvement measures in transport-related areas.

The Government's overall transport objectives, promulgated in the comprehensive Transport Strategy in October 1999, are to ensure that the safe, efficient and reliable transport system is not only maintained in the years ahead but also improved significantly.

It drew up a Transport Strategy to achieve these objectives by:

- better integration of transport and land use planning;
- better use of railways as the backbone of the passenger transport system;
- better public transport services and facilities;
- better use of advanced technologies in transport management; and
- better environmental protection.

Railway Development and RDS-2000

Railways play a key role in Hong Kong's transport systems strategy as they are safe, efficient, reliable, comfortable and environmentally friendly mass carriers. The Government, therefore, accords high priority to railway development.

About $75 billion has been committed to five railways under construction for completion between 2003 and 2007. These are the West Rail, the Ma On Shan to Tai Wai Rail Link, the KCR Tsim Sha Tsui Extension, the Penny's Bay Rail Link and the Sheung Shui to Lok Ma Chau Spur Line. The 30.5-kilometre West Rail, which comprises nine stations and connects West Kowloon with Yuen Long and Tuen Mun, began operation on December 20.

To meet Hong Kong's increasing transport needs in a sustainable manner over the next two decades, the Government has formulated the Railway Development Strategy 2000 (RDS-2000) based on the findings of the Second Railway Development Study. The RDS-2000 provides a blueprint for the next phase of railway development, and following its recommendations, two new projects — the Kowloon Southern Link and the Shatin to Central Link — are targeted for completion within a window between 2008 and 2011. Other projects under consideration include the West Hong Kong Island Line, South Hong Kong Island Line, Northern Link and Regional Express Line.

Transport Infrastructure

Existing Road Network

At the end of 2003, Hong Kong had 1 934 kilometres of roads and 1 057 road structures, three immersed-tube cross-harbour tunnels, nine road tunnels and three major bridges. These facilities provide a comprehensive road network for Hong Kong.

Major projects completed during the year included:

* Widening of Fo Tan Road between Yuen Wo Road and Kwei Tei Street from dual two-lane to dual three-lane with improvements to the capacities of the adjoining junctions. The project caters for the traffic demand arising from the industrial and residential developments in the Fo Tan and Sui Wo areas.

* Widening of the section of Tolo Highway between the Island House Interchange and the Ma Liu Shui Interchange by adding one traffic lane in each direction.

* The improvement to the Island Eastern Corridor section between the North Point Interchange and Sai Wan Ho to alleviate the problem caused by weaving and merging traffic.

Existing Tunnels

The Cross-Harbour Tunnel, Eastern Harbour Crossing, Tate's Cairn Tunnel, Western Harbour Crossing and Tai Lam Tunnel were built by the private sector under 'Build, Operate and Transfer' franchises.

The 1.9-kilometre Cross-Harbour Tunnel connects Causeway Bay on Hong Kong Island and Hung Hom in Kowloon. The franchise for the tunnel, which was opened in 1972, ended on August 31, 1999, and the facility was handed back to the Government. With a daily patronage of 119 800 vehicles in 2003, it is one of the world's busiest four-lane road tunnels. The tolls ranged from $8 to $30 for different types of vehicles.

The two-kilometre Eastern Harbour Crossing was opened in 1989. It links Quarry Bay on Hong Kong Island and Cha Kwo Ling in Kowloon. A daily average of 71 300 vehicles used the tunnel in 2003. Tolls ranged from $8 to $45.

The two-kilometre Western Harbour Crossing is the first six-lane cross-harbour road tunnel in Hong Kong. Opened in 1997, it links Sai Ying Pun on Hong Kong Island and the West Kowloon Reclamation near Yau Ma Tei in Kowloon. It was used by an average of 37 300 vehicles daily in 2003. Statutory tolls ranged from $30 to

$185. The tunnel company offers concessionary tolls and the actual tolls ranged from $20 to $100.

The four-kilometre Tate's Cairn Tunnel, the longest road tunnel in Hong Kong, was opened to traffic in 1991, providing an additional direct road link between the north-eastern New Territories and Kowloon. It was used by an average of 60 900 vehicles daily in 2003. Tolls ranged from $10 to $20.

The 3.8-kilometre Tai Lam Tunnel, together with the 6.3-kilometre Yuen Long Approach Road, forms the Route 3 (Country Park section), which extends from Ting Kau to Au Tau. Opened in May 1998, it was used by an average of 44 300 vehicles daily in 2003. Statutory tolls ranged from $20 to $90. The tunnel company offers concessionary tolls and the actual tolls ranged from $17 to $75.

The 2.4-kilometre Discovery Bay Tunnel Link, which comprises a 630-metre single tube two-way tunnel and a 1 770-metre approach road, is operated and maintained by the Discovery Bay Road Tunnel Company Limited, which also built it. It extends from Discovery Bay through Yi Pak Au to Cheung Tung Road. The tunnel link is only open to Discovery Bay residents' services and goods vehicles providing delivery of goods or a servicing function. Opened in May 2000, the tunnel link was used by an average of 700 vehicles daily in 2003. It has a one-way toll collection arrangement. The vehicles are charged a single journey toll when they enter Discovery Bay. The tolls ranged from $50 to $250.

The Government owns seven of the road tunnels (Lion Rock, Aberdeen, Airport, Shing Mun, Tseung Kwan O, Cheung Tsing and Cross-Harbour) which are managed and operated by private companies under management contracts. Tolls are set and monitored by the Government. The use of the Airport Tunnel and the Cheung Tsing Tunnel is free of charge.

The 1.4-kilometre Lion Rock Tunnel, linking Kowloon and Sha Tin, began single-tube operation in 1967, with a second tube added in 1978. The tunnel was used by 88 000 vehicles daily in 2003. The toll was $8.

The 1.9-kilometre Aberdeen Tunnel, opened in 1982, links the northern and southern parts of Hong Kong Island. It was used by 56 500 vehicles daily in 2003. The toll was $5.

The 1.3-kilometre toll-free Airport Tunnel between Hung Hom and Kowloon Bay passes under the former airport site at Kai Tak and was opened in 1982. It was used by 58 400 vehicles daily in 2003.

The 2.6-kilometre Shing Mun Tunnel between Sha Tin and Tsuen Wan was opened in 1990. A daily average of 53 000 vehicles paid a $5 toll in 2003.

The 900-metre Tseung Kwan O Tunnel, opened in 1990, links Kowloon and the new town at Tseung Kwan O. It was used by 65 400 vehicles daily in 2003. The toll was $3.

The 1.6-kilometre toll-free Cheung Tsing Tunnel was opened in 1997 and links Kwai Chung and Tsing Yi. It was used by 75 200 vehicles daily in 2003.

Existing Rail Network

Besides the network of road tunnels and highways, railways also form a vital part of Hong Kong's transport network. The rail system comprises a heavily utilised Mass Transit Railway (MTR) system, a dedicated express rail passenger service connecting the urban areas with the airport (the Airport Express Line (AEL)) and the Kowloon-Canton Railway (KCR) which includes the East Rail (ER), the West Rail (WR) and the Light Rail (LR). Cross-boundary service is also provided by the East Rail. The system now covers about 190 kilometres and has three MTR harbour crossings.

There is also a tramway serving as a local distributor on the northern shore of Hong Kong Island and a funicular tramway running between Central (Garden Road) and the Peak.

Railway Projects Under Construction

The four railway projects under construction are:

* The 11.4-kilometre Ma On Shan to Tai Wai Rail Link (MOS Rail) that connects the Ma On Shan town to the existing KCR East Rail at Tai Wai Station. Construction started in November 2000 for completion in 2004.

* The one-kilometre Hung Hom to Tsim Sha Tsui Extension (TST Extension) that extends the KCR East Rail from the existing Hung Hom terminus to a new station at Tsim Sha Tsui East. Construction started in March 2001 for completion in 2004.

* The 3.5-kilometre Penny's Bay Rail Link that connects a new Sunny Bay Station on the existing MTR Tung Chung Line to Penny's Bay where Hong Kong Disneyland is being built. Construction started in August 2002 for completion in 2005, to tie in with the opening of the Disneyland.

* The 7.4-kilometre Sheung Shui to Lok Ma Chau Spur Line (Spur Line) connects the KCR East Rail at Sheung Shui with a new passenger boundary crossing at Lok Ma Chau/Huanggang. Construction started in October 2002 for completion before mid-2007.

Railway Projects Under Planning

The seven railway projects under planning are:

* The Kowloon Southern Link (KSL) that will connect the KCR East Rail and West Rail at the southern tip of the Kowloon Peninsula. Upon completion, passengers will be able to interchange between the East Rail and the West Rail at Hung Hom. The project is in the detailed planning and design stage, with completion envisaged around 2009.

* The 17-kilometre Shatin to Central Link (SCL) that will be a strategic corridor from the New Territories to Hong Kong Island, via south-eastern Kowloon. The KCRC, which was awarded the project, is firming up the scheme with a view to completing the link within the window of 2008-2011 as recommended in the RDS-2000.

* The South Hong Kong Island Line (SIL) that links up the northern and southern parts of Hong Kong Island. The MTRCL is carrying out a preliminary study to develop various schemes for integrating the SIL and the WIL Phase 1.

* The Island Line Extensions that will comprise a new North Hong Kong Island Line (NIL) and a new West Hong Kong Island Line (WIL). The NIL will be an extension of the existing MTR Tung Chung Line eastwards along the north shore of Hong Kong Island to join up with the eastern half of the MTR Island Line (ISL) at Fortress Hill. At the same time, the MTR Tseung Kwan O Line (TKL) will be connected with the ISL's western half at Tin Hau. The WIL will be an extension of the existing ISL from Sheung Wan to Kennedy Town. The Government decided in January 2003 that the NIL would be deferred beyond 2016 because of a slower build-up of population along the northern shore of Hong Kong Island, and that the route

would be protected administratively. Also, the WIL would be planned in conjunction with the SIL.

* The Northern Link that will link the West Rail to the Lok Ma Chau boundary crossing. It will also link up the East Rail and the West Rail to enable passengers to travel more widely in the northern parts of the New Territories. Its implementation will depend on the growth of cross-boundary traffic from the western part of the HKSAR and developments in the north-western New Territories. The situation is being closely monitored.

* The Regional Express Line (REL) that will provide a new express connection between the boundary and the urban area. It will form part of the Guangzhou-Shenzhen-Hong Kong Express Rail Link, which is intended to shorten the journey time between Hong Kong and Guangzhou to within 60 minutes. A joint expert group comprising representatives from the Mainland and Hong Kong authorities has been formed to study the feasibility of this rail link.

* The Port Rail Line (PRL) that will be a freight rail connection from Lo Wu to a new terminal at Kwai Chung. The PRL will allow freight from the deep hinterland of the Mainland (i.e. beyond the Pearl River Delta) to access the container port at Kwai Chung. Its implementation depends on cross-boundary freight build-up. The KCRC is studying the viability of the project.

Road Projects Under Construction

Major road projects being implemented include:

* Deep Bay Link (DBL) and Hong Kong-Shenzhen Western Corridor (HK-SWC): construction of the DBL and the HK-SWC commenced in June and August, respectively, for completion in end-2005. The HK-SWC will become Hong Kong's fourth vehicular boundary crossing while the DBL will link it with the local transport network.

* New Boundary Bridge between Lok Ma Chau and Huanggang: to relieve the traffic burden on the existing boundary bridge between Lok Ma Chau and Huanggang, a new dual two-lane bridge is being built, and due to be completed by end-2004.

* Widening of Yuen Long Highway between Lam Tei and the Shap Pat Heung Interchange: this section of Yuen Long Highway is being widened to a dual three-lane carriageway to cope with the anticipated growth in traffic. Works commenced in August for completion by end-2005.

* Route 8 (previously known as Route 9 (Cheung Sha Wan to Sha Tin)): construction commenced in October 2002 for completion in mid-2007. This dual three-lane carriageway will serve as an additional link between Sha Tin and Kowloon and relieve traffic on existing links including the Lion Rock Tunnel and the Tate's Cairn Tunnel.

* Route 8 (previously known as Route 9 (Tsing Yi and Cheung Sha Wan)): construction commenced in April 2002 for completion in 2008. This dual three-lane carriageway will provide an alternative route to the Route 3 Tsing Yi and Kwai Chung sections and access to the Container Terminals 8 and 9.

* Trunk Road T3: this dual two-lane trunk road in Tai Wai links Route 8 (previously known as Route 9 (Cheung Sha Wan to Sha Tin)) with the existing Tai Po Road and will help relieve traffic congestion by providing a bypass for several congested sections of Tai Po Road. Construction commenced in March for completion in 2007.

* Route 9 (previously known as Route 5) between Shek Wai Kok and Chai Wan Kok: this dual two-lane carriageway will provide a direct link between the Shing Mun Tunnel and Tuen Mun Road as well as a local link to western Tsuen Wan. Construction commenced in September 2002 for completion in 2006.

* Trunk Road T7: this dual two-lane trunk road linking Ma On Shan Road and Sai Sha Road will serve as a bypass for Ma On Shan Road and allow traffic to avoid the busy Ma On Shan Town Centre. Construction commenced in January 2001 for completion in mid-2004.

* Widening of the section of Sai Sha Road between Kam Ying Road and its junction with Trunk Road T7: to cope with future growth in traffic demand from adjoining private developments, this section of Sai Sha Road is being widened to dual two-lane standard. Work started in August 2002 for completion in end-2004.

* Chok Ko Wan Link Road (Penny's Bay section): this dual three-lane carriageway will be the access road to developments at Penny's Bay, including Hong Kong Disneyland. Construction started in August 2002 for completion in August 2005.

* Castle Peak Road between Sham Tseng and Ka Loon Tsuen, Tsuen Wan: this section of Castle Peak Road is being widened to a dual two-lane carriageway to cater for increasing traffic demand. Works commenced in November 2001 for completion in 2006.

* Salisbury Road Underpass: this dual two-lane underpass along Salisbury Road will improve the traffic capacity at the junction of Salisbury Road and Chatham Road South. Works started in March 2001 for completion in 2004. The project also involves widening the section of Salisbury Road between Wing On Plaza and Canton Road.

Road Projects Under Planning

A number of road construction/improvement projects are under planning to further expand and improve the existing road network:

* A Hong Kong-Zhuhai-Macao Bridge Advance Work Co-ordination Group has been formed to take forward planning for the project.

* Improvement to Castle Peak Road between Ka Loon Tsuen and Siu Lam by upgrading it to dual two-lane carriageway standard would commence in March 2004 for completion in May 2007.

* Reconstruction and improvement of Tuen Mun Road would commence tentatively in end-2005 for completion in end-2011. The project is intended to upgrade the carriageway to current expressway standard so as to enhance road safety and to cater for the growing traffic demand. Design and site investigation works would start in mid-2004.

* Planning of the Central-Wan Chai Bypass and the Island Eastern Corridor Link is under way. This dual three-lane carriageway aims at relieving traffic congestion along the existing Connaught Road Central/Harcourt Road/Gloucester Road, which is the key east-west traffic route along the northern shore of Hong Kong Island linking the Central, Wan Chai and Causeway Bay areas.

The KCR West Rail, which opened on December 20, provides a rapid 30.5-kilometre link between West Kowloon and the new towns of Tsuen Wan, Yuen Long and Tuen Mun. *Previous page:* Connaught Road Central, a main artery through the business district of Hong Kong Island.

More walkways have been built to facilitate the movement of pedestrians through the busy Central business district.

* On Lantau Island, it is planned to upgrade the existing Tung Chung Road between Lung Tseng Tau and Cheung Sha to a single two-lane road to improve the island's north-south access and to enhance the safety and capacity of the existing substandard Tung Chung Road. Detailed design has been completed. Construction works are expected to commence in early 2004 for completion in 2006-07.

* Elsewhere, planning is at an advanced stage for the construction of a new boundary bridge at the Sha Tau Kok crossing, which is intended to improve traffic flow and increase capacity. Works are expected to commence in early 2004 for completion in early 2005.

Road Opening Works

Besides serving as carriageways for vehicles and pedestrians, roads also accommodate various utility services, such as water and gas mains, sewers and electricity and telephone cables. To cope with the increasing demand for utility services and maintenance work, utility companies often have to excavate the carriageways and footpaths to lay more pipes, cables and ducts, and to carry out repair work. There were about 230 new road openings each day in 2003. Road openings are coordinated and controlled by the Highways Department through a permit system, under which utility companies are required to carry out work to a required standard and within a time limit.

To coordinate and monitor road opening works more effectively and to minimise traffic disruption, the Highways Department has established a three-tier communication system with participants ranging from high level management to working level staff of utility companies and relevant government departments. A computerised utility management system has been in use since 1997 to further improve coordination and minimise inconvenience to road users.

Existing Control Area

The Tsing Ma Control Area (TMCA), which was opened to traffic in May 1997, is a 21-kilometre expressway network comprising the Tsing Kwai Highway, Cheung Tsing Tunnel, Cheung Tsing Highway, North-West Tsing Yi Interchange, Tsing Yi North Coastal Road, Lantau Link, Ting Kau Bridge, part of the North Lantau Highway as well as Ma Wan Road. The TMCA is operated and maintained by a private management contractor.

The Lantau Link has a one-way toll collection arrangement. Vehicles travelling on the Lantau Link are charged twice the single journey toll when they return from Lantau Island or enter Ma Wan. The double toll ranges from $20 to $80 for different types of vehicles. A daily average of 40 500 vehicles used the Lantau Link in 2003.

Public Transport

Rail, bus, ferry and other public transport services offer Hong Kong commuters a good choice of different transport modes at reasonable fares and different levels of comfort, speed and convenience.

Railways

Rail travel accounts for some 30 per cent of the total daily public transport volume. The railways are built and operated by the two railway corporations, the Kowloon-Canton Railway Corporation (KCRC) and the MTR Corporation Limited (MTRCL).

The KCRC is wholly owned by the Government. The MTRCL was formerly wholly owned by the Government but was privatised in 2000 to become a listed company with the Government remaining as a major shareholder. Both corporations operate on prudent commercial principles providing efficient, reliable and safe passenger rail services to the public.

The KCR was commissioned in 1910. It is the first and oldest railway system in Hong Kong. The railway was formerly operated by the Government until the KCRC was established in 1982. The KCRC now runs both the East Rail and the West Rail as well as a Light Rail System. The East Rail runs from Hung Hom to Lo Wu at the boundary. There are 13 stations along the 34-kilometre route and the railway carried an average of 763 000 passengers daily in 2003. In recent years, the KCRC has made rapid progress in a number of capital projects on the East Rail, including the train refurbishment project, commissioning of new trains, noise reduction project and upgrading the signalling system. The newly commissioned West Rail runs from West Kowloon to Yuen Long and Tuen Mun. There are nine stations along the 30.5-kilometre route and the railway has been serving approximately 100 000 passengers daily since its opening on December 20. The KCRC also operates inter-city through train services from Hong Kong to cities in Guangdong as well as to Shanghai and Beijing. Apart from passenger services, the KCRC provides rail freight transportation and intermodal services, covering some 60 cities in the Mainland. The corporation has also made significant progress on projects designed to expand its railway network, including the East Rail Extensions, the Kowloon Southern Link and the Shatin to Central Link.

The KCRC operates the Light Rail (LR), which started operation in the north-western New Territories in 1988. The LR carried an average of 291 000 passengers daily in 2003. To enable the Light Rail to be effectively integrated with the West Rail, three stops were upgraded and a new one was built to provide convenient interchanges with the West Rail. An extension of the Light Rail to the newly developed Tin Shui Wai Reserve Zone went into operation on December 7. The Light Rail was also grade-separated on Pui To Road in Tuen Mun to facilitate traffic flow.

The former Mass Transit Railway Corporation was established by statute in 1975 to operate the MTR. The first passenger train service on the Kwun Tong Line of the MTR began in 1979. The MTR was subsequently expanded to include the Tsuen Wan Line (1982), the Island Line (1985), the Eastern Harbour Crossing rail tunnel connecting Kwun Tong Line to Quarry Bay (1989), the Tung Chung Line (1998) and the Tseung Kwan O Line (2002). The MTR carried a weekday average of about 2.2 million passengers in 2003. The company also operates the Airport Express Line, a dedicated rail link between the airport and the city centre. The Airport Express Line carried a daily average of about 19 000 passengers in 2003.

In February 2000, the Legislative Council passed legislation to privatise a portion of the Government's shares in the company. The MTR Corporation Limited was listed on the Hong Kong Stock Exchange in October that year.

Tramway

Electric trams have been operating on Hong Kong Island since 1904. The Hong Kong Tramways Limited operates six routes on 13 kilometres of double track along the northern shore of Hong Kong Island between Kennedy Town and Shau Kei Wan, and about three kilometres of single track around Happy Valley.

The company's 164 trams, including two open-balcony trams for tourists and private hire and one special maintenance tram, make up the world's only fully double-decker tram fleet. The trams recorded an average of 223 744 passenger trips daily in 2003. Fares were $2 for adults and $1 for children aged under 12 and senior citizens aged 65 or above.

Peak Tram

Hong Kong's other tramway is a cable-hauled funicular railway operated by the Peak Tramways Company Limited from Central (Garden Road) to the Peak. The 1.4-kilometre tramway began operation in 1888 and was modernised in 1989. It served an average of 8 471 passengers a day in 2003, mostly tourists and local sightseers. One-way fares for adults, children aged under 12 and senior citizens aged 65 or above were $20, $6 and $7, respectively.

The period of right granted to the Peak Tramways Company Limited to run and operate the Peak Tramway was due to expire at the end of 2003. Taking account of the company's provision of stable and satisfactory service in terms of safety and service aspects and its plans to further improve its operation and passenger facilities, the Chief Executive in Council approved a 10-year extension of the company's operating right.

Other Road-based Passenger Transport

The other road-based passenger transport modes — comprising mainly franchised buses, public light buses, taxis and residents' services — account for 66 per cent of all public transport journeys. Franchised buses are the largest road-based carriers and account for about 38 per cent of the total daily public transport volume.

Franchised Buses

Local bus services in Kowloon and the New Territories are largely provided by the Kowloon Motor Bus Company (1933) Limited (KMB). At year-end, the company operated 393 bus routes in Kowloon and the New Territories; 23 and 29 cross-harbour routes jointly with Citybus Limited (CTB) and New World First Bus Services Limited (NWFB) respectively; and 11 cross-harbour routes on its own.

The KMB fleet comprised 4 284 licensed vehicles at year-end; 3 509 were air-conditioned and 1 444 wheelchair-accessible. KMB recorded 1.06 billion passenger trips (a daily average of 2.91 million passenger trips) and covered 344.3 million kilometres during the year. Fares ranged from $1.20 to $38 for its regular routes. Children aged under 12 and elderly passengers were offered concessionary fares on all the company's routes.

Local bus services on Hong Kong Island are provided by NWFB and CTB. At year-end, NWFB operated 59 bus routes on Hong Kong Island, 10 serving Kowloon and Tseung Kwan O and 33 cross-harbour routes, 29 of which were operated jointly with KMB. It had a licensed fleet of 730 buses: 729 were air-conditioned and 583 wheelchair-accessible.

NWFB recorded 180.5 million passenger trips (a daily average of 494 624 passenger trips) and covered 59.4 million kilometres during the year. Its fares ranged from $3 to $34.20 on regular routes. Concessionary fares were offered on all routes to children aged under 12 and elderly passengers.

CTB operates two bus networks under two franchises. One of the franchises comprises 66 bus routes on Hong Kong Island and 31 cross-harbour routes, 23 of which are operated jointly with KMB. Another franchise comprises a network of 16 routes linking major districts in Hong Kong Island and Kowloon with Tung Chung and the airport.

At year-end, CTB had a licensed fleet of 940 buses, all of which were air-conditioned, and 124 wheelchair-accessible. The company recorded 207.3 million passenger trips (a daily average of 568 044 passenger trips) and covered 82.8 million kilometres during the year. Fares ranged from $2.50 to $45 for its regular routes. Concessionary fares were offered to children aged under 12, and elderly passengers on Hong Kong Island routes (except recreational routes) and on cross-harbour and Tung Chung/airport routes.

The Long Win Bus Company Limited (LW) provides bus services between the New Territories and Tung Chung/the airport. The company recorded 19.3 million passenger trips (a daily average of 52 766 passenger trips) and covered 22.7 million kilometres in 2003. At year-end, 145 buses were serving a total of 15 routes: all were air-conditioned and 136 wheelchair-accessible. Fares ranged from $3.50 to $28 for its regular routes. The company also offers concessionary fares for children aged under 12 and elderly passengers on all routes.

The New Lantao Bus Company (1973) Limited (NLB) mainly provides bus services on Lantau Island. The company recorded 9.7 million passenger trips (a daily average of 26 523 passenger trips) and covered five million kilometres during the year. It runs 25 routes with a licensed fleet of 80 vehicles. Fares ranged from $2.50 to $40 for its regular routes. Children aged under 12 and elderly passengers are offered concessionary fares on all routes.

Bus-Bus Interchange schemes are being introduced to encourage more efficient use of bus resources and limited road space and to allow more choice for passengers. Fare discounts are offered to passengers when interchanging among designated bus routes. By year-end, a total of 120 Bus-Bus Interchange schemes had been implemented, involving a total of 368 routes.

Non-franchised Buses

Non-franchised bus services perform a supplementary role in the public transport system. They mainly serve tourists, groups of residents, employees and students, and help to reduce peak hour demand for other public transport services. At year-end, there were 7 296 licensed non-franchised buses in operation.

Minibuses

Hong Kong's minibuses are licensed to carry a maximum of 16 passengers. At year-end, there were 6 266 licensed minibuses. Of these, 4 343 were public light buses (PLBs), and 1 923 were private light buses. Private light buses are authorised to carry only group passengers and are not allowed to collect separate fares.

There are two types of PLBs: 'green' and 'red' minibuses. Green minibuses (GMBs) provide scheduled services with fixed routeing, fares, vehicle allocation and timetables stipulated by the Transport Department. There were 2 625 GMBs operating 349 routes which recorded a daily average of 1 141 000 passengers trips in 2003. Red minibuses (RMBs) are not required to operate on fixed routes or timetables and they may set their own fares, but they are subject to certain restrictions on their operating areas. There were 1 718 RMBs in operation and they recorded a daily average of 482 000 passengers trips during the year.

In 2003, the Transport Department and the Quality Public Light Bus Service Steering Committee continued to launch a series of schemes to improve the quality of PLB service. In the first half of the year, the Transport Department launched a campaign to issue standard PLB driver identity plates to about 14 000 PLB drivers free of charge. The department also promulgated the 'Public Light Bus Service Standards' in June, listing the principal standards for compliance by PLB drivers. In addition, three Driving Improvement Schools were appointed in August to provide a 'Public Light Bus Driver Training Course'. To arouse awareness of the importance of vehicle maintenance and repair, a workshop on 'Vehicle Servicing and Maintenance of Public Light Buses' was organised for the PLB trade in November.

A *PLB Newsletter* was published every four months to enhance communication with the trade. The department continued to promote and facilitate the provision of on-board facilities for passengers including electronic payment systems, passenger call bells, driver name plates and display of passenger hotlines numbers.

The Government introduced incentive schemes in August 2002 to encourage the early replacement of diesel light buses by vehicles operating on liquefied petroleum gas (LPG) or electricity. PLB owners who replace their diesel vehicles with those using LPG or electricity may apply for a one-off grant of $60,000 or $80,000, respectively. Owners of diesel private light buses who opt to switch to LPG vehicles will be exempted from the first registration tax (electricity-driven vehicles are already exempted from the tax). The deadlines for applications are the end of 2004 for diesel light buses that are 10 years old or over and the end of 2005 for those that are less than 10 years old at the time of de-registration. At year-end, 642 LPG public light buses and 57 LPG private light buses were operating on the roads. One electricity-driven private light bus was in operation.

Taxis

At year-end, there were 15 250 urban taxis (coloured red), 2 838 New Territories taxis (green) and 50 Lantau taxis (blue) in operation, and they carried about one million passengers trips per day.

To improve the operating environment for taxis, the Transport Department introduced a temporary arrangement in May to allow all taxis to pick up and set down passengers in all 'peak hours' and '7 am to 7 pm' restricted zones on roads with a speed limit below 70 kilometres per hour. At year-end, a total of 148 taxi pick-up/drop-off points and 51 taxi drop-off points had been designated. In addition, from February a taxi stand was designated at Happy Valley Racecourse on race days to facilitate picking up and setting down of passengers. In addition, a trial scheme was launched in March to allow urban and New Territories taxis to operate at Lok Ma Chau Control Point from midnight to 6.30 am daily.

The cash grant scheme introduced in August 2000 as an incentive for operators to convert taxis to LPG was completed on December 31. A total of 18 112 taxis had been converted, representing 99.9 per cent of the entire fleet.

During the year, the Transport Department and the Quality Taxi Services Steering Committee (QTSSC) continued to launch schemes to improve the quality of taxi service. The prize presentation ceremony of the Taxi Driver Commendation Scheme 2003 was held in December. A total of 12 Quality Taxi Drivers and some 1 200

Meritorious Taxi Drivers were commended on their good conduct and provision of quality taxi service. To further enhance the provision of useful information to taxi drivers and passengers, two new taxi passenger and fare information LED (light emitting diode) display panels, in addition to the existing five LED panels at various taxi stands, were erected at the taxi stands outside the KCR Hung Hom Station. Three taxi passenger and fare information plates were also installed at taxi stands in Pak Tam Chung and Sai Kung Town Centre. In addition, the department has published 11 issues of *Taxi Newsletters* and distributed 40 000 copies per issue to taxi drivers free of charge. Also, leaflets were distributed to tourists/taxi passengers to provide useful information on taxi services. A total of 150 000 and 20 000 leaflets were distributed at the airport and the Lok Ma Chau Control Point, respectively.

Ferries

Ferries provide essential transport links to outlying islands where no land transport alternatives are available, and an alternative service within the inner harbour and to other areas in Hong Kong.

At year-end, one ferry operator provided two cross-harbour franchised passenger ferry services and 11 ferry operators provided 28 licensed passenger ferry services to the outlying islands and across the harbour. These franchised/licensed services were supplemented by about 78 *kaito* services which provide services to relatively remote parts of Hong Kong.

In 2003, ferries recorded a daily average of about 89 000 passenger trips across the harbour and about 58 000 passenger trips to/from the outlying islands.

Transport Management

Effective transport management is essential for the orderly and safe operation of the transport system. The Government's regulatory powers are provided under the Road Traffic Ordinance. Every effort is made to improve the efficiency and effectiveness of transport management through the use of modern technology in the various areas elaborated below.

Licensing

By the end of 2003, Hong Kong had 1 659 249 licensed drivers and 524 253 licensed vehicles and government vehicles. There were 338 930 licensed private cars, and 22 821 new private cars were registered during the year. Registered goods vehicles totalled 121 587, of which 75 987 were light goods vehicles. The average number of new learner-drivers was 4 369 per month. Since the introduction of the Driving-offence Points System in August 1984, 68 734 disqualifications have been ordered by the courts and 648 838 notices served under the Road Traffic (Driving-offence Points) Ordinance. The figures for 2003 were 2 992 and 35 545, respectively. Over the past five years, 426 402 drivers have incurred Driving-offence Points for committing scheduled offences under the Driving-offence Points System.

Driver Improvement Scheme

The Government launched the Driver Improvement Scheme in September 2002 to promote road safety through the improvement of the participants' driving attitude/behaviour and reminding them of the requirement to comply with traffic regulations. Four driving improvement schools were designated to provide the driving improvement course. A driver is allowed to join a driving improvement course voluntarily and the courts are also empowered to direct drivers who have committed relevant offences to attend the course. A driver will have three driving-offence points deducted from his/her total driving-offence points already incurred, subject to satisfactory completion of the course and issue of a certificate by one of the designated driving improvement schools.

From September 2002 to December 2003, nearly 2 000 drivers had attended the driving improvement course. The feedback from the course participants was encouraging and positive. They found the course useful in improving driving practices and fostering good driving attitudes. Statistics also showed that about 80 per cent of the participants did not incur new driving-offence points within six months of the completion of the course, reflecting its usefulness.

Computerisation of Written Test

To provide better customer service and to streamline arrangements concerning the written test that is part of the procedure for obtaining a driving licence, the Transport Department computerised the written test from October 20. Under the new user-friendly environment, candidates will know their results as soon as they have completed the written test, and successful applicants will be able to make appointments for road tests in 15 minutes. The average waiting time for taking written tests has been shortened from 40 days to 30 days.

Vehicle Examination

Vehicles are examined to ensure that they are roadworthy and properly maintained. Compulsory annual inspection applies to all public service vehicles, goods vehicles and trailers. In 2003, 195 900 vehicles were examined at the four government vehicle examination centres. Private cars over six years old and light goods vehicles not exceeding 1.9 tonnes are inspected annually at 23 designated car testing centres operated by the private sector. These centres conducted 148 300 vehicle examinations during the year. In addition, 3 594 spot checks were conducted on franchised buses to ensure their safety, roadworthiness and service standards.

A chassis dynamometer has been installed in the Kowloon Bay Vehicle Examination Centre to perform random checks of smoke emissions from loaded diesel vehicles. Another chassis dynamometer will be installed in the same Vehicle Examination Centre in 2004.

New vehicle models imported into Hong Kong are required to undergo type approval to ensure their compliance with the relevant statutory requirements. In 2003, 449 vehicle types were approved. To facilitate type approval application by authorised vehicle dealers, a 'one-stop' approval service was implemented in July. In the past, applicants had to submit applications separately to the Transport Department, Electrical and Mechanical Services Department and Environment Protection Department. The 'one-stop' mechanism now enables dealers to make a single submission to the Transport Department, greatly simplifying the application process.

Booking of examination appointments on the Internet has been extended to include trailers, and electronic payment is now possible at all vehicle examination centres, providing additional convenience for users. Vehicle Appointment Status Display Systems have been installed at the New Kowloon Bay Vehicle Examination Centre, Kowloon Bay Vehicle Examination Centre and To Kwa Wan Vehicle Examination

Centre showing the available examination slots in the next five months, assisting the public in making appointments.

Traffic Control and Surveillance

The use of closed-circuit television (CCTV) cameras continues to provide real-time traffic information to government departments for monitoring traffic and allowing them to react quickly in case of a traffic disruption or an emergency. There are 146 cameras installed in the urban areas of Hong Kong Island, Kowloon, Sha Tin and Tsuen Wan and another 48 cameras are operating along Tuen Mun Road, West Kowloon Highway, North Lantau Highway, San Tin Highway and Fanling Highway and along roads leading to boundary crossings.

The Transport Department commenced the construction of a Traffic Control Centre (TCC) in mid-2002 for completion by early 2004. The TCC will accommodate Area Traffic Control (ATC) systems in the new towns, the Emergency Transport Coordination Centre (ETCC) and the monitoring system of the Tsing Ma Communication Centre (TMCC) to facilitate traffic management, incident management and dissemination of information. This project is progressing satisfactorily. The major component systems, including the ATC, ETCC and TMCC, have been operating in the TCC since October. Their respective CCTV facilities will be integrated by early 2004.

The ATC system is being expanded to 122 signalised junctions in Tai Po and North District. This project will also include 30 CCTV cameras. Delivery of the system components will commence in early 2004 for testing and system commissioning later in the year.

At year-end, 1 660 signalised junctions were in operation, and 1 156 of them were controlled by ATC systems.

Use of Information Technology in Transport

Reliable and comprehensive transport information enables commuters to make informed choices of routes and modes of transport resulting in more efficient use of road space, smoother traffic flow, enhanced road safety and improved accessibility.

A contract for the implementation of the Transport Information System (TIS) was awarded in May. Upon completion, the TIS will become a central data warehouse which will provide more transport information to the public and enhance the operation of the Transport Department and other departments. It will also facilitate the development of services in the private sector such as car navigation and fleet management. The system is scheduled for commissioning in phases from mid-2004.

Under the Journey Time Indication System, journey time indicators are provided along the approach roads to the three cross-harbour tunnels on Hong Kong Island to inform motorists of the estimated travel time to the Kowloon exits, so that they may make a more informed choice concerning the route to be taken. The first indicator on Gloucester Road, located near Revenue Tower, was put into service in June and the remaining two on the Island Eastern Corridor and the Canal Road Flyover were commissioned in December.

Automatic Toll Collection

Automatic toll collection systems (autotoll systems) were installed at the Cross-Harbour and Aberdeen Tunnels in August 1993, Lion Rock Tunnel in August 1994,

Eastern Harbour Crossing in September 1995, Tate's Cairn Tunnel in May 1996, Western Harbour Crossing in April 1997, Shing Mun Tunnels and Tseung Kwan O Tunnel in October 1997, Tai Lam Tunnel in June 1998 and Lantau Link in July 1998. They allow motorists to pay tolls by driving through designated toll booths without stopping. Since October 1998, the autotoll systems were unified so that a subscriber needs only one tag to use all tunnels and toll roads fitted with the system. In 2003, about 49 per cent of motorists used autotoll when passing through the tunnels and toll roads.

Parking

On-street parking is provided where there is parking demand and traffic conditions permit. At year-end, Hong Kong had about 17 700 metered parking spaces, with electronic parking meter charging in operation mainly between 8 am and midnight from Mondays to Saturdays, and 10 am to 10 pm on Sundays and public holidays. The management and operation of on-street metered parking spaces is contracted out to a private operator.

The Government owns 13 multi-storey carparks which together provide about 7 000 parking spaces. They are operated and managed by two private operators under management contracts with the Government.

Off-street public parking is provided by the Airport Authority at the airport at Chek Lap Kok and by the Housing Department in its housing estates. Park-and-Ride facilities have been operating at the Hong Kong, Kowloon and Tsing Yi Stations of the Airport Express, at Choi Yuen Road near the East Rail Sheung Shui Station, West Rail Kam Sheung Road Station in Yuen Long, and some commercial carparks located near the Olympic Station of the Tung Chung Line and the Hang Hau Station of the Tseung Kwan O Line. Private sector multi-storey and open-air public carparks in commercial/residential buildings and open-air lots provide about 184 500 parking spaces.

Road Safety

In 2003, there were 14 436 traffic accidents that resulted in casualties, including 173 fatal accidents and 2 674 involving serious injury. The number represented an overall decrease of 7.3 per cent compared with the 15 576 accidents in 2002 (162 fatal and 3 118 involving serious injury). In-depth investigations were carried out at 150 traffic accident 'black spots' to identify common accident causes. Remedial measures were recommended at 123 of these locations.

By year-end, 111 signalised road junctions were fitted with red light cameras to deter motorists from disobeying traffic signals and 85 locations on strategic routes were fitted with speed enforcement cameras to deter speeding. Further expansion of the red light camera and speed enforcement camera systems will be considered in 2004.

A legislative amendment to extend the rear seat belt requirement to public light bus passengers was endorsed by the Legislative Council and will come into effect in August 2004.

As part of efforts to promote road safety, an open competition for the Road Safety Vision was launched in November. The objectives were to devise a road safety vision for Hong Kong and to motivate the public towards achieving the common goal of road safety. In addition, a slogan will be selected to illustrate and supplement the Road Safety Vision.

Road safety campaigns continued to play an important role in reducing traffic accidents. The main theme chosen for 2003 was 'Smart Driving'. The message was conveyed through television and radio announcements, printed materials and on the Internet.

Transport and Environment

In planning for transport infrastructure projects, the Government is guided by sustainable development principles. It strives to ensure a better integration of transport provision with land use planning so as to reduce the number of motorised trips generated. It is also the Government's policy to accord priority to railways as the backbone of the transport system. Four railway lines or extensions will come into operation before 2008.

Less reliance on road-based transport will alleviate the pressure on transport systems and, in turn, lessen the impact on the environment. At the same time, the rationalisation of bus routes and stops and implementation of pedestrian schemes will continue. These will help reduce the impact of vehicle emissions and noise pollution on pedestrians.

Since late 1998, about 2 300 daily bus trips have been eliminated from the busy corridors on the northern shore of Hong Kong Island through service cancellation, frequency reduction, route truncation and amalgamation. In Nathan Road in Kowloon, about 360 daily bus trips have been eliminated since August 2002, enhancing the efficiency of bus operations. Bus stops have also been rationalised to reduce the number of stops on busy corridors.

The environmental impact of new transport projects both during the construction and the operation phases is also carefully examined. Environmental mitigation measures are implemented where necessary to minimise the environmental impact of transport projects. These include landscaping, artificial contouring of surrounding hillsides, depressed roads, laying of noise-reducing road surfacing and the installation of noise barriers or other forms of noise insulation.

To improve the environment for pedestrians, more pedestrian schemes and walkway systems are being planned and implemented. These help minimise conflict between pedestrians and vehicles, reduce traffic congestion and air pollution, as well as providing a more pleasant environment for pedestrians. A consultancy study on the detailed design of a pedestrian walkway system in Wan Chai, planned in conjunction with the pedestrian scheme for the district, commenced in 2003.

In 2002 and 2003, pedestrian schemes have been implemented in a number of streets including Paterson Street, Great George Street and Lee Garden Road in Causeway Bay; Canton Road, Hankow Road, Lock Road, Ashley Road and Ichang Street in Tsim Sha Tsui; Fa Yuen Street and Shan Tung Street in Mong Kok; Queen's Road Central, Chiu Lung Street, Lan Kwai Fong and D'Aguilar Street in Central; Johnston Road in Wan Chai; Kweilin Street and Apliu Street in Sham Shui Po; Temple Street and Nanking Street in Yau Ma Tei, and Stanley Market Street, New Street and Main Street in Stanley. In addition, the Mong Kok Road-Sai Yee Street Footbridge System, a private-public partnership project, was successfully commissioned and opened to the public in January. Situated in the heart of one of the busiest shopping areas in Mong Kok, this 360-metre elevated covered walkway segregates vehicles and pedestrians, thereby providing a safe, comfortable and convenient pedestrian environment conducive to relieving pressure on the narrow, crowded streets in the vicinity. It also directly interconnects the Mong Kok MTR and KCR stations, facilitating passenger interchange between the two rail systems under all weather conditions.

A study in 2001 to examine the feasibility of introducing trolleybus operation concluded that the introduction of trolleybuses was not recommended in existing built-up areas, while the possibility of trolleybus operation in new development areas could be further explored. In this connection, the merits of introducing trolleybuses among other environmentally friendly transport modes in the South-East Kowloon Development are being examined to determine the best choice of transport mode for this new development area.

Since 1993, franchised bus companies have been purchasing buses with environmentally friendly engines that meet the European emission standards (and known as 'Euro engines'). By year-end, about 78.7 per cent of the franchised buses were equipped with Euro engines while the remaining buses were all retrofitted with catalytic converters. To improve the environment, the franchised bus companies have been deploying only Euro II or Euro III engine buses to operate routes along Yee Wo Street in Causeway Bay, the busiest shopping area on Hong Kong Island. The Government is working with the companies to deploy cleaner vehicles along other busy corridors.

To enhance passengers' comfort at public transport interchanges, the franchised bus companies and the Government have been working to improve the overall quality of the interchanges. Electronic route information panels and customer service centres have been installed at some interchanges to enhance customer service. The Government has also implemented a number of improvement works, including upgrading the physical appearance of some interchanges and improving their ventilation systems.

As part of action to minimise air pollution, since August 1, 2001 all newly registered taxis have to run on LPG to meet the tighter emission standards. Incentive schemes to encourage the early replacement of diesel light buses by LPG or electricity-driven vehicles were introduced on August 27, 2002. The Government also implemented a mandatory dynamometer smoke test for all vehicles above 5.5 tonnes with effect from January 1, 2002, if they are reported to emit excessive smoke.

Cross-boundary Traffic

Overall Cross-boundary Traffic

In 2003, the cross-boundary vehicular traffic flow averaged 35 800 vehicles a day, 6 per cent higher than in the previous year. The overall cross-boundary passenger traffic by rail, road and ferry decreased by 3 per cent, comprising 332 000 passengers a day.

Rail Service to Lo Wu

Lo Wu, the only rail boundary crossing to the Mainland, which operates between 6.30 am and midnight every day, handled an average of 233 000 passengers daily in 2003. During festive seasons, the daily volume of passengers exceeded 266 000. A number of improvement projects at the Lo Wu Boundary Control Point are in progress, including the expansion of the Departure Hall and the widening of passageways, and scheduled to be completed in phases by 2005.

Road Crossings

There are three road crossings between Hong Kong and the Mainland — Lok Ma Chau, Man Kam To and Sha Tau Kok. The Lok Ma Chau crossing has been open round-the-clock to goods vehicles since November, 1994 and to passenger traffic since January 27, 2003. The Man Kam To and Sha Tau Kok crossings open daily to both goods vehicles and passenger traffic from 7 am to 10 pm and from 7 am to 8 pm, respectively.

In 2003, goods vehicles constituted 75 per cent of the traffic using the three road crossings. The average daily vehicular flows were 25 800 at Lok Ma Chau, 7 700 at Man Kam To and 2 300 at Sha Tau Kok. Of these, some 1 300 were approved cross-boundary coach trips that were operated by 82 companies.

For passenger traffic, the average daily flows were 67 000 at Lok Ma Chau, 5 200 at Man Kam To and 4 800 at Sha Tau Kok.

The shuttle bus service between Huanggang in Shenzhen and the Public Transport Interchange in San Tin, introduced in March 1997, carried 31 870 passengers daily in 2003. Before 24-hour operation of the Lok Ma Chau Control Point began on January 27, the shuttle bus service operated between 6.30 am and midnight. To tie in with the extended opening hours of the Control Point, the shuttle bus service also began to provide a 24-hour service. Two additional buses were introduced in September and another four buses will be introduced in the first quarter of 2004. There will then be 26 buses in the fleet. Improvement works to the shuttle bus terminus in San Tin commenced at the end of the year for completion in the fourth quarter of 2004. These works will improve the environment for passengers. A bus-only exit at the interchange and the widening of the adjacent section of Castle Peak Road were also completed during the year.

In connection with the 24-hour operation of the Lok Ma Chau Control Point, a trial scheme for taxi and GMB operations at the Control Point during the extended period, i.e. between midnight and 6.30 am, has been in effect since March 20. Passengers are able to board taxis and GMBs to go directly to the Lok Ma Chau Control Point during the extended period. The trial scheme will be reviewed in 2004.

To further facilitate cross-boundary traffic, since October 8 private cars with Man Kam To and Sha Tau Kok Closed Road Permits have been allowed to use the Lok Ma Chau facility between midnight and 6.30 am, when the former two crossings are closed. By year-end, 500 private cars with Man Kam To and Sha Tau Kok Closed Road Permits had used the Lok Ma Chau crossing within the specified hours.

Phase II of the improvement works at the Lok Ma Chau Control Point were completed in September. These works included the expansion of the Control Point Building with an increase in the number of passenger counters, provision of a one-lane northbound flyover to segregate goods and passenger vehicles before they go onto the boundary bridge, installation of X-ray machines for inspection of goods/container vehicles, provision of additional coach holding spaces and lay-bys, and a coach parking information system at both the northbound and southbound pick-up areas to help passengers to find and board their coaches after immigration clearance.

New Boundary Crossings Under Construction or Planning

To meet the anticipated growth in cross-boundary traffic, new road and rail passenger crossings have been planned in coordination with the Mainland authorities. The fourth land crossing, the Hong Kong-Shenzhen Western Corridor, is targeted for completion at the end of 2005. The second rail passenger crossing at Lok Ma Chau/Huanggang is planned to be completed together with the Sheung Shui to Lok Ma Chau Spur Line by mid-2007. A joint study is being conducted with the Mainland authorities on the feasibility of an express rail link connecting Guangzhou, Shenzhen and Hong Kong. Also, an Advance Work Co-ordination Group has been set up by the respective provincial and SAR governments to take forward preparatory work for the Hong Kong-Zhuhai-Macao Bridge.

Cross-boundary Ferries

Cross-boundary ferry services link Hong Kong with about 20 Mainland ports and Macau. In 2003, the passenger throughput by this mode of transport totalled 16.6 million.

The Port

Hong Kong set a new record in its container throughput in 2003 by handling 20.4 million 20-foot equivalent units (TEUs) of containers, making it the world's busiest container port for the 11th time in the last 12 years.

About 436 100 vessels arrived in and departed from Hong Kong during the year. These vessels carried 207.6 million tonnes of cargo and about 17 million passengers. Most of these passengers commuted on the world's largest fleet of high-speed ferries, including jetfoils and jet catamarans, to and from Macau and other ports in southern China.

Being the junction of two different forms of maritime transport — the large ocean-going vessels from the Pacific Ocean and the smaller, coastal and river trade craft from the Pearl River — Hong Kong is a modern, fully developed deep-water harbour and the focal point of all maritime trading activities in southern China.

On an average day there are around 100 ocean-going ships working in the port; nearly 500 river trade craft entering or leaving the port; and many river ferries and local craft working in or passing through the harbour. Ship turnaround performance is among the best in Asia: container ships at terminal berths are routinely turned round in 10 hours or less, while conventional vessels working cargo at buoys are in port for only 1.2 days on average.

Port Development

Container handling facilities are a key part of the infrastructure in the logistics sector, one of the four pillar industries of Hong Kong. Matching the supply of port facilities with demand will ensure and facilitate economic growth for the community. To meet the growing demand, Hong Kong is completing the construction of a new container terminal, Container Terminal 9 (CT9), on Tsing Yi Island opposite the eight terminals at Kwai Chung. Covering an area of 68 hectares, the CT9 has six berths and the first two came into operation in July and October. The whole terminal is expected to be completed by the end of 2004. The CT9 will help maintain Hong Kong's role as the premier port for southern China well into the 21st century.

Competition among the container terminals and among alternative modes of container handling motivates the operators to heighten efficiency and improve their quality of service. The continuing investment in upgrading equipment and systems in the existing terminals at Kwai Chung over the past few years has enabled the port to enhance its productivity.

The container port is vital, not only for Hong Kong, but also for southern China — one of the fastest industrialising areas in the world. Some 78 per cent of container traffic handled by Hong Kong is related to southern China. The port of Hong Kong, therefore, is likely to remain as the Asia-Pacific region's hub port.

Strategic Planning

To ensure that the port facilities in Hong Kong meet the demands and there is timely provision of sufficient facilities to handle the port's cargo growth following China's accession to the World Trade Organisation, a 'Study on Hong Kong Port — Master Plan 2020' has commenced with the objective of formulating a competitive strategy and master plan for port development in the next 20 years and beyond. The study focuses on strengthening the competitiveness of Hong Kong as a leading port in the region, the role of port operation in the development of transportation and logistics services in Hong Kong, and the preferred location of major container port and related infrastructure. The study is scheduled for completion in early 2004.

Hong Kong Port Development Council and Hong Kong Maritime Industry Council

The Hong Kong Port Development Council (PDC) and the Hong Kong Maritime Industry Council (MIC), two separate non-statutory bodies, were established in June to replace the Hong Kong Port and Maritime Board following the recommendation of the 'Study to Strengthen Hong Kong's Role as an International Maritime Centre'. Chaired by the Secretary for Economic Development and Labour, both the PDC and MIC are dedicated, high-level advisory bodies for key players from the private sector and the Government to discuss and coordinate matters in developing and promoting the port and maritime industries.

In Hong Kong, all port facilities are financed, developed, owned and operated by the private sector, a practice which few major international ports in the world adopt. The Government's role is to undertake long-term strategic planning for port facilities and to provide the necessary supporting infrastructure, such as by building roads and dredging access channels to the terminals.

The PDC advises the Government on the port development strategy and port facility planning to meet future demands. It also assists the Government in promoting Hong Kong as a regional hub port and a leading container port in the world.

A Port Development Advisory Group was formed in September, under the PDC, to assist the council in examining port cargo forecasts and assessing port development needs in the light of changing demand, port capacity, productivity, performance and competition both locally and regionally.

Hong Kong has a successful shipping industry with many well-known and experienced shipping-related companies. There are some 900 shipping-related companies operating in Hong Kong, providing a wide range of maritime services from ship owning/management, ship registration, financing, insurance and ship broking to maritime arbitration, survey, repairs, and ship replenishment.

The MIC advises the Government on the formulation of measures and initiatives to further develop the maritime industry and assists the Government in promoting the comprehensive maritime services provided in Hong Kong. It also focuses on the promotion of Hong Kong as an international maritime centre.

To further enhance Hong Kong's attractiveness as a base for international maritime enterprises, the MIC has set up a Human Resource Task Force to address the education, training and manpower supply issue. A Maritime Services Task Force was also set up to formulate measures to promote the various sectors in the maritime cluster.

The Hong Kong Shipping Register (HKSR) has gained a reputation as a world-class and quality register with excellent services. In order to further boost the quality standard and the reputation of the HKSR, a pre-registration quality control system was launched in July. Various improvement measures are also introduced regularly to heighten efficiency and user-friendliness. As a result, the Register's gross tonnage broke the 20-million mark in November, securing its position in the world's top 10 shipping registers.

Moreover, to enhance the competitiveness of the shipping industry, Hong Kong is proactive in negotiating double taxation relief arrangements covering shipping income with its trading partners. In 2003, Hong Kong signed Avoidance of Double Taxation Agreements (DTAs) on shipping income with Germany and Norway in January and October, respectively. Hong Kong also signed a DTA on shipping and air services incomes with Singapore in November. Together with similar arrangements with the Mainland, Belgium, the United States, the United Kingdom, the Netherlands as well as the confirmed provisions of reciprocal tax exemption with the tax authorities of New Zealand and the Republic of Korea, Hong Kong has made double taxation relief arrangements covering shipping income with 10 tax administrations.

Port Administration

The Marine Department administers the port. Its principal function is to ensure safety of navigation and efficiency of shipping activities in the waters of Hong Kong. This is achieved by comprehensive traffic management, harbour patrols, vessel traffic services, provision of mooring buoys and rigorous enforcement of major international maritime conventions.

The department liaises closely with shipping and commercial organisations through a number of advisory and consultative committees. Users and operators of port facilities can provide their advice in relation to port administration matters through these channels. The Port Operations Committee advises on all matters related to the efficient operation of the port, the Pilotage Advisory Committee on matters relating to pilotage services, and the Port Area Security Advisory Committee on port security. Besides these, the Provisional Local Vessel Advisory Committee is concerned with local craft matters and the Shipping Consultative Committee advises on efficient operation of the HKSR and Hong Kong's participation in the International Maritime Organisation (IMO).

The Marine Department's website provides a wide range of information on the port and the HKSR. The home page also carries Marine Department notices and gives details of the department's services and facilities. Special features include a Hong Kong Shipping Directory in which Hong Kong-based marine services companies are listed, real-time movements of ocean-going vessels (OGVs) and river-trade cargo vessels in port, examination schedules for seafarers and verification of Port Clearance Permits issued to OGVs. Applications for certain port formalities can be submitted over the Internet. Phase I of a new electronic business portal — the Marine Department eBusiness System — was launched in December, permitting some 35 types of online submissions for notification or application.

Vessel Traffic Management

The department's Vessel Traffic Centre (VTC) provides vessel traffic services to vessels which are required to participate in the Vessel Traffic Service (VTS) and follow the VTC's directions.

The movements of vessels participating in the VTS are regulated by the VTC through a computer-aided radar network, VHF communications and a database information system, which provides surveillance over 95 per cent of Hong Kong waters. The VTS system has been upgraded to cater for the continual growth and future demands in marine traffic.

Harbour Patrol and Local Control Stations

The Harbour Patrol Section operates a fleet of 20 patrol launches and provides on-scene support to the Vessel Traffic Centre. The main duties of the patrol launches are law enforcement and maintenance of port and shipping safety, as well as responding to maritime emergencies.

In addition, the department operates a local traffic control station at Kwai Chung Container Terminal 8. The station, manned 24 hours a day and equipped with a dedicated patrol launch, provides navigational assistance to vessels in the vicinity. For enhanced traffic control in the Western Fairway, a surveillance station was set up and began operation in September.

Carriage of Dangerous Goods

The department conducts random shipboard inspections of vessels in Hong Kong waters in accordance with international and local standards. The dangerous goods legislation is being revised with a view to bringing it into conformity with the new requirements of the International Maritime Dangerous Goods Code.

Pilotage Service

Pilotage is compulsory in Hong Kong waters for vessels of 3 000 gross tonnes and above, oil tankers of 1 000 gross tonnes and above, and all gas carriers.

The Director of Marine is the authority regulating and monitoring the pilotage service through the assistance of the Pilotage Advisory Committee, whose membership covers a wide spectrum of port users and shipping interests.

Pilotage service is provided through the Hong Kong Pilots Association, which is a private company. The service is available round-the-clock throughout the year.

Local Craft

In 2003, 13 300 local craft — including passenger vessels, cargo vessels, fishing vessels and pleasure vessels — were licensed in Hong Kong to provide a variety of efficient and continuous services for the port as well as the community. The department plans to introduce new legislation in 2004 with a view to rationalising the licensing and management of these vessels.

Hydrographic Service

The Hydrographic Office carries out hydrographic surveys and produces bilingual nautical charts and publications. It also produces Electronic Navigational Charts. Notices to Mariners for updating of charts are issued once every two weeks. The office also provides real-time tidal information and tidal stream predictions through the Internet (*http://www.hydro.gov.hk*).

Port Planning and Development

The department's Planning and Development Branch provides professional advice on port and marine projects, and coordinates publicity on all marine development works. These include CT9, the Hong Kong Disneyland and West Kowloon Cultural District projects, developments in Tuen Mun Area 38, South-East Kowloon and Tseung Kwan O, and the proposed new links to the Pearl River Delta.

The Planning and Development Branch is also the executive arm of the Designated Authority to implement the IMO's International Ship and Port Facility Security (ISPS) Code in respect of port facilities in Hong Kong. The main tasks include assessing the security assessments and security plans of port facilities that are required to comply with the ISPS Code and undertaking the annual audit of these assessments and plans.

Safety Guide and Code of Practice on Cargo Handling

A *Safety Guide for Container Handling* is available from the Marine Department for cargo operators to enhance marine industrial safety. The Safety Guide provides guidance on matters such as managing safety at work, safety procedures for working on the top of containers and personal protective clothing and equipment. The Safety Guide will become a Code of Practice after the Merchant Shipping (Local Vessels) Ordinance enters into force (expected in 2004). A new *Code of Practice for Strength Calculations, Test and Examination of Derrick Cranes on Local Vessels* will also be ready for issue in 2004.

Port Services and Facilities

Mainland and Macau Ferry Services

The department manages two cross-boundary ferry terminals: the China Ferry Terminal (CFT) with 13 berths and the Macau Ferry Terminal (MFT) with 12 berths. The CFT is open from 7 am to 10 pm daily and the MFT operates round-the-clock.

Immigration and Quarantine Services

Immigration and quarantine services are available at the Western Quarantine and Immigration Anchorage and the Eastern Quarantine and Immigration Anchorage. A shipping agent may apply for immigration and quarantine services, including advance clearance, for a ship.

The Tuen Mun Immigration Anchorage operates 24 hours daily for river trade vessels plying between Hong Kong and Pearl River Delta ports. Pre-arrival clearance (PAC) has been extended to Mainland River/Coastal Trade Vessels (MRCTVs). All MRCTVs may apply for the PAC facilities. MRCTVs operators who are interested in the scheme may submit applications to the Harbour Control Section of the Immigration Department.

Mooring Buoys

The department provides 31 mooring buoys in the harbour area for ship operations. There are 19 class 'A' buoys for vessels up to 183 metres in length and 12 class 'B' buoys for vessels up to 137 metres in length. Booking of these mooring buoys is made through the Vessel Traffic Centre.

Bunkering

Bunkering is readily available at commercial wharves and oil terminals or from a large fleet of private bunkering barges. Fresh water may also be provided alongside berths or from a private fleet of water boats.

Ship Repair and Dry-docking

The port has extensive facilities for repairing, docking and slipping all types of vessels of sizes up to 300 metres in length and 42 metres in beam. Local shipyards are able to build and maintain ferries, cargo boats, workboats and pleasure vessels. The department's Marine Industrial Safety Section provides free services in carrying out safety inspections of vessels and issuing permits for vessels to undergo repairs. As part of its safety advisory service, the section publishes free leaflets and pamphlets that promote safe working practices in ship-repairing, ship-breaking and cargo-handling afloat as well as in marine construction work.

Local Vessels Safety Certification Service

The Local Vessel Safety Section provides a certification service for all types of local vessels, except pleasure vessels, to ensure they comply with requirements in construction safety, life-saving appliances, fire-fighting equipment, light and sound signals, and anti-pollution installations.

Public Cargo Working Areas

The department manages eight Public Cargo Working Areas (PCWA), in which licensed cargo operators are allowed to load and unload cargo onto and from barges and coasters. The total length of berths available in these working areas is 6 992 metres. The Wan Chai PCWA was decommissioned on October 3 for local development but the Chai Wan PCWA was reopened on the same day to take over the cargo activities of Wan Chai.

Reception of Marine Wastes

The department provides contractor services to collect domestic and operational refuse from ocean-going vessels and local vessels. The Chemical Waste Treatment Centre on Tsing Yi Island provides facilities for handling oily and chemical wastes from ships. Registered contractors collect such wastes from ships and deliver them to the centre.

Combating Oil Pollution

The department maintains a maritime oil spill response plan to ensure a timely and effective response to oil spills in Hong Kong waters.

There is also a regional maritime oil spill response plan for the Pearl River Estuary. The aim of this plan is to enhance the regional cooperation in the event of a major oil spill incident occurring in Hong Kong or in any of the neighbouring ports in Shenzhen, Zhuhai, Macau and Guangzhou.

In October, the department's Pollution Control Unit organised a large-scale oil spill clean-up exercise in which all concerned government departments and local oil companies took part.

Shipping

Hong Kong Shipping Register

The HKSR is administered by the Marine Department. The supporting legislation relating to the Register embodies international standards under the IMO, the International Labour Organisation and other international conventions applicable to Hong Kong.

Substantial growth in the HKSR continued in 2003. By year-end, the Register had grown to 879 vessels with a total of 20.69 million gross tonnage, representing a 27.5 per cent increase in tonnage over 2002. The HKSR is now ranked eighth in the world.

The Register has an excellent reputation for high quality and standards. Port State Control detention rates for the Hong Kong-registered ships continue to remain well below the world averages.

While statutory surveys of passenger ships are undertaken by Marine Department surveyors, statutory surveys of cargo ships are fully delegated to accredited classification societies. The department monitors the performance of Hong Kong-registered ships and their management companies as well as of classification societies by means of an innovative Flag State Quality Control (FSQC) System, which ensures the ships comply fully with the applicable international standards. Under the system, the performance of all ships and management companies in the HKSR is carefully monitored in accordance with established criteria. A computerised database is then used for selection of ships and companies for FSQC inspections. During the year, 39 FSQC inspections of ships and nine FSQC visits of companies were carried out by the department's surveyors.

Marine Accident Investigations

To discharge its obligations as a responsible maritime administration, the department's Marine Accident Investigation Branch (MAIB) investigates all serious marine accidents involving vessels in HKSAR waters. The department also investigates all major or serious accidents outside the HKSAR if a Hong Kong-registered ship is involved.

Investigations are carried out to identify the cause of accidents as well as the circumstances under which they occurred, in order to avoid similar accidents from happening again. Summaries of the investigation reports are posted on the department's website and copies of the reports are made available to the public upon request so as to promote and enhance maritime safety.

Depending upon the seriousness of the accident and the public interest involved, a public inquiry in the form of a Marine Court may be ordered by the Chief Executive, or, in case of an accident involving a licensed pilot, a Board of Investigation by the Director of Marine.

In 2003, the MAIB investigated 12 serious accidents.

Seafarers

The Merchant Shipping (Seafarers) Ordinance and its subsidiary legislation regulates the registration, employment, competence, discipline, health, safety and welfare of Hong Kong seafarers. The Marine Department's Mercantile Marine Office registers these seafarers and supervises their engagement on board ships.

In 2003, some 14 300 seafarers of various nationalities served on board 668 ocean-going ships flying the Hong Kong flag. About 1 000 officers and ratings served on passenger vessels plying within the river trade area.

The department's Seafarers' Certification Section monitors training provided to seafarers and examines candidates for the issue of certificates of competency. Towards this end, the section works closely with various training institutions in the training of seafarers.

Participation in International Shipping Activities

International Maritime Organisation

As an Associate Member in the name of Hong Kong, China, the HKSAR participates in the activities of the IMO. The Hong Kong maritime industry is consulted and kept well informed of all the issues discussed in the IMO that may affect the HKSAR. In 2003, the HKSAR attended one conference and 18 IMO meetings on various maritime issues in London. These issues related to the standards of training and certification for seafarers, fire protection, bulk carrier safety, radio communications, revision of the International Maritime Dangerous Goods Code, safety of navigation, prevention of marine pollution, casualty statistics and investigation, suppression of maritime piracy and maritime security.

Port State Control

The department is actively involved in the technical cooperation programmes under the Memorandum of Understanding on Port State Control (PSC) in the Asia-Pacific Region ('Tokyo MOU'). In 2003, it sent a Senior Surveyor to Yokohama, Japan, to give lectures on subjects relating to Port State Control inspections under the MOU's Expert Mission and Basic Training Course programmes.

The department also participated in various working groups under the MOU in formulating general policies, evaluation of technical cooperation programmes and improvement of a computerised information system and data exchange. Hong Kong is currently the leader of the Action Group on technical cooperation.

In 2003, the department introduced Port State Control inspections during weekends. PSC officers of the department conducted 915 inspections of ocean-going vessels, amounting to 20.3 per cent of ocean-going vessels visiting Hong Kong. About 89.5 per cent of these vessels had deficiencies which were required to be rectified.

Maritime Search and Rescue

The search and rescue responsibility for maritime distress situations occurring within Hong Kong waters and the major part of the South China Sea covering a sea area of about 450 000 square nautical miles, as agreed internationally, rests with the Maritime Rescue Coordination Centre (MRCC) of the Marine Department.

The MRCC is manned 24 hours a day by professional staff and is equipped with comprehensive communication equipment and a shore-based Global Maritime Distress and Safety System. It coordinates search and rescue operations in conjunction with other government departments and international ships on the high seas. Staff members of the MRCC regularly hold maritime safety seminars for fishermen's associations and yacht clubs and for the shipping communities in both Hong Kong and Guangdong Province.

In 2003, the centre handled 220 cases of vessel emergencies, 72 of which developed into search and rescue operations, including 21 medical evacuations. A total of 113 persons were rescued. During the year, the centre also presented safety seminars for the public.

In recognition of its expertise, the Hong Kong MRCC has been selected as a member of the IMO/International Civil Aviation Organisation Joint Working Group for Search and Rescue.

Government Fleet and Dockyard

Government Fleet

There are over 670 vessels of different types and sizes in the government fleet. About 135 vessels are major mechanised vessels serving 16 government departments including the Hong Kong Police Force (Marine Police region), Customs and Excise and Fire Services. These are mainly purpose-built vessels operated and manned by the user departments or the Marine Department. The department itself controls some 65 vessels which comprise mainly patrol launches, conveyance launches, pontoons and some specialised vessels such as hydrographic survey launches and explosives carriers.

The department's launches, apart from meeting traffic needs for its own port operations, also serve other government departments that do not have their own fleets. Vessels will be modified and deployed quickly from the fleet to suit the needs of large or important events.

Since 1999, the department has been outsourcing the provision of marine transport services, such as conveyance launches and tug boats, to private contractors. A trial outsourcing in 2002 of two harbour patrol vessels on day-time operations proved successful, and more harbour patrol vessels will be outsourced in 2004.

Government Dockyard

The Government Dockyard at Stonecutters Island occupies a land site of 9.8 hectares in addition to a protected water basin of 8.3 hectares. It serves as one of the operational bases for the Marine Department, the Police Force and the Customs and Excise Department.

The dockyard is also responsible for the design, procurement and maintenance of all vessels for the Government. In 2003, 19 new vessels costing $58 million were built and delivered to the Government. Twelve new building contracts, worth $115 million, were awarded to shipbuilders in Hong Kong and overseas.

Marine Facilities

The Civil Engineering Department is responsible for the planning, design and construction of public marine facilities including piers, beacons, breakwaters, seawalls, navigation channels and anchorage areas. In 2003, the department completed the reconstruction of the public piers at Tai Lam Chung, Hei Ling Chau and Kadoorie Piers. The department continued with the reconstruction of the public piers at Peng Chau, Cheung Chau, Kat O and Wu Kai Sha. It commenced the construction of a sheltered boat anchorage at Tai O and started the planning and design of reconstruction of the public piers at Sha Tau Kok, Wong Shek, Ko Lau Wan, Sham Chung and Lai Chi Chong. Work began on constructing a pier and boardwalk at Stanley.

The department is also responsible for the maintenance of public marine facilities. It operates a maintenance strategy that is aimed at extending the life of reinforced concrete piers by incorporating a specification for durable concrete, applying coating to protect the concrete against chloride penetration, and preventing corrosion of reinforcement bars by installing a cathodic protection system. In addition, the department carries out routine inspections and repairs of other public marine structures including seawalls, breakwaters and beacons. It provides maintenance dredging services in anchorage areas, typhoon shelters, rivers and navigation channels. In 2003, the department maintained 117 kilometres of seawalls, 298 piers and 18 000 hectares of seabed.

To make public piers more environmentally friendly, the department has advocated the use of rubber or recycled plastic as alternative materials for the fender system, to replace the traditional hardwood timber fenders. Replacement work has begun at some public piers.

International Transportation and Logistics Hub

'Transportation and Logistics' is an important sector of the economy, accounting for about 4.8 per cent of Hong Kong's Gross Domestic Product. Hong Kong is Asia's premier international transportation and logistics hub, and for many years has maintained its position as the world's busiest container port and a leading international air cargo handling centre. These achievements are due to the people who run the services and facilities — the investors as well as the efficient workforce. It is also the result of a productive blend of private and public sector cooperation.

Hong Kong has a port and an airport that are efficient, reliable and well-connected and facilitate the development of the logistics industry. In the case of air cargo, the airport handles an average of 50 810 tonnes every week. With its dual runways, the airport has ample capacity to handle anticipated increases in demand.

Hong Kong is also home to the most productive and efficient container terminals and the biggest private terminal operator in the world. A comprehensive network of container line services connects the port of Hong Kong with over 500 destinations world-wide. A new six-berth container terminal, Container Terminal 9, is nearing completion. The first two berths came into operation in July and October. When the terminal becomes fully operational by the end of 2004, Hong Kong's container terminals will have a total handling capacity of more than 17 million TEUs.

Necessary measures continued to be taken during the year to further strengthen the air transport infrastructure. The Government's Economic Development and Labour Bureau initialled two new Air Services Agreements (ASAs) in 2003. This brings the total number of signed and initialled ASAs to 60 and provides more opportunities for airlines to expand services. In March, the Logistics Centre at the Hong Kong International Airport commenced operation to provide various logistics and supply chain management services.

'Logistics Hong Kong' Initiative

The policy objective of the Government is to maintain and strengthen the role of Hong Kong as the preferred international transportation and logistics hub in Asia. The Government provides a conducive environment and necessary infrastructure to facilitate the development of the logistics sector. It also maximises the scope for cooperation and coordination with the Pearl River Delta (PRD) region in developing intermodal transportation links to achieve synergistic benefits.

The Steering Committee on Logistics Development (LOGSCOM), chaired by the Financial Secretary, provides policy directives and accelerates measures to foster logistics development. The Hong Kong Logistics Development Council (LOGSCOUNCIL), chaired by the Secretary for Economic Development and Labour, underpins LOGSCOM in fostering logistics development and carries out joint projects between the public and private sectors. It also provides a forum for government officials and industry players to discuss and coordinate matters concerning 'Logistics Hong Kong'. Five Project Groups are set up under LOGSCOUNCIL to develop and implement work programmes in specific areas, including physical infrastructure, information connectivity, human resource development, support for small and medium sized enterprises, as well as marketing and promotion.

During the year, LOGSCOUNCIL focused on the development of a Digital Trade and Transportation Network System, an open and neutral e-platform for the exchange of information and data among participants in the supply chain; and the development of a Value Added Logistics Park to provide a designated facility for handling high value, time-critical merchandise. The Government also conducted a joint study with the National Development and Reform Commission to explore the room for cooperation between Hong Kong and the Mainland (especially in the PRD) in logistics development.

LOGSCOUNCIL worked closely with the logistics sector to upgrade the quality of human resources by encouraging training institutes to organise tailor-made courses for logistics practitioners. It also organised roadshows to promote Hong Kong's logistics industry to the public, in particular the younger generation.

Civil Aviation

Hong Kong is a major international and regional aviation centre. The Hong Kong International Airport (HKIA) is one of the busiest airports in the world. At the end of 2003, 71 scheduled airlines were serving Hong Kong. These airlines together operated about 4 155 scheduled flights weekly between Hong Kong and some 130 cities world-wide. In addition, an average of about 79 non-scheduled flights was operated to and from the HKIA each week.

Air Traffic in 2003

The outbreak of SARS in Hong Kong in March and the subsequent issue of travel advisory notices against non-essential travel to affected areas, including Hong Kong, by the World Health Organisation (WHO) had a significant deterrent effect on air travel. Although passenger traffic and flight frequency had fully recovered to pre-SARS levels by year-end, the total of 27.43 million passengers (including 0.68 million in transit) that passed through the airport in 2003 represented a sharp decrease of 20.1 per cent from 2002. Aircraft movements also fell markedly by 9.43 per cent to a total of 187 508.

Despite the drop in passenger throughput and aircraft movements, the year saw continued growth in air cargo throughput at the HKIA. The airport handled a record-breaking 2.64 million tonnes of air cargo, representing a growth of 6.6 per cent from 2002. The corresponding value also increased by 18.1 per cent to $1,074.47 billion. The growth in air cargo was mainly attributed to a surge in exports to Europe and to other Asian cities.

Air transport continues to play an important role in Hong Kong's external trade. Goods carried by air accounted for about 34.5 per cent, 27.7 per cent and 25.8 per cent, in value terms, of Hong Kong's total imports, exports and re-exports respectively in 2003.

Airport Operations and Development

At the peak of the SARS outbreak, passenger throughput at the HKIA fell by as much as 80 per cent, although air cargo volume continued to grow satisfactorily. The swift implementation of effective SARS preventive measures at the HKIA, including the implementation of body temperature checks for all passengers and staff entering the airport restricted area, helped rebuild confidence in air travel. The incentive and revitalisation packages introduced by the Airport Authority (AA) in April and May also helped alleviate the difficulties faced by the aviation industry and facilitate a quick recovery in air traffic. By December, the passenger throughput at the HKIA had rebounded to the pre-SARS level.

Despite the temporary setback, the HKIA continued to win accolades for Hong Kong. The HKIA was voted 'Airport of the Year' in 2003 for the third time in a row by Skytrax Research of the United Kingdom. It was also named the 'Cargo Airport of the Year' for the second consecutive year by *Air Cargo News*.

With a view to expanding the catchment area of the HKIA, much progress has been made to further improve its transport connectivity with the Pearl River Delta (PRD) region. With the opening in 2003 of a new Airport-Mainland Coach Station as well as an airport ferry terminal named as SkyPier, the HKIA has been transformed into a fully multi-modal transportation hub integrating air, sea and land transport.

The new Airport-Mainland Coach Station, opened in February, has a waiting lounge for passengers and sheltered bays for 10 coaches. Some 100 buses daily transport passengers between the HKIA and 18 destinations in the PRD.

The HKIA's links to the PRD were further strengthened by the opening of the SkyPier in September, providing people in the delta region the opportunity of direct access to the airport for overseas travel. Under arrangements agreed by the relevant government authorities, PRD transit passengers arriving at the SkyPier by high-speed ferries are able to proceed by bonded buses directly to the passenger terminal for onward flights. Similar procedures apply for arriving air transit passengers en route home to the PRD. Like other transit passengers, these passengers have to stay within the airport's restricted area and are not subject to Customs and Immigration clearance. The arrangements reduce by up to half the usual four hours' transit time for PRD passengers to take connecting flights at the HKIA. At year-end, four PRD ports — Shenzhen, Shekou, Dongguan and Macau — were served by ferries operating from the SkyPier, and efforts were being made to extend the ferry service to more PRD ports.

To meet air passengers' requests for more retail and dining outlets, the East Hall of the Passenger Terminal Building was reconfigured during the year to accommodate a wider variety of retail shops and restaurants.

Construction of the Express Cargo Terminal at the HKIA began during the year. When completed in 2004, the terminal will be able to handle approximately 440 tonnes of express cargo a day. This dedicated facility will further enhance the airport's capability in handling express cargo.

In August, the Government, the AA and a private consortium signed a joint venture agreement for the construction of an international exhibition centre at the HKIA. Named the AsiaWorld-Expo, the easily accessible facility will be a major exhibition venue in Hong Kong, and will increase the flow of people through the HKIA. Phase 1 of the development, comprising 66 000 square metres of net usable area, will be completed for full operation by the first quarter of 2006.

To further enhance the competitiveness of the HKIA as well as expand its catchment area, the AA is fostering closer cooperation with other PRD airports through the PRD A5 Forum in areas such as emergency coordination, services promotion and joint studies to promote smooth passenger and cargo processing. Apart from the HKIA, airports in Guangzhou, Shenzhen, Zhuhai and Macau also participate in the Forum. Besides this, the AA engages in discussion with individual PRD airports on proposals for cooperation.

Privatisation of Airport Authority

In August, the Government announced its plan to commence work in preparation for the partial privatisation of the AA. A financial adviser was subsequently appointed to provide professional services and assistance. Privatisation will reinforce the airport's first-class operations, and bring about more commercial opportunities. It will enhance the AA's access to the capital market, and introduce an additional quality stock to add diversity to the local financial markets. In addition, it will offer an opportunity for Hong Kong people to participate in the success of a well-managed company with strong growth potential. Proceeds from privatisation will help strengthen the Government's finances in the short to medium term. The Government will devise a package of proposals including the future regulatory mechanism for the privatised AA, and will consult stakeholders on the proposals.

Air Services

In 2003, the Air Transport Licensing Authority (ATLA) granted six licences: one to Cathay Pacific Airways Limited (CPA), two to Hong Kong Dragon Airlines Limited (HDA), one to AHK Air Hong Kong Limited (AHK), and two to CR Airways Limited (CRK). At year-end, CPA held nine licences to operate scheduled services to 133 destinations, HDA held 10 licences to operate scheduled services to 106 destinations, AHK held eight licences to operate scheduled services to 57 destinations, CRK held two licences to operate scheduled services to five destinations, and Helicopters Hong Kong Limited (HHK) held two licences to operate scheduled services to two destinations.

CPA commenced some major codeshare services with American Airlines to operate passenger services to 20 cities in the United States in January. The codeshare services were further extended to five more US cities later in the year. However, the outbreak of SARS in March triggered a world-wide reduction in demand for passenger air travel. CPA cut its scheduled passenger flights by almost 50 per cent. After the travel advisory notice concerning Hong Kong was lifted by the WHO in May, the market quickly recovered and CPA's scheduled passenger air services were restored to the pre-SARS level by September. CPA commenced scheduled all-cargo services to Osaka and passenger services to Beijing in September and December, respectively. The frequency of scheduled passenger air services to Auckland, Johannesburg, London, Melbourne, Rome and Sapporo was also increased from October. There had been a sustained growth in cargo carriage, which was not affected by the SARS outbreak. In October, CPA carried a record monthly tonnage of air cargo. In July, CPA took delivery of its third long-range Airbus A340-600 aircraft. The airline also took delivery of three Airbus A330-300 and two Boeing B777-300 aircraft in the last quarter of the year. By year-end, CPA operated scheduled services to 49 destinations world-wide.

HDA's services were also severely affected by the outbreak of SARS. Up to 64 per cent of its scheduled flights were cancelled before the lifting of the WHO's travel advisory notice. From July, visitors from designated cities in the Mainland were able to travel to Hong Kong under the Individual Visit Scheme. This had a stimulating effect on the demand for HDA's services between Hong Kong and the Mainland, which returned to pre-SARS levels in August. The airline also launched new scheduled passenger services to Bangkok in November and resumed its passenger air services to Harbin in December. Its air cargo shipment continued to grow robustly during the year. The airline took delivery of two Airbus A321-200 aircraft in September and October. At year-end, HDA operated scheduled services to a total of 30 destinations, including 19 cities in the Mainland.

In June, the Civil Aviation Department (CAD) issued a varied Air Operator's Certificate (AOC) to CRK for the operation of its first Bombardier CRJ-200 regional jet. CRK thus became the third Hong Kong-based carrier that can operate scheduled air services to the Mainland using fixed-wing aircraft.

AHK focused on developing its network in Asia. The airline continued to operate scheduled all-cargo services to Osaka, Seoul and Tokyo. It expanded its services to Bangkok and Singapore in March and October, respectively. In March, DHL Worldwide Express increased its stake in AHK by 10 per cent, bringing it to a total of 40 per cent. CPA held the remaining 60 per cent.

At the end of 2003, the fleets of CPA, HDA, AHK and CRK were as follows:

Airline	Aircraft Type	Number in Service
CPA	Airbus A330-300	23
	Airbus A340-300	15
	Airbus A340-600	3
	Boeing B747-200 freighter	6
	Boeing B747-400	19
	Boeing B747-400 freighter	5
	Boeing B777-200	5
	Boeing B777-300	9
	Total	**85**
HDA	Airbus A320-200	8
	Airbus A321-200	6
	Airbus A330-300	9
	Boeing B747-300 freighter	3
	Total	**26**
AHK	Boeing B747-200 freighter	1
	Total	**1**
CRK	Bombardier CRJ-200	1
	Sikorsky S76C+	1
	Total	**2**

During the year, one new AOC was granted. Visions Balloons Limited was issued an AOC in March to operate a hot air balloon within the territorial boundaries of Hong Kong. It was the first AOC issued to a balloon operator by the CAD.

As regards non-Hong Kong airlines, three airlines commenced scheduled passenger services to Hong Kong in 2003: Mekong Airlines and President Airlines, respectively, between Phnom Penh and Hong Kong in March; and Kenya Airways between Nairobi and Hong Kong in September. In October, Transaero Airlines resumed its services between Moscow and Hong Kong, which had been suspended since April 1998. Also, Myanmar Airways International resumed its services between Yangon and Hong Kong in December after suspension of the services in January 2002. In addition, Saudi Arabian Airlines commenced scheduled all-cargo services between Jeddah, Riyadh and Hong Kong in January.

In the midst of the SARS outbreak, a number of airlines suspended their services to Hong Kong. However, most of them resumed services in the third quarter. Two airlines suspended their scheduled passenger services to Hong Kong, namely Mekong Airlines between Phnom Penh and Hong Kong in May and Air Philippines between Laoag and Hong Kong in October. Three other airlines suspended their all-cargo services: Mandala Airlines between Batam (Indonesia) and Hong Kong in March; Transmile Air between Kuala Lumpur, Penang and Hong Kong in August; and Pacific East Asia Cargo Airlines between Clark (Philippines) and Hong Kong in September.

A number of airlines operating in Hong Kong underwent reorganisation during the year. Air China took over the operations of China Southwest Airlines in January; China Southern Airlines took over China Northern Airlines whereas China Eastern Airlines took over both China Northwest Airlines and Yunnan Airlines in March. A new all-cargo carrier, Lufthansa Cargo AG, took over the all-cargo services of Lufthansa German Airlines in October.

As regards domestic helicopter services, the Government made available a temporary site at the southern tip of the West Kowloon Reclamation Area to facilitate the continuous development of commercial domestic helicopter services after the closure of the Central Heliport. The new West Kowloon Heliport was officially commissioned on December 7. The development and management rights for the facility were awarded to HHK through an open tender exercise conducted earlier in the year.

Air Traffic Control

The overall air traffic control (ATC) system continued to perform in a stable and reliable manner during the year. To handle effectively the projected growth in air traffic movements in Hong Kong and the Pearl River Delta area, it is necessary to further enhance the operational efficiency and increase the data processing capacities of the ATC system. In this regard, the CAD had implemented an enhancement programme on six major ATC equipment systems, namely Radar Data Processing and Display System, Flight Data Processing System, Radar Simulator, Speech Processing Equipment, Automatic Message Switching System and Aeronautical Information Database System. The programme was satisfactorily completed in March, as scheduled.

With regard to the replacement of the long-range primary Route Surveillance Radar at Mount Parker, the CAD started equipment installation in September and system acceptance tests in November. With satisfactory commissioning flight check results, the new radar underwent operational evaluation and further system optimisation began in December.

The CAD liaised with the General Administration of Civil Aviation of China (CAAC) on the relay of the secondary surveillance radar (SSR) data from Xisha to Hong Kong, and installation of Very High Frequency (VHF) communications facilities at Xisha for use by the department. The plan is to have these facilities available for testing in Hong Kong in mid-2004. With such provision, the ATC operational efficiency in the Hong Kong Flight Information Region will be greatly enhanced.

To ensure the provision of efficient ATC services in the Pearl River Delta area, the CAD continued to maintain close liaison with the civil aviation authorities of the Mainland and Macau. In 2003, a series of tripartite meetings on ATC operations was held and the flight procedures of airports in Hong Kong, Shenzhen, Zhuhai and Macau were refined for more effective use of airspace in the region.

Under the auspices of the International Civil Aviation Organisation (ICAO), the Reduced Vertical Separation Minimum programme has been adopted and successfully put into operation. As a result, aircraft operating in this region enjoyed better fuel economy, reduced ground delay as well as improvements in operational efficiency. Review meetings organised by the ICAO were also held regularly to ensure safe operations of the programme and to further streamline the operations.

Following the establishment of a Safety and Quality Section in the CAD, the department's Air Traffic Management Division continued to implement and adapt existing practice in accordance with the principles of Safety Management System on air traffic management and air traffic service operations. In December, a Safety Regulatory Audit on Control Aerodrome Competency Assurance was conducted with satisfactory results. Further efforts will be made to use the Safety Management System as a tool for enhancing safety and quality.

The CAD hosted an international Search and Rescue Seminar on November 24 and 25. The seminar provided a forum for experts of the Asia-Pacific region to discuss search and rescue matters, enhance coordination and cooperation between states, and update states on the latest developments in the field. Participants in the seminar were also invited to observe the annual search and rescue exercise conducted from November 26 to 29.

Satellite-based Communications, Navigation and Surveillance/Air Traffic Management (CNS/ATM) Systems

To comply with the Global and Regional Implementation Plans of the ICAO for Satellite-based CNS/ATM Systems, studies on the latest CNS/ATM developments and detailed investigations on various elements of the CNS/ATM Systems continued. Satisfactory progress and results were achieved in 2003 in various technical and operational trials including those on the Aeronautical Telecommunication Network, Air Traffic Services Message Handling System, VHF Digital Link, Air Traffic Services Inter-facility Data Communication, and Automatic Dependent Surveillance/Controller-Pilot Data Link Communications for downlinking meteorological data.

Following satisfactory system trials, certain mature CNS/ATM System elements were put into operational use so as to reap the benefits of early CNS/ATM applications. These included Digital-Automatic Terminal Information Services (D-ATIS), Digital-Meteorological Information for Aircraft in Flight (D-VOLMET) and Pre-Departure Clearance delivery via datalinks. At year-end more than 43 per cent of the departure traffic at the HKIA was using Pre-Departure Clearance delivery via datalinks.

Aircraft Noise Management

In Hong Kong, impact caused by aircraft noise is assessed on the basis of the internationally accepted Noise Exposure Forecast (NEF) Contour. The determination of the contour takes into account factors including the decibel levels of aircraft noise, the tonal characteristics as well as the duration and frequency of overflying flights at different times of the day. Currently, the aircraft noise standard adopted in Hong Kong is the NEF 25 contour, which is more stringent than the standards adopted by some other airports.

The Government is mindful of the concern of some residents about aircraft noise. The CAD continued its effort in exploring and implementing all practicable aircraft noise mitigating measures. These included noise abatement take-off and landing procedures, prohibition of landing/take-off of relatively noisy aircraft (i.e. subsonic jet aircraft which do not comply with the noise standards specified in Volume I, Chapter 3 of Annex 16 to the Convention on International Civil Aviation) and, whenever possible, use of flight paths which cover fewer residential areas.

The expansion and upgrading works to enhance the monitoring capability of the existing computer-based aircraft noise and flight track monitoring system was completed in 2003. Another stage of works to improve its data processing ability was under way.

Aircraft Operations and Airworthiness

Aircraft Accident

On August 26, a Government Flying Service EC155B1 helicopter crashed while crossing Tung Chung Pass near the HKIA. The two crew members on board the helicopter died in the crash. An Inspector's Investigation is being conducted to determine the causes of the accident.

Maintenance Arrangement

Satisfactory progress was made on the Cooperation Arrangement on mutual acceptance of approval of aircraft maintenance organisations established among the CAD, the CAAC, and the Civil Aviation Authority of Macau during the year. The main objective of the Cooperation Arrangement is to ensure a common aircraft maintenance standard throughout the Mainland, Hong Kong, and Macau. The maintenance release certificates issued by organisations recognised under the Cooperation Arrangement will be accepted without further investigation by the other participating authorities. In September and October, the Maintenance Standardisation Team (MAST), composed of airworthiness officers from the three authorities, visited all authorities concerned and inspected some of the maintenance organisations recommended for mutual recognition. The visit reports were accepted by the MAST in December.

Aviation Security

The Aviation Security Ordinance and Regulation constitute the comprehensive local legislation for implementation of the conventions and agreements on aviation security promulgated by the ICAO. The Hong Kong Aviation Security Programme (HKASP), which was developed by the Government and in consultation with the airport operators, airlines and other concerned parties, stipulates the aviation security requirements for the various operators at the HKIA. The implementation of these requirements is closely monitored by the Government to ensure that they meet international standards.

In January, the CAD assisted the ICAO in holding the first Aviation Security Auditors Course for the Asia-Pacific region in Hong Kong. Two officers from the department completed the course and qualified as ICAO-certified aviation security auditors.

In August, the department assisted the Asia Pacific Economic Cooperation in hosting a 'Symposium on the Promotion of Effective 100% Hold Baggage Screening' in Hong Kong. More than 100 delegates from 13 member economies attended the symposium to share their knowledge and discuss the latest development in baggage screening technologies.

To further enhance cockpit door security, the department issued a Flight Operations Notice and an Airworthiness Notice in 2002 to reflect the mandatory cockpit door security requirements in accordance with the ICAO standards. The two concerned Hong Kong operators, namely CPA and HDA, complied with such requirements in 2003.

Home Pages

Environment, Transport and Works Bureau: http://www.etwb.gov.hk
(links to major public transport operators)
Economic Development and Labour Bureau: http://www.edlb.gov.hk
Transport Department: http://www.gov.hk/td
Marine Department: http://www.mardep.gov.hk
Civil Aviation Department: http://www.gov.hk/cad
Airport Authority Hong Kong: http://www.hkairport.com

CHAPTER 14

The Environment

Development that is environmentally responsible will provide a sound foundation upon which the people of Hong Kong can seek to sustain a better quality of life, now and in the future. The Government and stakeholders in the community are taking determined action on many fronts to consolidate and build upon the achievements of the environmental protection framework already well established. For its part, the Government will continue to implement effective programmes and adopt forward-looking policies across the broad spectrum of environmental protection: from improving air and water quality to nature conservation, waste reduction and recycling.

HONG KONG'S 1 103 square kilometres of land contain 6.8 million people and one of the world's largest trading economies. Steep mountains and strong planning controls have led to most of the population being housed in 215 square kilometres of urban development, while over 400 square kilometres have been designated as 'protected areas' including country parks, special areas and conservation zonings. The concentration of population and economic activities in such a small area leads to intense pressures on the environment. This is compounded by the effects, particularly on air quality, from development across the Pearl River Delta region.

In October 1999, the Chief Executive announced a major programme to improve the quality of Hong Kong's environment, covering air pollution control measures, improvement in water quality, reform of waste management, strengthening of conservation, greening of the urban environment and development of regional pollution control mechanisms with Guangdong Province. On July 1, 2002, a new policy bureau, the Environment, Transport and Works Bureau, was established and it will continue the momentum of this programme.

Administrative Framework

The Environment, Transport and Works Bureau has overall policy responsibility for the environment, among other matters. It receives professional support from several government departments and advice from the Advisory Council on the Environment, which comprises 15 members appointed by the Chief Executive including members from environmental non-governmental organisations (NGOs), business groups, academic institutions and professional institutions.

Fun on the beach at
Shek O, one of Hong
Kong's most popular
bathing beaches.
People made 10 million
visits to the beaches
in 2003.

The Mai Po Marshes,
an internationally recognised
wildlife conservation site, is a
haven where bird-watchers
can observe a wide range of
species including avocets
(bottom right), black-faced
spoonbills *(above)* and little
egrets *(top right)*.

Youngsters learning about environmental
matters at the Fanling Environmental
Resource Centre, the third such centre to be
opened in Hong Kong. *Right:* there are
about 230 species of butterflies in Hong Kong,
including the *common tiger* shown here.

The Environmental Protection Department (EPD) executes environmental policies and programmes, vets environmental planning and assessment findings, enforces and reviews environmental laws, plans and develops facilities for liquid and solid waste disposal and promotes environmental management, audit and reporting. The EPD also promotes environmental awareness in the community.

The Agriculture, Fisheries and Conservation Department (AFCD) is the main agency for nature and wildlife conservation. It manages country parks, special areas, marine parks and a marine reserve, which are designated by the Chief Executive in Council for nature conservation, recreation and education purposes. The department also identifies and protects ecologically important areas by other means, enforces the law to protect wildlife and plants, and examines ecological aspects of environmental impact assessment reports and planning studies. It promotes public awareness of nature conservation.

The Planning Department plans future land use and controls developments throughout Hong Kong. The Drainage Services Department, assisted by the Territory Development Department, designs, builds, operates and maintains sewerage and sewage treatment facilities. The Civil Engineering Department provides outlets for the re-use of inert construction and demolition material. The Electrical and Mechanical Services Department promotes energy efficiency and conservation. The Marine Department clears floating refuse and oil in the sea and enforces the law on oil pollution.

Government spending on the environment in 2003-04 was budgeted at $6.13 billion, or about 2.14 per cent of total public expenditure.

Environmental Challenges

Hong Kong's older urban areas present considerable environmental challenges. These areas, partly being redeveloped, consist of dense housing mixed with commerce and industry and an infrastructure that needs continuous upgrading so as to meet development needs and rising public expectations. Factors such as scarce habitable land, concentrated transport networks and immense housing demand mean noise from road and rail traffic remains a problem despite improvement and control measures. Construction noise is also a concern for residents living near development sites.

Unplanned discharges from livestock farming, industrial, commercial and domestic sources had once been a serious threat to the environment. These are now kept under control through enforcement and implementation of various environmental programmes since the late 1980s. The pollution load on major rivers has been significantly reduced, by about 90 per cent. However, owing to the low base flow rate of these rivers and the remaining pollution load, further improvement work is still necessary.

The Government's pollution control strategy aims not to compromise industry and commerce, but work in partnership with the private sector firms in ensuring environmental compliance so that all may benefit from a better environment. Direct economic benefits can often be gained from activities such as recycling and the adoption of environmentally friendly technology. These methods are better than pollution control techniques that have to apply after a waste material has become a potential pollutant.

The Government encourages industry and commerce to recognise the benefits of waste minimisation and pollution prevention and to work to achieve these goals by taking their own initiatives. Statutory control guidelines are also provided with well-defined standards to ensure compliance.

Planning Against Pollution

The past decade has seen many achievements in Hong Kong's efforts to pre-empt environmental problems through the application of an environmental assessment process to policy, planning and project proposals. Development and policy proposals submitted to the Executive Council that involve environmental issues and all submissions to the Public Works Subcommittee of the Legislative Council's Finance Committee must contain an assessment of the environmental implications.

Environmental Impact Assessment Ordinance

The Environmental Impact Assessment Ordinance (EIAO) came into effect on April 1, 1998. It provides a systematic, clear and transparent framework for assessing the environmental impacts arising from major development projects and, where avoidance of the impacts is not practicable, for identifying effective measures to mitigate the impacts to an acceptable level. It is supplemented by a technical memorandum setting out clear and consistent technical guidelines and criteria. Information on applications made under the ordinance is available at the EPD's home page. Since the implementation of the ordinance, 75 EIA reports have been approved (as at December 31) and over one million people and many ecologically sensitive areas are protected against unacceptable environmental impacts.

The EIAO Support Section was established in July 2002 to provide support service to government project proponents on the implementation of the EIAO. The section implements an EIA training and capacity building programme for relevant government departments to enhance their understanding of the EIA mechanism.

Environmental Monitoring and Audit

Environmental monitoring and audit (EM&A) is an integral part of the EIA process to validate the assumptions made in the planning stage and to monitor the effectiveness of prescribed mitigation measures during project implementation. This is to ensure that every project delivers the environmental performance promised in the impact assessments. In 2003, the EPD managed about 154 EM&A programmes for major projects.

Starting from 1999, the EPD has been promoting EM&A reporting through the Internet — the Cyber EIA Process under the EIAO. For major projects, permit holders are required to set up dedicated websites to publish their project information including EM&A data and results in a user-friendly format. Since April 2002, major projects have been required to set up web camera systems to make live images of the site conditions accessible by the public through the dedicated website. The web-based reporting provides easier access to information on environmental performance and enhances public participation in the monitoring of the EIA process.

Land Use Planning

Environment concerns are incorporated into land use planning through the application of the environmental planning standards and guidelines. The Advisory

Council on the Environment considered the results of a strategic environmental assessment of the Territorial Development Strategy Review in 1996. In 1997, the Planning Department began further studies on some new development areas that the review identified. Environmental Impact Assessments form the integral part of these studies and have identified major environmental issues and possible mitigation measures for integration into the land use plans.

Environmental Sustainability

The assessment of the Territorial Development Strategy showed that continuing urbanisation would likely have implications on air and water quality, increase public exposure to noise and overload Hong Kong's waste disposal capacity. While the timely provision of resources and environmental mitigation measures could resolve some of these issues, others may require fundamental reconsideration of the proposals' implications on Hong Kong's long-term sustainability. The issue of environmental sustainability is being revisited in the new round of review of the Territorial Development Strategy (known as the Hong Kong 2030: Planning Vision and Strategy) which began in September 2000.

Environmental Management

The Government has been promoting environmental management in both the public and private sectors since 1992. A number of initiatives have been introduced, including the Green Manager Scheme, the adoption of environmental auditing, the environmental management systems (EMS) and environmental performance reporting. The Government leads by example: all bureaux and departments have appointed their Green Managers; most of them have regular environmental audit programmes; and some have been certified to ISO14001 standard. Since 2000, all bureaux and departments have been required to publish annual environmental performance reports on their operations, programmes and policy areas. To further improve the quality of their reports, a seminar workshop was launched together with the dissemination of a Benchmark guidebook in January 2003. Useful environmental management information is also available at the EPD's home page.

Cross-boundary Liaison on EIA and Environmental Planning

Environmental pollution transcends administrative boundaries. Hong Kong and Guangdong have worked together on environmental matters for nearly 20 years. In order to enhance the collaboration, a Joint Working Group on Sustainable Development and Environmental Protection was set up in 2000. Various special panels were formed under the Joint Working Group to examine specific environmental issues in which cooperation could be enhanced.

In combating regional air pollution, the HKSAR Government and the Guangdong Provincial Government are working together and have drawn up a regional air quality management plan that aims to reduce the regional pollutant emissions by 20 per cent to 55 per cent by 2010, taking 1997 as the base year. On the water quality front, Hong Kong and Shenzhen are undertaking a 15-year joint implementation programme to gradually reduce the pollution loads in Deep Bay with the objective of returning the water body to a clean and healthy state by 2015. In 2003, a regional strategy to protect the water environment of Mirs Bay was jointly developed by the two sides. In addition, Hong Kong and Guangdong are now working on a joint project to construct a numerical water quality model to provide an analytical tool and the

287

scientific basis for the two Governments to formulate water quality management plans for the Pearl River Delta region. The two sides are also working in collaboration to improve the water quality of the Dongjiang (East River) and to protect Chinese white dolphins and fishery resources.

Rural Developments ·

The Government is committed to improving the quality of life in rural areas and to ending or removing land uses that degrade the rural environment. Village sewage disposal has also improved in the rural areas of the New Territories.

Potentially Hazardous Installations

The Government has completed risk assessments of all potentially hazardous installations (PHI), such as liquefied petroleum gas and oil terminals and chlorine stores at water treatment works. It has completed or is implementing all its plans for risk reduction and has substantially reduced the risk to the public. However, the risk management of these sites is an ongoing process due to changes in dangerous goods inventories and population development near the sites. In addition to coverage of PHI sites, risk assessment is required under the EIAO for designated projects which manufacture, store, use or transport dangerous goods.

Legislation and Pollution Control

Hong Kong has seven main laws to control pollution. These are the Waste Disposal Ordinance, the Water Pollution Control Ordinance, the Air Pollution Control Ordinance, the Noise Control Ordinance, the Ozone Layer Protection Ordinance, the Dumping at Sea Ordinance and the Environmental Impact Assessment Ordinance. Most of these laws have subsidiary regulations and other statutory provisions, such as technical memoranda, to give effect to the principal laws.

The Government has adopted a system of environmental quality objectives as a general principle in its pollution control laws. The objectives are set at levels that will meet environmental goals, such as the protection of public health or the preservation of a natural ecosystem. The system aims to achieve the required environmental benefits in the most cost-effective and economically sustainable manner. Limits imposed on polluting emissions are no more stringent or costly than is necessary to achieve the conservation goal, which also makes the maximum safe use of the environment's natural capacity to absorb and recycle wastes.

In 2003, EPD inspectors made more than 68 720 inspections to enforce control on air, noise, waste and water pollution. These included regular checks on environmental compliance and investigations of pollution complaints from the community. The enforcement work resulted in more than 577 prosecutions and $5.03 million in fines. To streamline enforcement operation from a customer-oriented perspective, the EPD has set up multi-skilled teams to deal with all types of pollution problems in any single site inspection.

Apart from law enforcement, the department has organised seminars and formed partnerships with various trades such as the construction industry, the catering industry, the vehicle repair trade and the property management sector to promote good environmental practices and compliance with pollution control regulations.

Air Pollution

Air quality in Hong Kong is typical of any large modern city. Diesel emissions and fine dust in the urban areas are the most pressing problems. As a result of various measures taken to reduce emissions from motor vehicles, the roadside air quality is improving. Compared with 1999, the total number of hours that the roadside Air Pollution Index exceeded 100 in 2003 declined by 35 per cent. The concentrations of respirable suspended particulates and nitrogen oxides, the two major air pollutants at the roadside, declined by 13 per cent and 23 per cent, respectively.

Hong Kong's objectives for air quality, developed in 1987, are comparable with standards adopted in developed countries at that time. Hong Kong is closely monitoring the latest overseas developments in air quality standards.

Many factories and commercial activities produce air-borne emissions. The EPD operates a range of controls under the Air Pollution Control Ordinance and its subsidiary regulations, including licensing of some large industrial facilities and specific controls on furnace and chimney installations, dark smoke emissions, fuel quality, open burning, dust emissions from construction works, emissions from petrol filling stations and perchloroethylene emissions from dry-cleaning facilities. A regulation was being prepared to reduce vapour emissions from vehicle refuelling. The Air Pollution Control Ordinance has banned the import and sale of the more dangerous types of asbestos, namely amosite and crocidolite, from May 1996. Moreover, anyone intending to remove asbestos must engage registered professionals, and submit asbestos investigation reports and plans to the department.

Air pollution arouses much public concern, especially when factories are near homes. In 2003, the department handled complaints of air pollution allegedly caused by factories and issued legal notices instructing offenders to abate air pollution.

Joining a global effort, Hong Kong has taken up its obligations under the Montreal Protocol on substances that deplete the ozone layer. Apart from prohibiting both local manufacture and import of substances such as chlorofluorocarbons (CFCs) and halons for local consumption under the Ozone Layer Protection Ordinance, the EPD also sets a quota to control the import of hydrochlorofluorocarbons.

Transport

Vehicle emissions are the major source of the air pollution and nuisances experienced at the roadside. The Government's policy is to apply the most stringent motor vehicle fuel and emission standards whenever they are practicable and available.

Hong Kong is moving ahead of the European Union in raising its statutory standards for motor vehicle fuel. On this front, in July 2000, Hong Kong became the first city in Asia to introduce ultra low sulphur diesel, which has a sulphur content of less than 0.005 per cent, for use in motor vehicles. From April 2002, it became the statutory standard for motor diesel. Hong Kong is a few years ahead of the European Union in this regard, as the European Union's plan is to adopt ultra-lead sulphur diesel as a standard in 2005.

As regards emission standards, Hong Kong follows the steps of the European Union and has adopted Euro III emission standards since January 2001 for all newly registered vehicles except newly registered diesel private cars which must meet emission standards more stringent than the Euro III standards. Cleaner fuels and

289

tighter emission standards introduced in the past few years have significantly reduced the pollution from motor vehicles.

To deal with the problem of in-use diesel vehicles, grants were provided to encourage owners of the 18 000 diesel taxis to replace their vehicles with ones that run on liquefied petroleum gas (LPG). This incentive programme was completed at the end of 2003. Nearly all of Hong Kong's taxis are now running on LPG. A similar scheme was launched in August 2002 to encourage the early replacement of diesel light buses with LPG or electric light buses. Nearly 80 per cent of the newly registered public light buses are fuelled by LPG. A programme to retrofit pre-Euro diesel light vehicles with particulate reduction devices was completed in October 2001, with about 24 000 vehicles retrofitted. A similar retrofit programme for pre-Euro diesel heavy vehicles began in December 2002. A new regulation to mandate the installation for pre-Euro diesel light vehicles of up to four tonnes was introduced on December 1, 2003.

Another motor vehicle emission control strategy is to tighten the control against smoky vehicles. A Smoky Vehicle Control Programme has been operating since 1988. All vehicles reported under the scheme must be smoke tested by an advanced test method using a chassis dynamometer at designated vehicle emission testing centres to confirm that the vehicle owners have rectified the smoke defects. Under this scheme, 14 553 tests were conducted in 2003.

Apart from having cleaner vehicles and cleaner fuels, it is essential to promote mass transit systems that are pollution-free at street level. The Government has adopted a policy that gives priority to rail over road, and encourages innovation wherever practical.

Indoor Air Quality

To promote good indoor air quality (IAQ) and public awareness of its importance, the Government is implementing an IAQ Management Programme. One of the core elements of the programme is a voluntary IAQ Certification Scheme for Offices and Public Places. The certification scheme is for buildings or premises used as offices and public places that are served by mechanical ventilation and air-conditioning systems. It aims to recognise good indoor air quality management practices and to provide incentives for owners of buildings/premises or property management companies to pursue the best level of indoor air quality. The scheme opened for applications in September.

Noise

Road Traffic Noise

Hong Kong, like many metropolitan cities in the world, experiences various noise problems, one of which is road traffic noise. Under the existing policy, when planning new roads, the project proponent must ensure that traffic noise will stay below the established noise limits. If it is envisaged that traffic noise generated will exceed the noise limits, the project proponent must adopt all practicable direct measures such as adjusting the road alignment, surfacing the roads with low noise material or erecting noise barriers to reduce the noise impact on the neighbourhood. Where direct measures are inadequate, the project proponent has to provide the affected noise sensitive receivers with indirect mitigation measures in the form of good quality windows and air-conditioning.

To address the noise impact of existing roads, the mitigation measures including retrofitting of noise barriers and resurfacing with low noise material would be implemented where practicable at existing excessively noisy roads. The Government has identified some 30 existing road sections as targets for the retrofitting of noise barriers. The extensive retrofit programme is being carried out in phases having regard to the resource availability. So far, 72 local roads have also been identified as possible targets for resurfacing with low noise material. The resurfacing programme is in progress and will benefit about 40 000 residential units upon completion. In addition, all high-speed (70km/hr or above) roads have been resurfaced with low noise material where technically feasible.

To ensure that individual vehicles do not produce excessive noise, the Government tightened legislation in 2002 requiring all newly registered vehicles to comply with the latest internationally recognised noise standards. The noise standard will continue to be tightened in step with international developments.

Railway Noise

Various noise reduction programmes have been implemented by railway operators since the early 1990s to address noise problems along existing railways. So far, noise mitigation projects have brought relief to some 110 000 residents affected by train noise. New railway projects are required to undergo Environmental Impact Assessments to ensure that the noise impact would be properly addressed.

Aircraft Noise

The problem of aircraft noise has been substantially overcome with the relocation of the airport to Chek Lap Kok, where the surrounding sea is the only area affected by severe aircraft noise and only about 100 village houses are within the moderately affected area. Although aircraft noise has been controlled within the planning standard for almost all of the residents under the new flight paths, there is concern about the aircraft noise impact on residents who were previously unaffected. The Government is mindful of the concern and will continue its effort in exploring and implementing all practicable aircraft noise mitigation measures, details of which are given in Chapter 13 *(Transport: section on Aircraft Noise Management)*.

Noise from Industrial or Commercial Activities

Noise from industrial or commercial activities is controlled by means of noise abatement notices. The EPD will serve abatement notice to require the owners of premises emitting excessive noise to reduce it within a given period. In 2003, the department handled about 3 500 complaints and served some 150 abatement notices, which led to some 20 prosecutions.

Construction Noise

Noise from general construction work between 7 pm and 7 am, and on public holidays, is controlled through construction noise permits. The permits restrict the use of equipment according to strict criteria and ban noisy manual activities in built-up areas. Percussive piling is prohibited at night and on public holidays and requires a permit during daytime on any day not being a public holiday. In 2003, some 2 800 permits for general construction work and percussive piling were issued. There were 90 prosecutions for working without permits or violating permit conditions.

In addition, the Government has also phased out the use of noisy diesel, steam and pneumatic piling hammers. The law also requires hand-held percussive breakers and air compressors for construction to meet strict noise standards and to have a 'green' noise emission label before use. In 2003, about 800 labels were issued.

To deter repeated violations of industrial/commercial and construction noise offences, the Noise Control Ordinance was amended in 2002 to include explicit provisions to hold the top management of a body corporate liable for repeated offences committed by it.

Intruder Alarm and Neighbourhood Noise

The Police Force handles complaints on intruder alarm and neighbourhood noise from domestic premises and public places. In 2003, the police dealt with some 3 600 complaints and 17 offenders were convicted.

Water and Sewerage

Water pollution has increased with urban development and population growth, and Hong Kong now produces more than two million tonnes of sewage every day. The lack of proper treatment for most of the sewage from the generally older urban areas around Victoria Harbour in the past had resulted in poor water quality there. But starting from 2002, following the full commissioning of the first stage of the Harbour Area Treatment Scheme (HATS) at the end of 2001, there has been a marked improvement.

In addition, pollution control at source is now having a positive effect, and river quality is slowly improving. The percentage of rivers in the 'good' and 'excellent' categories increased from 34 per cent in 1986 to 76 per cent in 2003, and the percentage in the 'bad' and 'very bad' categories fell from 45 per cent in 1986 to 15 per cent in 2003.

Sewage Treatment and Disposal

To treat wastewater from the main urban area, sewage collected by the local sewerage network on both sides of Victoria Harbour will be directed to the HATS system for treatment and disposal. The HATS, previously known as the Strategic Sewage Disposal Scheme, is a huge project that was originally divided into four stages.

The first stage, which collects sewage from the urban areas of Kowloon, Tsuen Wan, Kwai Tsing, Tseung Kwan O and the north-eastern part of Hong Kong Island for treatment at a sewage treatment plant at Stonecutters Island, was brought into full operation at the end of 2001. In addition to the treatment plant, which some experts considered as one of the most efficient of its kind in the world, the first stage comprises a number of preliminary treatment works at collection nodes, 23.6 kilometres of transfer tunnels up to 150 metres deep, and a tunnelled outfall which disperses the treated effluent into the western anchorage area away from core Victoria Harbour.

Since commissioning, the system has performed well. The Stonecutters Island Sewage Treatment Works, which employs a chemical treatment process, has been consistently removing about 70 per cent of the organic pollutants and 80 per cent of the solids from the sewage prior to discharge. Since the first stage actually treats about

75 per cent of the wastewater generated in the harbour catchment, it has thus reduced the total pollution load on the harbour waters by about 50 per cent. The sludge that once flowed into the harbour each day, amounting to about 600 tonnes, is now effectively being removed at the treatment works and sent to Hong Kong's modern landfills for disposal. This has brought about marked improvements in water quality in the harbour. At the eastern end of Victoria Harbour, the levels of sewage bacteria have declined up to 95 per cent, significantly reducing public health risks. Throughout the core harbour area dissolved oxygen has increased by 10 to 20 per cent and ammonia has declined by 20 to 50 per cent, helping to restore water quality to a more natural and ecologically healthier condition.

The original proposal for the subsequent stages of the scheme envisaged collection of the remainder of the untreated sewage around the harbour (from northern and western parts of Hong Kong Island) using a similar system of deep tunnels, centralised treatment at the works at Stonecutters Island, and eventual discharge of the treated effluent, after disinfection, through a long tunnelled outfall into the deep, oceanic waters to the south of Hong Kong.

This concept was reviewed in 2000 by a panel of international experts. In their report to the Government, the experts confirmed the use of deep tunnels and centralised treatment as an acceptable and cost-effective way of dealing with sewage. However, in the light of recent developments in sewage treatment technology, they recommended that, rather than pursuing the long outfall, the Government should consider upgrading the treatment level to a very high standard, and discharging the treated effluent into the harbour on a long-term basis.

The proposal to adopt a different procedure for the treatment of sewage raised a number of issues that require further study. The most important of these was whether compact sewage treatment technology developed and applied in temperate climates can treat wastewater effectively under Hong Kong conditions, and whether it was an environmentally sustainable proposition for the relatively congested Victoria Harbour to receive large volumes of effluent, although highly treated, on a long-term basis. In late 2001, the Government initiated a series of trials and studies to address these issues. The work is substantially complete and the results will be reported around the second quarter of 2004, at which time the community will have an opportunity to discuss the findings and express views on the general preference for a way forward. More details are available at the 'A Clean Harbour for Hong Kong' website, *http://www.cleanharbour.gov.hk*.

Sewerage Master Plans

Hong Kong has been divided into 16 areas for which sewerage master plans (SMPs) have been drawn up. The improvement works recommended under these SMPs are being carried out in a phased sewage programme so as to cater for the present and future development needs of Hong Kong. The first sewage construction works were completed in 1997 under the Chai Wan and Shau Kei Wan SMP, while the other recommended works under various SMPs are being implemented progressively.

In light of the revised population forecasts and development proposals, the sewerage master plans for Yuen Long, Kam Tin, Central and East Kowloon, Tuen Mun, Tsing Yi, the Outlying Islands, Hong Kong Island, North District and Tolo Harbour areas have been reviewed and proposals for further upgrading works are being made.

293

Sewer connections to individual properties are still in progress. Improvements in several parts of Hong Kong Island, Kowloon and the New Territories continue. Under the Water Pollution Control (Sewerage) Regulation, the EPD requires house owners to connect their wastewater pipes to new public sewers. In 2003, wastewater from premises housing 5 000 people was directed to public sewers so as to avoid water pollution. Since the regulation came into force at the end of 1995, wastewater from premises housing 56 000 people has been connected to public sewers.

Sewage Charges

All water users who discharge their sewage to public sewers pay a basic sewage charge. In addition, 30 trades and industries whose effluent strength well exceeds that of domestic sewage also pay a trade effluent surcharge to reflect the additional cost for treating their stronger effluent. These charges aim at recovering partially the operation and maintenance costs of sewage collection, treatment, and disposal facilities. The Government continues to provide funds for capital costs for these facilities from its Capital Works Reserve Fund. The household sewage charge in 2003 was a modest $1.20 per cubic metre of water consumed, with an exemption for the first 12 cubic metres consumed in a four-month billing period. As a one-off concession in the 2002-03 financial year, the sewage charge payable by each registered customer during the financial year was reduced by an amount not exceeding $200 and $800 for domestic and non-domestic purposes respectively, whereas the trade effluent surcharge payable was reduced by a flat rate of 30 per cent.

In addition, owing to the SARS outbreak, the Government decided that the levels of the sewage charge and the trade effluent surcharge should be reduced consecutively for a four-month billing period starting from August 2003, as part of the package of relief measures to help the community tide over the difficulties caused by the disease. The sewage charge payable by each registered customer in the billing period covering the four months from August to November 2003 has been reduced by an amount not exceeding $67 and $533 for domestic and non-domestic accounts, respectively. The trade effluent surcharge payable during the four-month billing period has been reduced by a flat rate of 60 per cent.

Livestock Waste Pollution

Indiscriminate disposal of waste from the livestock industry was formerly one of the main causes of pollution in streams and rivers in the New Territories. Before the livestock waste control scheme began in 1987, the pollution load from livestock waste — equivalent to raw sewage from more than 1.6 million people — ended up in Hong Kong's rivers and eventually the sea. Since 1988, the Waste Disposal Ordinance has banned livestock-keeping in new towns and environmentally sensitive areas. Where they are allowed, livestock farms must have proper waste treatment systems.

Under the control scheme, livestock farmers who chose to continue in business applied for a grant and a loan to help pay for pollution-control facilities. Since the start of the scheme in 1987, about $63 million has been paid out in capital grants. Farmers who chose to cease business applied for an allowance, and about $883 million has been paid. Livestock waste pollution has been reduced by 97 per cent since the inception of the control scheme.

The Government has been providing a free livestock waste collection service since 1996. A monthly average of about 5 178 tonnes of livestock waste was collected in 2003.

Bathing Beaches

Bathing beaches are an important recreational resource. To protect the health of swimmers, the Government has adopted strict standards for water quality control at bathing beaches. These standards relate to pollution measured as *E.coli* (the bacteria that can indicate the presence of sewage) and were devised after a thorough study of the health risk facing local bathers. The following table shows how beaches were classified in 2002 and 2003. Beaches in the 'good' and 'fair' categories meet the Government's water quality objective for bathing.

Beach water quality ranking	Bathing season geometric means of *E.coli* count per 100ml of beach water	Minor health risk cases per 1 000 swimmers	Number of beaches	
			2002	2003
Good	Up to 24	Undetectable	23	23
Fair	25 to 180	10 or less	10	11
Poor	181 to 610	11 or 15	2	1
Very Poor	More than 610	More than 15	6	6

Since 1998, beach water quality gradings for open beaches have been made available weekly through the mass media and the EPD's home page.

Waste Management

Waste Reduction

In November 1998, the Government launched a 10-year Waste Reduction Framework Plan. This was a response to the rapid growth in the amount of waste being dumped in the landfills, leading to a significant reduction in their expected lifespan. Given the shortage of land in Hong Kong and the keen competition for any available space, it will be difficult to find sites for any new landfills. The plan aims to reduce the amount of waste produced, to encourage re-use and recycling, to promote greater efficiency and economy in the management of waste, and to prolong the usable life of Hong Kong's landfills.

Waste recovery continues to play an important role in waste management, resulting in the export of substantial quantities of recovered waste materials for re-manufacturing outside Hong Kong. In all, more than 2.1 million tonnes of waste materials — including waste paper, metals and plastic — were exported in 2003, generating export earnings of about $2.5 billion.

Waste prevention and recovery has been the Government's main focus in tackling the waste problem. The Government introduced a package of initiatives in 2001 to further promote waste prevention and recycling and has been making progress in this regard.

Charging for waste disposal is an important element in the waste management strategy adopted in Hong Kong. It can provide economic incentives for waste producers to reduce waste and to carry out sorting to facilitate re-use and recycling which will, in turn, help conserve landfill capacity. As a first step, the Government intends to levy charges for the disposal of construction waste at landfills, sorting facilities and public fill reception facilities. In December, it introduced the Waste Disposal (Amendment) (No.2) Bill into the Legislative Council to give effect to the scheme for charging for construction waste disposal. Subject to the passage of the bill and related regulations, the Government intends to implement the charging scheme in late 2004.

Landfills

All municipal solid waste is disposed of at three large modern landfills in the New Territories. Specialist waste management contractors operate these landfills to high environmental standards.

The community disposed of about 9 440 tonnes of municipal solid wastes every day in 2003. Of this, 7 400 tonnes comprised domestic waste and 2 040 tonnes comprised commercial and industrial waste. On average, each person in Hong Kong disposed of about 1.38 kilograms of municipal solid waste daily.

Rapid development in Hong Kong over the past decade has contributed to a dramatic increase in the amount of construction and demolition (C&D) material. The material generated every day amounted to some 52 000 tonnes, on average, and about 87 per cent of it was suitable for re-use in reclamation projects.

The current three landfills have a remaining lifespan of only eight to 12 years. In 2003, the Government completed a study to explore the feasibility of extending the existing landfills and to identify potential new landfill sites. Extension schemes for the existing landfills have been proposed. Planning and development work will soon proceed to ensure the continuity of waste disposal outlets.

Hong Kong has 13 old landfills. For safety and environmental reasons, restoration measures have been taken at these landfills, and restoration of 12 of them has been completed. It is intended to restore the last landfill, at Pillar Point Valley, by late 2005. After full restoration, the sites may be used primarily for community and recreational activities.

Refuse Transfer Stations

The network of refuse transfer stations forms an important component of the Government's waste disposal facilities. Waste collected in urban centres is delivered to these stations, where it is compacted into sealed containers for delivery to the three landfills.

Seven modern transfer stations and one set of Outlying Island Transfer Facilities (OITF) handle a total of 5 720 tonnes of waste every day. This is mostly domestic waste, and represents around 74 per cent of Hong Kong's total daily domestic waste production. Six of these transfer facilities — the stations at Hong Kong Island East, Hong Kong Island West, West Kowloon, North Lantau and North-West New Territories and the OITF on Ma Wan — also provide service to private waste collectors.

Chemical and Special Wastes

Comprehensive controls on the handling and disposal of chemical waste have been in place since 1993. The former widespread malpractice of dumping chemical waste into sewers and surface waters has stopped. All chemical waste producers are required to properly pack, label and store their chemical wastes before disposal at proper treatment facilities. A trip ticket system — involving the waste producers, licensed collectors and licensed disposal points — tracks the movement of chemical waste from its origin to the final disposal point.

In 2003, a daily average of 117 tonnes of chemical waste, including waste from sea-going vessels, was treated at the Chemical Waste Treatment Centre on Tsing Yi Island, the main treatment facility for chemical waste. A government contractor operates the treatment centre. Waste producers using its services are required to pay part of the treatment cost.

Clinical Waste

In recognition of the public health risks associated with the improper handling of clinical waste generated by health-care activities, the Government plans to implement legal controls on the handling, collection and disposal of this type of waste. The Government also proposes to modify the Chemical Waste Treatment Centre so that it can receive clinical waste for proper treatment, replacing the current practice of disposing of untreated clinical waste at landfills. The health-care sectors and other related parties have been consulted and they generally supported the proposal. The Waste Disposal (Amendment) Bill 2003, providing for the control of clinical waste, was introduced into the Legislative Council in June. Subject to the passage of the bill and related subsidiary legislation, the Government intends to implement the controls in 2005.

Large-scale Waste Treatment Facilities

No matter how effective it is in dealing with waste prevention and recycling, Hong Kong still has to deal with a large volume of non-recyclable waste. New facilities to treat waste and reduce its volume will have to be put in place. Such facilities would need to meet the highest international environmental standards and be cost-effective. In April 2002, the Government invited the local and international waste management industries to express their interest in proposing latest technologies for the development of large-scale waste treatment facilities in Hong Kong. An Advisory Group, comprising mainly non-officials, is now considering various waste management technologies and options that are potentially suitable to Hong Kong. However, even with such large-scale waste treatment facilities, there are residual wastes that must be handled safely. Hence, Hong Kong will continue to require landfills for final disposal of waste.

Import and Export of Waste

Controls on the import and export of waste under the Waste Disposal Ordinance (WDO) came into operation on September 1, 1996. A ban on the importation of hazardous waste from developed countries (mainly of the Organisation for Economic Cooperation and Development and the European Union) was introduced on December 28, 1998. The controls are in line with the Basel Convention on the Control of Transboundary Movements of Hazardous Wastes and their Disposal.

The convention's main control mechanism requires notification and consent by authorities of the states of origin, destination and transit before the shipment of hazardous or non-recyclable waste can begin. The import or export of hazardous waste into or out of Hong Kong without a permit, regardless of the purpose of the import or export, is an offence under the WDO. Maximum penalties include a fine of $200,000 and six months' imprisonment for the first offence, and a fine of $500,000 and two years' imprisonment for subsequent offences. In 2003, there were six prosecutions for illegal import or export of waste, with fines totalling $130,000.

In January 2000, a memorandum of understanding with the State Environmental Protection Agency was signed on the control of hazardous waste shipments between the Mainland and the HKSAR.

Floating Refuse in the Harbour

The Marine Department deploys a fleet of seven government vessels and 68 contractors' vessels to collect floating refuse. In 2003, 13 926 tonnes of floating refuse were collected. The Government has also tackled the floating refuse problem by raising public awareness through publicity and educational activities, and deterring marine littering by means of enforcement action.

Marine Dumping

Hong Kong's development projects continue to generate vast quantities of dredged mud that is unsuitable for reclamation or other uses (38.3 million cubic metres in 2003). It is dumped at sea in specified mud disposal areas under a permit system. Regular monitoring is undertaken by the Government to make sure that dumping operations would not create an unacceptable impact on the marine environment. Because of the serious potential impact illegal dumping has on the marine environment, the EPD maintains strict control over dumping operations under the Dumping at Sea Ordinance. These operations follow the requirements of the London Convention on marine dumping.

Marine dumping permits only allow operations to be carried out by a vessel equipped with an automatic self-monitoring device. This device tracks all marine dumping operations by recording the position and draught of the vessel, so that the authorities can trace any illegal dumping in a cost-effective manner. Moreover, the department's inspectors operate frequent patrols. There were seven convictions for illegal dumping offences in 2003.

Monitoring and Investigation

The assessment of progress towards achieving policy goals is one of the EPD's key activities. Its routine monitoring and special investigations form the basis for much of the strategic planning, provision of facilities and statutory controls aimed at improving the environment. The department has 94 sampling stations in the marine waters, including enclosed bays and typhoon shelters, and another 82 stations for inland waters. It also keeps 41 bathing beaches under surveillance.

The current water quality monitoring programme was started in 1986. It provides a comprehensive record of the chemical, physical and microbiological quality of Hong Kong's waters. The monitoring data are depicted in the annual water quality reports which are available on the EPD's home page. Members of the public are usually more interested in the latest water quality of bathing beaches. Details of open beaches are issued to the mass media and updated in the department's home page every week.

Government Laboratory

The Government Laboratory supports the implementation of the various environmental programmes and the enforcement of environmental protection legislation through the provision of analytical and advisory services. It analyses environmental pollutants in a wide range of samples including air, water, sediment, biota and trade effluents. On-site support is also provided round-the-clock to assist in the handling of emergencies involving chemical spills or suspected emission of noxious or irritating gases.

In 2003, the Laboratory performed a total of 274 184 tests on environmental samples, exceeding the original estimate by around 4 per cent. The increase in workload reflects the active participation of the Laboratory in various ad hoc projects. A notable one involves the study of the volatile organic compounds emitted during the refuelling process in petrol filling stations. The data generated is essential, and has to be studied before new measures can be introduced for the long-term reduction of total volatile organic emissions in the vicinity of the stations. Another project was carried out in collaboration with the Hong Kong Polytechnic University to analyse the trace organic pollutants in particulates collected in road tunnels. Results obtained will help to provide a better understanding of the air quality in tunnels that have heavy traffic.

As a continuous commitment to the marine monitoring in the area, the Laboratory works closely with the EPD and the Mainland's State Oceanic Administration (SOA). In 2003, the Laboratory participated in the method validation exercise and the annual national inter-laboratory calibration work with satisfactory results. The technical meeting held in Dalian in March provided a firm basis for future participation in the National Marine Environment Monitoring Network.

Flora

Hong Kong is near the northern limit of the distribution of tropical South-East Asian flora, sharing similar species and structure with the flora of Guangdong Province. Despite its small size, Hong Kong has a rich flora with about 3 100 species of vascular plants. Various conservation measures have transformed the formerly bare hillsides and slopes into impressive woodlands. Besides greening and beautifying the countryside, woodlands are important habitats for wildlife and are essential for protecting water catchments from soil erosion. They also provide recreational opportunities for the public.

Remnants of the original forest cover, either scrub forest or well-developed woodlands, are still found in steep ravines. They have survived destructive human influences and hill fires through their location in precipitous topography and the moist winter micro-climate.

Terrestrial Fauna

Hong Kong's climate and physical environment provides a wide range of habitats and supports a rich and varied fauna. These include about 450 species of birds, 50 species of mammals, 80 species of reptiles, 23 species of amphibians, 230 species of butterflies and 110 species of dragonflies.

The Mai Po Marshes form one of the most important wildlife conservation sites in Hong Kong. Together with the Inner Deep Bay area, the Mai Po Marshes area was listed as a 'Wetland of International Importance' under the Ramsar Convention in September 1995. About 1 500 hectares of mudflats, fish ponds, marshes, reedbeds and dwarf mangroves provide a rich habitat for migratory and resident birds, particularly ducks and waders. Some 300 species of birds have been observed in this area, many of which are considered globally threatened and endangered, such as the black-faced spoonbill, Oriental stork, Nordmann's greenshank and Saunders' gull. The AFCD implements a wetland conservation and management plan to conserve the ecological value of the area.

The traditional *fung shui* woods near old villages and temples and the secondary forests provide important habitats for many woodland birds. Sightings in wooded areas include warblers, flycatchers, robins, bulbuls and tits.

Areas around the Kowloon reservoirs are inhabited by monkeys descended from individuals that had been released or had escaped from captivity. There are breeding groups of long-tailed macaques and rhesus macaques, and their hybrids. Feeding of monkeys has been prohibited since July 1999 to prevent unnatural growth of the monkey population. Other mammals like barking deer, leopard cats, Chinese porcupines, Chinese ferret badger, masked palm civets, small Indian civets, wild boar and bats are quite common in the countryside. Sightings of less common species such as Eurasian otters, Javan mongooses and Chinese pangolins are occasionally reported.

Hong Kong has over 100 species of amphibians and reptiles. There are 23 species of amphibians and three of them — Hong Kong cascade frog, Hong Kong newt and the endemic Romer's tree frog — are protected by the Wild Animals Protection Ordinance due to their endemic status or very restricted distribution in Hong Kong. Most of the 50 species of snakes are harmless and reports of people being bitten by highly venomous snakes are very rare in Hong Kong. Among the nine native species of chelonians, the green turtle is of particular interest as it is the only known species of sea turtle breeding locally. The AFCD has been satellite-tracking green turtles nesting in Hong Kong to better understand their migration biology. The results have shown that the two turtles under study migrated to feeding grounds in the coastal waters off Hainan Island.

Marine Fauna

Hong Kong is in the sub-tropical region, and its marine environment supports species of both tropical and temperate climates. Local waters contain a wide diversity of fishes, crustaceans, molluscs and other marine life, of which at least 150 species are of significance.

Set on the eastern bank of the Pearl River's estuary, Hong Kong receives freshwater discharged from the river, especially in its western waters. The eastern waters, on the other hand, are little influenced by the Pearl River outflow and have a predominantly oceanic characteristic. This special hydrographic condition helps to contribute to the diversity of marine life found in Hong Kong.

Despite being close to the northern limit for hard corals, Hong Kong supports some 80 stony coral species. This diversity of corals is considered quite rich by international standards. A variety of marine fishes also breed in Hong Kong waters. Typical of eastern waters is the red sea bream, one of the several sea bream varieties whose fry are abundant along the shore of Mirs Bay in early spring.

Top left and bottom: visitors from the Mainland surged in number to a remarkable eight million in 2003, with the Peak and the Peak Tram ride being popular attractions. *Above:* the Chief Executive joined The Walt Disney Company's Chief Executive Officer, Mr Michael Eisner (right), in a ground-breaking ceremony for Hong Kong Disneyland in January. *Lower left:* the 'CLP Lights Up Hong Kong' multimedia show during the Lunar New Year, and a 'Caribbean Street Carnival' in Lan Kwai Fong. *Previous page:* the 'Strato-Fantasia' multimedia show lighting up the harbour. *Overleaf:* Hong Kong's 'welcome' message taking to the air.

Despite the small extent of Hong Kong waters, two marine mammal species can be found locally throughout the year. The better-known one is the Indo-Pacific humpback dolphin, also known as the Chinese white dolphin. The other is the finless porpoise. The humpback dolphin prefers the estuarine environment and inhabits the western waters of Hong Kong while the finless porpoise lives in the eastern and southern areas, which are predominantly oceanic waters.

There has been concern over the degradation of the marine environment by pollution, coastal development works, over-fishing and destructive fishing practices. To counteract the disturbance to inshore marine resources, the AFCD has installed artificial reefs to enhance fisheries resources and the biodiversity of the marine environment. The Marine Parks programme continues to serve as an important scheme in protecting and conserving sites of special ecological and conservation value.

Legislation and Nature Conservation

The Director of Agriculture, Fisheries and Conservation, who is also the Country and Marine Parks Authority, is responsible for the conservation of the terrestrial and marine ecological resources, as well as for the enforcement of legislation on nature conservation issues.

The Forests and Countryside Ordinance provides for the general protection of vegetation, and gives special protection to certain rare plants, including native camellias, magnolias, orchids, azaleas and the Chinese New Year flower.

The Wild Animals Protection Ordinance prohibits the hunting of wild animals and the possession, sale or export of protected wild animals taken in Hong Kong. It also restricts entry by unauthorised persons to three designated important wildlife habitats: the Mai Po Marshes, the Yim Tso Ha Egretry and the green turtle nesting beach at Sham Wan.

The Country Parks Ordinance provides for the designation, control and management of the countryside as country parks and special areas for nature conservation, education, scientific research purposes while country parks can also be designated for compatible recreation and tourism uses.

The Marine Parks Ordinance provides for the designation, protection and management of the ecologically important marine environment as marine parks and marine reserves for nature conservation, education and scientific research purposes. Compatible recreational activities such as swimming and diving are allowed in marine parks.

Besides general conservation of the countryside, the Government has been identifying and conserving sites of special scientific interest, such as those that are natural habitats of rare plant or animals species through exercising strict development controls. In all, 64 sites have been listed.

The Fisheries Protection Ordinance provides for the regulation of fishing practices and the prevention of destructive fishing activities such as using explosive or toxic substances for the purpose of fishing.

Protected Areas

There are 23 country parks and 15 special areas (four of which are located outside country parks) with a total area of 41 582 hectares (about 38 per cent of the total land area of Hong Kong). They cover scenic hills, woodlands, reservoirs, islands, indented coastlines, marshes and uplands. All are carefully protected for the purposes of nature conservation, countryside education and compatible scientific studies. Management measures include protection of woodland and vegetation against fire, control of development, tree planting, litter collection, provision of educational and recreational facilities, education and promoting better understanding of the countryside.

There are four marine parks and one marine reserve covering a total area of 2 430 hectares. They cover scenic coastal areas, seascapes and important biological habitats. Similar to country parks, marine parks are managed for the purposes of conservation, education, recreation and scientific studies. Marine reserves are dedicated to conservation, education and scientific studies. Fishing in marine parks is controlled through a permit system which is confined to local villagers and bona fide fishermen while such activity is totally banned in marine reserves. Publicity and educational activities are organised for students and other members of the public.

Topography and Geology

Hong Kong's natural terrain is dominated by mountains and hills with steep slopes, many of which descend directly into the sea. The seabed is relatively flat. The highest point in Hong Kong is Tai Mo Shan in the New Territories at 957 metres above Principal Datum. The deepest point is 66 metres below Principal Datum in Lo Chau Mun (Beaufort Channel) north of Po Toi Island.

The mountains consist primarily of volcanic rocks, with some of the lower hills formed of granite. Low-lying areas tend to be formed of granite or sedimentary rocks. In places, hill-slope debris forms a mantle over the bedrock and alluvium fills some of the valleys. Much of the seabed is covered by marine mud with some scattered sand banks.

Hong Kong lies on the southern edge of an ancient land mass. The oldest exposed rocks are Devonian fluvial sediments that were deposited 400 million years ago. The region was subsequently inundated by a shallow sea. Sediments from this period are represented by the carboniferous marble of Yuen Long and Ma On Shan. The sandy and muddy sediments of the Permain rocks of Tolo Harbour are of alternate marine and continental deposits.

From the Jurassic to Cretaceous periods, between 170 and 140 million years ago, Hong Kong was the scene of violent volcanic activity. Thick accumulations of lava and ash were deposited. The eruptions were associated with the development of several giant craters (calderas). At deeper levels, the volcanic deposits were intruded by molten magma, which slowly crystallised to form granite.

Igneous activity had ceased by 60 million years ago. Rocks now seen on the island of Ping Chau represent sediments laid down in a lake on the edge of a desert.

During the Quaternary period, spanning the last two million years, major glaciations in polar regions affected global sea level, which fell to 120 metres below the present level, leaving the site of present-day Hong Kong as much as 130 kilometres from the coast. At that time, the flat areas between what are now the islands of Hong Kong were part of an extended Pearl River flood plain. In interglacial periods, such as at the present time, the global sea level rose to its present level and higher, and marine sediments were deposited.

Detailed information of the geology of Hong Kong can be found in a series of 15 geological maps at a scale of 1:20 000 and six accompanying memoirs. These were produced by the Hong Kong Geological Survey, a part of the Geotechnical Engineering Office. The Hong Kong Geological Survey has also recently published two new memoirs and a set of 1:100 000 geological and thematic maps that synthesise and summarise the current state of knowledge of the geology of Hong Kong.

Hydrography and Oceanography

Hong Kong's waters are characterised by the interaction of oceanic and estuarine water masses which vary in relative effect throughout the year. The variable freshwater discharge from the Pearl River has a marked influence on Hong Kong waters.

During the summer, an oceanic flow from the south-west to the north-east brings the warm, high-salinity water of the Hainan Current into Hong Kong waters. This interacts with fresh water from the Pearl River and divides Hong Kong into three distinct zones. In the west, where the fresh water influence is greatest, the environment is estuarine and the water is brackish. In the east, the water is mainly oceanic with relatively minor dilution from rainfall and runoff from streams. The limits of the central transitional zone vary depending upon the relative influence of Pearl River water and marine currents.

During the winter dry season, the Kuroshio oceanic current brings warm water of high salinity from the Pacific through the Luzon Strait. The freshwater discharge of the Pearl River is much lower than in the summer and salinity is more uniform across Hong Kong. The coastal Taiwan current also brings cold water from the north-east down the South China coast, affecting inshore waters.

The normal tidal range in Hong Kong waters is between one and two metres, depending on the relative influence of the moon and sun. The tidal pattern is complex due to the relative effects of the diurnal and semi-diurnal components. The basic pattern during flood tides is for oceanic water to flow north into Mirs Bay and west through Lei Yue Mun into Victoria Harbour and through Kap Shui Mun and the Ma Wan Channel. This flow is reversed during the ebb tide. Maximum tidal currents generally range from 0.5 to 1.5 knots, peaking at up to five knots in narrow channels.

Climate

Hong Kong's climate is sub-tropical, tending towards the temperate for nearly half the year. November and December are generally regarded as the best months of the year with pleasant breezes, plenty of sunshine and comfortable temperatures.

January and February are cloudier, with occasional cold fronts bringing in cold northerly winds. Temperatures can drop below 10 degrees Celsius in urban areas. Sub-zero temperatures and frost occur on high ground infrequently.

March and April can be mild and pleasant but humid. Fog sometimes disrupts air traffic and ferry services because of reduced visibility.

The months from May to August are hot and humid with occasional showers and thunderstorms. Afternoon temperatures often exceed 31 degrees, but at night temperatures generally stay around 26 degrees.

Hong Kong is more likely to be affected by tropical cyclones between June and October. When a tropical cyclone is some 1 000 kilometres south-east of Hong Kong, the weather is usually fine and exceptionally hot. If the centre of the tropical cyclone comes closer to Hong Kong, winds will increase and rain may become heavy and widespread. Landslips and flooding sometimes cause considerably more damage than the winds.

About 80 per cent of the annual rainfall falls between May and September. August is the wettest month and January is the driest.

Severe weather phenomena in Hong Kong include tropical cyclones, strong winter and summer monsoon winds, monsoon troughs and thunderstorms with associated squalls. Waterspouts and hailstorms occur infrequently, while snow and tornadoes are rare.

The Year's Weather

The year 2003 was the fifth warmest since records began in 1884. It was largely due to milder weather in the first few months when there was more sunshine and fewer cold surges than normal. The year was also relatively dry, with rainfall about 12 per cent below normal. It was also notable for having the driest July on record.

Tropical cyclones occurring in the western North Pacific in 2003 were fewer than normal. In Hong Kong, the tropical cyclone season started late in the year. The first tropical cyclone warning signal was issued on July 20, a month later than normal. Only four tropical cyclones, against the mean of six, necessitated the issuance of tropical cyclone warnings locally.

January was sunnier and slightly warmer than usual. It was warmer and drier than usual from February to April. An area of active thunderstorms affected Hong Kong in the evening of April 8 and the Thunderstorm Warning and the Amber Rainstorm Warning were issued for the first time in the year. May was slightly drier than usual and June was wetter than usual.

July was warmer and drier than usual. The monthly mean minimum temperature of 27.6 degrees equalled the record high value set in 1993. The monthly rainfall of 101.8 millimetres, less than one third of the normal figure of 323.5 millimetres, was the lowest on record. Waterspouts and funnel clouds occurred over Hong Kong waters on July 1, 6, 9 and 31. With the approach of Severe Tropical Storm Koni, the first Tropical Cyclone Warning Signal of the year was issued on July 20. The first No. 3 signal and later the first No. 8 Tropical Cyclone Warning Signal of the year were issued on July 23 as Typhoon Imbudo approached Hong Kong.

August was cloudier and wetter than usual. Typhoon Krovanh necessitated the issuance of the No. 3 Strong Wind Signal in Hong Kong. It was wetter than usual again in September. As Typhoon Dujuan skirted the north of Hong Kong about 30 kilometres from the Hong Kong Observatory on September 2, the Increasing Gale or Storm Signal No. 9 was issued for the first time since 1999.

October was sunnier and much drier than normal. November was wetter than normal. December was drier than normal with only a trace of rainfall recorded.

Meteorological Services

Hong Kong Observatory

The Hong Kong Observatory was established in 1883, mainly to provide scientific information for the safe navigation of ships. Since then, it has evolved in line with community needs providing services in and studies on weather forecasting, hydrometeorology, climatology, physical oceanography, aviation and marine meteorology, and radiation monitoring and assessment. The Observatory also administers the official time standard for Hong Kong, provides basic astronomical information and maintains a seismological monitoring network.

The Observatory issues weather forecasts and warnings of hazardous weather to the public, mariners, the civil aviation community as well as special users such as port and container terminal operators.

Whenever Hong Kong is threatened by tropical cyclones, frequent warnings are widely disseminated through the mass media. A colour-coded rainstorm warning system warns people of heavy rain. The Observatory also issues warnings on thunderstorms, landslips, fire danger, strong monsoon, cold and very hot weather, and frost. An advisory service on the ultraviolet (UV) index is also provided.

To promote public education and awareness regarding hazardous weather, the Observatory began in 2003 to run basic meteorological courses for members of the public and government personnel, and organised guided tours of the Observatory, exhibitions, popular scientific lectures and Open Days.

Besides presenting regular weather programmes on television, the Observatory's meteorologists also give interviews and briefings on the radio and television during adverse weather.

While the Dial-a-Weather service provides recorded weather messages to the public, the Telephone Information Enquiry System serves as an interactive means for the public to obtain a variety of meteorological, geophysical and time information by phone or by fax.

The Observatory operates a website displaying a great variety of information. The website also features an audio version for the visually impaired and a WAP (Wireless Application Protocol) version for mobile phone users. In 2003, weather information at Victoria Peak and at Ngong Ping on Lantau Island was added to the website to enhance the coverage of regional weather information for the public and tourists. The Observatory website recorded over 330 million hits in 2003. The Observatory also manages two websites set up on behalf of the World Meteorological Organisation to make available official weather warnings and forecasts around the world to the international community.

Weather Monitoring and Forecasting

The Observatory exchanges weather observations and forecasts with the rest of the world under the framework of the World Meteorological Organisation. In addition, it exchanges weather radar imageries and observations of automatic weather stations with the meteorological bureaux of Guangdong and Macau. The Observatory monitors the weather using a wide range of equipment including meteorological satellites ground stations, Doppler weather radars, automatic weather stations, weather buoys, radiosondes carried by balloons as well as wind profilers. These are augmented by observations from aircraft and Voluntary Observing Ships. The Observatory also operates tide gauges to monitor raised sea levels and coastal flooding caused by tropical cyclones.

To mitigate damage due to floods and landslips, rainstorm and landslip warnings are issued based on the objective guidance provided by a 'nowcasting' system developed by the Observatory. This system automatically analyses radar and raingauge data and forecasts the rainfall distribution within Hong Kong in the next few hours.

High-resolution numerical weather prediction models operated by the Observatory as well as those of meteorological centres overseas are the backbone of weather forecasting. Taking advantage of the improvement in forecasting techniques, the five-day forecast issued by the Observatory was extended to seven days in December. The Observatory also enhanced its tropical cyclone warning service during the year, by extending the forecast period from 48 to 72 hours.

Aviation Weather Services

The Observatory's Airport Meteorological Office at the Hong Kong International Airport provides weather services for civil aviation for a designated airspace over the northern part of the South China Sea. It provides aviation users with flight documents, aerodrome forecasts and warnings, and other information such as radar and satellite pictures.

A Light Detection and Ranging System and a terminal Doppler weather radar help to monitor windshear around the approaches to the airport under fine and rainy conditions, respectively.

Radiation Measurement and Assessment

The Observatory operates a network of 10 radiation monitoring stations to continuously monitor radiation levels in Hong Kong. Samples of air, water, soil and food are regularly collected over various parts of Hong Kong and their radiological contents measured.

In 2003, a review of data obtained since 1987 showed no significant difference in Hong Kong's environmental radiation levels before and after the operation of the nuclear power station at Daya Bay.

If a nuclear emergency occurs or is likely to occur, the Observatory will immediately intensify radiation monitoring, collect relevant information for assessing the radiological consequences and provide technical advice to the relevant government policy bureaux regarding the appropriate protective actions to take.

To promote public understanding of environmental radiation and preparedness for nuclear emergencies, the Observatory produced a video and launched an educational web page on the Daya Bay Contingency Plan in 2003.

Climatological, Oceanographic and Geophysical Services

The Hong Kong Observatory provides climatological information to meet the needs of users in various activities ranging from recreation through engineering design and environmental impact analysis to litigation. It also conducts research on short-range climate forecast and long-term climate change in Hong Kong. A forecast of the annual rainfall and number of tropical cyclones affecting Hong Kong is issued early in the year.

The Observatory produces an annual tide table for Hong Kong. It also provides assessments of the probabilities of occurrence of extreme storm surges and advice on oceanographic matters to other government departments and the engineering

community.

To monitor earthquake activities in the vicinity of Hong Kong, the Observatory operates a network of eight short-period seismograph stations. Long-period seismographs at the Observatory's headquarters detect tremors world-wide and information on significant tremors is made public through the media. On average, Hong Kong experiences about two minor earth tremors every year.

The Hong Kong Time Standard is provided by a caesium beam atomic clock. Accuracy within fractions of a microsecond a day is maintained. A six-pip time signal is sent to Radio Television Hong Kong for broadcast at quarter-hour intervals. The time checking service is also available to the public through the Observatory's Telephone Information Enquiry System as well as through a Network Time Service at its home page. The Network Time Service provided about 270 million checks in 2003.

Home Pages

Environment, Transport and Works Bureau: http://www.etwb.gov.hk
Economic Development and Labour Bureau: http://www.edlb.gov.hk
Agriculture, Fisheries and Conservation Department: http://www.afcd.gov.hk
Environmental Protection Department: http://www.epd.gov.hk
Hong Kong Observatory: http://www.hko.gov.hk and http://www.weather.gov.hk

CHAPTER 15

Travel and Tourism

Total visitor numbers have risen by 38 per cent since 1997, an increase largely attributable to the surge in visitor arrivals from the Mainland. These have soared from 2.36 million in 1997 to 8.47 million in 2003, making the Mainland Hong Kong's largest source market. To maintain and further enhance Hong Kong's position as the premier city tourist destination in Asia, the Government is committed to enhancing tourist attractions and facilities, upgrading service standards, promoting a hospitable culture in the community and facilitating the entry of visitors. It will continue to work closely with the Hong Kong Tourism Board and the trade to promote tourism development.

TOURISM is one of the major economic pillars of Hong Kong: the most popular city destination in Asia.

After a record-breaking 16.5 million arrivals in 2002, the tourism industry performed well in the first two months of 2003. Unfortunately, with the SARS outbreak in March, visitor arrivals fell dramatically to a new low of only 427 254 in May, a decrease of 68 per cent compared with May 2002. At the same time, the hotel occupancy rate fell from an average of 84 per cent in 2002 to 18 per cent.

With the lifting of the World Health Organisation's travel advisory concerning Hong Kong on May 23, the tourism sector rebounded quickly. From a 68 per cent year-on-year decline in May, arrivals reached almost 10 per cent year-on-year growth by August. The growth momentum was sustained in the last quarter of the year. Overall visitor arrivals for 2003 totalled 15.5 million, a moderate decrease of 6 per cent compared with the previous year but still representing a remarkable achievement when set against the challenges that arose around the middle of the year. Hotel occupancy also climbed to 85 per cent in October and to over 90 per cent in November. The rebound was mainly due to the success of the Global Tourism Revival Campaign spearheaded by the Hong Kong Tourism Board (HKTB) as well as by a significant growth in visitor arrivals from the Mainland. Long-haul markets are gradually recovering and the outlook for 2004 is positive.

Tourism Infrastructure, Facilities and Products

In December 1999, the Government and The Walt Disney Company announced the development of Hong Kong Disneyland at Penny's Bay on Lantau Island. Work on various fronts has progressed well and is on schedule. Reclamation for Hong Kong

Disneyland Phase 1 was completed in December 2002. Three major infrastructure contracts to support the development of Hong Kong Disneyland are on track for completion by 2005. Construction of the theme park superstructure commenced in January 2003.

Hong Kong Disneyland Phase 1 is targeted to open in 2005 as a world-class theme park for local residents and international visitors. It will strengthen Hong Kong's position as Asia's most popular city tourist destination. Upon opening, it will occupy an area of 126 hectares, comprising a Disney park with four different theme areas, two Disney-themed hotels with 1 000 rooms, as well as retail, dining and entertainment facilities. In its first year of operation, the number of tourist visitors is estimated at 3.4 million, rising to 7.4 million after about 15 years. Additional spending by tourists is expected to amount to some $8.3 billion in Year 1, rising to $16.8 billion per annum in Year 20 and beyond.

Beyond Disneyland, the Government is committed to building on Hong Kong's attractiveness as a tourist destination through the development of major new tourist attractions and the enhancement of existing facilities:—

- A 30-year franchise for the MTR Corporation Limited (MTRCL) to develop and operate the Tung Chung Cable Car System linking Tung Chung and Ngong Ping on Lantau Island commenced on December 24. In addition, the MTRCL will also develop a Buddhist 'Theme Village' at Ngong Ping to provide complementary facilities to meet the needs of visitors to the area. By early 2006, visitors will be able to enjoy a spectacular view of the South China Sea, the Pearl River Delta and the natural scenery of Lantau during a 17-minute ride on the Cable Car System;

- In May, the Government awarded the tender for a private sector development at the site of the former Marine Police Headquarters compound in Tsim Sha Tsui. This is the first project in which the private sector has been given the rights to preserve, restore and convert historic buildings as a tourism-themed development to enable local residents and visitors alike to appreciate Hong Kong's unique cultural heritage. The developer plans to turn the site into a heritage hotel, with food and beverage outlets, and retail facilities. The project is expected to be completed in early 2007;

- In April, the Government announced plans to involve the private sector in another heritage tourism project encompassing the Central Police Station, Victoria Prison and the former Central Magistracy. The intention is to invite tenders for the project in the first half of 2004 and hand over the site in phases in 2005;

- Construction work on Phase 2 of the Hong Kong Wetland Park at Tin Shui Wai, which is scheduled to be completed in late 2005, is proceeding smoothly. The park will be Hong Kong's first major ecotourism facility. Upon the opening of Phase 2, it is expected the park will attract some 500 000 nature lovers every year to appreciate the unique natural heritage of Hong Kong;

- A large outdoor wood inscription of the Chinese calligraphy masterpiece by renowned scholar Professor Jao Tsung I, the *Prajna Paramita Hrdaya Sutra* (the *Heart Sutra*), will be erected at a site at the foot of Lantau Peak, near Ngong Ping. The project is targeted for completion in early 2005;

- To further the objective of increasing the range of tourism attractions in Hong Kong, the Government is developing plans for a tourism node with a new world-class cruise terminal capable of meeting the needs of the new generation of large cruise ships. The Government is also assisting Ocean Park in its long-term strategic review, which will help shape future development at the Aberdeen Harbour tourism node surrounding the park;

- *A Symphony of Lights* — this world-class multimedia light and sound show, combining interactive light and musical effects to tell the story of Hong Kong through showcasing the major buildings along the waterfront of Victoria Harbour, was given a successful preview on December 20 prior to its official commencement on January 17, 2004. It will become a permanent tourism attraction, and be enhanced over the years as more buildings are included in the show;

- A consultancy study on the development of tourism in the northern New Territories was completed in December 2002. Based on the study report, which focused on opportunities to develop for green and heritage tourism in the area, the Government conducted a consultative forum with local representatives and relevant stakeholders. An inter-departmental committee has been formed to consider the feedback and take forward the recommendations as appropriate.

Tourism Friendliness

Visitor Signage and Tourist District Enhancement Improvements

The visitor signage improvement programme, which was introduced in Central and Stanley in 2001, is being extended to other districts in phases, beginning with Wong Tai Sin, Sha Tin and Sai Kung in early 2002. The programme, covering all 18 districts, will be completed in 2004. In the urban area, signs are intended to be eye-catching while in rural districts signage will blend in harmoniously with the natural environment.

The district-based enhancement projects at the Sai Kung Waterfront and Lei Yue Mun were completed in 2003, while those in the Central and Western District will be completed in 2004. Enhancement works include repaving of streets, redesigning street-lighting and erecting directional and information signage. Improvement works for the Stanley Waterfront and the Peak will be carried out in 2004 and 2005, respectively.

The scope of the Tsim Sha Tsui Promenade Beautification Project was expanded to cover the site to be vacated by the relocation of the existing Public Transport Interchange outside the Tsim Sha Tsui Star Ferry Pier. The promenade, stretching from the Cultural Centre Piazza to Tsim Sha Tsui East, will be enhanced with better access, new landscaping and improved lighting and open space. When completed in phases from 2005 to 2009, it will offer a much better place for residents and visitors to enjoy Victoria Harbour. As an advance part of the project, work on the 'Avenue of Stars' project started in June and will be completed in the second quarter of 2004.

Service Quality

To promote high standards of service in shops and restaurants, the HKTB launched the Quality Tourism Services (QTS) Scheme in 1999. It has been widely supported by the tourism industry and has helped to upgrade professionalism and service standards offered to visitors. At year-end, more than 1 100 businesses representing 3 557 outlets had received QTS accreditation.

In December, the QTS Scheme was enhanced to further strengthen Hong Kong's reputation for quality services. The new criteria tighten the entry requirements for applicant merchants, emphasise the provision of clear product information to consumers, improve the complaint handling system of the scheme and reinforce surveillance of participating merchants.

It is essential to upgrade hospitality standards generally to meet visitors' expectations and build for future growth. The Tourism Orientation Programme, a two-year project organised by the HKTB with $40 million in government funding, is designed to enhance Hong Kong's hospitality culture and provide an opportunity for those keen to pursue careers in the tourism industry to gain front-line experience in it. The first year of the programme was successfully completed in mid-2003 with 133 participants graduating as Tourism Hosts. More than 80 per cent of them subsequently joined the industry, and a further 220 people are undergoing training as part of the programme's second year.

The Tourism Commission launched a territory-wide public education campaign entitled 'A Hospitable Hong Kong' in 2001, with young people among the main targets. The campaign continued in 2003. In collaboration with the Hong Kong Federation of Youth Groups, the Tourism Commission set up the Hong Kong Young Ambassador Scheme to groom a cadre of young leaders who can serve as 'ambassadors' to overseas visitors and provide an effective medium through which to spread hospitality messages among young people. During the year, a series of TV announcements was broadcast to promote a hospitality culture among the public.

Facilitation of Visitor Entry

With effect from July 28, 2003, the Mainland authorities have implemented an Individual Visit Scheme in four Guangdong cities (Dongguan, Zhongshan, Jiangmen and Foshan) to allow residents there to visit Hong Kong in a personal capacity. The scheme has been extended to cover Guangzhou, Shenzhen, Zhuhai and Huizhou from August 20, and Beijing and Shanghai from September 1. It will be extended to the whole of Guangdong Province by May 1, 2004. The scheme has been well received, with some 667 000 Mainland visitors coming to Hong Kong under its auspices by year-end.

The Tourism Commission took the lead in coordinating action among various government departments and the tourism industry to draw up measures to cope with the upsurge in Mainland visitors, especially during the National Day 'Golden Week' holiday period in October. The measures adopted demonstrated the city's capability to receive a large number of visitors during the peak holiday season.

Hong Kong Tourism Board

The HKTB is a subvented organisation responsible for marketing and promoting Hong Kong internationally as a destination for leisure and business travel. With a board of 20 non-executive members drawn from the local community, and representing all major sectors of the tourism and related trades, it operates through a Head Office in Hong Kong, 13 world-wide offices and seven representative offices.

Through its various marketing activities, the HKTB strives to reinforce Hong Kong's standing as a world-class city and the most preferred tourism destination in Asia. It aims not only to increase the number of visitors to Hong Kong, but also to enhance their experience and satisfaction when they arrive and during their stay.

The HKTB undertakes extensive market research and monitoring to assess industry trends, perceptions of Hong Kong in the overseas markets and feedback from departing visitors. The board shares this data with the Government and its tourism industry partners to enable visitor facilities, products and services to be planned most effectively and the industry to capitalise on new business opportunities.

A wide range of marketing strategies is employed to target different market segments world-wide. In 2003, the HKTB hosted 1 350 international media visitors and over 2 000 travel trade representatives on familiarisation trips.

Major travel agents and wholesalers are kept informed of the latest tourism information and given assistance to develop attractive travel packages. To add value to travel itineraries and provide new experiences for visitors, 16 new local tour products were introduced or repackaged during the year, with a number of them targeted at individual travellers from the Mainland or elsewhere. The HKTB also works with other tourism offices in the Mainland and around Asia to promote visits to Hong Kong as part of multi-destination itineraries.

Information Network

In 2003, the HKTB helped over 1.1 million visitors, either directly through its Visitor Information and Services Centres or by responding to enquiries received by mail, over the Internet, through its Visitor Hotline or at information counters set up at major international conventions and exhibitions. About 11.6 million pieces of HKTB literature were distributed during the year by the board and its partner organisations.

The *discoverhongkong.com* consumer website now receives over seven million page views a month. The HKTB also maintains a specialised website, *PartnerNet*, to provide information to the local and international travel trade.

To cater for the growth in Mainland visitor arrivals, a new Visitor Information and Services Centre was opened at the Lo Wu boundary crossing in October. This supplements the existing HKTB information centres in Central on Hong Kong Island, at Tsim Sha Tsui in Kowloon and at Hong Kong International Airport. Self-service information racks are also provided at some 150 other entry points, hotels, shopping centres and tourist attractions.

Marketing

Following the SARS outbreak, the HKTB launched a major Global Tourism Revival Campaign in late June, under the aegis of the Government's Economic Relaunch Campaign.

The campaign adopted a two-stage approach. The first phase was designed to attract visitors back to Hong Kong through generous travel offers and special welcome privileges, to help local businesses achieve a swift recovery. The second phase focused on sustaining long-term growth and reinforcing Hong Kong's destination image through a series of spectacular mega events and a new global advertising campaign.

Phase 1 took the form of a two-month promotion from mid-July to mid-September, entitled *Hong Kong Welcomes You!* With extensive support from the airline and hotel industries, the HKTB and its travel trade partners were able to launch a wide range of consumer promotions world-wide, and brought over 580 media and 1 930 trade representatives to Hong Kong on *Seeing is Believing* familiarisation visits. At the same time, some 1 360 local travel trade members joined overseas market visits and roadshows organised by the HKTB. The highlight of the *Hong Kong Welcomes You!* promotion was a special 'Welcome Day' on August 17 with more than 3 500 VIP guests coming from around the world to attend a series of events, including the launch of the *Strato-Fantasia* multimedia show on the Wan Chai waterfront. These activities generated positive international publicity.

Phase 2 began in mid-September with the launch of a new global advertising campaign on the theme *Hong Kong — Live it, Love it!* The campaign is designed to broaden and revitalise Hong Kong's image by showing the depth and diversity of attractions that the city offers beyond its reputation for shopping and dining. The campaign was rolled out across 16 key markets world-wide, spearheaded by a television commercial featuring international film star Jackie Chan, Hong Kong's official Tourism Ambassador. The HKTB also staged a series of themed mega events, including the *Mid-Autumn Lantern Celebration*, the *Hong Kong International Musical Fireworks Competition* and the *Hong Kong WinterFest* during the second half of 2003.

A number of special initiatives were taken in response to the launching by the Mainland authorities of the Individual Visit Scheme for visitors from designated Mainland cities. These included briefings for the travel trade in these cities and joint promotions with travel agents and local media. The HKTB also encouraged local tour operators to develop new itineraries targeted at individual travellers. It also stepped up its 'Meet and Greet' services and distribution of visitor information at border points.

Convention and Exhibition Travel

To attract leading international events, the HKTB continues to provide comprehensive support services to organisations planning to stage major events in the city.

Although a number of conventions and exhibitions in the second quarter of 2003 were postponed due to the SARS outbreak, many were simply rescheduled to later in 2003 or 2004. So far, more than 120 international conferences and exhibitions have been scheduled between 2004 and 2010.

Hong Kong is an ideal meeting point for companies wishing to do international business with companies from the Mainland. Continued growth is anticipated in this high-yield sector with China's accession to the World Trade Organisation and Hong Kong's trading advantages under the Mainland/Hong Kong Closer Economic Partnership Arrangement. The opening of the new AsiaWorld-Expo exhibition centre at the airport in 2006 will strengthen Hong Kong's attractiveness to host major events.

Cruise Travel

Hong Kong is becoming an increasingly popular centre for cruise travel. Several cruise liners are home based and provide the opportunity for the HKTB and its trade partners to market Hong Kong as a fly-cruise centre, while many international cruise liners make annual stopovers in Hong Kong.

Following the recommendations of a cruise marketing study conducted in 2002, a joint public and private sector Cruise Forum was convened to share market intelligence, expand cooperation between the various parties and promote Hong Kong as a cruise destination. In early 2003, Hong Kong hosted a visit by 27 leading international cruise executives to view the city's cruise facilities, discuss cooperation with local partners and meet government officials.

Protection for Travellers

Travel agents providing outbound travel services departing from Hong Kong and inbound travel services for visitors coming to Hong Kong are regulated under the Travel Agents Ordinance. The aim of the ordinance is to minimise the occurrence of fraud and loss to travellers in the event of defaults by outbound travel agents, and to protect the interests of visitors by enhancing the service standards of inbound travel agents. The present regulatory system is made up of two components: a licensing system and a self-regulatory mechanism by the trade.

The licensing function is carried out by the Registrar of Travel Agents appointed under the ordinance. All travel agents providing outbound or inbound travel services must be licensed under the ordinance. This requirement provides the first line of protection for travellers and visitors against default and malpractice. Travel agents may also face suspension or revocation of their licences if they are found to be operating against the public interest. At year-end, the number of licensed travel agents totalled 1 323.

The self-regulatory function is performed by the Travel Industry Council of Hong Kong (TIC), an approved organisation under the ordinance. The ordinance requires travel agents to become, and remain, members of the TIC in order to obtain and hold a licence. The TIC sets and enforces codes of conduct and issues directives from time to time to regulate business operations. It also handles public complaints about the services of its members. Members who breach the council's rules are subject to disciplinary action.

A Travel Industry Compensation Fund (TICF) has been set up under the ordinance to provide *ex gratia* compensation of up to 90 per cent of the loss of tour fares to outbound travellers in the event of a default by an outbound travel agent. The TICF derives its income from contributions from licensed travel agents in the form of a levy on outbound package tours and from investments and bank interest. At year-end, the TICF had a balance of about $366 million. During the year, four cases of default on cessation of business by travel agents occurred, affecting 528 travellers. The affected travellers received a total of about $1.5 million in *ex gratia* compensation from the fund.

The TICF also provides emergency financial assistance in respect of outbound travellers injured or killed in accidents in the course of an activity arranged or organised by a Hong Kong travel agent. In 2003, four outbound tour group accidents (involving one fatality and 32 cases of injury) were reported. Payments under the scheme amounted to about $43,000.

As a complement to the licensing of inbound travel agents which took effect on November 1, 2002, a training and certification system to ensure the service quality of serving tourist guides has been developed by the trade. This system requires serving tourist guides to attend specified training courses, pass an examination and obtain a Tourist Guide Pass before they may work as tourist guides. With effect from July 1, 2004 all travel agents will be required to assign only those tourist guides possessing a valid Tourist Guide Pass to receive visitors to Hong Kong.

Home Pages

Tourism Commission: http://www.tourism.gov.hk
Hong Kong Tourism Board: http://www.discoverhongkong.com

CHAPTER 16

Public Order

Committed to keeping Hong Kong safe and secure, the Disciplined Services comprise the Hong Kong Police Force, Correctional Services Department, Customs and Excise Department, Fire Services Department, Immigration Department and Government Flying Service. The regular emergency services are augmented by the Auxiliary Medical Service and the Civil Aid Service. These departments operate under the policy direction of the Security Bureau.

HONG KONG is one of the safest cities in the world. The overall crime rate, that is, the total number of crimes per 100 000 population, is lower than that of many other metropolitan cities. The overall law and order situation remained stable in 2003. The violent crime rate was the fourth lowest in the past 10 years, and the number of various serious crimes registered a significant drop. There was, however, an increase in the overall crime rate, by 16 per cent over 2002, primarily due to the increase in minor and opportunistic theft cases.

The Government has continued to participate actively in international cooperation in the fight against terrorism. The international situation and its impact on Hong Kong are closely monitored. While there is no intelligence suggesting that Hong Kong may be the target of a terrorist attack, all law enforcement units have remained vigilant to counter possible threats.

Fight Crime Committee

Chaired by the Chief Secretary for Administration, the Fight Crime Committee provides advice and recommends measures to prevent and reduce crime. It also coordinates crime-fighting efforts and monitors their results.

In 2003, the committee discussed a number of crime-related issues. It examined the data in significant areas of commercial crime, and noted that most commercial crimes committed in Hong Kong were small-scale, often involving habitual criminals. As a result of law enforcement action in 2001 and 2002, once prevalent frauds such as 'Loco-London gold', 'modelling agency' and 'pyramid scheme related fraud' were successfully contained at low levels.

With the relaxation of restrictions on Mainland residents visiting Hong Kong in recent years, the committee registered concern over crimes and illegal activities, including illegal employment, illegal gambling, prostitution and overstaying, committed by Mainland visitors. The committee welcomed the setting up of an inter-departmental task force in April to tackle the problem. It noted the adoption of a three-pronged approach by the task force, in collaboration with the Mainland authorities, to impose an effective and stringent application process for the issue of two-way permits and passports, to tighten up screening at Hong Kong immigration control points and to enhance enforcement.

In addition, the committee noted the considerable increase in criminal anti-social behaviour, including assaults on and verbal abuse of police officers while executing their duties, during the year. The Police Force has provided front-line officers with clear guidelines and enhanced training to handle these situations. It has also stepped up publicity and education to remind members of the public of their civic responsibilities. The committee considered that good law and order was important to Hong Kong's position as an international business centre, and was supportive of the Police Force's strategies in tackling the problem and would continue to closely monitor the situation.

The committee noted the findings of the Customer Satisfaction Survey 2002 of various police services. As part of the Police Force's quality improvement strategy, the survey was conducted by the University of Hong Kong in October 2002 as the second survey within the four-year survey cycle from 1999 to 2002, which showed that members of the public having contacts with the police held a high opinion of the services rendered. The committee also noted that another survey on the effectiveness of the fight crime publicity campaign in 2001-02, commissioned by the Information Services Department, had found the campaign successful in soliciting public support in fighting crime.

On the rehabilitation of offenders, the committee was informed of the Correctional Services Department's plan for undertaking various publicity activities in 2003-04, targeting four community groups including students, the general public, employers and the individual district communities. The committee would continue to monitor the effectiveness of such activities.

District Fight Crime Committees (DFCCs) continue to play an important role in the fight against crime. These committees monitor the crime situation in districts and reflect community concerns on law and order issues. They help foster community awareness regarding crime prevention and encourage community participation in combating crime and, in addition, launch district fight crime publicity campaigns with funding support from District Councils and other sponsorship. To reinforce the close link between the committee and the DFCCs, the FCC members took turns to attend DFCC meetings and functions.

Police Role in Combating SARS

The Police Force played an active role in the fight against SARS by seconding senior officers to the Health, Welfare and Food Bureau as members of the bureau's internal task force and the SARS Inter-Departmental Action Coordinating Committee. The force also worked closely with the Department of Health and other government departments in enforcing the Quarantine and Prevention of Disease Ordinance.

The Major Incident Investigation Disaster Support Section of the Police Force assisted the medical authorities in tracing SARS contacts by using computer technology. This assistance drew praise from Hong Kong's own medical and health authorities and also the World Health Organisation.

Officers also took part in escort duties for residents of Amoy Gardens who were moved to the designated isolation centre in Lei Yue Mun, and undertook security duty at the centre throughout the quarantine period.

Police Force

The Hong Kong Police Force is committed to protecting the public, preventing and detecting crime, maintaining law and order, ensuring smooth traffic operations and reducing the number of accidents, as well as stamping out illegal immigration.

At year-end, the Police Force had an establishment of about 28 000 police officers supported by more than 5 400 civilian staff and reinforced by some 4 500 volunteers serving in the Hong Kong Auxiliary Police Force.

During the year, Hong Kong remained one of the safest cities in the world, with the police sparing no effort in combating violent crime, triad activities and drug offences.

In meeting one of the Commissioner's operational targets for the year, the force accorded priority to working closely with Mainland authorities to clamp down on crimes committed by illegal immigrants and two-way permit holders.

On other fronts, the Police Force maintained exchanges of intelligence with overseas law enforcement agencies in combating terrorism. A large-scale counter terrorist exercise, codenamed 'Spellbinder', was held in October to enhance police contingency plans and ensure an effective response to any terrorist threat.

To better meet various challenges, the 'Three Year Strategic Action Plan' of the Police Force was revised and republished in September, setting out the focus of police work from 2003 to 2006 with the addition of a further 20 projects. These projects include a review on the alignment of the New Territories regions in the light of demographic changes, the enhancement of force members' language capability and the development of a training strategy to facilitate better understanding of and response to Mainland-related issues.

Crime

Reported crimes in 2003 totalled 88 377, an increase of 16.5 per cent compared with 75 877 crimes recorded in 2002. The crime rate stood at 1 297 cases per 100 000 population, a rise of 16 per cent compared with 1 118 cases in 2002. The increase was mainly due to the rise in non-violent crimes such as theft and criminal damage.

Violent crimes increased to 14 542 cases, a rise of 2.8 per cent compared with 14 140 cases in 2002. Robbery, wounding and serious assault accounted for 71.3 per cent of the total number of violent crimes in 2003. There was a decrease in the relatively more serious violent crimes such as murder, rape, wounding, kidnapping and robbery.

Altogether, there were 3 215 cases of robbery in 2003, a drop of 8 per cent compared with 3 493 cases in 2002. There were no cases of robbery with genuine firearms, compared with four in 2002. The number of bank robbery cases remained the same at 34. Most of these were perpetrated by lone culprits and did not involve serious violence.

Regarding non-violent crimes, burglary increased from 8 211 cases in 2002 to 9 076 in 2003, a rise of 10.5 per cent. Serious narcotics offences decreased from 2 243 in 2002 to 2 142 in 2003, a decline of 4.5 per cent. Theft increased from 32 025 cases in 2002 to 40 887 in 2003, an increase of 27.7 per cent. Deception increased slightly from 4 656 cases to 4 732 over the same period, a rise of 1.6 per cent.

Of the 88 377 crimes in 2003, 39.2 per cent or 34 672 crimes were detected, with 42 051 people arrested for various criminal offences. Of those arrested, 5 156 were juveniles (aged below 16) and 6 018 were young persons (aged 16 to 20). Most of the juveniles and young persons were arrested for shop theft, miscellaneous theft, wounding, serious assault and robbery. Drug-related offences were also prevalent among the crimes committed by young offenders.

Violent Crime Involving Firearms

In 2003, there were four cases involving the use of firearms compared with eight in 2002. There were 28 firearm seizures, compared with 23 in the previous year. The majority of the seizures were the direct result of intelligence-based operations conducted by the Police Force. Increased cooperation between the force and other law enforcement agencies, especially those on the Mainland, continued to yield an effective exchange of information on the activities of cross-boundary criminal syndicates, which is important in combating crimes involving firearms.

Vehicle Crime

In 2003, a total of 2 301 vehicles were reported missing. This represented a decrease of 4.6 per cent compared with 2 412 vehicles in 2002. The number of luxury vehicles and high-performance vehicles reported missing continued to decline. Rigorous local enforcement action, enhanced boundary control, intelligence sharing with overseas and neighbouring jurisdictions and the Mainland authorities' ban on right-hand drive vehicles continued to contribute towards the downward trend in vehicle theft.

Organised Crime and Triads

The situation with regard to organised crime and triads remained stable as in previous years. There were 2 471 triad-related cases in 2003, accounting for only 2.8 per cent of the 88 377 total reported crimes. Persistent and proactive enforcement by the Police Force has resulted in a steady decline in the number of triad-related crimes reported over the last few years.

The Organised and Serious Crimes Ordinance, enacted in 1994, has given law enforcement agencies enhanced powers against organised crime and syndicates. The ordinance includes provisions governing confiscation of crime proceeds and enhanced sentencing of criminals upon conviction. During the year, 21 persons were charged with offences under this legislation and confiscation orders issued by the courts resulted in the confiscation of $380,000. Restraining orders have frozen a total of $164.25 million pending court proceedings.

The Police Force has been proactive in maintaining closer ties with Mainland and overseas law enforcement agencies. The success of numerous high-profile operations such as Operation 'Twilight', which targeted many facets of organised crime and triad activities in Macau, Hong Kong and the Mainland, has highlighted the effectiveness of collaborative enforcement action in combating organised crime.

Witness Protection

The Witness Protection Programme is administered by the Police Witness Protection Unit. The unit provides a wide range of protective measures tailor-made to suit the needs of individual witnesses assessed as being exposed to a genuine threat of serious physical injury or death. These include, as permitted by the Witness Protection

Ordinance, a change of identity. The unit also assists and advises other units and divisions in the Police Force on protection of witnesses who are under a lesser threat.

Child Protection

In 2003, the five Regional Child Abuse Investigation Units investigated a total of 104 child abuse cases (99 involving sexual abuse and five serious physical abuse). The figure decreased by 11.9 per cent compared with a total of 118 cases in 2002. To protect the welfare of children, a multi-disciplinary approach has been adopted in handling child abuse cases. Joint investigations have been conducted with officers of the Social Welfare Department (SWD) in cases that required immediate social work intervention.

Interviews of children are conducted in confidential and child-friendly video interview suites situated in non-police premises. These interview suites are equipped with advanced facilities for forensic examinations in a more caring environment. In 2003, the Police Force and the SWD jointly organised two basic training programmes including advanced programmes for trainers, police officers and SWD officers in special investigations relating to child abuse cases.

Officers from the Child Protection Policy Unit (CPPU) continued to give lectures on public education and to organise publicity programmes on the prevention and handling of child abuse cases for parents and concerned professionals from both the Government and non-governmental organisations.

The Prevention of Child Pornography Ordinance took effect on December 19, 2003. This ordinance further protects children from exploitation in the form of child pornography and child sex tourism. Although child pornography and child sex tourism are not widespread in Hong Kong, police officers will continue to be vigilant in guarding against such criminal activities.

In March, the Juvenile Offenders (Amendment) Bill 2001 was passed by the Legislative Council, raising the minimum age of criminal responsibility from seven to 10 years.

To strengthen support services for children or juveniles who come to the attention of the police due to non-law abiding behaviour, the Police Force and the SWD jointly introduced a 'Family Conference' arrangement in October. A 'Family Conference' will be conducted for children or juveniles who are cautioned under the Police Superintendent's Discretion Scheme. It brings together family members of cautioned juveniles and professionals from relevant government departments and agencies to assess the youngsters' needs, and prepare a follow-up welfare plan for them. The SWD will make the decision on whether or not a 'Family Conference' is required.

In compliance with Article 37(d) of the United Nations Convention on the Rights of the Child that every child deprived of his or her liberty shall have the right to prompt access to legal and other appropriate assistance, the Legal Representation Scheme took effect on October 1. Under the scheme, free legal representation will be made available to children or juveniles involved in care or protection proceedings who are deprived of their liberty and detained in a place of refuge. The Administration has commissioned the Duty Lawyer Service to run the scheme.

Commercial Crime

The number of reports of syndicated and serious fraud handled by the Commercial Crime Bureau (CCB) during the year declined by 17.8 per cent (83 compared with 101 in 2002), while the reported total financial losses increased by 0.6 per cent ($1,514 million compared with $1,505 million in 2002).

The successful conclusion of a number of court cases concerning 'pyramid scheme related fraud', with offenders receiving jail sentences of up to three years and nine months, has had a substantial deterrent effect on such crimes. Action taken against a syndicate involved in the fraudulent transfer of bank funds resulted in the arrest of 46 persons and prevented a potential loss of $41 million. A number of defendants have been sentenced to imprisonment for periods of up to six years and three months. There was also a series of mortgage frauds, in which suspects obtained mortgage loans from banks by providing false personal and credit information. Proactive action was taken with the cooperation of the banking industry and this resulted in the neutralisation of a syndicate, preventing a potential loss of $49 million.

In 2003, after strategic and coordinated action by the CCB and the Hong Kong Association of Banks, together with wide publicity in the media, the number of complaints of suspected fraud related to personal bankruptcy was contained. However, given the increasing number of complaints of suspected company insolvency fraud and abuse of the Protection of Wages on Insolvency Fund, the CCB is working with other concerned departments to take action to investigate all incidents.

In preparation for the operation of the Securities and Futures Ordinance from April 1, 2003, the CCB enhanced cooperation with the Securities and Futures Commission in taking enforcement action and sharing experience and knowledge. The successful prosecution and conviction in a high-profile market manipulation case was testimony to this cooperation. The CCB has also maintained close liaison and partnership with other agencies, such as the Hong Kong Monetary Authority, the Companies Registry, the Labour Department and the Official Receiver's Office.

There were a total of 588 cases of technology crime reported in 2003, compared with 272 in 2002. Over 49 per cent of the cases reported are attributable to minor crimes associated with online games, such as the unauthorised use of passwords of other persons to 'steal' or remove virtual weapons or tools earned while engaged in role-playing games.

The examination of computer systems for the purpose of searching, retrieving and preserving digital evidence (computer forensics) continues to provide the greatest challenge due to the increasing size and variety of the data storage media.

The Technology Crime Division continued its efforts to foster closer ties with overseas law enforcement agencies. In October, the division hosted a successful 'Computer Crime Investigation and Training Seminar' which was attended by representatives from eight different jurisdictions. It continued to play a leading role in the Interpol Asia-South Pacific Working Party on Information Technology Crime by assuming the group's Vice Chair.

Narcotics

In 2003, the Police Force continued to accord high priority to tackling the trafficking and abuse of psychotropic substances, especially in respect of young persons and the use of ketamine. At the same time, an upsurge in the trafficking and abuse of heroin in divans was a major target for enforcement.

There was some success in reducing the psychotropic substance abuse problem. However, it was clear that sustained enforcement action would be necessary. The

Police Force recorded some impressive results during operations to prevent psychotropic substances from reaching abusers, and quell abuse. A total of 39.49 kilograms of ketamine and 95 650 'ecstasy'-type tablets were seized. In 2003, a total of 1 770 persons were arrested for offences connected to ketamine and 639 were arrested in cases related to 'ecstasy'-type tablets. In a significant case, officers dismantled a fairly sophisticated 'ecstasy'-type tablet production enterprise based in Hung Hom, Kowloon. In operations targeting narcotic drugs, the Police Force seized a total of 40.17 kilograms of heroin and dismantled three heroin cutting centres. Officers also neutralised the operation of a large number of premises used as divans where heroin was sold and abused. Traffickers and abusers had switched to supplying and abusing narcotics in divans on account of stringent police enforcement at street-level 'black spots'.

In addition, the Police Force seized 215.61 kilograms of herbal cannabis, 4.3 kilograms of cannabis resin and 35.32 kilograms of methamphetamine ('ice'). A small amount of gamma hydroxybutyric acid (GHB), an illegally produced central nervous system depressant, was seized.

In 2003, the number of persons arrested for drug offences totalled 8 652, compared with 9 413 in 2002. Among those persons arrested, 1 081 were aged 16 to 20 years and 132 were aged under 16. Compared with 2002, there was a 23.1 per cent decrease in the number of arrested persons aged under 21.

Numerous complex financial investigations were conducted, either related to drug trafficking proceeds from local cases or to assist overseas law enforcement agencies.

Throughout the year, the Narcotics Bureau continued efforts to enhance the Police Force's drug abuse prevention work, particularly the work aimed at young persons.

Crime Prevention

The Crime Prevention Bureau continued to provide a public advisory service and 29 445 security surveys were conducted for both the public and private sectors.

The bureau continued its educational role through campaigns and seminars, its call-fax and web page services and the deployment of the Robotcop and the crime prevention bus.

In 2003, a total of 320 000 leaflets on crime prevention were distributed to tourists from the Mainland, especially upon the commencement of the Individual Visitor Scheme and during the National Day 'Golden Week' holiday period in October.

Appeals through the media are regularly made to heighten public awareness of prevalent trends in street deception. For example, a radio programme alerted the public to the most prevalent *modus operandi* used by swindlers in targeting the elderly.

The bureau also deals with the regular inspection of over 860 security companies and provides briefings to new companies.

Criminal Information

The Criminal Records Bureau maintains criminal records on people convicted of certain criminal offences in local courts. In addition, the 'Enhanced Police Operational Nominal Index Computer System' contains information on wanted persons, missing persons, warrants of arrest issued by courts, and an index of persons convicted of serious arrestable offences, from whom DNA samples have been taken. The bureau also maintains central indices on stolen or missing vehicles, a computerised suspect album library, an index of crime information sent to the Police Force by members of the public and a system that can assist in identifying suspects by their criminal methods and descriptions.

Forensic Firearms Examination

The Forensic Firearms Examination Bureau continued to play an important role in the investigation of firearms-related crimes by enhancing the quality of services it provides within the Police Force and to other disciplined services. Since 2000, the bureau has been an accredited laboratory with the American Society of Crime Laboratory Directors (ASCLD) and ranked in equal status with other overseas facilities, such as the FBI Laboratory in the United States.

The bureau's Scanning Electron Microscope and the computerised Integrated Bullet and Cartridge Identification System have heightened the force's capability in solving firearms-related crimes.

Identification

The Identification Bureau continued its key role in the investigation and detection of crime by applying the latest fingerprint detection techniques in crime scenes and subsequent fingerprint identification.

The Scene of Crime Section provides fingerprint services at crime scenes on a 24-hour basis. Through efficient coordination, Scene of Crime Officers attended 89.3 per cent of crime scenes within 45 minutes of being called. To implement the provisions of the DNA legislation that took effect in 2001, a dedicated cadre of Scene of Crime Officers has been responsible for DNA sampling since June of that year. With effect from June 2003, the responsibility for the collection of DNA samples has been divided into two groups of officers. About 1 000 front-line officers, including Uniform Branch and Crime, are now trained for taking DNA samples (normally buccal swabs) from suspects, volunteers and convicted persons. Scene of Crime Section officers recover both fingerprint and DNA evidence from crime scenes. The number of DNA profiles stored in the database exceeds 4 500 and, in total, DNA evidence has linked over 280 cases.

The advanced technology applied in recovery of fingerprints from crime scenes and exhibits, together with the sophisticated Computer Assisted Fingerprint Identification System, contributes substantially to the bureau's success by achieving a consistently high level of identification. In 2003, the bureau identified 1 688 suspects involved in 1 493 cases. The Photographic Section also assists in the gathering of valuable evidence from crime scenes, and its officers attended 4 275 crime scenes. During the year, the section produced 1 286 689 photographs and slides. Apart from conventional photographic services, the section provided video crime scene re-enactments and the printing of photographs from bank surveillance films and videotapes.

Liaison

The Liaison Bureau acts as a coordination centre in dealing with all police-related inquiries from overseas police organisations and local consulate officials.

The bureau's Liaison Division is responsible for liaison with Mainland and Macau police authorities. Close liaison has been maintained with the Interpol China National Central Bureau in Beijing, the Guangdong Liaison Office, the Shenzhen and Zhuhai Liaison Sub-Offices of Guangdong, and the newly established Shanghai

Liaison Office. Since 1990, 236 criminal fugitives and 287 stolen vehicles have been returned to Hong Kong from the Mainland.

The bureau represents the Hong Kong Police Force in the International Criminal Police Organisation (ICPO), better known as Interpol, as a sub-bureau of the China National Central Bureau. A Hong Kong police officer is seconded to the ICPO General Secretariat in Lyon, France, to work in one of its specialised groups, to enhance international cooperation in combating crime.

During the year, with the assistance and cooperation provided by overseas enforcement agencies, two persons were extradited to Hong Kong and nine were extradited from Hong Kong to other countries.

Public Order

The Police Tactical Unit (PTU) Headquarters provides training to Regional and District personnel to cope with internal security commitments. During the year, more than 1 400 officers received such training. The training provides officers with the capability to carry out a wide range of duties, including anti-crime patrols, anti-illegal immigration operations, security operations and crowd management for festive occasions, major international conferences, public gatherings, processions and demonstrations.

During the year, PTU officers played an important role in the successful policing of the Sixth Anniversary of the Establishment of the HKSAR, the Hong Kong International Musical Fireworks Competition in October, and various public processions.

On July 1, a public procession of the largest scale since 1989 was held on Hong Kong Island. Extensive police manpower was deployed and the demonstration was conducted in a peaceful and orderly manner.

The Special Duties Unit (SDU), which is the Police Force's counter-terrorist response unit, is also based at PTU Headquarters and during the year it was deployed on a number of occasions to assist other units in various operations. Although there is no specific intelligence to suggest that Hong Kong is likely to be a target for terrorism, the Police Force has continued to monitor the global situation to maintain its preparedness and response capabilities.

The Police Force's annual counter-terrorism exercise was significantly enhanced in scope and duration to allow participation by a large number of officers. Its final scenario not only involved the majority of force's counter-terrorism units, but also provided an opportunity for other government departments and outside agencies to participate, thereby assisting them in being prepared.

Explosive Ordnance Disposal Bureau

The Explosive Ordnance Disposal (EOD) Bureau is responsible for dealing with all explosive devices and weapons in Hong Kong. This remit includes dealing with Chemical, Biological, Radiological and Nuclear (CBRN) Weapons. The bureau is trained and equipped to deal with such items on dry land and underwater and is called out, on average, over three times per week. Items dealt with range from large World War II aircraft bombs and sea mines to improvised explosive devices.

In addition to EOD operations, the bureau is heavily involved in training. This includes lectures and demonstrations on bomb awareness, action at bomb scenes and 323 action at CBRN incidents for both the Police Force and outside agencies. As part of this effort, the bureau continues to maintain and build links with overseas organisations. During the year, a number of bomb disposal officers from other countries came to Hong Kong to participate in exercises and training in order to exchange knowledge and experience.

Illegal Immigration

There has been an overall downward trend since 1993 in illegal immigration from the Mainland. During the year, 3 809 illegal immigrants were arrested by the police, an average of 10 per day, representing a decrease of 29 per cent compared with 5 362 in 2002. Of these, 66 per cent crossed the land boundary and remaining 34 per cent claimed to have entered by sea.

Close liaison in the form of regular liaison meetings and exchange of intelligence was maintained with the Guangdong Border Defence Bureau. The Guangdong bureau has been working in partnership with the police in preventing cross-boundary crimes. The entire boundary fence is now monitored round-the-clock with the use of advanced technical equipment to intercept illegal immigrants from the Mainland.

Police Dog Unit

There are about 170 dogs in the Police Dog Unit, comprising general patrol dogs and 'sniffer' dogs. The unit is responsible for ensuring that all dogs and handlers are professionally trained and their skills are maintained at a high level of proficiency. The unit also provides training to drug detection dogs from the Customs and Excise Department.

Special 'sniffer' dogs are stationed at the Hong Kong International Airport and at the Kai Tak Operational Base to provide round-the-clock service in search operations. The unit's explosives detection dogs also play a key role in security operations undertaken by the Police Force.

Traffic

In 2003, there were 14 436 traffic accidents involving casualties, representing a 7.3 per cent decrease compared with 2002. The number of fixed penalty tickets issued for moving offences was 374 714, a decrease of 4 per cent. Police officers and traffic wardens issued 506 286 tickets for parking offences during the year, representing a marginal decrease of 1.2 per cent. The number of summonses issued to traffic offenders stood at 62 195, a decrease of 5.1 per cent.

Police Licensing Office

Within the licensing charter of the Police Licensing Office, there were 223 127 holders of valid Security Personnel Permits (SPP) in Hong Kong at year-end. Legislative amendments to the Criteria for Issuing Security Personnel Permits under the Security and Guarding Services Ordinance took effect on April 1. The amendments were aimed at tightening the criteria for issuing permits to persons with criminal records and to ensure that people who are granted permits have acquired the basic security knowledge required for discharging their duties, so as to further enhance the quality of the security service.

To facilitate legitimate business operations under the Massage Establishment Ordinance, the legislation was amended in December. The amendments provide for a reduction in the licence renewal fee. In addition, the processing time for licence applications has been shortened.

Marine Region

In line with the principles of the Police Force's Strategic Directions, the Marine Region has been carrying out extensive research into the operating protocols and priorities required for policing the waters of Hong Kong for the next 10 to 15 years, and making provision for adherence to the International Ship and Port Facility Security Code (ISPS Code) due for implementation in July 2004. Technologically advanced coastal surveillance systems, together with fast intercept craft linked by an enhanced radar system, are considered a practical and cost-efficient response to the future policing and security concepts identified. Enforcement action continued throughout the year, particularly with regard to illegal immigration and smuggling, as well as other forms of illegal activity in Hong Kong waters.

Public Relations

The Police Public Relations Branch (PPRB) plays a vital role in explaining police work to the media and the public as well as strengthening relationships in order to enlist the public's support in the maintenance of law and order.

Police Community Relations Officers attached to different districts work closely with representatives from government departments and organisations to keep the public well informed of police policies and operational priorities.

During the year, the Secondary School Liaison Officers Programme and the Junior Police Call Scheme continued to serve as bridges between the police and youngsters. Membership of the scheme stood at 144 043 at year-end.

In conjunction with Radio Television Hong Kong (RTHK), the Police Force produces two weekly television programmes, the 30-minute *Police Magazine* in Cantonese and the five-minute *Police Report* in English to keep the public abreast of prevalent crime trends and to appeal for information that will help officers in investigations.

Celebrating its 30th anniversary in 2003, *Police Magazine* continued to enjoy high ratings while enhancing cooperation between the Police Force and the community.

The PPRB and RTHK jointly produced a new television programme, *On the Beat*, which made its debut in January. It aimed to further enhance the image of the Police Force and promote public understanding of police work. One of its episodes, entitled *The Suddenness of Life*, won the Silver Plaque at the 39th Chicago International Television Awards.

Part II of *On the Beat* was launched in October to disseminate the messages of 'The evil will not prevail over the good' and 'Justice has a long arm'.

Both Part I and Part II of the programme enjoyed favourable ratings with as many as 1.5 million viewers aged four and above watching each episode, on average.

Police telephone hotlines and Crime Information Forms provide convenient channels for reporting crime. A total of 22 583 hotline phone calls (not including those made to the emergency hotline 999) as well as 2 049 returned Crime Information Forms were registered by year-end, resulting in 2 722 arrests.

To commend people's initiatives in helping in the fight against crime, the Police Force held two Good Citizen Award Scheme ceremonies in June and December, with sponsorship from the Hong Kong General Chamber of Commerce.

Information relating to police activities is disseminated to local and overseas media organisations round-the-clock. During the year, officers seconded from the Information Services Department (ISD) handled 290 468 media enquiries, issued 3 445 press releases, organised 321 press conferences and briefings and assisted media coverage at 235 serious crime scenes and other incidents.

Information Officers at PPRB also worked closely with their counterparts in the ISD and representatives from other government departments as well as the Fight Crime Committee in planning and implementing the Fight Crime Publicity Campaign 2003-04 which had two themes, namely, 'anti-street deception' and 'anti-miscellaneous theft'.

To further publicise police-related information effectively, the PPRB continued to update the contents and improve the presentation of force publications, including the biweekly newspaper *OffBeat*, the JPC monthly newsletter and the *Police in Figures* leaflet. The *Police Review 2002* won an Honourable Mention in the 2003 Best Annual Report Awards organised by the Hong Kong Management Association.

Planning and Development

The Police Force is about to complete a large-scale building programme, spearheaded by the construction of a new Police Headquarters which is scheduled for completion in April 2004. The headquarters complex will also accommodate the force's Central District Headquarters and the Central Division Police Station. This development will be a state-of-the-art complex equipped with modern technology and designed to be operationally and energy efficient.

Other major building projects include a new Police Dog Unit and Force Search Unit complex at Sha Ling, New Territories, which was completed in October 2003. A new Police Post at Penny's Bay on Lantau Island is scheduled for completion in late 2004.

Also being constructed is a new purpose-built Regional Police Headquarters and Operational Base for the New Territories South Region at Tsuen Wan due for completion in late 2005. The building of a new Marine Police Outer Waters District and North Division Base at Ma Liu Shui is expected to be completed in early 2006.

In conjunction with the expansion of Hong Kong's road and rail infrastructure and the construction of new control points to cater for the increasing cross-boundary traffic, facilities are being provided for the policing of the areas concerned. Construction works on the relevant facilities started in June and August and are due for completion in 2005-06.

The force-wide Station Improvement Project ended in mid-year. Enhancement works have revamped the public interface areas of all police stations into comfortable, clean and user-friendly facilities. This project benefits both the staff working in the stations and the members of the public who enter them. The Automated Station Security System was introduced to enhance the security of police stations while achieving manpower savings. The system was fully implemented in December.

Transport

The Police Force's land transport fleet stood at 2 500 which included some 900 police motorcycles. In 2003, light emitting diode (LED) lights were introduced to replace emergency vehicle beacons previously used on police vehicles as the new lights enhance performance, durability and reliability while consuming less power. Furthermore, the fitting of roof-mounted searchlights to selected cross-county vehicles has also enhanced the police operational response capability during the hours of darkness.

Communications

Design and implementation of the Police Force's third generation Command and Control Communications System is well in hand for a phased roll-out starting from the end of 2004. The new system will provide an integrated environment including encrypted radio, telephone, wireless data transmission, incident handling, and support for external interfaces to computer systems in other government departments. An Automatic Vehicle Location System (AVLS) will facilitate more flexible and efficient deployment of resources.

A state-of-the-art Internet Protocol-enabled telephone system comprising voice and fax mail, interactive voice response and network management sub-systems is being implemented for the new Police Headquarters Phase III building. Integration with the structured cabling system of the new building will provide an efficient and flexible communications platform able to meet the Police Force's dynamic and ever-changing requirements.

Following the launch of TETRA (Terrestrial Trunked Radio) voice services for the Marine Police, data transmission is now available over the same radio platform. This also allows the location of police vessels to be collected through the differential global positioning system (DGPS) for real-time display of location, speed and course in the Marine Police Control Centre.

Information Technology

Since July 2003, the Police Force has been testing a pilot records management and filing system in two districts. Running on the Lotus Notes platform, the system, known as GLORIA, promises to enhance efficiency in the running of office registries and in the day-to-day management of police formations. In addition to possible cost benefits, the system has proved highly adaptable.

Ongoing developments include an investigation management and monitoring system that will greatly enhance the supervision of criminal investigations and a training work-flow system to promote the Police Force as a learning organisation.

Service Quality

During the year, the Police Force continued to focus on service improvement by developing new initiatives to promote and reinforce a quality service and customer-oriented culture within all police formations. The excellent results obtained in the last Customer Satisfaction Survey conducted by an independent agency at the end of 2002 confirmed the high standard of police services provided to the public.

To further encourage officers to live out the Force Values, the fourth round of the Living-the-Values workshop was conducted between March and October, with 'professionalism' as its theme. In addition, the Police Force participated in the

327

Customer Service Excellence Award Scheme (2002-03) organised by the Civil Service Bureau and won the Silver Award of the Best Public Image and the Gold Award of the Most Impressive Booth Presentation. Both awards involved substantial public voting.

Continuous improvement is one of the key values and the Police Force organised a number of activities during the year to advance further the standard of service quality. Two force-wide competitions, the Force Service Quality Award and the Force Slogan Competition, were introduced to pay due recognition to high achievers in the area of service quality and consolidate efforts by all members of the force in preparing to confront the challenges ahead. The competitions also served to enhance the 'serving the community' spirit within the force.

The Research and Inspections Branch assists management at all levels in the Police Force to identify and realise practical opportunities for improved quality and performance, including better resource management. A new inspection process has been devised to enhance the efficiency, economy and effectiveness of the force as a whole.

Complaints Against Police

The Complaints and Internal Investigations Branch investigates public complaints against members of the Police Force, including traffic wardens, civilian staff and members of the Hong Kong Auxiliary Police Force. Such investigations are monitored by the Independent Police Complaints Council (IPCC), an independent body comprising leading members of the community appointed by the Chief Executive of the HKSAR.

In 2003, the Complaints Against Police Office (CAPO) received 3 384 complaints, a decrease of 438 cases, or 11.5 per cent, when compared with 2002. The most prevalent complaints received in 2003 in descending order were 'Neglect of Duty', 'Offensive Language & Misconduct/Improper Manner' and 'Assault' which decreased by 10.8 per cent or 171 cases, 13.5 per cent or 146 cases and 1 per cent or six cases, respectively, compared with 2002.

During the year, the IPCC endorsed the investigation results of 3 569 complaints cases, which involved 6 262 allegations. The rate of substantiation of complaint allegations that were fully investigated was 14.5 per cent; 43.9 per cent of the allegations were classified as 'withdrawn', 'not pursuable' and 'curtailed'. Complaints of a minor or trivial nature were dealt with by way of Informal Resolution, which was adopted in handling 24.6 per cent of the complaints. A total of 32 police officers were subject to disciplinary action arising from complaints made by members of the community.

Civilian Staff

A civilian establishment of more than 5 400 in 56 different grades is deployed throughout the Police Force, representing about 16 per cent of its total manpower. Civilian staff members play a vital role by performing a wide variety of functional duties to support police operations.

Training

All newly recruited police officers undergo basic training at the Police Training School (PTS). The training periods for constable and inspector recruits are 27 weeks and 36 weeks, respectively. In 2003, a total of 541 police constables and 28 inspectors graduated from the PTS.

The Continuation and Promotion Division of the PTS provides development and promotion courses to in-service and newly promoted junior police officers. In addition, the division provides mock court training for recruits, serving junior police officers and officers of other departments. It also trains newly recruited traffic wardens and traffic officers in various traffic-related subjects.

In 2003, the PTS continued to assist the Labour Department and the Education and Manpower Bureau in running youth training programmes. The programmes are aimed at developing young people's confidence, discipline, interpersonal skills and leadership potential. During the year, a total of 911 teenagers received such training at the school.

The Training Development Bureau continues to maintain its core responsibilities of planning, designing, updating and continuously reviewing the Police Force's training programmes. The use of e-learning and an Internet-accessible Knowledge Management system are being pursued in line with an overall plan to exploit opportunities available in information technology.

The successful Learning and Development plan that encourages participation in a lifelong learning culture is to be extended, providing more resources to officers pursuing self-development courses at selected universities and other institutions.

The Higher Training Division's role within the Training Wing has been revised to meet the increasingly complex demands of the police manager's role. Higher Training now focuses on competency-based training and the developmental training needs of all officers in the Police Force, from Constable to Assistant Commissioner level with the aim of introducing or enhancing managerial and leadership skills. A number of new modules have been introduced which cover basic managerial concepts for junior officers to more in-depth seminars for senior police managers. These modules will be continually developed to assist officers to equip themselves with the skills necessary to meet both internal and external customer expectations.

The Detective Training School successfully revamped all Detective Training Courses to bring the syllabi of courses in line with the changing needs of front-line officers. The new courses focus upon equipping trainees with practical working skills through problem-solving, scenario-based skills training.

The Weapons Training Division continued to design the most updated and practical use of training methodologies involving the application of force. The new technologies in crises resolution and resistance control training introduced in 2003 enabled the practical use of police tactics and the necessity and application of different levels of force to be demonstrated realistically in given training scenarios. The levels of force that could be practised included administering verbal commands, the application of OC Foam or an extendable baton, and use of firearms. The continuation tactics training for District personnel continued during the year, and was welcomed by all participants.

The Police Driving School provides high quality driving training to officers working in different formations. In order to meet the unique occupational characteristics, apart from running basic courses the school developed a series of Operational Driving Courses in car and motorcycle training. The school also set up Regional Driving

Examination Centres in different regions to facilitate participation in the five-year driving re-test.

The Information Technology Training Centre provides high quality user training courses on various major computer systems in the Police Force as well as microcomputer training with a view to enhancing the force's performance and capability. The centre has also developed a number of Computer Based Training modules to promote e-learning and a self-learning culture for all force members. A memorandum of understanding on e-learning was signed by the Hong Kong Police Force and the Singapore Police Force in August. The two police forces will share e-learning contents, development experience and expertise as well as explore the possibility of joint development of e-learning packages.

The Police Force is also aiming to play a more active role in police training in the international arena. Following its success in chairing the Interpol's 14th Symposium for Heads of Police Colleges held at the Interpol headquarters in Lyon, France, in December 2002, where around 100 delegates from 47 countries all over the world attended, the Police Force has been invited to co-host the 15th Symposium to be held in Hong Kong in early 2005. For the first time, the Police Force was also invited to give a presentation to the Interpol General Assembly, which was held in Spain in October.

Recruitment

There were 2 414 applications for Inspectorate posts in 2003, compared with 1 822 in 2002. Of the 17 officers who were appointed as Inspectors, two were serving officers promoted from within the ranks. Recruitment at the Constable rank remained satisfactory with 400 recruits out of 5 108 applicants.

Welfare

The Personnel Services Branch provides a wide range of support services in the areas of personal and family welfare, illness, financial protection, bursaries and scholarships for children, psychological consultations, assistance with retirement, sport, recreation, catering and the allocation and maintenance of departmental quarters. During the year, the major sources of funding for most welfare activities in the Police Force were the Police Welfare Fund, the Police Children's Education Trust and the Police Education and Welfare Trust, which were established with funds from public donations.

Welfare officers conducted casework interviews and visited officers in need of welfare counselling and support. Welfare loans and grants were provided to help needy officers and their families. Resettlement courses and job placement services were provided to retiring officers. Grants were offered to encourage officers to take up job-related academic courses after work. Family Life Education Programmes and Support Groups are organised to enhance relationship and problem-solving in police families.

The Police Healthy Lifestyle Working Committee continued to promote activities in prudent financial management, and physical and mental well-being. Under the Healthy Lifestyle Initiatives, volunteerism was promoted among police and civilian officers. Hundreds of officers responded to the appeal and registered themselves and their family members as volunteers with the Police Volunteer Services Corps. The

Boat Excursion Scheme was also revamped, and proved to be a popular healthy activity for officers and their families.

The Psychological Services Group provides professional counselling services for officers. The group also launched a series of promotional and training activities under the 'CARELINKS 2003 — Mental Health in the Workplace Campaign', with the aim of enhancing mental health and mutual support among force members.

Force Housing

Some 13 000 officers of various ranks are currently residing at departmental quarters maintained by the Police Force. In addition to quarters, serving officers can also choose to join various civil service housing benefit schemes, subject to their meeting the criteria of the particular scheme. Officers who are soon to retire may apply for their future accommodation through the Civil Service Public Housing Quota.

During the year, nearly 3 000 officers moved into new purpose-built Disciplined Services Quarters which provide an improved standard of living. The number accounts for over 23 per cent of the total police quarter occupation.

Hong Kong Auxiliary Police Force

The establishment of the Hong Kong Auxiliary Police Force (HKAPF) stands at 4 500. In an internal security situation, the HKAPF discharges duties to guard strategic and sensitive installations and to man command centres, and it also acts as a reserve to give assistance during natural disasters and civil emergencies. On a day-to-day basis, the HKAPF officers supports their regular counterparts at large-scale events requiring crowd management and in certain planned operations.

Independent Police Complaints Council

The Independent Police Complaints Council (IPCC) is responsible for monitoring and reviewing the investigations of public complaints against the Police Force, which are carried out by the Complaints Against Police Office (CAPO). The IPCC is an independent body comprising members who are appointed by the Chief Executive. It has a chairman, three vice-chairmen and 14 other members. The Ombudsman or her representative serves as an *ex officio* member.

During the year, the IPCC endorsed the investigation results of 3 569 complaint cases, involving 6 262 allegations. The number of IPCC Lay Observers rose to 65 with the appointment of another nine Observers. The Lay Observers could attend CAPO interviews and site visits on a scheduled or surprise basis to ensure that investigations were conducted in a thorough and impartial manner. The IPCC also organised a number of publicity programmes, which included talks at secondary schools and broadcasting of the IPCC corporate video on public transport, with a view to promoting public awareness of the operation of the police complaints system and the role the IPCC plays in it.

Customs and Excise

The Customs and Excise Department is primarily responsible for the collection of revenue on dutiable goods and the prevention of its evasion, the suppression of narcotics trafficking and abuse of narcotic drugs, the prevention and detection of smuggling, and the protection of intellectual property rights. It has an establishment of 4 989.

The department also enforces legislation to protect consumer interests, safeguard and facilitate legitimate trade and industry, uphold Hong Kong's trading integrity and fulfil international obligations (*See also Chapter 5*).

Revenue Collection

The department is responsible for the collection of excise duties derived from dutiable commodities stipulated in the Dutiable Commodities Ordinance. These are liquors, tobacco, hydrocarbon oil and methyl alcohol. During the year, the excise duties collected amounted to $6.48 billion, of which 53.5 per cent came from hydrocarbon oil, 34.2 per cent from tobacco, 12.2 per cent from liquors and 0.1 per cent from other alcohol products, representing a decrease of 2.35 per cent over 2002.

The department also assesses the taxable values of motor vehicles under the Motor Vehicles (First Registration Tax) Ordinance for the purpose of levying first registration tax. In 2003, the department registered a total of 46 motor traders and assessed the provisional taxable value on 36 536 vehicles.

Revenue Control

Dutiable commodities in Hong Kong are stored in warehouses licensed by the department (bonded warehouses) after import or local manufacture. Removal of dutiable commodities is subject to a permit being issued by the department, and the commodities can only be released for local consumption upon payment of duty.

Before April 1, 2003, the bonded warehouses for dutiable liquor and tobacco operated under the physical supervision of the department while the oil companies' and breweries' warehouses adopted the open system whereby no physical supervision by the department was necessary. The Government proposed in 2002 to phase out the physical supervision requirement with an open system, which control is based on risk management strategies including stricter licensing criteria, random checking, documentary verification, as well as post-transaction auditing. The proposal had the general support of the trade. The necessary legislative amendments were passed by the Legislative Council in February 2003 and the open system was implemented with respect to all liquor and tobacco bonded warehouses from April 1, 2003 and to distilleries bonded warehouses from October 1, 2003 onwards. The system has introduced a more flexible business environment for the warehouse operators and reduced their compliance cost.

Revenue Protection

To strengthen its work in revenue protection, the department has installed an Immigration Control Automation System at control points since February 2003 to verify the eligibility for duty-free concessions of incoming passengers travelling on Hong Kong Identity Cards. As provided for by amendments under a Dutiable Commodities (Exempted Quantities) Notice in July 2002 (Dutiable Commodities Ordinance, 109G), an incoming passenger aged 18 or above who travels on a Hong Kong Identity Card and has spent 24 hours or longer outside Hong Kong is eligible for the concession. Officers of the department stationed at control points can use the system to check quickly whether a passenger is eligible for the concession. The system has enhanced the efficiency and effectiveness of enforcement against abuse of the duty-free concession. In 2003, 53 228 incoming passengers declared possession of excessive duty-free goods and 1 547 passengers were arrested for undeclared excessive duty-free goods, representing increases of 133.4 per cent and 162.6 per cent over 2002.

The department continued its vigorous enforcement action against illicit cigarettes. During the year, 4 540 offenders were arrested and 152.6 million sticks were seized, an increase of 74 per cent and a decrease of 16 per cent, respectively, over 2002. The decline in the quantities of illicit cigarettes seized was attributed to the department's effectiveness in combating illicit cigarette activities, causing distributors and peddlers to reduce stock.

Illicit fuel including marked oil (commonly known as 'red oil'), detreated oil and illicit motor spirit continued to be used illegally as fuel for vehicles. To tackle the problem, in addition to enforcement action taken at sea and land boundaries sustained operations were mounted to eliminate filling stations, detreating plants and storage places for such fuel. Surprise checks were also conducted to detect the use of illicit fuel in road vehicles.

Resulting from the department's vigorous enforcement action, the number of 'black spots' for illicit fuel activities continued to be restricted to around 27. The department closed 897 illicit oil filling stations, 22 detreating plants and 32 storage places. A total of 974 persons were arrested. Altogether, 2.42 million litres of various types of illicit fuel, valued at $17.93 million, were seized. The duty potential of the seized illicit fuel amounted to $9.27 million, an increase of 18.4 per cent compared with 2002.

Anti-narcotics Operations

The department continued to take vigorous enforcement action to prevent and suppress the unlawful manufacture, distribution and trafficking of dangerous drugs, and to trace, confiscate and recover proceeds accrued in illegal drug activities. It also enforces the Control of Chemicals Ordinance, which aims at preventing the diversion of chemicals for illicit manufacture of dangerous drugs and psychotropic substances.

The Customs Drug Investigation Bureau is the department's major investigative arm in combating illicit drugs. The bureau's main functions are to conduct investigations and surveillance to combat illegal manufacture, trafficking or use of drugs. In addition, the department works closely with the Police Force and various drug enforcement agencies in other jurisdictions in exchanging intelligence and arresting drug criminals.

In 2003, the department dealt with 61 drug trafficking cases, and neutralised one heroin attenuating centre and eight drug distribution centres. Officers seized 12.7 kilograms of heroin, 4.3 kilograms of herbal cannabis, 13.7 kilograms of cannabis resin, 7.3 kilograms of cocaine, 3.5 kilograms of methamphetamine ('ice'), 12.2 kilograms of ketamine, 51 141 tablets of MDMA ('ecstasy') and 29 680 tablets of other psychotropic drugs. A total of 723 persons were arrested for drug-related offences. The department participated in joint operations with international drug enforcement agencies. As a result, 1 533 kilograms of various types of drugs were seized and 27 traffickers arrested in such joint operations overseas.

Boundary Control

In 2003, vehicular traffic movements through the three control points at Lok Ma Chau, Man Kam To and Sha Tau Kok increased by 6.1 per cent to 13.18 million compared with 2002.

The Lok Ma Chau Control Point Expansion Project Phase II was completed in the third quarter of 2003. Improvement works covered the expansion of the passenger terminal, improvement of the cargo examination facilities, reprovisioning of the existing vehicle processing kiosks, and the installation of two sets of a Vehicle X-ray Inspection System. In addition, the installation of a total of 42 sets of an Automatic Vehicle Recognition System (AVRS) at the Lok Ma Chau, Man Kam To and Sha Tau Kok Control Points to expedite the processing of vehicles was completed in May. The application of the AVRS shortens the Customs clearance time of each laden goods vehicle by three seconds, on average. Together with the implementation of a series of simplified Customs clearance procedures for vehicles, the average clearance time for a laden goods vehicle has been reduced from 45 seconds to 30 seconds and that for an empty goods vehicle from 20 seconds to 16 seconds.

To facilitate the flow of cross-boundary passenger traffic, the operating hours for passenger clearance at the Lok Ma Chau Control Point have been extended from 0630-2400 hours to round-the-clock operation since January 27, 2003.

To expand Hong Kong's air services network and to enhance its transport links with the Pearl River Delta region, the first cross-boundary ferry service for transit passengers between the Hong Kong International Airport and ports in the Pearl River Delta commenced operation in September. Passengers using this service do not need to go through Customs, Immigration and Quarantine clearance in Hong Kong. A new express cargo terminal to handle air-land-sea transhipment mails and cargo will commence operation in 2004. Simplified clearance procedures will be put in place to facilitate the express cargo flow.

Anti-smuggling Operations

In 2003, the department detected 282 smuggling offences, arrested 356 persons and seized contraband worth $525 million. The total value of seizures increased by 86 per cent compared with 2002. Smuggling between Hong Kong and the Mainland remained a cause for concern. The duty gradient leading to price differences between Hong Kong and the Mainland was still the main factor underlying the problem.

Goods commonly smuggled to the Mainland included computer parts, electrical and electronic appliances, marked oil and optical discs. Container tractors, box-type lorries and private cars were commonly used for smuggling on land. Apart from being stashed among declared cargoes, contraband of small size was concealed inside toolboxes and driving compartments of vehicles. Trailer chassis were sometimes modified to provide false compartments for concealing contraband. At sea, river trade vessels, fishing vessels and motorised sampans were commonly used for smuggling. The smuggled goods were usually hidden inside fuel tanks or secret compartments in these vessels.

A rising trend observed in 2003 was the smuggling to the Mainland of container loads of high-value merchandise such as computer parts and electrical and electronic appliances. During the year, the Customs detected 12 such cases and the value of seizures amounted to $232 million.

Cigarettes and meat were the main items smuggled into Hong Kong from the Mainland. Altogether, 65.94 million sticks of illicit cigarettes originating from the Mainland were seized. There was also an emerging trend in the smuggling of light diesel oil and motor spirit into Hong Kong. During the year, officers seized 21 670 litres of light diesel oil and 432 265 litres of motor spirit in the inbound traffic.

The department's anti-smuggling capability has been strengthened by the installation of the two sets of the Vehicle X-ray Inspection System at the Lok Ma Chau Control Point in March. These inspect vehicles and container lorries by means of instant X-ray scanning. The technology applied has proved efficient in curbing smuggling. Two additional sets of a Mobile X-ray Vehicle Scanning System are also being procured. For operations at sea, four high-speed pursuit craft were procured to reinforce the Customs fleet, enhancing the department's deterrent patrol and interception power in Hong Kong waters.

Two Explosive Detector Dog teams were formed in September to increase the department's capability in the detection of explosives.

The department continued to liaise closely with the Police Force and law enforcement agencies in other jurisdictions in exchanging intelligence and this contributed considerably to the successful interdiction of smuggling activities. Enhanced cooperation with Mainland counterparts in exchanging information and mounting parallel operations at the land boundary crossing points continued to produce satisfactory results.

Information Technology

Since April, carriers have been able to submit electronically their cargo manifests for air, ocean, river and rail modes, a service that facilitates trade and heightens the efficiency of government operations.

Performance Pledges

The department published its 10th set of performance pledges, together with its vision, mission and value statements. These reinforce the department's commitment to quality service. For better public accountability, the department regularly reviews the quality of its services with the four customer liaison groups connected with the air freight, sea freight, cross-boundary transport and dutiable commodities trades. A home page on the Internet provides comprehensive and updated departmental information to the public.

Effective Measures Against SARS

The department's priority task during the SARS outbreak was to maintain an uninterrupted service to the public including customs clearance at all control points and at the same time to provide sufficient protection to its staff, especially those on front-line duties.

The preventive measures taken included providing staff with protective gear such as face masks, gloves, gowns and shoe covers. Cleaning materials were provided to individual offices according to their respective operational needs. Safe and hygienic conditions were maintained at offices and workplaces, and public facilities were sterilised.

The department also ensured there was timely dissemination of relevant and useful information to staff, including information about the disease, precautionary measures to be taken, and guidelines on the proper use of protective gear, cleaning equipment, tools and vehicles, as well as the handling of any arrested persons having SARS symptoms.

In addition, the department set up a working group headed by an Assistant Commissioner to coordinate and monitor its preventive and follow-up measures, and it also established a system for staff to report on any matter involving SARS, such as contact with a person suspected to be infected. Overall, the department's preventive measures were successful, with no members of its staff contracting the disease through their daily work.

Independent Commission Against Corruption

The Independent Commission Against Corruption (ICAC) is a dedicated anti-corruption agency independent of the Civil Service. Its Commissioner is directly accountable to the Chief Executive of the HKSAR.

During the year, the ICAC continued to keep corruption effectively in check through its three-pronged strategy of investigation, prevention and community education.

The agency has continued to win international recognition. For example, at an international anti-corruption conference held in Hong Kong in January, the Secretary General of Interpol, Mr Ronald Noble, lauded Hong Kong as 'the anti-corruption capital' of the world and the ICAC as 'the No. 1 anti-corruption agency'.

A World Bank publication on fighting corruption in East Asia launched during the year also commended Hong Kong's comprehensive approach in tackling corruption in both the public and private sectors as well as its partnership with the private sector in weeding out graft.

In April, Hong Kong joined the Anti-Corruption Action Plan for Asia-Pacific jointly launched by the Asian Development Bank (ADB) and the Organisation for Economic Cooperation and Development (OECD), signifying the Government's long-term commitment to the anti-corruption cause.

An annual survey conducted by an independent research company in 2003 showed that the ICAC continued to enjoy a high degree of public confidence as an overwhelming 99 per cent of respondents expressed support for the anti-graft body.

Corruption Situation

In 2003, the ICAC received 4 310 corruption reports (excluding election-related complaints), a slight drop of 1 per cent over the previous year. Of these, 1 541 were made against government departments, down from 1 638 in 2002. There were 2 472 and 297 reports concerning the private sector and public bodies respectively, compared with 2 403 and 330 in 2002. Pursuable reports accounted for 76 per cent of all corruption reports.

A total of 711 election-related reports were received during the year, 666 of which were pursuable. They included 564 reports relating to the District Council Election and 132 about the Village Representative Election, which came under the regulation of the Elections (Corrupt and Illegal Conduct) Ordinance for the first time.

Investigation

In 2003, the Operations Department — the ICAC's investigative arm — continued to pursue a proactive strategy in unearthing corruption cases, rendering corruption a high-risk crime. It maintained close ties with disciplined services through Operational Liaison Groups. Liaison channels were also established with government departments, regulatory bodies and key industries for making joint efforts against corruption.

Major cases detected during the year included corruption-facilitated letter of credit frauds, investment and bank frauds, contract and tendering malpractices, fraudulent insurance claims and money laundering. There were also corruption allegations involving civil servants and misconduct in public office.

The number of corruption reports remained at a high level. At year-end, the Operations Department's case-load stood at 1 896 (including 435 investigations on election-related cases). A growing number of these cases featured a more sophisticated and complex *modus operandi*. During the year, 421 persons were prosecuted and 113 cautioned in accordance with the advice of the Department of Justice.

Prevention

The Corruption Prevention Department examines the practices and procedures of government departments and public bodies to identify corruption loopholes, and recommends measures to reduce opportunities for malpractice.

During the year, the department completed 101 detailed studies into corruption prone areas such as public procurement and outsourcing, law enforcement, contract administration, licensing and registration systems, public works and management of public funding schemes.

Priority of work was given to cases investigated by the Operations Department, corrupt practices commonly found in corruption complaints as well as corruption prone areas identified through established liaison with client departments.

The department continued to provide expeditious corruption prevention advice to government departments and public bodies in the formulation of new legislation, policies or procedures. During the year, the department undertook such consultation work on 294 occasions. Government departments were more ready to initiate corruption prevention studies and seek quick assistance from the department over their new work programmes and revised systems.

To promote good governance and management in the private sector, the Advisory Services Group of the department provided free, confidential and tailor-made corruption prevention advice to private organisations on 336 occasions.

In an effort to strengthen the corruption prevention capability of public and private sector organisations, the department continued to produce Best Practice Modules to provide guidance on ways to minimise corruption opportunities in common problem areas such as procurement, contract administration, staff management, outsourcing and construction. Seminars and workshops were arranged to promote best practices among these organisations.

Community Education

The Community Relations Department is tasked to educate the public against the evils of corruption and enlist the community's support in the fight against it. The department's work objectives are achieved mainly through the use of the mass media and direct liaison with various quarters of the community.

Maintaining a clean civil service remained a top priority for the department. It joined forces with the Civil Service Bureau to assist government departments in implementing the civil service integrity management programme with a view to building up an ethical culture. During the year, the department provided corruption prevention training for about 17 300 civil servants from 38 departments.

To enhance Hong Kong's competitiveness in tourism, an ethics promotion programme for the industry was launched jointly with six related organisations, with a trade-wide conference held for practitioners and training talks conducted for around 5 000 tourist guides. In addition, a practical guide on ethical management for managers and a self-learning training package for front-line employees were also produced.

Youth education remained a priority area in the work programme of the department. Positive values were promoted among young people through the mass media, the Internet, interactive drama performance and family-based programmes and activities. In 2003, a combined youth summit and study programme entitled 'Corporate Governance for the New Generation' project was organised, attracting hundreds of tertiary students from Singapore, the Mainland, Macau and Hong Kong.

During the year, education campaigns were launched to promote clean elections for the Village Representative, Rural Committee, Heung Yee Kuk and District Council elections. Apart from conducting 44 briefing sessions to help candidates, election agents and helpers understand the provisions of the Elections (Corrupt and Illegal Conduct) Ordinance, a 24-hour election hotline was also set up to handle related enquiries. In addition, a series of 66 roving exhibitions, a poster campaign and information booklets were also launched to promote the 'Clean Elections' message.

In media publicity, the department produced a 10-part TV spot series to raise the transparency of its work. Another six-episode series to recount Hong Kong's anti-graft history through the numerous TV commercials produced since the ICAC's inception was broadcast on the infotainment channel on buses.

International Cooperation

The ICAC maintains regular operational liaison with other overseas law enforcement agencies. During the year, it received 279 visitors from law enforcement agencies and other organisations from various countries.

The ICAC and Interpol joined hands to host a three-day international anti-corruption conference, entitled 'Partnership Against Corruption', in Hong Kong in January. The conference was attended by more than 500 local, Mainland and overseas delegates from 61 jurisdictions and eight international organisations. ICAC officers also attended overseas conferences and forums including the 11th International Anti-Corruption Conference and the 3rd Global Forum on 'Fighting Corruption and Safeguarding Integrity', both held in Seoul. With Hong Kong having endorsed in April the ADB/OECD Anti-Corruption Action Plan for Asia-Pacific, the ICAC's Commissioner and the Director of Administration attended the Steering Group meeting of the Action Plan in Kuala Lumpur in December, to report on Hong Kong's anti-corruption initiatives.

Cross-boundary Liaison

Cooperation between the ICAC and the Mainland anti-corruption authorities has become increasingly important with growing social and economic ties between Hong Kong and the Mainland.

The Mutual Case Assistance Scheme established to enable the ICAC and the Mainland procuratorate authorities to assist each other in interviewing voluntary witnesses in connection with corruption investigations continued to operate efficiently. Under the scheme, ICAC investigators visited the Mainland on 25 occasions to meet witnesses willing to assist in investigations while Mainland officers visited Hong Kong for the same purpose on 47 occasions during the year.

Checks and Balances

The operation of the ICAC is subject to a stringent system of checks and balances.

Apart from judicial supervision, the commission's work is scrutinised by four advisory committees — the Advisory Committee on Corruption, the Operations Review Committee, the Corruption Prevention Advisory Committee and the Citizens Advisory Committee on Community Relations.

An independent ICAC Complaints Committee, which comprises members of the Legislative Council and other prominent citizens, monitors the handling of non-criminal complaints against the ICAC and its officers.

Government Laboratory

The Forensic Science Division of the Government Laboratory provides a wide variety of specialist scientific analytical services to the criminal justice system. It is operationally divided into two groups: the Criminalistics and Quality Management Group and the Drugs, Toxicology and Documents Group.

The latter group comprises the Controlled Drugs Sections, the Forensic Toxicology Sections and the Questioned Documents Sections. In 2003, cases involving 'party drugs' such as ketamine, amphetamine-type stimulant tablets and nimetazepam constituted a large proportion of the submissions to the Controlled Drugs Sections. Requests for ketamine analysis in urine samples submitted to the Forensic Toxicology Sections continued to rise. To cope with the demand, a rapid method capable of analysing 200 samples per day has been developed for ketamine screening and confirmation. In addition to routine handwriting and document examinations, the Questioned Documents Sections also provide consultancy and scientific testing services in respect of the Immigration Department's project to introduce smart identity cards.

The eight specialist sections of the Criminalistics and Quality Management Group carry out various types of laboratory analysis and conduct crime scene examinations. A total of 702 scenes were attended in 2003. As a result of the recognition of the usefulness of DNA profiling in crime investigation, the number of cases submitted to the three Biochemical Sciences Sections for forensic DNA analysis increased from 3 959 in 2002 to 4 083 in 2003.

The DNA Database Section regularly receives outstanding DNA profile data from the Biochemical Sciences Sections, comparing them with those in the DNA database at two levels: (a) legally obtained individuals' DNA profiles against DNA profiles obtained from exhibits in unsolved cases, and (b) between DNA profiles derived from exhibits in unsolved cases. In 2003, there were, respectively, 126 and 54 matches, providing important investigative leads for the Police Force to follow.

The Parentage Testing Section conducts DNA tests for cases relating to Certificate of Entitlement applications under the Immigration Ordinance; the Chemical Sciences Section works mainly on cases requiring chemical analysis and investigates suspicious fires, while the Physical Sciences Section plays an important role in reconstruction of serious traffic accidents. Apart from managing crime scene attendance, the Scene of Crime and Quality Management Section is also responsible for ensuring adherence to the prescribed work standard.

Immigration Department

Immigration Control

The Immigration Department plays an important role in maintaining law and order by controlling entry into the HKSAR. Through examination at control points and vetting of entry applications, undesirable persons including international criminals and terrorists are detected and denied entry. In 2003, 20 521 such travellers and 7 134 other persons not in possession of proper documentation were refused permission to land, and 2 266 applications for entry were refused.

Detection of Forged Travel Documents

Strict measures were taken to guard against the use of forged travel documents. Officers detected 3 094 forged travel documents during the year, compared with 3 549 in 2002. Frequent contacts with local, Mainland and overseas law enforcement agencies and consulates were maintained to exchange information and intelligence on the use of such documents. Special operations were mounted against forgery syndicates.

Interception of Wanted Persons

In 2003, 212 608 wanted persons were intercepted at immigration control points and other offices. These persons were suspected to be connected with trafficking in dangerous drugs and other criminal offences such as murder and robbery.

Illegal Immigration and Unlawful Employment

In 2003, 4 052 illegal immigrants were apprehended and repatriated, compared with 6 545 in 2002.

Many illegal workers were visitors who breached their conditions of stay. The Immigration Task Force conducted frequent checks at targeted locations, including construction sites, factories, restaurants and other places of employment. In 2003, 5 739 operations were conducted and 16 548 illegal workers were arrested, compared with 3 580 operations and 11 990 arrests in 2002.

Illegal workers were prosecuted and either fined or jailed before being repatriated to their places of origin. Their employers were also prosecuted. In 2003, 445 employers of illegal workers were prosecuted, compared with 383 in 2002.

Deportation and Removal

The Immigration Department processes deportation and removal orders. During the year, 7 193 persons convicted of possessing or trafficking in dangerous drugs, deception, theft, forgery and other criminal offences were considered for deportation and 582 were deported. Another 1 555 were removed from the HKSAR under removal orders, covering 30 illegal immigrants and 1 525 people who had breached their conditions of stay.

Investigation and Prosecution of Immigration Offences

During the year, 23 040 charges were laid against persons who had committed various immigration offences. These offences included remaining in the HKSAR illegally, breaching conditions of stay, making false statements or representations, and using or possessing forged travel documents.

Measures Against SARS

During the SARS outbreak, the Immigration Department worked closely with the Department of Health, the Civil Aid Service and the Auxiliary Medical Service in implementing various health measures at immigration control points to guard against the disease.

At the airport, all travellers, including arriving, departing and transit passengers, were required to complete health declaration forms and be subject to temperature screening. All staff members were also given temperature checks before entering the restricted area of the Passenger Terminal Building.

At the boundary control points, all arriving passengers, including cross-boundary drivers, were required to submit health declaration forms and be subject to temperature screening. Passengers arriving on board overseas or locally based cruise liners on destination trips, and Mainland/Macau ferries were required to submit health declaration forms. All arriving and departing passengers travelling through the two cross-boundary ferry terminals were subject to temperature checks.

In order to provide better protection for the public and immigration staff, protective front panels were installed at clearance counters of all control points, crew counters at the airport and counters of public-oriented offices to prevent transmission of SARS by respiratory droplets.

In addition to the provision of sufficient protective gear to front-line staff in case of need, work in maintaining the cleanliness of office premises was stepped up. Procedures were also drawn up for handling suspected SARS patients.

Fire Services

The Fire Services Department fights fires, protects life and property in case of fires and other calamities, provides emergency ambulance services and gives fire protection advice to the public.

The department's establishment of staff comprises 8 688 uniformed and 659 civilian members. It is one of the world's finest fire brigades, with well-trained personnel, advanced communication systems, and modern equipment and appliances.

The department responded to 37 774 fire calls, 19 918 special service calls and 526 565 ambulance calls in 2003, representing an average of 1 600 calls a day.

Fire Suppression

Of the 37 774 fire calls received in 2003, 11 were classified as major fires of No. 3 alarm. Careless handling or disposal of smoking materials was still the major cause of fires, totalling 3 160 cases in all, followed by accidents involving the preparation of foodstuffs and electrical faults, which accounted for 2 563 and 863 cases, respectively. Unwanted alarms, caused mainly by faulty automatic alarm systems or poor positioning of such systems, contributed to 64.7 per cent of the total number of fire calls.

Two fatal fires involving improper use and excessive storage of inflammable substances in industrial buildings occurred on April 25 and May 10, both in Kwai Chung. The two No. 3 alarm fires caused the deaths of four people and injuries to 14 others, including two firemen.

The powers of Fire Services personnel to investigate the cause of fires have been strengthened under the Fire Services (Amendment) Ordinance 2003 and the Fire Services (Fire Hazard Abatement) Regulation, which take effect on January 1, 2004.

Special Services

The department also provides a wide range of rescue services in incidents such as traffic accidents, people trapped in lifts or locked in rooms, gas leakages, house collapses, flooding, landslides, industrial accidents and attempts by people to jump from a height. The department handled 19 918 emergency special service calls in 2003. Among the major incidents attended was a traffic accident on July 10 in which a double-decker bus plunged 40 metres from Tuen Mun Road on to a hill slope at Ting Kau Village, killing 21 people and injuring 22 others. In another major incident, a Government Flying Service helicopter crashed on a hill slope at Pak Kung Pass, about 300 metres from Tung Chung Road, on August 26. The pilot and the crewman were killed.

Ambulance Services

The Ambulance Command handled 475 407 patients during the year, representing 1 302 patients per day. A total of 7 175 suspected or confirmed SARS cases were handled by ambulances during the outbreak of the disease.

The department is committed to developing paramedic ambulance services for the public. About 80 per cent of the ambulance fleet has been equipped and manned at paramedic level. All ambulances and paramedic motorcycles are equipped with automatic external defibrillators. A fourth Mobile Casualty Treatment Centre was acquired to enhance efficiency in handling incidents with multiple casualties.

The department has also sought to improve the survival rate of casualties and patients before their arrival at hospital. A pilot 'first-responder programme', which trained front-line firemen to provide basic life support to casualties and patients before the arrival of an ambulance crew, was introduced in September.

Communications

The Fire Services Communication Centre, manned round the clock, is responsible for mobilising all fire-fighting and ambulance resources for providing efficient and effective fire and ambulance services to the community. The centre is also responsible for receiving complaints about fire hazards and dangerous goods. It acts as an emergency coordinator for other government departments and public utilities in large-scale emergencies or major incidents.

In order to meet the projected growth of emergency calls over the next 10 years, a $445 million Third Generation Mobilising System is being developed to replace the current Second Generation Mobilising System. The cutover to the system is expected to start in August 2004, and be implemented in phases.

Fire Safety

The Community Relations Division under the Fire Safety Command is responsible for enhancing the public's knowledge of fire safety and for coordinating actions with other government departments and District Fire Safety Committees in stepping up fire prevention publicity in the community. In 2003, 1 997 fire drills at various locations and 5 055 fire safety talks and seminars were conducted by the division and local fire stations for various community sectors.

The Commercial Buildings and Premises Division enforces the Fire Safety (Commercial Premises) Ordinance with the objective of upgrading fire safety measures in respect of specified commercial buildings and prescribed commercial premises. The Director of Buildings administers a Building Safety Loan Scheme, which provides non-means tested loans to individual owners who require financial assistance in carrying out building safety (including fire safety) improvement works, either on a voluntary basis or as required by law. Owners are required to pay interest calculated in accordance with the no-gain, no-loss principle. Those facing hardship, such as the elderly or people with very low income, may apply for interest-free loans and longer repayment periods.

In order to enlist more people to assist in reporting fire hazards and disseminating fire prevention messages, the Fire Safety Ambassador Scheme has been extended to 201 organisations, including schools, public transport companies, major property management companies, government departments, homes for the elderly and hotels. A total of 11 131 people were trained as Fire Safety Ambassadors during the year.

A major fire prevention publicity programme was launched on December 7, focusing on the safe use of inflammable substances. A series of publicity activities, including broadcasting fire safety messages on television and radio, and fire station open days, was organised. A mobile publicity unit was widely used for promoting fire safety and conducting roving exhibitions at schools and public housing estates.

To improve building fire safety and heighten the public's awareness of the need to maintain fire service installations and equipment in buildings, the Fire Service Installation Task Force stepped up monitoring efforts. A total of 45 888 inspections were made. The Task Force also monitors the performance of registered fire service installation contractors, with 445 random checks carried out. Legal action was taken against 17 contractors who had contravened the Fire Service (Installation Contractors) Regulations or the Fire Service (Installations and Equipment) Regulations.

With the construction of Hong Kong Disneyland and its associated projects well under way, the Theme Park Projects Division, which is responsible for formulating fire safety requirements, maintains close liaison and meets regularly with all parties concerned to give advice. The commissioning of the KCRC's West Rail in December involved the deployment of additional manpower to the Railway Development Strategy Division to carry out acceptance tests on the new railway's fire service installations.

The Licensing and Certification Command sets fire services requirements for buildings and various types of licensed premises as well as dangerous goods stores and vehicles to ensure proper protection for the public. Some 10 008 submissions of building plans were processed during the year. Fire Services personnel conducted 173 139 fire safety inspections of all types of premises and issued 12 523 fire hazard abatement notices requiring the removal of fire hazards. These helped to ensure that fire prevention measures met the required standards and enhanced public awareness of fire safety. There were 709 prosecutions in cases of contravention of the Fire Services Ordinance, the Dangerous Goods Ordinance and the Fire Safety (Commercial Premises) Ordinance, with fines amounting to $1,605,410. Direct prosecutions for obstructing the means of escape in buildings resulted in 59 convictions, with fines totalling $280,010.

The newly enacted Fire Services (Amendment) Ordinance 2003 and its subsidiary Fire Services (Fire Hazard Abatement) Regulation enhance the regulatory framework in tackling new forms of fire hazards, such as those arising from illicit fuel activities and the improper conveyance or stowage of vehicle parts stained with fuel.

Appliances and Equipment

In 2003, the department operated 820 fire appliances and supporting vehicles fitted with up-to-date fire-fighting and rescue equipment. Fire appliances procured during the year included nine hydraulic platforms, eight major pumps, one rescue tender, one lighting tender, six light rescue units, four 37-metre turntable ladders, three hook-lift trucks, three workshop vans and one mobile casualty treatment centre. A new diving support vessel was commissioned in February to enhance the department's maritime search and rescue capability.

Training

The Fire Services Training School provides initial training courses for new recruits to the Station Officer and Fireman ranks. The training programme covers basic fire-fighting techniques, compartment fire behaviour training, operation of fire appliances and equipment, breathing apparatus, ambulance aid and physical training. Subjects covering fire protection, legislation, physics and science of combustion are included. Altogether, 154 recruits completed the initial training during the year. A total of 2 138 in-service members also attended continuation training courses.

Apart from providing basic initial training for recruits, the school also provided training courses for 497 staff of other government departments and private organisations on basic fire-fighting techniques and the use of breathing apparatus. The school also co-organised with the Labour Department and the Education and Manpower Bureau a Youth Pre-employment Training Programme and a Smart Teen Challenge Project, respectively. These programmes aim at providing discipline, leadership and fire prevention training to young people and secondary school students. During the year, a total of 102 young people and 2 026 students attended the courses.

The Ambulance Command Training School provides a 26-week basic training programme for recruit ambulance officers and ambulancemen on ambulance aid, anatomy and physiology, mountain rescue and physical training; cardiac-pulmonary resuscitation training and refresher training for the staff of homes for the elderly, schools, community organisations and other government departments; advanced ambulance aid training and automated external defibrillator training for fire personnel; and paramedic training at Emergency Medical Assistant (EMA) II level for ambulance personnel. The school trained 63 new recruits and ran 12 EMA II recertification courses and 10 advanced airway management courses for 249 ambulance personnel during the year.

In-service training was provided to 5 983 fire and 3 247 ambulance personnel, while 31 officers were selected to attend various training programmes in the United Kingdom, United States, Canada, Germany and the Mainland.

New Stations and Depots

In line with the Government's policy to provide an emergency response to all areas within minimum set times according to the category of risk, the department continued to plan and build fire stations and ambulance depots at strategic locations to cope with local development and service needs. During the year, the Lau Fau Shan Fire Station cum Ambulance Depot and the new Sha Tau Kok Fire Station were commissioned.

Public Liaison Group

The Public Liaison Group was set up to encourage public participation in monitoring and improving the delivery of emergency fire and ambulance services. Thirty members of the public from all walks of life were randomly selected from among 100 applicants to form the group's ninth-term membership during the year.

Correctional Services

The Correctional Services Department (CSD) runs a comprehensive range of services for adult and young offenders, drug addicts and offenders with psychiatric problems. The services fall broadly under two programme areas: prison management and reintegration of offenders into society.

In 2003, the CSD managed 24 correctional institutions, three halfway houses and two custodial wards in public hospitals. It also runs an extensive community-based after-care service. In all, 6 814 staff were looking after a daily average of 12 381 inmates, 148 detainees and 2 920 persons under supervision after discharge from custody.

Offenders sentenced to imprisonment are assigned to institutions according to their gender, age and security rating. The last factor takes into account, among other things, the risk they pose to the community and whether they are first-time offenders. Basically, separate institutions are provided for males and females, and for adults and young offenders. Male and female young offenders aged between 14 and 20 may be admitted to a training centre or a rehabilitation centre. A detention centre programme is available for male offenders aged between 14 and 24. Drug addicts found guilty of an offence punishable by imprisonment may be sentenced to a drug addiction treatment centre. Separate sections are available for young addicts aged between 14 and 20. Offenders requiring psychiatric treatment will be accommodated in the Siu Lam Psychiatric Centre.

Inmates are properly cared for in their daily living. The diet for inmates follows approved scales of nutritional values and has regard to health and religious requirements. All adult inmates, unless certified physically unfit by a medical officer, are required by law to work six days a week. They are assigned to different work posts according to factors such as their fitness and security ratings, personal background and balance of sentence. They receive earnings for the work done and may use their earnings to buy approved personal items twice a month. Television, newspapers and library books are available to inmates. They may send out and receive an unrestricted number of letters, receive regular visits and participate in the religious services available. Compulsory education and vocational programmes are provided for inmates aged under 21 whereas voluntary programmes are provided for adults. Voluntary organisations such as the Prisoners' Friends Association may visit inmates who are not visited by their families.

Prisoners released under the Pre-release Employment Scheme, offenders released under supervision from training centres, detention centre, rehabilitation centres and drug addiction treatment centres, and those having special needs may be accommodated in halfway houses for varying lengths of time. Thereafter, they are permitted to live at home or in other places while they continue to receive after-care supervision.

Penal Institutions

The CSD manages 12 prisons for adult males, consisting of three maximum, five medium and four minimum security institutions. Female prisoners are accommodated in three prisons. For young offenders, the department operates three prisons (one maximum and two minimum security), two male training centres, two male rehabilitation centres and two female rehabilitation centres. A training centre section for young females is provided in the Tai Tam Gap Correctional Institution, a multi-function institution for females. There is also one detention centre for young males. Two drug addiction treatment centres are also provided, one each for male and female drug addicts. The Siu Lam Psychiatric Centre is a maximum security prison which separately houses male and female prisoners of all categories (sentenced or on remand) and detainees who require psychiatric observation, treatment or assessment. Of all these institutions, five cater for remanded males and females of different age groups. Facilities in a penal institution normally include dormitories, kitchens, dining rooms, laundries, workshops, exercising and recreational areas, library and hospital. Victoria Prison, the oldest prison and in use since 1841, will be reprovisioned by the end of 2005.

Three halfway houses operated by the CSD provide group counselling sessions and other activities for inmates to assist their reintegration into society.

Vietnamese illegal immigrants who arrive in Hong Kong are now detained in Victoria Prison after an initial period of quarantine.

To cope with the perennial overcrowding problem in correctional institutions, the department has drawn up a long-term prison development plan. In order to handle the increasing number of female adult offenders, Ma Hang Prison was converted from a male prison to a female institution in October 2003.

Penal Population

In 2003, the penal population remained high and averaged 10 per cent over the certified accommodation, with prisons for adults, particularly females, being the major pressure points. The female penal population continued to rise in 2003, and the female adults sentenced to imprisonment and remanded in custody increased by 21 per cent and 31 per cent, respectively, over 2002. A record high of 3 007 was registered in October, representing an occupancy rate of 197 per cent. Despite overcrowding which stretched resources, the CSD continued to implement its correctional programmes effectively.

During the year, 22 600 adult offenders (11 992 males and 10 608 females) were sentenced to imprisonment, and 8 878 adult remands (6 577 males and 2 301 females) were received for custody. The number of young offenders sentenced to imprisonment totalled 2 046 (473 males and 1 573 females), and 824 young remands (665 males and 159 females) were received for custody. In addition, 730 young offenders (671 males and 59 females) were sentenced to detention in training centres, rehabilitation centres or the detention centre, and 1 283 offenders (1 083 males and 200 females) to drug addiction treatment centres.

Certain categories of inmates have to undergo different periods of statutory supervision. They are inmates discharged from training centres, detention centre, rehabilitation centres and drug addiction treatment centres, discharged young prisoners subject to supervision under the Criminal Procedure Ordinance, prisoners discharged under the Release under Supervision Scheme, Pre-release Employment Scheme and Post-release Supervision Scheme, as well as prisoners discharged under a conditional release order or a post-release supervision order. During the year, 2 538 offenders were discharged under supervision. They, together with those discharged in previous years and who had yet to complete their supervision period, added up to a total of 2 907 persons (2 601 males and 306 females) under the CSD's supervision at the end of 2003. During the year, 668 persons (575 males and 93 females) were recalled for breach of supervision conditions.

Pre-sentence Assessment Panel

Young persons aged between 14 and 20, who are convicted of an offence punishable by imprisonment, may be remanded in custody for a period not exceeding three weeks for assessment of their suitability for admission to a training centre, rehabilitation centre, detention centre or drug addiction treatment centre. Young male adults aged between 21 and 24 may be similarly remanded for admission to the detention centre.

The CSD runs the Pre-sentence Assessment Panel that makes recommendations to the courts on the suitability of offenders for detention in a detention centre, training centre, rehabilitation centre or drug addiction treatment centre. The panel investigates all cases referred by the courts, and prepares suitability reports for them. In 2003, 5 455 offenders were remanded for suitability reports, and the panel found 1 459 males and 293 females suitable for admission to a rehabilitation centre, a training centre or detention centre, and 1 459 males and 261 females suitable for a drug addiction treatment centre.

Young Offender Assessment Panel

The Young Offender Assessment Panel, comprising representatives from the CSD and the Social Welfare Department, makes recommendations to magistrates and judges on the most appropriate rehabilitation programmes for young male offenders aged between 14 and 24 and females aged 14 to 20. In 2003, the panel received a total of 390 referrals from judges and magistrates and 84 per cent of its recommendations were accepted.

Training Centres, Detention Centre and Rehabilitation Centres

Training centres provide correctional training for young offenders for periods ranging from a minimum of six months to a maximum of three years. These offenders attend half-day educational classes and receive half-day vocational training. They also receive character development training in the form of scouting or guiding, Hong Kong Award for Young People activities and Outward Bound training. On Sundays and public holidays, visits are made to youth centres, factories, sports centres and country parks. Activities to provide social service for the elderly, and the mentally and physically handicapped are arranged for inmates nearing discharge to better prepare them for reintegration into society. The parent-inmate centre at the Tai Tam Gap Correctional Institution helps inmates to gain family support and to develop a better family relationship. Upon release, inmates must have suitable employment, education or vocational training and are subject to a statutory period of supervision of three years.

The detention centre programme is carried out at the Sha Tsui Detention Centre for young male offenders aged between 14 and 20, and young male adults aged between 21 and 24. It emphasises strict discipline, strenuous training, hard work and a vigorous routine. After release, detainees are subject to a statutory supervision period of one year.

In operation since July 2002, the rehabilitation centres provide an additional sentencing option for the courts to deal with young offenders aged between 14 and 20, and in need of a short-term residential rehabilitation programme. The programme consists of two phases with a total period of detention ranging from three to nine months. The first phase of the programme provides two to five months' training in a correctional institution. It focuses on discipline training with the aim of helping the young offenders learn to exercise better self-control and develop a regular living pattern through half-day basic work skills training and half-day educational/ counselling programmes. During the second phase of the programme, young offenders are accommodated in an institution with a halfway house setting for a period of one to four months. They may go out for work, attend vocational training and educational courses, and participate in community service programmes. Discharged young offenders are subject to a statutory period of supervision of one year.

An Enhanced Reintegration Programme, providing full-time voluntary vocational training for male prisoners aged between 21 and 24, was introduced in September. It aims at broadening the knowledge on work skills of those prisoners with at least junior secondary education. By year-end, 10 inmates were enrolled in this programme.

Education

Inmates aged under 21 are required to attend educational classes conducted by qualified teachers. Textbooks approved by the Education and Manpower Bureau and supplementary materials compiled by the CSD are used. To match the development of inmates at different levels and ages, a wide spectrum of curricula is offered. Guidance is provided to adult inmates who participate in educational studies on a voluntary basis. Self-study packages and distance learning courses, including degree courses offered by local and overseas academic institutes, are also available.

All inmates are encouraged to take part in both local and overseas public examinations organised by the Hong Kong Examinations and Assessment Authority as well as other local and overseas authorities. Young inmates may attend formal classes up to certificate level and sit for the Hong Kong Certificate of Education Examination as school candidates. Adult inmates may sit for the examination as private candidates. Inmates may obtain accreditation by way of public examinations held by the Pitman Qualifications or the London Chamber of Commerce and Industry Examination Board.

A Prisoners' Education Trust Fund, set up with charitable donations in 1995, provides financial assistance to prisoners in educational pursuits, in the form of grants to cover course or examination fees, and expenses on reference books.

Students learn about
corporal punishment
(abolished by Hong Kong
in 1990) at the Correctional
Services Museum in
Stanley, which has a wide
range of exhibits depicting
more than 160 years of
penal history.

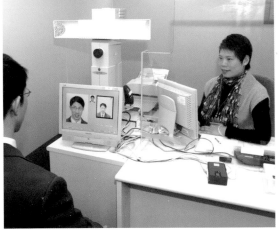

The Immigration Department began a region-wide Identity Card Replacement Exercise in August, introducing for the first time a 'smart' card which has the capacity for immigration and non-immigration applications through the innovative use of an embedded computer chip. The exercise will continue for four years, and streamlined procedures are adopted for the public in applying for the card, which is produced in a strict security environment by a specially designed card personalisation machine.

An X-ray inspection system operated by the Customs and Excise Department at the Lok Ma Chau Control Point enhances customs clearance procedures and also strengthens the department's capability in detecting smuggling. *Right:* immigration clearance kiosks at the same control point.

Vocational Training

To help young offenders to reintegrate smoothly into society as law abiding citizens, the department provides vocational training programmes for inmates aged under 21 to enable them to learn job skills, obtain accreditation and develop work habits.

The CSD offers various training courses that match with the inmates' learning ability and needs. All vocational training courses meet the demands of the business and industrial sectors in Hong Kong, so that inmates can have a better opportunity for employment upon discharge. Some courses help inmates to obtain qualifications of the City and Guilds International or the Pitman Qualifications. Other training courses are also provided to prepare inmates for trade tests or examinations conducted by the Vocational Training Council, the Construction Industry Training Authority and the Clothing Industry Training Authority.

Correctional Services Industries

The Correctional Services Industries (CSI) provide work to adult prisoners as required by law. Employment keeps all convicted inmates, except those who are physically unfit for work, purposefully and gainfully occupied, thus reducing the risk of unrest due to boredom. Through work, prisoners develop good working habits and a sense of responsibility, build up self-confidence and learn the spirit of teamwork. This will also help them acquire the basic skills for different trades and improve their reintegration after release.

In 2003, a daily average of about 7 240 prisoners engaged in industrial work. Workshops in penal institutions provide a wide range of goods and services mainly for government departments and public organisations. Examples are government furniture, staff uniforms and leather accoutrement, hospital linen, litter containers, mailboxes and traffic signs. They also make pre-cast concrete products such as paving blocks and slabs and kerbing blocks for highways and infrastructure projects. Prisoners provide laundry services for the Hospital Authority, the Department of Health and the ambulance depots. They also bind books for public libraries, undertake printing work and make file jackets and envelopes for some government departments.

Production and services provided by the CSI to government departments and public organisations amounted to the equivalent of $442 million in commercial value in 2003.

Prisoners' Welfare Services

Prisoners' Welfare Officers in the CSD look after the welfare of detainees and prisoners, and help them to deal with personal problems and difficulties arising from detention or imprisonment. Apart from conducting individual and group counselling sessions, Prisoners' Welfare Officers assist in the establishment and running of hobby groups. They also organise activities such as Pre-release Re-integration Orientation courses and meetings with family members of prisoners with the aim of helping inmates to reintegrate smoothly into society upon release and supplying them with information on community resources.

Drug Addiction Treatment

The CSD runs a compulsory treatment programme for convicted drug addicts which provides the courts with an alternative to imprisonment. Male inmates are accommodated at the Hei Ling Treatment Centre and the Lai Sun Correctional Institution, and females at the Chi Ma Wan Drug Addiction Treatment Centre. Adult and young inmates are accommodated separately. An inmate undergoes in-centre treatment from two to 12 months, followed by one year's statutory after-care supervision. The programme is based on therapeutic treatment, discipline, work programmes, outdoor physical activities and comprehensive after-care service.

Medical Services

All institutions have their own hospitals providing basic medical treatment, health and dental care to inmates. Those requiring specialist treatment are either referred to visiting consultants or to specialist clinics in public hospitals. HIV and AIDS have not caused any problem in the institutions. However, the department has established guidelines for its staff on handling such cases, as well as a programme of education and prevention.

Ante-natal and post-natal care is provided in institutions for female inmates, but babies are normally delivered in public hospitals. The Siu Lam Psychiatric Centre treats prisoners with mental health problems, and offers psychiatric consultations and assessments for inmates on referral from other institutions and the courts.

To guard against any SARS infection within the penal institutions, the department closely monitored the development of the outbreak in Hong Kong. Screening procedures were strictly followed and all newly admitted inmates had their body temperature checked as well as being placed under observation for a certain period. Medical consultations were arranged for any inmates showing suspected symptoms of SARS. The concerted efforts of front-line staff and management of the institutions proved effective as no SARS infection was recorded in any of the institutions.

Psychological Services

Psychological services are provided to inmates to enhance their psychological well-being and to correct their offending behaviour. Clinical psychologists and trained officers provide special treatment programmes for inmates such as sex offenders, violent offenders, inmates with addiction problems and young offenders. They also provide assessment reports to the courts, review boards and institutional management to assist decision-making on the management and rehabilitation of offenders.

After-care Services

After-care supervision is provided to persons discharged from training, rehabilitation, detention and drug addiction treatment centres, young prisoners and prisoners discharged under the Release Under Supervision, Pre-release Employment and Post-release Supervision Schemes, as well as prisoners discharged under a conditional release order or post-release supervision order. The aim of after-care services is to facilitate supervisees' rehabilitation and reintegration into society. Rapport among the supervisees, their families and the after-care staff is cultivated to help the supervisees to tackle obstacles in their path to rehabilitation. Throughout the statutory supervision period, regular contacts are maintained between the after-care staff and their respective supervisees to ensure that the supervisees settle well into the community and comply with the conditions of the supervision orders. Any breach of the supervision conditions may result in the supervisee being recalled for a further period of training, treatment or imprisonment.

Under the Release Under Supervision and Pre-release Employment Schemes, successful applicants may be discharged directly from prison for after-care supervision or permitted to go out to work and live in a hostel with after-care services. Both schemes aim at enabling suitable, eligible and motivated prisoners to serve their sentences in an open environment with supervision.

The Post-release Supervision Scheme provides after-care supervision for certain categories of adult prisoners to facilitate their rehabilitation and reintegration into society. Prisoners breaching the supervision conditions may be recalled to serve the balance of their unexpired supervision period. Prisoners with indeterminate sentences may, before the Long-term Prison Sentences Review Board makes recommendations as to whether their indeterminate sentences should be converted to determinate ones, be conditionally released under supervision for a specific period to test their determination and ability to lead a law-abiding life. Prisoners whose indeterminate sentences have been converted to determinate ones may also be ordered by the board to be placed under post-release supervision.

Success rates of the after-care programmes are measured by the percentage of supervisees completing supervision without reconviction and, as the case may be, remaining drug-free. In 2003, the success rates were 96 per cent for detention centre inmates; 69 per cent for male training centre inmates; 100 per cent for female training centre inmates; 92 per cent for young male prisoners; 86 per cent for young female prisoners; 64 per cent for male drug addiction treatment centre inmates; 77 per cent for female drug addiction treatment centre inmates; 100 per cent for the Release Under Supervision Scheme; 100 per cent for the Pre-release Employment Scheme; 91 per cent for the Post-release Supervision Scheme and 100 per cent for those prisoners discharged under a conditional release order or supervision after release order. There were no supervisees who completed their supervision period under the Rehabilitation Centres Ordinance in 2003. Altogether, there were 2 601 males and 306 females under after-care supervision at year-end.

Services Provided by Non-governmental Organisations

Non-governmental organisations such as the Society of Rehabilitation and Crime Prevention, Hong Kong, Buddhas' Light International Association of Hong Kong, Caritas Lok Heep Club, Hong Kong Christian Kun Sun Association, Christian Prison Pastoral Fellowship, Save the Children Hong Kong and Wu Oi Christian Centre provide services to help offenders and discharged inmates reintegrate into the community. They provide services such as case work, counselling, hostel accommodation, employment assistance, recreational activities and looking after children whose parents are in custody.

Community Support

Community acceptance and support is of paramount importance to the rehabilitation of offenders and their reintegration into society. Comprising representatives of non-governmental organisations, government departments and professionals from various sector of society, the Committee on Community Support for Rehabilitated Offenders advises the Commissioner of Correctional Services on rehabilitation programmes and publicity strategies.

A series of publicity activities has been launched since 1999 to appeal for public support for rehabilitated offenders. The major activities in 2003 included joint community activities organised with the 18 District Fight Crime Committees, an inter-institutional band contest, a musical performance highlighting scouting activities of inmates of the training centres, and the production of a VCD for the second series of the TV documentary-drama *The Road Back*. An increasing number of community groups share the view that the community as a whole will benefit from the successful transition of rehabilitated offenders, and express interest in rendering support to them after learning of their needs and the efforts they have made towards rehabilitation.

Information Technology and Management Services

Information technology is used extensively in the CSD to improve its efficiency in daily operation and record-keeping. Computer systems are used in the management of the movement of persons in custody, their daily provisions, work flow of the Correctional Services Industries, as well as staff management and administration. Continuous efforts are being made to enhance the quality and efficiency of prison management and rehabilitation services through the introduction of new technologies.

The Quality Assurance Division of the department initiates quality management to improve operations by carrying out management studies, inspections and evaluation of services as well as updating departmental practices to bring them in line with the prevailing policy and the changing needs of the community.

Staff Training

To strive for excellence in the delivery of quality custodial and rehabilitative services, the department is committed to providing staff with comprehensive training in modern correctional services and management skills. The department uses information technology to enhance efficacy both in the provision of training information and in the management of training resources. To promote self-learning, an e-learning platform has been established where staff can access various web-based training materials.

The Staff Development Theme for the year was 'Organisational Learning' which was an extension of the Corporate Culture Change Project that started in 2000 to advocate flexibility in the management of the department. As a learning organisation, the department encourages participation in the learning process at both individual and team levels. Apart from training new recruits, the Staff Training Institute (STI) offers serving staff with a wide range of job-related and professional training courses. Weekly in-service training is provided at team level at each correctional institution. The training curricula place equal emphasis on theory and practice, and include laws of the HKSAR, departmental rules and regulations, counselling, management, psychology, criminology, penology, first aid, foot drill, anti-riot drill, self-defence, tactical training, adventure training, field training, Putonghua, writing skills and information technology.

Customised training courses are scheduled from time to time to upgrade officers' professional knowledge and to develop their competencies for higher responsibilities. Some examples include the 'Diploma in Penology' jointly organised by the department and the School of Continuing Education of the Chinese University of Hong Kong and the course on 'Disciplinary Proceedings and Practices' organised by the Law Division of the School of Professional and Continuing Education of the University of Hong Kong. The 'Leadership Development Scheme' arranged by the department and the Civil Service Training and Development Institute provides selected senior officers with an opportunity to attend leadership and management training programmes organised by reputable academic institutions and training bodies in Hong Kong.

In an effort to broaden the horizon of staff and keep them abreast of contemporary correctional issues, overseas training and visits are arranged regularly. For example, the department has been sending suitable officers of middle and senior ranks to attend exchange programmes and attachment training at Correctional Services Canada since 2001.

Visiting Justices

Each penal institution is visited by Justices of the Peace fortnightly or monthly, depending on the type of institutions. The Justices of the Peace receive and investigate complaints from prisoners, inspects diets and examine living and working conditions.

Complaints

The Complaints Investigation Unit is responsible for handling and investigating complaints in relation to the department's work. All investigation reports are subject to the scrutiny of the Correctional Services Department Complaints Committee chaired by the department's Civil Secretary. This unit acquired the ISO 9001:2000 Certificate in August 2002 for its complaints handling services.

Inmates may also lodge complaints with visiting senior officers or utilise other channels for redress of grievances, such as by making complaints to visiting Justices of the Peace, The Ombudsman and Legislative Councillors.

Drug Abuse and Trafficking

The Government is committed to reducing both the supply of and the demand for illicit drugs through a wide range of action and programmes. It is also committed to reducing the prevalence and incidence of drug abuse by adopting a multi-modality approach in the provision of treatment and rehabilitation services for drug abusers and dissuading people, in particular the young, from taking or experimenting with drugs.

Overall Strategy and Coordination

In combating drug trafficking and abuse, the Government adopts a five-pronged approach which covers legislation and law enforcement, preventive education and publicity, treatment and rehabilitation, research, and international cooperation.

Effective law enforcement curtails illicit drug supply and also ensures compulsory treatment for many who are convicted of an offence and have a drug dependency. A wide range of treatment and rehabilitation services is provided to meet the changing drug abuse trends and varying needs of drug abusers from different backgrounds.

Preventive education and publicity programmes are organised on a territory-wide basis and at district level to increase public awareness of the harm caused by drug abuse and to encourage people to adopt a healthy lifestyle. Research studies are conducted on various aspects of the drug abuse problem and the evidence-based findings facilitate the planning and launching of suitable anti-drug strategies and programmes. Cooperation at the international level, through exchanges of information and experience as well as joint action against illicit trafficking, enhances the effectiveness of efforts in all these areas.

Composed of experts in various fields of social, community and other areas of anti-drug work, the Action Committee Against Narcotics (ACAN) is a non-statutory body which advises the Government on anti-drug policies and activities. Headed by a chairman, it has 17 unofficial members, three government officials including the Commissioner for Narcotics and a representative from the Department of Health and from the Hong Kong Police Force. Under a scheme of reciprocal appointment to advisory committees between the Singapore and Hong Kong Governments, the Director of Singapore's Central Narcotics Bureau is also invited to sit on the committee to exchange experience with ACAN members.

During the year, the Government continued to step up efforts to combat psychotropic substance abuse, particularly among young people, by adopting comprehensive measures to tackle the problem recommended in the Report of the Task Force on Psychotropic Substance Abuse.

Legislation and Law Enforcement

To fulfil its international obligations under the 1988 United Nations Convention against Illicit Traffic in Narcotic Drugs and Psychotropic Substances, Hong Kong enacted the Drug Trafficking (Recovery of Proceeds) Ordinance and the Organised and Serious Crimes Ordinance which provide for the tracing, freezing, confiscation and recovery of the proceeds of drug trafficking and other serious crimes.

The Drug Trafficking and Organised Crimes (Amendment) Ordinance was enacted in July 2002 to further enhance the effectiveness of Hong Kong's anti-money laundering regime through amendments to the Drug Trafficking (Recovery of Proceeds) Ordinance and the Organised and Serious Crimes Ordinance. These amendments took effect on January 1, 2003.

Since the enactment of the Drug Trafficking (Recovery of Proceeds) Ordinance and the Organised and Serious Crimes Ordinance, assets valued at $383 million have been confiscated and paid to the Government. As at year-end, assets amounting to $101 million had been ordered to be confiscated and were pending recovery and a further $1,278 million was restrained pending confiscation proceedings under these two ordinances.

The Places of Public Entertainment Ordinance (Amendment of Schedule 1) Regulation 2002, which came into operation in January 2003, brings dance parties at unlicensed premises under licensing control. To dovetail with the implementation of the new licensing arrangement, the Narcotics Division issued a revised *Code of Practice for Dance Party Organisers* to promote self-regulation by party organisers or venue providers.

The law enforcement agencies, i.e. the Police Force and the Customs and Excise Department, continued to take strong and sustained enforcement action to suppress drug trafficking and related crimes. Both agencies further enhanced cooperation and communication with external authorities and achieved fruitful results in the disruption and halting of transnational trafficking activities and arrest of criminals. Furthermore, cooperation with Guangdong Province and Macau was strengthened through the mounting of parallel law enforcement actions, sharing of intelligence, and exchange activities.

Treatment and Rehabilitation

Hong Kong adopts a multi-modality approach in providing treatment and rehabilitation services to cater for the different needs of drug abusers from varying backgrounds.

The major drug treatment and rehabilitation services include a compulsory drug treatment programme operated by the Correctional Services Department, a voluntary methadone out-patient treatment programme provided by the Department of Health, and voluntary residential programmes run by non-governmental organisations including Christian therapeutic drug treatment agencies. Medical and psychiatric treatment for psychotropic substance abusers is provided by six substance abuse clinics under the Hospital Authority. There are also five Counselling Centres for Psychotropic Substance Abusers operated by non-governmental organisations which are subvented by the Social Welfare Department.

The Drug Dependent Persons Treatment and Rehabilitation Centres (Licensing) Ordinance, which came into operation on April 1, 2002, provides for the control of treatment centres catering for voluntary residential treatment of four or more persons, through a licensing scheme administered by the Social Welfare Department. By year-end, 29 out of 44 Certificates of Exemption issued to treatment centres operating before commencement of the ordinance had been renewed and one licence issued to a new treatment centre.

During the year, good progress continued to be made in implementing the recommendations of the Second Three-year Plan on Drug Treatment and Rehabilitation Services (2000-2002). In June, a new centre providing a combined residential programme and out-patient service for young male substance abusers began operation in Tuen Mun. In October, a set of protocols for screening and assessment of poly-drug abusers was issued to front-line anti-drug workers.

A working group was formed in February to advise the Narcotics Division on the preparation of the Third Three-year Plan on Drug Treatment and Rehabilitation Services (2003-05). Following consultation with relevant government departments and drug treatment agencies, the Plan was promulgated in December. Apart from giving an overall view of the drug abuse trends and major developments in the past years, the Plan has formulated new strategies to improve the provision of drug treatment and rehabilitation services. A working group comprising representatives of relevant government departments will be set up in 2004 to follow up on its implementation.

During the year, various measures were adopted to improve the services of the methadone clinics pursuant to the recommendations of the Report on the Review of the Methadone Treatment Programme. Individual and group counselling services for methadone patients and their families were enhanced. Following a pilot project at three methadone clinics between July and September, the Department of Health decided to implement universal HIV urine testing at all methadone clinics with effect from January 2004. In October, the United Nations (UN) Regional Task Force on Drug Use and HIV Vulnerability organised a Training Workshop on Methadone Treatment for HIV Prevention in Hong Kong. The three-day workshop attracted over 100 health care workers from the South-East Asia and Pacific region.

Preventive Education and Publicity

The Narcotics Division adopted a multi-faceted approach in publicising the anti-drug message during the year. To sustain drug education for students, the division has continued to provide school programmes to students from Primary 5 to Senior Secondary levels as well as those in the Hong Kong Institute of Vocational Education (HKIVE). Further to an extension of the service to schools of the English Schools Foundation and international schools in September 2001, the provision of school drug education programmes was expanded to reach students of South Asian origin in 2003. During the year, 1 365 education programmes for 102 800 students in 217 primary schools and 123 secondary schools were delivered. Another 117 programmes were conducted for 5 500 students of the HKIVE. Apart from programmes targeting students, drug talks and seminars were also conducted for 5 400 teachers, social workers and members of uniformed youth groups.

Preparation for the commissioning of Hong Kong's first-ever exhibition centre on drug education continued, and it is scheduled to open in mid-2004. The Hong Kong Jockey Club Drug InfoCentre (DIC) comprises two levels. The ground level is home to the main exhibition areas — the Host, Agent and Environment areas. The mezzanine level houses functional areas including an interactive theatre, a classroom, an info-cafe and a library. Apart from graphic displays, the DIC makes use of multimedia exhibits to disseminate anti-drug messages to young people.

In view of the popularity of the Internet among young people, the Narcotics Division launched an interactive role-play game at its revamped website which contains more interactive elements and user-friendly navigation, as well as a special section giving anti-drug information and detailing the harmful effects of psychotropic substance abuse. The game was also produced as a CD-ROM for distribution to primary and secondary schools, tertiary institutes, anti-drug agencies, youth centres and public libraries.

Particular emphasis has been placed on the harm caused by psychotropic substance abuse. Other than in the electronic media, the year's anti-drug campaign messages were also publicised in buses, public light buses, the MTR, and the KCRC East Rail and new West Rail. Posters and anti-drug messages on the same theme were disseminated at sea and land boundary control points. In addition, a new series of the well-received TV documentary entitled *Anti-drugs Special II* was produced by Radio Television Hong Kong under the sponsorship of the Beat Drugs Fund to arouse public awareness of the harmful effects of drug abuse.

The Community Against Drugs Scheme continued to provide sponsorship of $600,000 to 20 anti-drug projects organised by District Fight Crime Committees, schools and community organisations. Anti-drug carnivals, competitions and district publicity functions were held.

The Anti-drug Volunteer Group had 230 individual and 90 corporate volunteers. Individual volunteers participated in 21 anti-drug community and publicity activities, including district carnivals, exhibitions and seminars. Corporate volunteers also helped promote the anti-drug message during the year. The Star Ferry Company Limited provided a venue for staging an anti-drug exhibition at the Kowloon Point Pier. The CLP Power Hong Kong Limited assisted by distributing anti-drug leaflets to customers as bill inserts. On December 24, volunteers stepped up publicity by staging anti-drug games at the 38th Hong Kong Products Expo held at Victoria Park.

The Anti-drug Abuse Hotline *(2366 8822)*, which was revamped in March, received more than 16 000 enquiry calls.

Drug Abuse, Statistics and Trends

Statistics on drug abuse are supplied by the Central Registry of Drug Abuse (CRDA). Information on drug abusers is collated by the Registry through a wide network of reporting agencies, including law enforcement departments, treatment and welfare agencies, hospitals and clinics. During the year, about 15 600 drug abusers were reported to the Registry. Of these, 28 per cent were newly reported cases, 14 per cent were aged under 21 and 84 per cent were male. The proportion of drug abusers in the general population remained relatively small at about 2.6 per thousand.

Heroin remained the drug most commonly abused in Hong Kong. It was abused by 75 per cent of the persons reported to the Registry. In comparison with the past, the trend is that more people who were reported to the Registry abused psychotropic substances (37 per cent) when compared with five years ago (22 per cent). The most common psychotropic substances of abuse included ketamine (14 per cent), triazolam/midazolam (11 per cent), cannabis (7 per cent), and 'ecstasy' (7 per cent). About 21 per cent of the drug abusers were reported to have abused more than one drug.

Research

Drug-related research studies are coordinated by the ACAN Subcommittee on Research. The findings of these studies provide useful reference materials to facilitate the Government's planning of anti-drug strategies and programmes. During the year, one new project was identified for implementation. Another five studies were carried forward and two studies were completed.

The computerised CRDA serves to monitor changes in trends and characteristics of the drug abuser population in Hong Kong, and produces statistics for in-depth analyses. Two half-yearly reports on characteristics of drug abusers were published.

International Action and Regional Cooperation

The Government participates in international forums against drug abuse, drug trafficking and money laundering. Apart from fulfilling its obligations under the three major UN conventions concerning narcotic drugs and psychotropic substances, the Government also maintains close links with the UN and the World Health Organisation, the International Criminal Police Organisation (Interpol), the World Customs Organisation and other governments, so as to ensure Hong Kong's anti-drug and anti-money laundering work on various fronts remains in step with current international standards and requirements.

In April, representatives from the Narcotics Division attended the 46th session of the UN Commission on Narcotics Drugs, held in Vienna, as members of the delegation of China. The meeting helped keep Hong Kong abreast of the world drug abuse situation, as well as trends in illicit drug trafficking and supply.

In response to the big increase in traffic and passenger flows between the Mainland and Hong Kong in recent years, the Narcotics Division has developed close ties with the Bureau of Narcotics Control of the Ministry of Public Security in order to align anti-drug policies and strategies. Furthermore, the Police Force and the Customs and Excise Department have also established cooperative mechanisms with their Mainland counterparts. The scope of cooperation includes exchange of information and intelligence, assistance in investigation, and mounting of joint operations as well as experience-sharing seminars which are conducted from time to time.

The Guangdong Narcotics Control Commission hosted the second Guangdong, Hong Kong and Macau Tripartite Conference on Policy to Tackle Drug Abuse and Trafficking in Zhongshan in February. The conference was attended by more than 120 anti-drug officials and professionals who had useful exchanges on the latest drug abuse and trafficking trends, and on strategies to tackle the problem.

On the anti-money laundering front, Hong Kong is a member of the Financial Action Task Force on Money Laundering (FATF) as well as a founding member of the Asia/Pacific Group on Money Laundering (APG). Over the years, Hong Kong has put in place effective legal and financial systems to tackle money laundering, and has implemented most of the FATF's 1996 Forty Recommendations — the international standards and practices in combating money laundering designed for universal application — either by legislation or through guidelines issued by the financial regulators. Apart from being its president in 2001-02, Hong Kong also served from 2000 to 2003 as a member of FATF's Steering Group, an advisory body which sets the direction and priority of the work of the Task Force.

Hong Kong contributes to all the important activities of the FATF. It participated in the work of the Working Group on the Review of the Forty Recommendations which culminated in the adoption of the revised set of Forty Recommendations by the FATF at its Berlin Plenary in June. The revised set forms the new international benchmark against which efforts by jurisdictions world-wide in the areas of anti-money laundering and countering financing of terrorism are assessed. Preparatory work has begun on implementing the revised Forty Recommendations in Hong Kong.

Hong Kong took part in the work of the FATF's Working Group on Terrorist Financing (WGTF) and the Working Group on International Financial Institutions (WGIFI). The work of the WGTF led to the issue in 2003 of various Interpretative Notes and Best Practice Papers on Special Recommendations concerning freezing and confiscating terrorist assets, alternative remittance, and wire transfer. Besides this, Hong Kong, through active involvement in the work of the WGIFI, assisted in the development of a new common assessment methodology for anti-money laundering and countering financing of terrorism for use by the FATF and the International Monetary Fund/World Bank.

In the context of the Non-Cooperative Countries and Territories (NCCT) exercises, Hong Kong has acted as the principal contact in the NCCT review exercise of Indonesia since 2000, and was part of the FATF delegation to the Philippines in March 2003. In both cases, the FATF succeeded in convincing the two jurisdictions to enhance their anti-money laundering regimes.

In September, Hong Kong was selected as a member of the APG's newly formed Steering Group, and it took part in the APG's mutual evaluation of the Philippines in November. Mutual evaluations are the primary means by which the APG monitors the progress made by members in implementing the FATF Forty Recommendations. The mutual evaluation process is designed to give due recognition where standard benchmarks are met, and to identify weaknesses and make appropriate recommendations.

Hong Kong has also joined the newly formed APG Typologies Working Group. The Working Group is to undertake a series of coordinated and intensive examinations of measures to counter money laundering and terrorist financing methods or trends. It will also develop and support a network of APG experts on key typological issues and act as an advisory body to provide practical assistance in planning and running typologies workshops.

To combat transnational crimes effectively, Hong Kong continued to support mutual legal assistance between jurisdictions. By year-end, it had entered into 15 agreements and signed 13 bilateral agreements with other jurisdictions on surrender of fugitive offenders.

In sharing experience and expertise, anti-drug personnel took part in various international meetings, seminars, and workshops concerned with anti-drug policies, law enforcement, treatment and rehabilitation, and preventive education.

Beat Drugs Fund

To promote community efforts to beat drugs, the Government established a Beat Drugs Fund in 1996 with a capital outlay of $350 million. During the year, a total of $5.52 million was allocated to 16 projects. Apart from education and publicity projects, treatment and rehabilitation and research works were also sponsored. For example, a substance abuse clinic was allotted funds to provide professionally led vocational assessment and counselling services to high-risk youths and young substance abusers through outreaching programmes. Another community organisation was funded to train up high-risk youths to serve as peer instructors in outreaching anti drug activities.

Civil Aid Service

The Civil Aid Service (CAS) is a government auxiliary emergency service established under the Civil Aid Service Ordinance. It has an establishment of 3 634 adult volunteers, 3 232 cadets and 115 civil servants.

The primary duty of the CAS is to provide civil support services during emergencies. Members of the volunteer service are trained to perform emergency duties during typhoons, flooding and landslips; to search for and rescue people in distress in the mountains; to help evacuate or rescue victims trapped under collapsed buildings or buried in landslips; and to combat vegetation fires and also oil pollution at sea.

In 2003, CAS members were moblised twice during typhoons, once for a flood rescue operation, 58 times for mountain search and rescue duties, and 47 times for vegetation fire-fighting operations. At the peak of the SARS outbreak, between March and June, the CAS was mobilised to man the medical surveillance posts at all land control points; to assist the Health, Welfare and Food Bureau in managing the isolation centres; to distribute daily necessities to residents under home confinement at the Amoy Gardens housing estate; and to escort suspected SARS contacts to the isolation centres.

The CAS continued to deploy more than 200 members for vegetation fire-fighting and hiking trail/country park patrol duties on Sundays and public holidays during the dry season periods (January to April and October to December). In other duties, such as providing assistance in crowd management, the CAS assigned members to 233 public events and also deployed 35 members daily at the Lo Wu Control Point.

During the year, the CAS continued to provide safety and skills training to other government departments, non-governmental organisations and organised groups. The training included 10 talks on mountain safety, and 24 courses covering basic mountain search and rescue work, safe movements on slopes and at heights, and crowd management. In support of the Pre-employment Training Programme and the

Smart Teen Challenge Camp Scheme, the CAS organised under these two programmes, respectively, a disciplinary module training course for 35 school leavers and five training camps for 450 secondary students.

The CAS endeavours to develop leadership potential and cultivate civic awareness among youngsters by recruiting persons in the 12 to 17 age group for the Cadet Corps. Apart from participating in recreational activities, cadets are trained in a wide variety of disciplines and skills including foot drill, basic emergency rescue, mechanical and electrical knowledge, printing and binding, fibreglass moulding, crowd management, rock climbing and expeditions. Cadets aged over 14 are also encouraged to participate in crowd management duties at major community events and to carry out hiking trail/country park patrol duties.

Government Flying Service

The Government Flying Service (GFS) is a disciplined service department. It provides the community of Hong Kong with a broad range of flying services, including round-the-clock search and rescue coverage and casualty and medical evacuation, fire fighting, and support for the law enforcement agencies and other government departments.

To perform these tasks, the GFS has an establishment of 178 disciplined and 60 civilian personnel and operates a mixed aircraft fleet of two Jetstream J-41 aeroplanes and seven helicopters — three Eurocopter AS332 L2s (Super Pumas) and four Eurocopter EC155B1s (Dauphines).

In 2003, the GFS flew a total of 6 956 hours and assisted in 377 search and rescue operations and transported 2 003 patients to hospital by helicopter. The auxiliary 'flying doctors' and 'flying nurses' flew a total of 530 hours in 713 operations. The GFS also flew 10 462 government officers and official visitors in the course of their duties or programmes.

During the year, the GFS enhanced its emergency air medical service by introducing the 'Helicopter Roadside Rescue' in which helicopters will land on roads, close to the scene of serious traffic accidents. The on-board medical team will prepare casualties for direct transfer to hospital.

The GFS maintained its high standard of emergency flying service, such as search and rescue and air ambulance service, to the community during the SARS outbreak. In particular, its helicopters transferred 10 suspected SARS patients from clinics on outlying islands to hospital. The GFS also assisted the Federation of Hong Kong Film Workers in shooting a short film which aimed at encouraging Hong Kong people at a difficult time.

Home Pages

Security Bureau: http://www.gov.hk/sb (links to Disciplined Services)
Independent Commission Against Corruption: http://www.icac.org.hk

CHAPTER 17

Communications, the Media and Information Technology

Hong Kong is a leading communications centre. It has:

— *over 3.8 million fixed telephone lines*

— *7.2 million mobile phone subscribers (106 per cent of the population)*

Hong Kong is an early adopter and mature user of information technology:

— *68 per cent of households have installed personal computers*

— *60 per cent of households are connected to the Internet*

— *broadband coverage reaches virtually all commercial buildings and households*

— *over 10 million e-payment smart cards are in circulation*

— *90 per cent of public services which are amenable to the electronic mode of delivery are provided with an e-option*

— *70 per cent of Internet users have used E-government services*

EXCELLENT communications have been an essential element in Hong Kong's development as an international business and financial centre. The HKSAR has one of the most sophisticated telecommunications markets in the world, and its people are kept well informed by a vigorous media.

The HKSAR already has a fully liberalised telecommunications market. In 2003, legislation was enacted to regulate merger and requisition authorities in the telecommunications market. The Government also started a review of the policy and regulatory regime of the Type II interconnection arrangement among operators' fixed networks to effect the last mile coverage to reach customers' premises. The review aims at, among other things, encouraging investment in the telecommunications network, thereby furthering the goal of developing Hong Kong into a leading digital city.

In broadcasting, the Government has liberalised the television market. The new services have brought in many more television programme channels. The Government is also set to introduce digital terrestrial broadcasting in Hong Kong and is reviewing the broadcasting regulatory regime to facilitate technological convergence. A vibrant television market will not only widen viewers' choice, but also enhance Hong Kong's position as a regional broadcasting hub.

The Government is building up a major population-wide information infrastructure for the further development of E-government and e-commerce through the issue of smart identity cards starting in 2003. The card has a number of different functions and the public can opt to embed a digital certificate in it.

The Mass Media

Hong Kong's mass media at the end of 2003 included 52 daily newspapers, a number of electronic newspapers, 864 periodicals, two free-to-air commercial television companies, five subscription television licensees, 12 non-domestic television programme licensees, one government radio-television station and two commercial radio stations.

The availability of the latest telecommunications technology and keen interest in Hong Kong's affairs have attracted many international news agencies, newspapers with international readership and overseas broadcasting corporations to establish regional headquarters or representative offices here. The successful regional publications produced in Hong Kong underline its important position as a financial, industrial, trading and communications centre.

The Press

The Hong Kong press registered at year-end included 28 Chinese-language dailies, 11 English-language dailies (one of them in Braille and one an Internet edition), eight bilingual dailies and five in other languages. Of the Chinese-language dailies, 20 cover mainly local and overseas general news; five specialise in finance; and the rest cover horse racing. The larger papers include overseas Chinese communities in their distribution networks, and some have editions printed outside Hong Kong, in particular in the United States, Canada, the United Kingdom and Australia.

One of the English dailies publishes a daily Braille edition, in conjunction with the Hong Kong Society for the Blind, and also an Internet edition. Three Chinese dailies and four bilingual dailies are published on the Internet. Hong Kong is the base for a number of regional publications such as the *Far Eastern Economic Review* and business and trade magazines. The *Financial Times, Asian Wall Street Journal, USA Today, International Herald Tribune* and *Nihon Keizai Shimbun* are printed here.

Several organisations represent and cater for people working in the news media in Hong Kong. The Newspaper Society of Hong Kong represents Chinese and English newspaper proprietors. It is empowered to act in matters that affect the interests of its members. The Hong Kong Journalists Association is the biggest industry-wide union of journalists in the HKSAR and one of the most active. Formed in 1968, it has around 600 members and promotes the right to freedom of expression, and focuses its attention on a range of press freedom and ethics concerns as well as on professional training. Among media organisations formed more recently are the Hong Kong News Executives' Association, the Hong Kong Federation of Journalists, and the Hong Kong Press Photographers Association. The long-established Foreign Correspondents' Club offers its members social facilities and a range of professional activities, including news conferences, briefings and films.

During the year, the Mass Communication Training Board of the Vocational Training Council continued to organise upgrading training for people working in the media, advertising and public relations sectors. An allocation of $290,000 from the council enabled the board to arrange various courses, talks and seminars with professional bodies such as the Hong Kong News Executives' Association, the Hong Kong Journalists Association, the Newspaper Society of Hong Kong, the Hong Kong Advertisers Association, the Association of Accredited Advertising Agents of Hong Kong and the Hong Kong Public Relations Professionals' Association. Popular activities included a management course for managerial or supervisory level staff of media organisations, a knowledge enhancement programme for journalists entitled 'China Today', and a 'Marketing, Advertising and PR Symposium' for advertising executives and public relations professionals.

Information Policy

The Secretary for Home Affairs has overall responsibility for policy formulation on information and related matters while the Director of Information Services advises the Government on the presentation of its policies, and on public relations matters generally, within Hong Kong and overseas. The main aims are to ensure an open exchange of information in the community and to keep the media fully informed of the Government's plans, policies and activities, and to promote Hong Kong's image abroad.

Information Services Department

The Information Services Department (ISD) serves as the Government's public relations consultant, news agency, publisher and advertising agent. It provides the link between the Administration and the media and, through the latter, enhances public understanding of government policies, decisions and activities.

The department is organised into five divisions: Local Public Relations, Publicity, Overseas Public Relations, Visits and Promotions Outside Hong Kong, and Administration. At year-end, it had a staff of 509, of whom 317 were Information Grade officers. A significant number of these information officers — 187 — operated outside ISD headquarters to provide information, publicity and public relations services to policy bureaux and their departments.

The ISD has been implementing progressively an information system to improve the quality of its services through computer links. It issues press releases to news organisations through the computerised Government News Information System and to the public through the Government Information Centre (GIC) (*http://www.gov.hk*), the Government's Internet home page. The GIC also provides links to more than 150 home pages of government agencies and related organisations. The Digital Photo System allows news organisations to search online and download government photographs round-the-clock.

All major government press conferences and briefings — in particular those given by the Chief Executive, the Chief Secretary for Administration and the Financial Secretary — are webcast live on the Internet, and the proceedings kept for reference in a video archive that is accessible through the GIC. Major events such as the annual Policy Address by the Chief Executive and the Budget Speech by the Financial Secretary are also webcast live, and can be heard in Chinese or English. Dissemination of government news is strengthened by way of a government electronic bulletin (*http://www.news.gov.hk*).

Local Public Relations Division

The division oversees the work of Information Grade officers seconded to various government bureaux and departments. It identifies and monitors controversies and advises these officers in helping their client bureaux and departments to formulate and develop public relations strategies. It also coordinates the officers' work regarding complex issues to ensure consistency. It has responsibility for the overall management of Information Grade officers in the units and ensures effective deployment and utilisation of staff resources.

While some Information Grade officers serve as Press Secretaries to Directors of Bureaux, most are seconded to 36 information units operating in government bureaux and departments. These units work closely with ISD headquarters on information, public relations and publicity aspects concerning the work of their bureaux or departments. They play a major role in maintaining the flow of information and helping to improve relations with the public.

The News Subdivision maintains direct contact with the media on a 24-hour basis. It disseminates government information to 60 newspapers, news agencies, television and radio stations, and other organisations. The subdivision processes press releases in Chinese and English and dispatches them to media organisations through a computerised broadcast system. These press releases are automatically uploaded to the GIC within a few minutes to give the public direct access. News photographs are issued to media organisations through the online Digital Photo System. The subdivision operates a 24-hour press enquiry service. During typhoons, severe rainstorms or any other emergency, extra teams of officers working in shifts operate a Combined Information Centre to disseminate the latest information on the situation to the media and the public.

The Media Research Subdivision keeps the Government fully informed of public opinion as expressed in the news media. It produces daily reports summarising news and editorial comments in the Chinese and English press as well as on radio and television. It also produces special reports on subjects of interest to the Government.

Publicity Division

The Publicity Division is responsible for publicity campaigns, government publications and advertising, and much of the Government's creative design and photographic work. The larger campaigns conducted or supported by the division during the year covered a wide range of subjects: from Brand Hong Kong, Fire Safety, Fight Crime, Anti-drug, Road Safety and New ID Card to Prevention of SARS and Dengue Fever, Voter Registration and District Council Election.

The division handles about 5 000 separate titles and produces a wide variety of government publications, including the Hong Kong Annual Report and its Internet version. A large number of free publications such as booklets, leaflets, fact sheets, brochures, posters and government forms are distributed by the division each year. Associated with this output, the division in 2003 sold some 715 220 copies of books and miscellaneous printed items through its sales outlet and online bookstore. The online 'Government Bookstore', developed under the Electronic Service Delivery Scheme, became operational in November 2001. Photographs are also sold by the division. Turnover from all sales amounted to $17.2 million in 2003.

Overseas Public Relations Division

The division advises on and helps develop and implement the Government's overseas public relations and communications strategy. It works closely with the Government's Economic and Trade Offices (ETOs) to monitor and promote Hong Kong's image overseas, and runs a programme under which journalists are invited to visit Hong Kong to gain a better understanding of the SAR. The division provides services to 95 locally based foreign media organisations and assists visiting journalists seeking information or interviews. It also coordinates the production of promotional material on Hong Kong for distribution world-wide.

The division is connected to the ETOs and the HKSAR Government Office in Beijing through a video conferencing system. It arranges for senior government officials to give briefings on major policy initiatives and issues of current interest to the heads of these offices and their interlocutors such as think tank members, analysts, academics and professionals.

The Editorial Production team drafts speeches for senior government officials, in particular the Chief Executive, the Chief Secretary for Administration and the Financial Secretary. It also provides English and Chinese writing and editing services for government offices for material ranging from feature articles and letters to the editor to advertising copy and TV/radio scripts.

The Brand Management Unit is responsible for Brand Hong Kong, the visual identity of the HKSAR. The brand provides a platform for promoting Hong Kong as Asia's world city. This is done through activities organised in conjunction with government departments and the private sector for international audiences overseas and in Hong Kong. The programme serves to showcase Hong Kong's assets as a world-class city and its attractions for visitors and the business community.

Visits and Promotions Outside Hong Kong Division

The Visits and Promotions Outside Hong Kong Division promotes a favourable image of Hong Kong abroad through the efforts of three subdivisions: Incoming Visits Subdivision, International Visits and Conferences Subdivision and International Promotions Subdivision.

The Incoming Visits Subdivision runs the department's sponsored VIP visitors programme, which targets opinion-formers and decision-makers for visits as guests of the Government, with a view to enhancing their understanding of Hong Kong. The subdivision also arranges visit programmes for other, non-sponsored VIPs coming to Hong Kong on private visits.

The International Visits and Conferences Subdivision runs an Overseas Speakers Programme with the aim of reinforcing foreign investors' confidence in Hong Kong and promoting Hong Kong as Asia's world city. Arrangements are made for senior government officials and prominent local personalities to address targeted audiences abroad. The subdivision also assists bureaux and departments in identifying suitable international conferences that could be hosted in Hong Kong.

The International Promotions Subdivision organises major promotional activities outside Hong Kong, covering principal cities in target countries. The promotions employ a multi-faceted approach comprising high-level business conferences, keynote addresses, political calls, tourism promotions as well as social, networking and cultural events.

Publicity to Combat SARS

During the SARS outbreak, the ISD played a key role in the Government's campaign to raise the public's awareness of the disease and how to guard against infection.

The Publicity Division produced a wide range of multimedia materials which included leaflets, posters, signage, and radio and TV Announcements in the Public Interest (APIs). Advertisements were placed in newspapers and health messages were displayed on public transport and at outdoors areas frequented by the public.

Altogether, 21.5 million leaflets were published in a total of nine languages (including Chinese and English) to ensure the anti-SARS advice reached all sectors of the community. The seven foreign languages were Filipino, Indonesian, Japanese, Nepali, Sinhalese, Thai and Urdu. The radio and TV announcements were also broadcast in different languages by arrangement with the consuls general or honorary consul of the countries concerned.

In addition, leaflets giving information on SARS were provided to visitors on arrival at the airport. These leaflets were published in Filipino, Hindi, Indonesian, Japanese, Korean, Malay and Thai for visitors from Asia and in Dutch, French, German and Italian for visitors from Europe.

By the end of March, six TV and five radio APIs had been given saturation airtime to convey SARS-related messages. During the course of the outbreak, 17 TV APIs and 20 radio APIs were broadcast over 12 000 minutes of TV airtime and 16 000 minutes of radio airtime. Altogether, 158 000 posters were produced, and these were displayed at prominent locations throughout Hong Kong.

The Internet proved a direct and effective means to disseminate SARS-related information to the public. A dedicated website launched in mid-March contained all press releases, updates and public health information released during the outbreak. Press releases and updates for public viewing were carried on the Government's home page and its dedicated news website.

In addition, the department produced a bilingual daily *SARS Bulletin* between April and June to convey key messages in a consistent and coordinated manner. The bulletin was sent electronically to chambers of commerce, consulates, business organisations, the tourism sector, and the transport and logistics sector.

The bulletin provided a ready source of factual information to update interlocutors, local and overseas stakeholders and overseas contacts and media on measures being taken in Hong Kong to contain the spread of the disease and, later, to relaunch Hong Kong economically.

Promoting Hong Kong Overseas

Europe

The Chief Executive, Mr Tung Chee Hwa, visited London and Paris in November to renew ties with political and business leaders there and to brief them on Hong Kong's latest economic, political and social developments.

In London, Mr Tung met the Prime Minister, Mr Tony Blair, and stressed Hong Kong's importance as a business hub, underlining the significance of Hong Kong as the leading platform for British companies wanting to enter the enormous and fast-growing Mainland market. The Chief Executive delivered a keynote speech at the Hong Kong Trade Development Council (HKTDC) Annual Dinner and officiated at the finale of the *Hong Kong — Live It, Love It!* promotion organised by the Hong Kong Tourism Board (HKTB). He also attended a concert presented by the Hong Kong Chinese Orchestra at the Natural History Museum.

In France, Mr Tung had discussions with President Jacques Chirac in an hour-long meeting at the Elysee Palace in Paris, and held separate meetings with the Minister of Economy, Finance and Industry, Mr Francis Mer; senior members of the Government, and business leaders. He also visited the *Confucius at the Dawn of Chinese Humanism* exhibition at the Guimet National Museum of Asian Art.

Also visiting Europe during the year were the Secretary for Economic Development and Labour, Mr Stephen Ip, the Secretary for Financial Services and the Treasury, Mr Frederick Ma, the Secretary for the Civil Service, Mr Joseph Wong, the Secretary for Home Affairs, Dr Patrick Ho, and Mr Henry Tang, then Secretary for Commerce, Industry and Technology.

Mr Ma visited London, Frankfurt and Zurich in July as part of the Economic Relaunch Campaign to promote Hong Kong post-SARS. Mr Ip took the relaunch message to London, Denmark and the Netherlands in September in the course of a visit aimed at promoting Hong Kong's logistics and maritime services as well as its position as the premier hub port of Asia.

Mr Wong visited Brussels in Belgium and Salzburg in Austria in June, his visit coming after Hong Kong had successfully contained the SARS outbreak and been removed from the World Health Organisation's (WHO) list of areas with recent local transmission of the disease. He also attended the three-day programme of the Salzburg Seminar, a prestigious international educational centre.

As Secretary for Commerce, Industry and Technology, Mr Tang visited Brussels in January, having useful exchanges on further cooperation with a number of Belgian Government ministers, and representatives of European institutions. In March, he led a business delegation of information and communications technology executives from Hong Kong on a visit to Ireland, Germany and Finland.

Dr Ho visited London in February to exchange views on heritage preservation with policy-makers and expert advisers on the subject. He inspected a number of heritage sites, and hosted a pre-concert reception for the Hong Kong Philharmonic Orchestra's European debut at the Barbican Hall.

North America

The Chief Secretary for Administration, Mr Donald Tsang, visited the United States in September to promote Hong Kong's role as an international business hub and the ideal strategic partner for accessing the Mainland market.

In Washington DC, Mr Tsang met the Secretary of State, Mr Colin Powell, to discuss the implementation of the 'one country, two systems' principle, developments on Article 23 of the Basic Law, measures to counter any future outbreak of SARS and Hong Kong's cooperation in the global fight against terrorism. In New York and San Francisco, Mr Tsang delivered keynote speeches at business lunches and launched the *Hong Kong — Live it, Love it!* promotion. He also met members of the think tank communities and briefed editors of major media organisations.

The Secretary for Constitutional Affairs, Mr Stephen Lam, visited Boston in April to speak at the *Harvard China Review's* sixth annual conference on 'Transition: Exploring China's Path Forward'.

The Secretary for Health, Welfare and Food, Dr Yeoh Eng-kiong, attended the 2003 Leadership Summit and the 33rd International Hospital Congress in San Francisco in August. During his visit, he spoke at a business luncheon, on 'Hong Kong: Ensuring a Healthy Climate for Business'. Dr Yeoh also met the US Secretary of Health and Human Services, Mr Tommy Thompson, and the Director of the Centres for Disease Control and Prevention, Dr Julie Gerberding.

During the year, the New York HKETO continued to publicise Hong Kong at the various dragon boat festivals held in New York, Atlanta and Boston as well as at the Canoe 2003 World Championship held at Lake Lanier, Georgia. The Washington HKETO also organised a number of events to promote Hong Kong, including the eighth annual *Made in Hong Kong* film festival co-sponsored by the Smithsonian Institution's Freer Gallery of Art.

In Canada, messages on Hong Kong's Economic Relaunch Campaign and the Mainland/Hong Kong Closer Economic Partnership Arrangement (CEPA) formed the main thrust of the Toronto HKETO's promotions across the country which, like Hong Kong, was seriously affected by SARS.

In recognition of the selfless medical and health care workers in Hong Kong and Canada involved in the fight against SARS, the office supported a nation-wide signature campaign organised by the alumni associations of the University of Hong Kong, the Chinese University of Hong Kong, the Hong Kong Polytechnic University, and the Hong Kong Baptist University in Vancouver and Toronto, with the backing of the HKTB, the HKTDC, the Chinese Cultural Centre of Greater Toronto and the Community Coalition Concerned About SARS in Toronto.

The Chinese media in Toronto, Vancouver and Montreal also supported the two-week signature campaign by helping spread the message throughout the community. The campaign won the support of the Ontario Health Ministry, the Health Ministry of British Columbia and hundreds of major business corporations, chambers of commerce and trade associations, resulting in over 11 000 signatures being collected in support of the health care workers.

A Hong Kong Film Festival, entitled 'Gems from Asia's Hollywood — A Retrospect of John Woo' was launched in Toronto in early June as the first promotional event to relaunch Hong Kong in Canada after the SARS outbreak. Featuring a selection of eight of the best earlier works of John Woo, the series symbolised the 'Hong Kong Spirit' in overcoming adversity. The film festival was also held in Calgary and Vancouver.

The Toronto HKETO launched its first ever large-scale promotional event 'Hong Kong and Quebec City — Friendship and Partnership' in Quebec City in August to inform the business community about Hong Kong's business opportunities under the CEPA framework. The popular promotion was extended to Montreal in October.

The Secretary for Justice, Ms Elsie Leung, paid her first official visit to Canada in November to enhance ties between Hong Kong and Canada. Her six-day visit covered Ottawa, Toronto and Vancouver where she met government officials, think tank members, legal professionals, academics and local Chinese business and community leaders. The visit proved useful in updating Canadians on the successful implementation of the 'one country, two systems' principle, the rule of law and constitutional development in Hong Kong as well as the business opportunities created by CEPA.

North Asia

The Chief Secretary for Administration visited Seoul in October to promote Hong Kong's role as an international business and financial hub and a strategic partner for accessing the Mainland market. During his visit, he called on the Deputy Prime Minister and Minister of Finance and Economy, Mr Kim Jin-pyo, and delivered a keynote speech at a business luncheon organised by the HKTDC. Besides briefing business and finance leaders, he officiated at the opening of the *Hong Kong — Live It! Love It!* tourism promotion and the opening ceremony of a Hong Kong Film Festival.

Mr Henry Tang, now Financial Secretary, addressed the first investment environment seminar jointly organised by the HKSAR Government and the Guangdong authorities in Tokyo in October, focusing on the opportunities under CEPA for Hong Kong and Japanese companies. He also called on the Minister of State in charge of Financial Services, Economic and Fiscal Policy, Mr Heizo Takenaka, and the Governor of the Bank of Japan, Mr Toshihiko Fukui.

The Secretary for Economic Development and Labour led a delegation of leading representatives of the shipping industry to Tokyo and Imabari in September to promote Hong Kong's maritime industry and the Hong Kong Shipping Register. The new Secretary for Commerce, Industry and Technology, Mr John Tsang, visited Seoul in October as head of the HKSAR delegation in the investment environment seminar there jointly organised by the HKSAR and Guangdong Governments. The Secretary for Home Affairs visited Tokyo in November to launch a 'Hong Kong Week' campaign, an economic relaunch project.

South-East Asia

The Chief Executive attended the 11th Asia Pacific Economic Cooperation (APEC) Economic Leaders Meeting in Bangkok, Thailand, on October 20-21 at which the leaders reaffirmed their strong commitment to finalising the current round of global trade negotiations known as the Doha Development Agenda. While in Bangkok, Mr Tung had a meeting with President Hu Jiantao. He also held bilateral meetings with the Prime Minister of Thailand, Mr Thaksin Shinawatra; the Prime Minister of Singapore, Mr Goh Chok Tong; and the President of Chile, Mr Richardo Lago Escobar.

Preceding the Economic Leaders Meeting, the Secretary for Commerce, Industry and Technology attended the APEC 15th Ministerial Meeting held in Bangkok. The Secretary also delivered a speech at the CEO Summit on intellectual property rights protection. In September, the Secretary for Financial Services and the Treasury attended the APEC Finance Ministers' Meeting in Phuket, and gave an address on 'Regional Bond Market Development'.

The Chief Executive, as a main member of China's delegation, travelled to Bangkok in April to attend the Association of Southeast Asian Nations (ASEAN) — China Leaders' Special Meeting on the SARS outbreak. Mr Tung had a meeting with Premier Wen Jiabao and briefed him on the latest situation in the fight against the disease in Hong Kong. The Chief Executive and the Secretary for Health, Welfare and Food also had a meeting with the WHO's Executive Director for Communicable Diseases, Dr David Heymann, and updated him on the proactive steps Hong Kong had taken to fight SARS.

The Secretary for the Civil Service attended the Civil Service College Advisory Panel Meeting in Singapore in January. In the same month, the Secretary for Home Affairs also visited Singapore and exchanged views with officials on policies relating to heritage preservation, promotion of arts, culture and sports, football betting and community development.

In June, the Secretary for Health, Welfare and Food attended the WHO's Global Conference on SARS held in Kuala Lumpur, Malaysia. Dr Yeoh told delegates about Hong Kong's strategy and achievements in containing the outbreak.

The Secretary for Economic Development and Labour visited Kuala Lumpur and Singapore in August. In Kuala Lumpur, Mr Ip visited the Multimedia Super Corridor in Cyberjaya and in Singapore he inspected air freight and container terminal facilities. While in the Malaysian capital, Mr Ip officiated at a 'Hong Kong Gala Dinner' being held as part of a series of *Hong Kong Welcomes You* fairs staged in various capital cities to publicise Hong Kong post-SARS, and emphasise it continued to be an attractive destination for tourists and business travellers. The Chinese Music Ensemble of the Hong Kong Academy for Performing Arts (HKAPA) performed at the dinner to showcase Hong Kong's culture and talented young musicians.

The Secretary for Health, Welfare and Food visited Manila in September to attend the WHO Western Pacific Meeting. The same month, the Secretary for Home Affairs visited Manila for a meeting of the Asia Pacific Philanthropy Consortium. Dr Yeoh also led a delegation to Singapore in November, meeting health officials and sharing experiences in the control measures taken against SARS and other communicable diseases. The delegation visited the Tan Tock Seng Hospital, Singapore's dedicated hospital for SARS patients. The Secretary for Economic Development and Labour also visited Singapore in November, and signed an Avoidance of Double Taxation Agreement on Shipping Income and Air Services Income with the Government.

In summer, the Singapore HKETO in collaboration with the HKTB and the HKTDC staged a *Hong Kong Welcomes You* fair to publicise how Hong Kong was moving forward as a vibrant place in which to live and work, post-SARS. The fair featured a Brand Hong Kong Photo Exhibition, a demonstration of traditional Hong Kong craftsmanship, and cultural performances led by students of the HKAPA. *Hong Kong Welcomes You* fairs were also held in Manila and Bangkok.

Australia

In September, the Secretary for Constitutional Affairs visited Australia and updated Australian Government officials, business leaders and the media on developments in Hong Kong, including the implementation of the 'one country, two systems' principle and constitutional development. He also had meetings with members of two think tanks, the Asia-Australia Institute and the Gilbert and Tobin Centre for Public Law.

In October, as part of the Economic Relaunch Campaign, the Secretary for Economic Development and Labour visited Sydney, Melbourne and Adelaide to promote Hong Kong as a leading business hub and tourist destination in Asia. Mr Ip delivered a keynote address at two business conferences in Sydney and Melbourne. He also officiated at the launching of the Hong Kong Food Festival organised by the HKTB.

In November, the Secretary for Commerce, Industry and Technology visited Melbourne, Sydney and Canberra, where he met a number of political and business leaders, as well as media representatives and briefed them on business opportunities in Hong Kong, especially following the signing of CEPA.

He visited the IT Cooperative Research Centre at the University of Victoria and toured the Australian Centre for the Moving Image in Melbourne and the Australian Technology Park in Sydney.

Government Home Pages on the Internet

Among other measures for ensuring openness, transparency and accountability, the Government uses the Internet to disseminate information on its policies, services and activities and to communicate with the public. All bureaux and departments produce their home pages in Chinese and English. Thematic home pages are produced for special events and topics.

These home pages can be accessed through the Government Information Centre (GIC) at *http://www.gov.hk*. Hyperlinks to the home pages of the Chief Executive, Executive Council, Legislative Council, the 18 District Councils, the Judiciary and other related organisations are provided.

The GIC provides 24-hour news updates, live broadcasts of government press conferences, consultation papers and topical information to enable the public to keep track of local developments and important announcements. It is also a portal to a wide range of electronics services of various departments and agencies, including the submission of tax returns, registration as a voter, payment of government fees and the purchase of government publications.

The Government's e-bulletin, *http://www.news.gov.hk*, is another effective means of presenting to the public a comprehensive spread of government news, views and information. Being a website with interactive and multimedia features, it has become a valuable tool in enhancing the transparency of the Government.

Code on Access to Information

The authorities believe in open and accountable government. This requires reasonable access to government information. An administrative Code on Access to Information now applies to all bureaux and departments, which are committed to making information available to the public.

The code sets out the types of government information to which the public has access. It also lists categories of exemptions to ensure appropriate confidentiality of sensitive information held by the Government, and information involving personal privacy and commercial sensitivity.

The public may complain to The Ombudsman about government departments that fail to respond to requests for information in accordance with the code. It represents a major step in meeting public expectations of greater transparency from the Government.

Protection of Privacy with Respect to Personal Data

The Personal Data (Privacy) Ordinance was enacted on August 3, 1995 to protect the privacy of individuals in relation to personal data. The core provisions of the ordinance came into force on December 20, 1996. The ordinance provides for the appointment of a Privacy Commissioner for Personal Data to monitor, supervise and promote compliance with the ordinance.

Information Technology

'Digital 21' IT Strategy

The Government is committed to keeping Hong Kong at the forefront of information technology (IT) development. In May 2001, it published an updated version of the Digital 21 IT Strategy, which was first promulgated in November 1998. The updated Strategy aimed at positioning Hong Kong as a leading e-business community and digital city. Since then great strides have been made in putting in place the right environment, infrastructure, skills and culture to encourage the development and adoption of IT by the whole community.

To sustain the momentum created in the last five years and to harness the benefits of IT for business, the community and Hong Kong's position in the world, the Government has reviewed the implementation of the 2001 Strategy and drafted an updated Strategy for public consultation from October to December 2003. The Government would, taking into account the public views received, finalise the updated Strategy for issue in early 2004.

Driving E-business

The Government is committed to providing the necessary infrastructure for e-business to prosper. It has reviewed the Electronic Transactions Ordinance and introduced amendments to the ordinance in June with a view to keeping the legal framework up-to-date with technological advancements and international e-business developments. The aim is to have the amendments enacted by the legislature in mid-2004.

There are now one public and two private certification authorities (CAs) recognised under the ordinance, which issue digital certificates for use by the community to conduct electronic transactions in a secure manner. In June, the public CA, the Hongkong Post Certification Authority, started to offer smart identity card holders one-year free use of its digital certificates. This will create a critical mass of digital certificate holders, providing the incentive for the industry to develop further applications and services using digital certificates.

The Government also works with industry support organisations to provide technical support, advisory services, financial support and training to encourage and assist the business sector, especially small and medium enterprises (SMEs), to adopt e-business to enhance efficiency and productivity.

E-government

The Government met its E-government targets in 2003. It provided an e-option for 90 per cent of public services which are amenable to the electronic mode of service delivery and attained its e-procurement target to carry out 80 per cent of government procurement tenders through electronic means. Its efforts were also widely recognised. Locally, a public opinion survey conducted in the first half of the year found that among the surveyed Internet users, 70 per cent had used E-government services before, and among them over 60 per cent rated E-government services as 'very good' or 'quite good'. Internationally, Hong Kong was ranked seventh in terms of

E-government leadership by Accenture[1]. In an international ranking[2] of the official websites of 100 cities, Hong Kong came second world-wide in terms of 'digital governance'. In addition, the flagship E-government project — the Electronic Service Delivery (ESD) Scheme — was selected as a winner of the Asia Best Practice Award in the category of E-government in the World Summit Award, in terms of e-content and creativity.

To ensure the community and the Government can reap the full benefits from the E-government programme, the following principles have been rigorously applied: exploit business process re-engineering opportunities to streamline e-services; participate in joined-up initiatives across departments to deliver more customer-centric and efficient services; and deploy customer relations management principles and features to enhance user-friendliness of services. The major E-government projects outlined below demonstrate how these key principles were put into practice in 2003:—

(a) The ESD Scheme

The ESD Scheme provides a one-stop portal (*http://www.esd.gov.hk*) to deliver integrated public and commercial services in a customer-oriented way. As at late 2003, the ESD portal provided some 180 online public services from over 50 government departments/public agencies. Its service scope has been broadened and service quality enhanced. Measures have been implemented to improve usage. The combined efforts of 12 departments has facilitated the roll-out of the 'Easy Change of Address' service, which is a joined-up initiative enabling citizens and businesses to notify any or all of the 12 departments of a change of address by using a single online form. The online appointment booking service for the smart identity card replacement exercise has brought much convenience to the public and reduced queues at Immigration Department counters. The online booking service for sports facilities was enhanced to incorporate a personalised feature, helping sportsmen and women to select their preferred venue and time slot in a faster and easier way. The 25 per cent discount offer for selected statistical and other government publications has significantly increased the usage of the online bookstores.

(b) Multiple Applications on the Smart Identity Card

The Immigration Department started issuing the smart identity (ID) card in 2003. This is another joined-up project that offers a number of public services through the single interface of the smart identity card. In addition to using the card for traditional immigration functions (as a means of identification), holders of the smart ID cards may choose to use their ID cards for library services; they may also opt to embed in their ID cards a digital certificate (the personal e-Cert) issued by Hongkong Post to carry out secure online transactions. Moreover, it can be used for automated immigration clearance in the near future and can be used to replace a driving licence around 2006. There is reserved capacity in the chip of the smart identity card for an e-purse function. This initiative is creating a critical mass of citizens who are ready to

---

[1] 'eGovernment Leadership: Engaging the Customer.' Accenture (a global management consulting and technology services company), 2003

[2] 'Digital Governance in Municipalities Worldwide: An Assessment of Municipal Web Sites throughout the World' by the E-Governance Institute/National Centre for Public Productivity (an institute of a US university) and Global e-Policy e-Government Institute (an institute of a Republic of Korea university), 2003

make use of e-services and it will serve as a population-wide platform for the further development of E-government and e-commerce in Hong Kong.

(c) Other Joined-up and Government-wide Projects

The Government is proceeding with a number of other joined-up projects. For example, the Business Entry Portal will assist existing and prospective businesses by providing a single entry point for coordinated business information from over 100 government bureaux, departments, public bodies, trade associations and other organisations. The Property Information Hub will provide one-stop access to property-related information held by the Rating and Valuation Department, Land Registry, Lands Department and Buildings Department. The Integrated Criminal Justice Processes will enhance efficiency and accuracy in transferring information among a number of departments and agencies involved in the criminal justice process.

(d) Common Look and Feel

In March, a 'Common Look and Feel' website design initiative was introduced to all bureaux and departments. By year-end, over 50 government websites had been revamped. By providing a more consistent navigation experience to surfers, it is aimed to enhance the online brand image and improve the public's accessibility to information as well as improve the user-friendliness of browsing through government websites.

With the solid foundation laid by the first wave of E-government, the E-government programme is being deepened with the intention of focusing more sharply on service quality and effectiveness. The next wave will bring greater value to customers as well as to the Government, by increasing utilisation through a better understanding of what customers need, encouraging customer relations management, and promoting service transformation towards customer-centric and quality-oriented service delivery with more effective business process re-engineering.

IT Manpower

The Government is committed to providing adequate and quality IT manpower to meet the demand in the community. Apart from implementing the measures recommended by the Task Force on IT Manpower set up under the Information Infrastructure Advisory Committee, the Government has implemented new initiatives in collaboration with the IT industry and academia during the year. Specific projects include a Secondary Schools IT Training Scheme and Exhibition to provide opportunities for students to demonstrate their IT and multimedia capability in web page design, video production, image display, and Flash demonstration, and a Young IT Leader Awards Scheme to recognise young people's achievements in learning and applying IT in their studies and daily life. (*Other educational and training measures are mentioned in Chapter 7: Education*)

The Government will continue to work with the academic sector and the IT industry on other longer term measures to ensure that the IT workforce meets the local manpower needs and enhance Hong Kong competitiveness in the globalised market. Where necessary, talented persons and professionals in IT from elsewhere, including the Mainland, may be admitted to Hong Kong to fill gaps or shortages in specific areas.

Building a Digitally Inclusive Society

The Government encourages citizens to embrace and use IT so as to enhance their quality of life. It will continue to organise various activities and initiatives to promote wider adoption and raise public awareness of IT in the community. These include district IT promotion activities, a dedicated website and 'infotainment' TV programmes to disseminate information on the Government's IT initiatives and latest developments in IT, free IT awareness courses providing basic training to different sectors of the community, over 5 300 public computers with Internet connection across Hong Kong for free use by the public, and a free public enquiry service on the use of basic IT applications called IT Easy Link. All government websites are now in compliance with universal accessibility guidelines so as to facilitate access and navigation by people with visual disabilities.

IT Cooperation

Hong Kong has concluded cooperative arrangements in information and communications technology with 11 countries, namely, Canada, Finland, France, Germany, India, Ireland, Israel, Italy, Republic of Korea, the Netherlands, and the United Kingdom. The Government has been working closely with these partners under the aegis of such cooperative arrangements to promote and support inter-governmental exchanges, business partnerships, investment cooperation and joint research and development in the areas of IT and telecommunications. It will continue to explore the opportunities of fostering further cooperation in the field of information and communications technology with these partners.

Cyberport

In March 1999, the Financial Secretary announced the Government's intention to develop the Cyberport at Telegraph Bay in the Southern District of Hong Kong Island. Being an IT infrastructure, the Cyberport aims to create a strategic cluster of quality IT and IT-related companies. The Cyberport is wholly owned by the Government through three private companies set up under the Financial Secretary Incorporated.

The Cyberport is a comprehensive development comprising 100 000 square metres of Grade A office space, a shopping arcade and a five-star hotel. This commercial portion is scheduled for completion in four phases between mid-2002 and late 2004. The ancillary residential development, to be completed between 2004 and 2007, provides an intelligent home environment for professionals who choose to live near their offices.

By year-end, 26 tenants had signed leases with the Cyberport, taking up 63 per cent of the office space available in the completed Phases I and II. These are companies specialising in IT applications, information services and multimedia content creation. Tenants are admitted based on the advice of a committee comprising local and international experts. Companies such as Microsoft, GXS International, Sybase, PCCW, CSL, ESRI, Centro Digital Pictures and SmarTrust have signed up with the Cyberport.

The University of Hong Kong, together with six corporate/industry partners, has set up a Cyberport Institute in the Cyberport to provide market-driven IT programmes. The campus-like environment of the Cyberport makes it an ideal place for nurturing professional talent. The Cyberport campus of the institute was officially opened in November.

The Cyberport also contributes to the technological development in Hong Kong and provides the necessary infrastructure and technical support for small and medium sized enterprises (SMEs). Its initial foci include the development of wireless applications and digital entertainment. Funded by the Innovation and Technology Fund, the Hong Kong Wireless Development Centre was opened on December 15 to provide central testing and demonstration facilities for wireless developers in Hong Kong. The Digital Media Centre at the Cyberport, which provides state-of-the-art post-production facilities and technical support for the digital media industries, is scheduled to open in March 2004.

Telecommunications

The Government's telecommunications policy aims to facilitate the development of the telecommunications industry and enhance Hong Kong's position as a regional telecommunications hub.

Supported by the Office of the Telecommunications Authority (OFTA), the Telecommunications Authority (TA) oversees the regulation of the telecommunications industry in Hong Kong and administers the ordinances governing the establishment and operation of telecommunications services.

Since 2000, the Government has opened to competition all sectors of the telecommunications market — local and external, services-based and facilities-based.

To provide a comprehensive and clear legislative framework for the regulation of merger and acquisition activities in the telecommunications market, the Telecommunications (Amendment) Ordinance 2003 was enacted in July. The ordinance would promote fair and effective competition in the market and facilitate informed decision-making by businesses on mergers and acquisitions. The Government was consulting the industry on the relevant guidelines before bringing the ordinance into force.

Local Fixed Telecommunications Network Services

Businesses and consumers in Hong Kong enjoy an excellent telecommunications infrastructure. In 2003, the telephone density was 56 exchange lines per 100 population — one of the highest in the world. Also serving Hong Kong's needs in data communications were more than 491 195 dedicated facsimile lines.

The local fixed network market was fully liberalised as from January 2003. Under the full liberalisation policy, there is no pre-set limit on the number of licences to be issued, nor on timing for submission of applications for licences. By year-end, there were altogether 14 local fixed telecommunications network services (FTNS) operators. They included nine local wireline-based FTNS operators, two local wireless-based FTNS operators, one cable television operator which provides telecommunications services over its hybrid fibre coaxial network and two FTNS operators for distribution of domestic free TV programme services.

In 2003, the Government started a review of the policy and regulatory regime for Type II interconnection. Type II interconnection refers to interconnection between two fixed telecommunications networks at the customer access network level. It enables operators without a customer access network to also provide services to customers through the networks of other operators. The review aimed to examine whether the arrangement remained appropriate and sufficiently updated in encouraging investment in the telecommunications network and facilitating effective competition in the current market conditions. In particular, it is the Government's aim to have a competitive, advanced and high bandwidth telecommunications infrastructure that is capable of supporting demanding, new and innovative services to meet future needs and challenges, thereby furthering the goal of developing Hong Kong into a leading digital city. The first consultation was conducted in May to August. In December, the Government initiated a second-round consultation with a view to promulgating an updated policy in 2004.

Broadband and Internet Access Services

By year-end, virtually all households and commercial buildings were covered by the broadband network. The number of broadband accounts increased significantly during the year to 1 230 607 or 18 broadband accounts per 100 inhabitants, representing an annual increase of 24 per cent. In addition, 52 per cent of households had broadband Internet access. The number of registered customer accounts with dial-up access was 1 084 368, or 16 dial-up access accounts per 100 inhabitants. Internet Service Providers (ISPs) numbered 201 at year-end.

According to a report issued by the International Telecommunication Union (ITU) in September, Hong Kong ranks second in the world in terms of broadband penetration. On the ITU's Digital Access Index published in November, Hong Kong ranks No. 1 in the world in terms of affordability of Internet access.

Public Mobile Phone Service

The market for public mobile phone services is highly competitive in Hong Kong. At year-end, six firms were operating a total of 11 digital systems, serving a customer base of over 7.2 million. This represented an annual growth rate of 16 per cent. The penetration rate of public mobile phone services was about 106 per cent, one of the highest in the world.

In October 2001, the Government issued four 3G licences under an innovative royalty scheme. The Government also spearheaded the introduction of an open network access requirement whereby 3G network operators are required to make available 30 per cent of their network capacity for interconnection to, or access by, non-affiliated Mobile Virtual Network Operators and/or content providers on a non-discriminatory basis. This would facilitate the development of innovative applications and services through effective competition. (*3G services began in January 2004*).

The existing licences for second generation mobile services would expire in 2005 and 2006. To facilitate long-term investment and business planning by industry participants, as well as planning for any necessary transitional or migration arrangements, the Government consulted the industry on future licensing arrangements in August to October. It planned to embark on a second round of consultation in early 2004.

External Telecommunications Services

Competition in the external telecommunications services market was introduced from January 1, 1999. Competition in the market has led to a significant drop in International Direct Dialling (IDD) call rates. Consumer savings in the four years from 1999 to 2002 amounted to an estimated $25.5 billion.

377

Competition in the external facilities market was introduced from January 1, 2000. Operators who bring in new submarine or overland cables, or use non-cable based means of transmission (primarily satellite) to provide external telecommunications facilities-based service may apply for a licence. At year-end, there were 18 licensees providing cable-based external telecommunications facilities and four providing non-cable based external telecommunications facilities.

Satellite Communications

Two Hong Kong companies, APT Satellite Company Limited and Asia Satellite Telecommunications Company Limited (AsiaSat), hold licences under the Telecommunications Ordinance and the Outer Space Ordinance to operate and provide satellite communication services. At year-end, the two satellite companies were operating a total of six satellites.

International Activities

Hong Kong continued to participate in the activities of international and regional telecommunications organisations. As a member of China's delegation, Hong Kong was represented in conferences and meetings convened by the ITU. Hong Kong participated in its own right in the meetings of the Asia-Pacific Telecommunity and the Telecommunications and Information Working Group of the Asia-Pacific Economic Cooperation (APEC). Hong Kong also took part in the initiative to implement the APEC Mutual Recognition Arrangement for Conformity Assessment of Telecommunications Equipment.

The work of the OFTA in the regulation of the development and operation of the telecommunications industry of Hong Kong is well recognised at the international level. The OFTA was named the 'Best Asian Regulator' of 2003 by a leading telecommunications journal in Asia, for the fifth time since 1998.

Broadcasting

Broadcasting Policy and Regulation

The broadcasting policy objective is to enhance Hong Kong's position as a regional broadcasting hub by promoting programme choice and diversity through competition and facilitating innovation and investment in the industry.

The Government opened up the television market and put in place a technology-neutral, pro-competition regulatory framework with the commencement of the Broadcasting Ordinance in mid-2000. It separated the licensing and regulation of 'carriage' and 'provision' of television programme services under the technology-neutral regime. A television programme service provider may hire operators of any transmission networks to transmit its television programme service instead of investing in transmission infrastructure itself. Such a framework facilitates entry to the television programme service market and is flexible enough to embrace new services made possible by emerging technologies and convergence.

Under the Broadcasting Ordinance, the four categories of television programme services — domestic free, domestic pay, non-domestic and other licensable television programme services that may be licensed — are regulated in accordance with the nature and pervasiveness of the services rather than the transmission mode. The former two categories of licences are issued by the Chief Executive in Council, and the latter two by the Broadcasting Authority (BA).

New Developments

In the light of emerging media and technological convergence, the Government is conducting a review of the broadcasting regulatory regime to ensure that the regulatory framework remains conducive to new business developments in the broadcasting industry. It is planned to consult the public on the outcome of the review in 2004.

The Government encourages the deployment of digital terrestrial broadcasting technology in Hong Kong to enhance spectrum efficiency and enable new and better services such as high-definition television broadcasting to be introduced. The Government published a second consultation paper on digital terrestrial broadcasting in December 2003 for a three-month consultation. It was proposed that the existing two terrestrial television broadcasters should start simulcasting their existing television services in analogue and digital forms in 2006 with a view to achieving territory-wide digital coverage by 2008.

Broadcasting Authority

Licensed broadcasters are regulated by the BA which comprises members from various sectors of the community and three public officers. The BA's major functions are to make recommendations to the Chief Executive in Council with respect to the licensing and renewal of domestic free and domestic pay television programme services and sound broadcasting services; to issue non-domestic and other licensable television programme service licences; to administer the provisions of licences; and to safeguard proper standards of television and sound broadcasting with regard to both programme content (including advertisements) and technical performance.

During the year, the BA submitted its recommendations to the Chief Executive in Council on the renewal of the sound broadcast licences of Hong Kong Commercial Broadcasting Company Limited and Metro Broadcast Corporation Limited, and the licensing arrangement for PCCW-VOD to replace its video-on-demand service by a multi-channel service, the subscription of which is on an innovative 'a la carte' basis. It also commenced the licence renewal exercise of the Domestic Pay Television Programme Service of Hong Kong Cable Television Limited (HKCTV) and commissioned an opinion survey and conducted a public hearing to collect public views on the service of HKCTV.

In 2003, the BA's Complaints Committee dealt with 32 complaint cases involving a total of 613 complaints. Having considered the recommendations of the Complaints Committee, the BA issued five warnings.

Television

Hong Kong's television viewers have access to over 159 domestic and non-domestic television programme service channels in various languages. These include four free-to-air terrestrial TV channels, 130 pay TV channels and a variety of free-to-air satellite channels.

Domestic Free Television Programme Services

The two domestic free television programme service licensees — Television Broadcasts Limited and Asia Television Limited — are each licensed to broadcast one Cantonese and one English channel. Both stations are required to broadcast programmes produced by the publicly funded Radio Television Hong Kong (RTHK).

Domestic Pay Television Programme Services

There were five domestic pay television programme service licensees in Hong Kong in 2003 — Hong Kong Cable Television Limited (HKCTV), PCCW VOD Limited (PCCW VOD), Yes Television (Hong Kong) Limited (Yes TV), TV Plus (HK) Corp. Limited (TV Plus) and Galaxy Satellite Broadcasting Limited (Galaxy). At year-end, a total of 130 pay TV channels were available in Hong Kong. The total number of subscribers exceeded 860 000.

Non-domestic Television Programme Services

Many regional and international broadcasters have chosen Hong Kong as their broadcasting centre in Asia, attracted by the excellent infrastructure and world-class telecommunications facilities, as well as the other advantages that make Hong Kong the best place to do business in Asia. There are 12 non-domestic television programme service licensees providing 59 satellite TV channels to the region, of which 24 channels are receivable in Hong Kong.

The licensees are: Starvision Hong Kong Limited, Galaxy Satellite Broadcasting Limited, APT Satellite TV Development Limited, Starbucks (HK) Limited, Asia Plus Broadcasting Limited, MATV Limited, China Entertainment Television Broadcast Limited, Turner International Asia Pacific Limited, Pacific Satellite International Limited, i-Cable Satellite Television Limited, Sun Television Cybernetworks Enterprise Limited and Pacific Century Matrix (HK) Limited.

Radio

Hong Kong has 13 radio channels — seven operated by RTHK, three by Hong Kong Commercial Broadcasting Company Limited and three by Metro Broadcast Corporation Limited.

Radio Television Hong Kong (RTHK)

RTHK is a publicly funded, editorially independent broadcaster whose mission is to provide quality programmes that inform, educate and entertain the people of Hong Kong. RTHK's online Cyberstation provides a 24-hour live webcast of six of its radio channels and its TV programmes, plus an online archive service for programmes broadcast in the past 12 months. The daily average access rate of the Cyberstation has reached a record of 16 million website hits, with about 45 per cent of them logging in from overseas. In 2003, RTHK commemorated 75 years of broadcasting in Hong Kong.

Film Industry

Hong Kong is a major film production centre. During the year, a total of 79 films produced in Hong Kong were released. Action films, romance and comedies were the main genres.

In 2003, there were 57 cinemas (with 188 screens) compared with 61 cinemas (with 184 screens) in 2002. The box-office hits of the year included *Finding Nemo* ($31.89 million), *Twins Effect* ($28.42 million) and *Infernal Affairs III* ($28.04 million)[3].

3 Box office up to December 31, 2003

The variety of exciting rides at the World Carnival held at the Tamar Site attracted thousands of visitors from December to January.

Lanterns large and small were lit up all over Hong Kong for the Mid-Autumn Festival in September. But pride of place went to the Hong Kong Tourism Board's spectacular giant lantern *(above)* erected in Victoria Park — it measured 35 metres wide and 15 metres tall. The structure won the President's Prize in the 2003 Annual Awards of the Hong Kong Institute of Architects.

The Hong Kong Flower Show continues to grow in popularity, with the 2003 show in March attracting a record attendance of 550 000 people. The floral displays were notable for their imaginative designs, and the Brand Hong Kong Dragon was again a popular backdrop for photographs.

Christmas and New Year brought forth an array of dynamic lighting and innovative decorations conveying a spirit of goodwill, whether at the Ocean Terminal in Tsim Sha Tsui, Maritime Square on Tsing Yi or Taikoo Shing in Quarry Bay.

Thousands of people crowded into Times Square in Causeway Bay for the traditional countdown to close out 2003 and welcome 2004. *Right:* the colourful International Chinese New Year Parade on February 1.

Film Classification System

Hong Kong has a three-tier film classification system: Category I (suitable for all ages); Category II, which is subdivided into Category IIA (not suitable for children) and Category IIB (not suitable for young persons and children); and Category III (for persons aged 18 and above only). The objective is to allow adults wide access to films while protecting persons under the age of 18 from exposure to potentially harmful material.

Category IIA and IIB classifications are advisory (no statutory age restriction is imposed) and are intended to give more information to movie-goers, parents in particular, to help them select films for themselves or their children. Age restriction is mandatory for Category III films.

During the year, 1 555 films were submitted for classification, compared with 1 944 films in 2002. Of these, 689 were classified Category I (12 with excisions), 362 Category IIA (none with excisions), 335 Category IIB (eight with excisions), and 169 Category III (21 with excisions). Film trailers, instructional films and cultural films intended for public exhibition also require censorship but do not need to be classified into any category. During the year, 3 309 such items were approved for exhibition.

Film classification standards are kept in line with society's standards by regular surveys of community views and consultation with a statutory panel of advisers, comprising about 250 members drawn from a wide cross-section of the population. A public opinion survey on the film classification system conducted in 2002 showed that the vast majority (97 per cent) of the public considered the current film classification standards acceptable.

Decisions on film classifications may be reviewed by the Board of Review (Film Censorship), a statutory body established under the Film Censorship Ordinance. The board comprises nine non-official members appointed by the Chief Executive, with the Secretary for Commerce, Industry and Technology as an *ex officio* member. There was one case of reviewing the censor's decisions in 2003.

Government Support

The Government is committed to providing a favourable environment conducive to the healthy and long-term development of the film industry in Hong Kong. The Film Services Advisory Committee was established in May 1998 to provide a conduit for dialogue between the industry and the Government and to advise on the work of the Film Services Office, set up under the Television and Entertainment Licensing Authority, which facilitates film production in Hong Kong and promotes Hong Kong films locally and abroad. The committee is appointed by the Chief Executive and comprises the Secretary for Commerce, Industry and Technology who is the chairman, four representatives from the Government and public bodies and nine non-official members.

Since its establishment in April 1998, the Film Services Office has obtained the agreement of over 1 130 organisations, including government departments, to let their premises for location filming and has published reference materials in this regard for the industry. To facilitate film production in Hong Kong, the office provides one-stop service to the film industry on location filming requests of a more complicated nature. During the year, it dealt with 463 such requests, with a 99 per cent success rate. To assist the film industry in applying for lane closures for location filming purposes, the Film Services Office, in consultation with the Police Force, Transport Department and

Highways Department, promulgated a set of guidelines in March 2001. Under this mechanism, the office is responsible for coordinating the processing of such applications by other departments; 102 applications for lane closures were approved in 2003.

To promote Hong Kong films internationally, the Film Services Office facilitated the organisation of Hong Kong Film Festivals in Antwerp, Toronto, Calgary, Vancouver, Washington DC and Seoul. The Film Services Office also promoted Hong Kong as a choice for location filming at the global expositions 'Locations 2003' and 'Busan International Film Commission & Industry Showcase'. During the year, 157 overseas crews, including the production team of the Hollywood film *Lara Croft Tomb Raider: The Cradle of Life*, carried out location filming in Hong Kong.

The Film Development Fund, which was established in 1999, provides financial support to a wide variety of projects that can enhance the professional and technological capabilities of the film industry so as to strengthen its competitiveness. By year-end, a total of $47 million had been approved for 68 projects to promote the development of the local film industry. They included training courses, workshops, seminars, consultancy studies, surveys, film awards presentation ceremonies, overseas promotional projects as well as sponsorship for Hong Kong films' participation in overseas film festivals.

The $50 million Film Guarantee Fund was established in April 2003 on a pilot basis for two years. It seeks to assist local film production companies to obtain loans from local lending institutions for film production. It also serves to stimulate the establishment of a film financing infrastructure in Hong Kong. The fund provided loan guarantees for four film projects and the total amount guaranteed was $8.63 million.

With the commencement of the Entertainment Special Effects Ordinance and its subsidiary legislation on March 16, 2001, a streamlined regulatory system is now in place to facilitate the use of pyrotechnic materials for producing special effects for films, television and theatrical productions. Under this legislation, the Commissioner for Television and Entertainment Licensing is the Entertainment Special Effects Licensing Authority responsible for licensing special effects operators; issuing discharge permits; registering and regulating the supply, conveyance and storage of pyrotechnic special effects materials. In 2003, the Authority processed a total of 1 192 applications, representing an increase of 42 per cent and 73 per cent over 2002 and 2001, respectively. This indicates that the regulatory system has been well received and utilised by the industry.

Postal Services

Hongkong Post provides reliable, efficient and universal postal services at affordable prices to meet the needs of Hong Kong and its international postal obligations. Since August 1, 1995, Hongkong Post has operated as a trading fund department. This gives it a higher degree of flexibility in resource management and enables it to respond more effectively to changes in markets and customer needs, improve productivity, efficiency and customer service, and introduce new services to its customers.

Leadership and Vision

Hongkong Post recognises that clear leadership and vision are essential to the evolution from a traditional, operationally focused government department to a forward-looking, customer-focused and market-oriented organisation. To this end, Hongkong Post established its corporate purpose as *Linking People, Delivering Business* in 2003. The words neatly define its dual responsibilities of firstly continuing to provide an affordable, universal service linking individuals and organisations in Hong Kong and across the globe through the delivery of correspondence and merchandise, and secondly adding value to the economy by delivering business solutions to the different sectors and maintaining the viability of Hongkong Post through diversification into new business arenas. Supported by the vision, mission and values set, the corporate purpose points to the organisation's long-term direction.

Mail Volumes

During the year, Hongkong Post handled 1.27 billion items of mail, or a daily average of 3.5 million items, representing a slight decrease of 0.3 per cent over 2002. Local mail accounted for 85.4 per cent of the items processed and overseas mail for 14.6 per cent. Some 11 217 tonnes of letter mail and 1 762 tonnes of parcels were dispatched overseas by air, representing an increase of 2 per cent on 2002. The United States, the Mainland, the United Kingdom, Japan and Australia were Hongkong Post's major partners in letter mail while Japan, the United States, Canada, the United Kingdom and Australia were its major partners in parcels.

Performance Pledges

Performance pledges are published for the delivery of mail, philatelic, counter and public Certification Authority services. Hongkong Post achieved a very high performance level in most of its pledges. In particular, it was able to achieve a success rate of 99.71 per cent for next-day delivery of local letters.

Perception Survey

In March, an independent firm was appointed to conduct the seventh annual public perception survey of Hongkong Post's services. The overall satisfaction levels remained high, with some 97 per cent, 96 per cent and 97 per cent of customers in the general public, business and philately groups, respectively, being satisfied or very satisfied with Hongkong Post's services. The survey also found that Hongkong Post has ranked the first runner-up among the best service organisations in every year since 2000.

Hong Kong Public Key Infrastructure Forum

In September, the Hong Kong Public Key Infrastructure Forum (HKPKIF) hosted an international conference on 'The Usage of PKI in e-Business'. The conference, chaired by the Postmaster General, was organised to position Hong Kong as a leading e-business community. Some 250 senior executives participated in the conference, 70 of whom were delegates of member PKI forums from across the Asia-Pacific region. Ideas were exchanged on various subjects relating to the development of business applications using PKI technology.

E-Cert in Smart ID Card

Anticipating the commencement of the region-wide ID Card replacement exercise in August, show business celebrities were appointed as e-Cert ambassadors to raise public awareness and encourage residents to learn more about e-Cert and the option to embed a Hongkong Post e-Cert, for one year's free usage, in their smart ID cards.   383

Those who elected to take advantage of this offer are now experiencing the convenience of performing secure online services and transactions.

Speedpost

A number of enhancements were added to Speedpost — Hongkong Post's international courier service — throughout the year. In January, the network was extended to Iran, Kenya, Mozambique and Myanmar, bringing the total number of destinations served to 96. A number of incentives were introduced to expand the account customer base. These included rebates and supermarket gift coupons for sending Speedpost items to the Republic of Korea. Under the bonus point scheme introduced in March, Speedpost account customers redeemed accumulated points for a wide range of items including PostShop souvenirs, supermarket, clothing chain and restaurant coupons as well as electrical and electronic appliances.

Collection and Delivery Management System

Hong Kong's role as a leading digital city was further affirmed at the launch in March of Hong Kong's first collection and delivery management system (CDMS) in a Hongkong Post-Hutchison Telecom cooperation. This advanced infrastructural system thrusts Hongkong Post to the forefront in courier service for its use of innovative resource allocation technology. The system was successfully tried out during the year and utilises Hutchison's advanced GPRS (General Packet Radio Service) and personal digital assistants equipped with a barcode scanning function to track package deliveries. It is expected to be fully implemented in April 2004.

Special Stamp Issues

Eleven sets of special stamps were issued in 2003, and comprised Hong Kong Disneyland; Year of the Ram; Traditional Trades and Handicrafts; Miniature Landscapes; Pet Fish; Heartwarming; Waterbirds — a joint issue by Hong Kong, China and Sweden; the successful flight of China's first manned spacecraft; Chinese Percussion Instruments; World Heritage in China; and Development of Public Housing in Hong Kong.

The special stamps featured a range of designs, exquisitely rendered and reflecting a variety of cultural, nostalgic and contemporary themes. Hongkong Post became the first postal administration in the world to print on flock paper, making its 'Year of the Ram' series a historic first. The 'Pet Fish' stamps incorporated a fish-shaped die-cut. The issue of the pentagonal 'Development of Public Housing' series was Hong Kong's first *tête-bêche* issue meaning the stamps were printed with an upright image attached to an inverted image. The 'Heartwarming' stamp was the first set of Hong Kong stamps without a value indicator and printed with 'Local Mail Postage' or 'Air Mail Postage'. The stamp tabs next to the stamps allow senders to add a warm and unique touch by printing a photographic portrait.

Philately Promotions

Philatelists of all ages continued to benefit from the Local Standing Order service which in 2003 introduced a customer loyalty programme for customers to enjoy various incentive schemes with attractive souvenir items. In March, a children's stamp design competition with the theme of 'My Favourite Toys and Games' attracted entries from hundreds of children. To reinforce young collectors' interest in producing stamp exhibits and to promote philately among students, Hongkong Post organised the fourth Inter-School Stamp Exhibitions Competition with the support of the Education and Manpower Bureau. The competition attracted a favourable response with 164 entries.

PostalPlus for SMEs

Amid a fast-changing business environment and intense competition, small and medium enterprises (SMEs) operating on limited resources are challenged to promote their businesses and streamline operations. The PostalPlus for SME programme was established to offer a simple, cost-efficient solution to Hong Kong's 300 000-plus SMEs by providing postal services, logistics, direct marketing and e-commerce support. Over 3 000 members were recruited by year-end.

Network Expansion

The post office network was extended with new post offices opened in the Cyberport development in Pok Fu Lam and Yau Tong in January and December, respectively. In June, the Yuen Long Post Office was included in the counter network for accepting bulk postings, Hongkong Post circulars, permit mail, and postage prepayment in money.

Health and Safety at Work

In February, Hongkong Post sanctioned its Occupational Safety Charter during Occupational Health and Safety Week 2003. It endorsed the shared responsibility of employers and employees to create and maintain a safe and healthy work environment, and achieved the 'Continual Improvement Safety Programme Recognition of System' Level 2 Certification of the Occupational Safety and Health Council in November.

Community Support

The PostCare Club consists of Hongkong Post staff who support the organisation's values of caring for colleagues and the community by undertaking a range of voluntary work. In May, the club saluted the community's efforts to combat SARS by issuing a 'One Heart, One Mind, Bless Hong Kong' souvenir cover. It was issued to encourage members of the public to send their appreciation and blessing to those persons engaged in combating SARS. The cover was distributed free of charge to the public on a first-come first-served basis and its production was funded by donations from staff. The Hong Kong Red Cross donation box in support of the 'SARS Prevention' Campaign was also made available at each of the 39 philatelic offices. Donations collected were spent on the provision of SARS preventive kits to the needy and vulnerable people as well as on health education projects for the community.

Participation in International Postal Arena

Hongkong Post's high standing in the international postal arena is clear from its re-election as a board member of the Universal Postal Union Express Mail Service Cooperative (UPU EMSC) in 2002 and the Asia Pacific Post Cooperative (APPC) in 2003. It participated in activities organised by the Universal Postal Union (UPU) including the UPU Postal Operations Council meetings and the Council of Administration meetings in Berne, Switzerland, and the Asian Pacific Postal Union (APPU) Executive Council meetings in Hainan as a member of China's delegation. In addition, Hongkong Post participated in the board meetings of the UPU EMSC and

APPC, the meetings of the UPU Advanced Electronic Services Group and the UPU Terminal Dues Action Group and the UPU and APPU workshops.

Gold Level Certification for EMS Performance

Hongkong Post achieved Gold Level Certification among over 100 postal administrations for outstanding Express Mail Service (EMS) performance during 2002. This represents a major step forward in its continuing efforts to strive for excellence in EMS performance, after achieving Silver Level Certification in both 2000 and 2001. This award for EMS (known as Speedpost in Hong Kong) was based on the UPU EMSC's Audit and Measurement Programme conducted by an independent consultant in areas including delivery performance and timely provision of tracking data.

Cooperation with Overseas Postal Administrations

By collaborating with overseas postal administrations, Hongkong Post is able to streamline business and personal communications. In May, the reciprocal postal remittance service was expanded from the existing postal administrations (the Mainland, the Philippines and Canada) to include Japan Post. In addition, under the International Fulfilment Service for Australian Natural Products launched in July, Hongkong Post and Australia Post teamed up with Western Australian merchants to arrange the posting, customs clearance and delivery, via Speedpost, to the recipient's door of a wide range of exclusive products from Western Australia including natural pollen, avocado oil, medicated honey, sandalwood oil, wildflowers and premium boutique wines.

Home Pages

Communications and Technology Branch: http://www.info.gov.hk/citb/ctb
Information Services Department: http://www.isd.gov.hk
Hongkong Post: http://www.hongkongpost.com
E-government in Hong Kong: http://www.egov.gov.hk

CHAPTER 18

Religion and Custom

Buddhism and Taoism have large numbers of adherents in Hong Kong. These adherents worship according to their individual purposes at temples and shrines spread throughout the HKSAR. Some of the temples are old while others are quite new, and built in the style of traditional Chinese architecture.

RELIGIOUS freedom is one of the fundamental rights enjoyed by Hong Kong residents. It is protected by the Basic Law and the relevant legislation. The various religious traditions practised in Hong Kong embrace, among others, Buddhism, Taoism, Confucianism, Christianity, Islam, Hinduism, Sikhism and Judaism. All of these traditions have a considerable number of adherents. Apart from offering religious instruction, many major religious bodies have established schools and provide health and welfare facilities.

Traditional Festivals

Five major Chinese festivals offer occasions for family union and feasting. Foremost is the Lunar New Year, celebrated in the first few days of the first moon of the year. Friends and relatives visit each other and exchange gifts while children and unmarried adults receive *lai see*, or 'lucky' money.

The Dragon Boat Festival is celebrated on the fifth day of the fifth moon in memory of an ancient Chinese poet, Qu Yuan, who committed suicide by jumping into a river rather than compromise his honour. The festival has developed into an annual event characterised by dragon boat races and eating of rice dumplings wrapped in lotus leaves.

For the Mid-Autumn Festival on the 15th day of the eighth moon, adults and children gather under the full moon with colourful lanterns, which nowadays reflect a variety of objects rather than only the animals of the lunar calendar, and eat mooncakes — a traditional festival delicacy.

The Ching Ming Festival in spring and the Chung Yeung Festival on the ninth day of the ninth moon are occasions for visiting ancestral graves. Many people mark Chung Yeung by climbing hills in remembrance of an ancient Chinese family that escaped plague and death by fleeing to a mountain-top.

Buddhism and Taoism

Buddhism and Taoism, traditional Chinese religions, have a large local following with more than 600 Chinese temples in the HKSAR. The major festival of Buddhism is the Buddha's Birthday, which falls on the eighth day of the fourth moon.

Buddhist and Taoist deities are often honoured together in the same temple. Leading deities include Buddha, Kwun Yum (the Buddhist Goddess of Mercy) and Lui Cho (a Taoist god). Besides this, deified mortals such as Che Kung and Kwan Tai are revered in recognition of their feats. Tin Hau, the Queen of Heaven and Protector of Seafarers, is worshipped widely. During the Tin Hau Festival, which falls on the 23rd day of the third moon, many worshippers visit the most famous Tin Hau temple, at Joss House Bay on the Clear Water Bay Peninsula. Other leading deities include Pak Tai (Supreme Emperor of the Dark Heaven and local patron of the island of Cheung Chau) and Hung Shing (God of the South Seas and a weather prophet).

Notable temples in Hong Kong include the Wong Tai Sin Temple, named after a Taoist deity, Wong Tai Sin, located in the Wong Tai Sin District in Kowloon. Nearby, the Chi Lin Nunnery in Diamond Hill is a group of temple structures built in the architectural style of the Tang Dynasty. The Po Lin Monastery on Lantau Island is famous for the Tian Tan Buddha, a majestic bronze seated Buddha believed to be the largest outdoor Buddha statue of this style in the world. It attracts many visitors, especially during the weekends and holidays. Other well-known temples include the Che Kung Temple in Sha Tin in the New Territories, and the Man Mo Temple in Hollywood Road on Hong Kong Island.

Confucianism

Confucianism is a belief in the teachings of Confucius, who lived in ancient China from 551 to 479 BC. His teachings were based on a moral code for human relations with emphasis on the importance of tradition and rites. He was one of the most eminent thinkers of the time, a great sage and educator whose philosophy has deeply influenced the political, economic and social systems of China through the ages. He has also been hailed as an exemplary mentor for all ages. The major festival of Confucianism is the birthday of Confucius, which falls on the 27th day of the eighth moon.

Christianity

The Christian community — largely Protestant and Roman Catholic — is estimated to number close to 540 000. The Protestant and Roman Catholic churches maintain a spirit of fellowship, with the Hong Kong Christian Council and the Roman Catholic Diocese joining together on special occasions. In recent years, the Orthodox Church has established a Metropolitanate of Hong Kong and South East Asia, which is based in Hong Kong.

Protestant Community

The presence of the Protestant community dates from 1841. About 300 000 Protestant Christians live in Hong Kong. The Protestant Church is made up of over 1 300 congregations in more than 50 denominations with many independent churches. The Baptists form the largest denomination, followed by the Lutherans. Other major denominations are Adventist, Anglican, Christian and Missionary Alliance, Church of Christ in China (representing the Presbyterian and Congregational traditions),

Methodist, Pentecostal and Salvation Army. With their emphasis on youth work, many congregations have a high proportion of young people.

Protestant organisations operate three post-secondary institutions: Chung Chi College at the Chinese University of Hong Kong, Hong Kong Baptist University and Lingnan University. They are also active in secondary, primary and pre-primary education, in 2003 operating 158 secondary schools, 206 primary schools, 273 kindergartens and 116 nurseries. There were 16 theological seminaries and Bible institutes, 16 Christian publishing houses and 69 Christian bookshops.

In health and welfare, Protestant organisations run seven hospitals with about 3 750 beds, and 18 clinics. There are also some 59 social service organisations. These social service organisations provided a wide range of services in 2003, including 227 community, family service and youth centres, 74 day care centres, 17 children's homes, 35 homes for the elderly, 106 centres for the elderly, two schools for the deaf and one for the blind, and 47 training centres for the mentally handicapped and disabled. There were also 15 camp sites. In addition, five international hotel-type guest houses are managed by the YMCA and the YWCA.

More than 70 para-church agencies and various Christian action groups minister to the Protestant community and respond to current issues and concerns within Hong Kong society at large. The church supports emergency relief and aid projects in developing countries. Two weekly newspapers, *The Christian Weekly* and *The Christian Times*, present news and comments from a Christian perspective.

Two ecumenical bodies facilitate cooperative work among the Protestant churches in Hong Kong. The older one, dating from 1915, is the Hong Kong Chinese Christian Churches Union with a membership of 275 congregations. The second cooperative body is the Hong Kong Christian Council, formed in 1954. Major mainline denominations and ecumenical services constitute the membership core of the council, which is committed to building closer relationships among all churches in Hong Kong as well as with churches in the Mainland and overseas. The council also encourages local Christians to play an active part in the development of Hong Kong society. It seeks to serve the wider community through its auxiliary agencies such as the Hong Kong Christian Service, Christian Industrial Committee, United Christian Hospital, Pamela Youde Nethersole Eastern Hospital and Alice Ho Min Yee Nethersole Hospital and the Christian Family Service Centre. The council runs weekly 'Alternative Tours', which give visitors and residents an opportunity to see how the church serves the community.

Roman Catholic Community

The Roman Catholic Church in Hong Kong was established as a Mission Prefecture in 1841 and as an Apostolic Vicariate in 1874. It became a diocese in 1946.

The present Bishop, Joseph Ze-kiun Zen, was installed in 2002, becoming the fourth Chinese bishop of the diocese. Bishop Zen is assisted by two Vicars General, John Hon Tong, who is also Auxiliary Bishop, and Father Dominic Chan.

Bishop Zen became head of the diocese upon the death of Cardinal John Baptist Cheng-chung Wu who had served since 1975. The first Chinese bishop was Francis Chen-ping Hsu, who was installed in 1969 and succeeded in 1973 by Peter Wang-kei Lei.

About 239 400 people are Catholics. They were served in 2003 by 309 priests, 60 brothers and 519 sisters. There are 52 parishes, comprising 40 churches, 31 chapels and 28 halls for religious service. Services are conducted in Chinese with three-fifths of the parishes also providing services in English, and in Tagalog in some cases.

The diocese has established its own administrative structure while maintaining close links with the Pope and other Catholic communities around the world. It has the same creed, scripture, liturgy and organisation as the other Catholic communities world-wide. The assistant secretary-general of the Federation of Asian Bishops' Conference has his office in Hong Kong.

Along with its apostolic work, one of the prime concerns of the diocese has been the well-being of the community as a whole. In education, there are 320 Catholic schools and kindergartens which have about 286 000 pupils. There is the Catholic Board of Education to assist in this area. The medical and social services include six hospitals, 15 clinics, 13 social centres, 15 hostels, 12 homes for the aged, 15 rehabilitation service centres and many self-help clubs and associations. Caritas is the official social welfare arm of the church in Hong Kong.

These services are open to all people. Indeed, 95 per cent of those who have benefited from the wide range of services provided by the diocese are not Catholics.

To reach people through the media, the diocese publishes two weekly newspapers, *Kung Kao Po* and *The Sunday Examiner*. In addition, the Diocesan Audio-Visual Centre produces tapes and films for use in schools and parishes and, overall, the Hong Kong Catholic Social Communications Office acts as an information and public relations channel for the diocese.

Muslim Community

The Muslim community in Hong Kong is estimated to number up to 70 000. More than half are Chinese, with the rest being either locally born non-Chinese or believers from Pakistan, India, Malaysia, Indonesia and Middle Eastern and African countries. The Chinese Muslim Cultural & Fraternal Association is the major body representing the Chinese Muslims in Hong Kong. It was established in 1922 at No. 7 Chan Tong Lane, Wan Chai, and was incorporated as a charity organisation in 1963. Apart from conducting religious activities for the Chinese Muslims, the association manages and maintains six non-profit making schools including one college, two primary schools and three kindergartens.

Four principal masjids are used daily for prayers. The oldest is the Jamia Masjid in Shelley Street on Hong Kong Island, which was established in 1849 and rebuilt in 1915. It can accommodate a congregation of 400.

The Masjid Ammar and Osman Ramju Sadick Islamic Centre, occupying eight storeys, was opened in 1981 and houses a masjid on two floors, a community hall, a library, a medical clinic, classrooms and offices. The masjid is managed by the Islamic Union of Hong Kong and accommodates 700 people but, if necessary, can hold up to 1 500 by using other space in the centre.

The Kowloon Masjid and Islamic Centre, in Nathan Road, was opened in 1984 and replaced a masjid built in 1896. This imposing building, with white marble finishing, is a landmark in Tsim Sha Tsui. The masjid can accommodate about 2 000 worshippers and has three prayer halls, a community hall, a medical clinic and a library.

Hong Kong Island has two Muslim cemeteries, one at Happy Valley and the other at Cape Collinson, Chai Wan. The Cape Collinson cemetery also has a masjid. The coordinating body for all Islamic religious affairs is the Incorporated Trustees of the Islamic Community Fund of Hong Kong, a public charity. A board of trustees nominated by the Islamic Union of Hong Kong, the Pakistan Association, the Indian Muslim Association and the Dawoodi Bohra Association, manages and maintains masjids and cemeteries. The trustees are also responsible for organising the celebration of Muslim festivals and other religious events. Charitable work among the Muslim community, including financial aid for the needy, medical facilities and assisted education, is conducted through various local Muslim organisations.

Hindu Community

The religious and social activities of the 15 000-strong Hindu community in Hong Kong are centred on the Hindu Temple in Happy Valley. The Hindu Association of Hong Kong is responsible for the upkeep of the temple, which is also used for meditation, spiritual lectures, yoga classes and other community activities as well as the observance of major Hindu festivals such as *Diwali*, *Dussehra* and *Holi*. Naming, engagement and marriage ceremonies are performed at the temple according to Hindu rites. Devotional music sessions and religious discourses are held every Sunday morning and Monday evening. The Sunday sessions are followed by a free community meal.

The Hindu Temple is an approved place of worship for the performance of marriages under the Marriage Ordinance.

Other important services provided by the temple include administration of last rites, arrangements for cremation and related ceremonies and the maintenance of the Hindu crematorium at Cape Collinson.

Sikh Community

The Sikhs came to Hong Kong from the Punjab, in North India, as part of the British Armed Forces in the 19th century. Because of their generally strong physique, they also formed a large segment of the Hong Kong Police Force before World War II.

Today, the community numbers about 8 000 and its members are engaged in a variety of occupations. The centre of their religious and cultural activities is the Sikh Temple at 371 Queen's Road East, Wan Chai, Hong Kong Island. A special feature of the temple, which was established in 1901, is the provision of free meals and short-term accommodation for overseas visitors of any faith.

Religious services, which include hymn-singing, readings from the *Guru Granth* (the Sikh Holy Book) and sermons by the priest, are held every Sunday morning. The temple houses a library containing a selection of books on the Sikh religion and culture, and runs a 'Starters' school for Indian children aged between four and six to prepare them for English primary schools in Hong Kong.

The main holy days and festivals observed by the Sikh community are the birthdays of Guru Nanak (founder of the faith), Guru Gobind Singh (the 10th Guru) and *Baisakhi* (the birthday of all Sikhs).

Jewish Community

The Jewish community of Hong Kong dates from about the 1840s and comprises families from various parts of the world. There are three main synagogues — Ohel Leah Synagogue, the United Jewish Congregation of Hong Kong and the Chabad Lubavitch. Daily, Sabbath and festival services are held at the Ohel Leah Synagogue (Orthodox). Sabbath and festival services are also held at the United Jewish Congregation of Hong Kong (Reform). The Ohel Leah Synagogue and the United Jewish Congregation of Hong Kong are both located in the same building complex in Robinson Road on Hong Kong Island. Daily services are also held at the Chabad Lubavitch (located in premises at 51 Garden Road, Hong Kong Island). These all fulfil important roles in the religious, cultural and social life of Jewish people in Hong Kong.

The Ohel Leah Synagogue was built in 1901 on land given by Sir Jacob Sassoon and his family and includes a *mikvah* (ritual bath). There is also a Jewish Cemetery, which was built in 1857, in Shan Kwong Road, Happy Valley.

The site adjoining the Ohel Leah Synagogue, now containing a residential complex, also houses the Jewish Community Centre which serves all three congregations in the HKSAR. The centre offers its 600 member families supervised kosher dining and banquet, cultural and recreational facilities, a wide range of activities and classes, as well as a specialist library covering all aspects of Judaica. The centre functions as the focal point of social and cultural life for the community.

The community also operates the Carmel School, as well as other supplementary religious educational classes. There are several charity organisations and cultural societies — including the Jewish Women's Association, United Israel Appeal, Israeli Chamber of Commerce, and the Jewish Historical Society — which all combine to create a vibrant Jewish community in Hong Kong.

Other Faiths

As well as the major religions practised in Hong Kong, faiths such as that of the Baha'is and Zoroastrianism have also found their place here.

CHAPTER 19

Recreation, Sport and the Arts

Hong Kong people enjoy access to a wide range of recreational, sports and cultural facilities. Many of these are built and managed by the Leisure and Cultural Services Department. The main objective of the department is to enrich the community's quality of life through the promotion and provision of recreational, sports and cultural facilities and activities.

RECREATION, sport and the arts provide opportunities for the people of Hong Kong to enrich the quality of their lives. The Government aims to nurture an environment in which freedom of creativity, pluralistic development of the arts, sporting excellence and recreation for the community can thrive.

The Government's policies on sport, recreation, culture and heritage matters are coordinated by the Home Affairs Bureau. A number of expert bodies contribute to the development of these policies, including the Hong Kong Sports Development Board, the Culture and Heritage Commission, the Hong Kong Arts Development Council and the Antiquities Advisory Board.

The continued development of Hong Kong's sporting and artistic culture is in part entrusted to the Hong Kong Sports Development Board and the Hong Kong Arts Development Council, both of which are statutory bodies. These two organisations have continued to implement plans for the development of their respective fields. Specific projects have been funded by grants from the $300 million Arts and Sport Development Fund, which was set up in 1997 to help the board and the council implement the initiatives in their strategic plans. The Home Affairs Bureau is now reviewing the overall sports policy in Hong Kong. A Sports Policy Review report was published for public consultation in May, and the bureau is considering the way forward in the light of comments received.

In the field of sport and recreation, the Leisure and Cultural Services Department (LCSD) is responsible for promoting and developing recreation and sport at the community level. In 2003, the department continued to coordinate the provision of high-quality recreational and sports facilities and to support and organise training programmes and sports competitions so that talented individuals could be identified and sports standards improved.

The department also works closely with the District Councils, the National Sports Associations under the Sports Federation and Olympic Committee of Hong Kong, China, district sports associations and schools to promote the concept of

'Sport-for-All' and to encourage people of all ages and from all walks of life to participate in sports and recreational activities.

The sports promotion and development programmes in 2003 included the Young Athletes Training Scheme, School Sports Programme, Community Sports Club Project, District Sports Teams and Age Group Competitions. The department also administered a Sports Subsidy Scheme to provide financial assistance to National Sports Associations to organise sports programmes for the community, as well as designated sports venues for use by National Sports Associations as National Squad Training Centres.

To provide better service to the public, the LCSD has implemented in phases a new mode of operation at recreational venues since 2002. Venue managers have been deployed to provide one-stop service at recreational venues. Members of the public may book facilities, register and pay charges for recreation programmes, and obtain professional advice and assistance on using facilities and sports programming at 144 venues.

To further improve the booking service, a number of enhancements were made to the 'LCSD Leisure Link' booking system in 2003. The enhancements offer convenience to members of the public in making online and telephone bookings of leisure facilities and enrolment in recreation and sports programmes. People are no longer required to make prior registration with the LCSD and can simply input their Hong Kong identity card number at the time of booking. The enhancements also provide additional booking information about each facility, enabling patrons to make their selection more easily.

In support of the Government's policy to make Hong Kong green, the LCSD in 2003 carried out extensive tree planting programmes in parks and playgrounds, as well as on roadsides. In addition, various educational and community activities were organised to promote public awareness of the importance of greening. In cultural services, good progress continued to be made in reviewing the existing policy on built heritage conservation. The department will provide additional funds for preservation of Hong Kong's cultural heritage and thereby also support the development of tourism.

Concerted Action Against SARS

The LCSD joined hands with other government departments in taking concerted action against SARS when the disease broke out early in the year. Three of the department's holiday camps — Lei Yue Mun Park and Village, Lady MacLehose Holiday Village and Sai Kung Outdoor Recreation Centre — were closed temporarily so they could serve as isolation centres for people evacuated from their homes during the outbreak, particularly the residents of Amoy Gardens in Ngau Tau Kok. The department's Kowloon Bay Sports Centre in Kwun Tong District was also made available for use as a support centre for the Inter-departmental Operation Team that was working in Amoy Gardens.

Preventive and operational measures were undertaken in all the department's leisure and cultural venues and facilities to prevent the disease spreading. These included strengthening the routine cleansing and maintenance of air-conditioning systems, issue of specific guidelines, and the provision of face masks to staff and visitors.

To cope with the demand for a large quantity of cleansing materials and face masks within a short period of time, the department's Supplies staff worked tirelessly to procure sufficient quantities of stock. Incoming consignments were received beyond midnight and, in addition, the operating hours of the Kwai Chung Main Store were extended during Saturdays and Sundays to ensure there was an uninterrupted supply of materials to staff, especially during the peak period of the outbreak.

Responding to the call from the Government's newly formed Team Clean, for widespread action to improve the environment, the LCSD strengthened its enforcement action against unhygienic behaviour, such as littering and spitting at leisure and cultural venues and facilities, particularly during public holidays and weekends, in all 18 districts. Officers of the department issued some 170 fixed penalty tickets to littering/spitting offenders and served 15 summonses on spitting offenders during the period from March to June.

The Arts

It is the Government's policy to create an environment that is conducive to freedom of expression and artistic creation and that encourages free participation in all aspects of cultural life.

Culture and Heritage Commission

The Culture and Heritage Commission was established by the Government in 2000. It is a high-level advisory body responsible for advising the Government on cultural policies as well as funding priorities in culture and the arts. The commission's key responsibility is to formulate a set of principles and strategies to promote the long-term development of culture in Hong Kong.

The commission published its first consultation report entitled 'Gathering of Talents for Continual Innovation' and the second consultation paper 'Identity with Diversity: Evolution through Innovation' in March 2001 and November 2002, respectively. After two rounds of consultation, the commission submitted its Policy Recommendation Report to the Government in April 2003. The Government accepted 90 per cent of the recommendations put forth in the report and would study the rest.

Hong Kong Arts Development Council

The Hong Kong Arts Development Council (HKADC) was established by ordinance in 1995 to plan, promote and support the broad development of the arts including literary, performing, visual and film arts as well as arts education in Hong Kong.

In addition to providing financial assistance to local artists and arts organisations, the HKADC is dedicated to creating a conducive environment for arts development. During the year, the HKADC, in collaboration with various public and private organisations as well as government departments, organised a variety of projects, with the aim of bringing the arts closer to the public. These included the 4th Hong Kong Literature Festival, jointly organised with the LCSD; the Hong Kong Book Fair, co-presented with the Hong Kong Trade Development Council; the Art Boutiques, co-organised with the MTR Property Management; the Arts Education Expo, organised in association with the Hong Kong Heritage Museum; Gallery Ferry, jointly organised with the LCSD's Art Promotion Office, New World First Ferry Services Ltd and New World First Bus Services Ltd; and the Arts Appreciation Zone, a regular newspaper column jointly presented with *Ming Pao*.

The introduction of the 'Artwork on Loan' Scheme was a milestone in promoting the arts in Hong Kong. In collaboration with the Hong Kong Central Library, the

HKADC pioneered an innovative lending service, allowing members of the public to borrow over 100 pieces of reproductions by 27 local artists. Besides individual and group borrowers, the council also encouraged schools to invite artists to host in-house arts appreciation activities and workshops in order to stimulate a greater interest in art among students. Over 100 pieces of artwork are lent out every month.

In April, the HKADC organised the 27th Hong Kong International Film Festival. During the 16-day programme, a total of 330 films from more than 40 countries were screened. Twenty selected films were also shown in Macau concurrently. In addition, 55 fringe events were organised including seminars, exhibitions and 'Meet the Audience' activities. More than 220 000 people attended the festival.

Hong Kong Academy for Performing Arts

Established by ordinance in 1984 with an autonomous governing council, the Hong Kong Academy for Performing Arts offers professional training in music, dance, drama, technical arts, film and television and Chinese traditional theatre.

The academy secured the Bethanie, a Grade II historical building in Pok Fu Lam, as its second campus. Funding was approved by the Legislative Council's Finance Committee in March for restoration and conversion works on the building.

Although a number of planned overseas tours were postponed or cancelled due to the SARS outbreak, Academy students participated and won prizes in several important international piano competitions overseas — in Ukraine, Germany and Italy. Students from the Cantonese Opera Programme and the Chinese Dance Department also won awards at competitions held in Guangdong and Chengdu during the year. From July to September, music students were invited by the Government's Economic and Trade Offices in Europe and Asia to perform there, helping to revive the image of Hong Kong.

The Academy's Extension and Continuing Education for Life (EXCEL) Unit celebrated its second anniversary. During the year, the unit enrolled 5 000 participants in over 200 courses across the spectrum of disciplines taught at the Academy.

Hong Kong Arts Centre

The Hong Kong Arts Centre was established by ordinance in 1974, with an objective to nurture creativity, and arts and cultural engagement through its two-pronged approach in promoting contemporary performing arts, visual arts as well as film and video arts and in providing lifelong and life-wide arts education.

Home to artists' bold and creative explorations, the Arts Centre featured numerous presentations in various art forms in 2003, including film and video arts programmes *When Cinema Meets Fashion* and the 9th Hong Kong Independent Short Film and Video Awards; visual arts programmes *Cheng Ming in All Directions: 40 Years Arts at CUHK*; and performing arts programmes *WAVE 2003* and *Little Asia Dance Exchange Network 2003*.

Established in 2000, the Art School, which is the Art Centre's education arm, offers integrated programmes ranging from short courses to certificate, diploma, higher diploma, associate degree, first degree and higher degree courses, covering the humanities and five academic areas: fine arts, applied arts, media arts, arts education and arts management. There were more than 8 800 students enrolled in 2003. Activities included the *Residency Project for International Renowned Visual Artists (Phase II): The Position of HK in the Cross-cultural Context of Contemporary Chinese*

Happy youngsters turned their talents to sketching horses, and having a 'ride' on the life-size equine statues, at a 'Kiddie Draw Contest' held in Tsim Sha Tsui in November; the event was staged by the Hong Kong Jockey Club as part of its activities to publicise the Hong Kong International Races the next month.

Drum beats reverberated through Causeway Bay in July at the Opening Rally of the Hong Kong Drum Festival in Victoria Park; the event featured the world's largest Peace Drum and a record number of over 3 000 drummers. *Left:* an inaugural Cantonese Opera Day was held at the Hong Kong Cultural Centre in November to promote development and appreciation of this traditional art form.

The Harbour Fest at the Tamar Site in October and November drew enthusiastic audiences eager to see local and international singing stars help to revitalise Hong Kong, post-SARS.

Art; Forum on Media Arts and Creative Industries — Digital Now 2003; Artist Survival Workshop, and a public art lecture series.

The Fringe Club

The Fringe Club was established in 1983. It mounts a fringe festival in January every year. Its open-access policy allows local and overseas artists to produce various performances and exhibitions. The Fringe Club is the venue for the Hong Kong International Literary Festival, 'Le French May' Festival, Faust Festival and others. It runs a diverse programme of theatre, dance, music, and the visual arts year-round. It also has its own theatre productions, and organises art exhibitions and site-specific work with a Hong Kong heritage theme.

The Fringe Club is housed in a cold storage warehouse built in 1890, which has been listed as a historic monument. Since 1983, the building has undergone seven major renovations, providing a vibrant contemporary arts space. In 2001, the Fringe Club was given the Heritage Award by the Government for its outstanding cultural use of space in this historical building. It has two studio theatres, three exhibition areas (including a photography gallery), a pottery workshop and showroom, a rehearsal studio, a restaurant, two bars, an outdoor cafe, and offices.

Performing Arts Groups

Chung Ying Theatre

Chung Ying Theatre was established in 1979. Its mission is to nurture artistic excellence through the development of new plays, theatre-in-education projects and training of theatre practitioners. In 2003, members of its creative team created four original plays including *Far away . . . yet so close, Angel Aurora, Action! Mr. Lai,* and *When Snow Falls* (a musical play). A theatre performance entitled *The Arctic Saviour* was touring in secondary schools. A rerun of *Alive in the Mortuary* was the final performance of the season. Moreover, Chung Ying was commissioned as a Community Cultural Ambassador by the LCSD, to further its promotion of theatre performances.

City Contemporary Dance Company

The City Contemporary Dance Company was established in 1979. It is a professional modern dance company that endeavours to rally the best Chinese talents in creating dance in the contemporary context of China. In 2003, the company produced five new works including *Autumn Sonata*, a double bill by its resident choreographer Helen Lai and Pun Siu-fai; *The Enigma of Desire* by its associate choreographer Mui Cheuk-yin and resident artist Xing Liang; and two mixed bills by young choreographers from Hong Kong and the Mainland. The company's Education and Outreach Department offered year-round comprehensive dance courses for both adults and children, and presented outdoor performances as part of its activities to reach out to the community.

Hong Kong Ballet

The Hong Kong Ballet was established in 1979. It mission is to promote the finest ballet art forms of East and West. In 2003, the Hong Kong Ballet commissioned a new production, *Turandot*, a dramatic ballet based on the Puccini opera. It was created by the internationally acclaimed choreographer Natalie Weir. During the year, the company performed six other ballets: *Swan Lake; Coppelia; Ballet Extravaganza* (which consisted of three short works: *Dreams of Tenderness and Solitude*, a neo-classical piece by the award-winning American choreographer David Allan, *The Rite of Spring*, a reworking by Natalie Weir of this still-controversial piece; and *Tango Ballet Tango*, a dance narrative by the company's artistic director Stephen Jefferies); *The Sleeping Beauty; Beauty and the Beast,* and *The Nutcracker*.

With a view to extending its audience base beyond Hong Kong, the company accepted an invitation to stage two performances of *Turandot* in Macau in September. The company's Education and Outreach Unit continued its work promoting dance to people of all ages and backgrounds through more than 10 projects during the year.

Hong Kong Chinese Orchestra

Founded in 1977, the Hong Kong Chinese Orchestra was incorporated as a non-profit-making company in April 2001. The orchestra is a professional Chinese music orchestra that has gained international recognition. Under the leadership of artistic director Yan Huichang, it has made notable achievements in promoting the development of Chinese orchestral music. During the year, it gave a total of 100 regular, outreach and special concerts. A highlight was the Hong Kong Drum Festival, organised by the orchestra and held from July to October. The festival's Opening Rally was staged at Victoria Park as an event in the Government's post-SARS Economic Relaunch Campaign. More than 3 000 residents took part in a drum piece *The Earth Shall Move,* under the baton of Yan and featuring the debut of the world's biggest Peace Drum. The event has been registered for an entry in the *Guinness Book of World Records.*

Hong Kong Dance Company

The Hong Kong Dance Company, founded in 1981, was incorporated as a non-profit-making organisation in April 2001. It is committed to promoting the art of Chinese dance and has also performed in Australia, the United Kingdom, Republic of Korea, Japan, Singapore and Canada as well as Beijing, Shanghai and Taipei. Besides producing five productions each season, the company also organises outreach and educational events for the community, especially young people.

Hong Kong Philharmonic Orchestra

The Hong Kong Philharmonic Orchestra, with 89 members, is the city's oldest and largest orchestra. It gave a total of 130 concerts during the year. The orchestra provides the community with classical music of an international standard, and inspires and cultivates creativity through its multi-faceted commissioning and music education programmes. As a Cultural Ambassador for Hong Kong, the orchestra made its debut in Europe in 2003, performing in London, Belfast, Dublin and Paris. The tour, in February and March, began with performances in Macau and in the Korean cities of Seoul, Busan and Gwangju.

Hong Kong Repertory Theatre

Founded in 1977, the Hong Kong Repertory Theatre was incorporated as a non-profit-making organisation in April 2001. The company is the first professional drama theatre in Hong Kong. Its extensive repertoire is performed mostly in Cantonese and sometimes in Putonghua. Other than original works, the company also performs translated classics. During the year, the company staged nine productions of different genres in 122 performances, including 15 student performances. Apart from its major productions, the company toured 128 schools, organised six summer camp classes for students and gave 52 sessions of theatre workshops for the community.

Hong Kong Sinfonietta

Established in 1990, the Hong Kong Sinfonietta strives to integrate the art of music with the lives of people. The orchestra hopes to achieve the best quality of music with the use of local and regional talent as well as elevating the status of the art of music and musicians in Hong Kong through classical music. Under music director Yip Wing-sie, the orchestra continued to bring quality music to its audiences. It initiated a special joint performance, *Arts Relief for SARS*, with five other performance groups to raise funds for SARS victims. The orchestra's concert at the Hong Kong Arts Festival, continued participation in the 'Le French May' Festival, International Arts Carnival and 'Legends of China' Festival highlighted the year's activities. The orchestra also broke new ground and collaborated for the first time with local pop stars — Andy Hui and William So.

Theatre Ensemble

Established in 1993 under the joint artistic directors Jim Chim and Olivia Yan, the Theatre Ensemble has endeavoured to create quality theatre works that are 'physical', 'creative' and 'humorous'. To commemorate its 10th anniversary, the company organised a variety of activities during the year including a physical stand-up comedy *Sure Wine*; a children's theatre *Oops! Belle the Witch is Gone* (a live music version); an interactive seminar for parents called *School of Jim Jim*; the 10th anniversary exhibition *10 • The Bounds • The Boundless*; the launching of PIP (Pleasure In Play) school with a PIP Festival; and a school touring programme of 200 performances of *Smokeland Adventure*.

Zuni Icosahedron

Zuni Icosahedron is a multimedia experimental theatre group. Since its inception in 1982, it has played an important role in developing new frontiers for Hong Kong's cultural scene. It has been active in video, sound experimentation and installation arts, as well as in the areas of arts education, arts criticism and arts policy research. In 2003, Zuni created five experimental performances. These were the multimedia music theatre, *A Lover's Discourse* and *18 Springs*; the experimental traditional Chinese opera series *Good Wind Like Water*; and the socio-political theatre *East Wing West Wing*. Popularising experimental arts and culture has always been the group's main focus. In 2003, it continued to organise a series of multimedia theatre workshops and joint-school performances for students, published a new supplementary booklet, *Book*, together with an arts and cultural magazine, *E+E*. Zuni was also invited to take part in international cultural exchange activities, including a performance of its *Sigmund Freud In Search of Chinese Matter and Mind* in Tokyo's Performing Art Market and launching the *Black Box Exercise* installation exhibition in the 'Images of Asia' Festival in Denmark.

Visual Arts Groups

1A Group

1A Group was established by a group of local art workers in 1998. Its objective is to promote research and creative works concerning international and local contemporary art. During the year, major exhibitions organised by the 1A Group included *Tree • Man, Frame Work* and *Video Cafe*.

Artist Commune

Artist Commune was established in 1997. It is devoted to the establishment of a new Asian art network with Hong Kong as the centre. In 2003, it organised exhibitions entitled *Via Cattle Depot . . . (The Artist Village)* and *sARTs*.

Asia Art Archive

Established in 2000, the Asia Art Archive is dedicated to cataloguing and preserving materials on Asian contemporary art. To raise awareness of and stimulate interest in contemporary local and regional art, it launched in 2003 an online database/catalogue and carried out research and collated related materials on artists based in Hong Kong, the Mainland, Taiwan, Macau, Singapore, Thailand and the Philippines.

Hong Kong Society for Education in Art

The Hong Kong Society for Education in Art was established in 1982. It promotes the development of visual arts education in schools and in the community. During the year, the society initiated and organised *Art in Teaching 2003: Teachers' Art-works and Interactive Creation by Teachers and Students* and *Visual Culture Teaching Training Course*. It also published a CD-ROM on *Integrative Learning and Life-wide Learning Project: Design a School-based Art Teaching Unit*.

Para/Site Art Space

Para/Site Art Space was established in 1996. It promotes multi-disciplinary projects and contemporary local arts by organising exhibitions for both emerging and established artists. It participated in the 50th Venice Biennale in June. Its exhibitions included *Housewarming* and *Did you know that Hong Kong was still last night?*

The Hong Kong Jockey Club Music and Dance Fund

The Hong Kong Jockey Club Music and Dance Fund was set up in 1980 with a donation of $10 million from the Hong Kong Jockey Club for the promotion and development of music and dance. It is a non-statutory trust fund, administered by a board of trustees. In 1994, the Jockey Club provided a further capital injection of $22 million to meet the increasing demand for support.

During the year, the fund awarded $2 million for eight scholarships and $0.86 million for 71 grants. The scholarships enabled young people to pursue an integrated programme of post-diploma/post-graduate studies or professional training in music or dance studies at leading institutions outside Hong Kong. The grants helped local secondary and primary schools to procure musical instruments and dance equipment for training purposes, and to organise new training classes for students.

Music Office

The main objectives of the Music Office are to promote general music education in the community, especially for young people; to develop public interest in music; and to foster sharing of music among local young musicians and their counterparts all over the world. The Music Office runs 18 youth orchestras/bands/choirs that have 1 300 members. In 2003, it organised an instrumental music training scheme for 4 200 trainees, short-term music interest courses for 2 000 participants, and 340 musical activities for audiences that totalled 190 000. Other major events included a music camp, youth music 'interflows', and music youth exchange programmes for local, Mainland and overseas young musicians.

Cultural Venues

Hong Kong Cultural Centre

Since its inauguration in 1989, the Hong Kong Cultural Centre has established itself as Hong Kong's premier performing arts venue, attracting leading artists from around the world. It has three main performing venues: Concert Hall, Grand Theatre and Studio Theatre with seating capacities of 2 019, 1 734 and 303/496, respectively. In 2003, a total of 537 496 people attended 671 performances in these venues. An Arts and Crafts Fair is organised at the Piazza every Sunday and on selected public holidays with the aim of enhancing the cultural atmosphere of the venue and attracting visitors.

Hong Kong City Hall

The Hong Kong City Hall has commanded a special place in Hong Kong's cultural life since its establishment in 1962. It is a major multi-purpose complex comprising a Concert Hall, Theatre, Recital Hall, Exhibition Hall and Exhibition Gallery. A total of 1 630 events were held during the year, attracting 340 175 people.

Regional and District Civic Centres

In addition to the Hong Kong Cultural Centre, Hong Kong City Hall and the two indoor stadia, the LCSD operates 11 regional and district civic centres: the Sheung Wan Civic Centre and Sai Wan Ho Civic Centre on Hong Kong Island; the Ngau Chi Wan Civic Centre and Ko Shan Theatre in Kowloon; and the Sha Tin Town Hall, Tsuen Wan Town Hall, Tuen Mun Town Hall, Kwai Tsing Theatre, Yuen Long Theatre, North District Town Hall and Tai Po Civic Centre in the New Territories.

Through the 'Artist-in-residence' Scheme, 12 local arts groups made use of these 11 venues for a designated period in 2003 to develop and promote their creative works and education programmes among the district communities.

The 'Programme Partnership' Scheme, first launched in 2002 at the Yuen Long Theatre and the North District Town Hall, was extended to the Sheung Wan Civic Centre and the Ngau Chi Wan Civic Centre. Under this scheme, facilities and resources were provided to selected arts groups so they could organise audience-building programmes and create new works. In this way, the arts community is offered the opportunity to be involved in organising programmes and to fully utilise the facilities at these civic centres.

West Kowloon Cultural District

A waterfront site of about 40 hectares at the southern tip of the West Kowloon Reclamation has been earmarked for development by the private sector into a world-class integrated arts, cultural, entertainment and commercial district to enhance Hong Kong's position as a centre of arts, culture and entertainment in Asia. Following announcement of the results of an Open International Concept Plan Competition for the development in February 2002, the Government had decided to adopt the concept plan of the first prize-winner as the basis for the master plan of the development, to become the West Kowloon Cultural District (WKCD).

The identifying features include an open-sided Canopy partially cladded with various types of solid or transparent panels, which unifies the many different land uses within the development and creates a comfortable environment for outdoor performances and leisure activities. It will be a fully integrated development which will include major arts and cultural facilities in a 'Cultural Headland' to the west, shopping and entertainment facilities in a central 'Retail and Entertainment Spine' and high-rise office and hotel buildings in the 'Commercial Gateway' to the east.

The Chief Secretary for Administration announced an Invitation For Proposal (IFP) on September 5, 2003, to invite the private sector to submit proposals for the WKCD development, to be submitted by June 19, 2004. Construction is anticipated to commence by 2007 and the core arts and cultural facilities will come into operation in phases starting from 2011.

Indoor Stadia

The Hong Kong Coliseum and the Queen Elizabeth Stadium are two of the largest multi-purpose indoor stadia in Hong Kong. The 12 500-seat coliseum is a leading venue for pop concerts, musicals, entertainment spectaculars, international sporting events, cultural programmes, large-scale celebrations and conventions. The 3 600-seat stadium is suitable for holding sports events, cultural and entertainment performances, school ceremonies, conferences and variety shows.

In 2003, 392 performances were staged in the two indoor stadia, attracting around 1 732 400 people.

URBTIX — Computerised Ticketing System

URBTIX, launched in 1984, has become the most popular ticketing system through which members of the public may purchase tickets at any of the 31 outlets as well as through its telephone reservation and Internet ticketing services. In 2003, some 3.5 million tickets for over 6 384 performances were sold, with a total sales value of $467 million.

The LCSD is proceeding to outsource the back-end ticketing system, i.e. hardware and software with enhanced features, to the private sector for development of an advanced ticketing system targeted to be completed in 2005. The department will maintain the operation of ticket outlets and services for venue hirers.

Cultural Presentations

LCSD Cultural Presentations

During the year, the LCSD presented 1 795 performances, covering a rich variety of performing arts programmes featuring local and visiting artists. These attracted a total audience of 660 113 people.

Musical highlights by visiting artists included the St Petersburg Philharmonic Orchestra with Yuri Temirkanov, English Chamber Orchestra with Sarah Chang and a commissioned production of Verdi's opera *Macbeth*. Thematic programmes presented included the *Encore Series*, the *Music Rendezvous — City Hall Concert Hall Series*, the *Hong Kong City Hall Theatre Recital Series*, the *Guqin Music Series*, the *Chinese Ethnic Music and Dance Series* and the *Jazz Up Series*.

Highlights of contemporary dance programmes included the distinguished Ultima Vez from Belgium, Taipei's Crossover Dance Company and Hong Kong's City Contemporary Dance Company. There was also a series of dance performances from the Mainland including the Guangzhou Ballet, Song and Dance Ensemble of the People's Liberation Army, and Xinjiang Song and Dance Troupe, all of which were well received.

On the multi-arts front, the projects included independent concerts and music theatre productions by local artists, and mime and puppetry performances by Switzerland's Mummenschanz, Guangxi Puppet Art Troupe of China and Canada's Theatre de L'oeil. Highlighting the year were the pantomime performances by France's legendary Marcel Marceau. Collaboration with local theatre groups continued; many of the works presented or sponsored were new creations.

The promotion of the appreciation of Chinese opera has always been a key objective. A Cantonese Opera Working Group formed under the Greater Pearl River Delta Cultural Cooperation Conference has enhanced cultural cooperation in the region in promoting Cantonese opera. The first Cantonese Opera Day was organised on the last Sunday in November. Throughout the year, the LCSD presented newly commissioned Cantonese opera works as well as Chinese opera highlights from other regions, including the *Heroic Heroines of Peking Opera* series performed by artists from Shanghai, Shenyang and Guiyang City.

The department continues to cooperate with other bodies, and has sponsored or jointly organised cultural activities with consulates general and cultural institutions to promote cultural exchange. With a view to promoting contemporary music, the department sponsored the Chinese Composers' Festival, a joint venture with the Hong Kong Arts Development Council, Hong Kong Composers' Guild and the Composers and Authors Society of Hong Kong. It also collaborated with the Hong Kong Harmonica Association in organising the 1st Hong Kong Harmonica Festival.

Entertainment Programmes

During the year, a total of 656 carnivals and entertainment programmes were organised by the LCSD in parks, playgrounds, community halls as well as in the department's cultural venues. These covered a variety of performing arts presentations and attracted more than one million people.

Outdoor entertainment extravaganzas included the Spring Lantern Festival, Summer Fun Gala, Mid-Autumn Lantern Carnival, Christmas Fun Gala and New Year's Eve Countdown Carnival. Celebrating the Spring Lantern and Mid-Autumn

403

Festivals, the department staged spectacular lantern displays at the Hong Kong Cultural Centre Piazza to promote traditional Chinese culture among tourists and local residents. Thematic programmes such as the *Concert in the Park* and the *Asian Ethnic Cultural Programmes* drew an enthusiastic response from local people and tourists as well as Asian nationals living in Hong Kong.

Arts Education and Audience-building Projects

The LCSD places emphasis on promoting and increasing public access to the arts through educational and audience-building programmes.

During the year, the department held a total of 812 arts education and audience-building activities. The 'School Culture Day' Scheme mobilised schools to bring their students to the department's performing venues, museums and libraries during school hours. The 'School Arts Animateur' Scheme sought collaboration with local performing arts groups to offer arts training programmes at schools.

Arts education and audience-building activities organised for the community included the 'Artist-in-residence' Scheme which offered workshops and arts training programmes at performing venues, the 'Community Cultural Ambassador' Scheme which reached out to the public and the 'District Cantonese Opera Parade' organised to promote Cantonese opera at the community level.

The 'Cultural Services Volunteers' Scheme, well into its second year, encouraged members of the public to make better use of their leisure time to perform voluntary work in promoting arts and culture. Some 1 800 volunteers were recruited under the scheme.

Hong Kong International Film Festival

Presented by the Hong Kong Arts Development Council and sponsored by the LCSD, the 27th Hong Kong International Film Festival offered a wide range of programmes. The highlights of the 16-day festival included retrospectives on local film-maker Jeff Lau and overseas directors Jean-Pierre and Luc Dardenne and Marco Bellocchio; a tribute to Ozu Yasujiro in commemoration of the 100th anniversary of his birth; and *The Direct Cinema of Rob Nilsson*, about his experimental Direct Action Cinema. The Hong Kong Film Archive, which organised the retrospective section, contributed *Shaws on Screen*. In addition to the FIPRESCI (International Film Critics Federation) Award, three international competitions were introduced for the first time: Firebird Awards for Young Cinema, Asian DV Competition and Humanitarian Awards for Documentaries.

Altogether, 330 films from over 40 countries were showcased under special topics such as *Directors in Focus, Indie Power* and *Hong Kong Panorama (2002-03)*. Seminars, forums and exhibitions were also organised.

Hong Kong Independent Short Film and Video Awards

This annual competition, organised by the Hong Kong Arts Centre and sponsored by the LCSD, aims to encourage creative non-commercial independent productions of short film and video as well as to promote public interest in film and video as an artistic and expressive media. Activities included screenings, workshops and community programmes.

Film and Video Programmes

The film and video programmes, presented either solely by the LCSD or jointly with local consulate offices, cultural and film institutions, continued to provide a variety of alternative film programmes and workshops for the public. Major programmes included *Shaws on Screen, The Psychic Labyrinth of Friedrich Wilhelm Murnau, 2-D dancing: movement in image, Foci — Microwave International Media Art Festival 2003, Looking Back: 50 Years of Korean Films* and *Early European Cinema — Italy 1909-1927*. In addition, film programmes from the Mainland and Israel as well as from France, Germany and other European Union countries were presented for the appreciation of local audiences. In order to enable children and young people to develop an interest in film, the International Children Film Carnival, being part of the International Arts Carnival, was organised in the summer and provided a series of film screenings and video workshops.

Cultural Events

Hong Kong Arts Festival

Held annually in February and March, the Hong Kong Arts Festival is the most important international festival in the Asia and has become highly regarded world-wide since it began in 1973. With a fine array of performers taking part, the 2003 festival sold over 98 000 tickets in 108 performances, with the average attendance exceeding 90 per cent. The programmes included the Stuttgart Opera's *The Abduction from the Seraglio*, Orchestre National de France with Yundi Li, Laurie Anderson's *Happiness, Directions in Music* featuring Herbie Hancock, Michael Brecker and Roy Hargrove, the Hamburg Ballet, the Ballet Flamenco of Antonio Canales, Robert Lepage's *The Far Side of the Moon* and the Edward Lam Dance Theatre's production of *The Happy Prince.*

International Arts Carnival

To provide children and families of Hong Kong with cultural and entertainment programmes of a healthy and educational nature, the LCSD presented the six-week International Arts Carnival in summer. Prior to the carnival, three drama outreach teams were sent to promote arts activities at various schools and kindergartens to arouse community interest. In addition to a rich series of stage performances, new interactive performances and seminars for parents and adults were included in the carnival for the first time. Apart from a Graphic Design Competition open to all primary and secondary school students, the carnival also featured a creative writing competition for young people which was jointly organised with the *Young Post* of the *South China Morning Post*. In addition, intensive arts workshops and day camps were held. About 134 000 people took part in 449 events that featured 22 local groups and three overseas groups.

'Legends of China' Festival

Following the success of the 'Legends of China' Festival in 2001, the LCSD presented the same thematic festival again from mid-October to November with the aim of enhancing public awareness, understanding and appreciation of the arts and culture of Asia, the Mainland and Hong Kong. The festival opened with the commissioned opera *Legend of Yao Ji* which featured leading artists, and creative and production personnel from the Mainland, Hong Kong and Taiwan. In order to appeal to younger audiences, the festival brought in new theatrical and multimedia productions like the *Seventh Drawer* and the *18 Springs*. Other popular shows included *Chanting from Mountains Afar, Majestic Drums II* and *Ancient Dance and Music of Dunhuang*. Alongside the stage performances, various extension activities were organised, and these included a performance tour to secondary schools and universities, exhibitions, lectures, demonstrations, forums, and free outdoor performances. A total of 94 cultural events, featuring eight local groups and 17 overseas groups, were presented for some 77 000 participants.

Heritage

Antiquities Advisory Board and Antiquities and Monuments Office

The LCSD's Antiquities and Monuments Office continued to preserve Hong Kong's heritage and promote public awareness of it through exhibitions, guided tours, publications and community involvement projects.

The Antiquities Advisory Board comprises 21 appointed members. It advises the Government on sites and structures that merit protection by declaring them as monuments and on other matters related to antiquities and monuments.

In 2003, the Antiquities and Monuments Office continued to undertake restoration and repair works at various historical buildings, including the Hau Mei Fung Ancestral Hall in Sheung Shui, the Tin Hau Temple in Causeway Bay, the Old House at Wong Uk Village in Sha Tin, the Pak Mong Watchtower and its Gate House on Lantau Island, and the Lawson's Bunker and Former West Brigade Headquarters in Wong Nai Chung Gap.

To encourage and assist owners of private historical buildings to participate in conservation works, the office provided technical advice and support to such owners in their maintenance and restoration projects. In a restoration project concerning the Liu Ying Lung Study Hall in Sheung Shui, a technical team from the Guangdong Provincial Institute of Cultural Relics and Archaeology was invited with the assistance of the office to conduct a cartographic survey of the historical building, and give advice on the conservation plan.

In its endeavours to preserve cultural heritage in the face of impending development projects, the office conducted Environment Impact Assessment (EIA) and various conservation studies. Examples were the heritage impact assessment study concerning the Extension of the North Point Low Level Salt Water Supply System, and the consultancy study on the feasibility of protecting the Tat Tak Communal Hall in Ping Shan, Yuen Long from the threat of serious flooding, and on the conservation plan for the hall. Other heritage conservation studies included a feasibility study on the preservation of Old Cable House in Telegraph Bay in Southern District, feasibility study on the preservation of Lee Tat Bridge and realignment of a new bridge in Shui Tsan Tin Tsuen in Pat Heung, Yuen Long, and a conservation assessment of the built heritage of Tung Ping Chau.

The office continued to contribute to the EIA for development projects, and monitored field investigations and implementation of mitigation measures under the Heritage Impact Assessment. For example, terrestrial and marine archaeological investigations and studies were conducted for the Shatin to Central Rail Link and the South-East Kowloon Development plan.

To save the archaeological heritage from destruction by development projects at the former Tai Hom Village in Kowloon and Telegraph Bay on Hong Kong Island, rescue excavations were launched in October 2002 and May 2003, respectively. Ceramic vessels of the Song and Ming dynasties were retrieved from the village and a kiln structure dating to the Tang dynasty was discovered at the bay.

Rescue excavations were carried out at Ngau Hom Shek, Tsing Chuen Wai and Lam Tei to facilitate implementation of the approved EIA reports and relevant conditions in the Environmental Permits concerning two major road projects, the Hong Kong-Shenzhen Western Corridor and the Deep Bay Link. Archaeological investigations and rescue excavations were also arranged before works began on village house developments in areas such as Tuen Mun and Sha Tau Kok, and road improvement projects at Chi Ma Wan Road on Lantau Island and at Tuen Mun Road.

Lord Wilson Heritage Trust

The Lord Wilson Heritage Trust was established in 1992, following the enactment of an ordinance bearing the same name. It aims to promote the preservation and conservation of Hong Kong's heritage.

During the year, apart from sponsoring $1.85 million for eight heritage-related activities and research projects, the trust granted $160,290 to the Summer Youth Programme Committee for organising heritage-related activities in local districts. Participation in these activities helps young people to develop an interest in preserving Hong Kong's heritage.

Museums

Hong Kong Museum of Art

The Hong Kong Museum of Art focuses on local and Chinese art collections, including Chinese painting and calligraphy, Chinese antiquities, historical paintings and contemporary art. In order to enhance the public's interest and knowledge in the arts of the world, the museum presented a variety of thematic exhibitions, covering ancient and modern works as well as Chinese and Western themes.

In 2003, the museum staged 12 exhibitions, comprising seven special exhibitions and five permanent ones. Three of the major special exhibitions were presented jointly by the museum with renowned Chinese and overseas museums, featuring art objects and cultural relics from the Mainland and overseas. *The Private Life of An Old Red Army Man*, jointly organised with the Shenzhen Sculpture House, was a 'social sculpture' exhibition rarely seen in Hong Kong. Through a display of old photographs and personal manuscripts of an 'old Red Army man', the exhibition intended to reinterpret the revolution of 20th century China.

The *Selection from the Guoyun Lou Collection of the Shanghai Museum* exhibition was another successful collaboration with the Shanghai Museum. It featured a rich collection of Chinese paintings and calligraphic works by well-known ancient masters from the collection of Gu Wenbin, an acclaimed scholar, connoisseur and owner of the *Guoyun Lou*, and his eminent Gu family in Suzhou. *Desire and Devotion: Art from India, Nepal and Tibet in the John and Berthe Ford Collection*, a thematic exhibition jointly organised with an American museum, the Walters Art Museum in Baltimore, displayed paintings and sculptures that reflected the uniqueness of the arts of the Indian subcontinent and Tibet.

Other special exhibitions were presented to cover noted local artists. *Hong Kong Cityscapes — Ink Painting in Transition*, a rerun of an exhibition held during the Hong Kong Festival in London, provided an overview of ink painting and its evolution in Hong Kong in recent decades. *Sun Xingge: An Exhibition of Chinese Painting and Calligraphy*, featuring a new museum collection generously donated by the family of Sun, reflected the unique artistic accomplishments of this well-known Guangdong painter who settled in Hong Kong in the early years. *Hong Kong Art Biennial 2003*, a region-wide event, featured works by local artists selected from over a thousand entries. The exhibition, covering a wide range of media, fully illustrated the recent development of contemporary Hong Kong art and the creativity of local artists. Also on display was *Navigating the Dot — Collective in Progress*, a new version of the Hong Kong exhibition at the 50th Venice Biennale.

In order to enrich people's knowledge of its collections, the museum updated its permanent exhibitions with new exhibits from time to time. The Chinese Antiquities Gallery featured a new exhibition *The Art of Rhinoceros Horn Carving*, which cast light on the artefacts of the Ming and Qing dynasties in the *Metal, Wood, Water, Fire and Earth: Gems of Antiquities Collections in Hong Kong* exhibition series. For Chinese painting and calligraphy, *Selection of 20th Century Chinese Figure Paintings from the Museum's Collection* showed the faces of people in the new era as seen by Chinese artists in the past century. The *Xubaizhai* Gallery also featured *Selection from the Xubaizhai Collection of Chinese Calligraphy* with a fine selection of over 50 works of calligraphy from the 'Six Dynasties' period to the 20th century.

To enhance the public's interest in art, the museum also organised a wide range of education and extension programmes, including video shows, special lectures, family programmes, art workshops and guided tours. During the year, the museum took part in various major art extension programmes such as the International Museum Day and the 'School Culture Day'. Moreover, the museum liased with 26 different art organisations, groups, tertiary institutions and galleries and presented over 20 fringe exhibitions and programmes for the *Hong Kong Art Biennial 2003*.

The exhibitions, together with various education and extension programmes, attracted over 207 000 visitors and participants during the year.

Flagstaff House Museum of Tea Ware

The collection of this museum comprises various kinds of teaware and related vessels from the collection of the late Dr K.S. Lo and rare Chinese ceramics and seals donated by the K.S. Lo Foundation. Two special exhibitions were held in 2003: *Far Beyond Teapots* featured various vessels for tea and wine, of periods ranging from the Neolithic period to the 20th century; *Yuanyang: An Exhibition of Coffee and Tea Vessels* illustrated items of coffee and tea vessels tailor-made by noted Hong Kong artists to associate with the theme *yuanyang* (a mixture of milk tea and coffee).

The museum organised a variety of educational activities, such as demonstrations of Chinese tea drinking, tea gatherings for parents and children, tea gatherings with instrumental music, tea classes and video shows. During the year, over 182 000 visitors were entertained.

Hong Kong Museum of History

Throughout the year, in addition to *The Hong Kong Story* permanent exhibition, the Museum of History presented four thematic exhibitions: namely *A Tribute to*

Heritage: Discovering Hong Kong's Culture and Tradition, 75 Years of Broadcasting in Hong Kong, We Shall Overcome: Plagues in Hong Kong, and *Sun Yat-sen: from Cuiheng to Hong Kong.* These exhibitions presented in detail the different facets of the history and heritage of Hong Kong. Moreover, four major thematic exhibitions were jointly presented with museums and cultural institutions from the Mainland and overseas. They were *War and Peace: Treasures of the Qin and Han Dynasties; Napoleon Bonaparte: Emperor and Man; National Flag, Emblem and Anthem of the People's Republic of China;* and *Boundless Learning: Foreign-educated Students of Modern China.* The joint presentations broadened the public's cultural horizons, and also facilitated the academic and cultural 'interflow' between Hong Kong, the Mainland and foreign countries. The museum attracted 973 231 visitors during the year.

To foster public interest in local history and cultural heritage, the museum organised diversified educational activities and extension services, like guided tours, audio-guides, lectures, workshops, demonstrations, performances, field trips, in-house video programmes, 'School Culture Day' programmes, loan of educational resources, travelling exhibitions, briefing sessions, an international symposium, seminars, a quiz competition, and an Inter-school Competition of Study Projects on Hong Kong's History and Culture. The museum and the Hong Kong Institute of Education jointly conducted the 2nd Junior Curator Training Course, which was successfully concluded with a small display assembled by the student-participants at the museum in November.

Apart from the Museum of Coastal Defence, the Museum of History also manages two other branch museums — the Lei Cheng Uk Han Tomb Museum in Sham Shui Po and the Law Uk Folk Museum in Chai Wan. They attracted 37 065 and 30 977 visitors, respectively.

Hong Kong Museum of Coastal Defence

Converted from the old Lei Yue Mun Fort in Shau Kei Wan, the Hong Kong Museum of Coastal Defence comprises three main areas: Reception Building, Redoubt and Historical Trail. The permanent exhibition galleries are located in the Redoubt, and feature the standing exhibition *600 Years of Coastal Defence in Hong Kong* that depicts Hong Kong's history of coastal defence from the Ming and Qing period, the British period and the Japanese invasion to the period after Hong Kong's reunification with the Mainland. Visitors may also explore the historical military relics in the Redoubt and on the Historical Trail, such as the gun batteries, the torpedo station, caponiers and magazines.

The museum presented three thematic exhibitions during the year — *Cultural Relics of the Zhongshan Gun Boat, Cultural Relics of the Fireboat Alexander Grantham* (jointly organised with the Fire Services Department) and *Archery Traditions of Asia.*

To arouse public interest in the history of Hong Kong's coastal defence, the museum organised a variety of educational activities, such as guided tours to the galleries and the Historical Trail, lectures on specific topics, family workshops, demonstrations and field trips. The museum's exhibitions and activities attracted 213 895 visitors during the year.

Hong Kong Heritage Museum

'Food Culture' was the theme of the Hong Kong Heritage Museum's programmes in 2003-04. A series of exhibitions and educational activities was organised, including thematic exhibitions entitled *More Than Just Food — Ceramic Art Exhibition* and *Hong Kong's Food Culture*. In the former exhibition, 12 local artists in ceramics produced appetising menus specially designed for each month of the year as well as some imaginative ware on which to serve the food. The latter exhibition reviewed the history of local food, investigated the changes that had taken place in eating establishments, and examined food packaging in Hong Kong.

Other thematic exhibitions staged during the year included *Life in China Around the May Fourth Movement: Sidney D. Gamble's Photographs of China 1908-1932; Huizhou Vernacular Architecture; Alan Chan: The Art of Living; 'Woman' Wanted; Fashion Parade: Women's Wears in Changing Hong Kong*; and *Mapping Asia — the 18th Asian International Art Exhibition*.

A total of 1 138 educational and extension activities were organised for the public such as lectures, field trips, video programmes, demonstrations, art camps for children, workshops, performances, guided tours and an international symposium. A new initiative, the *MuseKids*, was introduced in July to provide children from kindergarten level through to Primary 6 with opportunities to explore the history, art and culture of Hong Kong. Specially designed educational programmes would be regularly arranged for them. By year-end, 4 549 children had become members of the scheme.

The museum's exhibition programmes, together with its educational and extension activities, attracted 455 629 visitors and participants.

The Heritage Museum also manages three branch museums — Sam Tung Uk Museum, Hong Kong Railway Museum and Sheung Yiu Folk Museum. The Sam Tung Uk Museum in Tsuen Wan was originally a Hakka walled village built in 1786. It was declared a monument in 1981 and later converted into a museum for public viewing. Located in Tai Po, the Railway Museum consists of the old Tai Po Market Railway Station building, a narrow-gauge steam locomotive and various historical coaches. The station building, in Chinese style, was built in 1913 and declared a monument in 1984. The Sheung Yiu Folk Museum, situated in the Sai Kung Country Park, is housed in a Hakka village built in the late 19th century. It comprises eight domestic units, pig pens, an open courtyard and an entrance gate-tower. The village and a nearby lime kiln were gazetted as monuments in 1981.

In 2003, the Sam Tung Uk Museum, Hong Kong Railway Museum and Sheung Yiu Folk Museum attracted 154 933, 197 415 and 44 434 visitors, respectively.

Hong Kong Science Museum

On loan from a supplier in the United States, *Grossology: The (Impolite) Science of the Human Body* was held between November 2002 and March 2003. Animatronics and interactive exhibits were used to engage visitors. A total attendance of 153 797 was registered during the exhibition period.

The exhibition *Albert Einstein: Man of the Century* was held in the foyer of the Science Museum between February and April. Based on original material housed in the Albert Einstein Archives, the Jewish National and University Library and the Hebrew University of Jerusalem, the exhibition portrayed Albert Einstein both as an outstanding scientist and as a humanitarian. The exhibition consisted of rare photographs and film footage.

The *Sciencetunnel Exhibition* between May and August attracted 64 870 visitors. It was developed by the Max Planck Society of Germany. Featuring a 170-metre multimedia tunnel, the exhibition guided visitors through the new dimensions of modern-day research. As visitors passed through the 12 linked stations, they were able to appreciate the latest achievements and discoveries that help to explain the emergence and evolution of all kinds of things in the universe, including human life, as well as the importance of science in enhancing the well-being of humankind.

To complement the International Museum Day initiated by the International Council of Museums, the LCSD presented an International Museum Day programme in May with 'Discovering Museums' as its theme. Taking the role of event coordinator, the Science Museum worked with 20 public museums and cultural institutions to organise over 200 entertaining and educational programmes including a three-day 'Museum Panorama' held at the Hong Kong Cultural Centre Piazza which attracted about 20 000 participants. The museums, offering free admission to the public during the period, received 64 200 visitors.

The exhibition *SARS and Viruses* was held in the foyer of the Science Museum from June 30, and was originally intended to close in September. In view of the public response, the exhibition was extended to the end of October and attracted a total of 177 976 visitors. Entirely developed and produced in-house, the exhibition aimed at educating the public on the scientific aspects of SARS as well as of viruses in general. Among the exhibits was a 3D model of a coronavirus and an infrared forehead temperature scanner.

The *Wildlife Photographer of the Year* exhibition was presented between October and December and featured the winning entries in the 2001 and 2002 Wildlife Photographer of the Year competitions organised by the Natural History Museum of the United Kingdom. Combining artistic perspective, technical expertise and the natural beauty of animals across the spectrum of deserts, mountains, forests and oceans, the 200 images portrayed the harmony of nature and conveyed the message of environmental protection.

To commemorate China's first successful manned space flight in mid-October, the *Exhibition on China's First Manned Space Mission* was held from November 1 to November 4 in the Special Exhibition Hall. Among the exhibits was the re-entry module of the Shenzhou-5 spaceship that carried Colonel Yang Liwei into space on October 15 and the spacesuit he wore during his epic mission. The exhibition attracted more than 103 000 visitors during the continuous 76-hour exhibition period.

In late December, the museum began a three-month follow-up exhibition entitled *China's First Manned Space Mission Exhibition II — Gifts for Hong Kong* to display the items presented by the Space Mission Delegation that visited Hong Kong, including the training suit donated by Colonel Yang and two large satellite images covering the Hong Kong SAR and the Pearl River Delta. The exhibition also featured memorabilia produced for earlier aerospace exhibitions held in the museum.

From October to December, the museum joined hands with the Hong Kong Observatory to organise a series of six lectures presented by distinguished meteorologists from the United States, the Mainland and Hong Kong. The series, introducing meteorological topics of public concern like *El Nino,* typhoons and climate change, attracted a total audience of 1 380 people.

With the aim of introducing to the public scientific research projects currently conducted in local universities and disseminating knowledge of 'frontier' technology, the Science News Corner staged three thematic exhibitions in 2003: *Automatic Face Image and Sketch Recognition, Fruit Fly — Drosophila* and *Extremes of the Universe*. The exhibitions, jointly developed by the universities and the museum, represented a valuable collaboration between researchers and museum professionals in promoting science. The exhibition will be renewed regularly to keep abreast of scientific advancement and technological breakthroughs.

As in the previous year, the LCSD's 'Teacher Museum Pass' Scheme served to encourage teachers to visit museums and make use of museum resources to support their work. The museum, serving as coordinator of the scheme, arranged orientation visits for teachers and processed applications for around 2 000 schools.

The museum continued to work with educational institutions and professional bodies on a number of special projects to promote science. Popular examples were the Fun Science Competition in February, the Symposium on Environmental Issues for Schools and 6th Primary Science Project Competition in July, the 36th Joint School Science Exhibition in August, and the Joint Schools Robotic Olympiad in November.

The museum's exhibitions and extension activities attracted more than 870 000 visitors and participants during the year.

Hong Kong Space Museum

The Hong Kong Space Museum is dedicated to promoting astronomy and space science to the public. During the year, the museum strengthened its astronomical observation activities. A special occasion was the week from August 27 when the planet Mars was at its closest to the Earth in 60 000 years. The museum remained open until late at night to enable members of the public to view the planet through astronomical telescopes. More than 5 000 people took advantage of the opportunity.

In addition, the museum and the Hong Kong Astronomical Society jointly organised a *Sidewalk Astronomy* session for the public at the Tsim Sha Tsui waterfront in October. In this activity, about 50 astronomical telescopes were set up for use by interested passers-by, and more than 1 500 people took advantage of the opportunity to observe celestial objects.

To mark China's first manned space flight in October, the museum organised a number of activities including exhibitions, display of a model of the Shenzhou spacecraft and workshops. Related educational materials were also produced.

During the year, the museum published the *Astrocalendar 2004*. The museum's two Sky Shows, four Omnimax films, and six School Shows attracted some 290 100 people. The museum also organised 190 extension activities that had over 40 700 participants. Fourteen temporary special exhibitions, together with the permanent exhibits in the Hall of Astronomy and in the Hall of Space Science, attracted more than 317 700 visitors.

Hong Kong Film Archive

The Hong Kong Film Archive's major functions are to acquire, preserve, catalogue and document Hong Kong films and related materials. With a gross floor area of 7 200 square metres, its major facilities include a cinema, an exhibition hall, a resource centre and a number of temperature-controlled collection stores. It has already acquired more than 5 600 films and 994 000 items of related materials, mainly through donations and deposits.

During the year, nine thematic exhibitions such as the *Shaws Galaxy of Stars, The Psychic Labyrinth of Friedrich Wilhelm Murnau, In the Footsteps of Lai Man-wai,* and *Attraction and Magic — Early European Cinema* were organised and more than 460 screenings were held at the Film Archive. To complement the exhibitions and screening activities, the Film Archive also held a number of joint projects with local educational and cultural institutions in organising seminars and workshops for film students, researchers and the public. In research on the history of Hong Kong cinema, the Film Archive conducted oral history interviews with film veterans and produced a number of film-related publications.

The resource centre, equipped with computers, independent video booths and a rich collection of film-related reading materials, was well patronised by the public, attracting a daily average of 156 users. Overall, the Film Archive attracted more than 160 000 visitors during the year.

Art Promotion Office

The Art Promotion Office aims to promote local visual arts through wide-ranging activities focusing on public and community art. The office places importance on undertaking projects with different partners, which helps to further enhance art appreciation and participation among members of the public.

The Public Art Scheme 2002 was completed during the year with selected artworks installed in four public libraries and two town halls. The Gallery Ferry Project was jointly organised with the Hong Kong Arts Development Council, New World First Ferry Services Ltd and New World First Bus Services Ltd. In this project, three installation works and 20 two-dimensional works were displayed on board three ferries and at Pier 5 in Central from May until year-end.

The second 'Artists in the Neighbourhood' Scheme was another partnership project. In 2003, works of 12 artists and one art group were displayed at different LCSD venues, MTR stations, hospitals and shopping malls. Because of the success of the 'Art • Care' project in 2002, the office launched another community art project entitled *A New Beginning/A New Day* with the local arts organisation Art in Hospital, to sustain the efforts in introducing visual arts to hospitals.

Hong Kong Visual Arts Centre

The Art Promotion Office is also responsible for the management of the Hong Kong Visual Arts Centre. Nine art studios, a lecture theatre, an exhibition hall and a multi-purpose room were open for public hiring at subsidised rates. The centre focuses on providing professional hiring facilities and training in the visual arts and promoting them. The second Art Specialist Course, which covered five disciplines — ceramics, printmaking, painting, sculpture and ink painting — was specially designed for general art lovers who would wish to pursue structured professional art training. The course began in October 2002 and lasted nine months. A graduation exhibition was held in the centre in October to celebrate the graduation of 62 participants by displaying artworks they created during the course.

Central Conservation Section

The Central Conservation Section devises, implements and evaluates conservation programmes for museum artefacts and heritage objects. In 2003, the section administered conservation treatment to 2 633 cultural objects including paintings, paper artefacts, textiles, photographs, metals, ceramics, organic materials and archaeological finds. It continued to provide the necessary technical support for 79 thematic exhibitions and the management of some 200 000 collection items pertaining to 12 public museums, the Art Promotion Office, and assisted in the preservation of repository items for the Antiquities and Monuments Office.

As an essential part of its education and extension programmes, the section received five schools for behind-the-scene laboratory visits under the 'School Culture Day' Scheme and organised 14 workshops and guided tours for the International Museum Day. Adding together other lecture programmes and laboratory visits, the section received over 5 000 visitors during the year.

With a view to preserving the fireboat *Alexander Grantham* upon its decommissioning after 50 years of service and mounting it for public viewing, the section has been engaged in the necessary project planning and conservation work for the vessel and its more than 500 relics.

To follow on from the success of the first phase of staging cultural displays at the Hong Kong International Airport, the section undertook to organise another standing exhibition there, in cooperation with the Airport Authority, for the enjoyment of travellers and people working at the airport. Entitled *Formal Dialogue — Sculptures by Hong Kong Masters* the exhibition began in April and featured 28 acclaimed works by two local master sculptors.

Public Libraries

The LCSD operates the Hong Kong Public Library System which comprises 70 public libraries, including eight mobile libraries. It also manages the Books Registration Office. The Public Library System provides free public library services to meet community needs for information, research, informal education and the profitable use of leisure time. The aim is to promote reading and the literary arts and support lifelong learning.

The libraries have a comprehensive library collection of 8.98 million books and 1.19 million multimedia materials and a total of 2.97 million registered borrowers. In 2003, 58.62 million items of library materials were borrowed from the libraries and 3.91 million reference enquiries were handled by staff, representing an increase of 10.04 per cent and 3.97 per cent, respectively, over 2002.

Hong Kong Central Library

Since its opening in May 2001, the Hong Kong Central Library has developed into a major information and cultural centre in Hong Kong. Occupying a gross floor area of 33 800 square metres with a total stock of 1.82 million items, the 12-storey building provides a wide range of facilities. Special features include a Multimedia Information System, a Central Reference Library with six subject departments, an Arts Resource Centre, Hong Kong Literature Room, Basic Law Reference Collection Room, Map Library, Language Learning Centre, Young Adult Library and a Toy Library. There are also hiring facilities including a 1 500 square-metre Exhibition Gallery, a 293-seat Lecture Theatre, two Activity Rooms, a Music Practice Room and a number of

Discussion Rooms. On average, the Hong Kong Central Library is visited by about 16 000 users daily.

In addition to regular cultural activities and subject talks, a wide range of notable events was organised region-wide during the year. The 'Distinguished Contemporary Chinese Scientists Seminar', which was a joint programme with the China Association for Science and Technology and the Beijing-Hong Kong Academic Exchange Centre, was held in October, attracting an audience of over 800 and many others on the Internet through live webcasting. The *Exhibition on Heinrich Boll: Life and Work*, featuring photographs, manuscripts, awards and newspaper clippings concerning the winner of the 1972 Nobel Prize for Literature was jointly presented with the Cologne Public Library in Germany.

The *Exhibition on a Tribute to Heritage: Discovering Hong Kong's Culture and Tradition*, which was co-organised by the Hong Kong Museum of History and the Antiquities and Monuments Office, showcased over 100 cultural pieces. The *Music Encounter: Exhibition of Ng Tai-kong's Works* presented a collection of the works of this renowned music master, donated by his descendants. To promote public awareness and research in local history, the *Exhibition on Treasure of Literature* was organised with a display of over 280 pieces of historical documents selected from the 70 000 items collected by the library through the Documents Collection Campaign. The *Exhibition on Guqin Culture* highlighted the development of qin music and its culture, and displayed 20 rare examples of qin instruments.

New Initiatives in Library Services

The Hong Kong Public Libraries system has made dedicated efforts to improve service to the public through enrichment of library stock and reference and information services, use of information technology, promotion of reading habits in the community as well as enhancement of the accessibility of public library services.

With the expansion of the library stock and of the number of patrons, a total of 58.62 million items of library materials were borrowed from the public libraries, an increase of 10.04 per cent on 2002.

The public libraries continued to promote and support lifelong learning in the community. The 'Library Cards for all School Children' Scheme was continued in collaboration with the Education and Manpower Bureau to encourage primary school students to use library services. Regular meetings were held with school librarians on the provision of library services to support the school curriculum. Moreover, public libraries continued to provide supporting services to the Project Yi Jin education programme and 15 public libraries stocked course materials of the Open University of Hong Kong, facilitating the pursuit of self-learning by many in the community. Plans were also under way to set up an Education Resource Centre at the Kowloon Public Library.

In January, two new libraries were opened: a full-scale district library in Fanling and a small library in Fu Shan. Plans were in hand to open two more new libraries in Tung Chung and Ma On Shan and a new mobile library, as well as to reprovision the existing Tai Po Public Library in leased premises to the new Tai Po Complex in 2004.

An 'Artwork on Loan' Scheme was launched jointly with the Hong Kong Arts Development Council which allowed each reader to borrow two pieces of artwork and institutions to borrow a maximum of five pieces of artwork for a loan period of 30 days from the Arts Resources Centre of the Hong Kong Central Library.

Reference and Information Services

Reference and information services are provided at the Central Library and the five major libraries — the City Hall, Kowloon, Sha Tin, Tsuen Wan and Tuen Mun Public Libraries. The Central Reference Library has a total collection of 760 000 items, providing comprehensive reference and information services through its six subject departments. It features a comprehensive collection of electronic materials including CD-ROMs, online databases, electronic books, electronic journals and multimedia programmes, all of which are available for online access by the public. The library also holds the depository collection of books required under the Books Registration Ordinance. During the year, a total of 3.91 million reference enquiries were handled by library staff.

During the year, the City Hall Reference Library was renovated into a specialised reference library in business and industry subjects and further enhanced with the setting up of the Creativity and Innovation Resource Centre in November, a joint project with the Creative Initiatives Foundation. The centre helped further strengthen education in innovative and creative thinking and foster a deeper understanding of the potential of creativity, thereby enriching the creative culture in Hong Kong.

Information Technology Initiatives and Digital Library Initiatives

The Library Automation System of the public libraries is one of the world's largest computerised library systems with both Chinese and English capabilities. It provides 24-hour Internet library services for online searching, reservation and renewal of library materials. In 2003, the use of 14.10 million items of library material was renewed through the Internet and Telephone Renewal Services. With the growing popularity of online public library services, the Hong Kong Public Libraries home page (*http://www.hkpl.gov.hk*) was ranked sixth among the most popular websites in Hong Kong.

With the Government's launching in mid-year of a new generation of identity cards, utilising 'smart' technology, the public libraries provided residents the option of using their smart ID cards as library cards to borrow, renew and reserve library materials. Moreover, a number of computer terminals with Internet access were installed with e-Cert compatible smart card readers for public use to promote wider use of information technology and electronic services. In December, an e-mail notification service was introduced to enable registered readers to receive overdue and reservation notices by e-mail, thereby enhancing service efficiency and economy of paper. Plans were also in hand to install more self-charging terminals to further promote self-services in the libraries.

The successful implementation of the Multimedia Information System (MMIS), which provides audio and video on demand, online CD-ROM and reference resources, as well as searching and viewing of documents through the workstations at the libraries and on the Internet, was a milestone in the development of digital library services. The system was also extended from the Hong Kong Central Library to 24 major and district libraries which significantly expanded the network to a total of 592 workstations across the HKSAR. To further improve accessibility, the service hours of the MMIS on the Internet were extended to midnight from November. At the beginning of the year, the system was linked up with the International Children's Digital Library's Books Project, a programme which collects in digital format children's books and literature written and published in different countries and offers them free to readers world-wide through the Internet. With its strong archival feature, the MMIS has been included since April in the Archives Portal of the United Nations Educational, Scientific and Cultural Organisation, a website through which archivists and researchers may study the history and culture of different nations.

Outreach Programmes and Promotion of Reading and Literary Arts

Outreach programmes form an integral part of library services. Regular programmes like children's hours, book displays and exhibitions, thematic talks and seminars, interest clubs and group visits were organised throughout the year. In line with the digital library initiative, educational programmes on teaching the public to use the Online Public Access Catalogue, online databases, CD-ROMs, MMIS and the Internet were also held regularly. The libraries organised a total of 15 248 library outreach programmes during the year.

A variety of reading programmes and reading-related activities were organised to promote reading. A month-long reading promotion programme was organised during the summer holidays. The event included a Children's Poetry and Rhyme Exhibition and a series of children's reading programmes such as musical drama, mini concerts, film shows, reading talks, storytelling sessions, poetry writing workshops, workshops on paired reading, children's and parents dramatisation competition and children's musical rhyme competition.

Moreover, the Teens' Reading Clubs were extended from the Hong Kong Central Library and the five major libraries to 25 district libraries. A number of activities, including 'Meet-the-Author' talks, were held to support the reading clubs, and these drew an enthusiastic response. Apart from the regular block loan service which provided books and audio-cassettes to schools, not-for-profit organisations, rehabilitation and penal institutions, homes for the aged and the physically handicapped, a special mobile library loan programme was launched in collaboration with the Po Leung Kuk and the Education and Manpower Bureau to provide books to schools without library facilities. The 'Ten Recommended Good Books' programme continued to be held jointly with Radio Television Hong Kong, for the 10th year.

To encourage people to share books and support recycling, the Book Donation and Sale Campaign was held again in February, raising $677,000 for the Community Chest. The unsold books were donated to local schools and organisations.

A number of special programmes and large-scale competitions aimed at promoting creative writing and appreciation and development of the literary arts were held. The major activities included the Chinese Poetry Writing Competition, Competition on Story Writing in Chinese for Students, and Hong Kong Biennial Awards for Chinese Literature jointly organised with the Hong Kong Arts Development Council. The winning entries in these competitions were published. So far, the public libraries have published 99 Chinese literary books.

Cultural Exchange

The year saw the strengthening of cooperation with public libraries outside Hong Kong. A Memorandum of Understanding for a series of cooperative activities in library development, resource sharing and professional staff training was organised with the Cologne Public Library in Germany.

The cultural link with libraries in the Mainland, especially in the Greater Pearl River Delta, was also strengthened particularly in the areas of training, exchange of publications, library visits, reference service and organisation of joint functions such as talks and exhibitions. As part of the professional exchanges, a delegation of 16 librarian staff from the Shenzhen Library underwent an attachment programme at the Hong Kong Public Libraries.

Books Registration Office

The main functions of the Books Registration Office are to help preserve Hong Kong's literary heritage through the registration of local publications and to monitor the use of the International Standard Book Number (ISBN) system. A Catalogue of Books Printed in Hong Kong is published quarterly by the Books Registration Office in the *Government Gazette*, which can be accessed through the Internet. In 2003, the office registered a total of 13 075 books and 13 427 periodicals, and 669 new publisher prefixes conforming to the ISBN.

Sport and Recreation

A growing number of Hong Kong people enjoy a varied selection of sports and recreational facilities and activities. The LCSD develops and manages facilities such as sports grounds, playgrounds, sports centres, holiday camps, swimming pools and beaches. It also organises training courses, sporting competitions and other activities for people of all ages and abilities, and encourages passive recreation by providing parks and landscaped open spaces.

In addition, the department administers subventions provided to camps run by non-governmental organisations. There are 25 camps run by 12 separate organisations receiving subventions, and about 662 970 people participated in the activities organised by these camps during the year.

Hong Kong Sports Development Board

The Hong Kong Sports Development Board is the statutory body responsible for the development of sport and physical recreation in Hong Kong. In 2002-03, the board received a government subvention of $188.4 million, which included a contribution towards the Elite Training Programme for the HKSAR's top athletes at the Hong Kong Sports Institute. The board allocated $122.14 million to this programme in 2002-03, to provide to 314 scholarship athletes high-level coaching, squad training programmes, meals and accommodation, support in sports science and medicine, education and career guidance and use of training facilities. The key sports in the training programme are athletics, badminton, cycling, fencing, rowing, squash, swimming, table tennis, tennis, tenpin bowling, triathlon, windsurfing and wushu. Separately, the board provided $1.23 million to 13 athletes under the Individual Athletes Support Scheme, and $0.5 million under the Disabled Sports Elite Training Programme, to the Hong Kong Sports Association for the Physically Disabled and the Hong Kong Sports Association for the Mentally Handicapped.

Sporting Achievements

HKSAR athletes achieved significant success in 2003, winning a total of 244 gold, 222 silver and 181 bronze medals at their respective National, Asian and International Championships.

In the 5th National Intercity Games of China, held in Changsha, Hunan, the HKSAR team won two gold medals — in the men's cycling 120-kilometre road race and the men's tennis singles — and a bronze medal in women's windsurfing. The team ranked 35th among the 78 participating cities in the medal tally.

In the Inaugural FESPIC Youth Games held in Hong Kong, the SAR's disabled athletes won a total of 29 gold, 46 silver and 39 bronze medals. Hong Kong ranked fourth among the 15 competing countries and territories in the medal tally. The SAR's mentally disabled athletes also performed very well in the 2003 Special Olympics World Summer Games held in Dublin, Ireland, winning 50 medals — 31 gold, 13 silver and six bronze.

Sports Federation and Olympic Committee of Hong Kong, China

The Amateur Sports Federation and Olympic Committee (SF&OC) of Hong Kong was founded in 1949-50 and reorganised as a National Olympic Committee (NOC) in 1951. It changed to its present name of Sports Federation and Olympic Committee of Hong Kong, China with effect from March 8, 1999. The federation is a member of the International Olympic Committee, the Olympic Council of Asia and the Association of National Olympic Committees and has been responsible for organising Hong Kong's participation in such major multi-sports games as the Olympic, Asian, East Asian, Pacific and National Games. With a membership of 72 National Sports Associations (NSAs), it represents the collective voice of the Hong Kong sports community. Office-bearers, elected biennially, include the President, eight Vice-Presidents, the Honorary Secretary General, a maximum of three Honorary Deputy Secretaries, and the Honorary Treasurer.

Members of the SF&OC are NSAs, which are in turn affiliated to their International Federations (IFs) and Asian Federations (AFs). They have the responsibility to develop and promote their specific sports and are managed by elected officers under either the limited company or registered society ordinances. They are empowered to coordinate and conduct a wide range of activities related to their sports, from organising sports and recreation programmes for beginners to training of elite athletes; organising and sanctioning participation in local and overseas competitions and tournaments and the training of coaches and referees. NSAs implement and enforce local and international rules and regulations, and they represent Hong Kong in meetings of the IFs and the AFs.

The elected officers of the SF&OC and the NSAs are volunteers of high standing and expertise in their respective fields of sport. They are also the cornerstones in safeguarding the autonomy of the NOC/NSAs and in assuring a high quality of sports and recreation in Hong Kong.

For half a century, the federation has coordinated a comprehensive three-month Festival of Sport, commencing in March every year. It also organises extensive education programmes for sports leaders, administrators, coaches and technical officials free of charge, notably through the Hong Kong Olympic Academy which offers free sports management and sport science courses and programmes.

With the support of sponsors, the federation organises each year the Hong Kong Sports Stars Awards, the 'Oscars' of local sport, to recognise the achievements of top sportsmen and women. The 2002 prize presentation was held on March 10 in conjunction with the federation's annual spring dinner, which attracted a large turnout at the Hong Kong Convention and Exhibition Centre.

In October, Hong Kong sent a total of 87 young athletes and 31 officials to the 5th National Intercity Games held in Changsha. The delegation competed in 13 out of 29 events and won two gold medals and one bronze medal. Prior to its departure, a combined flag presentation ceremony and torch relay was held to publicise the Games locally; the torch relay began at the Golden Bauhinia Square in Wan Chai and finished at the Hong Kong Cultural Centre Piazza in Tsim Sha Tsui, where the flag was presented.

In June, Hong Kong submitted a bid to the East Asian Games Association to host the 5th East Asian Games in 2009. The sports sector and the Government joined hands in this endeavour, with a Bid Committee being formed under the chairmanship of the federation's President. The committee's hard work in campaigning bore fruit on November 3 when the East Asian Games Association, meeting in Macau, chose Hong Kong as the host city.

Paralymic Sports Associations

The Hong Kong Sports Association for the Physically Disabled (SAP) was founded in 1972 to promote and organise sports training and competition for physically disabled people. It aims at developing their full potential through taking part in sport, as well as promoting a community of equal opportunity and full participation for physically disabled persons.

Being one of the pioneers in advocating promotion and development of disabled sports in the Far East and South Pacific (FESPIC) Region, the SAP hosted the Inaugural FESPIC Youth Games in Hong Kong from December 21 to 28. A total of 480 athletes and officials from 15 nations/territories in the FESPIC Region took part. Hong Kong won a total of 114 medals (29 gold, 46 silver and 39 bronze) and ranked fourth overall in the medal tally.

Playing the role of the National Paralympic Committee of Hong Kong, the SAP is the only sports entity recognised by the International Paralympic Committee in the selection of disabled elite athletes for major international competitions such as the Paralympics and the World Championships. With the commitment and hard work of its athletes and coaches, the SAP again achieved impressive results internationally during the year. Athletes won a total of 215 medals (69 gold, 74 silver and 72 bronze) in international competitions.

The Hong Kong Sports Association for the Mentally Handicapped (SAM) was founded in 1978. It aims to develop, promote and organise sports activities for persons with intellectual disability in order to fully develop their potential in sports abilities, to cultivate positive attitudes in sportsmanship and to facilitate their integration into the community. The association provides sports training and competitions for more than 25 000 persons, and through the years has been steadily developing a training programme from the grass roots to an elite level.

Athletes took part in numerous international competitions during the year and made the most of these opportunities to polish their skills. Altogether, they won 79 gold, 56 silver and 47 bronze medals in the competitions, including the 2003 Special Olympics World Summer Games in Dublin during the SARS period and the world swimming championships hosted by the association in Hong Kong. Among the other competitions in which athletes competed successfully were the athletics world championships in Tunisia, rowing world championships in Italy, open swimming championships in Australia, tenpin bowling competition in Malaysia, world table tennis championships in Mexico, Special Olympics national winter games in Japan, and athletics world indoor championships in Hungary.

Hong Kong Jockey Club

The Hong Kong Jockey Club enjoyed another good year in racing, and for the 13th successive year donated more than $1 billion to charity organisations and community projects, testimony to the strength of its non-for-profit model, 'Racing for Charity'.

Hong Kong horses dominated the year's international races in December with two winners in the four international events. *Silent Witness* triumphed in the Hong Kong Sprint and *Lucky Owners* won the Hong Kong Mile. Both horses were trained by Tony Cruz, a former multiple champion jockey in Hong Kong, and ridden by South African jockey Felix Coetzee.

During the year, Hong Kong was elected chairman of the Asian Racing Federation, in which it leads the action against illegal gambling as well as off-shore betting operators with the promotion of the 'Good Neighbour Policy'. Hong Kong is also vice chairman of the International Federation of Horseracing Authorities.

The club continues to enhance its wide range of racecourse facilities. Construction has begun on a new Sha Tin paddock with a retractable roof, and a huge Diamond Vision Screen is now in use at Sha Tin. The *Guinness Book of World Records* cited this as the world's largest outdoor television screen. In addition, the club is advancing rapidly with a programme called STRIDE (for Sectional Timing Racing Information Dynamic Entertainment), which utilises technology similar to global positioning satellite technology to continuously track horses in a race.

To assist the Government in combating illegal gambling, football betting under a club subsidiary began on August 1. The Legislative Council passed the necessary amendments to the Betting Duty Ordinance on July 10 to allow this development.

Despite a drop in turnover in its financial year ended in June, the club donated $1,012 million to 126 charitable and community projects.

When SARS struck Hong Kong early in the year, the club donated $100 million to help schools provide a clean environment for their students and teachers, by undergoing thorough cleansing, when classes resumed after the outbreak waned. The club also made a supplementary grant of $25 million to help non-profit kindergartens and non-governmental organisations operating day and home-based social service units maintain cleaner environments to help stop the spread of the disease.

Besides this, the club also allocated $500 million towards the establishment of a Centre for Health Protection to strengthen the public health infrastructure in Hong Kong.

The betting duty paid by the club amounted to 11.7 per cent of the total revenue collected by the Inland Revenue Department in the 2002-03 fiscal year. The betting duty comprised $9,726 million in horse racing and $1,195 million in Mark Six lotteries.

Recreation and Sports Programmes

With the aim of promoting sport at all levels of the community, the LCSD organised some 27 600 recreation and sports programmes for over 1 620 000 participants of all ages and abilities in 2003. The total cost of these programmes was $105 million.

District Sports Teams

In order to generate more community interest in sport and enhance a stronger sense of belonging among residents, the LCSD — with the assistance of the respective National Sports Associations — set up district sports teams in basketball, football, badminton and table tennis in the 18 districts. About 4 000 youngsters participated in 408 activities organised in 2003.

'Healthy Exercise for All' Campaign

To enhance public awareness of the importance of exercising regularly in pursuit of a healthy lifestyle, the LCSD and the Department of Health continued to co-organise the 'Healthy Exercise for All' Campaign. Fitness schemes and roving exhibitions promoted the message of 'daily exercise keeps us fit, people of all ages can do it'. In 2003, over 85 000 people took part in some 1 500 programmes.

Region-wide Events

The Corporate Games, aimed specially at the working population, attracted 9 500 participants from 210 industrial and commercial organisations in 11 activities. The Masters Games, held for the 35 and above age group, attracted about 2 100 participants in five competitions. The three region-wide Age Group Competitions, which aimed to encourage people of all ages to take part in sports activities, attracted over 16 000 participants.

Young Athletes Training Scheme

With the assistance of the respective National Sports Associations, 812 activities were organised under the Young Athletes Training Scheme, which provided training in badminton, table tennis, football, basketball and swimming at district level for more than 22 100 participants. Talented young players were referred to the relevant National Sports Associations for further training.

School Sports Programme

The School Sports Programme is a sports promotion scheme specifically designed for students. The programme aims at providing more opportunities for primary, secondary and special school students to participate in sport. To raise the standard of sport in schools, progressive training is provided for students with potential in sport. The School Sports Programme comprises five subsidiary programmes, namely Sport Education Programme, Easy Sport Programme, Outreach Coaching Programme, Sport Captain Programme and Joint School Sport Training Programme. In 2003, about 5 400 sports activities were organised for 418 800 students from 1 000 schools. The LCSD will work closely with schools and National Sports Associations to improve the programme and to serve more schools and students.

Community Sports Club Project

The Community Sports Club Project was implemented in partnership with the National Sports Associations. It aims to provide sports development opportunities for young players, enhance the standard of sport at community level and promote lifelong participation in sport. During the year, 176 community sports clubs joined the project. A total of $3 million was spent on 645 sports training programmes for 17 300 participants. Seminars and management development programmes were organised for 568 sports volunteers with a view to improving the administration of the clubs.

Sports Subsidy Scheme

The LCSD continued to run the Sports Subsidy Scheme, which provides financial assistance to sports associations for organising sports events, training programmes and competitions. In 2003, the department spent $38.4 million on 5 524 sports programmes which attracted over 537 000 participants. Among the most popular programmes were the Youth Football Scheme, New Generation Table Tennis Training Courses, Youth Windsurfing Promotion Scheme and Youth Wushu Training Scheme.

During the year, the National Sports Associations concerned were given subsidies under the scheme to organise the World Hong Kong Luminous Dragon Dance and Lion Dance Championships and the Asian School Volleyball (Boys) Championships.

Economic Relaunch Campaign

In order to revitalise the economy post-SARS, the LCSD and the National Sports Associations concerned joined hands to organise top-class spectacular sports events, including the International Super Stars Diving and Synchronised Swimming Extravaganza, Hong Kong International Basketball Challenge, Real Madrid Asia Tour 2003 — Hong Kong, Euro-Asia Snooker Masters Challenge, International Volleyball Challenge, Hong Kong Open Badminton Championships, Around the Island Race in yachting, World Women's Open in squash, Women's Table Tennis World Cup and the Hong Kong Open in golf. These events strengthened Hong Kong's position as a major sports events capital in Asia and promoted its global exposure.

Sports and Recreational Venues

Hong Kong Stadium

This is Hong Kong's largest sports venue with 40 000 seats. The stadium is used mainly for football and international rugby matches, while large-scale religious gatherings and fund-raising events for charity are also held. In total, 504 000 spectators attended 37 events at the venue in 2003.

Water Sports and Holiday Camps

The LCSD manages four water sports centres (Chong Hing, Tai Mei Tuk, the Jockey Club Wong Shek and St Stephen's Beach) and four holiday camps (Lady MacLehose Holiday Village, Sai Kung Outdoor Recreation Centre, Tso Kung Tam Outdoor Recreation Centre, and Lei Yue Mun Park and Holiday Village). During the year, 86 500 people participated in water sports programmes held at the water sports centres and 382 890 enjoyed the facilities at the holiday camps. To allow more people at work to enjoy camping facilities after office hours, the department provided 'Evening Camp' programmes for 20 730 people in 2003.

Other Sports and Recreational Venues

The LCSD manages 83 sports centres, 36 swimming pool complexes, 268 tennis courts, 323 squash courts, 24 sports grounds, four golf driving ranges and two public riding schools.

Three new recreation and sport venues and one improvement projects were completed in 2003: Local Open Space in Area 44 Tuen Mun, Jordan Valley

Playground (Phase II, Stage 2), Aldrich Bay Promenade and Improvement Works to the Lady MacLehose Holiday Village and the Sai Kung Outdoor Recreation Centre.

Works were in progress on 23 other projects:

Tai Po Complex, Indoor Recreation Centre/Library in Area 100 Ma On Shan, Tai Kok Tsui Complex (Phase 2), Local Open Space in Areas 18 and 21 Fanling, Kowloon Bay Recreation Ground, Local Open Space in Area 14 (Mouse Island) Tuen Mun, District Open Space in Areas 3 and 8 Tsing Yi, Ma On Shan Sports Ground — Phase II, District Open Space in Area 5 Tai Po, Football Pitch in Area 5 Tai Po; and

Local Open Space in Area 15 Tin Shui Wai, Water Sports Centre at Stanley Main Beach, Improvement to Lok Wah Playground Kwun Tong, Local Open Space in Ping Shan Yuen Long, District Open Space in Area 7 Tung Chung, Provision of a Multi-purpose Grass Pitch on Sai Tso Wan Former Landfill, District Open Space Area 18 Tuen Mun, Stanley Complex, Hammer Hill Road Park Diamond Hill, Renovation of the Wu Kwai Sha Youth Village of YMCA Ma On Shan, Cherry Street Park Tai Kok Tsui, Additional Open Space adjacent to Tsuen Wan Town Hall and Indoor Recreation Centre in Area 17 Tin Shui Wai.

Beaches and Swimming Pools

Swimming is one of Hong Kong's most popular summer pastimes. In 2003, people made 10.12 million visits to the beaches, and there were 9.15 million visits to the public swimming pools managed by the LCSD. There are 41 gazetted bathing beaches — 12 on Hong Kong Island and 29 in the New Territories and outlying islands. The LCSD manages 36 public swimming pool complexes in the urban areas and the New Territories.

As sharks are occasionally sighted in Hong Kong waters, shark prevention nets have been installed for the safety of swimmers at 30 of the more popular and more accessible beaches.

All the public bathing beaches under the management of the LCSD will normally be closed in winter. However, lifeguard services are still provided at Clear Water Bay 2nd Beach, Golden Beach and Silverstrand Beach in the New Territories from 8 am to 5 pm from November to March and at Deep Water Bay Beach from 8 am to 5 pm from December to February. Shark prevention nets are also retained at these beaches during the period they are open.

Parks Managed by LCSD

The LCSD manages more than 1 350 parks and gardens of various sizes, including 22 major parks.

Hong Kong Zoological and Botanical Gardens

The Hong Kong Zoological and Botanical Gardens, the oldest public gardens in Hong Kong, occupy a total area of 5.4 hectares that overlooks Central. The gardens were established between 1861 and 1871. Divided by Albany Road, the eastern garden houses an extensive bird collection while the western garden, opened in 1871, is home to mammal and reptile exhibits. The botanical section is mainly in the eastern garden.

Despite the urban environment, the gardens provide a viable conservation centre for endangered species, and in 2003 accommodated 17 endangered species of mammals, birds and reptiles. The bird collection is one of the most comprehensive in Asia, with over 500 birds of 177 species. Fifteen of these species have reared offspring. The mammal collection, which specialises in primates, has 63 animals representing 20 species. More than 750 species of trees, shrubs, creepers and foliage plants thrive in the gardens. The medicinal plant collection established in 1987 and a new greenhouse built in 1993 have generated particular interest. These facilities contain about 500 species of herbs, orchids, ferns and indoor plants. There are continuing programmes for upgrading the animal enclosures and facilities in the gardens.

Hong Kong Park

Opened in 1991, the Hong Kong Park is situated on the site of a former military barracks in Central covering an area of about eight hectares. With the blending of modern design into the natural landscape as its main characteristic, the park also features flowing water, which is the thematic motif. Artificial waterfalls, streams and ponds adorn the park, integrating the varying scenery into a harmonious combination.

Major facilities in the park include an aviary, conservatory, vantage point, garden plaza, squash centre, sports centre, children's playground and a restaurant. The aviary is designed to imitate a tropical rain forest environment in which over 700 birds of 100 different species are kept. The conservatory comprises three parts: Humid Plant House, Dry Plant House and Display Plant House. Adjustable environmental control equipment is installed in these houses to simulate climatic conditions in areas such as tropical rain forests and deserts. The vantage point is a 30-metre tower from which visitors can have a panoramic view of the park and the surrounding area.

Apart from enjoying the passive recreation facilities of the park, visitors can also use the facilities in the sports centre and the squash centre.

Ocean Park

Ocean Park, situated on the southern side of Hong Kong Island, is one of the world's premier sea life and animal theme parks, covering more than 87 hectares of land. Operated by the Ocean Park Corporation — a statutory board — it is a not-for-profit organisation providing elements of entertainment and education.

Over three million people visit Ocean Park each year. Residents of Hong Kong as well as tourists enjoy the park's facilities and services. With 26 years of history, Ocean Park has established itself as one of the major tourist attractions in Hong Kong and Asia. Apart from entertainment through thrill rides and a wide variety of shows, the park prides itself on its education and conservation programmes. Over 30 000 school children in Hong Kong visit the park each year and learn about animals through structured programmes and behind-the-scenes tours.

The park's research activities on marine mammals and artificial insemination have also produced the world's first successful births of two Pacific Bottle Nose dolphins conceived through artificial insemination in May and June 2001. Among the animals at the park are two giant pandas, *An An* and *Jia Jia*, which the Central People's Government presented to Hong Kong in 1999. Both have adapted well in their Giant Panda Habitat. The park was awarded an accreditation by the American Zoo and Aquarium Association in 2002, making it the first animal facility in Asia to achieve a world-class status among an elite group of internationally acclaimed zoos and aquariums.

Ocean Park comprises two sections — the Headland and the Lowland — connected by a 1.5-kilometre cable car system which offers spectacular panoramic views of the southern side of Hong Kong and the South China Sea. At the Headland, the park has many of its many thrill rides including the Abyss Turbo Drop, Mine Train, Dragon, Eagle, Crazy Galleon and Flying Swing. Complementing the rides is the Ocean Theatre where performances by dolphins and sea lions both entertain and educate visitors. Providing more enjoyment and education are the Atoll Reef Aquarium, Shark Aquarium, and the Pacific Pier that features California sea lions and harbour seals. At the park's Tai Shue Wan site, there is the entrance to the Middle Kingdom and a 225-metre outdoor escalator leading to the Headland.

A prime exhibit at the Lowland is the Goldfish Pagoda that has more than 100 goldfish of various species. It is located adjacent to the Giant Panda Habitat. Other major attractions include the Kid's World, a dedicated area for junior visitors and the Dolphin University where visitors are able to have a closer encounter with the park's dolphin families.

Ocean Park continues to provide new attractions for visitors. These include the Amazing Birds Show at the newly developed Amazon Birds Theatre, which has more than 18 colourful and rare species, and the Dinosaurs Now and Then exhibit showing the endangered Chinese alligator, salamander and Chinese sucker fish from the Chang Jiang (Yangtze River). Another new attraction is the Whiskers' Wild Ride, located near the cable car station at the Lowland, which provides a thrilling and innovative simulation ride with special multi-sensory elements.

Apart from the mechanical rides and marine mammal attractions, Ocean Park also presents special events during the year, such as the Halloween Bash, Summer Daze, Christmas Sensation, Chinese New Year programme and Easter Education Week.

Outward Bound Hong Kong

Outward Bound Hong Kong is a registered charity established in 1970. The Outward Bound organisation is the world leader and originator of outdoor experiential education which, after some 60 years, is now operating more than 50 schools in over 30 countries.

With a mission 'to help people discover and develop their potential to care for themselves, others and the world around them through challenging experiences in unfamiliar settings', Outward Bound provides training for people from all walks of life. Participants include executives, managers, professionals, civil servants, general staff, students and teachers as well as the underprivileged and people who need special attention. The training aims at fostering confidence, responsibility, independent and creative thinking, leadership, teamwork, problem-solving skills, interpersonal relationships and social responsibility.

Outward Bound uses the experiential learning model that is 'learning-by-doing' through the process of 'plan, do, review, apply'. The outdoors is the classroom, resembling the changing and unpredictable world. Through involving close-knit teams in different learning activities and problem-solving situations, participants experience a series of physical, mental, social and emotional challenges. As a result of these real personal experiences and continuous reviews and reflection under trainers' guidance, participants are able to gain insights and learn skills that eventually can apply to work and real-life situations. Every year, more than 6 000 people join the courses.

The Tai Mong Tsai headquarters in Sai Kung and the Wong Wan Chau training base in Double Haven, Mirs Bay, have a total capacity of 174. Training facilities such as sailing boats, kayaks, ropes course, rock wall and a jetty are maintained to international standard to ensure training safety.

Public courses designed with different training objectives have been run for 30 years to serve people of different ages and needs. International courses covering the Mainland's 'Silk Road', Japan, Sabah and Nepal are also organised for those who wish to engage in cross-cultural experiences.

In cooperation with schools, universities and various charitable organisations, Outward Bound continues to deliver programmes for students, teachers, social workers and many others. Such programmes are gaining in popularity as they can contribute to the all-round development of individuals, helping to create motivated, caring and competent community leaders.

Two courses subsidised by the Government's Continuing Education Fund with the objective of strengthening employees' capabilities and developing their teamwork skills are provided for the public. The courses emphasise the development of important skills and attitudes that enable employees to deal with today's challenges, and to become more capable and better working partners.

A wide variety of customised programmes are also designed for groups from corporations, government departments and special groups including the mentally and physically disabled, the socially deprived, youth at risk and former drug addicts. These programmes aim at helping the physical, mental and social development of individuals.

Outward Bound Hong Kong continues to support the corporate programmes and activities of Outward Bound China, by providing professional trainers and resources.

Adventure-Ship

Adventure-Ship is a registered charity that maintains the 27.5-metre sailing junk, the *Huan*, and provides nautical training programmes for underprivileged children and children with disabilities. Adventure-Ship is a member of the Hong Kong Council of Social Service and is funded mainly by the Community Chest and the Hong Kong Jockey Club Charities Trust.

Each year, more than 6 000 young people from children and youth centres, institutions for the disabled, outreach teams and schools benefit from the training programmes offered. The training consists of day or overnight trips (up to three days and two nights) within the waters of Hong Kong. The ship can accommodate 60 youngsters on day trips and 50 on overnight voyages.

Challenge through 'disciplined entertainment' is the main theme of training. Once on board, participants are regarded as members of the ship's crew and take part in the operational routines. Under the guidance of experienced instructors, they are trained to face new challenges and participate in activities that build team spirit and self-confidence.

The training programmes have been devised to cope with various weather conditions and the special requirements of children of different aptitudes and backgrounds. In 2002, a Shore-based Reinforcement Programme was introduced to help children with special needs — such as those with disabilities, newly arrived children and those from broken families — to consolidate what they learn from the training experience so that there is a positive and lasting effect on their lifestyle. The programme is supported in part by a grant from the Government's Quality Education Fund.

Adventure-Ship is making good progress with its programme to build a training vessel to replace the *Huan*, which has been in service for more than 26 years. Building of the new vessel is due to be completed in late 2004. The vessel will be named the *Jockey Club Huan*, in recognition of the Hong Kong Jockey Club's donation of $24 million to fund construction.

The vessel will be a 34.5-metre three-masted sailing junk, with purpose-built facilities for training young people with disabilities. It will be able to accommodate up to 60 trainees on an overnight trip as well as up to 11 crew members and volunteer assistants from the Adventure-Ship Youth Association. Maintenance costs of the new vessel will be reduced significantly through the use of modern design techniques and materials, which will give the ship a design life of at least 50 years.

Hong Kong Youth Hostels Association

The Hong Kong Youth Hostels Association (HKYHA) celebrated 30 years of service to the community in 2003, having been established in September 1973.

At the time, the majority of the population lived in crowded public housing estates or squatter areas. The association's founders thus envisaged the establishment of a number of basic hostels in rural areas as a means whereby young people might escape temporarily from the restricting surroundings in which they lived.

The association is non-profit-making organisation that is entirely dependent upon the support of members and well-wishers to meet its day-to-day operating costs. The practice of tight financial control and careful husbandry has enabled it to maintain a sound financial position over the intervening years. The capital costs of developing the current hostel network together with the expenditure incurred in undertaking major upgrading and renovation works have been met through the receipt of generous financial contributions from a small number of benefactors.

The HKYHA is affiliated to the International Youth Hostels Federation and is governed by an Executive Committee whose members work on a voluntary, personal basis and are drawn from the private sector and the Government. The association has its principal office in Shek Kip Mei from where operational, administrative and marketing activities are carried out. Individual hostels are run by resident hostel managers who are given considerable latitude to stamp each with their own personality. Membership of the association in Hong Kong additionally entitles those joining to avail themselves of the facilities in over 4 200 hostels located in about 60 countries.

The aim of all the association's hostels is to provide a warm, welcoming and informal venue at which members from diverse backgrounds and differing countries can meet in comfort and fellowship. It is the association's policy to keep membership and overnight charges at the minimum level possible consistent with prudent financial management. This is intended to ensure that the hostels are accessible to all within the community so as to encourage succeeding generations to become better acquainted with the natural world that exists beyond the urban areas and to experience for themselves the beauty of the mountains and the coastal scenery that is so readily accessible within the HKSAR.

Left: the Hong Kong Stadium was sold out when England's Liverpool Football Club played a Hong Kong team in July as part of Hong Kong's economic relaunch programme; the Chief Executive met the visitors at a practice session, and was presented with a club jersey bearing a popular name *(top)*.

Enthusiastic football fans, young and old, again packed the Hong Kong
Stadium to see a Hong Kong team take on Spain's Real Madrid in August.
The Spanish side, featuring its array of international players, had earlier drawn
a large crowd to watch a training session *(above right)*.

Under the School Sports Programme launched in 2001, primary, secondary and special school students have the opportunity to take part in sports and recreational activities ranging from basketball and gymnastics to canoeing and windsurfing. Here, students learn the finer points of table tennis, tennis, climbing, fencing and tag rugby.

courtesy of Hong Kong Sports Association for the Physically Disabled

Top and bottom left: the inaugural FESPIC (Far East and South Pacific) Youth Games were held in Hong Kong in December and the events for physically disabled athletes ranged from swimming and table tennis to track and field competitions. The Government's School Sports Programme provides training in a variety of sports and recreational activities, including baseball, martial arts and dragon dancing.

The relaunch events included an exhibition basketball match between a Chinese national team and the Melbourne Tigers from Australia. The match, held at the Hong Kong Coliseum, featured the Mainland's international star, Yao Ming *(pictured ready to shoot)*.

Each of the seven hostels is appealing in its own way as a base for hiking, mountaineering, swimming, diving, kayaking, camping, barbecuing and the many other pastimes both active and passive that appeal to members. During the year, a new indoor activities hall was completed at the Sze Lok Yuen hostel on the slopes of Tai Mo Shan and fire-safety upgrading works were undertaken in the Mount Davis hostel on Hong Kong Island and the Mong Tung Wan hostel on Lantau Island. Other hostels are located at Pak Sha O and Chek Keng in Sai Kung, Ngong Ping on Lantau and Tai Mei Tuk in Tai Po. The HKYHA has an active volunteer services group drawn from within its membership and during the year this group organised a number of special events based on one or other of the association's hostels in addition to its work within the community at large.

Country and Marine Parks

Some 38 per cent of Hong Kong's total land area has been designated as country parks. The 23 country parks provide extensive hiking trails, barbecue sites, picnic sites, camp sites and visitor centres which attracted over 11 million visitors in 2003.

There are four marine parks and one marine reserve for the conservation of marine life. In these marine parks, visitors may appreciate and receive educational information on the beauty and diversity of marine life in Hong Kong. The Agriculture, Fisheries and Conservation Department manages the country parks, the marine parks and the marine reserve.

Green Promotion/Initiatives

Green Hong Kong Campaign

To enhance public awareness of the importance of 'greening' the environment, various community involvement projects and educational activities were organised in 2003. These included the District Green Hong Kong Ambassadors Scheme, community planting days, Greening Hong Kong Activities Subsidy Scheme, theme flower shows, horticultural courses and seminars. The Greening School Subsidy Scheme was also organised to promote greening initiatives at schools and it attracted the participation of 746 schools and kindergartens. In addition, 40 schools took part in the 'School Planting Plot in Park' Scheme and made arrangement for some of their students to practise gardening under the guidance of LCSD staff and their teachers. A total of 276 500 students from 934 schools participated in the 'One Person, One Flower' Programme in which impatiens seedlings were distributed to students for growing at home or in schools. The Best Landscape Award for Private Property Development was launched in December to promote greening in private property developments.

Hong Kong Flower Show

The Hong Kong Flower Show, an annual region-wide event, is organised for the enjoyment of the public and to promote a green culture in society. Participants range from horticultural associations and floral art clubs — both local and from the Mainland — to green groups, District Councils, schools and members of the public. The show has been growing in size, content and popularity every year. Apart from numerous pleasing landscape displays, artistic floral arrangements and colourful horticultural exhibits, the show provides many other fringe activities. These include talks and seminars, demonstrations, guided tours, musical and cultural performances, photographic and drawing competitions, horticultural workshops and family fun games. In addition, various types of plants and horticultural products are put on sale in commercial stalls inside the showground. More than 130 local and overseas horticultural organisations from 11 countries took part in the 2003 show held in March at Victoria Park, attracting a record attendance of over 550 000 visitors. For the first time in the history of the Flower Show, some 500 students and teachers joined hands and derived much enjoyment in preparing a 600-square-metre 'mosaiculture' display. The display was made up of 35 000 flowers of 20 species. It was designed in a 'Dreamy Wonderland' theme with features including colourful trees, a watermelon house, a beautiful butterfly, a snail, an earthworm burrowing out of the ground and mushrooms. The display proved to be a major attraction.

Horticulture and Landscape Services/Projects

The LCSD is responsible for improving the environment of Hong Kong through the planting of ornamental trees and shrubs in public gardens and roadside amenity areas, and the preservation of trees. It maintains all public open spaces in the form of parks, gardens, sports grounds, football pitches and children's playgrounds, and also amenity plots and soft landscape plantings alongside highways and public roads. The services provided include landscape planting, horticultural research, tree maintenance and conservation. During the year, the department planted 40 000 trees as well as three million shrubs and seasonal flowers at these places and carried out landscape improvement projects for 33 hectares of park land and roadside amenity areas, including footbridges.

Beautification of Footbridges

To enhance urban greenery and improve the environment of existing footbridges, the LCSD initiated an improvement programme at footbridges located in various districts by planting flowering plants in portable planters. The programme was completed in December, covering 19 footbridges at a cost of $1.52 million.

Summer Youth Programme

The Summer Youth Programme is a large-scale community building programme which provides a variety of activities in the summer vacation for children and young people aged from six to 25. With the slogan of *Treasure Yourself with Faith and Care; Pleasure will Fill your Life with Glare*, the Summer Youth Programme Committee focused in 2003 on sports, cultural and art activities with a view to inspiring and enhancing the self-confidence and creativity of Hong Kong's young people. In addition, all-round development training programmes were organised to help young people to better equip themselves for Hong Kong and the future.

In 2003, over 14 000 activities were organised, and more than two million young people took part. The total cost of the activities amounted to over $49 million of which $19.5 million was donated by the Hong Kong Jockey Club Charities Trust Fund and the balance was covered by subvention from the Government and District Councils, private donations and participants' fees.

Home Pages

Home Affairs Bureau: http://www.hab.gov.hk
Leisure and Cultural Services Department: http://www.lcsd.gov.hk
Agriculture, Fisheries and Conservation Department: http://www.afcd.gov.hk

CHAPTER 20

Population and Immigration

It has often been said that Hong Kong's greatest asset is its people. Their hard work, resilience and entrepreneurial spirit have transformed Hong Kong into one of the world's greatest economic success stories. But sustaining this success for future generations will be a major challenge as a low birth rate, an ageing population and longer life expectancies cause critical changes in demographic characteristics.

THE urgent need for Hong Kong to develop a comprehensive population policy was highlighted by the Chief Executive in his second-term Inaugural Speech on July 1, 2002. This population policy, he said, would be designed to fit Hong Kong's long-term social and economic development, complement family requirements and address the interests of different sectors of the community.

A Task Force on Population Policy, chaired by the Chief Secretary for Administration, was subsequently established to oversee the development of the proposed population policy. Its immediate task was to identify the major challenges to Hong Kong arising from its demographic trends and characteristics, setting the objectives of a population policy and recommending a set of policy initiatives that the Administration could explore in the short and medium term. The Task Force published its Report on February 26, 2003.

The Task Force stated that the key objective of a population policy must be to secure and nurture a population that would sustain Hong Kong's development as a knowledge-based economy and a world-class city.

In this context, Hong Kong should also aim to redress population ageing, foster the concept of active and healthy ageing, promote social integration of new arrivals, and ensure the long-term sustainability of economic growth. The attainment of these goals would lead to a steady improvement in the overall standard of living.

The Task Force advocated moving away from the proposition of achieving a simple optimum population both in terms of size and of composition. Rather, it would be more useful to ensure that sufficient flexibility was built into future policy formulation and implementation processes for Hong Kong to respond quickly to changing demographic conditions and market situations.

In 2001 the total fertility rate[1] in Hong Kong reached an extremely low level of 927 children per 1 000 women, well below the replacement level of 2 100 children per 1 000 women. At the same time, life expectancy at birth was projected to reach 82 years for men and 88 years for women in 2031, one of the longest in the world.

The continued ageing of the population was expected to result in a quarter of the population to be aged 65 or above by 2031. More significantly, the size of the workforce would shrink as the prime working age population declined.

The Report says. "One serious economic problem caused by an accelerated increase in the number of elderly people in the population is social security payments. More than 600 000 persons aged 60 or above receive financial assistance through either the Comprehensive Social Security Assistance or the Old Age Allowance. Both schemes are funded entirely from General Revenue and non-contributory. Steep increases in health care expenditure form another serious economic problem caused by an ageing population.

"As society spends more resources on caring for its elderly population, fewer resources can be devoted to productive investment or to the younger members of society. The result will be a prolonged period of slower economic growth, frustrated expectations and declining competitiveness against other economies with younger populations."

The growth of Hong Kong's population relied, apart from births, much on immigration, the bulk of which was admitted through the One Way Permit Scheme. From 1997 to 2001, more than 272 000 new arrivals from the Mainland were admitted under the scheme, equivalent to some 93 per cent of the population growth[2]. This compared with 266 000 births, equivalent to some 91 per cent of the population growth, during the same period. Between 1983 and 2002, over 720 000 Mainland new arrivals were admitted under the scheme, equivalent to about 11 per cent of the 6.72 million population in 2001.

The Task Force's recommendations concerned the continuation, enhancement or review of policies in several areas, such as: the One Way Permit Scheme, Training and Other Needs of New Arrivals, Education and Manpower Policy, Admission of Mainland Professionals and Talent, Investment Immigrants, Policies Impacting on Childbirth, Elderly Policy, the Growing Transient Population: Foreign Domestic Helpers, Eligibility for Public Benefits, and Portability of Benefits.

In addition, the Task Force recommended that resources be dedicated in the Administration to take forward the population policy and review annually the implementation of relevant decisions and programmes, with a view to publishing a report every two to three years.

(The Report of the Task Force on Population Policy is available on the Internet, at http://www.gov.hk/info/population)

---

[1] The total fertility rate refers to the average number of children that would be born alive to 1 000 women during their lifetime if they were to pass through their childbearing ages of 15-49 experiencing the age specific fertility rates prevailing in a given year.

[2] The population growth (292 400) equals births (266 000) and inflow of One Way Permit holders (272 100) minus deaths (164 100) and outflow of residents (81 600).

Population in 2003

The provisional figure for the population of Hong Kong at the end of 2003 was estimated at 6 810 100, up 0.4 per cent over a year earlier. This was due to 9 700 more births than deaths and a net inflow of 14 300 residents. Over the period 1998-2003, the average annual growth rate of the population was 0.7 per cent.

In 2003, the birth rate[3] was estimated at seven per 1 000, lower than that of eight per 1 000 in 1998. Yet the death rate held stable at about five per 1 000. Consequently, the rate of natural increase dropped from three to less than two per 1 000 over the same period.

Ageing of the population has continued. While the proportion of the people aged under 15 fell from 18 per cent in 1998 to 16 per cent in 2003, the proportion of people aged 65 and over rose from 11 per cent to 12 per cent. Correspondingly, the median age of the population rose from 35 to 38 over the same period.

The age composition of the population can be reflected from the dependency ratio. The ratio of people aged under 15 and aged 65 and over to the population of working age (aged 15-64), i.e. the overall dependency ratio, dropped from 394 per 1 000 in 1998 to 378 per 1 000 in 2003. This was attributable to a decline in the proportion of young persons aged under 15, which more than offset an increase in the proportion of older persons aged 65 and over in the same period.

Hong Kong continued to be one of the world's most densely populated places, with its land population density estimated at 6 300 persons per square kilometre in mid-2003. (*More statistics are given in the Appendices*).

Immigration Department

The Hong Kong Special Administrative Region (HKSAR) is a separate travel area with autonomy over its immigration policy. In accordance with the Basic Law, the HKSAR Government applies immigration controls on entry into, stay in and departure from the HKSAR by persons from foreign states and regions. The Basic Law also sets out the mechanism regulating the entry into the HKSAR of persons from other parts of China.

Apart from controlling the movement of people into and out of the HKSAR, the Immigration Department provides a wide range of services to local residents including the issue of HKSAR passports and other travel documents, visas and identity cards, the handling of nationality matters and the registration of births, deaths and marriages. To enhance these services, the Immigration Department is also in the process of implementing a long-term information systems strategy through the application of advanced technology. The policies aim on the one hand to keep at an acceptable level population growth brought about by immigration and, on the other hand, to facilitate the admission of persons, including those of outstanding talent, professionals and investors who would bring substantial benefits to help develop the economy. Immigration procedures for Hong Kong residents, tourists and business people are streamlined wherever possible, while efforts are also made to prevent the entry of undesirable persons and the departure of persons wanted for criminal offences, detect and prosecute immigration law offenders and remove illegal immigrants.

---

[3] The birth rate refers to the number of known live births occurring in a calendar year per thousand mid-year population.

Immigration Control

The HKSAR maintains a liberal visa policy for visitors. People from more than 170 countries and territories may come to the HKSAR visa-free for visits ranging from seven to 180 days. Passenger traffic dropped slightly in 2003 with 153 million people moving in and out of the HKSAR, representing a decrease of 5.6 per cent when compared with 162 million in 2002. The drop was mainly attributable to the outbreak of SARS in March. A total of 115.5 million land passengers and 13.1 million vehicular movements were recorded in 2003, representing a decrease of 1.8 per cent and an increase of 5.6 per cent over the figures of 2002 — 117.6 million and 12.4 million, respectively.

The number of visitors travelling to the HKSAR decreased from 16.57 million in 2002 to 15.54 million in 2003, down 6.2 per cent. These included 8.47 million from the Mainland and 1.85 million from Taiwan.

Legal Immigration

The Mainland is the major source of the HKSAR's immigrant population. During the year, about 53 500 Mainland residents came to settle and join their families in the HKSAR under the One-way Permit Scheme, which has a daily quota of 150.

Right of Abode

Article 24 of the Basic Law provides that permanent residents of the HKSAR shall have the right of abode in the HKSAR and be qualified to obtain, in accordance with the law of the Region, permanent identity cards which state their right of abode.

Certificate of Entitlement Scheme

Under Article 24(2)(3) of the Basic Law, persons of Chinese nationality born outside Hong Kong of Hong Kong permanent residents shall be permanent residents of the HKSAR and enjoy the right of abode. The Immigration Ordinance stipulates that in order for a person to qualify for the right of abode under Article 24(2)(3) of the Basic Law, at least one of his parents must be a Chinese citizen who has the right of abode at the time of his birth. The Government introduced the Certificate of Entitlement Scheme on July 10, 1997, under which a person's status as a permanent resident of the HKSAR under Article 24(2)(3) of the Basic Law can be established only by his holding a valid travel document (i.e. a One-way Permit) with a valid certificate of entitlement affixed to it. This arrangement enables systematic verification of right of abode claims and ensures orderly entry. Between July 1, 1997 and the end of 2003, some 146 000 certificate of entitlement holders have entered Hong Kong.

Entry for Employment

Hong Kong maintains an open and liberal policy towards entry for employment. Foreigners who possess special skills, knowledge or experience of value to and not readily available in Hong Kong, or who are in a position to make substantial contributions to its economy are welcome to come to work. In the light of social and economic developments in Hong Kong and elsewhere, the coverage of the policy was expanded in July 2003 to allow nationals/residents of more countries/territories to take up employment in Hong Kong. These people, after having ordinarily resided in Hong Kong for a continuous period of not less than seven years and having taken Hong Kong as their place of permanent residence, may apply to become Hong Kong permanent residents in accordance with the law. During the year, 15 774 professionals and persons with technical, administrative or managerial skills from more than 100 countries/territories were admitted for employment.

Admission Scheme for Mainland Talents and Professionals

The new Admission Scheme for Mainland Talents and Professionals was implemented on July 15, 2003, replacing the Admission of Talents Scheme and the Admission of Mainland Professionals Scheme. The conditions for admitting Mainland residents and foreigners for employment have been basically aligned upon the commencement of the new scheme. The objective of the scheme is to attract Mainland talent and professionals to work in Hong Kong in order to meet local manpower needs, so as to facilitate local economic and other development and to enhance Hong Kong's competitiveness in the globalised market.

There is no sectoral restriction or quota under the scheme. The applicant must possess professional skills or knowledge not readily available or in shortage locally. Apart from professionals in the commercial and financial fields, talented persons and professionals in the arts, culture and sports sectors as well as those in the culinary profession may also apply. The admission of these persons will enhance Hong Kong's status as an Asian world city.

Spouses and unmarried dependent children of persons admitted under the scheme are eligible to apply for entry into Hong Kong as dependants. Persons admitted under the scheme and their dependants may apply for the right of abode after having ordinarily resided in Hong Kong for a continuous period of not less than seven years in accordance with the law. Since the inception of the scheme, a total of 1 350 applications have been approved.

Admission of Mainland Student Graduated from University Grants Committee (UGC)-Funded Institutions in Hong Kong

With effect from August 1, 2001, Mainland students who have graduated from UGC-funded institutions since 1990 have been allowed to enter Hong Kong for employment. They should also possess skills or knowledge of value to, but not readily available in, Hong Kong. The objective of this arrangement is to attract outstanding Mainland students who have completed full-time studies at bachelor or above level to re-enter Hong Kong for employment after graduation, so as to increase Hong Kong's competitiveness in the knowledge-based global economy. During the year, 113 Mainland students received approval to enter through this channel.

Entry of Dependants

The review of the immigration policy governing the entry of dependants was completed in July 2003 to ensure that the policy continues to meet Hong Kong's needs and helps attract people with the right talent and skills to come to Hong Kong while minimising the associated immigration and security risks. Under the revised policy, spouses, unmarried dependent children under the age of 18 and dependent parents aged 60 or above of Hong Kong permanent residents are eligible to apply for entry into Hong Kong as dependants. In the case of capital investment entrants or persons admitted into Hong Kong to take up employment or study in full-time undergraduate or post-graduate programmes in local degree-awarding institutions, including those from the Mainland admitted under schemes or arrangements catering for them, their spouses and unmarried dependent children are eligible to apply for entry into Hong

Kong as dependants. Dependants of persons granted entry into Hong Kong to take up employment or study or as capital investment entrants are required to apply for permission from the Director of Immigration to take up employment in Hong Kong. Such applications would be considered on the basis of criteria similar to those under the policy governing the entry of foreigners for employment.

Capital Investment Entrant Scheme

The new 'Capital Investment Entrant Scheme' was launched in October 2003. The objective of the scheme is to facilitate the entry for residence by capital investment entrants, i.e. persons who make capital investment in Hong Kong but would not, in the context of the scheme, be engaged in the running of any business here. The new capital brought in by the entrants is beneficial to the economic development of Hong Kong. The scheme is generally applicable to foreign nationals, Macau SAR residents, Chinese nationals who have obtained permanent resident status in a foreign country, stateless persons who have obtained permanent resident status in a foreign country with proven re-entry facilities and residents of Taiwan. Successful applicants are required to invest in Hong Kong not less than $6.5 million in real estate or permissible financial assets, i.e. equities, debt securities, certificates of deposits, subordinated debt and other eligible Collective Investment Schemes. As at the end of 2003, a total of 150 applications had been received of which 19 formal approvals and 35 approvals-in-principle had been granted. The 19 entrants with formal approval had invested a total of $144.27 million.

Illegal Immigration

The HKSAR is vigilant in guarding against the entry of Mainland illegal immigrants. The total daily average arrest figure region-wide for 2003 was 10, a 33 per cent drop compared with 15 in 2002.

The Government maintains close liaison with the Mainland and overseas governments on matters relating to population movements and irregular migration. During the year, representatives from HKSAR law enforcement agencies participated in 'The 9th Pacific Rim Immigration Intelligence Conference' held in Singapore in October, a 'Legislation Workshop Ad Hoc Experts Group II — Bali Ministerial Conference on People Smuggling, Trafficking in Persons and Related Transnational Crime' held in Port Dickson, Malaysia in November and 'The 8th Plenary Meeting, Inter-governmental Asia-Pacific Consultations on Refugees, Displaced Persons and Migrants' held in Sydney, Australia in December.

Emigration

The estimated number of emigrants dropped from 10 600 in 2001 to 10 500 in 2002. The figure was 9 600 in 2003.

Personal Documentation

The issue of the HKSAR passport is strictly controlled by the Immigration Department. Under the HKSAR Passports Ordinance, eligibility is limited to Chinese citizens who are Hong Kong permanent residents holding permanent identity cards. The passport contains advanced anti-forgery design features. To further enhance the security features of the HKSAR passport, an enhanced version was introduced on January 1, 2003.

Applications can be made either by post or in person. Those from overseas can be sent to the Immigration Department through the nearest Chinese diplomatic or consular missions. All HKSAR passports are prepared centrally by the Immigration Department in Hong Kong, for collection either locally or at the relevant Chinese diplomatic or consular missions overseas. During the year, 476 739 applications were received, including 4 540 from overseas.

The HKSAR Passports Appeal Board was established on September 7, 1998 to handle appeals against refusal of applications for HKSAR passports. It received 22 appeals in 2003.

During the year, the Immigration Department continued its efforts in visa-free lobbying for HKSAR passport holders. Countries having agreed to grant visa-free access to HKSAR passport holders included Croatia, Central African Republic and Burkina Faso.

By year-end, a total of 126 countries/territories had agreed to grant visa-free access to HKSAR passport holders.

In September 2003, the Director of Immigration led a delegation to visit Finland, Slovenia, France, Belgium and United Kingdom. The visit has strengthened the links and cooperation between the Immigration Department and its counterparts in these countries in immigration matters, especially with regard to the global problem of human smuggling and forged documents.

During the visit to Europe, the Director of Immigration signed an immigration cooperation protocol with the Director-General of the Immigration Department of the Ministry of Interior of Finland on September 24. The protocol reflects the determination of two sides to work more closely and cooperatively to tackle immigration problems of common concern.

The Immigration Department will continue to lobby more countries for maximum travel convenience for HKSAR passport holders.

Other travel documents issued by the Immigration Department include Documents of Identity for Visa Purposes (DIs) and Re-entry Permits (REPs). DIs are issued for international travel and are valid for seven years. They are issued to Hong Kong residents who are not eligible for the HKSAR passport but are nevertheless unable to obtain a national passport or travel document of another country. With a view to automating the preparation process and enhancing the international acceptance of the DI, a new machine-readable DI with enhanced security features was launched on September 1. REPs are issued to Hong Kong residents for travelling to the Mainland and the Macau SAR. During the year, 49 214 DIs and 90 919 REPs were issued.

The Immigration Department also issues identity cards to Hong Kong residents. There are two types of identity cards: the Hong Kong Permanent Identity Card issued to persons who have the right of abode in Hong Kong, and the Hong Kong Identity Card issued to residents who do not have that right. During the year, 858 972 identity cards were issued, including 346 665 smart identity cards issued under the territory-wide replacement exercise for smart identity cards.

Issue of Smart Identity Card

On June 23, the Immigration Department introduced a new generation of identity cards for Hong Kong residents. The new identity card takes the form of a smart card and employs state-of-the-art technologies to make it more secure and fraud-resistant. While the personal particulars of the cardholder are engraved by laser on the card surface, the templates of his two thumbprints as well as his facial image are stored in the chip and protected by sophisticated cryptographic techniques. The smart identity cards enable the Immigration Department to use the fingerprint identification technology to quickly authenticate the cardholder's identity and make possible the introduction of an Automated Passenger Clearance System and Automated Vehicle Clearance System in the near future.

Pursuant to the Registration of Persons (Application for New Identity Cards) Order made by the Secretary for Security in mid-year, a territory-wide replacement exercise for the smart identity cards was launched on August 18. Existing identity card holders are being invited to have their identity cards replaced within specified periods according to age groups. The whole exercise is expected to be completed within four years.

To implement the replacement exercise, nine Smart Identity Card Centres have been set up at convenient locations on Hong Kong Island, in East Kowloon, West Kowloon, Tsuen Wan, Sha Tin, Tuen Mun, Sheung Shui, Yuen Long and Tseung Kwan O. For the convenience of the public, all centres are open from 8 am to 9.15 pm, Monday to Saturday and closed on Sunday and public holidays.

A simple and user-friendly appointment system for submitting applications under the replacement exercise is in place. People can make bookings round-the-clock through either the Internet under the Electronic Service Delivery Scheme or the Interactive Voice Response System. The booking service is well received and about 70 per cent of the applicants made appointments through the system.

Marriages

Marriage registration in Hong Kong is governed by the Marriage Ordinance. All marriages contracted under the ordinance involve the voluntary union for life of one man and one woman to the exclusion of all others. There is no residential or nationality requirement for marrying parties but neither of them can be under the age of 16 years.

Normally, the Registrar of Marriages should be given at least 15 days' notice of an intended marriage and the marriage must take place within three months of the giving of the notice. A marriage can take place in one of the five marriage registries, or any of the 246 licensed places of public worship. In 2003, 32 979 marriages were celebrated in the marriage registries and 2 453 in licensed places of public worship.

Since December 20, 2001, people may book an appointment for giving of the marriage notice through the Internet under the Electronic Service Delivery Scheme or the Interactive Voice Response System. The booking system has proved to be useful and convenient, with over 98 per cent of the parties who filed their marriage notices on the first day of the notice-giving period booking their appointments through the system.

The Registrar of Marriages is also responsible for issuing Certificates of Absence of Marriage Records. During the year, 14 357 such certificates were issued.

Births and Deaths

Births and deaths registrations in Hong Kong are governed by the Births and Deaths Registration Ordinance. Parents must report the birth of their child in Hong Kong to the Registrar of Births and Deaths within 42 days and the birth can be registered without any fee. A fee is charged if the birth is registered after 42 days and not later than one year. Beyond 12 months after the birth of the child, consent of the Registrar of Births and Deaths is required for post-registration. During the year, 63 births were post-registered.

There are four district birth registries providing birth registration service to the public.

Deaths from natural causes should be registered by the relatives within 24 hours. Hong Kong has three death registries providing a free service, and death may also be registered at one of the 15 designated police stations in the New Territories and outlying islands.

During the year, 47 687 live births and 36 422 deaths were registered, compared with 48 119 and 34 316 respectively in 2002. When adjusted for under-registration, the figures gave a natural population increase of about 0.14 per cent.

Verification of Eligibility for a Permanent Identity Card

Except those who are required to obtain Certificates of Entitlement, other persons who claim permanent resident status in the HKSAR must apply for verification of their eligibility for a permanent identity card. In 2003, 87 899 applications were received. Of these, 75 424 were approved.

Nationality Matters

The Immigration Department is authorised by the Central People's Government to handle Chinese nationality applications from Hong Kong residents. Applications can be made either by post or in person. With effect from February 1, 2000, those from overseas can be made through the nearest Chinese diplomatic or consular missions. Under the law, Hong Kong residents of Chinese descent born in Chinese territories (including Hong Kong) are Chinese nationals, regardless of whether they hold a foreign passport. Those who want to be treated as foreign nationals in the HKSAR must make a declaration of change of nationality to the Immigration Department. During the year, the Immigration Department received 49 applications for declaration of change of nationality, 702 applications for naturalisation as Chinese nationals, 94 applications for renunciation of Chinese nationality and 29 applications for restoration of Chinese nationality.

Assistance to Hong Kong Residents Outside Hong Kong

The Assistance to Hong Kong Residents Unit (AHU) of Immigration Department is tasked to provide practical assistance to Hong Kong residents in distress outside the territory. During the year, 1 470 requests were handled.

During the outbreak of SARS, the Immigration Department stayed alert to travel restrictions and screening procedures imposed by certain countries/places which might affect the travel convenience of Hong Kong residents. The Immigration Department kept close contacts with the Travel Industry Council, Department of Health, consular representations in Hong Kong, Chinese diplomatic and consular missions and overseas authorities in providing assistance to Hong Kong residents who met with difficulties when travelling abroad during the outbreak of SARS.

Establishment and Training

The Immigration Department had 4 439 disciplined staff and 1 567 civilian staff at the end of the year, compared with 4 235 and 1 565 respectively in 2002.

The Immigration Department provides training for new and serving officers. During the year, serving officers received various types of job-related and management training. In addition, 23 officers were sent for overseas or Mainland study and training.

Vietnamese Refugees and Migrants

Since 1975, Hong Kong has received more than 200 000 people from Vietnam. Up to the end of 2003, more than 143 000 Vietnamese refugees had resettled in other countries and more than 72 000 Vietnamese migrants had been repatriated.

With the formal conclusion of the internationally agreed Comprehensive Plan of Action and in view of the changed circumstances in Vietnam, the HKSAR ended the 'Port of First Asylum' policy for Vietnamese with effect from January 9, 1998.

In practice, it means the special statutory provisions on the screening for refugee status and related review procedures for Vietnamese ceased to have effect on new arrivals from that date. These people are treated in the same way as illegal immigrants from elsewhere and will be repatriated as soon as possible.

On February 22, 2000, the Government announced a Widened Local Resettlement Scheme to allow some 1 400 Vietnamese refugees and eligible Vietnamese migrants to apply for settlement in Hong Kong. As a corollary, the last refugee centre (Pillar Point Vietnamese Refugees Centre) in Hong Kong was closed on June 1, 2000. Thus the Vietnamese programme on which Hong Kong had worked for 25 years was concluded in an orderly, peaceful and humanitarian manner. By the end of 2003, a total of 960 Vietnamese refugees and 437 Vietnamese migrants had applied under the scheme to make Hong Kong their permanent home.

Home Pages

Security Bureau: http://www.gov.hk/sb
Immigration Department: http://www.immd.gov.hk
Census and Statistics Department: http://www.gov.hk/censtatd

CHAPTER 21

History

Hong Kong's modern history has been one of material and social improvement: the expansion of cities and towns by cutting into hillsides; reclaiming land from the sea; and the building of homes, schools, hospitals and other public facilities to meet the demands of the growing population.

HONG KONG became a Special Administrative Region (SAR) of the People's Republic of China on July 1, 1997. The Sino-British Joint Declaration, signed between China and Britain on December 19, 1984, provides that Hong Kong's lifestyle will remain unchanged for 50 years after 1997. Hong Kong will enjoy a high degree of autonomy, except in foreign and defence affairs, and China's socialist system and policies will not be practised in the SAR.

In recent years, Hong Kong's relationship with the Mainland has strengthened — not only in terms of business ties but also in the extent of government contacts and the flow of people. This close relationship is the product of culture, location and history.

Archaeological Background

Archaeological studies in Hong Kong began in the 1920s and have uncovered evidence of ancient human activities at many sites along the winding shoreline, testifying to events spanning more than 6 000 years. The interpretation of these events is still a matter of academic discussion. Archaeologically, Hong Kong is but a tiny part of the far greater cultural sphere of South China, itself as yet imperfectly known.

Despite suggestions that local prehistoric cultures developed out of incursions from North China or South-East Asia, a growing number of scholars believe that the prehistoric cultures within the South China region evolved locally, independent of any major outside influences. There is little dispute, on the other hand, that these earliest periods, from 4000 BC, must be seen within the framework of a changing environment in which sea levels rose from depths of 100 metres below the present — inexorably submerging vast tracts of coastal plain and establishing a basically modern shoreline and ecology to which human groups had to adapt if they were not to perish.

The stone tools, pottery and other artefacts relied on for an insight into the lives of Hong Kong's ancient inhabitants are for the most part preserved in coastal deposits. This pattern of coastal settlement points to a strong maritime orientation and an economy geared to the exploitation of marine resources. However, it would be unwise to over-emphasise this point, since the discovery of archaeological remains is influenced by many factors governing their survival. For example, the erosion of the hilly terrain has been severe and evidence of inland settlement is scanty, though not totally absent.

Recent excavations have revealed two main Neolithic cultures lying in stratified sequence. Coarse, cord-marked pottery has been found at the lower, older level together with a fine, soft, fragile pottery decorated with incised lines, perforations and occasionally painted. Chipped and polished stone tools are also present. Current indications suggest a fourth millennium BC date for this initial phase.

Cord-marked pottery and chipped stone tools continue into the higher, later levels, in which appears a new ceramic form decorated with a range of impressed geometric patterns. In this phase, beginning in the mid-third millennium BC, polished stone tools show better workmanship and a proliferation of forms, some with steps and shoulders — features probably connected with improvements in hafting techniques. Ornaments such as rings, some slotted, were also made from quartz and other suitable stones. These adornments came in a range of sizes, sometimes displaying exquisite craftsmanship.

The final phase of Hong Kong's prehistory was marked by the appearance of bronze about the middle of the second millennium BC. Bronze artefacts seem not to have been in common use, but fine specimens of weapons, knives, arrowheads and halberds, and tools such as fish hooks and socketed axes have been excavated from Hong Kong sites. There is evidence, too, in the form of stone moulds from Kwo Lo Wan on the original Chek Lap Kok Island, Tung Wan and Sha Lo Wan on Lantau Island and Tai Wan and Sha Po Tsuen on Lamma Island, that the metal was actually worked locally.

The pottery of the Bronze Age comprises a continuation of the earlier cord-impressed and geometric traditions and a new type of ware, fired at a much higher temperature leading to vitrification. This so-called hard geometric ware is decorated with designs, many of which are reminiscent of the geometric patterns of the late Neolithic period, but with their own distinctive style, including the 'Kui-dragon' or 'double F' pattern so characteristic of the region during this period.

Archaeology is silent on such questions as the ethnic and linguistic affinities of the ancient peoples. However, early Chinese literary records make references to maritime people known as 'Yue' occupying China's south-eastern seaboard. It is probable, therefore, that at least some of Hong Kong's prehistoric inhabitants belonged to the 'Hundred Yue', as this diverse group of peoples was often called.

The discovery of a prehistoric burial ground at Tung Wan Tsai North on Ma Wan Island in 1997 shed light on the ethnicity of prehistoric inhabitants in Hong Kong. Among the 20 burials discovered, 15 yielded human skeletal remains, seven of which were well preserved. Study of the human bones revealed that these early inhabitants were Asian Mongoloid with characteristics of a tropical racial group.

A Neolithic stone-working site discovered at Ho Chung, in Sai Kung, in 1999 was also of significance. Scattered around an activity floor, which covered about 200 square metres, were a number of stone cores, flakes, chipped stone tools such as oyster picks, carving tools and polished implements that included adzes, rings and slotted rings. The artefacts provide valuable data for the study of the stone-working technology of Hong Kong's Neolithic inhabitants.

To save the archaeological heritage from destruction by impending road construction, a joint local and Mainland team carried out a rescue excavation in Sha Ha, also in Sai Kung, between October 2001 and September 2002. This team, comprising experts from the archaeological institutes of Shaanxi, Hebei, Henan and Guangzhou as well as the Antiquities and Monuments Office, was the largest ever mobilised in Hong Kong. Important discoveries included artefacts and archaeological features of the Neolithic Period and the Bronze Age as well as the Tang/Song and Ming/Qing dynasties. These findings not only helped to portray the chronology of the local archaeological cultures, but also provided important clues to trace the prehistoric society and settlement patterns of the Pearl River Delta.

Interesting archaeological features, almost certainly made by those people, include the rock carvings, most of which are geometric in style, at Shek Pik on Lantau Island, on Kau Sai Chau, Po Toi, Cheung Chau and Tung Lung Chau; and at Big Wave Bay and Wong Chuk Hang on Hong Kong Island.

The military conquest of South China by the North during the Qin (221-207 BC) and Han (206 BC-AD 220) dynasties must have brought increasing numbers of Han settlers into the region and exerted a variety of influences on the indigenous populations. Testimony to this is the excavation of coins of the Han period but the outstanding monument to this turbulent period must undoubtedly be the fine brick-built tomb uncovered at Lei Cheng Uk, in Sham Shui Po, in 1955 with its array of typical Han tomb furniture, dateable from the early to middle Eastern Han period. Recent rescue excavations at Pak Mong on Lantau Island, on Kau Sai Chau, at Tung Wan Tsai on Ma Wan Island and at So Kwun Wat in Tuen Mun all yielded considerable quantities of Han Dynasty artefacts in well-stratified sequences. These included pottery vessels of various kinds, iron implements and a large quantity of bronze cash coins. They provide important clues to understanding the daily life and activities of the local people of that period.

Archaeological remains from later historic periods are still relatively rare. Recent work has thrown a welcome light on one aspect of life locally during the Tang Dynasty (AD 618-907) through a study of the dome-shaped lime kilns which are almost ubiquitous features of Hong Kong's beaches. Lime was a valuable commodity useful for caulking and protecting wooden boats against marine organisms, water-proofing containers, dressing the acid soils of agricultural fields, building, and salt production among other purposes. It clearly played an important role in the economy of the period. Strong traditions link Hong Kong with the events surrounding the Mongol incursions and the concluding chapters of the Song Dynasty in the 13th century AD. Several local finds are from this period: the Sung Wong Toi inscription, now relocated near the entrance to the former Hong Kong International Airport in Kowloon; the Song inscription in the grounds of the Tin Hau Temple at Joss House Bay; caches of Song coins from Shek Pik, Mai Po and Kellett Island; and celadons of Song type from various sites, especially Nim Shue Wan and Shek Pik on Lantau Island and Queen's Hill in Fanling.

Recent studies are beginning to shed fresh light on events in Hong Kong during the Ming (AD 1368-1644) and Qing (AD 1644-1911) dynasties. These include an analysis of considerable quantities of Ming blue-and-white porcelain collected and excavated from Penny's Bay, Lantau. It is very fine quality export ware of the kind that found its way to the courts of South-East Asia and further west, and dates from the first decades of the 16th century AD During another excavation in 2001, more Ming remains were retrieved, including building foundations and structures suggesting the presence of a Ming settlement in Penny's Bay. Archaeological investigations at the ancient kiln site at Wun Yiu in Tai Po suggested that potters probably began to manufacture blue-and-white wares locally early in the Ming Dynasty. The porcelain industry continued until the early 20th century, spanning a period of 500 years. The rescue excavation at So Kwun Wat in 2000 yielded a Ming Dynasty cemetery and more than 30 burials were found. The burial items — which include porcelain wares, bronze coins and iron implements — shed light on the life of local inhabitants in the Ming Dynasty.

The excavation of the Qing Dynasty fort on Tung Lung Chau has revealed fascinating details of the internal arrangements of the fortification and everyday utensils of the remote garrison during the final stages of Imperial China. Recent investigations at the Kowloon Walled City site also uncovered remnants of the old garrison wall and the two stone plaques above the original South Gate, which bore the Chinese characters 'South Gate' and 'Kowloon Garrison City', respectively.

A Place From Which to Trade

In its early days, Hong Kong was regarded as an uninviting prospect for settlement. A population of about 3 650 was scattered over 20 villages and hamlets, and 2 000 fishermen lived on board their boats in the harbour. Its mountainous terrain deficient in fertile land and water, Hong Kong possessed only one natural asset — a fine and sheltered anchorage. Largely the reason for the British presence, which began in the 1840s, Victoria Harbour was strategically located on the trade routes of the Far East, and was soon to become the hub of a burgeoning entrepôt trade with China.

Hong Kong's development into a commercial centre began with British settlement in 1841. At the end of the 18th century, the British dominated the foreign trade at Canton (Guangzhou) but found conditions unsatisfactory, mainly because of the conflicting viewpoints of two quite dissimilar civilisations. The Chinese regarded themselves as the only civilised people and foreigners trading at Canton were subject to residential and other restrictions. Confined to the factory area, they were allowed to remain only for the trading season, during which they had to leave their families at Macau. They were forbidden to enter the city or to learn the Chinese language. Shipping dues were arbitrarily varied and much bickering resulted between the British and Chinese traders. Yet, there was mutual trust and the spoken word alone was sufficient for even the largest transactions.

Trade had been in China's favour and silver flowed in until the growth of the opium trade — from 1800 onwards — reversed this trend. The outflow of silver became more marked from 1834, after the East India Company lost its monopoly of the China trade, and the foreign free traders, hoping to get rich quickly, joined the lucrative opium trade which the Chinese had made illegal in 1799. This led to the appointment of Lin Zexu (Lin Tse-hsu) in March 1839 as special Commissioner in Canton with orders to stamp out the opium trade. A week later, he surrounded the foreign factories with troops, stopped food supplies and refused to let anyone leave until all stocks of opium had been surrendered, and dealers and ships' masters had signed a bond not to import opium on pain of execution. Captain Charles Elliot, RN, the British Government's representative as Superintendent of Trade, was shut up with the rest and authorised the surrender of 20 283 chests of opium after a siege of six weeks.

Elliot would not allow normal trade to resume until he had reported fully to the British Government and received instructions. The British community retired to

Macau and, when warned by the Portuguese Governor that he could not be responsible for their safety, took refuge on board ships in Hong Kong harbour in the summer of 1839.

The British Foreign Secretary, Lord Palmerston, decided that the time had come for a settlement of Sino-British commercial relations. Arguing that, in surrendering the opium, the British in Canton had been forced to ransom their lives — though, in fact, their lives had never been in danger — he demanded either a commercial treaty that would put trade relations on a satisfactory footing, or the cession of a small island where the British could live under their own flag free from threats.

An expeditionary force arrived in June 1840 to back these demands, and thus began the so-called First Opium War (1840-42). Hostilities alternated with negotiations until agreement was reached between Elliot and Qishan (Keshen), the Manchu Commissioner who had replaced Lin after the latter was exiled in disgrace over the preliminaries of a treaty.

Under the Convention of Chuenpi (Chuanbi) signed on January 20, 1841, Hong Kong Island was ceded to Britain. A naval landing party hoisted the British flag at Possession Point (in the vicinity of present-day Hollywood Road Park in Sheung Wan) on January 26, 1841, and the island was formally occupied. In June, Elliot began to sell plots of land and settlement began.

Neither side accepted the Chuenpi terms. The cession of a part of China aroused shame and anger among the Chinese, and the unfortunate Qishan was ordered to Peking (Beijing) in chains. Palmerston was equally dissatisfied with Hong Kong, which he contemptuously described as 'a barren island with hardly a house upon it', and refused to accept it as the island station that had been demanded as an alternative to a commercial treaty.

'You have treated my instructions as if they were waste paper,' Palmerston told Elliot in a magisterial rebuke, and replaced him. Elliot's successor, Sir Henry Pottinger, arrived in August 1841 and conducted hostilities with determination. A year later, after pushing up the Yangtze River (Chang Jiang) and threatening to assault Nanking (Nanjing), he brought the hostilities to an end by the Treaty of Nanking, signed on August 29, 1842.

In the meantime, the Whig Government in England had fallen and, in 1841, the new Tory Foreign Secretary, Lord Aberdeen, issued revised instructions to Pottinger, dropping the demand for an island. Pottinger, who had returned to Hong Kong during the winter lull in the campaign, was pleased with the progress of the new settlement and, in the Treaty of Nanking, deviated from his instructions by demanding both a treaty and an island, thus securing Hong Kong.

Five Chinese ports, including Canton, were also opened for trade. The commercial treaty was embodied in the supplementary Treaty of the Bogue (Humen) in October 1843, by which the Chinese were allowed free access to Hong Kong Island for trading purposes.

Lease of the New Territories

The Second Anglo-Chinese War (1856-58) arose out of disputes over the interpretation of the earlier treaties and over the boarding by Chinese in search of suspected pirates of the Arrow, a British lorcha (a vessel with a European hull and Chinese rig). The Treaty of Tientsin (Tianjin) in 1858, which ended the war, gave the

British the privilege of diplomatic representation in China. The first British envoy, Sir Frederick Bruce, who had been the first Colonial Secretary in Hong Kong, was fired on at Taku (Dagu) Bar on his way to Peking to present his credentials, and hostilities were renewed from 1859-60.

Troops serving on this second expedition camped on Kowloon Peninsula, as Hong Kong's earliest photographs show. Finding it healthy, they wished to retain it as a military cantonment, with the result that Sir Harry Parkes, Consul at Canton, secured from the Viceroy a lease of the peninsula as far north as Boundary Street, including Stonecutters Island. The Convention of Peking in 1860, which ended the hostilities, provided for its outright cession.

Other European countries and Japan subsequently demanded concessions from China, particularly after Germany, France and Russia rescued China from the worst consequences of its defeat by Japan in 1895. In the ensuing tension, Britain felt that efficient defence of Hong Kong harbour demanded control of the land around it.

By a convention signed in Peking on June 9, 1898, respecting an extension of Hong Kong territory, the New Territories — comprising the area north of Kowloon up to the Shum Chun (Shenzhen) River and 235 islands — was leased for 99 years. The move was directed against France and Russia, not against China, whose warships were allowed to use the wharf at Kowloon City. There, Chinese authority was permitted to continue 'except insofar as may be inconsistent with the military requirements for the defence of Hong Kong'. However, an order-in-council of December 27, 1899, revoked this clause and the British unilaterally took over Kowloon City. There was some opposition when the British took over the New Territories in April 1899, but this eventually dissipated. The area was declared to be part of the overall territory of Hong Kong but was administered separately from the urban area.

Initial Growth

The new settlement did not go well at first. It attracted unruly elements, while fever and typhoons threatened life and property. Crime was rife. The population rose from 32 983 (31 463 or 95 per cent Chinese) in 1851 to 878 947 (859 425 or 97.8 per cent Chinese) in 1931. The Chinese influx was unexpected because it was not anticipated they would choose to live under a foreign flag.

The Chinese asked only to be left alone and thrived under a liberal British rule. Hong Kong became a centre of Chinese emigration and trade with Chinese communities abroad. Ocean-going shipping using the port increased from 2 889 ships in 1860 to 23 881 in 1939. The dominance of the China trade forced Hong Kong to conform to Chinese usage and to adopt the silver dollar as the currency unit in 1862. In 1935, when China went off silver, Hong Kong had to follow suit with an equivalent 'managed' dollar.

Hong Kong's administration followed the normal pattern for a British territory overseas, with a governor nominated by Whitehall and nominated Executive and Legislative Councils with official majorities. The first non-government members of the Legislative Council were nominated in 1850, and the first Chinese in 1880 (Singapore-born lawyer Ng Choy); the first non-government members of the Executive Council appeared in 1896, and the first Chinese in 1926 (Sir Shouson Chow). In 1972, the long-standing arrangement that two electoral bodies — the Hong

Kong General Chamber of Commerce and the Unofficial Justices of the Peace — were each allowed to nominate a member to the Legislative Council, was discontinued.

The British residents pressed strongly for self-government several times but the UK Government consistently refused to allow it, saying the Chinese majority would be subject to the control of a small European minority. A Sanitary Board was set up in 1883, became partly elected in 1887, and developed into an Urban Council in 1936.

The intention, at first, was to govern the Chinese through Chinese magistrates seconded from the Mainland. But this system of parallel administrations was only half-heartedly applied and broke down mainly because of the weight of crime. It was completely abandoned in 1865 in favour of the principle of equality of all races before the law. In that year, the Governor's instructions were significantly amended to forbid him to assent to any ordinance 'whereby persons of African or Asiatic birth may be subjected to any disabilities or restrictions to which persons of European birth or descent are not also subjected'. Government policy was *laissez-faire*, treating Hong Kong as a market place open to all and where the Government held the scales impartially.

Public and utility services developed — the Hong Kong and China Gas Company in 1861, the Peak Tram in 1885, the Hongkong Electric Company in 1889, China Light and Power in 1903, the electric tramways in 1904 and the Kowloon-Canton Railway, completed in 1910. Successive reclamations began in 1851 — notably one completed in 1904 in Central District, which produced Chater Road, Connaught Road and Des Voeux Road; and another in Wan Chai between 1921 and 1929.

Public education began in 1847 with grants to the Chinese vernacular schools. In 1873, the voluntary schools — mainly run by missionaries — were included in a grant scheme. The College of Medicine for the Chinese, founded in 1887 with Sun Yat Sen as one of its first two students, developed into the University of Hong Kong in 1911 and offered arts, engineering and medical faculties.

After the Chinese revolution of 1911, which overthrew the Qing Dynasty, there was a long period of unrest in China and many people found shelter in Hong Kong. Agitation continued after Chinese participation in World War I brought in its wake strong nationalist and anti-foreign sentiment — inspired both by disappointment over failure at the Versailles peace conference to regain the German concessions in Shantung (Shandong) and by the post-war radicalism of the Kuomintang.

The Chinese authorities sought to abolish all foreign treaty privileges in China. Foreign goods were boycotted and the unrest spread to Hong Kong, where a seamen's strike in 1922 was followed by a serious general strike in 1925-26 under pressure from Canton. This petered out, though not before causing considerable disruption in Hong Kong. Britain, with the largest foreign stake in China, was at that time a main target of anti-foreign sentiment, but Japan soon replaced it in this odious role.

The 1930s and World War II

During World War I, Japan presented its '21 demands' to China. In 1931, Japan occupied Manchuria and tried to detach China's northern provinces, leading to open war in 1937. Canton fell to the Japanese in 1938, resulting in a mass flight of refugees to Hong Kong. It was estimated that some 100 000 refugees entered in 1937, 500 000 in 1938 and 150 000 in 1939 — bringing Hong Kong's population at the outbreak of World War II to an estimated 1.6 million. It was thought that at the height of the influx, about 500 000 people were sleeping in the streets.

447

Japan entered World War II on December 7, 1941, when its aircraft bombed United States warships at Pearl Harbour. At about the same time, Japanese armed forces attacked Hong Kong (December 8, 1941, Hong Kong time). They invaded Hong Kong across the border from China and pushed the British from the New Territories and Kowloon on to Hong Kong Island. After a week of stubborn resistance on the island, the defenders — including the Hong Kong Volunteer Defence Corps — were overwhelmed and Hong Kong surrendered on Christmas Day.

The Japanese occupation lasted for three years and eight months. Trade virtually disappeared, currency lost its value, food supplies were disrupted, and government services and public utilities were seriously impaired. Many residents moved to Macau — the neutral Portuguese enclave hospitably opening its doors to them. Towards the latter part of the occupation, the Japanese sought to ease the food problems by organising mass deportations.

In the face of increasing oppression, the bulk of the community remained loyal to the allied cause. Chinese guerrillas operated in the New Territories and escaping allied personnel were assisted by the rural population. Soon after news of the Japanese surrender was received on August 14, 1945, a provisional government was set up by the Colonial Secretary, Mr (later Sir) Frank Gimson, who had spent the occupation imprisoned in Stanley Gaol. On August 30, Rear Admiral Sir Cecil Harcourt arrived with units of the British Pacific Fleet to establish a temporary military government. Civil government was formally restored on May 1, 1946, when Sir Mark Young resumed his interrupted governorship.

The Post-war Years

After the Japanese surrender, Chinese civilians — many of whom had moved into the Mainland during the war — returned at the rate of almost 100 000 a month. The population, which by August 1945 had been reduced to about 600 000, rose by the end of 1947 to an estimated 1.8 million. In 1948-49, as the forces of the Chinese Nationalist Government began to face defeat in civil war at the hands of the Communists, Hong Kong received an influx unparalleled in its history. Hundreds of thousands of people — mainly from Kwangtung (Guangdong) Province, Shanghai and other commercial centres — entered Hong Kong during 1949 and the spring of 1950. By mid-1950, the population had swelled to an estimated 2.2 million. It has continued to rise, reaching four million by 1970, five million by 1980, approaching six million by 1990, and now nearing seven million.

After a period of economic stagnation caused by the United Nations' embargo on trade with China, arising from the Korean War, Hong Kong began to industrialise. No longer could Hong Kong rely solely on its port to provide prosperity for its greatly increased population. From the start, the industrial revolution was based on cotton textiles, gradually adding woollens to the list and, in the late 1960s, man-made fibres and made-up garments. Textiles and clothing made up more than half of domestic exports by value during the 1960s.

Although Hong Kong has become increasingly a service-based economy over the past 10 years with domestic merchandise exports steadily declining, textiles and clothing still constitute over 50 per cent of domestic exports by value. Electronics, watches, clocks and jewellery are also major export items.

Over the years, the manufacturing sector has gradually moved from one concentrating on simple, labour-intensive products to one focusing on sophisticated, high value-added products. Taking advantage of the abundant supply of land and labour in the Pearl River Delta, industrialists have expanded their production bases across the boundary while maintaining headquarters operations in Hong Kong. This mode of operation has contributed to economic development in the region and facilitated the transformation of Hong Kong into a services centre.

Associated with events in the Mainland, 1966 saw mounting tension in Hong Kong. During 1967, this developed into a series of civil disturbances, affecting all aspects of life and temporarily paralysing the economy. But, by the year's end, the disturbances were contained and the community continued its tradition of peaceful progress.

Hong Kong continued to expand its role as an entrepôt with its neighbours and trade with the Mainland was no exception. Coupled with tourism, this has led to vast improvements in communications, with an increasing number of people entering the Mainland from or through Hong Kong, the natural gateway, each year. With the launch of the Individual Visit Scheme for Mainland people in 2003, there was a surge in the demand for air services between the Mainland and Hong Kong. On December 2, Cathay Pacific Airways commenced three weekly services to Beijing. Altogether, Cathay Pacific and Hong Kong Dragon Airlines (Dragonair) and four Mainland carriers — China Southern Airlines, Air China, China Eastern Airlines and Xiamen Airlines — operate more than 1 200 flight movements a week in scheduled and non-scheduled services between Hong Kong and about 40 destinations in the Mainland.

The Kowloon-Canton Railway Corporation operates frequent train services from Hung Hom in Kowloon to the Mainland boundary at Lo Wu. It also operates inter-city through train services between Hong Kong and cities in Guangdong as well as Shanghai and Beijing. Ten trains are available daily from Hung Hom to Guangzhou, six of which call at Dongguan, and one terminates at Zhaoqing via Foshan. Trains to Shanghai and Beijing operate on alternate days. Cross-boundary coach services operate different routes to Guangdong and other parts of southern China. There are frequent daily ferry services to Macau and there are also regular services to some 20 other ports in South China.

To keep pace with the development, the Government places strong emphasis on improving and expanding infrastructure. As a result, Hong Kong has been transformed into a modern city with efficient road and rail links, and first-class port and airport facilities. New highways have opened up previously remote areas, the railway networks are being expanded, and a new international airport has been in operation at Chek Lap Kok since 1998. Accommodating about 46 per cent of Hong Kong's population, the nine new towns in the New Territories have eased the pressure on developable land in Kowloon and on Hong Kong Island. Current and planned projects would continue to spur the economy, creating job opportunities and enhancing the environment for the community.

The development of Hong Kong's economic base has enabled the public sector to increase spending on housing, education, social welfare and health over the years — from $69.7 billion in 1993-94 to an estimated $155.3 billion in 2003-04.

Hong Kong's public housing programme started with an emergency measure to rehouse some 53 000 people made homeless overnight in a squatter fire on Christmas Day 1953. It has developed into a comprehensive programme that encompasses a wide range of rental and home ownership scheme flats with self-contained facilities.

The programme is in line with the Government's policy objectives to reduce the number of inadequately housed people, to help households gain access to affordable housing and to encourage home ownership in the community. The Hong Kong Housing Authority has primary responsibility for this programme. More than half of Hong Kong's families live in accommodation that they own.

The Government has been investing heavily in education to enhance Hong Kong's competitiveness in a knowledge-based and globalised economy. Free and compulsory primary and junior secondary education is provided to every student up to the age of 15 years. Senior secondary and tertiary education is also heavily subsidised and it is a government policy that no one is deprived of education for lack of financial means. Exemplifying this, starting from the 2002-03 school year, all Secondary 3 students from public sector schools who are able and willing to continue with their study may receive subsidised Secondary 4 education or vocational training.

The Government and non-governmental organisations have made major social welfare advances in the past decade, with expenditure increasing from $7.03 billion in 1992-93 to $32.76 billion in 2003-04. At the same time, social services have developed from providing emergency relief into today's diversified and comprehensive network.

Hong Kong's major health indicators such as life expectancy at birth and infant mortality rate are now among the best in the world. Important factors in this have been improvements in socio-economic conditions, education, housing, sanitation, nutrition and the introduction of a comprehensive childhood immunisation programme. With a high polio immunisation rate, coupled with a high level of vigilance, Hong Kong was certified polio-free in 2000. An effective disease surveillance system, which comprises clinics, hospitals and laboratories in public and private sectors, is in place and this is crucial to the effective prevention and control of diseases. In 2001, a new Public Health Laboratory Centre was established to enhance the provision of quality laboratory services

Medical and health services are undergoing continuous development programmes. The Government continues to invest in medical services and is aware of the international trend of developing ambulatory and community care programmes and replacing, where appropriate, in-patient treatment by ambulatory and out-patient services. In 2003, two projects were completed. The first project was the relocation of the Accident and Emergency Department of the Tang Shiu Kin Hospital to the Ruttonjee Hospital to make way for conversion of the former hospital into an ambulatory and day-care centre. The second was an improvement programme involving eight public hospitals. Construction works for other major hospital projects, at a total estimated cost of $5.9 billion, were to be completed over the next five years. In addition, all general out-patient services previously operated by the Department of Health were transferred to the Hospital Authority in 2003 to facilitate integration of the primary and secondary levels of care in the public sector.

A comprehensive system of labour legislation has been developed to provide for employees' benefits and protection, employees' compensation, occupational safety and health. Free employment services are provided to help job-seekers find work and employers to recruit staff. The Employees Retraining Board provides quality retraining courses and services to the unemployed and potentially unemployed in order to enhance their employability and meet the needs of employers and the Hong Kong economy.

Appendices

Note:

Figures presented in statistical appendices refer to those released up to end April 2004. Readers wishing to obtain current statistical information on Hong Kong are invited to visit the 'Hong Kong Statistics' section of the Census and Statistics Department's website (http://www.gov.hk/censtatd/eng/hkstat/index.html). The section is regularly updated and it also provides hyperlinks to relevant government websites for facilitating retrieval of other official statistics of Hong Kong.

Symbols:

The following symbols are used throughout the statistical appendices:

#	Provisional figures/estimates
@	Figures subject to revision
*	Revised figures
—	Not applicable
N.A.	Not available

APPENDIX 1
(Chapter 1: Constitution and Administration)

The Executive Council

Membership on January 2, 2004

Presided over by the Chief Executive the Honourable TUNG Chee Hwa

Members:

The Chief Secretary for Administration
The Honourable Donald TSANG Yam-kuen, GBM, JP

The Financial Secretary
The Honourable Henry TANG Ying-yen, GBS, JP

The Secretary for Justice
The Honourable Elsie LEUNG Oi-sie, GBM, JP

Member of the Executive Council
The Honourable LEUNG Chun-ying, GBS, JP

The Secretary for Housing, Planning and Lands
The Honourable Michael SUEN Ming-yeung, GBS, JP

The Secretary for Education and Manpower
Professor the Honourable Arthur LI Kwok-cheung, GBS, JP

The Secretary for Health, Welfare and Food
Dr the Honourable YEOH Eng-kiong, JP

Member of the Executive Council
The Honourable Jasper TSANG Yok-sing, GBS, JP

The Secretary for the Civil Service
The Honourable Joseph WONG Wing-ping, GBS, JP

Member of the Executive Council
The Honourable CHENG Yiu-tong, SBS, JP

The Secretary for Home Affairs
Dr the Honourable Patrick HO Chi-ping, JP

Member of the Executive Council
The Honourable Andrew LIAO Cheung-sing, SBS, SC, JP

The Secretary for Economic Development and Labour
The Honourable Stephen IP Shu-kwan, GBS, JP

The Secretary for the Environment, Transport and Works
Dr the Honourable Sarah LIAO Sau-tung, JP

The Secretary for Financial Services and the Treasury
The Honourable Frederick MA Si-hang, JP

The Secretary for Constitutional Affairs
The Honourable Stephen LAM Sui-lung, JP

The Secretary for Security
The Honourable Ambrose LEE Siu-kwong, IDSM, JP

The Secretary for Commerce, Industry and Technology
The Honourable John TSANG Chun-wah, JP

Member of the Executive Council
The Honourable Mrs Selina CHOW LIANG Shuk-yee, GBS, JP

APPENDIX 2

(Chapter 1: Constitution and Administration)

The Second Legislative Council of the Hong Kong Special Administrative Region

Membership on January 2, 2004

President:

The Honourable Mrs Rita FAN HSU Lai-tai, GBS, JP
(Election Committee)

Members:

Functional Constituencies

The Honourable Kenneth TING Woo-shou, JP (Industrial — First)
The Honourable James TIEN Pei-chun, GBS, JP (Commercial — First)
Ir Dr the Honourable Raymond HO Chung-tai, JP (Engineering)
Dr the Honourable Eric LI Ka-cheung, GBS, JP (Accountancy)
Dr the Honourable David LI Kwok-po, GBS, JP (Finance)
Dr the Honourable LUI Ming-wah, JP (Industrial — Second)
The Honourable Margaret NG (Legal)
The Honourable Mrs Selina CHOW LIANG Shuk-yee, GBS, JP
(Wholesale and Retail)
The Honourable CHEUNG Man-kwong (Education)
The Honourable HUI Cheung-ching, JP (Import and Export)
The Honourable CHAN Kwok-keung, JP (Labour)
The Honourable Bernard CHAN, JP (Insurance)
The Honourable Mrs Sophie LEUNG LAU Yau-fun, SBS, JP
(Textiles and Garment)
The Honourable SIN Chung-kai (Information Technology)
Dr the Honourable Philip WONG Yu-hong, GBS (Commercial — Second)
The Honourable WONG Yung-kan (Agriculture and Fisheries)
The Honourable Howard YOUNG, SBS, JP (Tourism)
The Honourable LAU Wong-fat, GBS, JP (Heung Yee Kuk)
The Honourable Miriam LAU Kin-yee, JP (Transport)
The Honourable Timothy FOK Tsun-ting, SBS, JP
(Sports, Performing Arts, Culture and Publication)
Dr the Honourable LAW Chi-kwong, JP (Social Welfare)
The Honourable Abraham SHEK Lai-him, JP
(Real Estate and Construction)
The Honourable LI Fung-ying, JP (Labour)
The Honourable Henry WU King-cheong, BBS, JP (Financial Services)
The Honourable Tommy CHEUNG Yu-yan, JP (Catering)
The Honourable Michael MAK Kwok-fung (Health Services)
The Honourable LEUNG Fu-wah, MH, JP (Labour)
Dr the Honourable LO Wing-lok, JP (Medical)

The Honourable IP Kwok-him, JP (District Council)
The Honourable LAU Ping-cheung (Architectural, Surveying and Planning)

Geographical Constituencies

The Honourable Cyd HO Sau-lan (Hong Kong Island)
The Honourable Albert HO Chun-yan (New Territories West)
The Honourable LEE Cheuk-yan (New Territories West)
The Honourable Martin LEE Chu-ming, SC, JP (Hong Kong Island)
The Honourable Fred LI Wah-ming, JP (Kowloon East)
The Honourable James TO Kun-sun (Kowloon West)
The Honourable CHAN Yuen-han, JP (Kowloon East)
The Honourable CHAN Kam-lam, JP (Kowloon East)
The Honourable LEUNG Yiu-chung (New Territories West)
The Honourable Andrew WONG Wang-fat, JP (New Territories East)
The Honourable Jasper TSANG Yok-sing, GBS, JP (Kowloon West)
Dr the Honourable YEUNG Sum (Hong Kong Island)
The Honourable LAU Chin-shek, JP (Kowloon West)
The Honourable LAU Kong-wah, JP (New Territories East)
The Honourable Emily LAU Wai-hing, JP (New Territories East)
The Honourable CHOY So-yuk (Hong Kong Island)
The Honourable Andrew CHENG Kar-foo (New Territories East)
The Honourable SZETO Wah (Kowloon East)
The Honourable TAM Yiu-chung, GBS, JP (New Territories West)
Dr the Honourable TANG Siu-tong, JP (New Territories West)
The Honourable Albert CHAN Wai-yip (New Territories West)
The Honourable WONG Sing-chi (New Territories East)
The Honourable Frederick FUNG Kin-kee (Kowloon West)
The Honourable Audrey EU Yuet-mee, SC, JP (Hong Kong Island)

Election Committee

Dr the Honourable David CHU Yu-lin, JP
The Honourable NG Leung-sing, JP
The Honourable YEUNG Yiu-chung, BBS
The Honourable Ambrose LAU Hon-chuen, GBS, JP
The Honourable MA Fung-kwok, JP

APPENDIX 3

(Chapter 1: Constitution and Administration)

The District Councils

Membership on January 15, 2004

Urban Areas

Central & Western District Council

Chairman:
Mr CHAN Tak-chor, MH (Elected member)

Vice Chairman:
Mr WU Chor-nam, JP (Appointed member)

Elected Members:
Mr CHAN Chit-kwai, Stephen, JP
Mr CHAN Choi-hi, Dominic
Ms CHENG Lai-king
Mr HO Chun-ki, Frederick
The Honourable HO Sau-lan, Cyd
Mr KAM Nai-wai
Dr KWOK Ka-ki
Dr LAI Kwok-hung
Mr LEUNG Yiu-cho, Henry
Mr Mark LIN, JP
Mr TAI Cheuk-yin, Leslie Spencer
Mr Victor S.Y. YEUNG
Mr YEUNG Wai-foon, MH
Mr YUEN Bun-keung

Appointed Members:
Mr CHUNG Yam-cheung
Mr LAM Kin-lai
Mr YOUNG Siu-chuen, Albert

Eastern District Council

Chairman:
Ms TING Yuk-chee, Christina, BBS, JP
  (Appointed member)

Vice Chairman:
Mr WONG Kwok-hing, MH (Elected member)

Elected Members:
Mr CHAN Bing-woon, SBS, JP
Ms CHAN Oi-kwan
Mr CHAN Tak-wai
Mr CHAN Tim-shing
Mr CHAN Yiu-tak
Mr CHAO Shing-kie
Mr CHIU Chi-keung
Mr CHOI Sai-chuen
Dr CHOW Kit-bing, Jennifer, MH
The Honourable CHOY So-yuk
Mr CHU Wai-joe
Mr CHUNG Shu-kun, Christopher, MH, JP
Mr FU Yuen-cheung, Alex
Mr HUI Ching-on
Mr HUI Ka-hoo, MH
Mr IP Chiu-shing
Mr KONG Chack-ho
Mr KONG Tze-wing, MH
Mr KUNG Pak-cheung
Mr LAI Chi-keong
Ms LAM Chui-lin
Mr LEE Yu-tai, Desmond
Mr LEUNG Siu-sun, Patrick
Ms LEUNG Suk-ching, Joanna
Dr LI Kin-yin, Mark
Ms LO Tip-chun, MH
Mr LO Wing-kwan, Frankie, MH
Mr LUI Chi-man
Mr MAK Shun-pong, MH
Mr SALAROLI Giuseppe, Joseph, MH
Mr TANG Lai-ming
Mr TO Boon-man
Mr TSANG Kin-shing
Mr TSO Hon-kwong
Mr WONG Kin-pan
Ms WONG Yuet-mui

Appointed Members:
Ms CHAN Kit-wing, Ellen, MH

The Honourable CHEUNG Yu-yan, Tommy, JP
Mr LAU Hing-tat, Patrick
Mr LO Sai-kwong
Ms PANG Melissa Kaye
Mr TSANG Heung-kwan
Dr WONG Kam-din
The Honourable WU King-cheong, Henry,
BBS, JP

Kowloon City District Council

Chairman:
Ir WONG Kwok-keung (Appointed member)

Vice Chairman:
Mr CHAN Ka-wai (Elected member)

Elected Members:
Mr AU Ka-shing, Ben
Mr CHAN King-wong
Ms CHAN Lai-kwan
Mr CHIANG Sai-cheong, MH
Miss FUNG King-man, Virginia
Mr HO Hin-ming
Mr IP Che-kin
Mr LAM Kin-man
Mr LAU Ting-pong
Mr LAU Wai-wing
Mr LEE Kin-kan
Ms LEE Wai-king, Starry
Ms LI Lin
Mr LIU Sing-lee
Mr MAN Tak-chuen
Miss MOK Ka-han, Rosanda
Mr NG Ching-man
Ms SIU Yuen-sheung, BBS, JP
Ms TSOI Lai-ling
Mr WEN Choy-bon
Dr WONG Yee-him

Appointed Members:
Mr CHAN Wing-lim
Mr HO Chi-kai
Mr LAU Yue-sun, BBS
Mr LEUNG Ying-piu, MH

Kwun Tong District Council

Chairman:
Mr CHAN Chung-bun, Bunny, JP
(Appointed member)

Vice Chairman:
Ms LEUNG Fu-wing, MH (Elected member)

Elected Members:
Ms AU Yuk-har, Grace
Mr CHAN Cheong
The Honourable CHAN Kam-lam, JP
Mr CHAN Kok-wah, Ben
Mr CHAN Man-kin
Mr CHAN Wah-yu, Nelson
Mr CHIN Danny Ching-man
Mr CHOY Chak-hung
Mr FAN Wai-kong
Mr FUNG Kam-yuen
Ms FUNG Mei-wan
Mr HO Wai-to
Mr LAI Wing-lin, Albert
Mr LAM Ka-keung
Mr LAU Ting-on
Mr LAW Chun-ngai
Ms LEE Ling, Alice
Mr LUI Tung-hai
Mr MAK Fu-ling
Mr NG Chung-tak, Philip
Mr NG Siu-cheung
Mr OR Chong-shing, Wilson
Mr POON Chun-yuen
Mrs POON YAM Wai-chun, Winnie, MH
Mr SO Ka-ho
Mr SO Koon-chung, Kevin
Ms SO Lai-chun
Mr TANG Chi-ho, Francis
Mr TSUI Wing-chuen, Ricky
Mr WONG Kai-ming
Mr WONG Wah-shun, David
Mr YIP Hing-kwok
Ms YU Sau-chun

Appointed Members:
Mr CHOW Yiu-ming
Mr FUNG Kam-chiu, MH
Ms KO Po-ling, MH
Mr LAI Shu-ho, Patrick, MH, JP

Mr So Kwan-hon
Mr Sun Kai-lit, Cliff, JP
Mr Wu Kwok-cheung, MH

Sham Shui Po District Council

Chairman:
Mr Tam Kwok-kiu, MH (Elected member)

Vice Chairman:
Mr Leung Lai (Elected member)

Elected Members:
Mr Chan Wai-ming
Mr Cheung Wing-sum, Ambrose, JP
Mr Chong Chi-tat
Mr Chum Tak-shing
The Honourable Fung Kin-kee, Frederick
Mr Kwun Sai-leung
Ms Lai Wai-lan, Tracy
Mr Lam Ka-fai, Aaron
Mr Leung Hon-wa
Mr Leung Kam-tao
Mr Leung Yau-fong
Ms Ng Mei, Carman
Mr Tai Yuen-ming
Mr Tam Kwok-hung
Mr Wai Woon-nam
Mr Wong Kam-kuen, MH
Ms Wong Kwai-wan
Mr Wong Tak-chuen, Joe
Mr Yan Kai-wing

Appointed Members:
Mr Chan Keng-chau
Mr Chan Tung, BBS, JP
Dr Chan Yan-chong
Mr Kwok Chun-wah, Jimmy, MH
Mr Li Hon-hung

Southern District Council

Chairman:
Ms Mar Yuet-har, MH (Elected member)

Vice Chairman:
Mr Chu Ching-hong (Elected member)

Elected Members:
Mr Au Lap-sing
Mr Chai Man-hon
Mrs Chan Lee Pui-ying
Mr Chu Chun-yin, Benny
Mr Ko Tam-kan
Mr Lam Kai-fai
Ms Lam Yuk-chun
Mr Law Kam-hung
Mr Miu Wah-chang
Mr Shek Kwok-keung
Mr Wong Che-ngai
Mr Wong King-cheung, JP
Mr Wong Man-kit, MH
Ms Yeung Siu-pik
The Honourable Howard Young, SBS, JP

Appointed Members:
Mr Chan Lee-shing, William
Mr Ko Kam-cheung, MH
Mr Leung Ho-kwan
Professor Zee Sze-yong, SBS

Wan Chai District Council

Chairman:
Ms Wong Ying-kay, Ada, JP
   (Elected member)

Vice Chairman:
Dr Tse Wing-ling, John (Elected member)

Elected Members:
Mr Chan Yiu-fai, Steve
Mr Cheng Ki-kin
Ms King Mary Ann Pui-wai
Mr Lee Hing-wai, Bonson
Mr Lee Kai-hung, Kennedy
Mr Lo Kin-ming, Tommy
Mr Ng Kam-chun, Stephen, MH
Ms Tang King-yung, Anna, MH
Mr Wong Wang-tai

Appointed Members:
Dr Siu Che-hung, Paul
Ms Tsui Wai-ling, Carlye, BBS, JP
Mr Yau How-boa, Stephen, MH, JP

Wong Tai Sin District Council

Chairman:
Mr WONG Kam-chi, MH (Elected member)

Vice Chairman:
Mr KAN Chi-ho, MH (Elected member)

Elected Members:
Mr CHAN Lee-shing
Ms CHAN Man-ki, Maggie
Mr CHAN On-tai
Mr CHAN Wai-kwan, Andie
Mr CHAN Yim-kwong, Joe
Mr CHENG Tak-kin, Michael, JP
Mr CHUI Pak-tai
Mr FUNG Kwong-chung, JP
Mr HO Yin-fai
Mr HUI Kam-shing
Ms KWOK Sau-ying
Mr LAI Wing-ho, Joe
Mr LAM Man-fai, JP
Mr LAU Kar-wah
Mr LEE Tat-yan
Mr MOK Ying-fan
Mr SO Sik-kin
Ms TAM Heung-man
Ms TAM Yuet-ping, Celia
Mr TO Kwan-hang, Andrew
Mr WONG Kwok-tung
Mr WONG Yat-yuk
Mr WU Chi-wai

Appointed Members:
Mr CHOW Ching-lam, Tony, MH
Dr LAU Chi-wang, James, JP
Ms LEE Ming-pui, Mavis
Dr LI Sze-bay, Albert, JP
Mr NG Yiu-man
Mr SHI Lop-tak

Yau Tsim Mong District Council

Chairman:
Mr CHAN Man-yu, Henry (Elected member)

Vice Chairman:
Mr LEUNG Wai-kuen, Edward
    (Elected member)

Elected Members:
Mr CHAN Kin-shing, Alexis
Mr CHAN Siu-tong
Mr CHOW Chun-fai, BBS, JP
Mr HUI Tak-leung, Eon
Mr IP Shu-on
Mr LAI Chi-lap, Albert
Mr LAM Ho-yeung
Mr LAU Chi-wing, David
Dr LAW Wing-cheung
Ms NG Po-shan, Austen
The Honourable TO Kun-sun, James
Mr TSUNG Po-shan
Mr WONG Che-ming
Mr WONG Chun-hung, Dennis

Appointed Members:
Mr KONG Wai-yeung
Ms KWAN Miu-mei
Mr SHING Yuen-hing, MH
Mr WU Man-keung, John, MH

New Territories

Islands District Council

Chairman:
Mr LAM Wai-keung, Daniel, BBS, JP
    (*Ex officio* member)

Vice Chairman:
Ms CHAU Chuen-heung, MH, JP
    (Elected member)

Elected Members:
Mr KWONG Kwok-wai, MH
Ms LEE Kwai-chun, MH
Mr LO Kwong-shing, Andy
Mr WONG Fuk-kan
Mr WONG Hoi-yue
Miss YU Lai-fan
Miss YUNG Wing-sheung, Amy

Appointed Members:
Mr LAM Kit-sing
Mr LEUNG Siu-tong
The Reverend SIK Chi-wai
Mr WAN Tung-lam, Tony

Ex Officio Members:
Mr CHOW Yuk-tong, MH
Mr FONG Kam-hung
Mr LAW Kam-fai, MH
Mr LEE Chi-fung, MH
Mr NG Kum-chuen
Mr WONG Chau-fuk
Mr YUNG Chi-ming

Kwai Tsing District Council

Chairman:
Mr CHOW Yick-hay, BBS (Elected member)

Vice Chairman:
Mr LEUNG Wing-kuen (Elected member)

Elected Members:
Mr CHAN Siu-man, Simon
Mr CHOW Lap-yan
Mr HUI Kei-cheung
Mr LAI Siu-tong
Mr LAM Siu-fai
Mr LAU Pik-kin
Mr LAU Wai-kit
Mr LEE Chi-keung, Alan
Mr LEE Wing-tat
Mr LEUNG Chi-shing
Mr LEUNG Kwong-cheong
Mr LEUNG Wai-man
The Honourable LEUNG Yiu-chung
Ms LO Wai-lan
Mr LUI Ko-wai
Miss MAK Mei-kuen, Alice
Mr NG Kim-sing
Ms POON Siu-ping, Nancy
Ms TAM Wai-chun
Mr TING Yin-wah
Mr TSUI Sang-hung, Sammy
Mr WAN Siu-kin, Andrew
Mr WONG Bing-kuen
Mr WONG Kwong-mo
Miss WONG Suet-ying
Mr WONG Yiu-chung

Appointed Members:
Ms CHAN Ka-mun, Carmen
Mr CHUI Chi-yun, Robert
Mr LAM Kin-ko

Mr POON Fat-lam, MH
Mr SO Hoi-pan, Edinson, BBS, JP
Mr WONG Chi-kwan, MH
Mr YUNG Wing-ki, Samuel, MH

Ex Officio Member:
Mr TANG Kwok-kong, MH

North District Council

Chairman:
Mr LI Kwok-fung (*Ex officio* member)

Vice Chairman:
Mr CHOW Kam-siu, Joseph (Elected member)

Elected Members:
Mr AU Wai-kwan
Mr CHAN Fat-hong
Mr CHAN Hing-fuk
Mr HAU Kam-lam
Ms IP Mei-ho
Mr LAU Tak-cheong, Adrian
Mr LIU Chiu-wa
Mr MOK Siu-lun
Mr POON Chung-yuen
Mr SHAM Wing-kan
Mr SO Sai-chi, MH
Mr WAN Wo-fai
Mr WONG Kam-sang
Mr WONG Leung-hi
Mr YU Chi-shing, Paul

Appointed Members:
Mr CHAN Yiu-wah
Ms CHEUNG Mui-seung, Emily
Mr KAN Wing-fai, Terry
Mr LUI Hing-chung
Mr YIP Yiu-shing, Chris, MH

Ex Officio Members:
Mr CHEUNG Fo-tai, MH
Mr LAU Tin-sang
Mr LAU Ying-wo

Sai Kung District Council

Chairman:
Mr NG Sze-fuk, BBS, JP (Elected member)

461

Vice Chairman:
Mr CHAU Yin-ming, Francis, MH
  (Elected member)

Elected Members:
Mr AU Ning-fat, Alfred
Mr CHAN Kwok-kai
Mr FAN Kwok-wai, Gary
Mr HIEW Moo-siew
Mr HO Man-kit, Raymond
Mr LAM Wing-yin
Mr LAU Wai-cheung, Peter
Dr LAW Cheung-kwok
Mr LING Man-hoi
Mr LUK Ping-choi
Mr LUK Wai-man
Mr NG Ping-yiu
Mr OR Yiu-lam, Ricky
Ms PHANG Shuk-yee, Zoe
Mr SHEK Chi-keung
Mr WAN Yuet-cheung
Mr WAN Yuet-kau, JP
Mr YAU Chi-wan

Appointed Members:
Mr CHAN Kwai-sang
Mr CHEUNG Chun-hoi, MH
Mr HIEW Chin, MH
Dr LAM Ching-choi, JP
Mr LAU Hing-kee

Ex Officio **Members:**
Mr LAU Wan-hei
Mr SING Hon-keung, MH

Sha Tin District Council

Chairman:
Mr WAI Kwok-hung, JP (Elected member)

Vice Chairman:
Mr PANG Cheung-wai, Thomas, JP
  (Elected member)

Elected Members:
Mr CHAN Kwok-tim
Ms CHAN Man-kuen
Mr CHENG Cho-kwong
Mr CHENG Tsuk-man

Mr CHING Cheung-ying
Mr CHOW Ka-kong, MH
Mr FONG Chun-bong, Stephen
Mr HO Hau-cheung
Mr HO Sau-mo
Ms HO Suk-ping, Shirley
Mr KAN Chung-nin, Tony, BBS, JP
Mr LAM Hong-wah
Mr LAU Tai-sang
Mr LAU Wai-lun
Mr LAW Kwong-keung
Mr LEE Chi-wing, Alvin
Mr LEE Kam-ming
Mr LEE Lap-hong, Almustafa
Dr LEE York-fai
Mr LEUNG Chi-kin, MH
Mr LEUNG Chi-wai
Mr LEUNG Wing-hung
Mr MOK Wai-hung
Mr PUN Kwok-shan
Mr SIU Hin-hong
Mr TANG Wing-cheong
Mr TING Tsz-yuen
Mr TSOI Ah-chung
Mr TSOI Yiu-cheong, Richard
Mr WAI Hing-cheung
Mr WONG Chak-piu, Philip
Mr WONG Kwok-hung
Ms YEUNG Sin-hung
Mr YIU Ka-chun

Appointed Members:
Mrs CHAN LO Yin-bing
Dr CHUI Hong-sheung
Dr FONG Yuk-fai, Ben
Professor KAN Wing-kay
Mrs LING LAU Yuet-fun, Laura, MH
Dr LO Wai-kwok, MH
Mr SIU Ka-keung
Dr TSO Wung-wai, BBS
Ms YU Sau-chu, MH

Ex Officio **Member:**
Mr MOK Kam-kwai

Tai Po District Council

Chairman:
Mr CHENG Chun-ping, JP (Elected member)

Vice Chairman:
Mr WAN Hok-lim, MH (Appointed member)

Elected Members:
Mr AU Chun-wah
Mr CHAN Siu-kuen
Mr CHENG Chun-wo
The Honourable CHENG Kar-foo, Andrew
Mr CHEUNG Kwok-yiu
Mr HO Tai-wai, David
Mr KWAN Wing-yip
Mr LEE Chi-shing, Edward
Mr LI Kwok-ying
Mr LO Sam-shing
Mr LO Sou-chour
Mr MAN Chen-fai
Mr WONG Chun-wai
Ms WONG Pik-kiu
Mr WONG Tin-lung
The Honourable WONG Yung-kan
Mr YAM Kai-bong
Ms YIK Kin-hing

Appointed Members:
Mr CHU King-yuen, MH
Ms HO On-nei, BBS, MH, JP
Mr LAM Luk-wing
Mr LI Yiu-ban, MH

Ex Officio **Members:**
Mr CHEUNG Hok-ming, SBS, JP
Mr TANG Kwong-wing, BBS

Tsuen Wan District Council

Chairman:
Mr CHAU How-chen, SBS, JP
  (Appointed member)

Vice Chairman:
Mr CHUNG Wai-ping, MH
  (*Ex officio* member)

Elected Members:
Mr CHAN Han-pan
Mr CHAN Kam-lam, Richard, MH
Mr CHAN Wai-ming, MH
The Honourable CHAN Wai-yip, Albert
Mr CHAN Yuen-sum, Sumly

Mr CHIU Ka-po
Mr CHOI Shing-for
Mr CHOW Ping-tim
Mr CHOY Tsz-man
Mr KWONG Kwok-chuen, Cosmas
Mr LAM Faat-kang
Mr LI Hung-por
Mr MAN Yu-ming
Mr TIN Sai-ming
Mr WONG Ka-wa
Mr WONG Yui-tak, Louis
Ms YOUNG Fuk-ki, Sarena

Appointed Members:
Mr CHAU Chun-wing, William
Mr KWONG Loi-hing, Kevin
Ms LEE Kit-ming
Ms TO Kwai-ying

Ex Officio **Member:**
Mr CHOW Kam-chuen

Tuen Mun District Council

Chairman:
The Honourable LAU Wong-fat, GBS, JP
  (*Ex officio* member)

Vice Chairman:
Mr LEUNG Kin-man, MH (Elected member)

Elected Members:
Mr AU Chi-yuen
Mr CHAN Man-wah
Ms CHAN Sau-wan
Ms CHAN Shu-ying, Josephine
Mr CHAN Wan-sang, MH
Mr CHAN Yau-hoi
Ms CHEUNG Yuet-lan, MH
Ms CHING Chi-hung
Mr CHU Yiu-wah
Ms FONG Lai-man
The Honourable HO Chun-yan, Albert
Ms HO Hang-mui
Ms KONG Fung-yi
Mr KWU Hon-keung
Mr KWUN Tung-wing
Mr LAM Chung-hoi
Mr LEE Hung-sham, Lothar

Ms LI Kwai-fong
Mr LO Man-hon
Ms LUNG Shui-hing
Mr NG Koon-hung
Ms SO Oi-kwan
Mr SO Shiu-shing
Mr TAI Yin-chiu
Mr TO Sheck-yuen
Mr TSUI Fan
Ms WONG Lai-sheung, Catherine
Mr YIM Tin-sang

Appointed Members:
Ms IP Shun-hing, MH
Dr LAU Chi-pang
Mr LAU Ip-keung, Kenneth, MH, JP
Ms LEE Ying, Robena
Mr PONG Chong, Edward, BBS, JP
Mr SIU Chor-kee, Caecage
Mr YING Yu-hing

Yuen Long District Council

Chairman:
Dr the Honourable TANG Siu-tong, JP
　(Appointed member)

Vice Chairman:
Mr LEUNG Che-cheung, MH
　(Elected member)

Elected Members:
Mr CHAM Ka-hung, Daniel, MH
Ms CHAN Mei-lin
Mr CHAN Siu-kay
Ms CHAN Wai-ching
Mr CHEUNG Man-fai
Mr CHEUNG Yin-tung
Ms CHIU Sau-han
Mr CHOW Wing-kan
Mr KWOK Keung
Mr LAI Wai-hung
Mr LAM Tim-fook
Mr LEE Yuet-man
Mr LIU Yam
Mr LUK Chung-hung
Mr MAK Ip-sing
Mr MAN Luk-sing
Mr TANG Hing-ip

Mr TANG Ka-leung
Mr TANG Kwai-yau
Mr TANG Tai-wah
Mr TSE Hoi-chau
Ms WONG Choi-mei
Mr WONG Kin-wing
Mr WONG Pak-yan
Mr WONG Shing-tong
Mr WONG Wai-yin, Zachary
Mr WONG Yu-choi
Miss YAU Tai-tai, MH

Appointed Members:
Ms FUNG Choi-yuk, MH
Ms KWONG Yuet-sum
Mr LAM Kwok-cheong, Alfred, JP
Mr SUNG Wai-ching
Mr TANG Chun-keung
Mr TANG Wai-ming

Ex Officio **Members:**
Mr LEUNG Fuk-yuen
Mr MAN Fu-wan, BBS
Mr TANG Che-cheung
Mr TANG Kam-leung
Mr TSANG Hin-keung
Mr WONG Yiu-wing

APPENDIX 4

Overseas Representation in

Hong Kong *(as at November 2003)*

Countries	Represented by
Argentina	Consul-General
Australia	Consul-General
Austria	Consul-General
The Bahamas	Consul-in-charge
Bahrain	Honorary Consul
Bangladesh	Consul-General
Barbados	Honorary Consul
Belgium	Consul-General
Benin	Honorary Consul
Brazil	Consul-General
Cambodia	Consul-General
Cameroon	Honorary Consul
Canada	Consul-General
Central African Republic	Honorary Consul
Chile	Consul-General
Colombia	Consul-General
Congo	Honorary Consul
Croatia	Honorary Consul
Cuba	Honorary Consul
Cyprus	Honorary Consul
Czech Republic	Consul-General
Democratic Republic of Congo	Honorary Consul
Democratic People's Republic of Korea	Consul-General
Denmark	Consul-General
Egypt	Consul-General
Equatorial Guinea	Honorary Consul
Estonia	Honorary Consul
Ethiopia	Honorary Consul
Fiji	Honorary Consul
Finland	Consul-General
France	Consul-General
Gabon	Honorary Consul
Germany	Consul-General
Ghana	Honorary Consul
Greece	Consul-General
Guinea	Honorary Consul
Hungary	Consul-General
Iceland	Honorary Consul
India	Consul-General
Indonesia	Consul-General
Iran	Consul-General
Ireland	Honorary Consul
Israel	Consul-General
Italy	Consul-General
Jamaica	Honorary Vice Consul
Japan	Consul-General
Jordan	Honorary Consul
Kazakhstan	Consul-General
Republic of Korea	Consul-General
Kuwait	Consul-General
Laos	Consul-General
Latvia	Honorary Consul
Lesotho	Honorary Consul
Lithuania	Honorary Consul
Luxembourg	Honorary Consul
Madagascar	Honorary Consul
Malaysia	Consul-General
Maldives	Honorary Consul
Mali	Honorary Consul
Malta	Honorary Consul
Mauritius	Honorary Consul
Mexico	Consul-General

Countries	Represented by
Monaco	Honorary Consul
Mongolia	Honorary Consul
Morocco	Honorary Consul
Mozambique	Honorary Consul
Myanmar	Consul-General
Namibia	Honorary Consul
Nepal	Consul-General
The Netherlands	Consul-General
New Zealand	Consul-General
Niger	Honorary Consul
Nigeria	Consul-General
Norway	Honorary Consul
Oman	Honorary Consul
Pakistan	Consul-General
Papua New Guinea	Honorary Consul
Peru	Consul-General
The Philippines	Consul-General
Poland	Consul-General
Portugal	Consul-General
Russia	Consul-General
Rwanda	Honorary Consul
Saudi Arabia	Consul-General
Seychelles	Honorary Consul
Singapore	Consul-General
Slovak Republic	Honorary Consul
Slovenia	Honorary Consul
South Africa	Consul-General
Spain	Consul-General
Sri Lanka	Honorary Consul
Sweden	Consul-General
Switzerland	Consul-General
Tanzania	Honorary Consul
Thailand	Consul-General
Togo	Honorary Consul
Tonga	Honorary Consul
Trinidad and Tobago	Honorary Consul
Tunisia	Honorary Consul
Turkey	Consul-General
Uganda	Honorary Consul
United Arab Emirates	Consul-General
United Kingdom	Consul-General
USA	Consul-General
Uruguay	Honorary Consul
Venezuela	Consul-General
Vietnam	Consul-General
European Union, Office of the European Commission	Head of Office
Bank for International Settlements, Representative Office for Asia and the Pacific	Chief Representative
International Finance Corporation Regional Office for East Asia and Pacific and the World Bank Private Sector Development Office for East Asia and Pacific	Regional Director
International Monetary Fund HKSAR Sub-Office	Resident Representative
United Nations High Commissioner for Refugees Sub-Office	Head of Sub-Office

APPENDIX 5

Hong Kong Representation

GOVERNMENT OFFICES

MAINLAND

Beijing
Office of the Government of the HKSAR
21/F., Office Tower 1
Henderson Centre
18 Jianguomen Nei Avenue
Dongcheng District
Beijing 100005
People's Republic of China.
Tel: (86)-10-6518-6318
Fax: (86)-10-6518-6321
E-mail: bjohksar@bjo-hksarg.org.cn

Guangdong
Hong Kong Economic and Trade Office
Flat 7101, 71/F., Citic Plaza
233 Tian He North Road
Guangzhou.
Postal Code: 510613
Tel: (86)-20-3891-1220
Fax: (86)-20-3891-1221
E-mail: general@gdeto.gov.hk
Website: http://www.gdeto.gov.hk

EUROPE

Brussels
Hong Kong Economic and Trade Office
Rue d'Arlon 118
1040 Brussels, Belgium.
Tel: (32)-2-775-0088
Fax: (32)-2-770-0980
     (32)-2-770-0793
E-mail: general@hongkong-eu.org
Website: http://www.hongkong-eu.org

Geneva
Hong Kong Economic and Trade Office
5 Allee David-Morse
1211 Geneva 20, Switzerland.
Tel: (41)-22-730-1300
Fax: (41)-22-730-1304
     (41)-22-730-1305
     (41)-22-730-1306
E-mail: hketo@hketogeneva.gov.hk
Website: http://www.gov.hk/cib/chtml/geneva.html

London
Hong Kong Economic and Trade Office
6 Grafton Street, London W1S 4EQ, UK.
Tel: (44)-207-499-9821
Fax: (44)-207-495-5033
     (44)-207-493-1964
     (44)-207-629-2199
     (44)-207-409-0647
E-mail: general@hketolondon.gov.hk
Website: http://www.hketolondon.gov.hk

NORTH AMERICA

New York
Hong Kong Economic and Trade Office
115 East 54th Street
New York, NY 10022, USA.
Tel: (1)-212-752-3320
Fax: (1)-212-752-3395
     (1)-212-752-3389
E-mail: hketony@hketony.gov.hk
Website: http://www.hongkong.org

San Francisco
Hong Kong Economic and Trade Office
130 Montgomery Street
San Francisco, CA 94104, USA.
Tel: (1)-415-835-9300
Fax: (1)-415-421-0646
     (1)-415-397-2276
     (1)-415-392-2963
     (1)-415-392-2964
     (1)-415-392-5255
E-mail: hketosf@hketosf.gov.hk
Website: http://www.hongkong.org

Washington
Hong Kong Economic and Trade Office
1520, 18th Street, N. W.
Washington DC 20036, USA.
Tel: (1)-202-331-8947
Fax: (1)-202-331-8958
     (1)-202-331-0318
E-mail: hketo@hketowashington.gov.hk
Website: http://www.hongkong.org

Toronto
Hong Kong Economic and Trade Office
174 St George Street, Toronto
Ontario M5R 2M7, Canada.
Tel: (1)-416-924-5544
Fax: (1)-416-924-3599
     (1)-416-924-3542
     (1)-416-924-6896
E-mail: info@hketotoronto.gov.hk
Website: http://www.hketo.ca

Vancouver Sub-Office
Suite 500, Park Place
666 Burrard Street,
Vancouver, British Columbia,
V6C 3P6, Canada.
Tel: (1)-604-331-1300
Fax: (1)-604-331-1368
E-mail: catherine_yuen@hketotoronto.gov.hk

APPENDICES

ASIA-PACIFIC

Tokyo
Hong Kong Economic and Trade Office
Hong Kong Economic and Trade Office Building
No. 30-1, Sanban-cho, Chiyoda-ku
Tokyo 102-0075, Japan.
Tel: (81)-3-3556-8980
Fax: (81)-3-3556-8968
     (81)-3-3556-8969
E-mail: mailbox@hketotyo.gov.hk
Website: http://www.hketotyo.or.jp

Singapore
Hong Kong Economic and Trade Office
34-01, Suntec Tower 2
9 Temasek Boulevard
Singapore 038989.
Tel: (65)-6338-1771
Fax: (65)-6339-2112
     (65)-6337-7297
E-mail: hketo_sin@hketosin.gov.hk
Website: http://www.hketosin.gov.hk

Sydney
Hong Kong Economic and Trade Office
Hong Kong House
80 Druitt Street, Level 1
Sydney, NSW 2000, Australia.
Tel: (61)-2-9283-3222
Fax: (61)-2-9283-3818
     (61)-2-9267-3560
E-mail: enquiry@hketosydney.gov.hk
Website: http://www.hketosydney.org.au

Investment Promotion Units

EUROPE

Brussels
Investment Promotion Unit
Hong Kong Economic and Trade Office
Rue d'Arlon 118
1040 Brussels
Belgium.
Tel: (32)-2-775-0088
Fax: (32)-2-770-0980
     (32)-2-770-0793
E-mail: general@hongkong-eu.org
Website: http://www.hketo.be

London
Investment Promotion Unit
Hong Kong Economic and Trade Office
6 Grafton Street, London W1S 4EQ
England.
Tel: (44)-207-499-9821
Fax: (44)-207-495-5033
     (44)-207-493-1964
     (44)-207-629-2199
     (44)-207-409-0647
E-mail: hk@hketo.co.uk

NORTH AMERICA

New York
Investment Promotion Unit
Hong Kong Economic and Trade Office
115 East 54th Street
New York, NY 10022, USA.
Tel: (1)-212-752-3320
Fax: (1)-212-752-3395
     (1)-212-752-3389
E-mail: hketony@hongkong.org
Website: http://www.hongkong.org

San Francisco
Investment Promotion Unit
Hong Kong Economic and Trade Office
130 Montgomery Street
San Francisco, CA 94104, USA.
Tel: (1)-415-835-9300
Fax: (1)-415-421-0646
     (1)-415-397-2276
     (1)-415-392-2963
     (1)-415-392-2964
     (1)-415-392-5255
E-mail: hketosf@hongkong.org
Website: http://www.hongkong.org

Toronto
Investment Promotion Unit
Hong Kong Economic and Trade Office
174 St George Street, Toronto, Ontario
M5R 2M7, Canada.
Tel: (1)-416-924-5544
Fax: (1)-416-924-3599
     (1)-416-924-3542
     (1)-416-924-6896
E-mail: etotor@hketo.ca
Website: http://www.hketo.ca

ASIA-PACIFIC

Tokyo
Investment Promotion Unit
Hong Kong Economic and Trade Office
Hong Kong Economic and Trade Office Building
No. 30-1, Sanban-cho, Chiyoda-ku
Tokyo 102-0075, Japan.
Tel: (81)-3-3556-8980
Fax: (81)-3-3556-8968
     (81)-3-3556-8969
E-mail: mailbox@hketotyo.gov.hk
Website: http://www.hketotyo.or.jp

Sydney
Investment Promotion Unit
Hong Kong Economic and Trade Office
Hong Kong House
80 Druitt Street, Level 1
Sydney, NSW 2000, Australia.
Tel: (61)-2-9283-3222
Fax: (61)-2-9283-3818
     (61)-2-9267-3560
E-mail: enquiry@hketosydney.gov.hk
Website: http://www.hketosydney.org.au

467

HONG KONG TRADE DEVELOPMENT COUNCIL

The Hong Kong Trade Development Council maintains branch and consultant offices round the world. The addresses of these offices are provided at the council's website.

Head Office
38/F., Office Tower
Convention Plaza
1 Harbour Road
Wan Chai, Hong Kong.
Tel: (852)-2584-4333
Fax: (852)-2824-0249
E-mail: hktdc@tdc.org.hk
Website: http://www.tdctrade.com

HONG KONG TOURISM BOARD

The Hong Kong Tourism Board also maintains offices or representative offices in various countries. The addresses of these offices are provided at the board's website.

Head Office
9-11/F., Citicorp Centre
18 Whitfield Road
North Point, Hong Kong.
Tel: (852)-2807-6543
Fax: (852)-2806-0303
E-mail: info@hktb.com
Website: http://www.discoverhongkong.com

APPENDIX 6

Table 1

(Chapter 3: The Economy)

(a) Gross Domestic Product (GDP)

	1998	*2002*@	*2003*@
GDP (HK$ billion)			
At current market prices	1,279.9	1,259.8	1,234.9
At constant (2000) market prices	1,130.8	1,323.7	1,367.6
Per capita GDP (HK$)			
At current market prices	195,585	185,615	181,527
At constant (2000) market prices	172,813	195,027	201,027

(b) GDP by Expenditure Component

	1998	*2002*@	*2003*@
Ratio of expenditure components to GDP at current market prices (%)			
Private consumption expenditure[1]	61.5	57.8	57.1
Government consumption expenditure	9.1	10.4	10.5
Gross domestic fixed capital formation	30.4	23.2	22.3
Changes in inventories	−1.2	0.2	0.6
Exports of goods (f.o.b.)	105.3	124.0	141.6
Exports of services[1]	20.1	26.8	28.4
Less: Imports of goods (f.o.b.)	*110.0*	*127.1*	*145.3*
Imports of services	*15.1*	*15.4*	*15.3*
GDP	100.0	100.0	100.0
Year-on-year rates of change of GDP and expenditure components (%)			
In nominal terms			
GDP	−4.8	−0.8	−2.0
Private consumption expenditure[1]	−4.6	−4.8	−3.1
Government consumption expenditure	+3.4	+1.8	−0.9
Gross domestic fixed capital formation	−14.0	−12.1	−6.0
Exports of goods (f.o.b.)	−7.4	+5.5	+12.0
Exports of services[1]	−5.6	+9.8	+3.7
Imports of goods (f.o.b.)	−11.4	+3.4	+12.0
Imports of services	−1.4	+0.5	−2.2
In real terms			
GDP	−5.0	+2.3	+3.3
Private consumption expenditure[1]	−6.8	−1.2	†
Government consumption expenditure	+0.7	+2.4	+1.9
Gross domestic fixed capital formation	−7.3	−4.3	−0.1
Exports of goods (f.o.b.)	−4.3	+8.7	+14.2
Exports of services[1]	−0.4	+12.2	+5.5
Imports of goods (f.o.b.)	−7.3	+7.9	+13.1
Imports of services	+1.6	+0.2	−4.4

(c) GDP by Economic Activity at Current Prices

	1998	2001	2002@
Percentage contribution of economic activities to GDP at current factor cost (%)			
Agriculture and fishing	0.1	0.1	0.1
Mining and quarrying	§	§	§
Manufacturing	6.0	5.2	4.5
Electricity, gas and water	3.0	3.3	3.4
Construction	5.9	4.9	4.4
Services	84.9	86.5	87.5
Wholesale, retail and import/export trades, restaurants and hotels	25.0	26.7	26.9
Transport, storage and communications	9.2	10.2	10.6
Financing, insurance, real estate and business services	24.6	22.5	22.2
Community, social and personal services	19.3	21.8	22.2
Ownership of premises	14.2	13.1	13.2
Less: Adjustment for financial intermediation services indirectly measured	*7.4*	*7.9*	*7.7*
Total	100.0	100.0	100.0
GDP at factor cost (HK$ billion)	1,205.3	1,215.4	1,205.9

(d) GDP by Economic Activity at Constant (2000) Prices

	2002@	2003@
Year-on-year rates of change in real terms of value added of major economic activities (%)		
Manufacturing	−9.8	−10.2
Construction	−0.8	−4.3
Services	+3.5	+3.7
of which:		
Wholesale, retail and import/export trades, restaurants and hotels	+4.4	+9.5
Transport, storage and communications	+6.2	−0.2
Financing, insurance, real estate and business services	+1.7	+3.6
Community, social and personal services	+0.6	−1.0

Notes: (1) Figures have been revised to incorporate the new data on destination consumption expenditure of incoming visitors and travellers released by the Hong Kong Tourism Board in November 2003. For details, please refer to the feature article 'Statistics on Inbound Tourism' in the December 2003 issue of the *Hong Kong Monthly Digest of Statistics*.

      † Change within ±0.05%

      § Less than 0.05%

Source: National Income Branches (1) and (2), Census and Statistics Department. (Enquiry Telephone No.: 2582 5077)

Table 2

(Chapter 3: The Economy)
Gross National Product (GNP)

HK$ Billion, unless otherwise specified

	1998	*2002*@	*2003*@
At constant (2000) market prices[1]			
GDP	1,130.8	1,323.7	1,367.6
Net external factor income flows	26.7	18.0	38.1
GNP	1,157.3	1,341.7	1,405.7
	(3.6)	(+0.4)	(+4.8)
Per capita GDP (HK$)	172,813	195,027	201,027
Per capita GNP (HK$)	176,858	197,682	206,631
	(–4.4)	(–0.5)	(+4.5)
At current market prices			
GDP	1,279.9	1,259.8	1,234.9
Net external factor income flows	28.8	16.7	34.1
GNP	1,308.6	1,276.5	1,269.1
	(–3.4)	(–2.6)	(–0.6)
Per capita GDP (HK$)	195,585	185,615	181,527
Per capita GNP (HK$)	199,980	188,076	186,543
	(–4.2)	(–3.5)	(–0.8)

Notes: Figures in brackets refer to percentage changes over the same period of the preceding year.

GNP is obtained by adding net external factor income flows to GDP of the same year.

(1) Owing to rebasing of GDP and GNP at constant prices to year 2000, there are slight discrepancies between figures on GNP at constant market prices and the sum of figures on GDP at constant market prices and net external factor income flows for reference periods before the base year of 2000.

Source: Balance of Payments Branch (2), Census and Statistics Department.
(Enquiry Telephone No.: 2116 5102)

Table 3

(Chapter 3: The Economy)
Balance of Payments Account

HK$ Billion

	1998	*2002*@	*2003*@
Current Account Balance[1]	19.6	107.0	135.5
Balance on goods	−60.7	−39.4	−45.0
Balance on services[4]	63.9	144.5	161.1
Net income flow	28.8	16.7	34.1
Net flow in current transfers	−12.4	−14.8	−14.7
Capital and Financial Account Balance[1]	−31.5	−151.2	−151.5
Net flow in capital transfers	−18.4	−15.7	−7.9
Net change[2] in financial non-reserve assets	−65.6	154.0	−135.9
Direct investment	−17.2	−60.7	76.2
Portfolio investment	171.1	−302.5	−237.1
Financial derivatives	25.6	51.6	79.6
Other investment	−245.1	157.6	−54.6
Net change[2] in reserve assets	52.6	18.5	−7.6
Net Errors and Omissions[3]	11.9	44.1	15.9
Overall Balance of Payments	−52.6	−18.5	7.6
	(in deficit)	(in deficit)	(in surplus)

Notes: (1) In accordance with the Balance of Payments accounting rules, a positive value for the balance figure in the current account represents a surplus whereas a negative value represents a deficit. For the capital and financial account, a positive value indicates a net capital and financial inflow and a negative value indicates a net outflow. As increases in external assets are debit entries and decreases are credit entries, a negative value for net change in reserve assets represents a net increase and a positive value represents a net decrease.

(2) The estimates on net change in reserve and non-reserve assets under the Balance of Payments framework are transaction figures. Effects from valuation changes (including price changes and exchange rate changes) and reclassifications are excluded.

(3) In principle, the *net sum* of credit entries and debit entries is zero. In practice, discrepancies between the credit and debit entries may however occur for various reasons as the data are collected from many sources. Equality between the sum of credit entries and debit entries is brought about by the inclusion of a balancing item which reflects *net errors and omissions*.

(4) Figures have been revised to incorporate the new data on destination consumption expenditure of incoming visitors and travellers released by the Hong Kong Tourism Board in November 2003. For details, please refer to the feature article 'Statistics on Inbound Tourism' in the December 2003 issue of the *Hong Kong Monthly Digest of Statistics*.

Source: Balance of Payments Branch (1), Census and Statistics Department.
(Enquiry Telephone No.: 2116 8677)

Table 4

(Chapter 3: The Economy)

Year-on-year Rates of Change in the Consumer Price Indices[1][2]

Percentages

	1998	2002	2003
Composite Consumer Price Index	+2.8	–3.0	–2.6
Food	+1.9	–2.1	–1.5
Housing[3]	+4.7	–5.7	–4.8
Consumer Price Index (A)	+2.6	–3.2	–2.1
Food	+1.9	–2.2	–1.6
Housing[3]	+3.1	–5.7	–3.0
Consumer Price Index (B)	+2.8	–3.1	–2.7
Food	+2.1	–2.1	–1.6
Housing[3]	+4.4	–5.9	–5.1
Consumer Price Index (C)	+3.2	–2.8	–2.9
Food	+1.9	–1.7	–1.3
Housing[3]	+6.4	–5.5	–6.5

Notes: (1) The year-on-year rate of change in the Consumer Price Index (CPI) is an important indicator of inflation affecting consumers.

      (2) The CPI(A), CPI(B) and CPI(C) respectively cover some 50%, 30% and 10% of households in Hong Kong. The average monthly household expenditure (in HK$) of these groups during the base period (i.e. Oct. 1999-Sep. 2000) were $4,500–$18,499, $18,500–$32,499 and $32,500–$65,999 respectively. After taking into account the impact of changes in price levels since the base period, the expenditure ranges of the different CPIs at 2003 prices are broadly equivalent to $4,200–$17,000 for the CPI(A), $17,000–$30,000 for the CPI(B) and $30,000–$60,900 for the CPI(C). The Composite CPI is compiled based on the expenditure patterns of all these households taken together.

      (3) 'Water and sewage charges' previously under 'Housing' section has been re-classified as a component of the 'Electricity, gas and water' section.

Source: Consumer Price Index Section, Census and Statistics Department.
(Enquiry Telephone No.: 2805 6403)

Table 5

(Chapter 3: The Economy)

Business Receipts Indices

(Quarterly average of 1996=100)

	1998	2002	2003
Service industry			
Wholesale/Retail	84.5	71.9	70.9
	(−18.6)	(−5.5)	(−1.4)
Import/Export trade	94.6	80.5	85.7
	(−14.6)	(+1.8)	(+6.5)
Restaurants	102.7	96.7	89.8
	(−4.6)	(−4.5)	(−7.1)
Hotels	58.8	60.1	54.4
	(−24.9)	(−2.5)	(−9.5)
Transport[1]	96.0	121.9	122.3
	(−10.2)	(+6.1)	(+0.3)
Storage	96.8	51.7	49.8
	(−4.8)	(−20.4)	(−3.7)
Communications	117.7	90.4	87.7
	(−6.1)	(−1.4)	(−3.1)
Banking	94.5	101.7	107.6
	(−13.1)	(−4.2)	(+5.8)
Financing (except banking)[2]	86.3	89.6	117.3
	(−47.1)	(−6.9)	(+30.9)
Insurance	109.4	165.9	208.0
	(−3.9)	(+9.8)	(+25.4)
Real estate[3]	80.9	56.8	67.2
	(−24.8)	(−8.4)	(+18.3)
Business services	102.1	78.8	79.4
	(−8.7)	(−5.0)	(+0.8)
Film entertainment	111.2	108.1	121.2
	(−1.6)	(−18.9)	(+12.1)
Service domain[4]			
Tourism, convention and exhibition	58.3	67.5*	64.6#
services[5]	(−20.9)	(+10.8)*	(−4.2)#
Computer and information services	109.5	135.8	143.9
	(−4.1)	(+6.9)	(+6.0)

Notes: Figures refer to the third quarter of the year. Figures in brackets refer to percentage changes over the same period of the preceding year.
  (1) Including business receipts from the Airport Authority as from the third quarter of 1998.
  (2) Not including investment and holding companies.
  (3) Not including real estate development.
  (4) A service domain differs from a service industry in that a domain comprises those economic activities straddling different industries but are somehow related to a common purpose. Tourism is a good example. It includes all activities of hotels and travel agents; and some (those involving visitors as customers) but not all of the activities of restaurants, retailers and transport operators.
  (5) Part of the data is obtained from the Hong Kong Tourism Board and figures have been revised to incorporate the new data on destination consumption expenditure of incoming visitors and travellers released by the Hong Kong Tourism Board in November 2003. For details, please refer to the feature article 'Statistics on Inbound Tourism' in the December 2003 issue of the *Hong Kong Monthly Digest of Statistics.*

Source: Business Services Statistics Sections, Census and Statistics Department.
  (Enquiry Telephone No.: 2802 1269)

Table 6
(Chapter 3: The Economy)
Public Expenditure by Function

$Million

Item	Actual 1998-1999			Actual 2002-2003			Revised Estimate 2003-2004		
	Recurrent	Capital	Total	Recurrent	Capital	Total	Recurrent	Capital	Total
Community and external affairs									
District and community relations	1,412	111	1,523	1,828	223	2,051	1,836	257	2,093
Recreation, culture and amenities	5,429	1,680	7,109	5,409	617	6,026	5,514	919	6,433
Sub-total	6,841	1,791	8,632	7,237	840	8,077	7,350	1,176	8,526
Economic	10,225	11,196	21,421	10,575	3,173	13,748	10,857	4,704	15,561
Education	40,892	7,587	48,479	46,992	7,793	54,785	46,761	10,987	57,748
Environment & food	7,931	5,415	13,346	8,512	2,931	11,443	8,315	2,898	11,213
Health	28,790	2,610	31,400	32,352	847	33,199	31,706	2,779	34,485
Housing	11,891	26,959	38,850	11,445	12,586	24,031	11,849	16,005	27,854
Infrastructure									
Buildings, lands and planning	2,578	5,683	8,261	3,157	6,228	9,385	3,129	6,557	9,686
Transport	2,664	3,992	6,656	2,987	4,745	7,732	2,928	6,992	9,920
Water supply	4,926	3,289	8,215	5,369	2,104	7,473	5,335	1,422	6,757
Sub-total	10,168	12,964	23,132	11,513	13,077	24,590	11,392	14,971	26,363
Security									
Immigration	1,988	46	2,034	2,252	279	2,531	2,291	514	2,805
Internal security	18,230	1,304	19,534	18,825	2,260	21,085	18,743	2,408	21,151
Other	3,240	307	3,547	3,363	89	3,452	3,449	51	3,500
Sub-total	23,458	1,657	25,115	24,440	2,628	27,068	24,483	2,973	27,456
Social welfare	25,327	1,050	26,377	31,264	1,018	32,282	32,512	1,485	33,997
Support	22,334	7,362	29,696	27,398	6,899	34,297	29,235	6,745	35,980
Total	187,857	78,591	266,448	211,728	51,792	263,520	214,460	64,723	279,183

Notes: Public expenditure comprises government expenditure (i.e. all expenditure charged to the General Revenue Account and financed by the Government's statutory funds excluding Capital Investment Fund), and expenditure by the Trading Funds, the Housing Authority, the Lotteries Fund and the previous Provisional Urban Council and Provisional Regional Council (up to 31 December 1999). Expenditure by institutions in the private or quasi-private sector is included to the extent of their subventions. But not included is expenditure by those organisations, including statutory organisations, in which the Government has only an equity position, such as the Airport Authority, the MTR Corp Ltd and the Kowloon-Canton Railway Corporation. Similarly, advances and equity investments from the Capital Investment Fund are excluded as they do not reflect the actual consumption of resources by the Government.

Where appropriate, historical figures have been adjusted to comply with the current classification of expenditure.

Source: Financial Services and the Treasury Bureau, Government Secretariat.
(Enquiry Telephone No.: 2810 3658)

Chart 1
(Chapter 3: The Economy)
Public Expenditure by Function

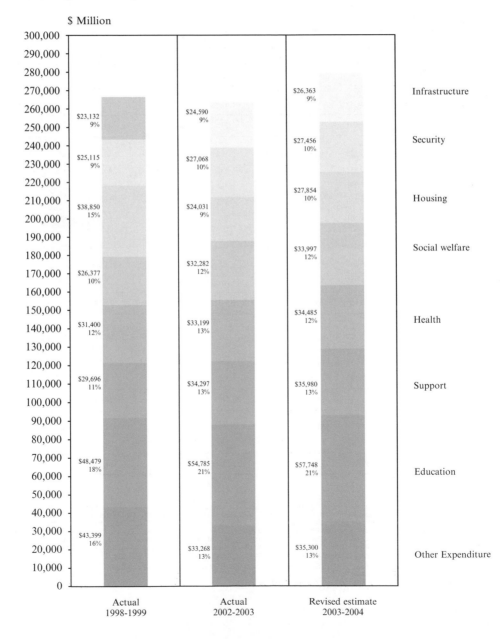

Table 7

(Chapter 3: Economy)

Government Expenditure and the Economy

$ Million

	Actual 1998-1999	Actual 2002-2003	Revised Estimate 2003-2004
Government Expenditure (see Table 8)			
Operating Expenditure	174,793 †	200,310	206,734
Capital Expenditure	41,405	35,927	41,873
Total Government Expenditure	216,198	236,237	248,607
Add other public sector bodies	50,250	27,283	30,576
Total Public Expenditure[(1)]	266,448	263,520	279,183
Gross Domestic Product (GDP) at current market prices (HK$ billion)[(2)]	1,279.9	1,259.8 @	1,234.9 @
Growth in GDP[(2)]:			
Nominal terms	–4.8%	–0.8% @	–2.0% @
Real terms	–5.0%	2.3% @	+3.3% @
Growth in Public Expenditure:			
Nominal terms	13.5%	–2.2%	4.8%
Real terms	8.0%	–0.2%	8.4%
Public Expenditure as percentage of GDP	20.8%	20.9%	22.6%

Notes: (1) Public expenditure comprises government expenditure (i.e. all expenditure charged to the General Revenue Account and financed by the Government's statutory funds excluding Capital Investment Fund), and expenditure by the Trading Funds, the Housing Authority, the Lotteries Fund and the previous Provisional Urban Council and Provisional Regional Council (up to 31 December 1999). Expenditure by institutions in the private or quasi-private sector is included to the extent of their subventions. But not included is expenditure by those organisations, including statutory organisations, in which the Government has only an equity position, such as the Airport Authority, the MTR Corp Ltd and the Kowloon-Canton Railway Corporation. Similarly, advances and equity investments from the Capital Investment Fund are excluded as they do not reflect the actual consumption of resources by the Government.

(2) Figures refer to calender years of 1998, 2002 and 2003.

† To avoid the double-counting of expenditure, this figure excludes government's payments to the two previous municipal councils.

Source: Financial Services and the Treasury Bureau, Government Secretariat.
(Enquiry Telephone No.: 2810 3658)

Table 8

(Chapter 3: Economy)

Total Government Revenue and Expenditure and Summary of Financial Position

$ Million

	Revenue		
	Actual 1998-1999	Actual 2002-2003	Revised Estimate 2003-2004
Operating Revenue			
Direct taxes			
Earnings and profits tax[1]	75,746	73,028	78,080
Indirect taxes			
Duties	7,698	6,620	6,539
General rates	3,614	8,923	11,131
Internal revenues[2]	23,404	19,464	22,595
Motor vehicle taxes	2,237	2,510	2,712
Royalties and concessions	1,286	1,726	1,654
Other revenue			
Fines, forfeitures and penalties	1,333	843	822
Properties and investments	8,335	8,015	7,708
Reimbursements and contributions	6,517	4,405	3,212
Utilities—			
Airport and air services	1,087	—	
Ferry terminals	198	225	207
Postal services	—		—
Water	2,415	1,458	2,093
Sewage services	700	385	550
Fees and charges	10,565	9,687	10,369
Investment Income			
General revenue account	21,568	2,766	5,886
Land Fund	10,080	13,281	17,150
Total Operating Revenue	176,783	153,336	170,708
Capital Revenue			
Indirect taxes			
Estate duty	1,237	1,403	1,500
Taxi concessions	—	—	—
Other revenue	2,453	2,760	2,866
Funds			
Capital Works Reserve Fund (Land sales and interest)	25,686	12,190	6,025
Capital Investment Fund	6,329	2,432	2,423
Civil Service Pension Reserve Fund	1,091	631	1,146
Disaster Relief Fund	3	2	3
Innovation and Technology Fund	—	271	422
Loan Fund	2,533	4,464	17,551
Lotteries Fund	—	—	1,193
Total Capital Revenue	39,332	24,153	33,129
Total Government Revenue	216,115	177,489	203,837

	Expenditure		
			$ Million
	Actual 1998-1999	Actual 2002-2003	Revised Estimate 2003-2004
Operating Expenditure			
Recurrent expenditure			
Personal emoluments	44,092	50,966	49,585
Personnel related expenses	4,708	4,830	4,938
Pensions	7,395	12,107	13,804
Departmental expenses	8,935	15,563	16,291
Other charges	28,568	33,655	35,209
Subventions—			
Education	21,082	25,894	25,921
Medical	26,562	29,553	29,111
Social welfare	5,419	6,818	7,031
University and Polytechnic	13,189	13,189	12,900
Vocational Training Council	1,968	2,005	1,926
Miscellaneous	2,359	3,424	3,312
Other non-recurrent	13,129	2,306	6,706
Total Operating Expenditure	177,406	200,310	206,734
Capital Expenditure			
General Revenue Account			
Plant, equipment and works	790	952	896
Capital subventions	1,454	953	1,088
Funds			
Capital Works Reserve Fund	31,267	30,919	35,593
Disaster Relief Fund	38	19	11
Innovation and Technology Fund	—	295	502
Loan Fund	7,856	2,789	2,710
Lotteries Fund	—	—	1,073
Total Capital Expenditure	41,405	35,927	41,873
Total Government Expenditure	218,811	236,237	248,607
Equity Investments (Capital Investment Fund)	20,545	2,940	4,253
Total Government Expenditure and Equity Investments	239,356	239,177	252,860

$ Million

	Summary of Financial Position		
	Actual 1998-1999	Actual 2002-2003	Revised Estimate 2003-2004
Total Government Revenue	216,115	177,489	203,837
Less total Government Expenditure and Equity Investments	239,356	239,177	252,860
Consolidated surplus/(deficit)	(23,241)	(61,688)	(49,023)
Reserve balance at 1 April	457,543	372,503	311,402
Lotteries Fund balance at 1 April[3]	—	—	4,069
Write-back of Provision for loss in investments with the Exchange Fund[4]	—	587	—
Reserve balance at 31 March	434,302	311,402	266,448

Notes: (1) Including salaries tax, profits tax, property tax and personal assessment.
(2) Including bets and sweeps tax, hotel accommodation tax, air passenger departure tax, Cross-Harbour Tunnel passage tax and stamp duties.
(3) The Lotteries Fund was included in the Consolidated Accounts of the Government with effect from 1 April 2003.
(4) In 2002-03, the amount refers to the balance of the provision to be written back.

Source: Financial Services and the Treasury Bureau, Government Secretariat.
(Enquiry Telephone No.: 2810 3658)

Chart 2
(Chapter 3: The Economy)
Major Sources of Revenue
(2002-03)

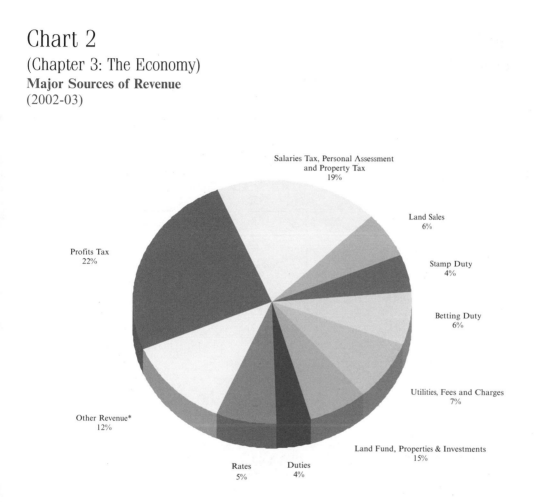

*Other Revenue includes:—

1. Loans, Reimbursements and Others
2. Estate Duty
3. Capital Works Reserve Fund (excluding land premium)
4. Motor Vehicle First Registration Tax
5. Air Passenger Departure Tax
6. Capital Investment Fund
7. Royalties and Concessions
8. Hotel Accommodation Tax
9. Fines, Forfeitures and Penalties
10. Loan Fund
11. Civil Service Pension Reserve Fund
12. Disaster Relief Fund
13. Innovation and Technology Fund

Table 9

(Chapter 4: Financial and Monetary Affairs)

Deposits, Loans and Advances of Authorised Institutions

	1998	*2002*	*2003*
Number of authorised institutions in operation			
Licensed banks	171	133	133
Restricted licence banks	60	46	41
Deposit-taking companies	101	45	39
Total	332	224	213
	(−7.8)	(−10.0)	(−4.9)
Deposits from customers[1][2] (HK$ billion)			
Licensed banks	2,954.0	3,275.8	3,523.3
Restricted licence banks	36.2	35.9	38.2
Deposit-taking companies	9.9	5.9	4.9
Total	3,000.0	3,317.5	3,566.4
	(+10.7)	(−2.6)	(+7.5)
Loans and advances for use in Hong Kong[1][3] (HK$ billion)			
Licensed banks	1,779.6	1,618.7	1,602.5
Restricted licence banks	126.3	98.9	83.1
Deposit-taking companies	54.4	25.3	22.9
Total	1,960.4	1,742.9	1,708.6
	(−3.8)	(−2.6)	(−2.0)
Total loans and advances to customers[1] (HK$ billion)			
Licensed banks	3,087.1	1,936.7	1,912.7
Restricted licence banks	150.2	112.3	97.5
Deposit-taking companies	67.1	27.3	25.0
Total	3,304.4	2,076.3	2,035.2
	(−19.8)	(−5.0)	(−2.0)

Notes: Figures in brackets refer to percentage changes over the same period of the preceding year.
(1) Figures are revised on a monthly basis to take into account any subsequent amendments submitted by authorised institutions.
(2) As from June 2002, short-term Exchange Fund placements of less than one month are included under time deposits as part of the monetary aggregates. The revised data series are backdated to April 1997.
(3) Excluding loans for trade financing.

Source: Hong Kong Monetary Authority.
(Enquiry Telephone No.: 2878 8222)

Table 10

(Chapter 4: Financial and Monetary Affairs)
Exchange Rates of the Hong Kong Dollar Against Selected Major Currencies

	Sterling	US dollar	Deutsche -mark	Euro[2]	Japanese yen	Special Drawing Right	*Effective exchange rate index for the HK dollar*[1] *Trade (import and export)-weighted (Jan. 2000 = 100)*
End of period			*(HK dollar to per unit of foreign currency)*				
1998	12.86	7.746	4.62	N.A.[2]	0.0682	10.90660	100.3
2002	12.51	7.798	N.A.[2]	8.17	0.0657	10.60154	102.0
2003	13.83	7.763	N.A.[2]	9.77	0.0726	11.53559	98.8

Notes: (1) New series released since 2 January 2002. The effective exchange rate index for the Hong Kong dollar is derived from the weighted average of nominal exchange rates of the Hong Kong dollar against 14 major currencies.

(2) Euro was launched on 1 January 1999. As from 1 January 2002, Euro has replaced national currencies of its participating countries (including Deutsche-mark).

Source: Hong Kong Monetary Authority.
(Enquiry Telephone No.: 2878 8222)

Table 11

(Chapter 4: Financial and Monetary Affairs)
Money Supply

HK$ Billion

	1998	2002	2003
M1@			
Hong Kong dollar	178.3	259.4	354.7
Foreign currency	19.4	36.2	58.7
Total	197.7	295.7	413.4
	(−5.2)	(+14.6)	(+39.8)
M3[1]@			
Hong Kong dollar[2]	1,840.8	2,004.2	2,122.8
Foreign currency[3]	1,327.4	1,557.9	1,734.6
Total	3,168.2	3,561.9	3,857.5
	(+10.3)	(−0.9)	(+8.3)

Notes: Figures in brackets refer to percentage changes over the same period of the preceding year.

Figures are revised on a monthly basis to take into account any subsequent amendments submitted by authorised institutions.

(1) As from June 2002, short-term Exchange Fund placements of less than one month are included under time deposits as part of the monetary aggregates. The revised data series are backdated to April 1997.

(2) Adjusted to include foreign currency swap deposits.

(3) Adjusted to exclude foreign currency swap deposits.

Source: Hong Kong Monetary Authority.
(Enquiry Telephone No.: 2878 8222)

Table 12
(Chapter 4: Financial and Monetary Affairs)

Exchange Fund Balance Sheet

$ Million

	As at end of year		
	1998	2002	2003
Assets[1]			
Foreign currency assets	701,239	891,632	929,625
Hong Kong dollar assets	211,036	63,433	82,020
	912,275	955,065	1,011,645
Liabilities[1]			
Certificates of Indebtedness[2]	86,465	118,475	134,215
Government issued currency notes and coins in circulation	5,778	5,891	6,297
Balance of the banking system[3]	2,527	525	28,277
Exchange Fund Bills and Notes	98,334	122,925	123,520
Placements by other HKSAR government funds[4]	424,562	301,669	252,296
Other liabilities[5]	52,364	78,406	82,161
	670,030	627,891	626,766
Accumulated Surplus	242,245	327,174	384,879

Notes: (1) (*a*) Investment
  The Fund is invested in interest-bearing placements with banks and other financial institutions both in Hong Kong and outside Hong Kong and in a variety of financial instruments, including bonds, notes, treasury bills and equities.
  (*b*) Foreign currency assets distribution
  A large proportion of the Fund's foreign currency assets is held in US dollars. Apart from US dollar assets, the Fund also holds assets denominated in fully convertible foreign currencies.
  (*c*) Location of assets
  The assets are held in deposit, trustee and safe-keeping accounts with banks, central banks and custodial organisations situated in Hong Kong and other major financial centres.
  (*d*) Valuation of assets and liabilities
  Debt securities, equities and Exchange Fund Bills and Notes are valued in the accounts at market value at the balance sheet date. Placements with banks and other financial institutions, certificates of deposit, consideration received or paid under repurchase and resale agreements, securities lending agreements, placements by banks and other financial institutions, placements by other HKSAR government funds for which interest is payable at market-based rates and placements by Hong Kong statutory bodies are valued according to a price matrix of discounted cash flows using applicable interest rates for discounting. The consequential change in value of the asset or liability is reflected in the carrying value of the relevant asset or liability in the Balance Sheet except in the case of placements by other HKSAR government funds for which interest is payable at market-based rates, which are stated in the Balance Sheet at the principal amounts payable at the balance sheet date with the revaluation differences included in other liabilities. Placements by other HKSAR government funds for which interest is payable at rates determined by reference to the investment income of the Fund are stated at the principal amounts payable at the balance sheet date.
  (*e*) Translation of foreign currency assets and liabilities
  Assets and liabilities denominated in foreign currencies are translated into Hong Kong dollars at the rates of exchange ruling at the balance sheet date. Exchange gains and losses on foreign currency translation are included in the Income and Expenditure Account. Certificates of Indebtedness, government-issued currency notes and coins in circulation, all of which are denominated in Hong Kong dollars but are issued and redeemed in US dollars at the linked exchange rate of US$1=$7.80, are stated in the accounts at their Hong Kong dollar face value. At the balance sheet date the difference between their Hong Kong dollar face value and the market value of the US dollars required for their redemption is included in other assets.
  (2) As backing for the bank note issued, each note-issuing bank is required to hold a non-interest bearing Certificate of Indebtedness issued by the Financial Secretary. Payments for the issuance and redemption of notes against these Certificates are made in US dollars at the fixed rate of US$1=HK$7.80.
  (3) Under the interbank payment system based on Real Time Gross Settlement principles, all licensed banks maintain a Hong Kong dollars clearing account with the Hong Kong Monetary Authority for the account of the Exchange Fund. The aggregate balance in these accounts represents the total level of liquidity in the interbank market.
  (4) These represent placements by other HKSAR government funds with the Exchange Fund. Until 31 March 1998, all placements by other HKSAR government funds bore interest at market-based rates. With effect from 1 April 1998, the basis of interest payable on certain placements by other HKSAR government funds was amended from market-based rates to rates determined by reference to the investment income of the Fund.
  (5) Other liabilities include placements by banks and other financial institutions, placements by Hong Kong statutory bodies, interest payable on Exchange Fund Notes and placements by other HKSAR government funds, revaluation losses on off-balance sheet items which are marked to market, other accrued expenses and provisions and the revaluation differences of placements by other HKSAR government funds for which interest is payable at market-based rates.

Source: Hong Kong Monetary Authority.
  (Enquiry Telephone No.: 2878 8222)

Table 13

(Chapter 5: Commerce and Industry)
(a) Merchandise Trade by Main Country/Territory

HK$ Billion

Type of trade/Main country/territory	1998	2002	2003
Imports	1,429.1	1,619.4	1,805.8
	(−11.5)	(+3.3)	(+11.5)
The mainland of China	580.6	717.1	785.6
Japan	179.9	182.6	214.0
Taiwan	104.1	115.9	125.2
United States	106.5	91.5	98.7
Singapore	61.5	75.7	90.6
Asia-Pacific Economic Co-operation	1,216.3	1,391.4	1,553.4
European Union	151.9	139.2	151.0
Domestic exports	188.5	130.9	121.7
	(−10.9)	(−14.7)	(−7.1)
United States	54.8	41.9	39.1
The mainland of China	56.1	41.4	36.8
United Kingdom	10.1	7.6	7.8
Germany	9.8	4.3	4.9
Taiwan	6.5	4.4	3.7
Asia-Pacific Economic Co-operation	143.5	105.2	95.8
European Union	35.2	20.4	20.9
Re-exports	1,159.2	1,429.6	1,620.7
	(−6.9)	(+7.7)	(+13.4)
The mainland of China	407.4	571.9	705.8
United States	259.9	291.0	285.1
Japan	64.2	80.7	91.2
Germany	42.2	44.6	51.4
United Kingdom	42.3	46.6	49.6
Asia-Pacific Economic Co-operation	880.4	1,146.7	1,303.7
European Union	176.5	186.4	210.1

Note: Figures in brackets refer to percentage changes over the same period of the preceding year.

Source: Trade Analysis Section (2), Census and Statistics Department.
(Enquiry Telephone No.: 2582 5042)

(b) Imports, Retained Imports and Re-exports by End-use Category

HK$ Billion

End-use category	1998	2002	2003
Foodstuffs			
Imports	64.6	59.1	58.3
Retained imports[1]	48.9	44.6	45.2@
Re-exports	21.0	16.2	14.7
Consumer goods			
Imports	511.3	543.2	575.8
Retained imports[1]	98.4	114.8	120.2@
Re-exports	541.1	580.4	617.3
Raw materials and semi-manufactures			
Imports	483.5	558.1	654.4
Retained imports[1]	182.4	159.1	179.8@
Re-exports	333.4	448.3	533.2
Fuels			
Imports	23.4	31.3	35.4
Retained imports[1]	15.9	29.7	33.5@
Re-exports	8.1	1.7	2.0
Capital goods			
Imports	346.4	427.7	481.8
Retained imports[1]	140.6	114.8	111.3@
Re-exports	255.5	383.0	453.5
Total			
Imports	1,429.1	1,619.4	1,805.8
Retained imports[1]	486.7	462.9	494.6@
Re-exports	1,159.2	1,429.6	1,620.7

Note: (1) Retained imports refer to those imported goods which are retained for use in Hong Kong rather than being re-exported to other places. The value of retained imports is derived by subtracting the estimated import value of re-exports from the value of imports. The former is obtained by removing an estimated re-export margin from the value of re-exports.

Source: Trade Analysis Section (1), Census and Statistics Department.
(Enquiry Telephone No.: 2582 4918)

(c) Domestic Exports by Principal Commodity

HK$ Billion

Principal commodity	1998	2002	2003
Articles of apparel and clothing accessories	74.9	65.0	63.9
Electrical machinery, apparatus and appliances, and electrical parts thereof	26.7	15.6	10.2
Textile yarn, fabrics, made-up articles and related products	10.8	7.6	5.9
Jewellery, goldsmiths' and silversmiths' waves, and other articles of precious or semi-precious materials	4.8	5.2	5.4
Printed matters	4.2	3.9	3.7

Source: Trade Analysis Section (2), Census and Statistics Department.
(Enquiry Telephone No.: 2582 5042)

Table 14

(Chapter 5: Commerce and Industry)

Exports and Imports of Services by Major Service Group

HK$ Billion

Major service group	1998	2002@	2003@
Exports of services			
Transportation	85.1	103.0	105.3
	(−2.6)	(+10.0)	(+2.2)
Travel[1]	44.0	58.8	55.4
	(−26.3)	(+26.9)	(−5.8)
Insurance services	3.1	3.7	4.0
	(+16.4)	(+5.1)	(+7.3)
Financial services	16.3	20.9	21.5
	(−13.9)	(−4.2)	(+2.9)
Merchanting and other trade-related services	76.9	117.2	130.0
	(+4.7)	(+10.1)	(+10.9)
Other services	32.1	34.2	34.1
	(+4.5)	(−4.3)	(−0.5)
Total	257.4	337.9	350.3
	(−5.6)	(+9.8)	(+3.7)
Imports of services			
Transportation	42.9	51.7	52.1
	(−14.7)	(+1.5)	(+0.8)
Travel	104.4	96.8	90.0
	(+6.3)	(+0.8)	(−7.0)
Insurance services	4.6	4.0	4.3
	(+2.2)	(−0.1)	(+7.5)
Financial services	6.7	5.3	5.8
	(+16.4)	(+2.0)	(+7.6)
Merchanting and other trade-related services	8.5	12.1	13.2
	(−13.7)	(+2.8)	(+9.1)
Other services	26.5	23.4	23.8
	(−4.8)	(−4.2)	(+1.6)
Total	193.6	193.4	189.2
	(−1.4)	(+0.5)	(−2.2)
Net exports of services	63.9	144.5	161.1

Notes: Figures in brackets refer to percentage changes over the same period of the preceding year.

(1) Figures have been revised to incorporate the new data on destination consumption expenditure of incoming visitors and travellers released by the Hong Kong Tourism Board in November 2003. For details, please refer to the feature article 'Statistics on Inbound Tourism' in the December 2003 issue of the *Hong Kong Monthly Digest of Statistics*.

Source: Trade in Services Statistics Section, Census and Statistics Department.
(Enquiry Telephone No.: 2802 1372)

Table 15

(Chapter 5: Commerce and Industry)

(a) Position and Flow of Inward Direct Investment by Major Investor Country/Territory

HK$ Billion

| Major investor country/territory [1] | Inward direct investment at market value | | | |
| | Position at end of year | | Inflow during the year [2] | |
	2001	*2002*	*2001*	*2002*
British Virgin Islands	943.6	779.4	74.7	59.4
The mainland of China	958.1	594.6	38.5	31.7
Bermuda	315.7	273.2	9.9	2.1
Netherlands	199.9	204.9	−2.3	10.3
United States	193.7	186.6	11.8	−11.0
Others	658.7	583.7	52.9	−17.1
Total	3,269.7	2,622.3	185.4	75.5

Notes: (1) Country/territory here refers to the immediate source economy. It does not necessarily reflect the country/territory in which the funds are initially mobilised.
(2) Negative inflow does not necessarily relate to equity withdrawal. It may be the result of repayment of loans to non-resident affiliates.

(b) Position and Flow of Outward Direct Investment by Major Recipient Country/Territory

HK$ Billion

| Major recipient country/territory [1] | Outward direct investment at market value | | | |
| | Position at end of year | | Outflow during the year [2] | |
	2001	*2002*	*2001*	*2002*
British Virgin Islands	1,437.0	1,148.3	25.4	10.1
The mainland of China	844.0	843.0	66.3	124.3
Bermuda	91.9	76.8	−19.2	−4.9
Panama	32.4	39.0	9.5	2.2
United States	24.8	32.2	−2.0	7.2
Others	319.1	273.6	8.5	−2.8
Total	2,749.2	2,412.9	88.5	136.2

Notes: (1) Country/territory here refers to the immediate destination economy. It does not necessarily reflect the country/territory in which the funds are ultimately used.
(2) Negative outflow does not necessarily relate to equity withdrawal. It may be the result of repayment of loans by non-resident affiliates.

Source: Balance of Payments Branch (2), Census and Statistics Department.
(Enquiry Telephone No.: 2116 5113)

Table 16

(Chapter 5: Commerce and Industry)

(a) Number of Companies that are Regional Headquarters by Major Country/Territory of Incorporation of the Parent Company

Major country/territory of incorporation of the parent company	1998		2002		2003	
	Number	%	Number	%	Number	%
United States	194	23.7	233	24.6	242	25.1
Japan	109	13.3	159	16.8	168	17.4
United Kingdom	95	11.6	80	8.4	86	8.9
The mainland of China	70	8.5	96	10.1	84	8.7
Germany	59	7.2	52	5.5	56	5.8
France	38	4.6	35	3.7	44	4.6
Switzerland	28	3.4	36	3.8	40	4.1
Netherlands	27	3.3	39	4.1	38	3.9
Singapore	17	2.1	26	2.7	22	2.3
Australia	16	2.0	13	1.4	22	2.3
Canada	13	1.6	23	2.4	19	2.0
Taiwan	26	3.2	21	2.2	18	1.9
Sweden	14	1.7	17	1.8	16	1.7
Republic of Korea	21	2.6	17	1.8	15	1.6
Denmark	**	**	11	1.2	10	1.0
Total number of companies that are regional headquarters	819		948		966	

(b) Number of Companies that are Regional Offices by Major Country/Territory of Incorporation of the Parent Company

Major country/territory of incorporation of the parent company	1998		2002		2003	
	Number	%	Number	%	Number	%
United States	285	17.5	437	20.1	498	22.2
Japan	347	21.3	471	21.7	442	19.7
United Kingdom	128	7.9	163	7.5	196	8.7
The mainland of China	135	8.3	170	7.8	148	6.6
Germany	74	4.5	96	4.4	122	5.4
Taiwan	85	5.2	121	5.6	111	5.0
France	76	4.7	91	4.2	101	4.5
Singapore	37	2.3	79	3.6	81	3.6
Switzerland	54	3.3	61	2.8	61	2.7
Republic of Korea	66	4.0	49	2.3	60	2.7
Netherlands	46	2.8	57	2.6	55	2.5
Australia	38	2.3	52	2.4	45	2.0
Italy	36	2.2	38	1.8	41	1.8
Canada	23	1.4	28	1.3	27	1.2
Austria	20	1.2	26	1.2	22	1.0
Total number of companies that are regional offices	1 630		2 171		2 241	

Notes: Figures refer to the 1st working day of June of the year.

Country/territory of incorporation of the parent company may be greater than one in the case of joint ventures.

**Indicates fewer than five companies.

Source: Business Expectation Statistics Section, Census and Statistics Department.
(Enquiry Telephone No.: 2805 6112)

Table 17

(Chapter 6: Employment)

Labour Force, Labour Force Participation Rate, Unemployment and Underemployment

	1998	*2002*	*2003@*
Labour Force[1] ('000)			
Age Group			
Under 25	460	401	383
25–44	1 992	2 049	2 001
45–64	817	1 016	1 063
65 and over	41	42	42
Overall	3 310	3 507	3 488
Sex			
Male	1 966	1 961	1 957
Female	1 344	1 546	1 532
Overall	3 310	3 507	3 488
Labour Force Participation Rate (%)			
Male	74.5	72.2	71.8
Female	49.0	52.5	51.3
Overall	61.5	61.9	61.1
Unemployment			
Unemployed persons ('000)	195	252	253
Unemployment rate (%)	5.9	7.2	7.3
Underemployment			
Underemployed persons ('000)	96	109	116
Underemployment rate (%)	2.9	3.1	3.3

Notes: Figures are averages of the figures obtained from the General Household Survey for the four quarters of the year.

    (1)   The labour force refers to the land-based non-institutional population aged 15 and over who satisfy the criteria for inclusion in the employed population or the unemployed population.

Source: General Household Survey Section (2), Census and Statistics Department.
    (Enquiry Telephone No.: 2887 5508)

Table 18

(Chapter 6: Employment)

Number of Establishments and Persons Engaged (other than those in the Civil Service) by Industry Sector, and Number of Construction Sites and Manual Workers at Construction Sites

Industry Sector/Sub-sector	1998		2002		2003	
	Establishments	Persons Engaged	Establishments	Persons Engaged	Establishments	Persons Engaged
Mining and quarrying	6	402	6	117	7	180
Manufacturing	22 414	245 457	19 106	184 503	16 272	168 348
Electricity and gas	21	9 302	17	8 406	16	8 337
Wholesale, retail and import/export trades, restaurants and hotels						
Wholesale	14 800	75 162	15 514	65 605	14 529	64 693
Retail	50 003	185 568	58 283	211 076	55 114	217 102
Import and export trades	85 852	452 539	103 383	499 735	96 834	490 700
Restaurants	8 582	171 541	10 856	180 547	10 574	177 164
Hotels and boarding houses	806	28 260	736	25 994	696	24 201
Transport, storage and communications						
Transport and storage	8 311	136 094	9 860	144 552	9 408	142 854
Communications	903	32 525	1 223	31 141	1 139	31 451
Financing, insurance, real estate and business services						
Financing and insurance	12 861	154 153	16 056	152 081	14 703	147 729
Real estate	11 217	77 795	10 435	87 234	8 645	85 946
Business services	19 992	158 506	29 952	201 990	27 327	190 158
Community, social and personal services	25 047	326 395	33 968	402 565	32 734	416 508
All industry sectors above	260 815	2 053 699	309 395	2 195 546	287 998	2 165 371
Construction sites	1 003	72 253	949	66 393	968	62 176

Notes: (a) Figures refer to December of the year.
     (b) Figures are based on the Quarterly Survey of Employment and Vacancies and the Quarterly Employment Survey of Construction Sites conducted by the Census and Statistics Department.
     (c) Figures in this table do not cover establishments and persons engaged in the following activities:
        (i) Agriculture and fishing.
        (ii) Construction (other than construction sites).
        (iii) Hawkers and retail pitches (other than market stalls).
        (iv) Taxis, public lights buses, goods vehicles, barges, lighters and stevedoring services.
        (v) Public administration, religious organisations, authors and other independents artists, domestic helpers and miscellaneous recreational and personal services.
     (d) Establishment in construction sites refer to number of sites, while persons engaged refer to manual workers only.
     (e) Manual workers at construction sites include craftsmen, semi-skilled and unskilled workers.
     (f) Starting from March 2002 round of Quarterly Survey of Employment and Vacancies, the survey coverage has been expanded to include five more industries in the community, social and personal services sector. They are veterinary services, billiard centres, bowling centres, electronic game centres and funeral services.

Source: Employment Statistics Section, Census and Statistics Department.
     (Enquiry Telephone No.: 2582 5076)

Table 19

(Chapter 6: Employment)

Wage Indices for Employees up to Supervisory Level (Excluding Managerial and Professional Employees) by Industry Sector

Industry sector	Wage index (September 1992=100)		
	1998	*2002*	*2003*
Nominal wage index			
Manufacturing	143.3 (+0.8)	147.3 (−1.5)	141.8 (−3.7)
Wholesale, retail and import/export trades, restaurants and hotels	148.9 (+1.3)	148.9 (−2.2)	145.1 (−2.6)
Transport services	156.2 (+4.3)	149.4 (§)	146.9 (−1.6)
Financing, insurance, real estate and business services	160.4 (+4.3)	157.8 (§)	157.3 (−0.3)
Personal services	154.6 (+3.7)	152.2 (−3.0)	146.0 (−4.1)
All selected industries[1]	150.6 (+2.2)	149.7 (−1.5)	146.6 (−2.1)
Real wage index			
Manufacturing	99.4 (−1.4)	115.9 (+2.8)	114.7 (−1.0)
Wholesale, retail and import/export trades, restaurants and hotels	103.3 (−0.9)	117.2 (+2.1)	117.4 (+0.2)
Transport services	108.3 (+2.0)	117.5 (+4.4)	118.9 (+1.1)
Financing, insurance, real estate and business services	111.2 (+1.9)	124.1 (+4.4)	127.3 (+2.5)
Personal services	107.2 (+1.4)	119.8 (+1.3)	118.2 (−1.3)
All selected industries[1]	104.4 (−0.1)	117.8 (+2.8)	118.6 (+0.7)

Notes: Figures refer to September of the year. Figures in brackets refer to percentage changes over the same period of the preceding year.
As from 2001, the Real Wage Indices are derived by deflating the Nominal Wage Indices by the 1999/2000-based CPI(A). To facilitate comparison, Real Wage Indices prior to 2001 have been re-compiled using the 1999/2000-based CPI(A).
(1) Figures refer to all industries covered by the Wage Enquiry of Labour Earnings Survey, including the electricity and gas sector.
§ Change within ±0.05%.

Source: Wages and Labour Costs Statistics Section, Census and Statistics Department.
(Enquiry Telephone No.: 2887 5550)

Table 20

(Chapter 6: Employment)

Average Wage Rates for Employees up to Supervisory Level (Excluding Managerial and Professional Employees) by Broad Occupational Group and by Industry Sector for September 2003

$

Industry sector	Craftsmen and operatives *Average daily wages*	Supervisory, technical, clerical and miscellaneous non-production workers *Average monthly salaries*	All selected occupations *Average monthly salaries*
Manufacturing	321	11,648	9,562
Wholesale, retail and import/export trades, restaurants and hotels	—	11,549	11,549
Transport services	496	12,796	12,841
Financing, insurance, real estate and business services	425	10,574	10,583
Personal services	524	5,983	6,164
All selected industries[1]	412	10,825	10,795

Note: (1) Figures refer to all industries covered by the Wage Enquiry Labour Earnings Survey, including the electricity and gas sector.

Source: Wages and Labour Costs Statistics Section, Census and Statistics Department.
(Enquiry Telephone No.: 2887 5550)

Table 21

(Chapter 6: Employment)

Employed Persons by Monthly Employment Earnings

Thousands

Monthly employment earnings ($)	*1998*	*2002*	*2003*
<3,000	67.0	125.8	149.7
3,000–3,999	169.6	244.6	255.7
4,000–4,999	84.9	115.8	144.5
5,000–5,999	121.5	169.2	187.5
6,000–6,999	177.4	220.1	227.0
7,000–7,999	209.0	208.3	213.8
8,000–8,999	278.8	246.1	243.4
9,000–9,999	228.2	171.0	177.4
10,000–14,999	765.2	666.0	606.7
15,000–19,999	358.4	343.1	323.1
20,000–29,999	345.9	360.1	344.9
≧30,000	316.0	361.6	349.6
Total	3 122.0	3 231.6	3 223.3
Median monthly employment earnings ($)	10,000	10,000	10,000

Note: Figures are averages of the figures obtained from the General Household Survey for the four quarters of the year.

Source: General Household Survey Section (2), Census and Statistics Department.
(Enquiry Telephone No.: 2887 5508)

Table 22

(Chapter 7: Education)

(a) Number of Educational and Training Institutions by Type

Number of institutions

Type	Academic year		
	1998-1999	*2002-2003*	*2003-2004*
Kindergarten	744	777	768
Primary school			
Day	830	803	785
Evening	2	—	—
Secondary school			
Day	471	499	501
Evening	36	43	36
Special school[1]	74	74	74
Vocational Training Council	1	1	1
Approved post-secondary college[2]	1	2	2
Other colleges[3]			
Day	6	7	8
Evening	5	4	4
University Grants Committee-funded institution	8	8	8
The Hong Kong Academy for Performing Arts	1	1	1
The Open University of Hong Kong	1	1	1
Construction Industry Training Authority	1	1	1
Clothing Industry Training Authority	1	1	1
Hospital Authority	1	1	1
Institute offering adult education/ tutorial/vocational courses			
Day	310	949	1 108
Evening	296	825	1 020

Notes: (1) Figures include special schools, practical schools and skills opportunity schools.

(2) Approved post-secondary college refer to colleges registered under the Post Secondary Colleges Ordinance.

(3) Other colleges refer to private schools which provide post-secondary courses, such as Chu Hai College, Hong Kong Adventist College, Hong Kong Buddhist College, etc.

(b) Number of Students by Type of Educational and Training Institution

Thousand

Institution/Programme	Academic year		
	1998-1999	*2002-2003*	*2003-2004*
Kindergarten	175.1	143.7	136.1
Primary school	477.1	483.2	468.8
Secondary school	468.0	465.9	470.5
Special education [1]	9.7	9.9	10.2
Vocational Training Council [2][3]	67.0	60.0	59.4 #
Approved post-secondary college [4]	2.3	4.0	4.0
Other colleges [5]	4.2	3.0	2.9
University Grants Committee (UGC)-funded institution [6][7]	80.9	85.6	90.4 #
The Hong Kong Academy for Performing Arts	0.7	0.7	0.7
The Open University of Hong Kong [3][8]	30.0	47.5	40.8 #
Construction Industry Training Authority	2.5	1.5	1.4 #
Clothing Industry Training Authority	0.5	0.6	0.9
Hospital Authority [9]	—	0.1	0.1
Project Yi Jin [10]	—	4.2	4.5
Institute offering adult education/tutorial/ vocational courses [5]	125.7	210.1	201.1
Total	1 443.8	1 520.0	1 491.9 #

Notes: The sum of figures may not be equal to the total due to rounding.

Student numbers are in head counts. Figures include both full-time and part-time students attending long programmes lasting for at least one academic year, except for 'institute offering adult education/tutorial/vocational courses' where long and short programmes are included.

(1) Figures also include students of special classes in ordinary schools and students of mainstreamed classes in practical schools and skills opportunity schools.

(2) Figures for the Vocational Training Council refer to students of the Hong Kong Institute of Vocational Education (formerly Technical Colleges and Technical Institutes before 1999), Training and Development Centres, and Continuing Professional Development Centre. Students attending full-time self-financing post-secondary programmes run by the Vocational Training Council School of Business and information Systems are also included since the school started to admit students in September 2001.

(3) Figures do not include students attending programmes of Project Yi Jin.

(4) Approved post-secondary colleges refer to colleges registered under the Post Secondary Colleges Ordinance.

(5) Other colleges refer to private schools which provide post-secondary courses, such as Chu Hai College, Hong Kong Adventist College, Hong Kong Buddhist College, etc.

(6) Figures refer to students attending UGC-funded programmes.

(7) Starting from 2001-2002, figures also include students attending full-time accredited self-financing post-secondary programmes.

(8) Figures also include students of Li Ka Shing Institute of Professional and Continuing Education.

(9) Figures refer to nurse training programmes and are available only since 2002.

(10) Project Yi Jin was launched in October 2000.

Source: Education and Manpower Bureau, Government Secretariat.
(Enquiry Telephone No.: 2117 7469)

Table 23

(Chapter 7: Education)

**Distribution of Educational Attainment of Population
Aged 15 and Over**

Percentages

Educational attainment	1998	2002	2003@
No schooling/Kindergarten	8.9	7.0	6.9
Primary	22.9	21.0	20.4
Secondary[1]	46.7	46.8	46.2
Matriculation[2]	4.1	4.7	5.3
Tertiary			
Non-degree course	7.0	7.6	7.8
Degree course	10.4	12.9	13.4
Total	100.0	100.0	100.0

Notes: Figures are averages of the figures obtained from the General Household Survey for the four quarters of the year.
　　(1) Secondary education refers to Form 1 to Form 5.
　　(2) Matriculation education refers to Form 6 to Form 7.

Source: General Household Survey Section (2), Census and Statistics Department.
　　(Enquiry Telephone No.: 2887 5508)

Table 24

(Chapter 7: Education)

Government Expenditure on Education

	Financial Year (April-March)		
	1998-1999	2002-2003	2003-2004#
Total expenditure ($ million)	48,479	54,937	57,748
As percentage of total government expenditure (%)	22.4	23.3	23.2
As percentage of Gross Domestic Product (%)	3.8	4.4	4.7
Recurrent expenditure ($ million)	40,892	46,976	46,761
Spent on (%)			
Primary education	20.6	23.1	23.2
Secondary education	32.6	34.3	34.6
Tertiary education	35.3	30.1	29.9
Others[1]	11.5	12.5	12.3

Note: (1) Figures include government recurrent expenditure on kindergarten, special education, adult education courses run or funded by the Education and Manpower Bureau (formerly Education Department), vocational education courses run by the Vocational Training Council and departmental support.

Source: Education and Manpower Bureau, Government Secretariat.
　　(Enquiry Telephone No.: 2117 7469)

Table 25

(Chapter 8: Health)

Population and Vital Events

	1998	2002	2003
Mid-year population	6 543 700	6 787 000	6 803 100
Crude birth rate (per 1 000 population)	8.1	7.1	6.8[#]
Crude death rate (per 1 000 population)	5.0	5.0	5.4[#]
Infant mortality rate[1] (per 1 000 registered live births)	3.2	2.4	2.3[#]
Neonatal (aged under four weeks) mortality rate[1] (per 1 000 registered live births)	1.5	1.3	1.1[#]
Post neonatal (aged from four weeks to under one year) mortality rate[1] (per 1 000 registered live births)	1.7	1.0	1.2[#]
Maternal mortality ratio[1] (per 100 000 registered live births)	1.9	2.1	4.2[#]
Expectation of life at birth (years)[2]			
Male	77.4	78.6	78.6[#]
Female	83.0	84.5	84.3[#]

Notes: (1) Figures are derived based on registered deaths.
(2) Figures on expectation of life at birth presented in this table may be different from those presented in earlier editions of this publication. The change is due to some enhancements made to the method of compiling expectation of life at birth.

Sources: Demographic Statistics Section, Census and Statistics Department.
(Enquiry Telephone No.: 2716 8345)
Department of Health.
(Enquiry Telephone No.: 2961 8569)

Table 26

(Chapter 8: Health)

Number of Deaths and Death Rate by Leading Cause of Death

	2002*		2003#	
Cause	Number	Rate[1]	Number	Rate[1]
Malignant neoplasms	11 658	171.8	11 907	175.0
Diseases of heart	4 969	73.2	5 236	77.0
Cerebrovascular disease	3 218	47.4	3 382	49.7
Pneumonia	3 194	47.1	3 770	55.4
Chronic lower respiratory diseases	2 075	30.6	2 157	31.7

Notes: Ranking of causes of death is according to year 2002's number of deaths.
(1) Death rate per 100 000 population.

Source: Department of Health.
(Enquiry Telephone No.: 2961 8569)

Table 27

(Chapter 8: Health)

Hospital Beds and Selected Types of Healthcare Professionals

	2002		2003#	
	Number	*Ratio[1]*	*Number*	*Ratio[1]*
Hospital beds	35 159*	5.2	35 566	5.2
Doctors[2]	10 731	1.6	11 016	1.6
Chinese medicine practitioners[3]	2 385	0.4*	4 738	0.7
Dentists[2]	1 907	0.3	1 848	0.3
Pharmacists	1 414	0.2	1 457	0.2
Nurses[4]	43 383	6.4	43 782	6.4
Midwives	5 136	0.8	4 791	0.7
Chiropractors[5]	—	—	67	†

Notes: Figures are as at end of the year.
  (1) Number of beds/healthcare professionals per 1 000 population.
  (2) Figures refer to doctors/dentists with full registration on the local and overseas lists.
  (3) Figures are available since 2002. They do not include 3 227 listed Chinese medicine practitioners who can practise lawfully in Hong Kong but are required to pass the Registration Assessment or Licensing Examination before they can apply for registration.
  (4) Figures refer to registered nurses and enrolled nurses.
  (5) It has become a mandatory requirement for registered chiropractors to practise only with valid practising certificates since February 2003.
  † Less than 0.05.

Sources: Department of Health.
  (Enquiry Telephone No.: 2961 8582)
  Hospital Authority.
  (Enquiry Telephone No.: 2300 6515)

Table 28

(Chapter 10: Social Welfare)

Social Security

	1998	2002	2003
Comprehensive Social Security			
Assistance Scheme			
Number of cases[1] ('000)	227	267	290
Amount of payment[2] (HK$ million)	9,441	14,405	16,131
Social Security Allowance Scheme			
Disability Allowance			
Number of cases[1] ('000)	81	105	107
Amount of payment[2] (HK$ million)	1,182	1,660	1,707
Old Age Allowance			
Number of cases[1] ('000)	444	456	457
Amount of payment[2] (HK$ million)	3,238	3,581	3,574
Traffic Accident Victims Assistance			
Scheme			
Number of cases authorised for payment	6 019	7 089	7 139
Amount of payment[2] (HK$ million)	137	142	151

Notes: (1) Figures are as at end of the year.
    (2) Figures refer to financial years of 1997-98, 2001-02 and 2002-03.

Source: Social Welfare Department.
  (Enquiry Telephone No.: 2892 5232)

Table 29

(Chapter 11: Housing)

Stock of Permanent Quarters and Estimated Persons Accommodated as at Mid 2003

Type of housing	Hong Kong Island	Kowloon	New Territories	Total
				Number of quarters[1]
Public rental housing	74 700	239 200	365 000	678 900
Subsidized sale flats	41 600	100 600	251 800	394 000
Private permanent housing	342 100	360 000	582 500	1 284 600
Total permanent housing	458 400	699 800	1 199 300	2 357 500

Type of housing	Hong Kong Island	Kowloon	New Territories	Total
				Estimated persons accommodated
Public rental housing	237 600	712 700	1 158 500	2 108 800
Subsidized sale flats	137 100	302 800	841 400	1 281 400
Private permanent housing	882 800	989 700	1 455 000	3 327 500
Total permanent housing	1 257 500	2 005 300	3 454 900	6 717 700
Marine				4 600
Other[2]	5 300	14 300	61 100	80 700
Total population				6 803 100

Notes: Figures may not add up to total due to rounding.
(1) The coverage of quarters excludes those in hotels and institutions.
(2) Including persons living in public temporary housing, private temporary squatters/huts, rooftop structures, unsheltered areas, etc.

Source: Census Planning Section (1), Census and Statistics Department.
(Enquiry Telephone No.: 2716 8006)

Table 30

(Chapter 12: Land, Public Works and Utilities)

Property Transactions

	1998	*2002*	*2003*
Value of registered agreements for sale and purchase of property (HK$ billion)			
Residential property	278.5	154.3	153.6
Non-residential property	62.4	31.1	35.8
Total	340.9	185.4	189.4
Property price index (1999 = 100)			
Private domestic units	117.1	69.9	61.3 [#]
Private offices (Grades A, B and C)	134.5	68.4	61.8 [#]
Property rental index (1999 = 100)			
Private domestic units	112.6	83.4	73.5 [#]
Private offices (Grades A, B and C)	135.9	85.4	73.7 [#]

Source: Land Registry.
(Enquiry Telephone No.: 2867 2882)

Table 31

(Chapter 12: Land, Public Works and Utilities)
Land Usage (as at 31 December 2003)

Class	Approximate Area (km²)	%	Remarks
Residential			
Private Residential	24	2.2	Residential land developed by private developers except village houses, HOS/PSPS and temporary housing areas
Public Residential	17	1.5	Include HOS/PSPS and temporary housing areas
Rural Settlement	26	2.3	Include temporary structures
Commercial			
Commercial/Business & Office	3	0.3	
Industrial			
Industrial Land	6	0.5	
Industrial Estates	3	0.3	
Warehouse and Storage	12	1.1	Include open storage areas
Institutional & Open Space			
Government, Institutions & Communities Facilities	21	1.9	
Open Space	20	1.8	Include parks, stadiums and playground
Transportation			
Roads	37	3.3	
Railways	2	0.2	
Airport	13	1.2	
Other Urban or Built-up Land			
Cemetery and Crematorium	6	0.5	
Utilities	6	0.5	
Vacant Development Land/ Construction in Progress	31	2.8	
Others	16	1.4	
Agricultural Land			
Agricultural Land	58	5.2	
Fish Pond/Gei Wais	13	1.2	
Woodland/Shrubland/Grassland/Wetland			
Woodland	285	25.7	
Shrubland	230	20.8	
Grassland	226	20.4	
Mangrove and Swamp	10	0.9	About 5 km² of Mangrove and Swamp, which is below the High Water Mark, is included in this figure but should not be counted in the total land area of the Territory.
Barren Land			
Badlands	11	1	
Quarries	2	0.2	
Rocky Shore	2	0.2	
Water Bodies			
Reservoirs	24	2.2	
Streams and Nullahs	4	0.4	
Total	1 108 (1 103)	100.0	According to Lands Department, the total land area of the Territory, i.e. land above the High Water Mark, is 1 103 km².

Source: Planning Department.
(Enquiry Telephone No.: 2231 5000)

Table 32
(Chapter 12: Land, Public Works and Utilities)
(a) Electricity Distribution

			Terajoules
	1998	*2002*	*2003*
Domestic	32 793	33 394	34 365
Commercial	73 857	87 241	88 834
Industrial	18 489	16 112	14 851
Street lighting	307	365	384
Export to the mainland of China	2 197	7 830	10 827
Total	127 643	144 942	149 262

Sources: CLP Power Hong Kong Limited,
The Hongkong Electric Company Limited.
(For enquiries, please call Census and Statistics Department. Enquiry Telephone No.: 2805 6167)

(b) Gas Distribution (Towngas)

			Terajoules
	1998	*2002*	*2003*
Domestic	12 519	14 794	15 446
Commercial	10 536	10 860	10 542
Industrial	888	987	1 015
Total	23 943	26 641	27 002

Source: Hong Kong and China Gas Company Limited.
(For enquiries, please call the Census and Statistics Department. Enquiry Telephone No.: 2805 6167)

(c) Local Sales of Liquefied Petroleum Gas (LPG)

			Tonnes
	1998	*2002*	*2003*
Local sales of liquefied petroleum gas (LPG)	139 382	342 312	367 795

Source: Industrial Production & Tourism Statistics Section, Census and Statistics Department.
(Enquiry Telephone No.: 2805 6167)

(d) Water Consumption

			Million cubic metres
	1998	*2002*	*2003*
Fresh water	916	949	974
Sea water (flushing purposes)	199	235	241

Source: Water Supplies Department.
(Enquiry Telephone No.: 2829 4709)

Table 33

(Chapter 13: Transport)

(a) Inward and Outward Movements of Aircraft and Vessels

	1998	2002	2003
Aircraft ('000)[1]	163	207	187
Ocean vessels (million N.R.T.)	416	584	591
River vessels (million N.R.T.)[1]	107	161	181

Note: (1) Including both cargo and passenger aircrafts and vessels.

Sources: Civil Aviation Department,
           (Enquiry Telephone No.: 2867 4237)
           Marine Department.
           (Enquiry Telephone No.: 2852 3661)

(b) Inward and Outward Movements of Cargo

'000 tonnes

	1998	2002	2003
Discharged			
By air	775	1 004	1 035 #
By water	106 851	119 729	126 500 #
By ocean	90 104	93 444	97 600 #
By river	16 747	26 284	28 900 #
By road[1]	18 465	21 085 *	20 606
By rail[2]	324	283	253
Total	126 414	142 101 *	148 394 #
Loaded			
By air	854	1 475	1 608 #
By water	60 319	72 782	77 500 #
By ocean	37 378	44 857	48 100 #
By river	22 941	27 925	29 400 #
By road[1]	17 688	18 288 *	18 846
By rail	138	102	76
Total	78 999	92 647 *	98 030 #

Notes: (1) Figures are compiled based on a new estimation method, which has been adopted as from April 2001.
        (2) Figures exclude livestock.

Sources: Civil Aviation Department.
          Shipping and Cargo Statistics Section, Census and Statistics Department,
          Kowloon-Canton Railway Corporation,
          Customs and Excise Department.
          (For enquiries, please call Census and Statistics Department. Enquiry Telephone No.: 2582 4068)

(c) Port Container Throughput

'000 TEUs

	1998	2002	2003
Container terminals	9 555	11 892	12 070
Inward	4 646	5 706	5 910
Outward	4 909	6 186	6 160
Other than container terminals	5 027	7 252	8 379
Ocean	2 641	3 326	3 904
Inward	1 458	1 775	1 988
Outward	1 183	1 551	1 917
River	2 386	3 926	4 475
Inward	1 180	2 011	2 288
Outward	1 206	1 916	2 186
Total	14 582	19 144	20 449
Inward	7 284	9 492	10 186
Outward	7 297	9 652	10 263

Source: Marine Department.
(Enquiry Telephone No.: 2852 3661)

(d) Arrivals and Departures of Passengers by Mode of Transport

'000

Mode of transport	1998	2002	2003
Arrivals			
By air	10 284	11 841	9 486
By sea [1]	8 855	10 048	8 879
By land	38 603	59 233	58 156
Total	57 742	81 122	76 521
Departures			
By air	10 209	11 722	9 361
By sea [1]	9 111	10 915	9 765
By land	38 425	58 402	57 353
Total	57 745	81 039	76 479

Note: (1) Including passengers to/from Macao by helicopters.

Source: Immigration Department.
(Enquiry Telephone No.: 2829 3407)

Table 34

(Chapter 13: Transport)
(a) Motor Vehicles Licensed by Type

Thousands

Type	1998	2002	2003
Private cars	318	341	339
Motor cycles (including motor tricycles)	23	28	30
Taxis	18	18	18
Buses, public and private	12	13	13
Light buses, public and private	7	6	6
Goods vehicles	115	111	110
Special purpose vehicles	†	1	1
Government vehicles (excluding military vehicles)	7	7	7
Total	501	526	524

Note: † Less than 500 vehicles.

(b) Public Transport: Average Daily Number of Passenger Journeys by Different Modes of Transport

Thousands

	1998	2002	2003
Franchised bus	3 808	4 327	4 047
KCRC Light Rail Transit Feeder Bus	104	70	71
Mass Transit Railway	2 185	2 153	2 130
Red Minibus[2] and Green Minibus	1 588	1 655	1 623 #
Taxi[2]	1 304	1 307	1 307
Kowloon-Canton Railway—Heavy Rail[3]	738	812	767
Tram	264	249	232
Kowloon-Canton Railway—Light Rail	314	314	291
Ferry	172	151	146
Residents' Services	110	170	167 #
Total[1]	10 586	11 206	10 782 #

Notes: (1) Figures may not add up to total due to rounding.
(2) Estimates.
(3) KCRC West Rail was introduced on 20 December 2003. Heavy Rail includes East Rail and West Rail from 2003 onwards.

Source: Transport Department.
(Enquiry Telephone No.: 2829 5354)

Table 35

(Chapter 14: The Environment)

Meteorological Observations

| | Normals (1961-1990)[1] | | | |
	January	July	Whole Year	2003
Air temperature (°C)				
Mean maximum	18.6	31.5	25.7	25.8
Mean	15.8	28.8	23.0	23.6
Mean minimum	13.6	26.6	20.9	21.9
Mean relative humidity (%)	71	80	77	77
Total rainfall (mm)	23.4	323.5	2 214.3	1 941.9
Total bright sunshine (hours)	152.4	231.1	1 948.1	2 116.5
Mean wind speed (km/h)	24.0	20.0	22.6	21.9

Note: (1) The World Meteorological Organization (WMO) defines climatological standard normals as averages of climatological data computed for the following consecutive periods of 30 years: 1 January 1901 to 31 December 1930, 1 January 1931 to 31 December 1960, 1 January 1961 to 31 December 1990, 1 January 1991 to 31 December 2020 etc.

Source: Hong Kong Observatory.
(Enquiry Telephone No.: 2926 8444)

Table 36

(Chapter 14: The Environment)

Environmental Statistics

	1998	2002	2003
Average daily solid waste (tonnes)[1]			
Municipal solid waste	8 730	9 420	9 440
Construction and demolition waste	7 030	10 200	6 730
Special waste	790	1 540	1 590
Recovered waste	4 270	5 370	5 480
Total	20 820	26 530	23 240
Pollution complaints handled (number of cases)			
Air	7 476	10 471	10 245
Noise	9 666	12 487	9 708
Waste	1 058	1 083	1 193
Water[2]	1 618	1 529	2 696
Miscellaneous	9	0	57
Total	19 827	25 570	23 899

Notes: (1) All figures are rounded off to the nearest ten.
(2) As from this edition, the previously used complaint categories 'Liquid' and 'Water' are combined into one single category 'Water' on the ground that both types of complaint are dealt with under the Water Population Control Ordinance.

Source: Environmental Protection Department.
(Enquiry Telephone No.: 2835 1018)

Table 37
(Chapter 15: Travel and Tourism)
Visitor Arrivals by Country/Territory of Residence

Thousands

Country/Territory of residence	1998	2002	2003
The mainland of China	2 672	6 825	8 467
Taiwan	1 886	2 429	1 852
South & Southeast Asia	1 273	1 905	1 360
North Asia	1 298	1 852	1 235
The Americas	1 105	1 347	926
Europe, Africa & the Middle East	1 126	1 263	946
Macao	442	535	444
Australia, New Zealand & South Pacific	358	410	306
Total	10 160	16 566	15 537

Source: Hong Kong Tourism Board.
(Enquiry Telephone No.: 2807 6543)

Table 38
(Chapter 16: Public Order)
Traffic Accidents by Area

Number of accidents

	1998	2002	2003[#]
Hong Kong Island[1]	2 945	3 044	2 927
Kowloon	6 182	6 037	5 556
New Territories[2]	4 887	6 495	5 953
Total	14 014	15 576	14 436

Notes: Figures represent the position as at 6 February 2004.
(1) Including traffic accidents occurred on outlying islands other than Lantau Island.
(2) Including traffic accidents occurred on Lantau Island.

Source: Hong Kong Police Force.
(Enquiry Telephone No.: 2186 1286)

Table 39

(Chapter 16: Public Order)

(a) Reported Crimes by Type of Offence

			Cases reported
Type of offence	*1998*	*2002*	*2003*
Violent crime	14 682	14 140	14 542
Non-violent crime	57 280	61 737	73 835
Total	71 962	75 877	88 377
Overall crime rate (per 100 000 population)	1 100	1 118	1 299
Violent crime rate (per 100 000 population)	224	208	214

(b) Persons Arrested for Crime by Type of Offence

			Persons arrested
Type of offence	*1998*	*2002*	*2003*
Violent Crime	9 207	8 781	9 080
Non-violent crime	31 215	30 884	32 971
Total	40 422	39 665	42 051
Rate of persons arrested for crime (per 100 000 population)	669	622	669

Source: Hong Kong Police Force.
(Enquiry Telephone No.: 2860 8448)

(c) ICAC Cases

			Number of persons prosecuted				
	1998	*2002*	*2003*				
			Pending	*Convicted*	*Acquitted*	*Others*[2]	*Total*
Involving individuals employed in government departments and policy bureaux	55	51	21	14	12	3	50
Private sector							
Civilians prosecuted in public sector cases	84	145	47	48	7	—	102
Civilians prosecuted in private sector cases	228	391	81	148	29	1	259
Sub-total	312	536	128	196	36	1	361
Public bodies[1]	15	17	3	7	—	—	10
Total	382	604	152	217	48	4	421

Notes: (1) As defined in the Prevention of Bribery Ordinance, Cap. 201.
(2) Including Nolle Prosequi entered against one defendant, and three defendants died before trial.

Source: Independent Commission Against Corruption.
(Enquiry Telephone No.: 2826 3273)

Table 40

(Chapter 17: Communications, the Media and Information Technology)
Communications and Internet Services

	1998	2002	2003
Postal services			
Letter mail (million articles)	1 257	1 274*	1 270
Parcels (thousands)	1 125	928*	946
Telecommunications and Internet Services			
Telephone lines (thousands)			
Business	1 549	1 708	1 701
Residential	2 159	2 134	2 119
Total	3 708	3 842	3 820
Number of fax lines (thousand working lines)	360	546	491
Telephone lines per 1 000 population	563	566*	561#
Public mobile radiotelephone subscribers per 1 000 population[1]	420 [440]	620* [916]*	647# [1 056]#
Public radio paging subscribers per 1 000 population	87	29	26#
Outward external telephone traffic (million minutes)	1 719	3 951	4 233
Number of licensed Internet Service Providers (ISPs)	133	236*	201
Number of customers of the licensed Internet Service Providers (ISPs)			
Registered customer accounts with dial-up[2] access (thousands)	—	1 372	1 084
Registered broadband Internet access customer accounts (thousands)	—	989	1 231
Internet traffic volume			
Customer access via public switched telephone networks[3] (million minutes)	5 359	5 550	3 564
Customer access via broadband networks (terabits)	—	215 296	933 728

Notes: (1) Excluding pre-paid SIM cards. Figures including pre-paid SIM cards are presented in square brackets.
(2) Excluding Internet pre-paid calling cards.
(3) Excluding customer access via leased circuits.

Sources: Hong Kong Post.
(Enquiry Telephone No.: 2921 2231)
Office of the Telecommunications Authority.
(Enquiry Telephone No.: 2961 6652)

Table 41

(Chapter 17: Communications, the Media and Information Technology)

(a) Penetration of Information Technology in the Household Sector

	2002	*Percentages* 2003
Households with personal computers at home[1]	62.1	67.5
Households with personal computers at home connected to Internet [1]	52.5	60.0

(b) Usage of Information Technology amongst Household Members

	2002	*Percentages* 2003
Persons aged 10 and over who had used personal computers during the twelve months before enumeration[2]	54.0	56.2
Persons aged 10 and over who had used Internet service during the twelve months before enumeration[2]	48.2	52.2

Notes: Figures for 2002 refer to May-Jul. 2002, while those for 2003 refer to May-Aug. 2003.
    (1) As a percentage of all households in Hong Kong.
    (2) As a percentage of all persons aged 10 and over in Hong Kong.

Source: Social Surveys Section, Census and Statistics Department.
      (Enquiry Telephone No.: 2887 5103)

(c) Penetration and Usage of Information Technology in the Business Sector

	2002	*Percentages* 2003
Establishments using personal computers[1]	54.5	54.8
Establishments with Internet connection[1]	44.2	47.5
Establishments with Web page/Web site[1]	11.8	13.5
Business receipts from selling goods, services or information through electronic means[2]	0.29	N.A.

Notes: (1) As a percentage of all establishments in the industries covered in the annual Survey of Information Technology Usage
      and Penetration in the Business Sector. Figures refer to Apr.-Jun. of the year.
    (2) As a percentage of the total business receipts. Figure for 2003 will be available in end 2004.

Source: Information Technology & Telecommunications Statistics Section, Census and Statistics Department.
      (Enquiry Telephone No.: 2887 5560)

Index